THE TRIBES AND CASTES OF THE CENTRAL PROVINCES OF INDIA

THE TRIBES AND CASTES OF THE CENTRAL PROVINCES OF INDIA

BY

R. V. RUSSELL

OF THE INDIAN CIVIL SERVICE
SUPERINTENDENT OF ETHNOGRAPHY, CENTRAL PROVINCES

ASSISTED BY

RAI BAHADUR HIRA LAL
EXTRA ASSISTANT COMMISSIONER

PUBLISHED UNDER THE ORDERS OF THE CENTRAL PROVINCES ADMINISTRATION

IN FOUR VOLUMES
VOL. III

GYAN

Published by

Gyan Publishing House
5, Ansari Road
Daryaganj, New Delhi-110002
Phone: 011-47034999, 9811692060
E-mail: books@gyanbooks.com

Distribution Network
gyanbooks.com
India, USA, Canada, UK, Australia, France

ISBN : 978-81-212-4168-7 (Set)
ISBN : 978-81-212-4705-4 (HB)
First Published, 1916

2nd Impression 2020

Printed at: Gyan Press, Delhi.

The
Tribes and Castes of the Central Provinces of India
Author: R. V. Russell

CONTENTS OF VOLUME III

ARTICLES ON CASTES AND TRIBES OF THE CENTRAL PROVINCES IN ALPHABETICAL ORDER

The articles which are considered to be of most general interest are shown in capitals

ILLUSTRATIONS IN VOLUME III

PRONUNCIATION

a has the sound of **u** in *but* or *murmur*.
ā „ „ **a** in *bath* or *tar*.
e „ „ **é** in *écarté* or **ai** in *maid*.
i „ „ **i** in *bit*, or (as a final letter) of **y** in *sulky*.
ī „ „ **ee** in *beet*.
o „ „ **o** in *bore* or *bowl*.
u „ „ **u** in *put* or *bull*.
ū „ „ **oo** in *poor* or *boot*.

The plural of caste names and a few common Hindustāni words is formed by adding *s* in the English manner according to ordinary usage, though this is not, of course, the Hindustāni plural.

NOTE.—The rupee contains 16 annas, and an anna is of the same value as a penny. A pice is a quarter of an anna, or a farthing. Rs. 1-8 signifies one rupee and eight annas. A lakh is a hundred thousand, and a krore ten million.

PART II

ARTICLES ON CASTES AND TRIBES

GADARIA—KOSHTI

GADARIA

LIST OF PARAGRAPHS

Gadaria, Gādri.[1]—The occupational shepherd caste of northern India. The name is derived from the Hindi *gādar* and the Sanskrit *gandhāra*, a sheep, the Sanskrit name being taken from the country of Gandhāra or Kandahār, from which sheep were first brought. The three main shepherd castes all have functional names, that of the Dhangars or Marātha shepherds being derived from *dhan*, small stock, while the Kuramwārs or Telugu shepherds take their name like the Gadarias from *kuruba*, a sheep. These three castes are of similar nature and status, and differ only in language and local customs. In 1911 the Gadarias numbered 41,000 persons. They are found in the northern Districts, and appear to have been amongst the earliest settlers in the Nerbudda valley, for they have given their name to several villages, as Gadariakheda and Gādarwāra. 1. General notice.

The Gadarias are a very mixed caste. They themselves say that their first ancestor was created by Mahādeo to tend his rams, and that he married three women who were fascinated by the sight of him shearing the sheep. These belonged to the Brāhman, Dhīmar and Barai castes respectively, and became the ancestors of the Nikhar, Dhengar and Barmaiyan subcastes of Gadarias. The Nikhar subcaste are the highest, their name meaning pure. Dhengar is probably, in reality, a corruption of Dhangar, the name of the Marātha shepherd 2. Subdivisions.

[1] This article is based on information collected by Mr. Hīra Lāl in Jubbulpore, and the author in Mandla.

caste. They have other subdivisions of the common territorial type, as Jheria or jungly, applied to the Gadarias of Chhattīsgarh; Desha from *desh*, country, meaning those who came from northern India; Purvaiya or eastern, applied to immigrants from Oudh; and Mālvi or those belonging to Mālwa. Nikhar and Dhengar men take food together, but not the women; and if a marriage cannot be otherwise arranged these subcastes will sometimes give daughters to each other. A girl thus married is no longer permitted to take food at her father's house, but she may eat with the women of her husband's subcaste. Many of their exogamous groups are named after animals or plants, as Hiranwār, from *hiran*, a deer; Sapha from the cobra, Moria from the peacock, Nāhar from the tiger, Phulsungha, a flower, and so on. Others are the names of Rājpūt septs and of other castes, as Ahirwār (Ahīr) and Bamhania (Brāhman).

Another more ambitious legend derives their origin from the Bania caste. They say that once a Bania was walking along the road with a cocoanut in his hand when Vishnu met him and asked him what it was. The Bania answered that it was a cocoanut. Vishnu said that it was not a cocoanut but wool, and told him to break it, and on breaking the cocoanut the Bania found that it was filled with wool. The Bania asked what he should do with it, and Vishnu told him to make a blanket out of it for the god to sit on. So he made a blanket, and Vishnu said that from that day he should be the ancestor of the Gadaria caste, and earn his bread by making blankets from the wool of sheep. The Bania asked where he should get the sheep from, and the god told him to go home saying '*Ehān, Ehān, Ehān*,' all the way, and when he got home he would find a flock of sheep following him; but he was not to look behind him all the way. And the Bania did so, but when he had almost got home he could not help looking behind him to see if there were really any sheep. And he saw a long line of sheep following him in single file, and at the very end was a ram with golden horns just rising out of the ground. But as he looked it sank back again into the ground, and he went back to Vishnu and begged for it, but Vishnu said that as he had looked behind him he had lost it. And this was the origin of the Gadaria caste, and the Gadarias always say '*Ehān, Ehān*,' as they lead their flocks of sheep and goats to pasture.

3. Marriage customs. Marriage within the clan is forbidden and also the union of first cousins. Girls may be married at any age, and are sometimes united to husbands much younger than themselves. Four castemen of standing carry the proposal of marriage from the boy's father, and the girl's father, being forewarned, sends others to meet them. One of the ambassadors opens the conversation by saying, 'We have the milk and you have the milk-pail; let them be joined.' To which the girl's party, if the match be agreeable, will reply, "Yes, we have the tamarind and you have the mango; if the *panches* agree let there be a marriage." The boy's father gives the girl's father five areca-nuts, and the latter returns them and they clasp each other round the neck. When the wedding procession reaches the bride's village it is met by their party, and one of them takes the *sarota* or iron nut-cutter, which the bridegroom holds in his hand, and twirls it about in the air several times. The ceremony is performed by walking round the sacred pole, and the party return to the bridegroom's lodging, where his brother-in-law fills the bride's lap with sweetmeats and water-nut as an omen of fertility. The *maihar* or small wedding-cakes of wheat fried in sesamum oil are distributed to all members of the caste present at the wedding. While the bridegroom's party is absent at the bride's house, the women who remain behind enjoy amusements of their own. One of them strips herself naked, tying up her hair like a religious mendicant, and is known as Bāba or holy father. In this state she romps with her companions in turn, while the others laugh and applaud. Occasionally some man hides himself in a place where he can be a witness of their play, but if they discover him he is beaten severely with *belnas* or wooden bread-rollers. Widow-marriage and divorce are permitted, the widow being usually expected to marry her late husband's younger brother, whether he already has a wife or not. Sexual offences are not severely reprobated, and may be atoned for by a feast to the caste-fellows.

The Gadarias worship the ordinary Hindu deities and

4. Religion and funeral rites. also Dishai Devi, the goddess of the sheep-pen. No Gadaria may go into the sheep-pen with his shoes on. On entering it in the morning they make obeisance to the sheep, and these customs seem to indicate that the goddess Dishai Devi[1] is the deified sheep. When the sheep are shorn and the fleeces are lying on the ground they take some milk from one of the ewes and mix rice with it and sprinkle it over the wool. This rite is called Jimai, and they say that it is feeding the wool, but it appears to be really a sacrificial offering to the material. The caste burn the dead when they can afford to do so, and take the bones to the Ganges or Nerbudda, or if this is not practicable, throw them into the nearest stream.

5. Social customs. Well-to-do members of the caste employ Brāhmans for ceremonial purposes, but others dispense with their services. The Gadarias eat flesh and drink liquor, but abstain from fowls and pork. They will take food cooked with water from a Lodhi or a Dāngi, members of these castes having formerly been their feudal chieftains in the Vindhyan Districts and Nerbudda valley. Brāhmans and members of the good cultivating castes would be permitted to become Gadarias if they should so desire. The head of the caste committee has the title of Mahton and the office is hereditary, the holder being invariably consulted on caste questions even if he should be a mere boy. The Gadarias rank with those castes from whom a Brāhman cannot take water, but above the servile and labouring castes. They are usually somewhat stupid, lazy and good-tempered, and are quite uneducated. Owing to their work in cleaning the pens and moving about among the sheep, the women often carry traces of the peculiar smell of these animals. This is exemplified in the saying, '*Ek to Gadaria, dusre lahsan khae*,' or 'Firstly she is a Gadaria and then she has eaten garlic'; the inference being that she is far indeed from having the scent of the rose.

6. Goats and sheep. The regular occupations of the Gadarias are the breeding and grazing of sheep and goats, and the weaving of country blankets from sheep's wool. The flocks are usually

[1] The word Dishai really means direction or cardinal point, but as the goddess dwells in the sheep-pen it is probable that she was originally the sheep itself.

tended by the children, while the men and women spin and weave the wool and make blankets. Goats are bred in larger numbers than sheep in the Central Provinces, being more commonly used for food and sacrifices, while they are also valuable for their manure. Any Hindu who thinks an animal sacrifice requisite, and objects to a fowl as unclean, will choose a goat; and the animal after being sacrificed provides a feast for the worshippers, his head being the perquisite of the officiating priest. Muhammadans and most castes of Hindus will eat goat's meat when they can afford it. The milk is not popular and there is very little demand for it locally, but it is often sold to the confectioners, and occasionally made into butter and exported. Sheep's flesh is also eaten, but is not so highly esteemed. In the case of both sheep and goats there is a feeling against consuming the flesh of ewes. Sheep are generally black in colour and only occasionally white. Goats are black, white, speckled or reddish-white. Both animals are much smaller than in Europe. Both sheep and goats are in brisk demand in the cotton tracts for their manure in the hot-weather months, and will be kept continually on the move from field to field for a month at a time. It is usual to hire flocks at the rate of one rupee a hundred head for one night; but sometimes the cultivators combine to buy a large flock, and after penning them on their fields in the hot weather, send them to Nāgpur in the beginning of the rains to be disposed of. The Gadaria was formerly the *bête noir* of the cultivator, on account of the risk incurred by the crops from the depredations of his sheep and goats. This is exemplified in the saying:

Ahīr, Gadaria, Pāsi,
Yeh tinon satyanāsi,

or, 'The Ahīr (herdsman), the Gadaria and the Pāsi, these three are the husbandmen's foes.' And again:

Ahīr, Gadaria, Gūjar,
Yeh tinon chāhen ujar,

or 'The Ahīr, the Gadaria and the Gūjar want waste land,' that is for grazing their flocks. But since the demand for manure has arisen, the Gadaria has become a popular personage in the village. The shepherds whistle to their flocks to guide them, and hang bells round the necks of goats but not of sheep. Some of them, especially in forest tracts, train ordinary pariah dogs to act as sheep-dogs. As a rule, rams and he-goats are not gelt, but those who have large flocks sometimes resort to this practice and afterwards fatten the animals up for sale. They divide their sheep into five classes, as follows, according to the length of the ears: Kanāri, with ears a hand's length long; Semri, somewhat shorter; Burhai, ears a forefinger's length; Churia, ears as long as the little finger; and Neori, with ears as long only as the top joint of the forefinger. Goats are divided into two classes, those with ears a hand's length long being called Bangalia or Bagra, while those with small ears a forefinger's length are known as Gujra.

7. Blanket-weaving. While ordinary cultivators have now taken to keeping goats, sheep are still as a rule left to the Gadarias. These are of course valued principally for their wool, from which the ordinary country blanket is made. The sheep[1] are shorn two or sometimes three times a year, in February, June and September, the best wool being obtained in February from the cold weather coat. Members of the caste commonly shear for each other without payment. The wool is carded with a *kamtha*, or simple bow with a catgut string, and spun by the women of the household. Blankets are woven by men on a loom like that used for cotton cloth. The fabric is coarse and rough, but strong and durable, and the colour is usually a dark dirty grey, approaching black, being the same as that of the raw material. Every cultivator has one of these, and the various uses to which it may be put are admirably described by 'Eha' as follows:[2]

"The *kammal* is a home-spun blanket of the wool of black sheep, thick, strong, as rough as a farrier's rasp, and of a colour which cannot get dirty. When the Kunbi (cultivator) comes out of his hole in the morning it is wrapped round his shoulders and reaches to his knees,

[1] The following particulars are taken from the *Central Provinces Monograph on Woollen Industries*, by Mr. J. T. Marten.

[2] *A Naturalist on the Prowl*, 3rd ed., p. 219. In the quotation the Hindustāni word *kammal*, commonly used in the Central Provinces, is substituted for the Marāthi word *kambli*.

guarding him from his great enemy, the cold, for the thermometer is down to 60° Fahrenheit. By-and-by he has a load to carry, so he folds his *kammal* into a thick pad and puts it on the top of his head. Anon he feels tired, so he lays down his load, and arranging his *kammal* as a cushion, sits with comfort on a rugged rock or a stony bank, and has a smoke. Or else he rolls himself in it from head to foot, like a mummy, and enjoys a sound sleep on the roadside. It begins to rain, he folds his *kammal* into an ingenious cowl and is safe. Many more are its uses. I cannot number them all. Whatever he may be called upon to carry, be it forest produce, or grain or household goods, or his infant child, he will make a bundle of it with his *kammal* and poise it on his head, or sling it across his back, and trudge away."

8. Sanctity of wool.

Wool is a material of some sanctity among the Hindus. It is ceremonially pure, and woollen clothing can be worn by Brāhmans while eating or performing sacred functions. In many castes the bridegroom at a wedding has a string of wool with a charm tied round his waist. Religious mendicants wear *jatas* or wigs of sheep's wool, and often carry woollen charms. The beads used for counting prayers are often of wool. The reason for wool being thus held sacred may be that it was an older kind of clothing used before cotton was introduced, and thus acquired sanctity by being worn at sacrifices. Perhaps the Aryans wore woollen clothing when they entered India.

1. Description and structure of the tribe.

Gadba, Gadaba.[1]—A primitive tribe classified as Mundāri or Kolarian on linguistic grounds. The word Gadba, Surgeon-Major Mitchell states, signifies a person who carries loads on his shoulders. The tribe call themselves Guthau. They belong to the Vizagapatam District of Madras, and in the Central Provinces are found only in the Bastar State, into which they have immigrated to the number of some 700 persons. They speak a Mundāri dialect, called Gadba, after their tribal name, and are one of the two Mundāri tribes found so far south as Vizagapatam, the other being

[1] This article is compiled from an excellent monograph contributed by Surgeon-Major Mitchell of Bastar State, with extracts from Colonel Glasfurd's *Report on Bastar* (Selections from the Records of the Government of India in the Foreign Department, No. 39 of 1863).

the Savars.[1] Their tribal organisation is not very strict, and a Bhatra, a Parja, a Muria, or a member of any superior caste may become a Gadba at an expenditure of two or three rupees. The ceremony consists of shaving the body of the novice, irrespective of sex, clean of hair, after which he or she is given to eat rice cooked in the water of the Ganges. This is followed by a feast to the tribe in which a pig must be killed. The Gadbas have totemistic exogamous septs, usually named after animals, as *gutāl* dog, *angwān* bear, *dungra* tortoise, *surangai* tiger, *gūmal* snake, and so on. Members of each sept abstain from killing or injuring the animal or plant after which it is named, but they have no scruple in procuring others to do this. Thus if a snake enters the hut of a person belonging to the Gūmal sept, he will call a neighbour of another sept to kill it. He may not touch its carcase with his bare hand, but if he holds it through a piece of rag no sin is incurred.

2. Marriage. Marriage is adult, but the rule existing in Madras that a girl is not permitted to marry until she can weave her own cloth does not obtain in the Central Provinces.[2] As a rule the parents of the couple arrange the match, but the wishes of the girl are sometimes consulted and various irregular methods of union are recognised. Thus a man is permitted with the help of his friends to go and carry off a girl and keep her as his wife, more especially if she is a relation on the maternal side more distant than a first cousin. Another form is the Paisa Mundi, by which a married or unmarried woman may enter the house of a man of her caste other than her husband and become his wife; and the Upaliya, when a married woman elopes with a lover. The marriage ceremony is simple. The bridegroom's party go to the girl's house, leaving the parents behind, and before they reach it are met and stopped by a bevy of young girls and men in their best clothes from the bride's village. A girl comes forward and demands a ring, which one of the men of the wedding party places on her finger, and they then proceed to the bride's house, where the bridegroom's presents, consisting of victuals, liquor, a cloth,

[1] *India Census Report* (1901), p. 283.

[2] *Madras Census Report* (1891), p. 253.

and two rupees, are opened and carefully examined. If any deficiency is found, it must at once be made good. The pair eat a little food together, coloured rice is applied to their foreheads, and on the second day a new grass shed is erected, in which some rice is cooked by an unmarried girl. The bride and bridegroom are shut up in this, and two pots of water are poured over them from the roof, the marriage being then consummated. If the girl is not adult this ceremony is omitted. Widow-marriage is permitted by what is called the *tīka* form, by which a few grains of rice coloured with turmeric are placed on the foreheads of the pair and they are considered as man and wife. There is no regular divorce, but if a married woman misbehaves with a man of the caste, the husband goes to him with a few friends and asks whether the story is true, and if the accusation is admitted demands a pig and liquor for himself and his friends as compensation. If these are given he does not turn his wife out of his house. A *liaison* of a Gadba woman with a man of a superior caste is also said to involve no penalty, but if her paramour is a low-caste man she is excommunicated for ever. In spite of these lax rules, however, Major Mitchell states that the women are usually very devoted to their husbands. Mr. Thurston [1] notes that among the Bonda Gadabas a young man and a maid retire to the jungle and light a fire. Then the maid, taking a burning stick, places it on the man's skin. If he cries out he is unworthy of her, and she remains a maid. If he does not, the marriage is at once consummated. The application of the brand is probably light or severe according to the girl's feelings towards the young man.

3. Religious beliefs and festivals.

The Gadbas worship Burhi Māta or Thākurāni Māta, who is the goddess of smallpox and rinderpest. They offer to her flowers and incense when these diseases are prevalent among men or cattle, but if the epidemic does not abate after a time, they abuse the goddess and tell her to do her worst, suspending the offerings. They offer a white cock to the sun and a red one to the moon, and various other deities exercise special functions, Bhandārin being the goddess of agriculture and Dharni of good health, while

1 *Ethnographic Notes in Southern India*, p. 22.

Bharwān is the protector of cattle and Dand Devī of men from the attacks of wild beasts. They have vague notions of a heaven and hell where the sinful will be punished, and also believe in re-birth. But these ideas appear to be borrowed from their Hindu neighbours. When the new rice crop is ripe, the first-fruits are cooked and served to the cattle in new bamboo baskets, and are then partaken of by men. The ripening of the mango crop is also an important festival. In the bright fortnight of Chait (March) the men go out hunting, and on their return cook the game before Mātideo, the god of hunting, who lives in a tree. In Madras the whole male population turn out to hunt, and if they come back without success the women pelt them with cowdung on their return. If successful, however, they have their revenge on the women in another way.[1] On festival days men and women dance together to the music of a pipe and drum. Sometimes they form a circle, holding long poles, and jump backwards and forwards to and from the centre by means of the pole; or the women dance singly or in pairs, their hands resting on each other's waists. A man and woman will then step out of the crowd and sing at each other, the woman reflecting on the man's ungainly appearance and want of skill as a cultivator or huntsman, while the man retorts by reproaching her with her ugliness and slatternly habits.[2]

4. Disposal of the dead.

The dead are buried with their feet to the west, ready to start for the region of the setting sun. On their return from the funeral the mourners stop on the way, and a fish is boiled and offered to the dead. An egg is cut in half and placed on the ground, and pieces of mango bark are laid beside it on which the mourners tread. The women accompany the corpse, and in the meantime the house of the dead person is cleaned with cowdung by the children left behind. On the first day food is supplied to the mourners by their relatives, and in the evening some cooked rice and vegetables are offered to the dead. The mourning lasts for nine days, and on the last day a cow or bullock is killed with the blunt head of an axe, the performance of

1 *Madras Census Report* (1891), p. 253.

2 *Report on the Dependency of Bastar*, p. 37.

this function being hereditary in certain families of the caste. Some blood from the animal and some cooked rice are put in leaf-cups and placed on the grave by the head of the corpse. The animal is cooked and eaten by the grave, and they then return to the cooking shed and place its jawbone under a stick supported on two others, blood and cooked rice being again offered. The old men and women bathe in warm water, and all return to the place where the dead man breathed his last. Here they drink and have another meal of rice and beef, which is repeated on the following day, and the business of committing the dead to the ancestors is complete. Liquor is offered to the ancestors on feast days.

5. Occupation and mode of living.

The caste are cultivators and labourers, while some are employed as village watchmen, and others are hereditary *pālki*-bearers to the Rāja of Bastar, enjoying a free grant of land. They practise shifting cultivation, cleaning a space by indiscriminate felling in the forest, and roughly ploughing the ground for a single broad-cast crop of rice; in the following year the clearing is usually abandoned. Their dress is simple, though they now wear ordinary cloth. Forty years ago it is said that they wore coverings made from the bark of the *kuring* tree and painted with horizontal bands of red, yellow and blue.[1] A girdle of the thickness of a man's arm made from fine strips of bark is still worn and is a distinguishing feature of the Gadba women. They also carry a circlet round their forehead of the seeds of *kusa* grass threaded on a string. Both men and women wear enormous earrings, the men having three in each ear. The Gadbas are almost omnivorous, and eat flesh, fish, fowls, pork, buffaloes crocodiles, non-poisonous snakes, large lizards, frogs, sparrows, crows and large red ants. They abstain only from the flesh of monkeys, horses and asses. A Gadba must not ride on a horse under penalty of being put out of caste. Mr. Thurston[2] gives the following reason for this prejudice :—"The Gadbas of Vizagapatam will not touch a horse, as they are palanquin-bearers, and have the same objection to a rival animal as a cart-driver has to a motor-car." They will eat the leavings of other castes and take food from all except the impure ones,

[1] *Report on the Dependency of Bastar*, p. 37.

[2] *Ethnographic Notes in Southern India*, p. 270.

but like the Mehtars and Ghasias elsewhere they will not take food or water from a Kāyasth. Only the lowest castes will eat with Gadbas, but they are not considered as impure, and are allowed to enter temples and take part in religious ceremonies.

1. Distribution and origin.

Gānda.—A servile and impure caste of Chota Nāgpur and the Uriya Districts. They numbered 278,000 persons in 1901, resident largely in Sambalpur and the Uriya States, but since the transfer of this territory to Bengal, only about 150,000 Gāndas remain in the Central Provinces in Raipur, Bilāspur and Raigarh. In this Province the Gāndas have become a servile caste of village drudges, acting as watchmen, weavers of coarse cloth and musicians. They are looked on as an impure caste, and are practically in the same position as the Mehras and Chamārs of other Districts. In Chota Nāgpur, however, they are still in some places recognised as a primitive tribe,[1] being generally known here as Pān, Pāb or Chik. Sir H. Risley suggests that the name of Gānda may be derived from Gond, and that the Pāns may originally have been an offshoot of that tribe, but no connection between the Gāndas and Gonds has been established in the Central Provinces.

2. Caste subdivisions.

The subcastes reported differ entirely from those recorded in Orissa. In the Central Provinces they are mainly occupational. Thus the Bajna or Bajgari are those who act as musicians at feasts and marriages; the Māng or Mangia make screens and mats, while their women serve as midwives; the Dholias make baskets; the Doms skin cattle and the Nagārchis play on *nakkāras* or drums. Panka is also returned as a subcaste of Gānda, but in the Central Provinces the Pankas are now practically a separate caste, and consist of those Gāndas who have adopted Kabīrpanthism and have thereby obtained some slight rise in status. In Bengal Sir H. Risley mentions a group called Patradias, or slaves and menials of the Khonds, and discusses the Patradias as follows:—"The group seems also to include the descendants of Pāns, who sold themselves as slaves or were sold as Merias or victims to the Khonds. We know that an extensive

[1] Risley, *Tribes and Castes of Bengal*, art. Pān.

traffic in children destined for human sacrifice used to go on in the Khond country, and that the Pāns were the agents who sometimes purchased, but more frequently kidnapped, the children, whom they sold to the Khonds, and were so debased that they occasionally sold their own offspring, though they knew of course the fate that awaited them.[1] Moreover, apart from the demand for sacrificial purposes, the practice of selling men as agricultural labourers was until a few years ago by no means uncommon in the wilder parts of the Chota Nāgpur Division, where labour is scarce and cash payments are almost unknown. Numbers of formal bonds have come before me, whereby men sold themselves for a lump sum to enable them to marry." The above quotation is inserted merely as an interesting historical reminiscence of the Pāns or Gāndas.

3. Marriage.

The Gāndas have exogamous groups or septs of the usual low-caste type, named after plants, animals or other inanimate objects. Marriage is prohibited within the sept, and between the children of two sisters, though the children of brothers and sisters may marry. If a girl arrives at maturity without a husband having been found for her, she is wedded to a spear stuck up in the courtyard of the house, and then given away to anybody who wishes to take her. A girl going wrong with a man of the caste is married to him by the ceremony employed in the case of widows, while her parents have to feed the caste. But a girl seduced by an outsider is permanently expelled. The betrothal is marked by a present of various articles to the father of the bride. Marriages must not be celebrated during the three rainy months of Shrāwan, Bhādon or Kunwār, nor during the dark fortnight of the month, nor on a Saturday or Tuesday. The marriage-post is of the wood of the mahua tree, and beneath it are placed seven cowries and seven pieces of turmeric. An elderly male member of the caste known as the Sethia conducts the ceremony, and the couple go five times round the sacred pole in the morning and thrice in the evening. When the bride and bridegroom return home after the wedding, an image of a deer is made with grass and placed behind the

[1] The human sacrifices of the Khonds were suppressed about 1860. See the article on that tribe.

ear of the bride. The bridegroom then throws a toy arrow at it made of grass or thin bamboo, and is allowed seven shots. If he fails to knock it out of her ear after these the bride's brother takes it and runs away and the bridegroom must follow and catch him. This is clearly a symbolic process representing the chase, of the sort practised by the Khonds and other primitive tribes, and may be taken as a reminiscence among the Gāndas of their former life in the forests. The remarriage of widows is permitted, and the younger brother of the deceased husband takes his widow if he wishes to do so. Otherwise she may marry whom she pleases. A husband may divorce his wife for adultery before the caste committee, and if she marries her lover he must repay to the husband the expenses incurred by the latter on his wedding.

4. Religion. The Gāndas principally worship Dūlha Deo, the young bridegroom who was carried off by a tiger, and they offer a goat to him at their weddings. They observe the Hindu fasts and festivals, and at Dasahra worship their musical instruments and the weaver's loom. Being impure, they do not revere the *tulsi* plant nor the banyan or pīpal trees. Children are named on the sixth day after birth without any special ceremony. The dead are generally buried from motives of economy, as with most families the fuel required for cremation would be a serious item of expenditure. A man is laid on his face in the grave and a woman on her back. Mourning is observed for three days, except in the case of children under three years old, whose deaths entail no special observances. On the fourth day a feast is given, and when all have been served, the chief mourner takes a little food from the plate of each guest and puts it in a leaf-cup. He takes another leaf-cup full of water and places the two outside the house, saying 'Here is food for you' to the spirit of the departed.

5. Occupation and social status. The Gāndas are generally employed either in weaving coarse cloth or as village musicians. They sing and dance to the accompaniment of their instruments, the dancers generally being two young boys dressed as women. They have long hair and put on skirts and half-sleeved jackets, with hollow anklets round their feet filled with stones to

make them tinkle. On their right shoulders are attached some peacocks' feathers, and coloured cloths hang from their back and arms and wave about when they dance. Among their musical instruments is the *sing-bāja*, a single drum made of iron with ox-hide leather stretched over it; two horns project from the sides for purposes of decoration and give the instrument its name, and it is beaten with thick leather thongs. The *dafla* is a wooden drum open on one side and covered with a goat-skin on the other, beaten with a cane and a bamboo stick. The *timki* is a single hemispherical drum of earthenware; and the *salnai* is a sort of bamboo flute. The Gāndas of Sambalpur have strong criminal tendencies which have recently called for special measures of repression. Nevertheless they are usually employed as village watchmen in accordance with long-standing custom. They are considered as impure and, though not compelled actually to live apart from the village, have usually a separate quarter and are not permitted to draw water from the village well or to enter Hindu temples. Their touch defiles, and a Hindu will not give anything into the hands of one of the caste while holding it himself, but will throw it down in front of the Gānda, and will take anything from him in the same manner. They will admit outsiders of higher rank into the caste, taking from them one or two feasts. And it is reported that in Raipur a Brāhman recently entered the caste for love of a Gānda girl.

Gandhmāli,[1] Thānāpati.—The caste of village priests of the temples of Siva or Mahādeo in Sambalpur and the Uriya States. They numbered about 700 persons in the Central Provinces in 1911. The caste appears to be an offshoot of the Mālis or gardeners, differentiated from them by their special occupation of temple attendants. In Hindustān the priests of Siva's temples in villages are often Mālis, and in the Marātha country they are Guraos, another special caste, or Phulmālis. Some members of the caste in Sambalpur, however, aspire to Rājpūt origin and wear

[1] This article is compiled from papers by Mr. Jhanjhan Rai, Tahsīldār, Sārangarh, and Satyabādi Misra of the Sambalpur Census office.

the sacred thread. These prefer the designation of Thānāpati or 'Master of the sacred place,' and call the others who do not wear the thread Gandhmālis. *Gandh* means incense. The Thānāpatis say that on one occasion a Rājpūt prince from Jaipur made a pilgrimage to the temple of Jagannāth at Puri, and on his return stopped at the celebrated temple of Mahādeo at Huma near Sambalpur. Mahādeo appeared before the prince and asked him to become his priest; the Rājpūt asked to be excused as he was old, but Mahādeo promised him three sons, which he duly obtained and in gratitude dedicated them to the service of the god. From these sons the Thānāpatis say that they are descended, but the claim is no doubt quite illusory. The truth is, probably, that the Thānāpatis are priests of the temples situated in towns and large villages, and owing to their calling have obtained considerable social estimation, which they desire to justify and place on an enduring basis by their claim to Rājpūt ancestry; while the Gandhmālis are village priests, more or less in the position of village menials and below the cultivating castes, and any such pretensions would therefore in their case be quite untenable. There are signs of the cessation of intermarriage between the two groups, but this has not been brought about as yet, probably owing to the paucity of members in the caste and the difficulty of arranging matches. Three functional subdivisions also appear to be in process of formation, the Pujāris or priests of Mahādeo's temples, the Bandhādias or those who worship him on the banks of tanks, and the Mundjhulas[1] or devotees of the goddess Somlai in Sambalpur, on whom the inspiration of the goddess descends, making them shake and roll their heads. When in this state they are believed to drink the blood flowing from goats sacrificed in the temple. For the purposes of marriage the caste is divided into exogamous groups or *bargas*, the names of which are usually titles or designations of offices. Marriage within the *barga* is prohibited. When the bride is brought to the altar in the marriage ceremony, she throws a garland of jasmine flowers on the neck of the bridegroom. This custom resembles

[1] *Mund-jhulānā*, to swing the head.

the old Swayamwāra form of marriage, in which a girl chose her own husband by throwing a garland of flowers round his neck. But it probably has no connection with this and merely denotes the fact that the caste are gardeners by profession, similar ceremonies typifying the caste calling being commonly performed at marriages, especially among the Telugu castes. Girls should be married before adolescence and, as is usual among the Uriya castes, if no suitable husband is forthcoming a symbolic marriage is celebrated; the Thānāpatis make her go through the form with her maternal grandfather or sister's husband, and in default of them with a tree. She is then immediately divorced and disposed of as a widow. Divorce and the remarriage of widows are permitted. A bachelor marrying a widow must first go through the ceremony with a flower. The Gandhmālis, as the priests of Mahādeo, are generally Saivas and wear red clothes covered with ochre. They consider that their ultimate ancestor is the Nāg or cobra and especially observe the festival of Nāg-Panchmi, abstaining from any cooked food on that day. They both burn and bury the dead and perform the *shrādhh* ceremony or the offering of sacrificial cakes. They eat flesh but do not drink liquor. Their social position is fairly good and Brāhmans will take water from their hands. Many of them hold free grants of land in return for their services at the temples. A few are ordinary cultivators.

Gārpagāri.[1]—A caste of village menials whose function it is to avert hailstorms from the crops. They are found principally in the Marātha Districts of the Nāgpur country and Berār, and numbered 9000 persons in 1911. The name is derived from the Marāthi *gār*, hail. The Gārpagāris are really Nāths or Jogis who have taken to this calling and become a separate caste. They wear clothes coloured with red ochre, and a garland of *rudrāksha* beads, and bury their dead in a sitting posture. According to their tradition the first Gārpagāri was one Rāut, a Jogi, who accompanied a Kunbi mālguzār on a visit to Benāres, and while there he 1. Origin of the caste.

[1] Based on notes taken by Mr. Hīrā Lāl at Chānda and the notices of the Gārpagāri in the District Gazetteers.

prophesied that on a certain day all the crops of their village would be destroyed by a hailstorm. The Kunbi then besought him to save the crops if he could, and he answered that by his magic he could draw off the hail from the rest of the village and concentrate it in his own field, and he agreed to do this if the cultivators would recompense him for his loss. When the two came home to their village they found that there had been a severe hailstorm, but it had all fallen in the Jogi's field. His loss was made good to him and he adopted this calling as a profession, becoming the first Gārpagāri, and being paid by contributions from the proprietor and tenants. There are no subcastes except that the Kharchi Gārpagāri are a bastard group, with whom the others refuse to intermarry.

2. Marriage. Marriage is regulated by exogamous groups, two of which, Watāri from the Otāri or brass-worker, and Dhankar from the Dhangar or shepherds, are named after other castes. Some are derived from the names of animals, as Harnya from the black-buck, and Wāgh from the tiger. The Diunde group take their name from *diundi*, the kotwar's[1] drum. They say that their ancestor was so named because he killed his brother, and was proclaimed as an outlaw by beat of drum. The marriage of members of the same group is forbidden and also that of the children of two sisters, so long as the relationship between them is remembered. The caste usually celebrate their weddings after those of the Kunbis, on whom they depend for contributions to their expenses. Widow-marriage is permitted, but the widow sometimes refuses to marry again, and, becoming a Bhagat or devotee, performs long pilgrimages in male attire. Divorce is permitted, but as women are scarce, is rarely resorted to. The Gārpagāris say, "If one would not throw away a vegetable worth a *damri* (one-eighth of a pice or farthing), how shall one throw away a wife who is 3½ cubits long." A divorced wife is allowed to marry again.

3. Religion. The caste worship Mahādeo or Siva and Mahābīr or Hanumān, and do not usually distinguish them. Their principal festival is called Māhi and takes place on the first day of Poush (December), this being the day from which

[1] Village watchman.

hailstorms may be expected to occur; and next to this Māndo Amāwas, or the first day of Chait (March), after which hailstorms need not be feared. They offer goats to Mahādeo in his terrible form of Kāl Bhairava, and during the ceremony the Kunbis beat the *dāheka*, a small drum with bells, to enhance the effect of the sacrifice, so that their crops may be saved. When a man is at the point of death he is placed in the sitting posture in which he is to be buried, for fear that after death his limbs may become so stiff that they cannot be made to assume it. The corpse is carried to the grave in a cloth coloured with red ochre. A gourd containing pulse and rice, a pice coin, and a small quantity of any drug to which the deceased may have been addicted in life are placed in the hands, and the grave is filled in with earth and salt. A lamp is lighted on the place where the death occurred, for one night, and on the third day a cocoanut is broken there, after which mourning ends and the house is cleaned. A stone brought from the bed of a river is plastered down on to the grave with clay, and this may perhaps represent the dead man's spirit.

The occupation of the Gārpagāri is to avert hailstorms, 4. Occupation.
and he was formerly remunerated by a customary contribution of rice from each cultivator in the village. He received the usual presents at seed-time and harvest, and two pice from each tenant on the Basant-Panchmi festival. When the sky is of mixed red and black at night like smoke and flame, the Gārpagāri knows that a hailstorm is coming. Then, taking a sword in his hand, he goes and stands before Mahābīr, and begs him to disperse the clouds. When entreaties fail, he proceeds to threats, saying that he will kill himself, and throws off his clothes. Sometimes his wife and children go and stand with him before Mahābīr's shrine and he threatens to kill them. Formerly he would cut and slash himself, so it is said, if Mahābīr was obdurate, but now the utmost he does is to draw some blood from a finger. He would also threaten to sacrifice his son, and instances are known of his actually having done so.

Two ideas appear to be involved in these sacrifices of the Gārpagāri. One is the familiar principle of atonement, the blood being offered to appease the god as a substitute for the crops which he seems about to destroy. But when the Gārpagāri threatened to kill himself, and actually killed his son, it was not merely as an atonement, because in that case the threats would have had no meaning. His intention seems rather to have been to lay the guilt of homicide upon the god by slaying somebody in front of his shrine, in case nothing less would move him from his purpose of destroying the crops. The idea is the same as that with which people committed suicide in order that their ghosts might haunt those who had driven them to the act. As late as about the year 1905 a Gond Bhumka or village priest was hanged in Chhindwāra for killing his two children. He owed a debt of Rs. 25 and the creditor was pressing him and he had nothing to pay. So he flew into a rage and exclaimed that the gods would do nothing for him even though he was a Bhumka, and he seized his two children and cut off their heads and laid them before the god. In this it would appear that the Bhumka's intention was partly to take revenge on his master for the neglect shown to him, the god's special servant. The Gārpagāri diverts the hail by throwing a handful of grain in the direction in which he wishes it to go. When the storm begins he will pick up some hailstones, smear them with his blood and throw them away, telling them to rain over rivers, hills, forests and barren ground. When caterpillars or locusts attack the crops he catches one or two and offers them at Mahābīr's shrine, afterwards throwing them up in the air. Or he buries one alive and this is supposed to stay the plague. When rust appears in the crops, one or two blades are in like manner offered to Mahābīr, and it is believed that the disease will be stayed. Or if the rice plants do not come into ear a few of them are plucked and offered, and fresh fertile blades then come up. He also has various incantations which are believed to divert the storm or to cause the hailstones to melt into water. In some localities, when the buffalo is slaughtered at the Dasahra festival, the Gārpagāri takes seven different kinds of spring-crop seeds and dips them in its blood. He buries them in a spot beside his hearth, and it is believed that when a hail-storm threatens the grains move about and give out a humming sound like water boiling. Thus the Gārpagāri has warning of the storm. If the Gārpagāri is absent and a storm comes his wife will go and stand naked before Mahābīr's shrine. The wives know the incantations, but they must not learn them from their husbands, because in that case the husband would be in the position of a *guru* or spiritual preceptor to his wife and the conjugal relation could no longer continue. No other caste will learn the incantations, for to make the hailstones melt is regarded as equivalent to causing an abortion, and as a sin for which heavy retribution would be incurred in a future life.

In Chhattīsgarh the Baiga or village priest of the aboriginal tribes averts hailstorms in the same manner as the Gārpagāri, and elsewhere the Barais or betel-vine growers perform this function, which is especially important to them because their vines are so liable to be injured by hailstorms. In ancient Greece there existed a village functionary, the *Chalazo phulax*, who kept off hailstorms in exactly the same manner as the Gārpagāri. He would offer a victim, and if he had none would draw blood from his own fingers to appease the storm.[1]

The same power has even been imputed to Christian priests as recorded by Sir James Frazer: "In many villages of Provence the priest is still required to possess the faculty of averting storms. It is not every priest who enjoys this reputation; and in some villages when a change of pastors takes place, the parishioners are eager to learn whether the new incumbent has the power (*pouder*) as they call it. At the first sign of a heavy storm they put him to the proof by inviting him to exorcise the threatening clouds; and if the result answers to their hopes, the new shepherd is assured of the sympathy and respect of his flock. In some parishes where the reputation of the curate in this respect stood higher than that of the rector, the relations between the two have been so strained in consequence that the bishop has had to translate the rector to another benefice."[2]

Of late years an unavoidable scepticism as to the Gārpagāri's efficiency has led to a reduction of his earnings, and the cultivators now frequently decline to give him anything, or

[1] Dr. Jevons, *Introduction to the History of Religion*, p. 171.

[2] *The Golden Bough*, 2nd ed. vol. i. p. 68, quoting from French authorities.

only a sheaf of corn at harvest. Some members of the caste have taken to weaving *newār* or broad tape for beds, and others have become cultivators.

5. Social status. The Gārpagāris eat flesh and drink liquor. They will take cooked food from a Kunbi, though the Kunbis will not take even water from them. They are a village menial caste and rank with others of the same position, though on a somewhat lower level because they beg and accept cooked food at the weddings of Kunbis. Their names usually end in *nāth*, as Rāmnāth, Kisannāth and so on.

Gauria.[1]—A small caste of snake-charmers and jugglers who are an offshoot of the Gond tribe. They number about 500 persons and are found only in Chhattīsgarh. They have the same exogamous septs as the Gonds, as Markām, Marai, Netām, Chhedaiha, Jagat, Purteti, Chichura and others. But they are no doubt of very mixed origin, as is shown by the fact that they do not eat together at their feasts, but the guests all cook their own food and eat it separately. And after a daughter has been married her own family even will not take food from her hand because they are doubtful of her husband's status. It is said that the Gaurias were accustomed formerly to beg only from the Kewat caste, though this restriction is no longer maintained. The fact may indicate that they are partly descended from the unions of Kewats with Gond women.

Adult marriage is the general rule of the caste and a fixed bride-price of sixteen rupees is paid. The couple go away together at once and six months afterwards return to visit the bride's parents, when they are treated as outsiders and not allowed to touch the food cooked for the family, while they reciprocally insist on preparing their own. Male Gaurias will take food from any of the higher castes, but the women will eat only from Gaurias. They will admit outsiders belonging to any caste from whom they can take food into the community. And if a Gauria woman goes wrong with a member of any of these castes they overlook the matter and inflict only a feast as a penalty.

[1] This article is based on papers by Mr. Jeorākhān Lāl, Deputy Inspector of Schools, Bilāspur, and Bhagwān Singh, Court of Wards Clerk, Bilāspur.

Their marriage ceremony consists merely in the placing of bangles on the woman's wrists, which is the form by which a widow is married among other castes. If a widow marries a man other than her husband's younger brother, the new husband must pay twelve rupees to her first husband's family, or to her parents if she has returned to them. If she takes with her a child born of her first husband with permission to keep it, the second husband must pay eight rupees to the first husband's family as the price of the child. But if the child is to be returned as soon as it is able to shift for itself the second husband receives eight rupees instead of paying it, as remuneration for his trouble in rearing the baby. The caste bury their dead with the feet to the south, like the Hindus. The principal business of the Gaurias is to catch and exhibit snakes, and they carry a *damru* or rattle in the shape of an hour-glass, which is considered to be a distinctive badge of the caste. If a Gauria saw an Ojha snake-charmer carrying a *damru* he would consider himself entitled to take it from the Ojha forcibly if he could. A Gauria is forbidden to exhibit monkeys under penalty of being put out of caste. Their principal festival is the Nāg-Panchmi, when the cobra is worshipped. They also profess to know charms for curing persons bitten by snakes. The following incantation is cried by a Gauria snake-doctor three times into the ears of his patient in a loud voice:

"The *bel* tree and the *bel* leaves are on the other side of the river. All the Gaurias are drowned in it. The breast of the *koil*; over it is a net. Eight snakes went to the forest. They tamed rats on the green tree. The snakes are flying, causing the parrots to fly. They want to play, but who can make them play? After finishing their play they stood up; arise thou also, thou sword. I am waking you (the patient) up by crying in your ear, I conjure you by the name of Dhanvantari[1] to rise carefully."

Similar meaningless charms are employed for curing the bites of scorpions and for exorcising bad spirits and the influence of the evil eye.

The Gaurias will eat almost all kinds of flesh, including pigs, rats, fowls and jackals, but they abstain from beef.

[1] The Celestial Physician.

Their social status is so low that practically no caste will take food or water from them, but they are not considered as impure. They are great drunkards, and are easily known by their *damrus* or rattles and the baskets in which they carry their snakes.

GHASIA

LIST OF PARAGRAPHS

Ghasia, Sais.[1]—A low Dravidian caste of Orissa and Central India who cut grass, tend horses and act as village musicians at festivals. In the Central Provinces they numbered 43,000 in 1911, residing principally in the Chhattīsgarh Division and the adjoining Feudatory States. The word Ghasia is derived from *ghās* (grass) and means a grass-cutter. Sir H. Risley states that they are a fishing and cultivating caste of Chota Nāgpur and Central India, who attend as musicians at weddings and festivals and also perform menial offices of all kinds.[2] In Bastar they are described as an inferior caste who serve as horse-keepers and also make and mend brass vessels. They dress like the Māria Gonds and subsist partly by cultivation and partly by labour.[3] Dr. Ball describes them in Singhbhūm as gold-washers and musicians. Colonel Dalton speaks of them as "An extra-ordinary tribe, foul parasites of the Central Indian hill tribes and submitting to be degraded even by them. If the Chandāls of the Purānas, though descended from the union of a Brāhmini and a Sūdra, are the lowest of the low, the Ghasias are Chandāls and the people further south who are called Pariahs are no doubt of the same distinguished lineage."[4]

1. Description of the caste.

[1] This article is compiled partly from papers by Munshis Pyāre Lāl Misra and Kanhya Lāl of the Gazetteer Office.

[2] *Tribes and Castes of Bengal,* art. Ghāsi.

[3] *Central Provinces Gazetteer* (1871), p. 273.

[4] *Descriptive Ethnology of Bengal,* p. 325.

2. Subcastes. The Ghasias generally, however, appear now to be a harmless caste of labourers without any specially degrading or repulsive traits. In Mandla their social position and customs are much on a par with those of the Gonds, from whom a considerable section of the caste seems to be derived. In other localities they have probably immigrated into the Central Provinces from Bundelkhand and Orissa. Among their subdivisions the following may be mentioned: the Udia, who cure raw hides and do the work of sweepers and are generally looked down on; the Dingkuchia, who castrate cattle and ponies; the Dolboha, who carry *dhoolies* or palanquins; the Nagārchi, who derive their name from the *nakkāra* or kettle-drum and are village musicians; the Khaltaha or those from Raipur; the Laria, belonging to Chhattīsgarh, and the Uria of the Uriya country; the Rāmgarhia, who take their name from Rāmgarh in the Mandla District, and the Mahobia from Mahoba in Bundelkhand. Those members of the caste who work as grooms have become a separate group and call themselves Sais, dropping the name of Ghasia. They rank higher than the others and marry among themselves, and some of them have become cultivators or work as village watchmen. They are also called Thānwar by the Gonds, the word meaning stable or stall. In Chota Nāgpur a number of Ghasias have become tailors and are tending to form a separate subcaste under the name of Darzi.

3. Exogamous sections. Their septs are of the usual low-caste type, being named after animals, inanimate objects or nicknames of ancestors. One of them is Pānch-biha or 'He who had five wives,' and another Kul-dīp or 'The sept of the lamp.' Members of this sept will stop eating if a lamp goes out. The Janta Ragda take their name from the mill for grinding corn and will not have a grinding-mill in their houses. They say that a female ancestor was delivered of a child when sitting near a grinding-mill and this gave the sept its name. Three septs are named after other castes: Kumhārbans, descended from a potter; Gāndbans, from a Gānda; and Luha, from a Lohār or blacksmith, and which names indicate that members of these castes have been admitted into the community.

Marriage is forbidden within the sept, but is permitted

between the children of brothers and sisters. Those members of the caste who have become Kabīrpanthis may also marry with the others. Marriages may be infant or adult. A girl who is seduced by a member of the caste is married to him by a simple ceremony, the couple standing before a twig of the *ūmar*[1] tree, while some women sprinkle turmeric over them. If a girl goes wrong with an outsider she is permanently expelled and a feast is exacted from her parents. The boy and his relatives go to the girl's house for the betrothal, and a present of various articles of food and dress is made to her family, apparently as a sort of repayment for their expenditure in feeding and clothing her. A gift of clothes is also made to her mother, called *dudh-sāri*, and is regarded as the price of the milk with which the mother nourished the girl in her infancy. A goat, which forms part of the bride-price, is killed and eaten by the parties and their relatives. The binding portion of the marriage is the *bhānwar* ceremony, at which the couple walk seven times round the marriage-post, holding each other by the little fingers. When they return to the bridegroom's house, a cock or a goat is killed and the head buried before the door; the foreheads of the couple are marked with its blood and they go inside the house. If the bride is not adult, she goes home after a stay of two days, and the *gauna* or going-away ceremony is performed when she finally leaves her parents' house. The remarriage of widows is permitted, no restriction being imposed on the widow in her choice of a second husband. Divorce is permitted for infidelity on the part of the wife. 4. Marriage.

5. Religion and superstitions.

Children are named on the sixth day after birth, special names being given to avert ill-luck, while they sometimes go through the ceremony of selling a baby for five cowries in order to disarm the jealousy of the godlings who are hostile to children. They will not call any person by name when they think an owl is within hearing, as they believe that the owl will go on repeating the name and that this will cause the death of the person bearing it. The caste generally revere Dūlha Deo, the bridegroom god, whose altar stands near the cooking place, and the goddess Devi.

[1] *Ficus glomerata.*

Once in three years they offer a white goat to Bura Deo, the great god of the Gonds. They worship the sickle, the implement of their trade, at Dasahra, and offer cocoanuts and liquor to Ghāsi Sādhak, a godling who lives by the peg to which horses are tied in the stable. He is supposed to protect the horse from all kinds of diseases. At Dasahra they also worship the horse. Their principal festival is called Karma and falls on the eleventh day of the second half of Bhādon (August). On this day they bring a branch of a tree from the forest and worship it with betel, areca-nut and other offerings. All through the day and night the men and women drink and dance together. They both burn and bury the dead, throwing the ashes into water. For the first three days after a death they set out rice and pulse and water in a leaf cup for the departed spirit. They believe that the ghosts of the dead haunt the living, and to cure a person possessed in this manner they beat him with shoes and then bury an effigy of the ghost outside the village.

6. Occupation. The Ghasias usually work as grass-cutters and grooms to horses, and some of them make loom-combs for weavers. These last are looked down upon and called Madarchawa. They make the *kūnch* or brushes for the loom, like the Kūchbandhias, from the root of the *babai* or khas-khas grass, and the *râchh* or comb for arranging the threads on the loom from the stalks of the *bharru* grass. Other Ghasias make ordinary hair combs from the *kathai*, a grass which grows densely on the borders of streams and springs. The frame of the comb is of bamboo and the teeth are fixed in either by thread or wire, the price being one pice (farthing) in the former case and two in the latter.

7. Social customs. The caste admit outsiders by a disgusting ceremony in which the candidate is shaved with urine and forced to eat a mixture of cowdung, basil leaves, *dub*[1] grass and water in which a piece of silver or gold has been dipped. The women do not wear the *choli* or breast-cloth nor the nose-ring, and in some localities they do not have spangles on the forehead. Women are tattooed on various parts of the body before marriage with the idea of enhancing their

[1] *Cynodon dactylon.*

beauty, and sometimes tattooing is resorted to for curing a pain in some joint or for rheumatism. A man who is temporarily put out of caste is shaved on readmission, and in the case of a woman a lock of her hair is cut. To touch a dead cow is one of the offences entailing temporary excommunication. They employ a Brāhman only to fix the dates of their marriages. The position of the caste is very low and in some places they are considered as impure. The Ghasias are very poor, and a saying about them is '*Ghasia ki jindagi hasia,*' or 'The Ghasia is supported by his sickle,' the implement used for cutting grass. The Ghasias are perhaps the only caste in the Central Provinces outside those commonly returning themselves as Mehtar, who consent to do scavenger's work in some localities.

8. Ghasias and Kāyasths.

The caste have a peculiar aversion to Kāyasths and will not take food or water from them nor touch a Kāyasth's bedding or clothing. They say that they would not serve a Kāyasth as horse-keeper, but if by any chance one of them was reduced to doing so, he at any rate would not hold his master's stirrup for him to mount. To account for this hereditary enmity they tell the following story:

On one occasion the son of the Kāyasth minister of the Rāja of Ratanpur went out for a ride followed by a Ghasia sais (groom). The boy was wearing costly ornaments, and the Ghasia's cupidity being excited, he attacked and murdered the child, stripped him of his ornaments and threw the body down a well. The murder was discovered and in revenge the minister killed every Ghasia, man, woman or child that he could lay his hands on. The only ones who escaped were two pregnant women who took refuge in the hut of a Gānda and were sheltered by him. To them were born a boy and a girl and the present Ghasias are descended from the pair. Therefore a Ghasia will eat even the leavings of a Gānda but will accept nothing from the hands of a Kāyasth.

This story is an instance of the process which has been called the transplantation of myth. Sir H. Risley tells a similar legend of the Ghasias of Orissa,[1] but in their case it was a young Kāyasth bridegroom who was killed, and before dying he got leave from his murderers to write a

[1] *Tribes and Castes of Bengal*, art. Ghāsi.

letter to his relatives informing them of his death, on condition that he said nothing as to its manner. But in the letter he disclosed the murder, and the Ghasias, who could not read, were duly brought to justice. In the Ratanpur story as reported from Bilāspur it was stated that "Somehow, even from down the well, the minister's son managed to get a letter sent to his father telling him of the murder." And this sentence seems sufficient to establish the fact that the Central Provinces story has merely been imported from Orissa and slightly altered to give it local colour. The real reason for the traditional aversion felt by the Ghasias and other low castes for the Kāyasths will be discussed in the article on that caste.

Ghosi.[1]—A caste of herdsmen belonging to northern India and found in the Central Provinces in Saugor and other Districts of the Jubbulpore and Nerbudda Divisions. In 1911 they numbered 10,000 persons in this Province out of a strength of about 60,000 in India. The name is said to be derived from the Sanskrit root *ghush*, to shout, the word *ghosha* meaning one who shouts as he herds his cattle. A noticeable fact about the caste is that, while in Upper India they are all Muhammadans—and it is considered to be partly on account of the difference in religion that they have become differentiated into a separate caste from the Ahīrs—in the Central Provinces they are nearly all Hindus and show no trace of Muhammadan practices. A few Muhammadan Ghosis are found in Nimār and some Muhammadans who call themselves Gaddi in Mandla are believed to be Ghosis. And as the Ghosis of the northern Districts of the Central Provinces must in common with the bulk of the population be descended from immigrants from northern India, it would appear that they must have changed their religion, or rather abandoned one to which their ancestors had only been imperfectly proselytised, when it was no longer the dominant faith of the locality in which they lived. Sir D. Ibbetson says that in the Punjab the name Ghosi is used only for Muhammadans, and

[1] This article is based partly on a paper by Khān Bahādur Imdād Ali, Pleader, Damoh.

is often applied to any cowherd or milkman of that religion, whether Gūjar, Ahīr or of any other caste, just as Goāla is used for a Hindu cowherd. It is said that Hindus will buy pure milk from the Musalmān Ghosi, but will reject it if there is any suspicion of its having been watered by the latter, as they must not drink water at his hands.[1] But in Berār Brāhmans will now buy milk and curds from Muhammadan milkmen. Mr. Crooke remarks that most of the Ghosis are Ahīrs who have been converted to Islām. To the east of the United Provinces they claim a Gūjar origin, and here they will not eat beef themselves nor take food with any Muhammadans who consume it. They employ Brāhmans to fix the auspicious times for marriage and other ceremonies. The Ghosis of Lucknow have no other employment but the keeping of milch cattle, chiefly buffaloes of all kinds, and they breed buffaloes.[2] This is the case also in Saugor, where the Ghosis are said to rank below ordinary Ahīrs because they breed and tend buffaloes instead of cows. Those of Narsinghpur, however, are generally not herdsmen at all but ordinary cultivators. In northern India, owing to the large number of Muhammadans who, other things being equal, would prefer to buy their milk and *ghī* from co-religionists, there would be an opening for milkmen professing this faith, and on the facts stated above it may perhaps be surmised that the Ghosi caste came into existence to fill the position. Or they may have been forcibly converted as a number of Ahīrs in Berār were forcibly converted to Islam, and still call themselves Muhammadans, though they can scarcely repeat the Kalma and only go to mosque once a year.[3] But when some of the Ghosis migrated into the Central Provinces, they would find, in the absence of a Musalmān clientele, that their religion, instead of being an advantage, was a positive drawback to them, as Hindus would be reluctant to buy milk from a Muhammadan who might be suspected of having mixed it with water; and it would appear that they have relapsed naturally into Hinduism, all traces of their profession of Islām being lost. Even so, how-

[1] *Punjab Census Report* (1881), para. 272.

[2] Crooke's *Tribes and Castes*, art. Ghosi.

[3] From a note by Mr. Hīra Lāl.

ever, in Narsinghpur they have had to abandon their old calling and become ordinary cultivators, while in Saugor, perhaps on account of their doubtful status, they are restricted to keeping buffaloes. If this suggestion turned out to be well founded, it would be an interesting instance of a religion being changed to secure a professional advantage. But it can only be considered as a guess. A parallel to the disadvantage of being unable to water their milk without rendering it impure, which attaches to the Ghosis of the Punjāb, may be adduced in the case of the Telis of the small town of Multai in Betūl District. Here the dairyman's business is for some reason in the hands of Telis (oilmen) and it is stated that from every Teli who engages in it a solemn oath is exacted that he will not put water in the milk, and any violation of this would be punished by expulsion from caste. Because if the Hindus once found that they had been rendered impure by drinking water touched by so low a caste as the Telis, they would decline any longer to purchase milk from them. It is curious that the strict rule of ceremonial purity which obtains in the case of water has apparently no application to milk.

In the Central Provinces the Ghosis have two subcastes, the Havelia or those living in open wheat country, and the Birchheya or residents of jungle tracts. In Saugor they have another set of divisions borrowed from the Ahīrs, and here the Muhammadan Ghosis are said to be a separate subcaste, though practically none were returned at the census. They have the usual system of exogamous groups with territorial names derived from those of villages. At their marriages the couple walk six times round the sacred post, reserving the seventh round, if the bride is a child, to be performed subsequently when she goes to her husband. But if she is adult, the full number may be completed, the ceremony known as *lot pata* coming between the sixth and seventh rounds. In this the bride sits first on the right of her husband and then changes seats so as to be on his left; and she is thus considered to become joined to her husband as the left part of his body, which the Hindus consider the wife to be, holding the same belief as that expressed in Genesis. After this the bride takes some child of the household into her lap and then makes it over to the bridegroom saying, 'Take care of the baby while I go and do the household work.' This ceremony, which has been recorded also of the Kāpus in Chānda, is obviously designed as an auspicious omen that the marriage may be blessed with children. Like other castes of their standing, the Ghosis permit polygamy, divorce and the remarriage of widows, but the practice of taking two wives is rare. The dead are burnt, with the exception that the bodies of young children whose ears have not been pierced and of persons dying of smallpox are buried. Children usually have their ears pierced when they are three or four years old. A corpse must not be taken to the pyre at night, as it is thought that in that case it would be born blind in the next birth. The caste have bards and genealogists of their own who are known as Patia. In Damoh the Ghosis are mainly cart-drivers and cultivators and very few of them sell milk. In Nimār there are some Muhammadan Ghosis who deal in milk. Their women are not secluded and may be known by the number of little rings worn in the ear after the Muhammadan custom. Like the Ahīrs, the Ghosis are considered to be somewhat stupid. They call themselves Ghosi Thākur, as they claim to be Rājpūts, and outsiders also sometimes address them as Thākur. But in Saugor and Damoh these aspirations to Kshatriya rank are so widespread that when one person asks another his caste the usual form of the question is 'What Thākur are you?' The questioner thus politely assumes that his companion must be a Rājpūt of some sort and leaves it to him to admit or deny the soft impeachment. Another form of this question is to say 'What *dudh*, or milk, are you?'

Golar,[1] **Gollam, Golla, Gola, Golkar.**—The great shepherd caste of the Telugu country, which numbers nearly $1\frac{1}{2}$ million of persons in Madras and Hyderābād. In the Central Provinces there were under 3000 Golars in 1901, and they were returned principally from the Bālāghāt and Seoni Districts. But 2500 Golkars, who belonged to Chānda and were classified under Ahīrs in 1901, may, in view of the

1 This article is compiled from papers by Kanhya Lāl of the Gazetteer Office, and Mādho Rao, Deputy Inspector of Schools, Bālāghāt.

information now available, be considered to belong to the Golar caste. Some 2000 Golars were enumerated in Berār. They are a nomadic people and frequent Bālāghāt, owing to the large area of grazing land found in the District. The caste come from the south and speak a dialect of Canarese. Hindus liken the conversation of two Golars to two cocks crowing at each other.[1] They seem to have no subcastes except that in Chānda the Yera and Nāna, or black and white Golkars, are distinguished. Marriage is regulated by the ordinary system of exogamous groups, but no meaning can be assigned to the names of these. In Seoni they say that their group-names are the same as those of the Gonds, and that they are related to this great tribe; but though both are no doubt of the same Dravidian stock, there is no reason for supposing any closer affinity to exist, and the statement may be explained by the fact that Golars frequently reside in Gond villages in the forest; and in accordance with a practice commonly found among village communities the fiction of relationship has grown up. The children of brothers and sisters are allowed to marry, but not those of two sisters, the reason stated for this prohibition being that during the absence of the mother her sister nurses her children; the children of sisters are therefore often foster brothers and sisters, and this is considered as equivalent to the real relationship. But the marriage of a brother's son to a sister's daughter is held, as among the Gonds, to be a most suitable union. The adult marriage of girls involves no stigma, and the practice of serving for a wife is sometimes followed. Weddings may not be held during the months of Shrāwan, Bhādon, Kunwār and Pūs. The marriage altar is made of dried cowdung plastered over with mud, in honour perhaps of the animal which affords the Golars their livelihood. The clothes of the bridegroom and bride are knotted together and they walk five times round the altar. In Bhandāra the marriages of Golars are celebrated both at the bride's house and the bridegroom's. The bridegroom rides on a horse, and on arrival at the marriage-shed is presented by his future mother-in-law with a cup of milk. The bride and bridegroom sit on a platform together, and

[1] *Bālāghāt District Gazetteer* (C. E. Low), p. 80.

each gets up and sits down nine times, whoever accomplishes this first being considered to have won. The bridegroom then takes the bride's little finger in his hand and they walk nine times round the platform. He afterwards falls at the girl's feet, and standing up carries her inside the house, where they eat together out of one dish. After three days the party proceeds to the bridegroom's house, where the same ceremonies are gone through. Here the family barbers of the bride and bridegroom take the couple up in their arms and dance, holding them, and all the party dance too. The remarriage of widows is permitted, a sum of Rs. 25 being usually paid to the parents of the woman by her second husband. Divorce may be effected at the option of either party, and documents are usually drawn up on both sides. The Golars worship Mahādeo and have a special deity, Hularia, who protects their cattle from disease and wild beasts. A clay image of Hularia is erected outside the village every five or ten years and goats are offered to it. Each head of a family is supposed to offer on the first occasion two goats, and on the second and subsequent ones, five, seven, nine and twelve goats respectively. But when a man dies his son starts afresh with an offering of two. The flesh of the animals offered is consumed by the caste-fellows. The name Hularia Deo has some connection with the Holias, a low Telugu caste of leather-workers to whom the Golars appear to be related, as they have the same family names. When a Golar dies a plate of cooked rice is laid on his body and then carried to the burning-*ghāt*. The Holias belonging to the same section go with it, and before arrival the plate of rice is laid on the ground and the Holias eat it. The Golars have various superstitions, and on Saturdays, Sundays and Mondays they will not give salt, fire, milk or water to any one. They usually burn the dead, the corpse being laid with the head to the south, though in some localities the Hindu custom of placing the head to the north has been adopted. They employ Brāhmans for religious and ceremonial purposes. The occupation of the caste is to breed and tend buffaloes and cattle, and they also deal in live-stock, and sell milk, curds and *ghī*. They were formerly addicted to dacoity and cattle-theft. They have a caste *panchāyat*, the head of which is designated as *Mokāsi*. Formerly the *Mokāsi* received Rs. 15 on the marriage of a widow, and Rs. 5 when a person temporarily outcasted was readmitted to social intercourse, but these payments are now only occasionally made. The caste drink liquor and eat flesh, including pigs and fowls, but not beef. They employ Brāhmans for ceremonial purposes, but their social status is low and they are practically on a level with the Dravidian tribes. The dialect of Canarese spoken by the Golars is known as Golari, Holia or Komtau, and is closely related to the form which that language assumes in Bijāpur;[1] but to outsiders they now speak Hindī.

[1] *Linguistic Survey of India*, vol. iv. *Dravidian Language*, p. 386.

GOND

[*Bibliography*.—The most important account of the Gond tribe is that contained in the Rev. Stephen Hislop's *Papers on the Aboriginal Tribes of the Central Provinces*, published after his death by Sir R. Temple in 1866. Mr. Hislop recorded the legend of Lingo, of which an abstract has been reproduced. Other notices of the Gonds are contained in the ninth volume of General Cunningham's *Archaeological Survey Reports*, Sir C. Grant's *Central Provinces Gazetteer of* 1871 (Introduction), Colonel Ward's *Mandla Settlement Report* (1868), Colonel Lucie Smith's *Chānda Settlement Report* (1870), and Mr. C. W. Montgomerie's *Chhīndwāra Settlement Report* (1900). An excellent monograph on the Bastar Gonds was contributed by Rai Bahādur Panda Baijnāth, Superintendent of the State, and other monographs by Mr. A. E. Nelson, C.S., Mandla; Mr. Ganga Prasād Khatri, Forest Divisional Officer, Betūl; Mr. J. Langhorne, Manager, Ahiri zamindāri, Chānda; Mr. R. S. Thākur, tahsīldār, Bālāghāt; and Mr. Dīn Dayāl, Deputy Inspector of Schools, Nāndgaon State. Papers were also furnished by the Rev. A. Wood of Chānda; the Rev. H. J. Molony, Mandla; and Major W. D. Sutherland, I.M.S., Saugor. Notes were also collected by the writer in Mandla. Owing to the inclusion of many small details from the different papers it has not been possible to acknowledge them separately.]

LIST OF PARAGRAPHS

(*a*) Origin and History

(*b*) Tribal Subdivisions

(*c*) Marriage Customs

(*c*) Marriage Customs—*continued*

19. *Wedding expenditure.*
20. *Special customs.*
21. *Taking omens.*
22. *Marriage by capture. Weeping and hiding.*
23. *Serving for a wife.*
24. *Widow remarriage.*
25. *Divorce.*
26. *Polygamy.*

(*d*) Birth and Pregnancy

27. *Menstruation.*
28. *Superstitions about pregnancy and childbirth.*
29. *Procedure at a birth.*
30. *Names.*
31. *Superstitions about children.*

(*e*) Funeral Rites

32. *Disposal of the dead.*
33. *Funeral ceremony.*
34. *Mourning and offerings to the dead.*
35. *Memorial stones to the dead.*
36. *House abandoned after a death.*
37. *Bringing back the soul.*
38. *The dead absorbed in Bura Deo.*
39. *Belief in a future life.*

(*f*) Religion

40. *Nature of the Gond religion. The gods.*
41. *Tribal gods, and their place of residence.*
42. *Household gods.*
43. *Nāg Deo.*
44. *Nārāyan Deo.*
45. *Bura Deo.*
46. *Charms and magic.*
47. *Omens.*
48. *Agricultural superstitions.*
49. *Magical or religious observances in fishing and hunting.*
50. *Witchcraft.*
51. *Human sacrifice.*
52. *Cannibalism.*
53. *Festivals. The new crops.*
54. *The Holi Festival.*
55. *The Meghnāth swinging rite.*
56. *The Karma and other rites.*

(*g*) Appearance and Character and Social Rules and Customs

57. *Physical type.*
58. *Character.*
59. *Shyness and ignorance.*
60. *Villages and houses.*
61. *Clothes and ornaments.*
62. *Ear-piercing.*
63. *Hair.*
64. *Bathing and washing clothes.*
65. *Tattooing.*
66. *Special system of tattooing.*
67. *Branding.*
68. *Food.*
69. *Liquor.*
70. *Admission of outsiders and sexual morality.*
71. *Common sleeping-houses.*
72. *Methods of greeting and observances between relatives.*
73. *The caste panchāyat and social offences.*
74. *Caste penalty feasts.*
75. *Special purification ceremony.*
76. *Dancing.*
77. *Songs.*
78. *Language.*

(*h*) Occupation

79. *Cultivation.*
80. *Patch cultivation.*
81. *Hunting. Traps for animals.*

(*a*) Origin and History

Gond.—The principal tribe of the Dravidian family, and perhaps the most important of the non-Aryan or forest tribes in India. In 1911 the Gonds were three million strong, and they are increasing rapidly. The Kolis of western India count half a million persons more than the Gonds, and if the four related tribes Kol, Munda, Ho, and Santāl were taken together, they would be stronger by about the same amount. But if historical importance be considered as well as numbers, the first place should be awarded to the Gonds. Of the whole caste the Central Provinces contain 2,300,000 persons, Central India, and Bihār and Orissa about 235,000 persons each, and they are returned in small numbers from Assam, Madras and Hyderābād. The 50,000 Gonds in Assam are no doubt immigrant labourers on the tea-gardens. **1. Numbers and distribution.**

In the Central Provinces the Gonds occupy two main tracts. The first is the wide belt of broken hill and forest country in the centre of the Province, which forms the Satpūra plateau, and is mainly comprised in the Chhindwārā, Betūl, Seoni and Mandla Districts, with portions of several others adjoining them. And the second is the still wider and more inaccessible mass of hill ranges extending south of the Chhattīsgarh plain, and south-west down to the Godāvari, which includes portions of the three Chhattīsgarh Districts, the Bastar and Kanker States, and a great part of Chānda. In Mandla the Gonds form nearly half the population, and in Bastar about two-thirds. There is, however, no District or State of the Province which does not contain some Gonds, and it is both on account of their numbers and the fact that Gond dynasties possessed a great part of its area that the territory of the Central Provinces was formerly known as Gondwāna, or the country of the Gonds.[1] The existing importance of the Central Provinces dates from recent years, for so late as 1853 it was stated before the Royal Asiatic Society that "at present the Gondwāna high- **2. Gondwāna.**

[1] The country of Gondwāna properly included the Satpūra plateau and a section of the Nāgpur plain and Nerbudda valley to the south and west.

lands and jungles comprise such a large tract of unexplored country that they form quite an oasis in our maps." So much of this lately unexplored country as is British territory is now fairly well served by railways, traversed almost throughout by good roads, and provided with village schools at distances of five to ten miles apart, even in the wilder tracts.

3. Derivation of name and origin of the Gonds.

The derivation of the word Gond is uncertain. It is the name given to the tribe by the Hindus or Muhammadans, as their own name for themselves is Koitūr or Koi. General Cunningham considered that the name Gond probably came from Gauda, the classical term for part of the United Provinces and Bengal. A Benāres inscription relating to one of the Chedi kings of Tripura or Tewar (near Jubbulpore) states that he was of the Haihaya tribe, who lived on the borders of the Nerbudda in the district of the Western Gauda in the Province of Mālwa. Three or four other inscriptions also refer to the kings of Gauda in the same locality. Gauda, however, was properly and commonly used as the name of part of Bengal. There is no evidence beyond a few doubtful inscriptions of its having ever been applied to any part of the Central Provinces. The principal passage in which General Cunningham identifies Gauda with the Central Provinces is that in which the king of Gauda came to the assistance of the ruler of Mālwa against the king of Kanauj, elder brother of the great Harsha Vardhana, and slew the latter king in A.D. 605. But Mr. V. A. Smith holds that Gauda in this passage refers to Bengal and not to the Central Provinces;[1] and General Cunningham's argument on the locality of Gauda is thus rendered extremely dubious, and with it his derivation of the name Gond. In fact it seems highly improbable that the name of a large tribe should have been taken from a term so little used and known in this special application. Though in the *Imperial Gazetteer*[2] the present writer reproduced General Cunningham's derivation of the term Gond, it was there characterised as speculative, and in the light of the above remarks now seems highly improbable. Mr. Hislop considered that the name Gond was a form of Kond, as he spelt the name of

[1] *Early History of India*, 3rd ed. p. 337.

[2] Art. Gondwāna.

Bemrose, Collo., Derby.

GOND WOMEN GRINDING CORN.

the Khond tribe. He pointed out that *k* and *g* are interchangeable. Thus Gotalghar, the empty house where the village young men sleep, comes from Kotal, a led horse, and *ghar*, a house. Similarly, Koikopāl, the name of a Gond subtribe who tend cattle, is from Koi or Gond, and *gopal*, a cowherd. The name by which the Gonds call themselves is Koi or Koitūr, while the Khonds call themselves Ku, which word Sir G. Grierson considers to be probably related to the Gond name Koi. Further, he states that the Telugu people call the Khonds, Gond or Kod (Kor). General Cunningham points out that the word Gond in the Central Provinces is frequently or, he says, usually pronounced Gaur, which is practically the same sound as *god*, and with the change of *G* to *K* would become Kod. Thus the two names Gond and Kod, by which the Telugu people know the Khonds, are practically the same as the names Gond and God of the Gonds in the Central Provinces, though Sir G. Grierson does not mention the change of *g* to *k* in his account of either language. It seems highly probable that the designation Gond was given to the tribe by the Telugus. The Gonds speak a Dravidian language of the same family as Tamil, Canarese and Telugu, and therefore it is likely that they come from the south into the Central Provinces. Their route may have been up the Godavāri river into Chānda; from thence up the Indravati into Bastar and the hills south and east of the Chhattīsgarh plain; and up the Wardha and Wainganga to the Districts of the Satpūra Plateau. In Chānda, where a Gond dynasty reigned for some centuries, they would be in contact with the Telugus, and here they may have got their name of Gond, and carried it with them into the north and east of the Province. As already seen, the Khonds are called Gond by the Telugus, and Kandh by the Uriyas. The Khonds apparently came up more towards the east into Ganjam and Kālāhandi. Here the name of Gond or Kod, given them by the Telugus, may have been modified into Kandh by the Uriyas, and from the two names came the English corruption of Khond. The Khond and Gondi languages are now dissimilar. Still they present certain points of resemblance, and though Sir G. Grierson does not discuss their connection, it appears from his highly interesting genealogical tree of the Dravidian languages that Khond or Kui and Gondi are closely connected. These two languages, and no others, occupy an intermediate position between the two great branches sprung from the original Dravidian language, one of which is mainly represented by Telugu and the other by Tamil, Canarese and Malayālam.[1] Gondi and Khond are shown in the centre as the connecting link between the two great branches. Gondi is more nearly related to Tamil and Khond to Telugu. On the Telugu side, moreover, Khond approaches most closely to Kolāmi, which is a member of the Telugu branch. The Kolāms are a tribe of Wardha and Berār, sometimes considered an offshoot of the Gonds; at any rate, it seems probable that they came from southern India by the same route as the Gonds. Thus the Khond language is intermediate between Gondi and the Kolāmi dialect of Wardha and Berār, though the Kolāms live west of the Gonds and the Khonds east. And a fairly close relationship between the three languages appears to be established. Hence the linguistic evidence appears to afford strong support to the view that the Khonds and Gonds may originally have been one tribe. Further, Mr. Hislop points out that a word for god, *pen*, is common to the Gonds and Khonds; and the Khonds have a god called Bura Pen, who might be the same as Bura Deo, the great god of the Gonds. Mr. Hislop found Kodo Pen and Pharsi Pen as Gond gods,[2] while Pen or Pennu is the regular word for god among the Khonds. This evidence seems to establish a probability that the Gonds and Khonds were originally one tribe in the south of India, and that they obtained separate names and languages since they left their original home for the north. The fact that both of them speak languages of the Dravidian family, whose home is in southern India, makes it probable that the two tribes originally belonged there, and migrated north into the Central Provinces and Orissa. This hypothesis is supported by the traditions of the Gonds.

4. History of the Gonds.

As stated in the article on Kol, it is known that Rājpūt dynasties were ruling in various parts of the Central Provinces

[1] *Linguistic Survey, Munda and Dravidian Languages*, iv. p. 285.
[2] *Notes*, p. 15.

from about the sixth to the twelfth centuries. They then disappear, and there is a blank till the fourteenth century or later, when Gond kingdoms are found established at Kherla in Betūl, at Deogarh in Chhīndwara, at Garha-Mandla,[1] including the Jubbulpore country, and at Chānda, fourteen miles from Bhāndak. It seems clear, then, that the Hindu dynasties were subverted by the Gonds after the Muhammadan invasions of northern India had weakened or destroyed the central powers of the Hindus, and prevented any assistance being afforded to the outlying settlements. There is some reason to suppose that the immigration of the Gonds into the Central Provinces took place after the establishment of these Hindu kingdoms, and not before, as is commonly held.[2] But the point must at present be considered doubtful. There is no reason however to doubt that the Gonds came from the south through Chānda and Bastar. During the fourteenth century and afterwards the Gonds established dynasties at the places already mentioned in the Central Provinces. For two or three centuries the greater part of the Province was governed by Gond kings. Of their method of government in Narsinghpur, Sleeman said: "Under these Gond Rājas the country seems for the most part to have been distributed among feudatory chiefs, bound to attend upon the prince at his capital with a stipulated number of troops, to be employed wherever their services might be required, but to furnish little or no revenue in money. These chiefs were Gonds, and the countries they held for the support of their families and the payment of their troops and retinue little more than wild jungles. The Gonds seem not to have been at home in open country, and as from the sixteenth century a peaceable penetration of Hindu cultivators into the best lands of the Province assumed large dimensions, the Gonds gradually retired to the hill ranges on the borders of the plains." The headquarters of each dynasty at Mandla, Garha, Kherla, Deogarh and Chānda seem to have been located in a position strengthened for defence either by a hill or a great river, and adjacent to an especially fertile plain tract, whose

[1] Garha is six miles from Jubbulpore.

[2] See article on Kol.

produce served for the maintenance of the ruler's household and headquarters establishment. Often the site was on other sides bordered by dense forest which would afford a retreat to the occupants in case it fell to an enemy. Strong and spacious forts were built, with masonry tanks and wells inside them to provide water, but whether these buildings were solely the work of the Gonds or constructed with the assistance of Hindu or Muhammadan artificers is uncertain. But the Hindu immigrants found Gond government tolerant and beneficent. Under the easy eventless sway of these princes the rich country over which they ruled prospered, its flocks and herds increased, and the treasury filled. So far back as the fifteenth century we read in Firishta that the king of Kherla, who, if not a Gond himself, was a king of the Gonds, sumptuously entertained the Bāhmani king and made him rich offerings, among which were many diamonds, rubies and pearls. Of the Rāni Dūrgavati of Garha-Mandla, Sleeman said: "Of all the sovereigns of this dynasty she lives most in the page of history and in the grateful recollections of the people. She built the great reservoir which lies close to Jubbulpore, and is called after her Rāni Talao or Queen's pond; and many other highly useful works were formed by her about Garha." When the castle of Chaurāgarh was sacked by one of Akbar's generals in 1564, the booty found, according to Firishta, comprised, independently of jewels, images of gold and silver and other valuables, no fewer than a hundred jars of gold coin and a thousand elephants. Of the Chānda rulers the Settlement officer who has recorded their history wrote that, "They left, if we forget the last few years, a well-governed and contented kingdom, adorned with admirable works of engineering skill and prosperous to a point which no aftertime has reached. They have left their mark behind them in royal tombs, lakes and palaces, but most of all in the seven miles of battlemented stone wall, too wide now for the shrunk city of Chānda within it, which stands on the very border-line between the forest and the plain, having in front the rich valley of the Wardha river, and behind and up to the city walls deep forest extending to the east." According to local tradition the great wall of Chānda and other buildings,

Bemrose, Collo., Derby.

PALACE OF THE GOND KINGS OF GARHA-MANDLA AT RĀMNAGAR.

such as the tombs of the Gond kings and the palace at Junona, were built by immigrant Telugu masons of the Kāpu or Munurwār castes. Another excellent rule of the Gond kings was to give to any one who made a tank a grant of land free of revenue of the land lying beneath it. A large number of small irrigation tanks were constructed under this inducement in the Wainganga valley, and still remain. But the Gond states had no strength for defence, as was shown when in the eighteenth century Marātha chiefs, having acquired some knowledge of the art of war and military training by their long fighting against the Mughals, cast covetous eyes on Gondwāna. The loose tribal system, so easy in time of peace, entirely failed to knit together the strength of the people when united action was most required, and the plain country fell before the Marātha armies almost without a struggle. In the strongholds, however, of the hilly ranges which hem in every part of Gondwāna the chiefs for long continued to maintain an unequal resistance, and to revenge their own wrongs by indiscriminate rapine and slaughter. In such cases the Marātha plan was to continue pillaging and harassing the Gonds until they obtained an acknowledgment of their supremacy and the promise, at least, of an annual tribute. Under this treatment the hill Gonds soon lost every vestige of civilisation, and became the cruel, treacherous savages depicted by travellers of this period. They regularly plundered and murdered stragglers and small parties passing through the hills, while from their strongholds, built on the most inaccessible spurs of the Satpūras, they would make a dash into the rich plains of Berār and the Nerbudda valley, and after looting and killing all night, return straight across country to their jungle fortresses, guided by the light of a bonfire on some commanding peak.[1] With the pacification of the country and the introduction of a strong and equable system of government by the British, these wild marauders soon settled down and became the timid and inoffensive labourers which they now are.

5. Mythical traditions. Story of Lingo.

Mr. Hislop took down from a Pardhān priest a Gond myth of the creation of the world and the origin of the

[1] Mr. Standen's *Betūl Settlement Report.*

Gonds, and their liberation from a cave, in which they had been shut up by Siva, through the divine hero Lingo. General Cunningham said that the exact position of the cave was not known, but it would seem to have been somewhere in the Himalayas, as the name Dhawalgiri, which means a white mountain, is mentioned. The cave, according to ordinary Gond tradition, was situated in Kachikopa Lohāgarh or the Iron Valley in the Red Hill. It seems clear from the story itself that its author was desirous of connecting the Gonds with Hindu mythology, and as Siva's heaven is in the Himalayas, the name Dhawalgiri, where he located the cave, may refer to them. It is also said that the cave was at the source of the Jumna. But in Mr. Hislop's version the cave where all the Gonds except four were shut up is not in Kachikopa Lohāgarh, as the Gonds commonly say; but only the four Gonds who escaped wandered to this latter place and dwelt there. And the story does not show that Kachikopa Lohāgarh was on Mount Dhawalgiri or the Himalayas, where it places the cave in which the Gonds were shut up, or anywhere near them. On the contrary, it would be quite consonant with Mr. Hislop's version if Kachikopa Lohāgarh were in the Central Provinces. It may be surmised that in the original Gond legend their ancestors really were shut up in Kachikopa Lohāgarh, but not by the god Siva. Very possibly the story began with them in the cave in the Iron Valley in the Red Hill. But the Hindu who clearly composed Mr. Hislop's version wished to introduce the god Siva as a principal actor, and he therefore removed the site of the cave to the Himalayas. This appears probable from the story itself, in which, in its present form, Kachikopa Lohāgarh plays no real part, and only appears because it was in the original tradition and has to be retained.[1] But the Gonds think that their ancestors were actually shut up in Kachikopa Lohāgarh, and one tradition puts the site at Pachmarhi, whose striking hill scenery and red soil cleft by many deep and inaccessible ravines would render it a likely place for the incident. Another version locates Kachikopa Lohāgarh at Dārekasa

[1] The argument in this section will be followed more easily if read after the legend in the following paragraphs.

in Bhandāra, where there is a place known as Kachagarh or the iron fort. But Pachmarhi is perhaps the more probable, as it has some deep caves, which have always been looked upon as sacred places. The point is of some interest, because this legend of the cave being in the Himalayas is adduced as a Gond tradition that their ancestors came from the north, and hence as supporting the theory of the immigration of the Dravidians through the north-west of India. But if the view now suggested is correct, the story of the cave being in the Himalayas is not a genuine Gond tradition at all, but a Hindu interpolation. The only other ground known to the writer for asserting that the Gonds believed their ancestors to have come from the north is that they bury their dead with the feet to the north. There are other obvious Hindu accretions in the legend, as the saintly Brāhmanic character of Lingo and his overcoming the gods through fasting and self-torture, and also the fact that Siva shut up the Gonds in the cave because he was offended by their dirty habits and bad smell. But the legend still contains a considerable quantity of true Gond tradition, and though somewhat tedious, it seems necessary to give an abridgment of Mr. Hislop's account, with reproduction of selected passages. Captain Forsyth also made a modernised poetical version,[1] from which one extract is taken. Certain variations from another form of the legend obtained in Bastar are included.

6. Legend of the creation.

In the beginning there was water everywhere, and God was born in a lotus-leaf and lived alone. One day he rubbed his arm and from the rubbing made a crow, which sat on his shoulder; he also made a crab, which swam out over the waters. God then ordered the crow to fly over the world and bring some earth. The crow flew about and could find no earth, but it saw the crab, which was supporting itself with one leg resting on the bottom of the sea. The crow was very tired and perched on the crab's back, which was soft so that the crow's feet made marks on it, which are still visible on the bodies of all crabs at present. The crow asked the crab where any earth could be found. The crab said that if God would make its body hard it would find

[1] *Highlands of Central India* (Chapman & Hall).

some earth. God said he would make part of the crab's body hard, and he made its back hard, as it still remains. The crab then dived to the bottom of the sea, where it found Kenchna, the earth-worm. It caught hold of Kenchna by the neck with its claws and the mark thus made is still to be seen on the earth-worm's neck. Then the earth-worm brought up earth out of its mouth and the crab brought this to God, and God scattered it over the sea and patches of land appeared. God then walked over the earth and a boil came on his hand, and out of it Mahādeo and Pārvati were born.

7. Creation of the Gonds and their imprisonment by Mahādeo.

From Mahādeo's urine numerous vegetables began to spring up. Pārvati ate of these and became pregnant and gave birth to eighteen threshing-floors[1] of Brāhman gods and twelve threshing-floors of Gond gods. All the Gonds were scattered over the jungle. They behaved like Gonds and not like good Hindus, with lamentable results, as follows:[2]

Hither and thither all the Gonds were scattered in the jungle.
Places, hills, and valleys were filled with these Gonds.
Even trees had their Gonds. How did the Gonds conduct themselves?
Whatever came across them they must needs kill and eat it;
They made no distinction. If they saw a jackal they killed
And ate it; no distinction was observed; they respected not antelope, sambhar and the like.
They made no distinction in eating a sow, a quail, a pigeon,
A crow, a kite, an adjutant, a vulture,
A lizard, a frog, a beetle, a cow, a calf, a he- and she-buffalo,
Rats, bandicoots, squirrels—all these they killed and ate.
So began the Gonds to do. They devoured raw and ripe things;
They did not bathe for six months together;
They did not wash their faces properly, even on dunghills they would fall down and remain.
Such were the Gonds born in the beginning. A smell was spread over the jungle
When the Gonds were thus disorderly behaved; they became disagreeable to Mahādeva,
Who said: "The caste of the Gonds is very bad;
I will not preserve them; they will ruin my hill Dhawalgiri."

Mahādeo then determined to get rid of the Gonds. With this view he invited them all to a meeting. When they sat

[1] *Deo-khulla* or threshing-floor of the gods. See section on Religion.
[2] Passage from Mr. Hislop's version.

down Mahādeo made a squirrel from the rubbings of his body and let it loose in the middle of the Gonds. All the Gonds at once got up and began to chase it, hoping for a meal. They seized sticks and stones and clods of earth, and their unkempt hair flew in the wind. The squirrel dodged about and ran away, and finally, directed by Mahādeo, ran into a large cave with all the Gonds after it. Mahādeo then rolled a large stone to the mouth of the cave and shut up all the Gonds in it. Only four remained outside, and they fled away to Kachikopa Lohāgarh, or the Iron Cave in the Red Hill, and lived there. Meanwhile Pārvati perceived that the smell of the Gonds, which had pleased her, had vanished from Dhawalgiri. She desired it to be restored and commenced a devotion. For six months she fasted and practised austerities. Bhagwān (God) was swinging in a swing. He was disturbed by Pārvati's devotion. He sent Nārāyan (the sun) to see who was fasting. Nārāyan came and found Pārvati and asked her what she wanted. She said that she missed her Gonds and wanted them back. Nārāyan told Bhagwān, who promised that they should be given back.

8. The birth and history of Lingo.

The yellow flowers of the tree Pahindi were growing on Dhawalgiri. Bhagwān sent thunder and lightning, and the flower conceived. First fell from it a heap of turmeric or saffron. In the morning the sun came out, the flower burst open, and Lingo was born. Lingo was a perfect child. He had a diamond on his navel and a sandalwood mark on his forehead. He fell from the flower into the heap of turmeric. He played in the turmeric and slept in a swing. He became nine years old. He said there was no one there like him, and he would go where he could find his fellows. He climbed a needle-like hill,[1] and from afar off he saw Kachikopa Lohāgarh and the four Gonds. He came to them. They saw he was like them, and asked him to be their brother. They ate only animals. Lingo asked them to find for him an animal without a liver, and they searched all through the forest and could not. Then Lingo told them to cut down trees and make a field. They tried to cut down the *anjan*[2] trees, but their hands were blistered

[1] Dhūpgarh in Pachmarhi might be indicated, which has a steep summit.

[2] *Terminalia arjuna.*

and they could not go on. Lingo had been asleep. He woke up and saw they had only cut down one or two trees. He took the axe and cut down many trees, and fenced a field and made a gate to it. Black soil appeared. It began to rain, and rained without ceasing for three days. All the rivers and streams were filled. The field became green with rice, and it grew up. There were sixteen score of *nīlgai* or blue-bull. They had two leaders, an old bull and his nephew. The young bull saw the rice of Lingo's field and wished to eat it. The uncle told him not to eat of the field of Lingo or all the *nīlgai* would be killed. But the young bull did not heed, and took off all the *nīlgai* to eat the rice. When they got to the field they could find no entrance, so they jumped the fence, which was five cubits high. They ate all the rice from off the field and ran away. The young bull told them as they ran to put their feet on leaves and stones and boughs and grass, and not on the ground, so that they might not be tracked. Lingo woke up and went to see his field, and found all the rice eaten. He knew the *nīlgai* had done it, and showed the brothers how to track them by the few marks which they had by accident made on the ground. They did so, and surrounded the *nīlgai* and killed them all with their bows and arrows except the old uncle, from whom Lingo's arrow rebounded harmlessly on account of his innocence, and one young doe. From these two the *nilgai* race was preserved. Then Lingo told the Gonds to make fire and roast the deer as follows:

He said, I will show you something; see if anywhere in your
Waistbands there is a flint; if so, take it out and make fire.
But the matches did not ignite. As they were doing this, a watch of the night passed.
They threw down the matches, and said to Lingo, Thou art a Saint;
Show us where our fire is, and why it does not come out.
Lingo said: Three koss (six miles) hence is Rikad Gawādi the giant.
There is fire in his field; where smoke shall appear, go there,
Come not back without bringing fire. Thus said Lingo.
They said, We have never seen the place, where shall we go?
Ye have never seen where this fire is? Lingo said;
I will discharge an arrow thither.
Go in the direction of the arrow; there you will get fire.
He applied the arrow, and having pulled the bow, he discharged one:
It crashed on, breaking twigs and making its passage clear.

Having cut through the high grass, it made its way and reached the old man's place (above mentioned).
The arrow dropped close to the fire of the old man, who had daughters.
The arrow was near the door. As soon as they saw it, the daughters came and took it up,
And kept it. They asked their father: When will you give us in marriage?
Thus said the seven sisters, the daughters of the old man.
I will marry you as I think best for you;
Remain as you are. So said the old man, the Rikad Gawādi.
Lingo said, Hear, O brethren! I shot an arrow, it made its way.
Go there, and you will see fire; bring thence the fire.
Each said to the other, I will not go; but (at last) the youngest went.
He descried the fire, and went to it; then beheld he an old man looking like the trunk of a tree.
He saw from afar the old man's field, around which a hedge was made.
The old man kept only one way to it, and fastened a screen to the entrance, and had a fire in the centre of the field.
He placed logs of the Mahua and Anjun and Sāj trees on the fire,
Teak faggots he gathered, and enkindled flame.
The fire blazed up, and warmed by the heat of it, in deep sleep lay the Rikad Gawādi.
Thus the old man like a giant did appear. When the young Gond beheld him, he shivered;
His heart leaped; and he was much afraid in his mind, and said:
If the old man were to rise he will see me, and I shall be eaten up;
I will steal away the fire and carry it off, then my life will be safe.
He went near the fire secretly, and took a brand of *tendu* wood tree.
When he was lifting it up a spark flew and fell on the hip of the old man.
That spark was as large as a pot; the giant was blistered; he awoke alarmed.
And said: I am hungry, and I cannot get food to eat anywhere; I feel a desire for flesh;
Like a tender cucumber hast thou come to me. So said the old man to the Gond,
Who began to fly. The old man followed him. The Gond then threw away the brand which he had stolen.
He ran onward, and was not caught. Then the old man, being tired, turned back.
Thence he returned to his field, and came near the fire and sat, and said, What nonsense is this?
A tender prey had come within my reach;
I said I will cut it up as soon as I can, but it escaped from my hand!
Let it go; it will come again, then I will catch it. It has gone now.
Then what happened? the Gond returned and came to his brethren.
And said to them: Hear, O brethren, I went for fire, as you sent me, to that field; I beheld an old man like a giant.
With hands stretched out and feet lifted up. I ran. I thus survived with difficulty.

The brethren said to Lingo, We will not go. Lingo said, Sit ye here.
O brethren, what sort of a person is this giant? I will go and see him.
So saying, Lingo went away and reached a river.
He thence arose and went onward. As he looked, he saw in front three gourds.
Then he saw a bamboo stick, which he took up.
When the river was flooded
It washed away a gourd tree, and its seed fell, and each stem produced bottle-gourds.
He inserted a bamboo stick in the hollow of the gourd and made a guitar.
He plucked two hairs from his head and strung it.
He held a bow and fixed eleven keys to that one stick, and played on it.
Lingo was much pleased in his mind.
Holding it in his hand, he walked in the direction of the old man's field.
He approached the fire where Rikad Gawādi was sleeping.
The giant seemed like a log lying close to the fire; his teeth were hideously visible;
His mouth was gaping. Lingo looked at the old man while sleeping.
His eyes were shut. Lingo said, This is not a good time to carry off the old man while he is asleep.
In front he looked, and turned round and saw a tree
Of the pīpal sort standing erect; he beheld its branches with wonder, and looked for a fit place to mount upon.
It appeared a very good tree; so he climbed it, and ascended to the top of it to sit.
As he sat the cock crew. Lingo said, It is daybreak;
Meanwhile the old man must be rising. Therefore Lingo took the guitar in his hand,
And held it; he gave a stroke, and it sounded well; from it he drew one hundred tunes.
It sounded well, as if he was singing with his voice.
Thus (as it were) a song was heard.
Trees and hills were silent at its sound. The music loudly entered into
The old man's ears; he rose in haste, and sat up quickly; lifted up his eyes,
And desired to hear (more). He looked hither and thither, but could not make out whence the sound came.
The old man said: Whence has a creature come here to-day to sing like the maina bird?
He saw a tree, but nothing appeared to him as he looked underneath it.
He did not look up; he looked at the thickets and ravines, but
Saw nothing. He came to the road, and near to the fire in the midst of his field and stood.
Sometimes sitting, and sometimes standing, jumping, and rolling, he began to dance.
The music sounded as the day dawned. His old woman came out in the morning and began to look out.
She heard in the direction of the field a melodious music playing.
When she arrived near the edge of her field, she heard music in her ears.
That old woman called her husband to her.

With stretched hands, and lifted feet, and with his neck bent down, he danced.
Thus he danced. The old woman looked towards her husband, and said, My old man, my husband,
Surely, that music is very melodious. I will dance, said the old woman.
Having made the fold of her dress loose, she quickly began to dance near the hedge.

Then Lingo disclosed himself to the giant and became friendly with him. The giant apologised for having tried to eat his brother, and called Lingo his nephew. Lingo invited him to come and feast on the flesh of the sixteen scores of *nīlgai.* The giant called his seven daughters and offered them all to Lingo in marriage. The daughters produced the arrow which they had treasured up as portending a husband. Lingo said he was not marrying himself, but he would take them home as wives for his brothers. So they all went back to the cave and Lingo assigned two of the daughters each to the three elder brothers and one to the youngest. Then the brothers, to show their gratitude, said that they would go and hunt in the forest and bring meat and fruit and Lingo should lie in a swing and be rocked by their seven wives. But while the wives were swinging Lingo and his eyes were shut, they wished to sport with him as their husbands' younger brother. So saying they pulled his hands and feet till he woke up. Then he reproached them and called them his mothers and sisters, but they cared nothing and began to embrace him. Then Lingo was filled with wrath and leapt up, and seeing a rice-pestle near he seized it and beat them all with it soundly. Then the women went to their houses and wept and resolved to be revenged on Lingo. So when the brothers came home they told their husbands that while they were swinging Lingo he had tried to seduce them all from their virtue, and they were resolved to go home and stay no longer in Kachikopa with such a man about the place. Then the brothers were exceedingly angry with Lingo, who they thought had deceived them with a pretence of virtue in refusing a wife, and they resolved to kill him. So they enticed him into the forest with a story of a great animal which had put them to flight and asked him to kill it, and there they shot him to death with their arrows and gouged out his eyes and played ball with them.

9. Death and resurrection of Lingo.

But the god Bhagwān became aware that Lingo was not praying to him as usual, and sent the crow Kageshwar to look for him. The crow came and reported that Lingo was dead, and the god sent him back with nectar to sprinkle it over the body and bring it to life again, which was done.

Lingo then thought he had had enough of the four brothers, so he determined to go and find the other sixteen score Gonds who were imprisoned somewhere as the brothers had told him. The manner of his doing this may be told in Captain Forsyth's version:[1]

10. He releases the Gonds shut up in the cave and constitutes the tribe.

And our Lingo redivivus
Wandered on across the mountains,
Wandered sadly through the forest
Till the darkening of the evening,
Wandered on until the night fell.
Screamed the panther in the forest,
Growled the bear upon the mountain,
And our Lingo then bethought him
Of their cannibal propensities.
Saw at hand the tree Niruda,
Clambered up into its branches.
Darkness fell upon the forest,
Bears their heads wagged, yelled the jackal
Kolyal, the King of Jackals.
Sounded loud their dreadful voices
In the forest-shade primeval.
Then the Jungle-Cock Gugotee,
Mull the Peacock, Kurs the Wild Deer,
Terror-stricken, screeched and shuddered,
In that forest-shade primeval.
But the moon arose at midnight,
Poured her flood of silver radiance,
Lighted all the forest arches,
Through their gloomy branches slanting;
Fell on Lingo, pondering deeply
On his sixteen scores of Koitūrs.
Then thought Lingo, I will ask her
For my sixteen scores of Koitūrs.
'Tell me, O Moon!' said Lingo,
'Tell, O Brightener of the darkness!
Where my sixteen scores are hidden.'
But the Moon sailed onwards, upwards,
And her cold and glancing moonbeams
Said, 'Your Gonds, I have not seen them.'

[1] This extract is reproduced by permission of the publishers, Messrs. Chapman & Hall, London.

And the Stars came forth and twinkled
Twinkling eyes above the forest.
Lingo said, "O Stars that twinkle!
Eyes that look into the darkness,
Tell me where my sixteen scores are."
But the cold Stars twinkling ever,
Said, 'Your Gonds, we have not seen them.'
Broke the morning, the sky reddened,
Faded out the star of morning,
Rose the Sun above the forest,
Brilliant Sun, the Lord of morning,
And our Lingo quick descended,
Quickly ran he to the eastward,
Fell before the Lord of Morning,
Gave the Great Sun salutation—
'Tell, O Sun!' he said, 'Discover
Where my sixteen scores of Gonds are.'
But the Lord of Day reply made—
"Hear, O Lingo, I a Pilgrim
Wander onwards, through four watches
Serving God, I have seen nothing
Of your sixteen scores of Koitūrs."
Then our Lingo wandered onwards
Through the arches of the forest;
Wandered on until before him
Saw the grotto of a hermit,
Old and sage, the Black Kumāit,
He the very wise and knowing,
He the greatest of Magicians,
Born in days that are forgotten,
In the unremembered ages,
Salutation gave and asked him—
'Tell, O Hermit! Great Kumāit!
Where my sixteen scores of Gonds are.
Then replied the Black Magician,
Spake disdainfully in this wise—
"Lingo, hear, your Gonds are asses
Eating cats, and mice, and bandicoots,
Eating pigs, and cows, and buffaloes;
Filthy wretches! wherefore ask me?
If you wish it I will tell you.
Our great Mahādeva caught them,
And has shut them up securely
In a cave within the bowels
Of his mountain Dewalgiri,
With a stone of sixteen cubits,
And his bulldog fierce Basmāsur;
Serve them right, too, I consider,
Filthy, casteless, stinking wretches!"
And the Hermit to his grotto

Back returned, and deeply pondered
On the days that are forgotten,
On the unremembered ages.
But our Lingo wandered onwards,
Fasting, praying, doing penance;
Laid him on a bed of prickles,
Thorns long and sharp and piercing.
Fasting lay he devotee-like,
Hand not lifting, foot not lifting,
Eye not opening, nothing seeing.
Twelve months long thus lay and fasted,
Till his flesh was dry and withered,
And the bones began to show through.
Then the great god Mahādeva
Felt his seat begin to tremble,
Felt his golden stool, all shaking
From the penance of our Lingo.
Felt, and wondered who on earth
This devotee was that was fasting
Till his golden stool was shaking.
Stepped he down from Dewalgiri,
Came and saw that bed of prickles
Where our Lingo lay unmoving.
Asked him what his little game was,
Why his golden stool was shaking.
Answered Lingo, "Mighty Ruler!
Nothing less will stop that shaking
Than my sixteen scores of Koitūrs
Rendered up all safe and hurtless
From your cave in Dewalgiri."
Then the Great God, much disgusted,
Offered all he had to Lingo,
Offered kingdom, name, and riches,
Offered anything he wished for,
'Only leave your stinking Koitūrs
Well shut up in Dewalgiri.'
But our Lingo all refusing
Would have nothing but his Koitūrs;
Gave a turn to run the thorns a
Little deeper in his midriff.
Winced the Great God: "Very well, then,
Take your Gonds—but first a favour.
By the shore of the Black Water
Lives a bird they call Black Bindo,
Much I wish to see his young ones,
Little Bindos from the sea-shore;
For an offering bring these Bindos,
Then your Gonds take from my mountain."
Then our Lingo rose and wandered,
Wandered onwards through the forest,

Till he reached the sounding sea-shore,
Reached the brink of the Black Water,
Found the Bingo birds were absent
From their nest upon the sea-shore,
Absent hunting in the forest,
Hunting elephants prodigious,
Which they killed and took their brains out,
Cracked their skulls, and brought their brains to
Feed their callow little Bindos,
Wailing sadly by the sea-shore.
Seven times a fearful serpent,
Bhawarnāg the horrid serpent,
Serpent born in ocean's caverns,
Coming forth from the Black Water,
Had devoured the little Bindos—
Broods of callow little Bindos
Wailing sadly by the sea-shore—
In the absence of their parents.
Eighth this brood was. Stood our Lingo,
Stood he pondering beside them—
"If I take these little wretches
In the absence of their parents
They will call me thief and robber.
No! I'll wait till they come back here."
Then he laid him down and slumbered
By the little wailing Bindos.
As he slept the dreadful serpent,
Rising, came from the Black Water,
Came to eat the callow Bindos,
In the absence of their parents.
Came he trunk-like from the waters,
Came with fearful jaws distended,
Huge and horrid, like a basket
For the winnowing of corn.
Rose a hood of vast dimensions
O'er his fierce and dreadful visage.
Shrieked the Bindos young and callow,
Gave a cry of lamentation;
Rose our Lingo; saw the monster;
Drew an arrow from his quiver,
Shot it swift into his stomach,
Sharp and cutting in the stomach,
Then another and another;
Cleft him into seven pieces,
Wriggled all the seven pieces,
Wriggled backward to the water.
But our Lingo, swift advancing,
Seized the headpiece in his arms,
Knocked the brains out on a boulder;
Laid it down beside the Bindos,

Callow, wailing, little Bindos.
On it laid him, like a pillow,
And began again to slumber.
Soon returned the parent Bindos
From their hunting in the forest;
Bringing brains and eyes of camels
And of elephants prodigious,
For their little callow Bindos
Wailing sadly by the sea-shore.
But the Bindos young and callow
Brains of camels would not swallow;
Said—"A pretty set of parents
You are truly! thus to leave us
Sadly wailing by the sea-shore
To be eaten by the serpent—
Bhawarnāg the dreadful serpent—
Came he up from the Black Water,
Came to eat us little Bindos,
When this very valiant Lingo
Shot an arrow in his stomach,
Cut him into seven pieces—
Give to Lingo brains of camels,
Eyes of elephants prodigious."
Then the fond paternal Bindo
Saw the head-piece of the serpent
Under Lingo's head a pillow,
And he said, 'O valiant Lingo,
Ask whatever you may wish for.'
Then he asked the little Bindos
For an offering to the Great God,
And the fond paternal Bindo,
Much disgusted first refusing,
Soon consented; said he'd go too
With the fond maternal Bindo—
Take them all upon his shoulders,
And fly straight to Dewalgiri.
Then he spread his mighty pinions,
Took his Bindos up on one side
And our Lingo on the other.
Thus they soared away together
From the shores of the Black Water,
And the fond maternal Bindo,
O'er them hovering, spread an awning
With her broad and mighty pinions
O'er her offspring and our Lingo.
By the forests and the mountains
Six months' journey was it thither
To the mountain Dewalgiri.
Half the day was scarcely over
Ere this convoy from the sea-shore

Lighted safe on Dewalgiri ;
Touched the knocker to the gateway
Of the Great God, Mahādeva.
And the messenger Nārāyan
Answering, went and told his master—
" Lo, this very valiant Lingo !
Here he is with all the Bindos,
The Black Bindos from the sea-shore."
Then the Great God, much disgusted,
Driven quite into a corner,
Took our Lingo to the cavern,
Sent Basmāsur to his kennel,
Held his nose, and moved away the
Mighty stone of sixteen cubits ;
Called those sixteen scores of Gonds out
Made them over to their Lingo.
And they said, " O Father Lingo !
What a bad time we've had of it,
Not a thing to fill our bellies
In this horrid gloomy dungeon."
But our Lingo gave them dinner,
Gave them rice and flour of millet,
And they went off to the river,
Had a drink, and cooked and ate it.

The next episode is taken from a slightly different local version :

And while they were cooking their food at the river a great flood came up, but all the Gonds crossed safely except the four gods, Tekām, Markām, Pusām and Telengām.[1] These were delayed because they had cooked their food with *ghī* which they had looted from the Hindu deities. Then they stood on the bank and cried out,

O God of the crossing,
O Boundary God !
Should you be here,
Come take us across.

Hearing this, the tortoise and crocodile came up to them, and offered to take them across the river. So Markām and Tekām sat on the back of the crocodile and Pusām and Telengām on the back of the tortoise, and before starting the gods made the crocodile and tortoise swear that they would not eat or drown them in the sea. But when they

[1] Tekām the teak tree, Markām the mango tree, and Telengām the Telugu. These are the names of well-known exogamous septs.

got to the middle of the river the tortoise and crocodile began to sink, with the idea that they would drown the Gonds and feed their young with them. Then the Gonds cried out, and the Raigīdhni or vulture heard them. This bird appears to be the same as the Bindo, as it fed its young with elephants. The Raigīdhni flew to the Gonds and took them up on its back and flew ashore with them. And in its anger it picked out the tongue of the crocodile and crushed the neck of the tortoise. And this is why the crocodile is still tongueless and the tortoise has a broken neck, which is sometimes inside and sometimes outside its shell. Both animals also have the marks of string on their backs where the Gond gods tied their necks together when they were ferried across. Thus all the Gonds were happily reunited and Lingo took them into the forest, and they founded a town there, which grew and prospered. And Lingo divided all the Gonds into clans and made the oldest man a Pardhān or priest and founded the rule of exogamy. He also made the Gond gods, subsequently described,[1] and worshipped them with offerings of a calf and liquor, and danced before them. He also prescribed the ceremonies of marriage which are still observed, and after all this was done Lingo went to the gods.

(*b*) Tribal Subdivisions

11. Sub-castes.

Out of the Gond tribe, which, as it gave its name to a province, may be considered as almost a people, a number of separate castes have naturally developed. Among them are several occupational castes such as the Agarias or iron-workers, the Ojhas or soothsayers, Pardhāns or priests and minstrels, Solāhas or carpenters, and Koilabhutis or dancers or prostitutes. These are principally sprung from the Gonds, though no doubt with an admixture of other low tribes or castes. The Parjas of Bastar, now classed as a separate tribe, appear to represent the oldest Gond settlers, who were subdued by later immigrants of the race; while the Bhatras and Jhādi Telengas are of mixed descent from Gonds and Hindus. Similarly the Gowāri caste of cattle-graziers

[1] See section on Religion.

Bemrose, Collo., Derby

GONDS ON A JOURNEY.

originated from the alliances of Gond and Ahīr graziers. The Mannewārs and Kolāms are other tribes allied to the Gonds. Many Hindu castes and also non-Aryan tribes living in contact with the Gonds have a large Gond element; of the former class the Ahīrs, Basors, Barhais and Lohārs, and of the latter the Baigas, Bhunjias and Khairwārs are instances.

Among the Gonds proper there are two aristocratic subdivisions, the Rāj-Gonds and Khatolas. According to Forsyth the Rāj-Gonds are in many cases the descendants of alliances between Rājpūt adventurers and Gonds. But the term practically comprises the landholding subdivision of the Gonds, and any proprietor who was willing to pay for the privilege could probably get his family admitted into the Rāj-Gond group. The Rāj-Gonds rank with the Hindu cultivating castes, and Brāhmans will take water from them. They sometimes wear the sacred thread. In the Telugu country the Rāj-Gond is known as Durla or Durlasattam. In some localities Rāj-Gonds will intermarry with ordinary Gonds, but not in others. The Khatola Gonds take their name from the Khatola state in Bundelkhand, which is said to have once been governed by a Gond ruler, but is no longer in existence. In Saugor they rank about equal with the Rāj-Gonds and intermarry with them, but in Chhindwāra it is said that ordinary Gonds despise them and will not marry with them or eat with them on account of their mixed descent from Gonds and Hindus. The ordinary Gonds in most Districts form one endogamous group, and are known as the Dhur or 'dust' Gonds, that is the common people. An alternative name conferred on them by the Hindus is Rāwanvansi or of the race of Rāwan, the demon king of Ceylon, who was the opponent of Rāma. The inference from this name is that the Hindus consider the Gonds to have been among the people of southern India who opposed the Aryan expedition to Ceylon, which is preserved in the legend of Rāma; and the name therefore favours the hypothesis that the Gonds came from the south and that their migration northward was sufficiently recent in date to permit of its being still remembered in tradition. There are several other small local subdivisions. The Koya Gonds live on the border of the Telugu country, and their name is apparently a corruption of Koi or Koitūr, which the Gonds call themselves. The Gaita are another Chānda subcaste, the word Gaite or Gaita really meaning a village priest or headman. Gattu or Gotte is said to be a name given to the hill Gonds of Chānda, and is not a real subcaste. The Darwe or Nāik Gonds of Chānda were formerly employed as soldiers, and hence obtained the name of Nāik or leader. Other local groups are being formed such as the Larhia or those of Chhattisgarh, the Mandlāha of Mandla, the Lānjiha from Lānji and so on. These are probably in course of becoming endogamous. The Gonds of Bastar are divided into two groups, the Māria and the Muria. The Māria are the wilder, and are apparently named after the Mad, as the hilly country of Bastar is called. Mr. Hīra Lāl suggests the derivation of Muria from *mur*, the *palās* tree, which is common in the plains of Bastar, or from *mur*, a root. Both derivations must be considered as conjectural. The Murias are the Gonds who live in the plains and are more civilised than the Mārias. The descendants of the Rāja of Deogarh Bakht Buland, who turned Muhammadan, still profess that religion, but intermarry freely with the Hindu Gonds. The term Bhoi, which literally means a bearer in Telugu, is used as a synonym for the Gonds and also as an honorific title. In Chhindwāra it is said that only a village proprietor is addressed as Bhoi. It appears that the Gonds were used as palanquin-bearers, and considered it an honour to belong to the Kahār or bearer caste, which has a fairly good status.[1]

12. Exogamy. The Gond rules of exogamy appear to preserve traces of the system found in Australia, by which the whole tribe is split into two or four main divisions, and every man in one or two of them must marry a woman in the other one or two. This is considered by Sir J. G. Frazer to be the beginning of exogamy, by which marriage was prohibited, first, between brothers and sisters, and then between parents and children, by the arrangement of these main divisions.[2]

Among the Gonds, however, the subdivision into small exogamous septs has been also carried out, and the class

[1] See also art. Kahār.

[2] The theory is stated and explained in vol. iv. of *Exogamy and Totemism.*

system, if the surmise that it once existed be correct, remains only in the form of a survival, prohibiting marriage between agnates, like an ordinary sept. In one part of Bastar all the septs of the Māria Gonds are divided into two great classes. There are ninety septs in A Class and sixty-nine in B Class, though the list may be incomplete. All the septs of A Class say that they are Bhaiband or Dādabhai to each other, that is in the relation of brothers, or cousins being the sons of brothers. No man of Class A can marry a woman of any sept in Class A. The septs of Class A stand in relation of Māmabhai or Akomāma to those of Class B. Māmabhai means a maternal uncle's son, and Akomāma apparently signifies having the same maternal grandfather. Any man of a sept in Class A can marry any woman of a sept in Class B. It will thus be seen that the smaller septs seem to serve no purpose for regulating marriage, and are no more than family names. The tribe might just as well be divided into two great exogamous clans only. Marriage is prohibited between persons related only through males; but according to the exogamous arrangement there is no other prohibition, and a man could marry any maternal relative. Separate rules, however, prohibit his marriage with certain female relatives, and these will be given subsequently.[1] It is possible that the small septs may serve some purpose which has not been elicited, though the inquiry made by Rai Bahādur Panda Baijnāth was most careful and painstaking.

In another part of Bastar there were found to be five classes, and each class had a small number of septs in it. The people who supplied this information could not give the names of many septs. Thus Class A had six septs, Class B five, Classes C and D one each, Class E four, and Class F two. A man could not marry a woman of any sept belonging to his own class.

The Muria Gonds of Bastar have a few large exogamous septs or clans named in Hindi after animals, and each of these clans contains several subsepts with Gondi names. Thus the *Bakaravans* or Goat race contains the Garde, Kunjami, Karrami and Vadde septs. The *Kachhimvans* or Tortoise race has the Netāmi, Kawachi, Usendi and

[1] See para. 15

Tekāmi septs; the *Nāgvans* or Cobra race includes the Marāvi, Potāri, Karanga, Nurethi, Dhurwa and others. Other exogamous races are the Sodi (or tiger), Behainsa (buffalo), Netām (dog in Gondi), Chamchidai (bat) and one or two more. In this case the exogamous clans with Hindi names would appear to be a late division, and have perhaps been adopted because the meaning of the old Gondi names had been forgotten, or the septs were too numerous to be remembered.

In Chānda a classification according to the number of gods worshipped is found. There are four main groups worshipping seven, six, five and four gods respectively, and each group contains ten to fifteen septs. A man cannot marry a woman of any sept which worships the same number of gods as himself. Each group has a sacred animal which the members revere, that of the seven-god worshippers being a porcupine, of the six-god worshippers a tiger, of the five-god worshippers the sāras crane, and of the four-god worshippers a tortoise. As a rule the members of the different groups do not know the names of their gods, and in practice it is doubtful whether they restrict themselves to the proper number of gods of their own group. Formerly there were three-, two- and one-god worshippers, but in each of these classes it is said that there were only one or two septs, and they found that they were much inconvenienced by the paucity of their numbers, perhaps for purposes of communal worship and feasting, and hence they got themselves enrolled in the larger groups. In reality it would appear that the classification according to the number of gods worshipped is being forgotten, and the three lowest groups have disappeared. This conjecture is borne out by the fact that in Chhindwāra and other localities only two large classes remain who worship six and seven gods respectively, and marry with each other, the union of a man with a woman worshipping the same number of gods as himself being prohibited. Here, again, the small septs included in the groups appear to serve no purpose for regulating marriages. In Mandla the division according to the number of gods worshipped exists as in Chānda; but many Gonds have forgotten all particulars as to the gods, and say only that those septs which worship the same number of gods are *bhaiband*, or related to each other, and therefore cannot intermarry. In Betūl the division by numbers of gods appears to be wholly in abeyance. Here certain large septs, especially the Uika and Dhurwa, are subdivided into a number of subsepts, within each of which marriage is prohibited.

Many of the septs are named after animals and plants. 13. Totemism.
Among the commonest septs in all Districts are Markām, the mango tree; Tekām, the teak tree; Netām, the dog; Irpāchi, the mahua tree; Tumrāchi, the tendu tree; Warkara, the wild cat, and so on. Generally the members of a sept do not kill or injure their totem animals, but the rule is not always observed, and in some cases they now have some other object of veneration, possibly because they have forgotten the meaning of the sept name, or the object after which it is named has ceased to be sacred. Thus the Markām sept, though named after the mango, now venerate the tortoise, and this is also the case with the Netām sept in Bastar, though named after the dog. In Bastar a man revering the tortoise, though he will not catch the animal himself, will get one of his friends to catch it, and one revering the goat, if he wishes to kill a goat for a feast, will kill it not at his own house but at a friend's. The meaning of the important sept names Marābi, Dhurwa and Uika has not been ascertained, and the members of the sept do not know it. In Mandla the Marābi sept are divided into the Eti Marābi and Padi Marābi, named after the goat and pig. The Eti or goat Marābi will not touch a goat nor sacrifice one to Bura Deo. They say that once their ancestors stole a goat and were caught by the owner, when they put a basket over it and prayed Bura Deo to change it into a pig, which he did. Therefore they sacrifice only pigs to Bura Deo, but apparently the Padi Marābi also both sacrifice and eat pigs. The Dhurwa sept are divided into the Tumrāchi and Nābalia Dhurwa, named after the tendu tree and the dwarf date-palm. The Nābalia Dhurwas will not cut a dwarf date-palm nor eat its fruit. They worship Bura Deo in this tree instead of in the sāj tree, making an iron doll to represent him and covering it with palm-leaves. The Uika sept in Mandla say that they revere no animal or plant, and can eat any animal

or cut down any plant except the *sāj* tree,[1] the tree of Bura Deo; but in Betūl they are divided into several subsepts, each of which has a totem. The Parteti sept revere the crocodile. When a marriage is finished they make a sacrifice to the crocodile, and if they see one lying dead they break their earthen pots in token of mourning. The Warkara sept revere the wild cat; they also will not touch a village cat nor keep one in their house, and if a cat comes in they drive it out at once. The Kunjām sept revere the rat and do not kill it.

14. Connection of totemism with the gods.

In Betūl the Gonds explain the totemistic names of their septs by saying that some incident connected with the animal, tree or other object occurred to the ancestor or priest of the sept while they were worshipping at the Deokhulla or god's place or threshing-floor. Mr. Ganga Prasād Khatri has made an interesting collection of these. The reason why these stories have been devised may be that the totem animals or plants have ceased to be revered on their own merits as ancestors or kinsmen of the sept, and it was therefore felt necessary to explain the sept name or sanctity attaching to the totem by associating it with the gods. If this were correct the process would be analogous to that by which an animal or plant is first held sacred of itself, and, when this feeling begins to decay with some recognition of its true nature, it is associated with an anthropomorphic god in order to preserve its sanctity. The following are some examples recorded by Mr. Ganga Prasād Khatri. Some of the examples are not associated with the gods.

Gajjāmi, subsept of Dhurwa sept. From *gaj*, an arrow. Their first ancestor killed a tiger with an arrow.

Gouribans Dhurwa. Their first ancestor worshipped his gods in a bamboo clump.

Kusadya Dhurwa. (*Kosa*, tasar silk cocoon.) The first ancestor found a silk cocoon on the tree in which he worshipped his gods.

Kohkapath. *Kohka* is the fruit of the *bhilawa*[2] or marking-nut tree, and *path*, a kid. The first ancestor worshipped his gods in a *bhilawa* tree and offered a kid to them. Members of this sept do not eat the fruit or flowers of the *bhilawa* tree.

[1] *Boswellia serrata*,

[2] *Semecarpus anacardian.*

Jaglya. One who keeps awake, or the awakener. The first ancestor stayed awake the whole night in the Deo-khulla, or god's threshing-floor.

Sariyām. (*Sarri*, a path.) The first ancestor swept the path to the Deo-khulla.

Guddām. Gudda is a place where a hen lays her eggs. The first ancestor's hen laid eggs in the Deo-khulla.

Irpāchi. The mahua tree. A mahua tree grew in the Deo-khulla or worshipping-place of this sept.

Admachi. The *dhaura* tree.[1] The first ancestor worshipped his gods under a *dhaura* tree. Members of the sept do not cut this tree nor burn its wood.

Sarāti Dhurwa. (*Sarāti*, a whip.) The first ancestor whipped the priest of the gods.

Suibadiwa. (*Sui*, a porcupine.) The first ancestor's wife had a porcupine which went and ate the crop of an old man's field. He tried to catch it, but it went back to her. He asked the name of her sept, and not being able to find it out called it Suibadiwa.

Watka. (A stone.) Members of this sept worship five stones for their gods. Some say that the first ancestors were young boys who forgot where the Deo-khulla was and therefore set up five stones and offered a chicken to them. As they did not offer the usual sacrifice of a goat, members of this sept abstain from eating goats.

Tumrecha Uika. (The *tendu* tree.[2]) It is said that the original ancestor of this sept was walking in the forest with his pregnant wife. She saw some *tendu* fruit and longed for it and he gave it to her to eat. Perhaps the original idea may have been that she conceived through swallowing a *tendu* fruit. Members of this sept eat the fruit of the *tendu* tree, but do not cut the tree nor make any use of its leaves or branches.

Tumdan Uika. Tumdan is a kind of pumpkin or gourd. They say that this plant grows in their Deo-khulla. The members drink water out of this gourd in the house, but do not carry it out of the house.

Kadfa-chor Uika. (Stealer of the *kadfa.*) *Kadfa* is the sheaf of grain left standing in the field for the gods when

[1] *Anogeissus latifolia.*

[2] *Diosypyros tomentosa.*

the crop is cut. The first ancestor stole the *kadfa* and offered it to his gods.

Gadhamār Uika. (Donkey-slayer.) Some say that the gods of the sept came to the Deo-khulla riding on donkeys, and others that the first ancestor killed a donkey in the Deo-khulla.

Eti-kumra. Eti is a goat. The ancestors of the sept used to sacrifice a Brāhman boy to their gods. Once they were caught in the act by the parents of the boy they had stolen, and they prayed to the gods to save them, and the boy was turned into a goat. They do not kill a goat nor eat its flesh, nor sacrifice it to the gods.

Ahke. This word means 'on the other side of a river.' They say that a man of the Dhurwa sept abducted a girl of the Uika sept from the other side of a river and founded this sept.

Tirgām. The word means fire. They say that their ancestor's hand was burnt in the Deo-khulla while cooking the sacrifice.

Tekām. (The teak tree.) The ancestor of the sept had his gods in this tree. Members of the sept will not eat food off teak leaves, but they will use them for thatching, and also cut the tree.

Manapa. In Gondi *mani* is a son and *apa* a father. They say that their ancestors sacrificed a Brāhman father and son to their gods and were saved by their being turned into goats like the Eti-kumra sept. Members of the sept do not kill or eat a goat.

Korpachi. The droppings of a hen. The ancestors of the sept offered these to his gods.

Mandani. The female organ of generation. The ancestor of the sept slept with his wife in the Deo-khulla.

Paiyām. *Paiya* is a heifer which has not borne a calf, such as is offered to the gods. Other Gonds say that the people of this sept have no gods. They are said not only to marry a girl from any other subsept of the Dhurwas and Uikas, but from their own sept and even their own sisters, though this is probably no longer true. They are held to be the lowest of the Gonds. Except in this instance, as already seen, the subsepts of the Dhurwa and Uika septs do not intermarry with each other.

(c) Marriage Customs

A man must not marry in his own sept, nor in one which worships the same number of gods, in localities where the classification of septs according to the number of gods worshipped obtains. Intermarriage between septs which are *bhaiband* or brothers to each other is also prohibited. The marriage of first cousins is considered especially suitable. Formerly, perhaps, the match between a brother's daughter and sister's son was most common; this is held to be a survival of the matriarchate, when a man's sister's son was his heir. But the reason has now been generally forgotten, and the union of a brother's son to a sister's daughter has also become customary, while, as girls are scarce and have to be paid for, it is the boy's father who puts forward his claim. Thus in Mandla and Bastar a man thinks he has a right to his sister's daughter for his son on the ground that his family has given a girl to her husband's family, and therefore they should give one back. This match is known as *Dūdh lautāna* or bringing back the milk; and if the sister's daughter marries any one else her maternal uncle sometimes claims what is known as 'milk money,' which may be a sum of Rs. 5, in compensation for the loss of the girl as a wife for his son. This custom has perhaps developed out of the former match in changed conditions of society, when the original relation between a brother and his sister's son has been forgotten and girls have become valuable. But it is said that the *dūdh* or milk money is also payable if a brother refuses to give his daughter to his sister's son. In Mandla a man claims his sister's daughter for his son and sometimes even the daughter of a cousin, and considers that he has a legitimate grievance if the girl is married to somebody else. Frequently, if he has reason to apprehend this, he invites the girl to his house for some ceremony or festival, and there marries her to his son without the consent of her parents. As this usually constitutes the offence of kidnapping under the Penal Code, a crop of criminal cases results, but the procedure of arrest without warrant and the severe punishment imposed by the Code are somewhat unsuitable for a case of this kind, which, according to Gond ideas, is rather in the nature of a civil

15. Prohibitions on intermarriage, and unions of relations.

wrong, and a sufficient penalty would often be the payment of an adequate compensation or bride-price for the girl. The children of two sisters cannot, it is said, be married, and a man cannot marry his wife's elder sister, any aunt or niece, nor his mother-in-law or her sister. But marriage is not prohibited between grandparents and grandchildren. If an old man marries a young wife and dies, his grandson will marry her if she is of proper age. In this there would be no blood-relationship, but it is doubtful whether even the existence of such relationship would prevent the match. It is said that even among Hindu castes the grandfather will flirt with his granddaughter, and call her his wife in jest, and the grandmother with her grandson. In Bastar a man can marry his daughter's daughter or maternal grandfather's or grandmother's sister. He could not marry his son's daughter or paternal grandfather's sister, because they belong to the same sept as himself.

16. Irregular marriages.

In the Māria country, if a girl is made pregnant by a man of the caste before marriage, she simply goes to his house and becomes his wife. This is called *Paithu* or entering. The man has to spend Rs. 2 or 3 on food for the caste and pay the price for the girl to her parents. If a girl has grown up and no match has been arranged for her to which she agrees, her parents will ask her maternal uncle's or paternal aunt's son to seize her and take her away. These two cousins have a kind of prescriptive claim to the girl, and apparently it makes no difference whether the prospective husband is already married or not. He and his friends lie in wait near her home and carry her off, and her parents afterwards proceed to his house to console their daughter and reconcile her to the match. Sometimes when a woman is about to become what is known as a Paisamundi or kept woman, without being married, the relations rub her and the man whose mistress she is with oil and turmeric, put marriage crowns of palm-leaves on their heads, pour water on them from the top of a post, and make them go seven times round a mahua branch, so that they may be considered to be married. When a couple are very poor they may simply go and live together without any wedding, and perform the ceremony afterwards when they have means, or they distribute little pieces of bread to the tribesmen in lieu of the marriage feast.

17. Marriage. Arrangement of matches.

Marriage is generally adult. Among the wild Māria Gonds of Bastar the consent of the girl is considered an essential preliminary to the union. She gives it before a council of elders, and if necessary is allowed time to make up her mind. The boy must also agree to the match. Elsewhere matches are arranged by the parents, and a bride-price which amounts to a fairly substantial sum in comparison with the means of the parties is usually paid. But still the girls have a considerable amount of freedom. It is generally considered that if a girl goes of her own accord and pours turmeric and water over a man, it is a valid marriage and he can take her to live in his house. Married women also sometimes do this to another man if they wish to leave their husbands.

18. The marriage ceremony.

The most distinctive feature of a Gond marriage is that the procession usually starts from the bride's house and the wedding is held at that of the bridegroom, in contradistinction to the Hindu practice. It is supposed that this is a survival of the custom of marriage by capture, when the bride was carried off from her own house to the bridegroom's, and any ceremony which was requisite was necessarily held at the house of the latter. But the Gonds say that since Dūlha Deo, the bridegroom god and one of the commonest village deities, was carried off by a tiger on his way to his wedding, it was decided that in future the bride must go to the bridegroom to be married in order to obviate the recurrence of such a calamity. Any risk incidental to the journey thus falls to the lady. Among the wilder Māria Gonds of Bastar the ritual is very simple. The bride's party arrive at the bridegroom's village and occupy some huts made ready for them. His father sends them provisions, including a pig and fowls, and the day passes in feasting. In the evening they go to the bridegroom's house, and the night is spent in dancing by the couple and the young people of the village. Next morning the bride's people go back again, and after another meal her parents bring her to the bridegroom's house and push her inside, asking the boy's father to take charge of her, and telling her that she now belongs to her husband's family and must not come back to them alone. The girl cries a little for form's sake and acquiesces, and the business is over, no proper marriage rite being apparently performed at all. Among the more civilised Mārias the couple are seated for the ceremony side by side under a green shed, and water is poured on them through the shed in imitation of the fertilising action of rain. Some elder of the village places his hands on them and the wedding is over. But Hindu customs are gradually being adopted, and the rubbing of powdered turmeric and water on the bodies of the bride and bridegroom is generally essential to a proper wedding. The following description is given of the Gonds of Kanker. On the day fixed for the marriage the pair, accompanied by the Dosi or caste priest, proceed to a river, in the bed of which two reeds five or six feet high are placed just so far apart that a man can lie down between them, and tied together with a thread at the top. The priest lies down between the reeds, and the bride and bridegroom jump seven times over his body. After the last jump they go a little way off, throw aside their wet clothes, and then run naked to a place where their dry clothes are kept; they put them on and go home without looking back. Among the Gonds in Khairagarh the pair are placed in two pans of a balance and covered with blankets. The caste priest lifts up the bridegroom's pan and her female relatives the bride's, and walk round with them seven times, touching the marriage-post at each time. After this they are taken outside the village without being allowed to see each other. They are placed standing at a little distance with a screen between them, and liquor is spilt on the ground to make a line from one to the other. After a time the bridegroom lifts up the screen, rushes on the bride, gives her a blow on the back and puts the ring on her finger, at the same time making a noise in imitation of the cry of a goat. All the village then indulge in bacchanalian orgies, not sparing their own relations.

19. Wedding expenditure.

In Bastar it is said that the expenses of a wedding vary from Rs. 5 to Rs. 20 for the bride's family and from Rs. 10 to Rs. 50 for the bridegroom's, according to their means.[1]

[1] One rupee = 1s. 4d.

In a fairly well-to-do family the expenditure of the bridegroom's family is listed as follows: liquor Rs. 20, rice Rs. 12, salt Rs. 2, two goats Rs. 2, chillies Rs. 2, *ghī* Rs. 4, turmeric Rs. 2, oil Rs. 3, three cloths for the bride Rs. 8, two sheets and a loin-cloth for her relatives Rs. 5, payment to the Kumhār for earthen pots Rs. 5, the bride-price Rs. 10, present to the bride's maternal uncle when she is not married to his son Rs. 2, and something for the drummers. The total of this is Rs. 76, and any expenditure on ornaments which the family can afford may be added. In wealthier localities the bride-price is Rs. 15 to 20 or more. Sometimes if the girl has been married and dies before the bride-price has been paid, her father will not allow her body to be buried until it is paid. The sum expended on a wedding probably represents the whole income of the family for at least six months, and often for a considerably longer period. In Chānda[1] the bride's party on arrival at the bridegroom's village receive the *Bara jawa* or marriage greeting, every one present being served with a little rice-water, an onion and a piece of tobacco. At the wedding the bridegroom has a ring either of gold, silver or copper, lead not being permissible, and places this on the bride's finger. Often the bride resists and the bridegroom has to force her fist open, or he plants his foot on hers in order to control her while he gets the ring on to her finger. Elsewhere the couple hold each other by the little fingers in walking round the marriage-post, and then each places an iron ring on the other's little finger. The couple then tie strings, coloured yellow with turmeric, round each other's right wrists. On the second day they are purified with water and put on new clothes. On the third day they go to worship the god, preceded by two men who carry a chicken in a basket. This chicken is called the Dhendha or associate of the bridal couple, and corresponds to the child which in Hindu marriages is appointed as the associate of the bridegroom. Just before their arrival at the temple the village jester snatches away the chicken, and pretends to eat it. At the temple they worship the god, and deposit before him the strings coloured with turmeric which had been tied on

[1] From Mr. Langhorne's monograph.

their wrists. In Chhindwāra the bride is taken on a bullock to the bridegroom's house. At the wedding four people hold out a blanket in which juāri, lemons and eggs are placed, and the couple walk round this seven times, as in the Hindu *bhānwar* ceremony. They then go inside the house, where a chicken is torn asunder and the blood sprinkled on their heads. At the same time the bride crushes a chicken under her foot. In Mandla the bride on entering the marriage-shed kills a chicken by cutting off its head either with an axe or a knife. Then all the gods of her house enter into her and she is possessed by them, and for each one she kills a chicken, cutting off its head in the same manner. The chickens are eaten by all the members of the bride's party who have come with her, but none belonging to the bridegroom's party may partake of them. Here the marriage-post is made of the wood of the mahua tree, round which a *toran* or string of mango leaves is twisted, and the couple walk seven times round this. In Wardha the bride and bridegroom stand on the heap of refuse behind the house and their heads are knocked together. In Bhandāra two spears are placed on the heap of refuse and their ends are tied together at the top with the entrails of a fowl. The bride and bridegroom have to stand under the spears while water is poured over them, and then run out. Before the bride starts the bridegroom must give her a blow on the back, and if he can do this before she runs out from the spears it is thought that the marriage will be lucky. The women of the bride's and bridegroom's party also stand one at each end of a rope and have a competition in singing. They sing against each other and see which can go on the longest. Brāhmans are not employed at a Gond wedding. The man who officiates is known as Dosi, and is the bridegroom's brother-in-law, father's sister's husband or some similar relative. A woman relative of the bride helps her to perform her part and is known as Sawāsin. To the Dosi and Sawāsin the bride and bridegroom's parties present an earthen vessel full of kodon. The donors mark the pots, take them home and sow them in their own fields, and then give the crop to the Dosi and Sawāsin.

Some years ago in Bālāghāt the bride and bridegroom

sat and ate food together out of two leaf-plates. When they had finished the bride took the leaf-plates, ran with them to the marriage-shed, and fixed them in the woodwork so that they did not fall down. The bridegroom ran after her, and if she did not put the plates away quickly, gave her one or two blows with his fist. This apparently was a symbolical training of the bride to be diligent and careful in her household work. Among the Rāj-Gonds of Saugor, if the bridegroom could not come himself he was accustomed to send his sword to represent him. The Sawāsin carried the sword seven times round the marriage-post with the bride and placed a garland on her on its behalf, and the bride put a garland over the sword. This was held to be a valid marriage. In a rich Rāj-Gond or Khatola Gond family two or three girls would be given with the bride, and they would accompany her and become the concubines of the bridegroom. Among the Māria Gonds of Chānda the wedded pair retire after the ceremony to a house allotted to them and spend the night together. Their relatives and friends before leaving shout and make merry round the house for a time, and throw all kinds of rubbish and dirt on it. In the morning the couple have to get up early and clear all this off, and clean up the house. A curious ceremony is reported from one part of Mandla. When a Gond girl is leaving to be married, her father places inside her litter a necklace of many strings of blue and yellow beads, with a number of cowries at the end, and an iron ring attached to it. On her arrival at the bridegroom's house his father takes out the necklace and ring. Sometimes it is said that he simply passes a stone through the ring, but often he hangs it up in the centre of a room, and the bridegroom's relatives throw stones at it until one of them goes through the ring, or they throw long bamboo sticks or shoot arrows at it, or even fire bullets from a gun. In a recent case it is said that a man was trying to fire a bullet through the ring and killed a girl. Until a stone, stick, arrow or bullet has been sent through the ring the marriage cannot take place, nor can the bridegroom or his father touch the bride, and they go on doing this all night until somebody succeeds. When the feat has been done they pour a

20. Special customs.

bottle of liquor over the necklace and ring, and the bride's relatives catch the liquor as it falls, and drink it. The girl wears the necklace at her wedding, and thereafter so long as her husband lives, and when he dies she tears the string to pieces and throws it into the river. The iron ring must be made by a Gondi Lohār or blacksmith, and he will not accept money in payment for it, but must be given a cow, calf, or buffalo. The symbolical meaning of this rite does not appear to require explanation.[1] In many places the bride and bridegroom go and bathe in a river or tank on the day after the wedding, and throw mud and dirt over each other, or each throws the other down and rolls him or her in the mud. This is called Chikhal-Mundi or playing in the mud. Afterwards the bride has to wash the bridegroom's muddy clothes, roll them up in a blanket, and carry them on her head to the house. A see-saw is then placed in the marriage-shed, and the bridegroom's father sits on it. The bride makes the see-saw move up and down, while her relations joke with her and say, 'Your child is crying.' Elsewhere the bridegroom's father sits in a swing. The bride and bridegroom swing him, and the bystanders exclaim that the old man is the child of the new bride. It seems possible that both customs are meant to portray the rocking of a baby in a cradle or swinging it in a swing, and hence it is thought that through performing them the bride will soon rock or swing a real baby.

21. Taking omens. In Bastar an omen is taken before the wedding. The village elders meet on an auspicious day as Monday, Thursday or Friday, and after midnight they cook and eat food, and go out into the forest. They look for a small black bird called Usi, from which omens are commonly taken. When anybody sees this bird, if it cries '*Sun, Sun*,' on the right hand, it is thought that the marriage will be lucky. If, however, it cries '*Chi, Chi*,' or '*Fie, Fie*,' the proposed match is held to be of evil omen, and is cancelled. The Koya Gonds of Bastar distil mahua liquor before arranging for a match. If the liquor is good they think the marriage

[1] The above rite has some resemblance to the test required of the suitors of Penelope in the *Odyssey* of bending the bow of Odysseus and shooting an arrow through the axes, which they could not perform.

will be lucky, and take the liquor with them to cement the betrothal; but if it is bad they think the marriage will be unlucky, and the proposal is dropped. Mondays, Wednesdays and Fridays are held to be lucky days for marriages, and they are celebrated in the hot-weather months of Baisākh, Jesth and Asār, or April, May and June, or in Pūs (December), and rarely in Māgh (January). A wedding is only held in Kārtik (October) if the bride and bridegroom have already had sexual intercourse, and cannot take place in the rains.

22. Marriage by capture. Weeping and hiding.

Survivals of the custom of marriage by capture are to be found in many localities. In Bastar the prospective bridegroom collects a party of his friends and lies in wait for the girl, and they catch her when she comes out and gets a little distance from her house. The girl cries out, and women of the village come and rescue her and beat the boys with sticks till they have crossed the boundary of the village. The boys neither resist nor retaliate on the women, but simply make off with the girl. When they get home a new cloth is given to her, and the boys have a carouse on rice-beer, and the marriage is considered to be complete. The parents do not interfere, but as a rule the affair is prearranged between the girl and her suitor, and if she really objects to the match they let her go. A similar procedure occurs in Chānda. Other customs which seem to preserve the idea that marriage was once a forcible abduction are those of the bride weeping and hiding, which are found in most Districts. In Bālāghāt the bride and one or two friends go round to the houses of the village and to other villages, all of them crying, and receive presents from their friends. In Wardha the bride is expected to cry continuously for a day and a night before the wedding, to show her unwillingness to leave her family. In Kanker it is said that before marriage the bride is taught to weep in different notes, so that when that part of the ceremony arrives in which weeping is required, she may have the proper note at her command. In Chhindwāra the bridegroom's party go and fetch the bride for the wedding, and on the night before her departure she hides herself in some house in the village. The bridegroom's brother and other men seek all through the village for her, and when they find her she runs and clings to the post of the house. The bridegroom's brother carries her off by force, and she is taken on a bullock to the bridegroom's house. In Seoni the girl hides in the same manner, and calls out 'Coo, coo,' when they are looking for her. After she is found, the bridegroom's brother carries her round on his back to the houses of his friends in the village, and she weeps at each house. When the bride's party arrive at the bridegroom's village the latter's party meet them and stop them from proceeding further. After waving sticks against each other in a threatening manner they fall on each other's necks and weep. Then two spears are planted to make an arch before the door, and the bridegroom pushes the bride through these from behind, hitting her to make her go through, while she hangs back and feigns reluctance. In Mandla the bride sometimes rides to the wedding on the shoulders of her sister's husband, and it is supposed that she never gets down all the way.

23. Serving for a wife. The practice of Lamsena, or serving for a wife, is commonly adopted by boys who cannot afford to buy one. The bridegroom serves his prospective father-in-law for an agreed period, usually three to five or even six years, and at its expiry he should be married to the girl without expense. During this time he is not supposed to have access to the girl, but frequently they become intimate, and if this happens the boy may either stay and serve his unexpired term or take his wife away at once; in the latter case his parents should pay the girl's father Rs. 5 for each year of the bridegroom's unexpired service. The Lamsena custom does not work well as a rule, since the girl's parents can break their contract, and the Lamsena has no means of redress. Sometimes if they are offered a good bride-price they will marry the girl to another suitor when he has served the greater part of his term, and all his work goes for nothing.

24. Widow remarriage. The remarriage of widows is freely permitted. As a rule it is considered suitable that she should marry her deceased husband's younger brother, but she may not marry his elder brother, and in the south of Bastar and Chānda

the union with the younger brother is also prohibited. In Mandla, if she will not wed the younger brother, on the eleventh day after the husband's death he puts the *tarkhi* or palm-leaf earrings in her ears, and states that if she marries anybody else he will claim *dawa-bunda* or compensation. Similarly in Bastar, if an outsider marries the widow, he first goes through a joint ceremony with the younger brother, by which the latter relinquishes his right in favour of the former. The widow must not marry any man whom she could not have taken as her first husband. After her husband's death she resides with her parents, and a price is usually paid to them by any outsider who wishes to marry her. In Bastar there is a fixed sum of Rs. 24, half of which goes to the first husband's family and half to the caste *panchāyat.* The payment to the *panchāyat* perhaps comes down from the period when widows were considered the property of the state or the king, and sold by auction for the benefit of the treasury. It is said that the descendants of the Gond Rājas of Chānda still receive a fee of Rs. 1-8 from every Gond widow who is remarried in the territories over which their jurisdiction extended. In Bastar when a widow marries again she has to be transferred from the gods of her first husband's sept to those of her second husband. For this two leaf-cups are filled with water and mahua liquor respectively, and placed with a knife between them. The liquor and water are each poured three times from one cup to the other and back until they are thoroughly mixed, and the mixture is then poured over the heads of the widow and her second husband. This symbolises her transfer to the god of the new sept. In parts of Bastar when a man has been killed by a tiger and his widow marries again, she goes through the ceremony not with her new husband but with a lance, axe or sword, or with a dog. It is thought that the tiger into which her first husband's spirit has entered will try to kill her second husband, but owing to the precaution taken he will either simply carry off the dog or will himself get killed by an axe, sword or lance. In most localities the ceremony of widow-marriage is simple. Turmeric is rubbed on the bodies of the couple and they may exchange a pair of rings or their clothes.

25. Divorce. Divorce is freely allowed on various grounds, as for adultery on the wife's part, a quarrelsome disposition, carelessness in the management of household affairs, or if a woman's children continue to die, or she is suspected of being a witch. Divorce is, however, very rare, for in order to get a fresh wife the man would have to pay for another wedding, which few Gonds can afford, and he would also have difficulty in getting a girl to marry him. Therefore he will often overlook even adultery, though a wife's adultery not infrequently leads to murder among the Gonds. In order to divorce his wife the husband sends for a few castemen, takes a piece of straw, spits on it, breaks it in two and throws it away, saying that he has renounced all further connection with his wife. If a woman is suspected of being a witch she often has to leave the village and go to some place where she is not known, and in that case her husband must either divorce her or go with her. There is no regular procedure for a wife divorcing her husband, but she can, if sufficiently young and attractive, take matters into her own hands, and simply leave her husband's house and go and live with some one else. In such a case the man who takes her has to repay to the husband the sum expended by the latter on his marriage, and the *panchāyat* may even decree that he should pay double the amount. When a man divorces his wife he has no liability for her maintenance, and often takes back any ornaments he may have given her. And a man who marries a divorced woman may be expected to pay her husband the expenses of his marriage. Instances are known of a bride disappearing even during the wedding, if she dislikes her partner; and Mr. Lampard of the Baihir Mission states that one night a Gond wedding party came to his house and asked for the loan of a lantern to look for the bride who had vanished.

26. Polygamy. Polygamy is freely allowed, and the few Gonds who can afford the expense are fond of taking a number of wives. Wives are very useful for cultivation as they work better than hired servants, and to have several wives is a sign of wealth and dignity. A man who has a number of wives will take them all to the bazār in a body to display his importance. A Gond who had seven wives in Bālāghāt

was accustomed always to take them to the bazār like this, walking in a line behind him.

(d) Birth and Pregnancy

In parts of Mandla the first appearance of the signs of puberty in a girl is an important occasion. She stays apart for four days, and during this time she ties up one of her body-cloths to a beam in the house in the shape of a cradle, and swings it for a quarter or half an hour every day in the name of Jhulān Devi, the cradle goddess. On the fifth day she goes and bathes, and the Baiga priest and his wife go with her. She gives the Baiga a hen and five eggs and a bottle of wine, and he offers them to Jhulān Devi at her shrine. To the Baigan she gives a hen and ten eggs and a bottle of liquor, and the Baigan tattoos the image of Jhulān Devi on each side of her body. A black hen with feathers spotted with white is usually chosen, as they say that this hen's blood is of a darker colour and that she lays more eggs. All this ceremonial is clearly meant to induce fertility in the girl. The Gonds regard a woman as impure for as long as the menstrual period lasts, and during this time she cannot draw water nor cook food, nor go into a cowshed or touch cowdung. In the wilder Māria tracts there is, or was till lately, a building out of sight of the village to which women in this condition retired. Her relatives brought her food and deposited it outside the hut, and when they had gone away she came out and took it. It was considered that a great evil would befall any one who looked on the face of a woman during the period of this impurity. The Rāj-Gonds have the same rules as Hindus regarding the menstrual periods of women.[1] 27. Menstruation.

No special rites are observed during pregnancy, and the superstitions about women in this condition resemble those of the Hindus.[2] A pregnant woman must not go near a horse or elephant, as they think that either of these animals would be excited by her condition and would assault her. 28. Superstitions about pregnancy and child-birth.

1 The information on child-birth is obtained from papers by Mr. Durga Prasād Pānde, Extra Assistant Commissioner, and the Rev. Mr. Franzen of Chhindwāra, and from notes taken in Mandla.

2 See articles on Kunbi, Kurmi, and Mehtar.

In cases where labour is prolonged they give the woman water to drink from a swiftly flowing stream, or they take pieces of wood from a tree struck by lightning or by a thunder-bolt, and make a necklace of them and hang it round her neck. In these instances the swiftness of the running water, or of the lightning or thunder-bolt, is held to be communicated to the woman, and thus she will obtain a quick delivery. Or else they ask the Gunia or sorcerer to discover what ancestor will be reborn in the child, and when he has done this he calls on the ancestor to come and be born quickly. If a woman is childless they say that she should worship Bura Deo and fast continually, and then on the termination of her monthly impurity, after she has bathed, if she walks across the shadow of a man she will have a child. It is thus supposed that the woman can be made fertile by the man's shadow, which will be the father of the child. Or she should go on a Sunday night naked to a *sāj* tree [1] and pray to it, and she may have a child. The *sāj* is the tree in which Bura Deo resides, and was probably in the beginning itself the god. Hence it is supposed that the woman is impregnated by the spirit of the tree, as Hindu women think that they can be made fertile by the spirits of unmarried Brāhman boys living in pīpal trees. Or she may have recourse to the village priest, the Bhumka or the Baiga, who probably finds that her barren condition is the work of an evil spirit and propitiates him. If a woman dies in the condition of pregnancy they cut her belly open before burial, so that the spirit of the child may escape. If she dies during or soon after delivery they bury her in some remote jungle spot, from which her spirit will find it difficult to return to the village. The spirit of such a woman is supposed to become a Churel and to entice men, and especially drunken men, to injury by causing them to fall into rivers or get shut up in hollow trees. The only way they can escape her is to offer her the ornaments which a married woman wears. Her enmity to men is due to the fact that she was cut off when she had just had the supreme happiness of bearing a child, and the present of these ornaments appeases her. The spirit of a woman whose engagement for marriage has

[1] *Boswellia serrata.*

been broken off, or who has deserted her husband's house for another man's, is also supposed to become a Churel. If an abortion occurs, or a child is born dead or dies very shortly after birth, they put the body in an earthen pot, and bury it under the heap of refuse behind the house. They say that this is done to protect the body from the witches, who if they get hold of it will raise the child's spirit, and make it a Bir or familiar spirit. Witches have special power over the spirits of such children, and can make them enter the body of an owl, a cat, a dog, or a headless man, and in this form cause any injury which the witch may desire to inflict on a human being. The real reason for burying the bodies of such children close to the house is probably, however, the belief that they will thus be born again in the same family. If the woman is fat and well during pregnancy they think a girl will be born, but if she is ailing and thin, that the child will be a boy. If the nipples of her breasts are of a reddish colour they think the birth of a boy is portended, but if of blackish colour, a girl. When a birth occurs another woman carefully observes the knots or protuberances on the navel-cord. It is supposed that the number of them indicates the further number of children which will be born to the mother. A blackish knot inclining downwards portends a boy, and a reddish one inclining upwards a girl. It is supposed that an intelligent midwife can change the order of these knots, and if a woman has only borne girl-children can arrange that the next one shall be a boy.

29. Procedure at a birth. Professional midwives are not usually employed at childbirth, and the women look after each other. Among the Māria Gonds of Bastar the father is impure for a month after the birth of a child and does not go to his work. A Muria Gond father is impure until the navel-cord drops; he may reap his crop, but cannot thresh or sow. This is perhaps a relic of the custom of the Couvade. The rules for the treatment of the mother resemble those of the Hindus, but they do not keep her so long without food. On some day from the fifth to the twelfth after the birth the mother is purified and the child is named. On this day its hair is shaved by the son-in-law or husband's or wife's brother-in-law. The mother and child are washed and rubbed with oil and turmeric, and the house is freshly whitewashed and cleaned with cowdung. They procure a winnowing-fan full of kodon and lay the child on it, and the mother ties this with a cloth under her arm. In the Nāgpur country the impurity of the mother is said to last for a month, during which time she is not allowed to cook food and no one touches her. Among the poorer Gonds the mother often does not lie up at all after a birth, but eats some pungent root as a tonic and next day goes on with her work.

30. Names. On the Sor night, or that of purification, the women of the village assemble and sing. The mother holds the child in her lap, and they each put a pice ($\frac{1}{4}$d.) in a dish as a present to it. A name is chosen, and an elderly woman announces it. Names are now often Hindu words, and are selected very much at random.[1] If the child was born on a Tuesday, Wednesday, Friday or Sunday the name of the day is often given, as Mangal, Budhu, Sukhiya, Itwāri; or if born in the month of Māgh (January), Phāgun (February), Chait (March), Baisākh (April), Jesth (May), or Pūs (December), the name may be from the month, as Māhu, Phāgu, Chaitia, Baisākhu, Jetha and Puso. The names of the other months are also given, but are less common. If any Government official is in the village when the child is born it may be named after his office, as Daroga, Havildar (head-constable), Vaccinator, Patwāri (village surveyor), Jemadār (head process-server), or Munshi (clerk). If a European officer is in the village the child may be called Gora (red) or Bhura (brown). Other names are Zamīndār (landholder) or Kirsān (tenant). Or the child may be named after any peculiarity, as Ghurman, fat, Kaluta, black, Chatua, one who kicks, and so on. Or it may be given a bad name in order to deceive the evil spirits as to its value, as Ghurha, a heap of cowdung, Jhāru, sweepings, Dumre or Bhangi, a sweeper, Chamari, a Chamār or tanner, and so on. If the mother has got the child after propitiating a spirit, it may be called Bhūta, from *bhūt*, a spirit or ghost. Nick-names are also given to people when they grow up, as

[1] The following examples of names were furnished by the Rev. Mr. Franzen and Mr. D. P. Pande.

Dariya, long-footed, Bobdi, fat and sluggish, Putchi, having a tail or cat-like, Bera, an idiot, and so on. Such names come into general use, and the bearers accept and answer to them without objection. All the above names are Hindi. Names taken from the Gond language are rare or non-existent, and it would appear either that they have been completely forgotten, or else that the Gonds had not advanced to the stage of giving every individual a personal name prior to their contact with the Hindus.

31. Superstitions about children.

If a child is born feet first its feet are supposed to have special power, and people suffering from pain in the back come and have their backs touched by the toes of the child's left foot. This power is believed to be retained in later life. If a woman gets a child when the signs of menstruation have not appeared, the child is called Lamka, and is held to be in danger of being struck by lightning. In order to avert this fate an offering of a white cock is made to the lightning during the month of Asārh (June) following the birth, when thunderstorms are frequent, and prayer is made that it will accept this sacrifice in lieu of the life of the child. They think that the ancestors who have been mingled with Bura Deo may be born again. Sometimes such an ancestor appears in a dream and intimates that he is coming back to earth. Then if a newborn child will not drink its mother's milk, they think it is some important male ancestor, and that he is vexed at being in such a dependent position to a woman over whom he formerly had authority. So they call the Gunia or sorcerer, and he guesses what ancestor has been reborn by measuring a stick. He says that if the length of the stick is an even number of times the breadth of his hand, or more or less than half a hand-breadth over, such and such an ancestor is reborn in the child. Then he measures his hand along the stick breadthwise, and when the measurement comes to that foretold for a particular ancestor he says that this one has been reborn; or if they find any mark on the body of the child corresponding to one they remember to have been borne by a particular ancestor, they identify it with this ancestor. Then they wash the child's feet as a token of respect, and pass their hands over its head and say to it, 'Drink milk, and we will give you a ring and clothes and jewels.' Sometimes they think that an ancestor has been born again in a calf, and the Gunia ascertains who he is in the same manner. Then this calf is not castrated if a bull, nor put to the plough if it is a cow, and when it dies they will not take off its hide for sale but bury it with the hide on.

It is believed that if a barren woman can get hold of the first hair of another woman's child or its navel-cord, she can transfer the mother's fertility to herself, so they dispose of these articles very carefully. If they wish the child to grow fat, they bury the navel-cord in a manure-heap. The upper milk teeth are thrown on to the roof, and the lower ones buried under a water-pot. They say that the upper ones should be in a high place, and the lower ones in a low place. The teeth thrown on the roof may be meant for the rats, who in exchange for them will give the child strong white teeth like their own, while those thrown under the water-pot will cause the new teeth to grow large and quickly, like the grass under a water-pot. Diseases of children are attributed to evil spirits. The illness called Sukhi, in which the body and limbs grow weak and have a dried-up appearance, is very common, and is probably caused by malnutrition. They attribute it to the machinations of an owl which has heard the child's name or obtained a piece of its soiled clothing. If a stone or piece of wood is thrown at the owl to scare it away, it will pick this up, and after wetting it in a stream, put it out in the sun to dry. As the stone or wood dries up, so will the child's body dry up and wither. In order to cure this illness they use charms and amulets, and also let the child wallow in a pig-sty so that it may become as fat as the pigs. They say that they always beat a brass dish at a birth so that the noise may penetrate the child's ears, and this will remove any obstruction there may be to its hearing. If the child appears to be deaf, they lay it several times in a deep grain-bin for about half an hour at a time; when it cries the noise echoes in the bin, and this is supposed to remove the obstruction to its power of hearing. If they wish the boy to be a good dancer, they get a little of the flesh of the kingfisher or hawk which hangs poised in the air over water by the rapid vibration of its wings, on the look-out for a fish, and give him this to eat. If they wish him to speak well, they touch his finger with the tip of a razor, and think that he will become talkative like a barber. If they want him to run fast, they look for a stone on which a hare has dropped some dung and rub this on his legs, or they get a piece of a deer's horn and hang it round his neck as a charm. If a girl or boy is very dark-coloured, they get the branches of a creeper called *malkangni*, and express the oil from them, and rub it on the child's face, and think it will make the face reddish. Thus they apparently consider a black colour to be ugly.

(*e*) Funeral Rites

Burial of the dead has probably been the general custom of the Gonds in the past, and the introduction of cremation may be ascribed to Hindu influence. The latter method of disposal involves greater expense on account of the fuel, and is an honour reserved for elders and important men, though in proportion as the body of the tribe in any locality becomes well-to-do it may be more generally adopted. The dead are usually buried with the feet pointing to the north in opposition to the Hindu practice, and this fact has been adduced in evidence of the Gond belief that their ancestors came from the north. The Māria Gonds of Bastar, however, place the feet to the west in the direction of the setting sun, and with the face upwards. In some places the Hindu custom of placing the head to the north has been adopted. Formerly it is said that the dead were buried in or near the house in which they died, so that their spirits would thus the more easily be born again in children, but this practice has now ceased. In most British Districts Hindu ceremonial[1] tends more and more to be adopted, but in Bastar State and Chānda some interesting customs remain. **32. Disposal of the dead.**

Among the Māria Gonds a drum is beaten to announce a death, and the news is sent to relatives and friends in other villages. The funeral takes place on the second or third day, when these have assembled. They bring some pieces of cloth, and these, together with the deceased's own clothes **33. Funeral ceremony.**

[1] See article on Kurmi.

and some money, are buried with him, so that they may accompany his spirit to the other world. Sometimes the women will put a ring of iron on the body. The body is borne on a hurdle to the burial- or burning-ground, which is invariably to the east of the village, followed by all the men and women of the place. Arrived there, the bearers with the body on their shoulders face round to the west, and about ten yards in front of them are placed three *sāj* leaves in a line with a space of a yard between each, the first representing the supreme being, the second disembodied spirits, and the third witchcraft. Sometimes a little rice is put on the leaves. An axe is struck three times on the ground, and a villager now cries to the corpse to disclose the cause of his death, and immediately the bearers, impelled, as they believe, by the dead man, carry the body to one of the leaves. If they halt before the first, then the death was in the course of nature; if before the second, it arose from the anger of offended spirits; if before the third, witchcraft was the cause. The ordeal may be thrice repeated, the arrangement of the leaves being changed each time. If witchcraft is indicated as the cause of death, and confirmed by the repeated tests, the corpse is asked to point out the sorcerer or witch, and the body is carried along until it halts before some one in the crowd, who is at once seized and disposed of as a witch. Sometimes the corpse may be carried to the house of a witch in another village to a distance of eight or ten miles. In Mandla in such cases a Gunia or exorciser formerly called on the corpse to go forward and point out the witch. The bearers then, impelled by the corpse, made one step forward and stopped. The exorciser then again adjured the corpse, and they made a step, and this was repeated again and again until they halted in front of the supposed witch. All the beholders and the bearers themselves thus thought that they were impelled by the corpse, and the episode is a good illustration of the power of suggestion. Frequently the detected witch was one of the deceased's wives. In Mandla the cause of the man's death was determined in the digging of his grave. When piling in the earth removed for the grave after burial, if it reached exactly to the surface of the ground, they thought that the dead man had died after living the proper span of his life. If the earth made a mound over the hole, they thought he had lived beyond his allotted time and called him Sīgpur, that is a term for a measure of grain heaped as high as it will stand above the brim. But if the earth was insufficient and did not reach to the level of the ground, they held that he had been prematurely cut off, and had been killed by an enemy or by a witch through magic.

Children at breast are buried at the roots of a mahua tree, as it is thought that they will suck liquor from them and be nourished as if by their mother's milk. The mahua is the tree from whose flowers spirits are distilled. The body of an adult may also be burnt under a mahua tree so that the tree may give him a supply of liquor in the next world. Sometimes the corpse is bathed in water, sprinkled over with milk and then anointed with a mixture of mahua oil, turmeric and charcoal, which will prevent it from being reincarnated in a human body. In the case of a man killed by a tiger the body is burned, and a bamboo image of a tiger is made and thrown outside the village. None but the nearest relatives will touch the body of a man killed by a tiger, and they only because they are obliged to do so. None of the ornaments are removed from the corpse, and sometimes any other ornaments possessed by the deceased are added to them, as it is thought that otherwise the tiger into which his spirit passes will come back to look for them and kill some other person in the house. In some localities any one who touches the body of a man killed or even wounded by a tiger or panther is put temporarily out of caste. Yet the Gonds will eat the flesh of tigers and panthers, and also of animals killed and partly devoured by them. When a man has been killed by a tiger, or when he has died of disease and before death vermin have appeared in a wound, the whole family are temporarily out of caste and have to be purified by an elaborate ceremony in which the Bhumka or village priest officiates. The method of laying the spirit of a man killed by a tiger resembles that described in the article on Baiga.

Mourning is usually observed for three days. The mourners abstain from work and indulgence in luxuries, and

34. Mourning and offerings to the dead.

the house is cleaned and washed. The Gonds often take food on the spot after the burial or burning of a corpse and they usually drink liquor. On the third day a feast is given. In Chhindwāra a bullock or cow is slaughtered on the death of a male or female Gond respectively. They tie it up by the horns to a tree so that its forelegs are in the air, and a man slashes it across the head once or twice until it dies. The head is buried under a platform outside the village in the name of the deceased. Sometimes the spirit of the dead man is supposed to enter into one of the persons present and inform the party how he died, whether from witchcraft or by natural causes. He also points out the place where the bullock's or cow's head is to be buried, and here they make a platform to his spirit with a memorial stone. Red lead is applied to the stone and the blood of a chicken poured over it, and the party then consume the bodies of the cow and chicken. In Mandla the mourners are shaved at the grave nine or ten days after the death by the brother-in-law or son-in-law of the deceased, and they cook and eat food there and drink liquor. Then they come home and put oil on the head of the heir and tie a piece of new cloth round his head. They give the dead man's clothes and also a cow or bullock to the Pardhān priest, and offer a goat to the dead man, first feeding the animal with rice, and saying to the dead man's spirit, 'Your son- or brother-in-law has given you this.' Sometimes the rule is that the priest should receive all the ornaments worn on the right side of a man or the left side of a woman, including those on the head, arm and leg. If they give him a cow or bullock, they will choose the one which goes last when the animals are let out to graze. Then they cook and eat it in the compound. They have no regular anniversary ceremonies, but on the new moon of Kunwār (September) they will throw some rice and pulse in front of the house and pour water on it in honour of the dead. The widow breaks her glass bangles when the funeral takes place, and if she is willing she may be married to the dead man's younger brother on the expiry of the period of mourning.

In Bastar, at some convenient time after the death, a stone is set up in memory of any dead person who was an adult, usually by the roadside. Families who have emigrated to other localities often return to their parent village for setting up these stones. The stones vary according to the importance of the deceased, those for prominent men being sometimes as much as eight feet high. In some places a small stone seat is made in front, and this is meant for the deceased to sit on, the memorial stone being his house. After being placed in position the stone is anointed with turmeric, curds, *ghī* and oil, and a cow or pig is offered to it. Afterwards irregular offerings of liquor and tobacco are made to the dead man at the stone by the family and also by strangers passing by. They believe that the memorial stones sometimes grow and increase in size, and if this happens they think that the dead man's family will become extinct, as the stone and the family cannot continue to grow together. Elsewhere a long heap of stones is made in honour of a dead man, sometimes with a flat-topped post at the head. This is especially done for men who have died from epidemic disease or by an accident, and passers-by fling stones on the heap with the idea that the dead man's spirit will thereby be kept down and prevented from returning to trouble the living. In connection with the custom of making a seat at the deceased's tomb for his spirit to sit upon, Mr. A. K. Smith writes: "It is well known to every Gond that ghosts and devils cannot squat on the bare ground like human beings, and must be given something to sit on. The white man who requires a chair to sit on is thus plainly akin to the world of demons, so one of the few effective ways of getting Gonds to open their mouths and talk freely is to sit on the ground among them. Outside every Gond house is placed a rough bench for the accommodation of any devils that may be flitting about at night, so that they may not come indoors and trouble the inmates."

35. Memorial stones to the dead.

36. House abandoned after a death.

If one or two persons die in a house in one year, the family often leave it and make another house. On quitting the old house they knock a hole in the back wall to go out, so as to avoid going out by the front door. This is usually done when the deaths have been due to an epidemic, and it is presumably supposed that the dead men's spirits will haunt the house and cause others to die, from spite at their own untimely end. If an epidemic visits a village, the Gonds will also frequently abandon it, and make a new village on another site.

37. Bringing back the soul.

They believe that the spirits of ancestors are reincarnated in children or in animals. Sometimes they make a mark with soot or vermilion on the body of a dead man, and if some similar mark is subsequently found on any newborn child it is held that the dead man's spirit has been reborn in it. In Bastar, on some selected day a short time after the death, they obtain two small baskets and set them out at night, placing a chicken under one and some flour of wheat or kutki under the other. The householder then says, "I do the work of those old men who died. O spirits, I offer a chicken to you to-day; be true and I will perform your funeral rites to-morrow." On the next morning the basket placed over the flour is lifted up, and if a mark resembling a footprint of a man or any animal be found, they think that the deceased has become incarnate in a human being or in that animal. Subsequently they sacrifice a cow to the spirit as described. In other places on the fifth day after death they perform the ceremony of bringing back the soul. The relatives go to the riverside and call aloud the name of the dead person, and then enter the river, catch a fish or insect and, taking it home, place it among the sainted dead of the family, believing that the spirit of the dead person has in this manner been brought back to the house. The brother-in-law or son-in-law of the dead man will make a miniature grass hut in the compound and place the fish or insect inside it. He will then sacrifice a pig, killing it with a rice-husker, and with not more than three blows. The animal is eaten, and next morning he breaks down the hut and throws away the earthen pots from the house. They will spread some flour on the ground and in the morning bring a chicken up to it. If the animal eats the flour they say that the soul of the deceased has shown his wish to remain in the house, and he is enshrined there in the shape of a stone or copper coin. If it does not eat, then they say that the spirit will not remain in the house. They take the stone or coin outside the village, sacrifice a chicken to it and bury it under a heap of stones to prevent it from returning.

Sometimes at the funeral ceremony one of the party is possessed by the spirit of the dead man, and a little white mark or a small caterpillar appears on his hand, and they say that it is the soul of the dead man come back. Then the caterpillar vanishes again, and they say that the dead man has been taken among the gods, and go home. Occasionally some mark may appear on the hand of the dead man's son after a period of time, and he says that his father's soul has come back, and gives another funeral feast. The good souls are quickly appeased and their veneration is confined to their descendants. But the bad ones excite a wider interest because their evil influences may be extended to others. And the same fear attaches to the spirits of persons who have died a violent or unnatural death. The soul of a man who has been eaten by a tiger must be specially propitiated, and ten or twelve days are occupied in bringing it back. To ascertain when this has been done a thread is tied to a beam and a copper ring is suspended from it, being secured by twisting the thread round it and not by a knot. A pot full of water is placed below the ring. Songs are then sung in propitiation and a watch is kept day and night. When the ring falls from the thread and drops into the water it is considered that the soul has come back. If the ring delays to fall they adjure the dead man to come back and ask where he has gone to and why he is tarrying. Animals are offered to the ring and their blood poured over it, and when it finally falls they rejoice greatly and say that the dead man has come back. The ancestors are represented by small pebbles kept in a basket in the kitchen, which is considered the holiest part of the house, or they may be pice copper coins ($\frac{1}{4}$d.) tied up in a little bundle. They are daubed with vermilion and worshipped occasionally. A man who has been killed by a tiger or cobra may receive general veneration, with the object of appeasing his spirit, and become a village god. And the same honour may be accorded to any prominent man, such as the founder of a village.

38. The dead absorbed in Bura Deo.

In Mandla the dead are sometimes mingled with Bura Deo or the Great God. On the occasion of a communal sacrifice to Bura Deo a stalk of *charra* grass is picked in the name of each of the dead ancestors, and tied to the little bundle containing a pice and a piece of turmeric, which represents the dead ancestor in the house. The stalk of grass and the bundle is called *kunda*; and all the *kundas* are then hidden in grass or under stones in the adjacent forest. Then Bura Deo comes on some man and possesses him, and he waves his arms about and goes and finds all the *kundas*. Some of them he throws down beside Bura Deo, and these they say have been absorbed in Bura Deo and are disposed of. Others he throws apart, and these are said not to have been absorbed into the god. For the latter, as well as for all persons who have died a violent death, a heap of stones should be made outside the village, and wine and a fowl are offered at the heap, and passers-by cast additional stones on it to keep down their spirits, which remain unquiet because they have not been absorbed in the god, and are apt to wander about and trouble the living.

39. Belief in a future life.

The Gonds seem originally to have had no idea of a place of abode for the spirits of the dead, that is a heaven or hell. So far as can be conjectured, their primary view of the fate of the spirits of the dead, after they had come to consider the soul or spirit as surviving the death of the body, was that they hung about the houses and village where they had dwelt, and were able to exert considerable influence on the lives and fortunes of their successors. An alternative or subsequent view was that they were reincarnated, most frequently in the bodies of children born in the same family, and less frequently in animals. Whether or no this doctrine of reincarnation is comparatively late and borrowed from Hinduism cannot be decided. In Bastar, however, they have now a conception of retribution after death for the souls of evil-doers. They say that the souls are judged after death, and the sinful are hurled down into a dense forest without any *sulphi* trees. The *sulphi* tree appears to be that variety of palm from which palm-liquor or toddy is obtained in Bastar, and the Gond idea of a place of punishment for departed sinners is, therefore, one in which no alcoholic liquor is to be had.

(*f*) Religion

The religious practices of the Gonds present much variety. The tribal divisions into groups worshipping seven, six, five and four gods, already referred to, are generally held to refer to the number of gods which a man has in his house. But very few Gonds can name the gods of their sect, and the prescribed numbers are seldom adhered to. The worship of ancestors is an integral part of their religion and is described in the section on funeral customs. Bura Deo, their great god in most localities, was probably at first the *sāj* tree,[1] but afterwards the whole collection of gods were sometimes called Bura Deo. He is further discussed subsequently. The other Gond gods proper appear to be principally implements and weapons of the chase, one or two animals, and deified human beings. A number of Hindu deities have now also been admitted into the Gond pantheon. The following account of the gods is largely taken from a note written by Mr. J. A. Tawney.[2] The worship of the Gonds may be summarised as that of the gods presiding over the village destinies, the crops, and epidemic disease, the spirits of their forefathers and the weapons and creatures of the chase. The village gods are generally common to the Gonds and Hindus. They consist of stones, or mud platforms, placed at a convenient distance from the village under the shade of some appropriate tree, and often having a red or white flag, made of a piece of cloth, tied to the end of a pole to indicate their position. The principal village gods have been given in the article on Kurmi. Besides these in Gond villages there is especially Bhīmsen, who is held to be Bhima, one of the five Pāndava brothers, and is the god of strength. Ghor Deo[3] is the horse god, and Holera, who is represented by a wooden bullock's bell, is the god of cattle. Ghansiām Deo is a god much worshipped in Mandla. He is said to have been a prince who was killed by a tiger on his way to his wedding like Dūlha Deo. In northern Bastar the Gonds worship the spirit of a

40. Nature of the Gond religion. The gods.

[1] *Boswellia serrata.*

[2] Deputy-Commissioner, Chhīndwāra. The note was contributed to the *Central Provinces Census Report* for 1881 (Mr. Drysdale).

[3] *Ghora*, a horse.

Muhammadan doctor under the name of Doctor Deo. A Gond of the place where the doctor died is occasionally possessed by his spirit, and on such occasions he can talk fluent Urdu. This man's duty is to keep off cholera, and when the epidemic breaks out he is ordered by the Rāja to drive it away. The local method of averting cholera is to make a small litter covered with cloth, and in it to place a brass or silver image of the cholera goddess, Marai Māta. When the goddess is thus sent from one village to another it is supposed that the epidemic is similarly transferred. The man possessed by Doctor Deo has the power of preventing the approach of this litter to villages in Bastar, and apparently also can drive away the epidemic, though his method of doing this is not explained. The dealings of the Gonds with the Government of India are mainly conducted through chuprāssies or peons, who come to collect their revenue, obtain supplies and so on. The peons have in the past been accustomed to abuse their authority and practise numerous petty extortions, which is a very easy business with the ignorant Gonds of the wilder tracts. Regarding the peons as the visible emblem of authority, the Gonds, like the Oraons, have similarly furnished the gods with a peon, who is worshipped under the name of Kalha Deo with offerings of liquor and fowls. Besides this if a tiger makes himself troublesome a stone is set up in his honour and he receives a small offering; and if a platform has been erected to the memory of the founder of the village he is included with the others. The cholera and smallpox deities are worshipped when an epidemic breaks out. The worship of the village gods is communal, and in Chhīndwāra is performed at the end of the hot weather before seed is sown, houses thatched, or the new mahua oil eaten by the Gonds. All the villagers subscribe, and the Bhumka or village priest conducts the rite. If in any year the community cannot afford a public worship they hang up a little grass over the god just to intimate that they have not forgotten him, but that he will have to wait till next year.

41. Tribal gods, and their place of residence.

Besides the village gods worshipped in common with the Hindus, the Gonds have also their special tribal gods. These are sometimes kept at a Deo-khulla, which is said to mean literally the threshing-floor of the gods, and is perhaps so called because the place of meeting of the worshippers is cleaned and plastered like a threshing-floor in the fields. The gods most commonly found are Pharsi Pen, the battle-axe god; Matiya, the great god of mischief; Ghangra, the bell god; Chāwar, the cow's tail, which is also used as a whisk; Pālo, who consists of a piece of cloth used to cover spear-heads; and Sale, who may be the god who presides over cattle-pens (*sāla*). The Deo-khulla of a six-god Gond should have six, and that of a seven-god Gond seven gods, but this rule is not regularly observed, and the Deo-khullas themselves now tend to disappear as the Gonds become Hinduised and attention is concentrated on the village and household gods. The collection of gods at a Deo-khulla, Mr. Tawney remarks, is called Bura Deo, and when a Gond swears by Bura Deo, he swears by all the gods of his sect. "The gods," Mr. Tawney writes, "are generally tied up in grass and fixed in the fork of the *sāj* tree, or buried in some recess in the forest, except Pālo, who is put in a bag to prevent his getting wet, and Chāwar the cow's tail. The Bhumkas or priests are somewhat shy of showing the gods at the Deo-khulla, and they may have some reason for this, for not long since, a young scamp of a Muhammadan, having determined to put to a test the reputed powers of the Gond gods for evil, hid himself in a tree near the Deo-khulla during a meeting, and afterwards took the gods out and threw them bag and baggage down a well. However, when I went there, the Bhumka at Mujāwar after some parley retired into the forest, and came out quite confidingly with an armful of gods. The Deo-khulla gods are generally all of iron, and those at Mujāwar were all spear-shaped except Pālo, who is a piece of cloth, and Ghangra, who is of bell-metal and in form like the bells ordinarily put round the necks of bullocks. When a spear-head has been lost, and another is not available, anything in the shape of a pike or spear will do, and it does not appear to make any difference so long as iron is the metal used. Women may not worship at the Deo-khulla. It seems clear that the original gods were, with the exception of Ghangra, hunting-weapons and representations of animals. Ghangra may be venerated because of his association with bullocks and also on account of the melodious sound made by bullock-bells. Of all the gods the most remarkable probably is Pālo. He is made of cloth and acts as a covering for the spear-heads at the time of worship. The one I saw was a small cloth, about 30 by 18 inches, and in the form of a shield. He is a very expensive god and costs from Rs. 50 to Rs. 80, his outside value perhaps being Rs. 5. When a new one is required it has to be made by a Katia or Rāj-Pardhān, who must live in a separate house and not go near his own till its completion. He must also be naked while he is working and may not eat, drink, smoke or perform natural functions till he has finished for the day. While engaged on the cloth he is well fed by the Gonds and supplied with fowls and spirits; it is not surprising, therefore, that the god is never finished in six months, though I would engage to make one in a week. The cloth is embroidered with figures in coloured silk, with a stitch or two of red silk in each animal, which will subsequently represent blood. The animals I saw embroidered were a bullock, some sort of deer, a gouty-looking snake with a body as thick as the elephant's, and the latter animal barely distinguishable from it by having two legs and a trunk. When ready the cloth Pālo is taken to the Deo-khulla and a great worship is held, during which blood is seen to flow from the figures on the cloth and they are supposed to be endowed with life." The animals embroidered on the cloth are probably those principally revered by the Gonds, as the elephant, snake, deer and bullock, while the worship of the cloth itself and the embroidery on it indicates that they considered the arts of weaving and sewing as divinely revealed accomplishments. And the fact that the other gods were made of iron shows a similar reverence for this metal, which they perhaps first discovered in India. At any rate the quarrying and refining of indigenous iron-ore is at present carried out by the Agarias, a caste derived from the Gonds. The spear-head shape of most of the gods and that of Pālo like a shield show their veneration for these weapons of war, which are themselves sacred.

42. Household gods.

"In almost every house," Mr. Tawney states, "there is also a set of gods for everyday use. They are often the same as the village gods or those of the Deo-khulla and also include deified ancestors. These household gods have a tendency to increase, as special occasions necessitate the creation of a new god, and once he is enthroned in the house he never seems to leave it of his own accord. Thus if a man is killed by a cobra ; he or the cobra becomes a household god and is worshipped for many generations. If a set of gods does not work satisfactorily, they are also, some or all of them, discarded and a new lot introduced. The form of the gods varies considerably, the only constant thing about them being the vermilion with which they are all daubed. They are sometimes all earthen cones and vary from that to miniature wooden tables. I may mention that it is somewhat difficult to get a Gond either to confess that he has any household gods or to show them. The best way is to send off the father of the family on some errand, and then to ask his unsuspecting wife to bring out the gods. You generally get them on a tray and some of the villagers will help her to name them." In Mandla in every Gond's house there is a Deothāna or god's place, where all the gods are kept. Those who have children include Jhulān Devi, or the cradle goddess, among their household deities. In the Deothāna there is always a vessel full of water and a stick, and when a man comes in from outside he goes to this and sprinkles a little water over his body to free himself from any impurity he may have contracted abroad.

On one of the posts of the house the image of Nāg Deo, the cobra god, is made in mud. In Asārh (June) the first month of the rains, which the Gonds consider the beginning of the year, snakes frequently appear. In this month they try to kill a cobra, and will then cut off the head and tail, and offer them to Nāg Deo, inside the house, while they cook and eat the body. They think that the eating of the snake's body will protect them from the effects of eating any poisonous substance throughout the year. 43. Nāg Deo.

Nārāyan Deo or the sun is also a household deity. He has a little platform inside the threshold of the house. He may be worshipped every two or three years, but if a snake appears in the house or any one falls ill they think that Nārāyan Deo is impatient and perform his worship. A 44. Nārāyan Deo.

young pig is offered to him and is sometimes fattened up beforehand by feeding it on rice. The pig is laid on its back over the threshold of the door and a number of men press a heavy beam of wood on its body till it is crushed to death. They cut off the tail and testicles and bury them near the threshold. The body of the pig is washed in a hole dug in the yard, and it is then cooked and eaten. They sing to the god, "Eat, Nārāyan Deo, eat this rice and meat, and protect us from all tigers, snakes and bears in our houses; protect us from all illnesses and troubles." Next day the bones and any other remains of the pig are buried in the hole in the compound and the earth is well stamped down over it.

45. Bura Deo. Bura Deo, the great god of the Gonds, is sometimes, as seen, a name for all the gods in the Deo-khulla. But he is usually considered as a single god, and often consists of a number of brass or iron balls suspended to a ring and hung on a *sāj* tree. Again, he may be represented by a few links of a roughly forged iron chain also hung on the tree, and the divine power of the chain is shown by the fact that it can move of itself, and occasionally descends to rest on a stone under the tree or migrates to a neighbouring nullah (stream). Nowadays in Mandla Bura Deo is found as an iron doll made by a neighbouring blacksmith instead of a chain. It would appear, however, that he was originally the *sāj* tree (*Boswellia serrata*), an important forest tree growing to a considerable height, which is much revered by the Gonds. They do not cut this tree, nor its branches, except for ceremonial purposes, and their most sacred form of oath is to swear by the name of Bura Deo, holding a branch of the *sāj* tree above the head. If Bura Deo was first the *sāj* tree, then we may surmise that when the Gonds discovered iron they held it more sacred than the tree because it was more important, as the material from which their axes and spears were made. And therefore Bura Deo became an iron chain hanging on the *sāj* tree. The axe is a Gond's most valuable implement, as with it he cut down the forest to clear a space for his shifting cultivation, and also provided himself with wood for hutting, fuel and other purposes. The axe and spear were also his weapons of war. Hence the discovery

of iron was an enormous step forward in civilisation, and this may account for the reverence in which it is held by the Gonds. The metamorphosis of Bura Deo from an iron chain to an iron doll may perhaps be considered to mark the arrival of the Gonds at the stage of religion when anthropomorphic gods are worshipped. Bura Deo is sometimes represented with Mahādeo or Siva and Pārvati, two of the greatest Hindu deities, in attendance on him on each side. Communal sacrifices of pigs and also of goats are made to him at intervals of one or two years; the animals are stretched out on their backs and killed by driving a stake of *sāj* or *tendu*[1] wood through the belly. Sometimes a goat is dedicated to him a year beforehand, and allowed to wander loose in the village in the name of Bura Deo, and given good food, and even called by the name of the god. It would appear that the original sacrificial animal was the pig, and the goat was afterwards added or substituted. Bura Deo is also worshipped on special occasions, as when a man has got vermin in a wound, or, as the people of the country say, when god has remembered him. In this case the sufferer must pay all the expenses of the ceremony which is necessary for his purification. The dead are also mingled in Bura Deo, as described in the section on funeral rites. Bura Deo is believed to protect the Gonds from wild animals; and if members of a family meet a tiger, snake or other dangerous animal several times within a fairly short period, they think that Bura Deo is displeased with them and have a special sacrifice in his honour. Ordinarily when the Panda or priest sacrifices an animal he severs its head with an axe and holds the head over the image or symbol of the god to allow the blood to drop on it. Before sacrificing a chicken he places some grain before it and says, 'If I have committed no fault, eat,' and if the chicken does not eat of itself he usually forces it to pick a grain. Then he says that the sacrifice is acceptable to the god.

46. Charms and magic.

When they think a child has been overlooked they fetch a strip of leather from the Chamār's house, make it into a little bag, fill it with scrapings from a clean bit of leather, and hang it round the child's neck. If a child is ill they

[1] *Diospyros tomentosa.*

sometimes fetch from the Chamār's house water which has been used for tanning and give it him to drink. If a man is possessed by an evil spirit, they will take some coins, silver for preference, and wave them round his head with a lamp, and take them out and bury them in a waste place. They throw one or two more rupees on the surface of the soil in which they have buried the coins. Then they think the spirit will leave the sufferer, and if any one picks up the coins on the surface of the ground the spirit will possess him. Hindus who find such buried coins frequently refuse to take them, even though they may be valuable, from fear of being possessed by the spirit. Occasionally a man of a treacherous disposition may transfer an evil spirit, which is haunting him, with a daughter in marriage. The husband's family suspect this if a spirit begins to trouble them. A Vaddai or magician is called, and he tries to transfer the spirit to a fowl or goat by giving the latter some rice to eat. If the spirit then ceases troubling they conclude that it was transferred by the bride's father, and go to him and reproach him. If he admits that he had a spirit in his family which has given no trouble lately, they ask him to take it back, even though he may not have intended its transfer. The goat or fowl to which the spirit was transferred is then sacrificed in its name and the meat is eaten only by the father-in-law's family, to whom the spirit thus returns. A miniature hut is built for the spirit in his yard, and a pot, a lamp and a knife are placed in the hut for its use, and an offering of a goat is made to the spirit occasionally at festivals.

In order to injure an enemy they will make an image of him in clay, preferably taken from underneath his foot-print, and carry it to the cemetery. Here they offer red lead, red thread, bangles, and various kinds of grain and pulse to the ghosts and say to them, "Male and female deities, old and newly buried, maimed and lame, spirits of the wind, I pronounce this charm with your help." Then they pierce the figure with arrows in the chest and cut it with a knife in the region of the liver and think that their enemy will die. Another method is to draw the likeness of an enemy on cloth with lime or charcoal, and bury it in a pot in front of his house on a Sunday or Tuesday night so that he may walk on it in the morning, when they hope that the same result will be achieved.

In order to breed a quarrel in an enemy's house they get the feathers of a crow, or the seeds of the *amaltās*,[1] or porcupine needles, and after smoking them over a fire in which some nails have been placed, tie them to the eaves of his house, repeating some charm. The seeds of the *amaltās* rattle in their pods in the wind, and hence it is supposed that they will produce a noise of quarrelling. Porcupine's quills are sharp and prickly, and crow's feathers are perhaps efficacious because the crow is supposed to be a talkative and quarrelsome bird. The nails in the fire, being sharp-pointed, may be meant to add potency to the charm. One who wishes to transfer sickness to another person obtains a cloth belonging to the latter and draws two human figures on it, one right side up and the other upside down, in lamp-black. After saying charms over the cloth he puts it back surreptitiously in the owner's house. When people are ill they make a vow to some god that if they recover they will sacrifice a certain number of animals proportionate to the severity of the illness. If the patient then recovers, and the vow is for a larger number of animals than he can afford, he sets fire to a piece of forest so that a number of animals may be burnt as an offering to the god, and his vow may thus be fulfilled. This practice has no doubt gone out owing to the conservation of forests.

If a Gond, when starting on a journey in the morning, 47. Omens.
should meet a tiger, cat, hare, or a four-horned deer, he will return and postpone his journey; but if he meets one of these animals when he is well on the way it is considered to be lucky. Rain falling at a wedding or some other festival is believed to be unlucky, as it is as if somebody were crying. In Mandla, if a cock crows in the night, a man will get up at once, catch it and twist its neck, and throw it over the house as far away as he can. Apparently the cock is supposed to be calling to evil spirits. If a hen cackles, or lays eggs at night, it is also considered inauspicious, and the bird is often killed or given away. They think they can acquire strength by carrying the shoulder-bones of a tiger

[1] *Cassia fistula*.

on their shoulders or drinking a little of the bone-dust pounded in water. If there is disease in the village, the Bhumka or village priest performs the ceremony of *Gaon bāndhna* or tying up the village. Accompanied by a party of men he drives a pig all round the village boundary, scattering grains of urad pulse and mustard seed on the way. The pig is then sacrificed, its blood is sprinkled on all the village gods, and it is eaten by the party. No man or animal may go outside the village on the day of this ceremony, which should be performed on a Sunday or Wednesday. When cattle disease breaks out the Bhumka makes an arch of three poles, to which is hung a string of mango leaves, and all the cattle of the village are driven under it to avert the disease.

48. Agricultural superstitions.

When there is drought two boys put a pestle across their shoulders, tie a living frog to it with a rag, and go from house to house accompanied by other boys and girls singing:

Mendak Bhai pāni de,
Dhān, kodon pakne de,
Mere byāh hone de,

or 'Brother Frog give rain; let the rice and kodon ripen; let my marriage be held.' The frog is considered to be able to produce rain because it lives in water and therefore has control over its element. The boy's point in asking the frog to let his marriage be held is that if the rains failed and the crops withered, his parents would be unable to afford the expense. Another method of obtaining rain is for two naked women to go and harness themselves to a plough at night, while a third naked woman drives the plough and pricks them with a goad. This does not appear capable of explanation on any magical basis, so far as I know, and the idea may possibly be to force the clemency of the gods by showing their extraordinary sufferings, or to show that the world is topsy-turvy for want of rain. A leather rope is sometimes tied to a plough and harrow, and the boys and girls pull against one another on the rope in a tug-of-war. If the girls win they think that rain will soon come, but if the boys win that it will not. In order to stop excessive rain, a naked bachelor collects water from the eaves in a new earthen pot, covers the pot with a lid or with mud, and buries it beneath the earth; or the pot may be filled with salt. Here it may perhaps be supposed that, as the water dries up in the pot or the salt gets dry, so the rain will stop and the world generally become dry. The reason for employing women to produce rain, and men to stop it, may be that women, as they give milk, will be more potent in obtaining the other liquid, water. Nakedness is a common element in magic, perhaps because clothes are considered a civilised appanage, and unsuitable for a contest with the powers of nature; a certain idea of impurity may also attach to them. If a crow in carrying a straw to build its nest holds it in the middle, they think that the rains will be normal and adequate; but if the straw is held towards one end, that the rains will be excessive or deficient. If the *titahri* or sandpiper lays four eggs properly arranged, they think that sufficient rain will fall in all the four monsoon months. If only one, two or three eggs are laid, or only this number properly placed in the nest and the others at the side, then the rains will be good only in an equivalent number of months.

At the beginning of the harvest they pluck an ear of corn and say, 'Whatever god is the guardian of this place, this is your share, take it, and do not interfere.' The last plants in the field are cut and sent home by a little girl and put at the bottom of the grain-bin of the house. Chitkuar Devi is the goddess of the threshing-floor, and before beginning to winnow the grain they sacrifice a pig and a chicken to her, cutting the throats of the animals and letting their blood drop on to the central post of the threshing-floor. When they are about to take the kodon home, they set aside a basketful and give it to the sister's son or sister's husband of the owner, placing a bottle of liquor on the top, and he takes it home to the house, and there they drink one or two bottles of liquor, and then begin eating the new grain.

49. Magical or religious observances in fishing and hunting.

In Mandla the Gonds still perform, or did till recently, various magical or religious rites to obtain success in fishing and hunting. The men of a village were accustomed to go out fishing as a communal act. They arrived at the river before sunrise, and at midday their women brought them *pej* or gruel. On returning the women made a mound or platform before the house of the principal man of the party.

All the fish caught were afterwards laid on this platform and the leader then divided them, leaving one piece on the platform. Next morning this piece was taken away and placed on the grave of the leader's ancestor. If no fish were caught on the first day, then on the next day the women took the men no food. And if they caught no fish for two or three days running, they went and dug up the platform erected in front of the leader's house and levelled it with the ground. Then the next morning early all the people of the village went to another village and danced the Sela dance before the tombs of the ancestors of that village. Sometimes they went on to a third village and did the same. The headman of the village visited levied a contribution from his people, and gave them food and drink and a present of Rs. 1-4. With this they bought liquor, and coming back to their own village, offered it in front of the platform which they had levelled, and drank it. Next morning they went fishing again, but said that they did not care whether they caught anything or not, as they had pleased their god. Next year all the people of the village they had visited would come and dance the Sela dance at their village the whole day, and the hosts had to give the visitors food and drink. This was said to be from gratitude to the headman of the other village for placating their god with an offering of Rs. 1-4. And the visit might even be repeated annually so long as the headman of the other village was alive. Apparently in this elaborate ritual the platform especially represented the forefathers of the village, whose spirits were supposed to give success in fishing. If the fishers were unsuccessful, they demolished the platform to show their displeasure to the spirits, and went and danced before the ancestors of another village to intimate the transfer of their allegiance from their own ancestors to these latter. The ancestors would thus feel themselves properly snubbed and discarded for their ill-nature in not giving success to the fishing party. But when they had been in this condition for a day or so the headman of the other village sent them an offering of liquor, and it was thus intimated to them that, though their own descendants had temporarily transferred their devotion, they were not entirely abandoned. It would be hoped that the ancestors would lay the lesson to heart, and, placated by the liquor, be more careful in future of the welfare of their descendants. The season for fishing was in Kunwār and Kārtik, and it sometimes extended into Aghan (September to November). During these months, from the time the new kodon was cut at the beginning of the period, they danced the Sela, and they did not dance this dance at any other time of the year.[1] At other seasons they would dance the Karma. The Sela dance is danced by men alone; they have sticks and form two circles, and walk in and out in opposite directions, beating their sticks together as they pass. Sometimes other men sit on the shoulders of the dancers and beat their sticks. Sela is said to be the name of the stick. In the Sela dance the singing is in the form of Dadaria, that is, one party recites a line and the other party replies; this is not done in the Karma dance, for which they have regular songs. It seems possible that the Sela dance was originally a mimic combat, danced before they went out to fight in order to give them success in the battle. Subsequently it might be danced before they went out hunting and fishing with the same object. If there was no stream to which they could go fishing they would buy some fish and offer it to the god, and have a holiday and eat it, or if they could not go fishing they might go hunting in a party instead. When a single Gond intends to go out hunting in the forest he first lights a lamp before his household god in the house, or if he has no oil he will kindle a fire, and the lamp or fire must be kept burning all the time he is out. If he returns successful he offers a chicken to the god and extinguishes the lamp. But if he is unsuccessful he keeps the lamp burning all night, and goes out again early next morning. If he gets more game this time he will offer the chicken, but if not he will extinguish the lamp, put his gun outside and not touch it again for eight days. A Gond never takes food in the morning before going out hunting, but goes out in a fasting condition perhaps in order that the god, seeing his hunger, may send

1 This is incorrect, at present at any rate, as the Karma is danced during the harvest period. But it is probable that the ritual observances for communal fishing and hunting have now fallen into abeyance.

him some game to eat. Nor will a Gond visit his wife the night before he goes out hunting. When a Baiga goes out hunting he bangs his liquor-gourd on the ground before his household god and vows that, if successful, he will offer to the god the gourd full of liquor and a chicken. But if he returns empty-handed, instead of doing this he fills the gourd with earth and throws it over the god to show his wrath. Then if he is successful on the next day, he will scrape off the earth and offer the liquor and chicken as promised. A Baiga should worship his god and go out hunting at the new moon, and then he will hunt the whole month. But if he has not worshipped his god at the new moon, and still goes out hunting and is unsuccessful, he will hunt no more that month. Some Gonds before they go hunting draw an image of Mahābīr or Hanumān, the monkey god and the god of strength, on their guns, and rub it out when they get home again.

50. Witchcraft. The belief in witchcraft has been till recently in full force and vigour among the Gonds, and is only now showing symptoms of decline. In 1871 Sir C. Grant wrote:[1] "The wild hill country from Mandla to the eastern coast is believed to be so infested by witches that at one time no prudent father would let his daughter marry into a family which did not include among its members at least one of the dangerous sisterhood. The non-Aryan belief in the power of evil here strikes a ready chord in the minds of their conquerors, attuned to dread by the inhospitable appearance of the country and the terrible effect of its malicious influences upon human life. In the wilds of Mandla there are many deep hillside caves which not even the most intrepid Baiga hunter would approach for fear of attracting upon himself the wrath of their demoniac inhabitants; and where these hillmen, who are regarded both by themselves and by others as ministers between men and spirits, are afraid, the sleek cultivator of the plains must feel absolute repulsion. Then the suddenness of the epidemics to which, whether from deficient water-supply or other causes, Central India seems so subject, is another fruitful source of terror among an ignorant people. When cholera breaks out in a wild part

[1] *C. P. Gazetteer* (1871), Introduction, p. 130.

of the country it creates a perfect stampede—villages, roads, and all works in progress are deserted; even the sick are abandoned by their nearest relations to die, and crowds fly to the jungles, there to starve on fruits and berries till the panic has passed off. The only consideration for which their minds have room at such times is the punishment of the offenders, for the ravages caused by the disease are unhesitatingly set down to human malice. The police records of the Central Provinces unfortunately contain too many sad instances of life thus sacrificed to a mad unreasoning terror." The detection of a witch by the agency of the corpse, when the death is believed to have been caused by witchcraft, has been described in the section on funeral rites. In other cases a lamp was lighted and the names of the suspected persons repeated; the flicker of the lamp at any name was held to indicate the witch. Two leaves were thrown on the outstretched hand of a suspected person, and if the leaf representing her or him fell above the other suspicion was deepened. In Bastar the leaf ordeal was followed by sewing the person accused into a sack and letting her down into shallow water; if she managed in her struggles for life to raise her head above water she was finally adjudged to be guilty. A witch was beaten with rods of the tamarind or castor-oil plants, which were supposed to be of peculiar efficacy in such cases; her head was shaved cross-wise from one ear to the other over the head and down to the neck; her teeth were sometimes knocked out, perhaps to prevent her from doing mischief if she should assume the form of a tiger or other wild animal; she was usually obliged to leave the village, and often murdered. Murder for witchcraft is now comparatively rare as it is too often followed by detection and proper punishment. But the belief in the causation of epidemic disease by personal agency is only slowly declining. Such measures as the disinfection of wells by permanganate of potash during a visitation of cholera, or inoculation against plague, are sometimes considered as attempts on the part of the Government to reduce the population. When the first epidemic of plague broke out in Mandla in 1911 it caused a panic among the Gonds, who threatened to attack with their axes any Government officer who should come to their village, in the belief that all of them must be plague-inoculators. In the course of six months, however, the feeling of panic died down under a system of instruction by schoolmasters and other local officials and by circulars ; and by the end of the period the Gonds began to offer themselves voluntarily for inoculation, and would probably have come to do so in fairly large numbers if the epidemic had not subsided.

51. Human sacrifice.[1]

The Gonds were formerly accustomed to offer human sacrifices, especially to the goddess Kāli and to the goddess Danteshwari, the tutelary deity of the Rājas of Bastar. Her shrine was at a place called Dantewāra, and she was probably at first a local goddess and afterwards identified with the Hindu goddess Kāli. An inscription recently found in Bastar records the grant of a village to a Medipota in order to secure the welfare of the people and their cattle. This man was the head of a community whose business it was, in return for the grants of land which they enjoyed, to supply victims for human sacrifice either from their own families or elsewhere. Tradition states that on one occasion as many as 101 persons were sacrificed to avert some great calamity which had befallen the country. And sacrifices also took place when the Rāja visited the temple. During the period of the Bhonsla rule early in the nineteenth century the Rāja of Bastar was said to have immolated twenty-five men before he set out to visit the Rāja of Nāgpur at his capital. This would no doubt be as an offering for his safety, and the lives of the victims were given as a substitute for his own. A guard was afterwards placed on the temple by the Marāthas, but reports show that human sacrifice was not finally stamped out until the Nāgpur territories lapsed to the British in 1853. At Chānda and Lānji also, Mr. Hislop states, human sacrifices were offered until well into the nineteenth century[2] at the temples of Kāli. The victim was taken to the temple after sunset and shut up within its dismal walls. In the morning, when the door was opened, he was found dead, much to the glory of the great goddess, who had shown her power by coming during the night and sucking his blood. No doubt there

[1] This section contains some information furnished by R. B. Hira Lāl.

[2] *Notes on the Gonds*, pp. 15, 16.

must have been some of her servants hid in the fane whose business it was to prepare the horrid banquet. It is said that an iron plate was afterwards put over the face of the goddess to prevent her from eating up the persons going before her. In Chānda the legend tells that the families of the town had each in turn to supply a victim to the goddess. One day a mother was weeping bitterly because her only son was to be taken as the victim, when an Ahīr passed by, and on learning the cause of her sorrow offered to go instead. He took with him the rope of hair with which the Ahīrs tie the legs of their cows when milking them and made a noose out of it. When the goddess came up to him he threw the noose over her neck and drew it tight like a Thug. The goddess begged him to let her go, and he agreed to do so on condition that she asked for no more human victims. No doubt, if the legend has any foundation, the Ahīr found a human neck within his noose. It has been suggested in the article on Thug that the goddess Kāli is really the deified tiger, and if this were so her craving for human sacrifices is readily understood. All the three places mentioned, Dantewāra, Lānji and Chānda, are in a territory where tigers are still numerous, and certain points in the above legends favour the idea of this animal origin of the goddess. Such are the shutting of the victim in the temple at night as an animal is tied up for a tiger-kill, and the closing of her mouth with an iron plate as the mouths of tigers are sometimes supposed to be closed by magic. Similarly it may perhaps be believed that the Rāja of Bastar offered human sacrifices to protect himself and his party from the attacks of tigers, which would be the principal danger on a journey to Nāgpur. In Mandla there is a tradition that a Brāhman boy was formerly sacrificed at intervals to the god Bura Deo, and the forehead of the god was marked with his hair in place of sandalwood, and the god bathed in his blood and used his bones as sticks for playing at ball. Similarly in Bindrānawāgarh in Raipur the Gonds are said to have entrapped strangers and offered them to their gods, and if possible a Brāhman was obtained as the most suitable offering. These legends indicate the traditional hostility of the Gonds to the Hindus, and especially to the

Brāhmans, by whom they were at one time much oppressed and ousted from their lands. According to tradition, a Gond Rāja of Garha-Mandla, Madhkur Shāh, had treacherously put his elder brother to death. Divine vengeance overtook him and he became afflicted with chronic pains in the head. No treatment was of avail, and he was finally advised that the only means of appeasing a justly incensed deity was to offer his own life. He determined to be burnt inside the trunk of the sacred pīpal tree, and a hollow trunk sufficiently dry for the purpose having been found at Deogarh, twelve miles from Mandla, he shut himself up in it and was burnt to death. The story is interesting as showing how the neurotic or other pains, which are the result of remorse for a crime, are ascribed to the vengeance of a divine providence.

52. Cannibalism.

Mr. Wilson quotes[1] an account, written by Lieutenant Prendergast in 1820, in which he states that he had discovered a tribe of Gonds who were cannibals, but ate only their own relations. The account was as follows: "In May 1820 I visited the hills of Amarkantak, and having heard that a particular tribe of Gonds who lived in the hills were cannibals, I made the most particular inquiries assisted by my clerk Mohan Singh, an intelligent and well-informed Kāyasth. We learned after much trouble that there was a tribe of Gonds who resided in the hills of Amarkantak and to the south-east in the Gondwāna country, who held very little intercourse with the villagers and never went among them except to barter or purchase provisions. This race live in detached parties and seldom have more than eight or ten huts in one place. They are cannibals in the real sense of the word, but never eat the flesh of any person not belonging to their own family or tribe; nor do they do this except on particular occasions. It is the custom of this singular people to cut the throat of any person of their family who is attacked by severe illness and who they think has no chance of recovering, when they collect the whole of their relations and friends, and feast upon the body. In like manner when a person arrives at a great age and becomes feeble and weak, the Halālkhor operates upon him,

[1] *Indian Caste*, i. p. 325.

Bemrose, Collo., Derby.

KILLING OF RĀWAN, THE DEMON KING OF CEYLON, FROM WHOM THE GONDS ARE SUPPOSED TO BE DESCENDED.

when the different members of the family assemble for the same purpose as above stated. In other respects this is a simple race of people, nor do they consider cutting the throats of their sick relations or aged parents any sin; but on the contrary an act acceptable to Kāli, a blessing to their relatives, and a mercy to their whole race."

It may be noted that the account is based on hearsay only, and such stories are often circulated about savage races. But if correct, it would indicate probably only a ritual form of cannibalism. The idea of the Gonds in eating the bodies of their relatives would be to assimilate the lives of these as it were, and cause them to be reborn as children in their own families. Possibly they ate the bodies of their parents, as many races ate the bodies of animal gods, in order to obtain their divine virtues and qualities. No corroboration of this custom is known in respect of the Gonds, but Colonel Dalton records[1] a somewhat similar story of the small Birhor tribe who live in the Chota Nāgpur hills not far from Amarkantak, and it has been seen that the Bhunjias of Bilāspur eat small portions of the bodies of their dead relatives.[2]

53. Festivals. The new crops.

The original Gond festivals were associated with the first eating of the new crops and fruits. In Chait (March) a festival called Chaitrai is observed in Bastar. A pig or fowl with some liquor is offered to the village god, and the new urad and *semi* beans of the year's crop are placed before him uncooked. The people dance and sing the whole night and begin eating the new pulse and beans. In Bhādon (August) is the Nawākhai or eating of the new rice. The old and new grain is mixed and offered raw to the ancestors, a goat is sacrificed, and they begin to eat the new crop of rice. Similarly when the mahua flowers, from which country spirit is made, first appear, they proceed to the forest and worship under a *sāj* tree.

Before sowing rice or millet they have a rite called Bījphūtni or breaking the seed. Some grain, fowls and a pig are collected from the villagers by subscription. The grain is offered to the god and then distributed to all the villagers, who sow it in their fields for luck.

[1] See article Birhor. [2] See article Bhunjia.

54. The Holi festival.

The Holi festival, which corresponds to the Carnival, being held in spring at the end of the Hindu year, is observed by Gonds as well as Hindus. In Bilāspur a Gond or Baiga, as representing the oldest residents, is always employed to light the Holi fire. Sometimes it is kindled in the ancient manner by the friction of two pieces of wood. In Mandla, at the Holi, the Gonds fetch a green branch of the *semar* or cotton tree and plant it in a little hole, in which they put also a pice (farthing) and an egg. They place fuel round and burn up the branch. Then next day they take out the egg and give it to a dog to eat and say that this will make the dog as swift as fire. They choose a dog whom they wish to train for hunting. They bring the ploughshare from the house and heat it red-hot in the Holi fire and take it back. They say that this wakes up the ploughshare, which has fallen asleep from rusting in the house, and makes it sharp for ploughing. Perhaps when rust appears on the metal they think this a sign of its being asleep. They plough for the first time on a Monday or Wednesday and drive three furrows when nobody is looking.

55. The Meghnāth swinging rite.

In the western Districts on one of the five days following the Holi the swinging rite is performed. For this they bring a straight teak or *sāj* tree from the forest, as long as can be obtained, and cut from a place where two trees are growing together. The Bhumka or village priest is shown in a dream where to cut the tree. It is set up in a hole seven feet deep, a quantity of salt being placed beneath it. The hole is coloured with *geru* or red ochre, and offerings of goats, sheep and chickens are made to it by people who have vowed them in sickness. A cross-bar is fixed on to the top of the pole in a socket and the Bhumka is tied to one end of the cross-bar. A rope is attached to the other end and the people take hold of this and drag the Bhumka round in the air five times. When this has been done the village proprietor gives him a present of a cocoanut, and head- and body-clothes. If the pole falls down it is considered that some great misfortune, such as an epidemic, will ensue. The pole and ritual are now called Meghnāth. Meghnāth is held to have been the son of Rāwan, the demon king of

Bemrose, Collo., Derby.

WOMAN ABOUT TO BE SWUNG ROUND THE POST
CALLED MEGHNĀTH.

Ceylon, from whom the Gonds are supposed by the Hindus to be descended, as they are called Rāwanvansi, or of the race of Rāwan. After this they set up another pole, which is known as Jheri, and make it slippery with oil, butter and other things. A little bag containing Rs. 1-4 and also a seer (2 lbs.) of *ghī* or butter are tied to the top, and the men try to climb the pole and get these as a prize. The women assemble and beat the men with sticks as they are climbing to prevent them from doing so. If no man succeeds in climbing the pole and getting the reward, it is given to the women. This seems to be a parody of the first or Meghnāth rite, and both probably have some connection with the growth of the crops.

56. The Karma and other rites.

During Bhādon (August), in the rains, the Gonds bring a branch of the *kalmi* or of the *haldu* tree from the forest and wrap it up in new cloth and keep it in their houses. They have a feast and the musicians play, and men and women dance round the branch singing songs, of which the theme is often sexual. The dance is called Karma and is the principal dance of the Gonds, and they repeat it at intervals all through the cold weather, considering it as their great amusement. A further notice of it is given in the section on social customs. The dance is apparently named after the tree, though it is not known whether the same tree is always selected. Many deciduous trees in India shed their leaves in the hot weather and renew them in the rains, so that this season is partly one of the renewal of vegetation as well as of the growth of crops.

In Kunwār (September) the Gond girls take an earthen pot, pierce it with holes, and put a lamp inside and also the image of a dove, and go round from house to house singing and dancing, led by a girl carrying the pot on her head. They collect contributions and have a feast. In Chhattīsgarh among the Gonds and Rāwats (Ahīrs) there is from time to time a kind of feminist movement, which is called the Stiria-Rāj or kingdom of women. The women pretend to be soldiers, seize all the weapons, axes and spears that they can get hold of, and march in a body from village to village. At each village they kill a goat and send its head to another village, and then the women of that village come and join them. During this time they leave their hair unbound and think that they are establishing the kingdom of women. After some months the movement subsides, and it is said to occur at irregular intervals with a number of years between each. The women are commonly considered to be out of their senses.

(g) Appearance and Character, and Social Rules and Customs

57. Physical type. Hislop describes the Gonds as follows:[1] "All are a little below the average size of Europeans and in complexion darker than the generality of Hindus. Their bodies are well proportioned, but their features rather ugly. They have a roundish head, distended nostrils, wide mouth, thickish lips, straight black hair and scanty beard and moustache. It has been supposed that some of the aborigines of Central India have woolly hair; but this is a mistake. Among the thousands I have seen I have not found one with hair like a negro." Captain Forsyth says:[2] "The Gond women differ among themselves more than the men. They are somewhat lighter in colour and less fleshy than Korku women. But the Gond women of different parts of the country vary greatly in appearance, many of them in the open tracts being great robust creatures, finer animals by far than the men; and here Hindu blood may fairly be expected. In the interior again bevies of Gond women may be seen who are more like monkeys than human beings. The features of all are strongly marked and coarse. The girls occasionally possess such comeliness as attaches to general plumpness and a good-humoured expression of face; but when their short youth is over all pass at once into a hideous age. Their hard lives, sharing as they do all the labours of the men except that of hunting, suffice to account for this." There is not the least doubt that the Gonds of the more open and civilised country, comprised in British Districts, have a large admixture of Hindu blood. They commonly work as farmservants, women as well as men, and illicit connections with their Hindu masters have been a natural result. This

[1] *Notes*, p. 1. [2] *Highlands of Central India*, p. 156.

Bemrose, Collo., Derby.

CLIMBING THE POLE FOR A BAG OF SUGAR.

interbreeding, as well as the better quality of food which those who have taken to regular cultivation obtain, have perhaps conduced to improve the Gond physical type. Gond men as tall as Hindus, and more strongly built and with comparatively well-cut features, are now frequently seen, though the broad flat nose is still characteristic of the tribe as a whole. Most Gonds have very little hair on the face.

58. Character.

Of the Māria Gonds, Colonel Glasfurd wrote[1] that "They are a timid, quiet race, docile, and though addicted to drinking they are not quarrelsome. Without exception they are the most cheerful, light-hearted people I have met with, always laughing and joking among themselves. Seldom does a Māria village resound with quarrels or wrangling among either sex, and in this respect they present a marked contrast to those in more civilised tracts. They, in common with many other wild races, bear a singular character for truthfulness and honesty, and when once they get over the feeling of shyness which is natural to them, are exceedingly frank and communicative." Writing in 1825 Sleeman said: "Such is the simplicity and honesty of character of the wildest of these Gonds that when they have agreed to a *jama*[2] they will pay it, though they sell their children to do so, and will also pay it at the precise time that they agreed to. They are dishonest only in direct theft, and few of them will refuse to take another man's property when a fair occasion offers, but they will immediately acknowledge it."[3] The more civilised Gonds retain these characteristics to a large extent, though contact with the Hindus and the increased complexity of life have rendered them less guileless. Murder is a comparatively frequent crime among Gonds, and is usually due either to some quarrel about a woman or to a drunken affray. The kidnapping of girls for marriage is also common, though hardly reckoned as an offence by the Gonds themselves. Otherwise crime is extremely rare in Gond villages as a rule. As farmservants the Gonds are esteemed fairly honest and hardworking; but unless well driven they are constitutionally averse to labour, and care nothing about provision for the

[1] *Report on Bastar Dependency*, p. 41.

[2] Assessment of revenue for land.

[3] Quoted in *C.P. Gazetteer* (1871), Introduction, p. 113.

future. The proverb says, 'The Gond considers himself a king as long as he has a pot of grain in the house,' meaning that while he has food for a day or two he will not work for any more. During the hot weather the Gonds go about in parties and pay visits to their relatives, staying with them several days, and the time is spent simply in eating, drinking when liquor is available, and conversation. The visitors take presents of grain and pulse with them and these go to augment the host's resources. The latter will kill a chicken or, as a great treat, a young pig. Mr. Montgomerie writes of the Gonds as follows:[1] "They are a pleasant people, and leave kindly memories in those who have to do with them. Comparatively truthful, always ready for a laugh, familiar with the paths and animals and fruits of the forest, lazy cultivators on their own account but good farmservants under supervision, the broad-nosed Gonds are the fit inhabitants of the hilly and jungly tracts in which they are found. With a marigold tucked into his hair above his left ear, with an axe in his hand and a grin on his face, the Gond turns out cheerfully to beat for game, and at the end of the day spends his beating pay on liquor for himself or on sweetmeats for his children. He may, in the previous year, have been subsisting largely on jungle fruits and roots because his harvest failed, but he does not dream of investing his modest beating pay in grain."

59. Shyness and ignorance.

In the wilder tracts the Gonds were, until recently, extremely shy of strangers, and would fly at their approach. Their tribute to the Rāja of Bastar, paid in kind, was collected once a year by an officer who beat a tom-tom outside the village and forthwith hid himself, whereupon the inhabitants brought out whatever they had to give and deposited it on an appointed spot. Colonel Glasfurd notes that they had great fear of a horse, and the sight of a man on horseback would put a whole village to flight.[2] Even within the writer's experience, in the wilder forest tracts of Chānda Gond women picking up mahua would run and climb a tree at one's approach on a pony. As displaying the ignorance of the Gonds, Mr. Cain relates[3] that about forty years ago a Gond

[1] *Chhīndwāra Settlement Report*. p. 43.

[2] *Report on Bastar Dependency*,

[3] *Ind. Ant.* (1876), p. 359.

was sent with a basket of mangoes from Palvatsa to Bhadrachalam, and was warned not to eat any of the fruit, as it would be known if he did so from a note placed in the basket. On the way, however, the Gond and his companion were overcome by the attraction of the fruit, and decided that if they buried the note it would be unable to see them eating. They accordingly did so and ate some of the mangoes, and when taxed with their dishonesty at the journey's end, could not understand how the note could have known of their eating the mangoes when it had not seen them.

The Gonds can now count up to twenty, and beyond that they use the word *kori* or a score, in talking of cattle, grain or rupees, so that this, perhaps, takes them up to twenty score. They say they learnt to count up to twenty on their ten fingers and ten toes.

60. Villages and houses. When residing in the centre of a Hindu population the Gonds inhabit mud houses, like the low-class Hindus. But in the jungles their huts are of bamboo matting plastered with mud, with thatched roofs. The internal arrangements are of the simplest kind, comprising two apartments separated from each other by a row of tall baskets, in which they store up their grain. Adjoining the house is a shed for cattle, and round both a bamboo fence for protection from wild beasts. In Bastar the walls of the hut are only four or five feet high, and the door three feet. Here there are one or two sheds, in which all the villagers store their grain in common, and no man steals another's grain. In Gond villages the houses are seen perched about on little bluffs or other high ground, overlooking the fields, one, two and three together. The Gond does not like to live in a street. He likes a large *bāri* or fenced enclosure, about an acre in size, besides his house. In this he will grow mustard for sale, or his own annual supply of tobacco or vegetables. He arranges that the village cattle shall come and stand in the *bāri* on their way to and from pasture, and that the cows shall be milked there for some time. His family also perform natural functions in it, which the Hindus will not do in their fields. Thus the *bāri* gets well manured and will easily give two crops in the year, and the Gond sets great store by this field. When building a new house a man plants as the first post a pole of the *sāj* tree, and ties a bundle of thatching-grass round it, and buries a pice ($\frac{1}{4}$d.) and a *bhilawa* nut beneath it. They feed two or three friends and scatter a little of the food over the post. The post is called Khirkhut Deo, and protects the house from harm.

A brass or pewter dish and *lota* or drinking-vessel of the same material, a few earthen cooking-pots, a hatchet and a clay *chilam* or pipe-bowl comprise the furniture of a Gond.

61. Clothes and ornaments. In Sir R. Jenkins' time, a century ago, the Gonds were represented as naked savages, living on roots and fruits, and hunting for strangers to sacrifice. About fifty years later, when Mr. Hislop wrote, the Māria women of the wilder tracts were said only to have a bundle of leafy twigs fastened with a string round their waist to cover them before and behind. Now men have a narrow strip of cloth round the waist and women a broader one, but in the south of Bastar they still leave their breasts uncovered. Here a woman covers her breasts for the first time when she becomes pregnant, and if a young woman did it, she would be thought to be big with child. In other localities men and women clothe themselves more like Hindus, but the women leave the greater part of the thighs bare, and men often have only one cloth round the loins and another small rag on the head. They have bangles of glass, brass and zinc, and large circlets of brass round the legs, though these are now being discarded. In Bastar both men and women have ten to twenty iron and brass hoops round their necks, and on to these rings of the same metal are strung. Rai Bahādur Panda Baijnāth counted 181 rings on one hoop round an old woman's neck. In the Māria country the boys have small separate plots of land, which they cultivate themselves and use the proceeds as their pocket-money, and this enables them to indulge in a profusion of ornaments sometimes exceeding those worn by the girls. In Mandla women wear a number of strings of yellow and bluish-white beads. A married woman has both colours, and several cowries tied to the end of the necklace. Widows and girls may only wear the bluish-white beads without cowries, and a remarried widow may not have any yellow beads, but she can have one cowrie on her necklace. Yellow beads are thus confined to married

Bemrose, Collo., Derby.

GONDS WITH THEIR BAMBOO CARTS AT MARKET.

women, yellow being the common wedding-colour. A Gond woman is not allowed to wear a *choli* or little jacket over the breasts. If she does she is put out of caste. This rule may arise from opposition to the adoption of Hindu customs and desire to retain a distinctive feature of dress, or it may be thought that the adoption of the *choli* might make Gond women weaker and unfitted for hard manual labour, like Hindu women. A Gond woman must not keep her cloth tucked up behind into her waist when she meets an elderly man of her own family, but must let it down so as to cover the upper part of her legs. If she omits to do this, on the occasion of the next wedding the Bhumka or caste priest will send some men to catch her, and when she is brought the man to whom she was disrespectful will put his right hand on the ground and she must make obeisance to it seven times, then to his left hand, then to a broom and pestle, and so on till she is tired out. When they have a sprain or swelling of the arm they make a ring of tree-fibre and wear this on the arm, and think that it will cure the sprain or swelling.

The ears of girls are pierced by a thorn, and the hole is enlarged by putting in small pieces of wood or peacock's feathers. Gond women wear in their ears the *tarkhi* or a little slab in shape like a palm-leaf, covered with coloured glass and fixed on to a stalk of hemp-fibre nearly an inch thick, which goes through the ear; or they wear the silver shield-shaped ornament called *dhāra*, which is described in the article on Sunār. In Bastar the women have their ears pierced in a dozen or more places, and have a small ring in each hole. If a woman gets her ear torn through she is simply put out of caste and has to give a feast for readmission, and is not kept out of caste till it heals, like a Hindu woman. 62. Ear-piercing.

Gond men now cut their hair. Before scissors were obtainable it is said that they used to tie it up on their heads and chop off the ends with an axe, or burn them off. But the wilder Gonds often wear their hair long, and as it is seldom combed it gets tangled and matted. The Pandas or priests do not cut their hair. Women wear braids of false hair, of goats or other animals, twisted into their own to improve their appearance. In Mandla a Gond girl should not have her hair 63. Hair.

parted in the middle till she is married. When she is married this is done for the first time by the Baiga, who subsequently tattoos on her forehead the image of Chandi Māta.[1]

64. Bathing and washing clothes.

Gonds, both men and women, do not bathe daily, but only wash their arms and legs. They think a complete bath once a month is sufficient. If a man gets ill he may think the god is angry with him for not bathing, and when he recovers he goes and has a good bath, and sometimes gives a feast. Hindus say that a Gond is only clean in the rains, when he gets a compulsory bath every day. In Bastar they seldom wash their clothes, as they think this impious, or else that the cloth would wear out too quickly if it were often washed. Here they set great store by their piece of cloth, and a woman will take it off before she cleans up her house, and do her work naked. It is probable that these wild Gonds, who could not weave, regarded the cloth as something miraculous and sacred, and, as already seen, the god Pālo is a piece of cloth.[2]

65. Tattooing.

Both men and women were formerly much tattooed among the Gonds, though the custom is now going out among men. Women are tattooed over a large part of the body, but not on the hips or above them to the waist. Sorcerers are tattooed with some image or symbol of their god on their chest or right shoulder, and think that the god will thus always remain with them and that any magic directed against them by an enemy will fail. A woman should be tattooed at her father's house, if possible before marriage, and if it is done after marriage her parents should pay for it. The tattooing is done with indigo in black or blue, and is sometimes a very painful process, the girl being held down by her friends while it is carried out. Loud shrieks, Forsyth says, would sometimes be heard by the

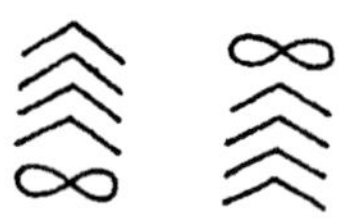

traveller issuing from a village, which proclaimed that some young Gondin was being operated upon with the tattooing-

[1] See *para.* 65, Tattooing.

[2] See *para.* 41, Religion.

needle. Patterns of animals and also common articles of household use are tattooed in dots and lines. In Mandla the legs are marked all the way up behind with sets of parallel lines, as shown above. These are called *ghāts* or steps, and sometimes interspersed at intervals is another figure called *sānkal* or chain. Perhaps their idea is to make the legs strong for climbing.

Tattooing seems to have been originally a magical means of protecting the body against real and spiritual dangers, much in the same manner as the wearing of ornaments. It is also supposed that people were tattooed with images of their totem in order the better to identify themselves with it. The following account is stated to have been taken from the Baiga priest of a popular shrine of Devi in Mandla. His wife was a tattooer of both Baigas and Gonds, and considered it the correct method for the full tattooing of a woman, though very few women can nowadays be found with it. The magical intent of tattooing is here clearly brought out:— **66. Special system of tattooing.**

On the sole of the right foot is the annexed device:

It represents the earth, and will have the effect of preventing the woman's foot from being bruised and cut when she walks about barefoot.

On the sole of the left foot is this pattern:

It is meant to be in the shape of a foot, and is called Padam Sen Deo or the Foot-god. This deity is represented by stones marked with two footprints under a tree outside the village. When they have a pain in the foot they go to him, rub his two stones together and sprinkle the dust from them on their feet as a means of cure. The device tattooed on the foot no doubt performs a similar protective function.

On the upper part of the foot five dots are made, one on each toe, and a line is drawn round the foot from the big toe to the little toe. This sign is said to represent Gajkaran

Deo, the elephant god, who resides in cemeteries. He is a strong god, and it is probably thought that his symbol on the feet will enable them to bear weight. On the legs behind they have the images of the Baiga priest and priestess. These are also supposed to give strength for labour, and when they cannot go into the forest from fever or weakness they say that Bura Deo, as the deified priest is called, is angry with them. On the upper legs in front they tattoo the image of a horse, and at the back a saddle between the knee and the thigh. This is Koda Deo the horse-god, whose image will make their thighs as strong as those of a horse. If they have a pain or weakness in the thigh they go and worship Koda Deo, offering him a piece of saddle-cloth. On the outer side of each upper arm they tattoo the image of Hanumān, the deified monkey and the god of strength, in the form of a man. Both men and women do this, and men apply burning cowdung to the tattoo-mark in order to burn it effectually into the arm. This god makes the arms strong to carry weights. Down the back is tattooed an oblong figure, which is the house of the god Bhimsen, with an opening at the lower end just above the buttocks to represent the gate. Inside this on the back is the image of Bhimsen's club, consisting of a pattern of dots more or less in the shape of an Indian club. Bhimsen is the god of the cooking-place, and the image of his club, in white clay stained green with the leaves of the *semar* tree, is made on the wall of the kitchen. If they have no food, or the food is bad, they say that Bhimsen is angry with them. The pattern tattooed on the back appears therefore to be meant to facilitate the digestion of food, which the Gonds apparently once supposed to pass down the body along the back. On the breast in front women tattoo the image of Bura Deo, as shown, the head on her neck and the body finishing at her

breast-bone. The marks round the body represent stones, because the symbol of Bura Deo is sometimes a basket

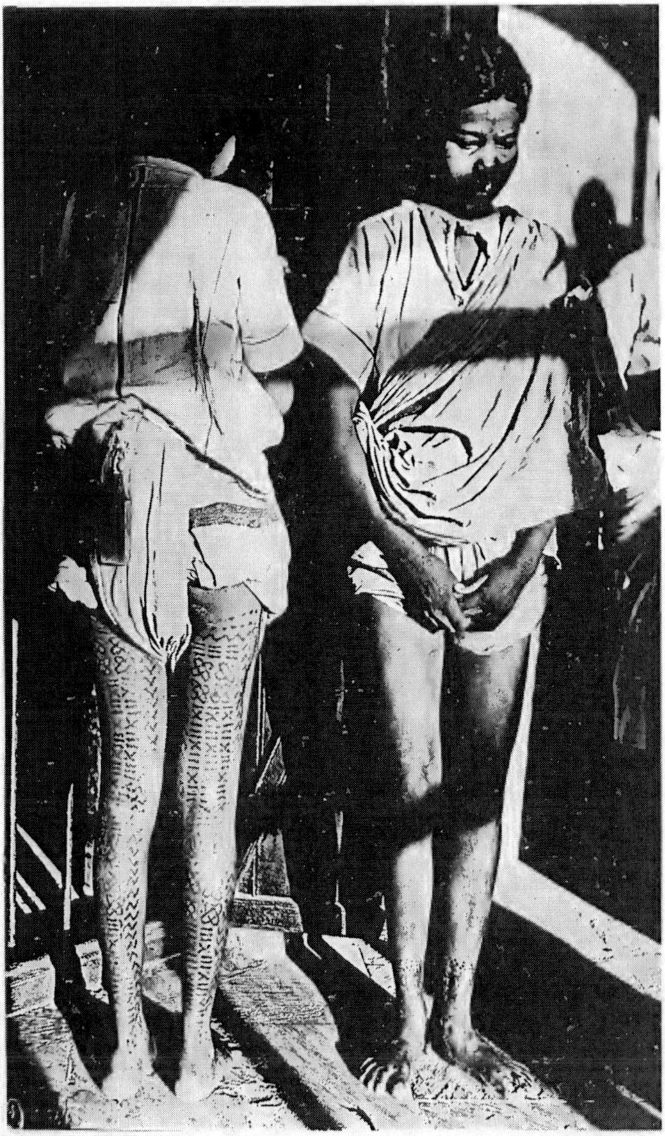

Bemrose, Collo., Derby.

GOND WOMEN, SHOWING TATTOOING ON BACKS OF LEGS.

plastered with mud and filled with stones. On each side of the body women have the image of Jhulān Devi, the cradle goddess, as shown by the small figures attached to Bura Deo. But a woman cannot have the image of Jhulān Devi tattooed on her till she has borne a child. The place where the image is tattooed is that where a child rests against its mother's body when she carries it suspended in her cloth, and it is supposed that the image of the goddess supports and protects the child, while the mother's arms are left free for work.

Round the neck they have Kanteshwar Māta, the goddess of the necklace. She consists of three to six lines of dots round the neck representing bead necklaces.

On the face below the mouth there is sometimes the image of a cobra, and it is supposed that this will protect them from the effects of eating any poisonous thing.

On the forehead women have the image of Chāndi Māta. This consists of a dot at the forehead at the parting of the hair, from which two lines of dots run down to the ears on each side, and are continued along the sides of the face to the neck. This image can only be tattooed after the hair of a woman has been parted on her marriage, and they say that Chāndi Māta will preserve and guard the parting of the hair, that is the life of the woman's husband, because the parting can only be worn so long as her husband is alive. Chāndi means the moon, and it seems likely that the parting of the hair may be considered to represent the bow of the moon.

The elaborate system of tattooing here described is rarely found, and it is perhaps comparatively recent, having been devised by the Baiga and Pardhān priests as their intelligence developed and their theogony became more complex.

Men are accustomed to brand themselves on the joints of the wrists, elbows and knees with burning wood of the *semar* tree from the Holi fire in order to render their joints supple for dancing. It would appear that the idea of suppleness comes from the dancing of the flames or the swift burning of the fire, while the wood is also of very light weight. Men are also accustomed to burn two or three marks on each wrist with a piece of hare's dung, perhaps to make the joints supple like the legs of a hare. 67. Branding.

8. Food. The Gonds have scarcely any restriction on diet. They will eat fowls, beef, pork, crocodiles, certain kinds of snakes, lizards, tortoises, rats, cats, red ants, jackals and in some places monkeys. Khatola and Rāj-Gonds usually abstain from beef and the flesh of the buffalo and monkey. They consider field-mice and rats a great delicacy, and will take much trouble in finding and digging out their holes. The Māria Gonds are very fond of red ants, and in Bastar give them fried or roasted to a woman during her confinement. The common food of the labouring Gond is a gruel of rice or small millet boiled in water, the quantity of water increasing in proportion to their poverty. This is about the cheapest kind of food on which a man can live, and the quantity of grain taken in the form of this gruel or *pej* which will suffice for a Gond's subsistence is astonishingly small. They grow the small grass-millets kodon and kutki for their subsistence, selling the more valuable crops for rent and expenses. The flowers of the mahua tree are also a staple article of diet, being largely eaten as well as made into liquor, and the Gond knows of many other roots and fruits of the forest. He likes to eat or drink his *pej* several times a day, and in Seoni, it is said, will not go more than three hours without a meal.

Gonds are rather strict in the matter of taking food from others, and in some localities refuse to accept it even from Brāhmans. Elsewhere they will take it from most Hindu castes. In Hoshangābād the men may take food from the higher Hindu castes, but not the women. This, they say, is because the woman is a wooden vessel, and if a wooden vessel is once put on the fire it is irretrievably burnt. A woman similarly is the weaker vessel and will sustain injury from any contamination. The Rāj-Gond copies Hindu ways and outdoes the Hindu in the elaboration of ceremonial purity, even having the fuel with which his Brāhman cook prepares his food sprinkled with water to purify it before it is burnt. Mr. A. K. Smith states that a Gond will not eat an antelope if a Chāmar has touched it, even unskinned, and in some places they are so strict that a wife may not eat her husband's leavings of food. The Gonds will not eat the leavings of any Hindu caste, probably on account of a traditional hostility arising out of their subjection by the Hindus. Very few Hindu castes will take water or food from the Gonds, but some who employ them as farmservants do this for convenience. The Gonds are not regarded as impure, even though from a Hindu point of view some of their habits are more objectionable than those of the impure castes. This is because the Gonds have never been completely reduced to subjection, nor converted into the village drudges, who are consigned to the most degraded occupations. Large numbers of them hold land as tenants and estates as zamīndārs; and the greater part of the Province was once governed by Gond kings. The Hindus say that they could not consider a tribe as impure to which their kings once belonged. Brāhmans will take water from Rāj-Gonds and Khatola Gonds in many localities. This is when it is freshly brought from the well and not after it has been put in their houses.

Excessive drinking is the common vice of the Gonds **69. Liquor.** and the principal cause which militates against their successfully competing with the Hindus. They drink the country spirit distilled from the flowers of the mahua tree, and in the south of the Province toddy or the fermented juice of the date-palm. As already seen, in Bastar their idea of hell is a place without liquor. The loss of the greater part of the estates formerly held by Gond proprietors has been due to this vice, which many Hindu liquor-sellers have naturally fostered to their own advantage. No festival or wedding passes without a drunken bout, and in Chānda at the season for tapping the date-palm trees the whole population of a village may be seen lying about in the open dead drunk. They impute a certain sanctity to the mahua tree, and in some places walk round a post of it at their weddings. Liquor is indispensable at all ceremonial feasts, and a purifying quality is attributed to it, so that it is drunk at the cemetery or bathing-*ghāt* after a funeral. The family arranges for liquor, but mourners attending from other families also bring a bottle each with them, if possible. Practically all the events of a Gond's life, the birth of a child, betrothals and weddings, recovery from sickness, the arrival of a guest, bringing home the harvest, borrowing money or hiring bullocks, and making contracts for cultivation, are celebrated by drinking. And when a Gond has once begun to drink, if he has the money he usually goes on till he is drunk, and this is why the habit is such a curse to him. He is of a social disposition and does not like to drink alone. If he has drunk something, and has no more money, and the contractor refuses to let him have any more on credit as the law prescribes, the Gond will sometimes curse him and swear never to drink in his shop again. Nevertheless, within a few days he will be back, and when chaffed about it will answer simply that he could not resist the longing. In spite of all the harm it does him, it must be admitted that it is the drink which gives most of the colour and brightness to a Gond's life, and without this it would usually be tame to a degree.

When a Gond drinks water from a stream or tank, he bends down and puts his mouth to the surface and does not make a cup with his hands like a Hindu.

70. Admission of outsiders and sexual morality.

Outsiders are admitted into the tribe in some localities in Bastar, and also the offspring of a Gond man or woman with a person of another caste, excepting the lowest. But some people will not admit the children of a Gond woman by a man of another caste. Not much regard is paid to the chastity of girls before marriage, though in the more civilised tracts the stricter Hindu views on the subject are beginning to prevail. Here it is said that if a girl is detected in a sexual intrigue before marriage she may be taken into caste, but may not participate in the worship of Bura Deo nor of the household god. But this is probably rather a counsel of perfection than a rule actually enforced. If a daughter is taken in the sexual act, they think some misfortune will happen to them, as the death of a cow or the failure of crops. Similarly the Māria Gonds think that if tigers kill their cattle it is a punishment for the adultery of their wives, and hence if a man loses a head or two he looks very closely after his wife, and detection is often followed by murder. Here probably adultery was originally considered an offence as being a sin against the tribe, because it contaminated the tribal blood, and out of this attitude marital jealousy has subsequently developed. Speaking generally, the enforcement of rules of sexual morality appears to be comparatively recent, and there is no doubt that the Baigas and other tribes who have lived in contact with the Gonds, as well as the Ahīrs and other low castes, have a large admixture of Gond blood. In Bastar a Gond woman formerly had no feelings of modesty as regards her breasts, but this is now being acquired. Laying the hand on a married woman's shoulder gives great offence. Mr. Low writes:[1] "It is difficult to say what is not a legal marriage from a Gond point of view; but in spite of this laxity abductions are frequent, and Colonel Bloomfield mentions one particularly noteworthy case where the abductor, an unusually ugly Gond with a hare-lip, was stated by the complainant to have taken off first the latter's aunt, then his sister and finally his only wife."

71. Common sleeping-houses.

Many Gond villages in Chhattīsgarh and the Feudatory States have what is known as a *gotalghar*. This is a large house near the village where unmarried youths and maidens collect and dance and sing together at night. Some villages have two, one for the boys and one for the girls. In Bastar the boys have a regular organisation, their captain being called Sirdār, and the master of the ceremonies Kotwār, while they have other officials bearing the designation of the State officers. After supper the unmarried boys go first to the *gotalghar* and are followed by the girls. The Kotwār receives the latter and directs them to bow to the Sirdār, which they do. Each girl then takes a boy and combs his hair and massages his hands and arms to refresh him, and afterwards they sing and dance together until they are tired and then go to bed. The girls can retire to their own house if they wish, but frequently they sleep in the boys' house. Thus numerous couples become intimate, and if on discovery the parents object to their marriage, they run away to the jungle, and it has to be recognised. In some villages, however, girls are not permitted to go to the *gotalghar*. In one part of Bastar they have a curious rule that all males, even the married, must sleep in the common house for the eight

[1] *Balaghat District Gazetteer*, p. 87.

months of the open season, while their wives sleep in their own houses. A Māria Gond thinks it impious to have sexual intercourse with his wife in his house, as it would be an insult to the goddess of wealth who lives in the house, and the effect would be to drive her away. Their solicitude for this goddess is the more noticeable, as the Māria Gond's house and furniture probably constitute one of the least valuable human habitations on the face of the globe.

72. Methods of greeting and observances between relatives.

When two Gond friends or relatives meet, they clasp each other in their arms and lean against each shoulder in turn. A man will then touch the knees of an elder male relative with his fingers, carrying them afterwards to his own forehead. This is equivalent to falling at the other's feet, and is a token of respect shown to all elder male relatives and also to a son-in-law, sister's husband, and a *samhdi*, that is the father of a son- or daughter-in-law. Their term of salutation is Johār, and they say this to each other. Another method of greeting is that each should put his fingers under the other's chin and then kiss them himself. Women also do this when they meet. Or a younger woman meeting an elder will touch her feet, and the elder will then kiss her on the forehead and on each cheek. If they have not met for some time they will weep. It is said that Baigas will kiss each other on the cheek when meeting, both men and women. A Gond will kiss and caress his wife after marriage, but as soon as she has a child he drops the habit and never does it again. When husband and wife meet after an absence the wife touches her husband's feet with her hand and carries it to her forehead, but the husband makes no demonstration. The Gonds kiss their children. Among the Māria Gonds the wife is said not to sleep on a cot in her husband's house, which would be thought disrespectful to him, but on the ground. Nor will a woman even sit on a cot in her own house, as if any male relative happened to be in the house it would be disrespectful to him. A woman will not say the name of her husband, his elder or younger brother, or his elder brother's sons. A man will not mention his wife's name nor that of her elder sister.

The tribe have *panchāyats* or committees for the settlement of tribal disputes and offences. A member of the *panchāyat* is selected by general consent, and holds office during good behaviour. The office is not hereditary, and generally there does not seem to be a recognised head of the *panchāyat*. In Mandla there is a separate *panchāyat* for each village, and every Gond male adult belongs to it, and all have to be summoned to a meeting. When they assemble five leading elderly men decide the matter in dispute, as representing the assembly. Caste offences are of the usual Hindu type with some variations. Adultery, taking another man's wife or daughter, getting vermin in a wound, being sent to jail and eating the jail food, or even having handcuffs put on, a woman getting her ear torn, and eating or even smoking with a man of very low caste, are the ordinary offences. Others are being beaten by a shoe, dealing in the hides of cattle or keeping donkeys, removing the corpse of a dead horse or donkey, being touched by a sweeper, cooking in the earthen pots of any impure caste, a woman entering the kitchen during her monthly impurity, and taking to wife the widow of a younger brother, but not of course of an elder brother.

73. The caste *panchāyat* and social offences.

In the case of septs which revere a totem animal or plant, any act committed in connection with that animal or plant by a member of the sept is an offence within the cognisance of the *panchāyat*. Thus in Mandla the Kumhra sept revere the goat and the Markām sept the crocodile and crab. If a member of one of these septs touches, keeps, kills or eats the animal which his sept reveres, he is put out of caste and comes before the *panchāyat*. In practice the offences with which the *panchāyat* most frequently deals are the taking of another man's wife or the kidnapping of a daughter for marriage, this last usually occurring between relatives. Both these offences can also be brought before the regular courts, but it is usually only when the aggrieved person cannot get satisfaction from the *panchāyat*, or when the offender refuses to abide by its decision, that the case goes to court. If a Gond loses his wife he will in the ordinary course compromise the matter if the man who takes her will repay his wedding expenses; this is a very serious business for him, as his wedding is the principal expense of a man's life, and it is probable that he may not be able to afford to buy another girl and pay for her wedding. If he cannot get his wedding expenses back through the *panchāyat* he files a complaint of adultery under the Penal Code, in the hope of being repaid through a fine inflicted on the offender, and it is perfectly right and just that this should be done. When a girl is kidnapped for marriage, her family can usually be induced to recognise the affair if they receive the price they could have got for the girl in an ordinary marriage, and perhaps a little more, as a solace to their outraged feelings.

The *panchāyat* takes no cognisance of theft, cheating, forgery, perjury, causing hurt and other forms of crime. These are not considered to be offences against the caste, and no penalty is inflicted for them. Only if a man is arrested and handcuffed, or if he is sent to jail for any such crime, he is put out of caste for eating the jail food and subjected in this latter case to a somewhat severe penalty. It is not clear whether a Gond is put out of caste for murder, though Hindu *panchāyats* take cognisance of this offence.

74. Caste penalty feasts.

The punishments inflicted by the *panchāyat* consist of feasts, and in the case of minor offences of a fine. This last, subject perhaps to some commission to the members for their services, is always spent on liquor, the drinking of which by the offender with the caste-fellows will purify him. The Gonds consider country liquor as equivalent to the Hindu Amrita or nectar.

The penalty for a serious offence involves three feasts. The first, known as the meal of impurity, consists of sweet wheaten cakes which are eaten by the elders on the bank of a stream or well. The second or main feast is given in the offender's courtyard to all the castemen of the village and sometimes of other villages. Rice, pulse, and meat, either of a slaughtered pig or goat, are provided at this. The third feast is known as 'The taking back into caste' and is held in the offender's house and may be cooked by him. Wheat, rice and pulses are served, but not meat or vegetables. When the *panchāyat* have eaten this food in the offender's house he is again a proper member of the caste. Liquor is essential at each feast. The nature of the penalty feasts is thus very clear. They have the effect of a gradual purification of the offender. In the first meal he can take no part, nor is it served in his house, but in some neutral place. For the second meal the castemen go so far as to sit in his compound, but apparently he does not cook the food nor partake of it. At the third meal they eat with him in his house and he is fully purified. These three meals are prescribed only for serious offences, and for ordinary ones only two meals, the offender partaking of the second. The three meals are usually exacted from a woman taken in adultery with an outsider. In this case the woman's head is shaved at the first meal by the Sharmia, that is her son-in-law, and the children put her to shame by throwing lumps of cowdung at her. She runs away and bathes in a stream. At the second meal, taken in her courtyard, the Sharmia sprinkles some blood on the ground and on the lintel of the door as an offering to the gods and in order that the house may be pure for the future. If a man is poor and cannot afford the expense of the penalty feasts imposed on him, the *panchāyat* will agree that only a few persons will attend instead of the whole community. The procedure above described is probably borrowed to a large extent from Hinduism, but the working of a *panchāyat* can be observed better among the Gonds and lower castes than among high-caste Hindus, who are tending to let it lapse into abeyance.

75. Special purification ceremony.

The following detailed process of purification had to be undergone by a well-to-do Gond widow in Mandla who had been detected with a man of the Panka caste, lying drunk and naked in a liquor-shop. The Gonds here consider the Pankas socially beneath themselves. The ritual clearly belongs to Hinduism, as shown by the purifying virtue attached to contact with cows and bullocks and cowdung, and was directed by the Panda or priest of Devi's shrine, who, however, would probably be a Gond. First, the offending woman was taken right out of the village across a stream; here her head was shaved with the urine of an all-black bullock and her body washed with his dung, and she then bathed in the stream, and a feast was given on its bank to the caste. She slept here, and next day was yoked to the same bullock and taken thus to the Kharkha or standing-place for the village cattle. She was rolled over the surface of the Kharkha about four times, again rubbed with cowdung, another feast was given, and she slept the night on the spot, without being washed. Next day, covered with the dust and cowdung of the Kharkha, she crouched underneath the black bullock's belly and in this manner proceeded to the gate of her own yard. Here a bottle of liquor and fifteen chickens were waved round her and afterwards offered at Devi's shrine, where they became the property of the Panda who was conducting the ceremony. Another feast was given in her yard and the woman slept there. Next day the woman, after bathing, was placed standing with one foot outside her threshold and the other inside; a feast was given, called the feast of the threshold, and she again slept in her yard. On the following day came the final feast of purification in the house. The woman was bathed eleven times, and a hen, a chicken and five eggs were offered by the Panda to each of her household gods. Then she drank a little liquor from a cup of which the Panda had drunk, and ate some of the leavings of food of which he had eaten. The black bullock and a piece of cloth sufficient to cover it were presented to the Panda for his services. Then the woman took a dish of rice and pulse and placed a little in the leaf-cup of each of the caste-fellows present, and they all ate it and she was readmitted to caste. Twelve cow-buffaloes were sold to pay for the ceremony, which perhaps cost Rs. 600 or more.

76. Dancing. Dancing and singing to the dance constitute the social amusement and recreation of the Gonds, and they are passionately fond of it. The principal dance is the Karma, danced in celebration of the bringing of the leafy branch of a tree from the forest in the rains. They continue to dance it as a recreation during the nights of the cold and hot weather, whenever they have leisure and a supply of liquor, which is almost indispensable, is forthcoming. The Mārias dance, men and women together, in a great circle, each man holding the girl next him on one side round the neck and on the other round the waist. They keep perfect time, moving each foot alternately in unison throughout the line, and moving round in a slow circle. Only unmarried girls may join in a Māria dance, and once a woman is married she can never dance again. This is no doubt a salutary provision

Bemrose, Collo., Derby.

MĀRIA GONDS IN DANCING COSTUME.

for household happiness, as sometimes couples, excited by the dance and wine, run away from it into the jungle and stay there for a day or two till their relatives bring them home and consider them as married. At the Māria dances the men wear the skins of tigers, panthers, deer and other animals, and sometimes head-dresses of peacock's feathers. They may also have a girdle of cowries round the waist, and a bell tied to their back to ring as they move. The musicians sit in the centre and play various kinds of drums and tom-toms. At a large Māria dance there may be as many as thirty musicians, and the provision of rice or kodon and liquor may cost as much as Rs. 50. In other localities the dance is less picturesque. Men and women form two long lines opposite each other, with the musicians in the centre, and advance and retreat alternately, bringing one foot forward and the other up behind it, with a similar movement in retiring. Married women may dance, and the men do not hold the women at any time. At intervals they break off and liquor is distributed in small leaf-cups, or if these are not available, it is poured into the hands of the dancers held together like a cup. In either case a considerable proportion of the liquor is usually spilt on to the ground.

All the time they are dancing they also sing in unison, 77. Songs.
the men sometimes singing one line and the women the next, or both together. The songs are with few exceptions of an erotic character, and a few specimens are subjoined.

a. Be not proud of your body, your body must go away above (to death).
Your mother, brother and all your kinsmen, you must leave them and go.
You may have lakhs of treasure in your house, but you must leave it all and go.

b. The musicians play and the feet beat on the earth.
A pice (¼d.) for a divorced woman, two pice for a kept woman, for a virgin many sounding rupees.
The musicians play and the earth sounds with the trampling of feet.

c. Rāja Darwa is dead, he died in his youth.
Who is he that has taken the small gun, who has taken the big bow?
Who is aiming through the *harra* and *bahera* trees, who is aiming on the plain?
Who has killed the quail and partridge, who has killed the peacock?

Rāja Darwa has died in the prime of his youth.
The big brother says, 'I killed him, I killed him'; the little brother shot the arrow.
Rāja Darwa has died in the bloom of his youth.

d. Rāwan[1] is coming disguised as a Bairāgi; by what road will Rāwan come?
The houses and castles fell before him, the ruler of Bhānwargarh rose up in fear.
He set the match to his powder, he stooped and crept along the ground and fired.

e. Little pleasure is got from a kept woman; she gives her lord *pej* (gruel) of kutki to drink.
She gives it him in a leaf-cup of laburnum;[2] the cup is too small for him to drink.
She put two gourds full of water in it, and the gruel is so thin that it gives him no sustenance.

f. *Man speaks:*

The wife is asleep and her Rāja (husband) is asleep in her lap.
She has taken a piece of bread in her lap and water in her vessel.
See from her eyes will she come or not?

Woman:

I have left my cow in her shed, my buffalo in her stall.
I have left my baby at the breast and am come alone to follow you.

g. The father said to his son, 'Do not go out to service with any master, neither go to any strange woman.
I will sell my sickle and axe, and make you two marriages.'
He made a marriage feast for his son, and in one plate he put rice, and over it meat, and poured soup over it till it flowed out of the plate.
Then he said to the men and women, young and old, 'Come and eat your fill.'

78. Language. In 1911 Gondi was spoken by 1,500,000 persons, or more than half the total number of Gonds in India. The other Gonds of the Central Provinces speak a broken Hindi. Gondi is a Dravidian language, having a common ancestor with Tamil and Canarese, but little immediate connection

[1] Rāwan was the demon king of Ceylon who fought against Rāma, and from whom the Gonds are supposed to be descended. Hence this song may perhaps refer to a Gond revolt against the Hindus.

[2] The *amaltas* or *Cassia fistula*, which has flowers like a laburnum. The idea is perhaps that its leaves are too small to make a proper leaf-cup, and she will not take the trouble to get suitable leaves.

with its neighbour Telugu; the specimens given by Sir G. Grierson show that a large number of Hindi words have been adopted into the vocabulary of Gondi, and this tendency is no doubt on the increase. There are probably few Gonds outside the Feudatory States, and possibly a few of the wildest tracts in British Districts, who could not understand Hindi to some extent. And with the extension of primary education in British Districts Gondi is likely to decline still more rapidly. Gondi has no literature and no character of its own; but the Gospels and the Book of Genesis have been translated into it and several grammatical sketches and vocabularies compiled. In Saugor the Hindus speak of Gondi as Farsi or Persian, apparently applying this latter name to any foreign language.

(*h*) Occupation

The Gonds are mainly engaged in agriculture, and the great bulk of them are farmservants and labourers. In the hilly tracts, however, there is a substantial Gond tenantry, and a small number of proprietors remain, though the majority have been ousted by Hindu moneylenders and liquor-sellers. In the eastern Districts many important zamīndāri estates are owned by Gond proprietors. The ancestors of these families held the wild hilly country on the borders of the plains in feudal tenure from the central rulers, and were responsible for the restraint of the savage hillmen under their jurisdiction, and the protection of the rich and settled lowlands from predatory inroads from without. Their descendants are ordinary landed proprietors, and would by this time have lost their estates but for the protection of the law declaring them impartible and inalienable. A few of the Feudatory Chiefs are also Gonds. Gond proprietors are generally easy-going and kind-hearted to their tenants, but lacking in business acumen and energy, and often addicted to drink and women. The tenants are as a class shiftless and improvident and heavily indebted. But they show signs of improvement, especially in the ryotwāri villages under direct Government management, and it may be hoped that primary education and more temperate

79. Cultivation.

habits will gradually render them equal to the Hindu cultivators.

80. Patch cultivation. In the Feudatory States and some of the zamīndāris the Gonds retain the *dahia* or *bewar* method of shifting cultivation, which has been prohibited everywhere else on account of its destructive effects on the forests. The Māria Gonds of Bastar cut down a patch of jungle on a hillside about February, and on its drying up burn all the wood in April or May. Tying strips of the bark of the *sāj* tree to their feet to prevent them from being burnt, they walk over the smouldering area, and with long bamboo sticks move any unburnt logs into a burning patch, so that they may all be consumed. When the first showers of rain fall they scatter seed of the small millets into the soft covering of wood ashes, and the fertility of the soil is such that without further trouble they get a return of a hundred-fold or more. The same patch can be sown for three years in succession without ploughing, but it then gives out, and the Gonds move themselves and their habitations to a fresh one. When the jungle has been allowed to grow on the old patch for ten or twelve years, there is sufficient material for a fresh supply of wood-ash manure, and they burn it over again. Teak yields a particularly fertilising ash, and when standing the tree is hurtful to crops grown near it, as its large, broad leaves cause a heavy drip and wash out the grain. Hence the Gonds were particularly hostile to this tree, and it is probably to their destructive efforts that the poor growth of teak over large areas of the Provincial forests is due.[1] The Māria Gonds do not use the plough, and their only agricultural implement is a kind of hoe or spade. Elsewhere the Gonds are gradually adopting the Hindu methods of cultivation, but their land is generally in hilly and jungly tracts and of poor quality. They occupy large areas of the wretched *barra* or gravel soil which has disintegrated from the rock of the hillsides, and covers it in a thin sheet mixed with quantities of large stones. The Gonds, however, like this land, as it is so shallow as to entail very little trouble in ploughing, and it is suitable for their favourite crops of the small millets, kodon and kutki, and the poorer oilseeds.

[1] Hislop, *Notes*, p. 2.

After three years of cropping it must be given an equal or longer period of fallow before it will again yield any return. The Gonds say it is *nārang* or exhausted. In the new ryotwāri villages formed within the last twenty years the Gonds form a large section, and in Mandla the great majority, of the tenantry, and have good black-soil fields which grow wheat and other valuable crops. Here, perhaps, their condition is happier than anywhere else, as they are secured in the possession of their lands subject to the payment of revenue, liberally assisted with Government loans at low interest, and protected as far as possible from the petty extortion and peculation of Hindu subordinate officials and moneylenders. The opening of a substantial number of primary schools to serve these villages will, it may be hoped, have the effect of making the Gond a more intelligent and provident cultivator, and counteract the excessive addiction to liquor which is the great drawback to his prosperity. The fondness of the Gond for his *bāri* or garden plot adjoining his hut has been described in the section on villages and houses.

81. Hunting: traps for animals.

The primary occupation of the Gonds in former times was hunting and fishing, but their opportunities in this respect have been greatly circumscribed by the conservation of the game in Government forests, which was essential if it was not to become extinct, when the native *shikāris* had obtained firearms. Their weapons were until recently bows and arrows, but now Gond hunters usually have an old matchlock gun. They have several ingenious devices for trapping animals. It is essential for them to make a stockade round their patch cultivation fields in the forests, or the grain would be devoured by pig and deer. At one point in this they leave a narrow opening, and in front of it dig a deep pit and cover it with brushwood and grass; then at the main entrance they spread some sand. Coming in the middle of the night they see from the footprints in the sand what animals have entered the enclosure; if these are worth catching they close the main gate, and make as much noise as they can. The frightened animals dash round the enclosure and, seeing the opening, run through it and fall into the pit, where they are easily despatched with clubs and axes. They also set traps across the forest paths frequented by animals. The method is to take a strong raw-hide rope and secure one end of it to a stout sapling, which is bent down like a spring. The other end is made into a noose and laid open on the ground, often over a small hole. It is secured by a stone or log of wood, and this is so arranged by means of some kind of fall-trap that on pressure in the centre of the hole it is displaced and releases the noose. The animal comes and puts his foot in the hole, thus removing the trap which secured the noose. This flies up and takes the animal's foot with it, being drawn tight in mid-air by the rebound of the sapling. The animal is thus suspended with one foot in the air, which it cannot free, and the Gonds come and kill it. Tigers are sometimes caught in this manner. A third very cruel kind of trap is made by putting up a hedge of thorns and grass across a forest-path, on the farther side of which they plant a few strong and sharply-pointed bamboo stakes. A deer coming up will jump the hedge, and on landing will be impaled on one of the stakes. The wound is very severe and often festers immediately, so that the victim dies in a few hours. Or they suspend a heavy beam over a forest path held erect by a loose prop which stands on the path. The deer comes along and knocks aside the prop, and the beam falls on him and pins him down. Mr. Montgomerie writes as follows on Gond methods of hunting:[1] "The use of the bow and arrow is being forgotten owing to the restrictions placed by Government on hunting. The Gonds can still throw an axe fairly straight, but a running hare is a difficult mark and has a good chance of escaping. The hare, however, falls a victim to the fascination of fire. The Gond takes an earthen pot, knocks a large hole in the side of it, and slings it on a pole with a counterbalancing stone at the other end. Then at night he slings the pole over one shoulder, with the earthen pot in front containing fire, and sallies out hare-hunting. He is accompanied by a man who bears a bamboo. The hare, attracted and fascinated by the light, comes close and watches it stupidly till the bamboo descends on the animal's head, and the Gonds have hare for

[1] *Chhindwāra Settlement Report.*

supper." Sometimes a bell is rung as well, and this is said to attract the animals. They also catch fish by holding a lamp over the water on a dark night and spearing them with a trident.

Gond-Gowāri.[1]—A small hybrid caste formed from alliances between Gonds and Gowāris or herdsmen of the Marātha country. Though they must now be considered as a distinct caste, being impure and thus ranking lower than either the Gonds or Gowāris, they are still often identified with either of them. In 1901 only 3000 were returned, principally from the Nāgpur and Chānda Districts. In 1911 they were amalgamated with the Gowāris, and this view may be accepted as their origin is the same. The Gowāris say that the Gond-Gowāris are the descendants of one of two brothers who accidentally ate the flesh of a cow. Both the Gonds and Gowāris frequent the jungles for long periods together, and it is natural that intimacies should spring up between the youth of either sex. And the progeny of these irregular connections has formed a separate caste, looked down upon by both its progenitors. The Gond-Gowāris have no subcastes, and for purposes of marriages are divided into exogamous septs, all bearing Gond names. Like the Gonds, the caste is also split into two divisions, worshipping six and seven gods respectively, and members of septs worshipping the same number of gods must not marry with each other. The deities of the six and seven god-worshippers are identical, except that the latter have one extra called Durga or Devi, who is represented by a copper coin of the old Nāgpur dynasty. Of the other deities Būra Deo is a piece of iron, Khoda and Khodāvan are both pieces of the *kadamb* tree (*Nauclea parvifolia*), Supāri is the areca-nut, and Kaipen consists of two iron rings and counts as two deities. It seems probable, therefore, from the double set of identical deities that two of the original ones have been forgotten. The gods are kept on a small piece of red cloth in a closed bamboo basket, which must not be opened except on days of worship, lest they should work some mischief; on these special days they are rendered harmless

[1] This article is based on a paper by Pandit Pyāre Lāl Misra.

for the time being by the homage which is rendered to them. Marriage is adult, and a bride-price of nine rupees and some grain is commonly paid by the boy's family. The ceremony is a mixture of Gond and Marātha forms; the couple walk seven times round a *bohla* or mound of earth and the guests clap their hands. At a widow-marriage they walk three and a half times round a burning lamp, as this is considered to be only a kind of half-marriage. The morality of the caste is very loose, and a wife will commonly be pardoned any transgression except an intrigue with a man of very low caste. Women of other castes, such as Kunbis or Barhais, may be admitted to the community on forming a connection with a Gond-Gowāri. The caste have no prescribed observance of mourning for the dead. The Gond-Gowāris are cultivators and labourers, and dress like the Kunbis. They are considered to be impure and must live outside the village, while other castes refuse to touch them. The bodies of the women are disfigured by excessive tattooing, the legs being covered with a pattern of dots and lines reaching up to the thighs. In this matter they simply follow their Gond ancestors, but they say that a woman who is not tattooed is impure and cannot worship the deities.

Gondhali.[1]—A caste or order of wandering beggars and musicians found in the Marātha Districts of the Central Provinces and in Berār. The name is derived from the Marāthi word *gondharne*, to make a noise. In 1911 the Gondhalis numbered about 3000 persons in Berār and 500 in the Central Provinces, and they are also found in Bombay. The origin of the caste is obscure, but it appears to have been recruited in recent times from the offspring of Wāghyas and Murlis or male and female children devoted to temples by their parents in fulfilment of a vow. Mr. Kitts states in the *Berār Census Report*[2] of 1881 that the Gondhalis are there attached either to the temple of Tukai at Tuljāpur or the temple of Renuka at Māhur, and in consequence form two

[1] This article is compiled from papers by Mr. Kesho Rao Joshi, Headmaster, City School, Nāgpur, and Pyāre Lāl Misra, Ethnographic Clerk.

[2] Page 67.

Bemrose, Collo., Derby.

GONDHALI MUSICIANS AND DANCERS.

subcastes, the Kadamrai and Renurai, who do not intermarry. In the Central Provinces, however, besides these two there are a number of other subcastes, most of which bear the names of distinct castes, and obviously consist of members of that caste who became Gondhalis, or of their descendants. Thus among the names of subcastes reported are the Brāhman, Marātha, Māne Kunbi, Khaire Kunbi, Teli, Mahār, Māng and Vidūr Gondhalis, as well as others like the Deshkars, or those coming from the Deccan, the Gangāpāre,[1] or those from beyond the Ganges, and the Hijade or eunuchs. It is clear, therefore, that members of these castes becoming Gondhalis attempt to arrange their marriages with other converts from their own caste and to retain their relative social position. There is little doubt that all Gondhalis are theoretically meant to be equal, a principle which at their first foundation applies to nearly all sects and orders, but here as elsewhere the social feeling of caste has been too strong to permit of its retention. It may be doubted, however, whether in view of the small total numbers of the caste all these groups can be strictly endogamous. The Kunbi Gondhalis can take food from the ordinary Kunbis, but they rank below them, as being mendicants. The caste has also a number of exogamous groups or *gotras*, the names of which may be classified as titular or territorial. Instances of the former kind are Dokiphode or one who broke his head while begging, Sukt (thin, emaciated), Muke (dumb), Jabal (one with long hair like a Jogī), and Panchānge (one who has five limbs). Girls are married as a rule before adolescence, and the ceremony resembles that of the Kunbis, but a special prayer is offered to the deity Renuka, and the boy is invested with a necklace of cowries by five married men of the caste. Till this has been done he is not considered to be a proper Gondhali. Celibacy is not a tenet of the order. The remarriage of widows is allowed, and the ceremony consists in the husband placing a string of small black glass beads round the woman's neck, while she holds out a pair of new shoes for him to put his feet

[1] In the Marātha Districts the term Ganges sometimes signifies the Wainganga.

into. The second wife often wears a small silver or golden image of the first wife round her neck, and worships it before she eats by touching it with food; she also asks its permission before going to sleep with her husband. The goddess Bhawāni or Devi is especially revered by the caste, and they fast in her honour on Tuesdays and Fridays. They worship their musical instruments at Dasahra with an offering of a goat, and afterwards sing and dance for the whole night, this being their principal festival. They also observe the nine days' fasts in honour of Devi in Chait (March) and Kunwār (September) and sow the Jawaras or pots of wheat. The Gondhalis are mendicant musicians, and are engaged on the occasion of marriages among the higher castes to perform their *gondhal* or dance accompanied by music. Four men are needed for it, one being the dancer who is dressed in a long white robe with a necklace of cowries and bells on his ankles, while the other three stand behind him, two of them carrying drums and the third a sacred torch called *dioti*. The torch-bearer serves as a butt for the witticisms of the dancer. Their instruments are the *chonka*, an open drum carrying an iron string which is beaten with a small wooden pin, and two *sambals* or double drums of iron, wood or earth, one of which emits a dull and the other a sharp sound. The dance is performed in honour of the goddess Bhawāni. They set up a wooden stool on the stage arranged for the performance, covered with a cloth on which wheat is spread, and over this is placed a brass vessel containing water and a cocoanut. This represents the goddess. After the performance the Gondhalis take away and eat the cocoanut and wheat; their regular fee for an engagement is Rs. 1-4, and the guests give them presents of a few pice (farthings). They are engaged for important ceremonies such as marriages, the Bārsa or name-giving of a boy, and the Shantik or maturity of a girl, and also merely for entertainment; but in this case the stool and cocoanut representing the goddess are not set up. The following is a specimen of a Gondhali religious song:

Where I come from and who am I,
This mystery none has solved;
Father, mother, sister and brother, these are all illusions.

I call them mine and am lost in my selfish concerns.
Worldliness is the beginning of hell, man has wrapped himself in it without reason.
Remember your *guru*, go to him and touch his feet.
Put on the shield of mercy and compassion and take the sword of knowledge.
God is in every human body.

The caste beg between dawn and noon, wearing a long white or red robe and a red turban folded from twisted strings of cloth like the Marāthas. Their status is somewhat low, but they are usually simple and honest. Occasionally a man becomes a Gondhali in fulfilment of a vow without leaving his own caste; he will then be initiated by a member of the caste and given the necklace of cowries, and on every Tuesday he will wear this and beg from five persons in honour of the goddess Devi; while except for this observance he remains a member of his own caste and pursues his ordinary business.

Gopāl, Borekar.—*Bibliography:* Major Gunthorpe's *Criminal Tribes*; Mr. Kitt's *Berār Census Report*, 1881.

A small vagrant and criminal caste of Berār, where they numbered about 2000 persons in 1901. In the Central Provinces they were included among the Nats in 1901, but in 1891 a total of 681 were returned. Here they belong principally to the Nimār District, and Major Gunthorpe considers that they entered Berār from Nimār and Indore.

They are divided into five classes, the Marāthi, Vīr, Pangul, Pahalwān, or Khām, and Gujarāti Gopāls. The ostensible occupation of all the groups is the buying and selling of buffaloes. The word Gopāl means a cowherd and is a name of Krishna. The Marāthi Gopāls rank higher than the rest, and all other classes will take food from them, while the Vīr Gopāls eat the flesh of dead cattle and are looked down upon by the others. The ostensible occupation of the Vīr Gopāls is that of making mats from the leaves of the date-palm tree. They build their huts of date-leaves outside a village and remain there for one or two years or more until the headman tells them to move on. The name Borekar is stated to have the meaning of mat-maker. The Pāngul Gopāls also make mats, but in addition to this they are mendicants, begging from off trees, and must be the same as the Harbola mendicants of the Central Provinces. The Pāngul spreads a cloth below a tree and climbing it sits on some high branch in the early morning. Here he sings and chants the praises of charitable persons until somebody throws a small present on to the cloth. This he does only between cock-crow and sunrise and not after sunrise. Others walk through the streets, ejaculating *dam !*[1] *dam !* and begging from door to door. With the exception of shaving after a death they never cut the hair either of their head or face. Their principal deity is Dāwal Mālik, but they also worship Khandoba; and they bury the bodies of their dead. The corpse is carried to the grave in a *jholi* or wallet and is buried in a sitting posture. In order to discover whether a dead ancestor has been reborn in a child they have recourse to magic. A lamp is suspended from a thread, and the upper stone of the grinding-mill is placed standing upon the lower one. If either of them moves when the name of the dead ancestor is pronounced they consider that he has been reborn. One section of the Pānguls has taken to agriculture, and these refuse to marry with the mendicants, though eating and drinking with them. The Pahalwān Gopāls live in small tents and travel about, carrying their belongings on buffaloes. They are wrestlers and gymnasts, and belong mainly to Hyderābād.[2] The Khām Gopāls are a similar group also belonging to Hyderābād; and are so named because they carry about a long pole (*khām*) on which they perform acrobatic feats. They also have thick canvas bags, striped blue and white, in which they carry their property. The Gujarāti Gopāls are lower than the other divisions, who will not take food from them. They are tumblers and do feats of strength and also perform on the tight-rope. All five groups, Major Gunthorpe states, are inveterate cattle-thieves; and have colonies of their people settled on the Indore and Hyderābād borders and between them along the foot of the Satpūra Hills. Buffaloes or other animals which they steal are passed along from post to post and taken to foreign territory in an incredibly short space of time. A

[1] *Dam* apparently here means life or breath.
[2] Gunthorpe, p. 91.

considerable proportion of them, however, have now taken to agriculture, and their proper traditional calling is to sell milk and butter, for which they keep buffaloes. Gopāl is a name of Krishna, and they consider themselves to be descended from the herdsmen of Brindāban.

GOSAIN

LIST OF PARAGRAPHS

1. Names for the Gosains.

Gosain, Gusain, Sanniāsi, Dasnāmi.[1]—A name for the orders of religious mendicants of the Sivite sect, from which a caste has now developed. In 1911 the Gosains numbered a little over 40,000 persons in the Central Provinces and Berār, being distributed over all Districts. The name Gosain signifies either *gao-swāmi*, master of cows, or *go-swāmi*, master of the senses. Its significance sometimes varies. Thus in Bengal the heads of Bairāgi or Vaishnava monasteries are called Gosain, and the priests of the Vishnuite Vallabhachārya sect are known as Gokulastha Gosain. But over most of India, as in the Central Provinces, Gosain appears to be a name applied to members of the Sivite orders. Sanniāsi means one who abandons the desires of the world and the body. Properly every Brāhman should become a Sanniāsi in the fourth stage or *ashrām* of his life, when after marrying and begetting a son to celebrate his funeral rites in the second stage, he should retire to the forest, become a hermit and conquer all the appetites and passions of the body in the third stage. Thereafter, when

[1] This article contains material from Mr. J. C. Oman's *Mystics, Ascetics and Saints of India*, Sir E. Maclagan's *Punjab Census Report*, 1891, and Dr. J. N. Bhattachārya's *Hindu Castes and Sects* (Calcutta, Messrs. Thacker, Spink and Co.).

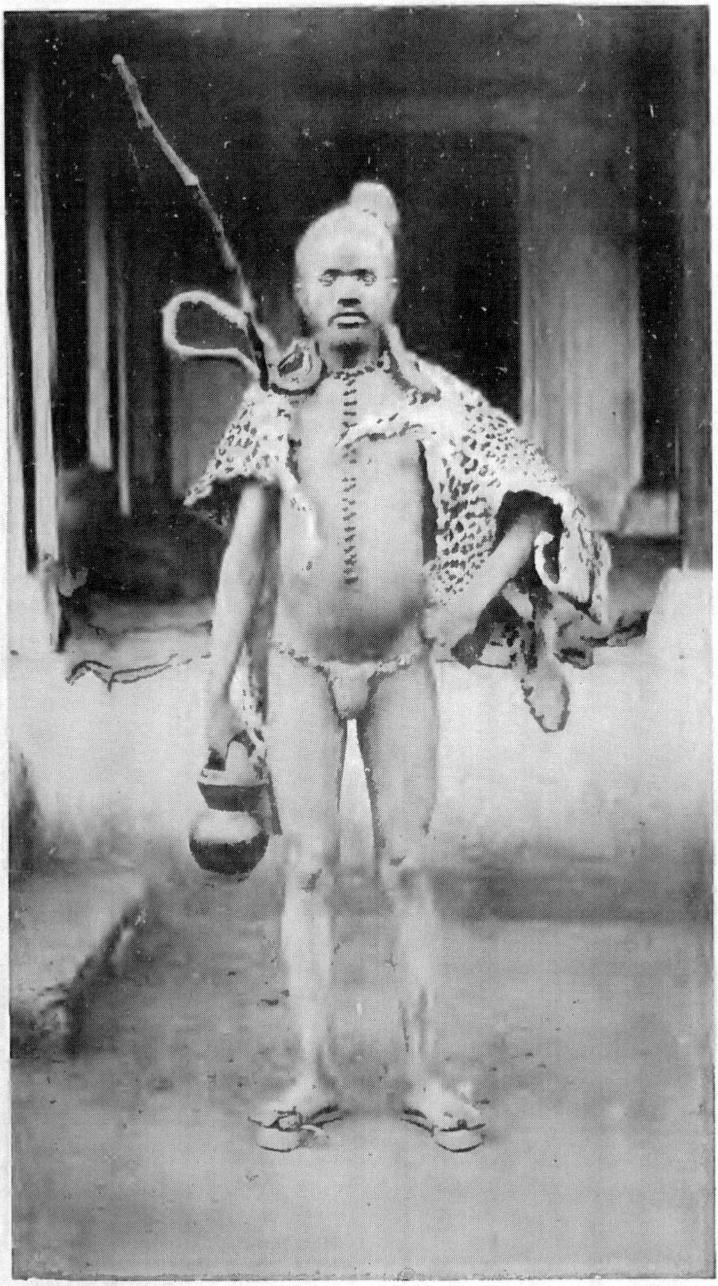

Bemrose, Collo., Derby.

GOSAIN MENDICANT.

the process of mortification is complete he should beg his bread as a Sanniāsi. But only those who enter the religious orders now become Sanniāsis, and the name is therefore confined to them. Dasnāmi means the ten names, and refers to the ten orders in which the Gosains or Sivite anchorites are commonly classified. Sādhu is a generic term for a religious mendicant. The name Gosain is now more commonly applied to the married members of the caste, who pursue ordinary avocations, while the mendicants are known as Sādhu or Sanniāsi.

The Gosains consider their founder to have been Shankar Achārya, the great apostle of the revival of the worship of Siva in southern India, who lived between the eighth and tenth centuries. He had four disciples from whom the ten orders of Gosains are derived. These are commonly stated as follows: **2. The ten orders.**

1. Giri (peak or top of a hill).
2. Puri (a town).
3. Parbat (a mountain).
4. Sāgar (the ocean).
5. Ban or Van (the forest).
6. Tīrtha (a shrine of pilgrimage).
7. Bhārthi (the goddess of speech).
8. Sāraswati (the goddess of learning).
9. Aranya (forest).
10. Ashrām (a hermitage).

The names may perhaps be held to refer to the different places in which the members of each order would pursue their austerities. The different orders have their head-quarters at great shrines. The Sāraswati, Bhārthi and Puri orders are supposed to be attached to the monastery at Sringeri in Mysore; the Tīrtha and Ashrām to that at Dwārka in Gujarāt; the Ban and Aranya to the Govardhan monastery at Puri; and the Giri, Parbat and Sāgara to the shrine of Badrināth in the Himalayas.

Dandi is sometimes shown as one of the ten orders, but it seems to be the special designation of certain ascetics who carry a staff and may belong to either the Tīrtha, Ashrām, Bhārthi or Sāraswati groups. Another name for Gosain ascetics is Abdhūt, or one who has separated himself from the world. The term Abdhūt is sometimes specially applied to followers of the Marātha saint, Dattatreya, an incarnation of Siva.

The commonest orders in the Central Provinces are Giri, Puri and Bhārthi, and the members frequently use the name of the order as their surname. Members of the Aranya, Sāgara and Parbat orders are rarely met with at present.

3. Initiation. A notice of the Gosains who have become an ordinary caste will be given later. Formerly only Brāhmans or members of the twice-born castes could become Gosains, but now a man of any caste, as Kurmi, Kunbi or Māli, from whom a Brāhman takes water, may be admitted. In some localities it is said that Gonds and Kols can now be made Gosains, and hence the social position of the Gosains has greatly fallen, and high-caste Hindus will not take water from them. It is supposed, however, that the Giri order is still recruited only from Brāhmans.

At initiation the body of a neophyte is cleaned with the five products of the sacred cow, milk, curds, *ghī*, dung and urine. He drinks water in which the great toe of his *guru* has been dipped and eats the leavings of the latter's food, thus severing himself from his own caste. His sacred thread is taken off and broken, and it is sometimes burned and he eats the ashes. All the hair of his head is shaved, including the scalp-lock, which every secular Hindu wears. A *mantra* or text is then whispered or blown into his ear.

4. Dress. The novice is dressed in a cloth coloured with *geru* or red ochre, such as the Gosains usually wear. It is probable that the red or pink colour is meant to symbolise blood and to signify that the Gosains allow the sacrifice of animals and the consumption of flesh, and on this account they are called Lāl Pādri or red priest, while Vishnuite mendicants, who dress in white, are called Sīta Pādri. He has a necklace or rosary of the seeds of the *rudrākhsa* tree,[1] sacred to Siva, consisting of 32 or 64 beads. These are like nuts with a rough indented shell. On his forehead he marks with *bhabhūt* or ashes three horizontal lines to

[1] *Elaeocarpus.*

Bemrose, Collo., Derby.

ALAKHWĀLE GOSAINS WITH FACES COVERED WITH ASHES.

represent the trident of Siva, or sometimes the eye of the god. Others make only two lines with a dot above or below, and this sign is said to represent the phallic emblem. A crescent moon or a triangle may also be made.[1] The marks are often made in sandalwood, and the Gosains say that the original sandalwood grows on a tree in the Himalayas, which is guarded by a great snake so that nobody can approach it; but its scent is so strong that all the surrounding trees of the grove are scented with it and sandalwood is obtained from them. Those who worship Bhairon make a round mark with vermilion between the eyes, taking it from beneath the god's foot. A mendicant usually has a begging-bowl and a pair of tongs, which are useful for kindling a fire. Those who have visited Badrināth or one of the other Himalayan shrines have a ring of iron, brass or copper on the arm, often inscribed with the image of a deity. If they have been to the temple of Devi at Hinglāj in the Lāsbela State of Beluchistan they have a necklace of little white stone beads called *thumra*; and one who has made a pilgrimage to Rāmeshwaram at the extreme southern point of India has a ring of conch-shell on the wrist. When he can obtain it a Gosain also carries a tiger- or panther-skin, which he wears over his shoulders and uses to sit and lie down on. Among the ancient Greeks it was the custom to sleep in a temple or its avenue either on the bare ground or on the skin of a sacred animal, in order to obtain visions or appearances of the god in a dream or to be cured of diseases.[2] Formerly the Gosains were accustomed to go about naked, and at the religious festivals they would go in procession naked to bathe in the river. At Amarnāth in the Punjab they would throw themselves naked on the block of ice which represented Siva.[3] The Nāga Gosains, so called because they were once accustomed to go naked into battle, were a famous fighting corps. Though they shave the head and scalp-lock on initiation the Gosains usually let the hair grow, and either have it hanging down

[1] Mr. Marten's *C.P. Census Report* (1911), p. 79.

[2] *Orphéus*, p. 137.

[3] Oman, *Mystics, Ascetics and Saints*, p. 269.

in matted locks over the shoulders, which gives them a wild and unkempt appearance, or wind it on the top of the head into a coil often thickened with strips of sheep's wool. They say that they let the hair grow in imitation of the ancient forest ascetics, who could not but let it grow as they had no means to shave it, and also of the matted locks of the god Siva. Sometimes they let the hair grow during the whole period of a pilgrimage, and on arrival at the shrine of their destination shave it off and offer it to the god. Those who are initiated on the banks of the Nerbudda throw the hair cut from their head into the sacred river.

5. Methods of begging and greetings.

They have various rules about begging. Some will never turn back to receive alms. They may also make a rule only to accept the surplus of food cooked for the family, and to refuse any of special quality or cooked expressly for them. One Gosain, noticed by Mr. A. K. Smith, always begged hopping, and only from five houses; he took from them respectively two handfuls of flour, a pinch of salt, and sufficient quantities of vegetables, spices and butter for his meal, and then went hopping home. Those who are performing the *perikrama* or circuit of the Nerbudda from its source to its mouth and back, do not cut their hair or nails during the whole period of about three years. They may not enter the Nerbudda above their knees nor wash their vessels in it. After crossing any tributary river or stream in their path they may not re-cross this; and if they have forgotten or left any article behind, must abandon it unless they can persuade somebody to go back and fetch it for them. Some carry a gourd with a single string stretched on a stick, on which they twang some notes; others have a belt of sheep's hair hung with the bells of bullocks which they tie round the waist, so that the tinkling of the bells may announce their coming. A common begging cry is Alakh, which is said to mean 'apart,' and to refer to themselves as being apart or separated from the world. The beggar gives this cry and stands at the door of the house for half a minute, shaking his body about all the time. If no alms are brought in this time he moves on.

When an ordinary Hindu meets a Gosain he says 'Nāmu Nārāyan' or 'I go to Nārāyan,' and the Gosain

Bemrose, Collo., Derby.

GOSAIN MENDICANTS WITH LONG HAIR.

answers 'Nārāyan.' Nārāyan is a name of Vishnu, and its use by the Gosains is curious. Those who have performed the circuit of the Nerbudda say 'Har Nerbudda,' and the person addressed answers 'Nerbudda Mai ki Jai' or 'Victory to Mother Nerbudda.'

6. The Dandis.

The Dandis are a special group of ascetics belonging to several of the ten orders. According to one account a novice who desires to become a Sanniāsi must serve a period of probation for twelve years as a Dandi. Others say that only a Brāhman can be a Dandi, while members of other castes may become Sanniāsis, and a Brāhman can only become one if he is without father, mother, wife or child.[1] The Dandi is so called because he has a *dand* or bamboo staff like the ancient Vedic students. He must always carry this and never lay it down, but when sleeping plant it in the ground. Sometimes a piece of red cloth is tied round the staff. The Dandi should live in the forest, and only come once a day to beg at a Brāhman's house for a part of such food as the family may have cooked. He should not ask for food if any one else, even a dog, is waiting for it. He must not accept money, or touch fire or any metal. As a matter of fact these rules are disregarded, and the Dandi frequents towns and is accompanied by companions who will accept all kinds of alms on his behalf.[2] Dandis and Sanniāsis do not worship idols, as they are themselves considered to have become part of the deity. They repeat the phrase 'Sevoham,' which signifies 'I am Siva.'

7. The Rāwanvansis.

Another curious class of Gosains are the Rāwanvansis, who go about in the character of Rāwan, the demon king of Ceylon, as he was when he carried off Sīta. The legend is that in order to do this, Rāwan first sent his brother in the shape of a golden deer before Rāma's palace. Sīta saw it and said she must have the head of the deer, and sent Rāma to kill it. So Rāma pursued it to the forest, and from there Rāwan cried out, imitating Rāma's voice. Then Sīta thought Rāma was being attacked and told his brother Lachman to go to his help. But Lachman had been left

[1] Bhattachārya, *Hindu Castes and Sects*, p. 380.

[2] Bhattachārya, *ibidem*, and Oman, *Mystics, Ascetics and Saints*, pp. 160, 161.

in charge of her by Rāma and refused to leave her, till Sīta said he was hoping Rāma would be killed, so that he might marry her. Then he drew a circle round her on the ground, and telling her not to step outside it until his return, went off. Then Rāwan took the disguise of a beggar and came and begged for alms from Sīta. She told him to come inside the magic circle and she would give him alms, but he refused. So finally Sīta came outside the circle, and Rāwan at once seized her and carried her off to Ceylon. The Rāwanvansi Gosains wear rings of hair all up their arms and a rope of hair round the waist, and the hair of their head hanging down. It would appear that they are intended to represent some animal. They smear vermilion on the forehead, and beg only at twilight and never at any other time, whether they obtain food or not. In begging they will never move backwards, so that when they have passed a house they cannot take alms from it unless the householder brings the gift to them.

8. Monasteries. Unmarried Sanniāsis often reside in Maths or monasteries. The superior is called Mahant, and he appoints his successor by will from the members. The Mahant admits all those willing and qualified to enter the order. If the applicant is young the consent of the parents is usually obtained; and parents frequently vow to give a child to the order. Many convents have considerable areas of land attached to them, and also dependent institutions. The whole property of the convent and its dependencies seems to be at the absolute disposal of the Mahant, but he is bound to give food, raiment and lodging to the inmates, and he entertains all travellers belonging to the order.[1]

9. The fighting Gosains. In former times the Gosains often became soldiers and entered the service of different military chiefs. The most famous of these fighting priests were the Nāga Gosains of the Jaipur State of Rājputāna, who are said to have been under an obligation from their *guru* or religious chief to fight for the Rāja of Jaipur whenever required. They received rent-free lands and pay of two pice ($\frac{1}{2}$d.) a day, which latter was put into a common treasury and expended on the purchase of arms and ammunition whenever needed

[1] Buchanan, *Eastern India*, i. pp. 197, 198.

Bemrose, Collo., Derby.

FAMOUS GOSAIN MAHANT, PHOTOGRAPH TAKEN AFTER DEATH.

for war. They would also lend money, and if a debtor could not pay would make him give his son to be enrolled in the force. The 7000 Nāga Gosains were placed in the vanguard of the Jaipur army in battle. Their weapons were the bow, arrow, shield, spear and discus. The Gosain proprietor of the Deopur estate in Raipur formerly kept up a force of Nāga Gosains, with which he used to collect the tribute from the feudatory chiefs of Chhattīsgarh on behalf of the Rāja of Nāgpur. It is said that he once invaded Bastar with this object, where most of the Gosains died of cholera. But after they had fasted for three days, the goddess Danteshwari appeared to them and promised them her protection. And they took the goddess away with them and installed her in their own village in Raipur. Forbes records that in Gujarāt an English officer was in command of a troop known as the Gosain's wife's troops. These Nāga Gosains wore only a single white garment, like a sleeveless shirt reaching to the knees, and hence it is said that they were called naked. The Gosains and Bairāgis, or adherents of Siva and Vishnu, were often engaged in religious quarrels on the merits of their respective deities, and sometimes came to blows. A favourite point of rivalry was the right of bathing first in the Ganges on the occasion of one of the great religious fairs at Allahābād or Hardwār. The Gosains claim priority of bathing, on the ground that the Ganges flows from the matted locks of Siva; while the Bairāgis assert that the source of the river is from Vishnu's foot. In 1760 a pitched battle on this question ended in the defeat of the Bairāgis, of whom 1800 were slain. Again in 1796 the Gosains engaged in battle with the Sikh pilgrims and were defeated with the loss of 500 men.[1] During the reign of Akbar a combat took place in the Emperor's presence between the two Sivite sects of Gosains, or Sanniāsis and Jogis, having been apparently arranged for his edification, to decide which sect had the best ground for its pretensions to supernatural power. The Jogis were completely defeated.[2]

[1] Nesfield, *Brief View of the Caste System*, p. 86.

[2] J. C. Oman, *Cults, Customs and Superstitions of India* (London, T. Fisher Unwin), p. 11.

10. Burial. A dead Sanniāsi is always buried in the sitting attitude of religious contemplation with the legs crossed. The grave may be dug with a side receptacle for the corpse so that the earth, on being filled in, does not fall on it. The corpse is bathed and rubbed with ashes and clad in a new reddish-coloured shirt, with a rosary round the neck. The begging-wallet with some flour and pulse are placed in the grave, and also a gourd and staff. Salt is put round the body to preserve it, and an earthen pot is put over the head. Sometimes cocoanuts are broken on the skull, to crack it and give exit to the soul. Perhaps the idea of burial and of preserving the corpse with salt is that the body of an ascetic does not need to be purified by fire from the appetites and passions of the flesh like that of an ordinary Hindu; it is already cleansed of all earthly frailty by his austerities, and the belief may therefore have originally been that such a man would carry his body with him to the afterworld or to absorption with the deity. The burial of a Sanniāsi is often accompanied with music and signs of rejoicing; Mr. Oman describes such a funeral in which the corpse was seated in a litter, open on three sides so that it could be seen; it was tied to the back of the litter, and garlands of flowers partly covered the body, but could not conceal the hideousness of death as the unconscious head rolled helplessly from side to side with the movement of the litter. The procession was headed by a European brass band and by men carrying censers of incense.[1]

11. Sexual indulgence. Celibacy is the rule of the Gosain orders, and a man's property passes in inheritance to a selected *chela* or disciple. But the practice of keeping women is very common, even outside the large section of the community which now recognises marriage. Women could be admitted into the order, when they had to shave their heads, assume the ochre-coloured shirt and rub their bodies with ashes. Afterwards, with the permission of the *guru* and on payment of a fine, they could let their hair grow again, at least temporarily. These women were supposed to remain quite chaste and live in nunneries, but many of them lived with men of the order. It is not known to what extent women are admitted at

[1] *Mystics, Ascetics and Saints of India*, pp. 156, 157.

present. The sons born of such unions would be adopted as *chelas* or disciples by other Gosains, and made their heirs by a reciprocal arrangement. Women who are convicted of some social offence, or who wish to leave their husbands, often join the order nominally and live with a Gosain or are married into the caste. Many of the wandering mendicants lead an immoral life, and scandals about their enticing away the wives of rich Hindus are not infrequent.[1] During their visits to villages they also engage in intrigues, and a ribald Gond song sung at the Holi festival describes the pleasure of the village women at the arrival of a Gosain owing to the sexual gratification which they expected to receive from him.

12. Missionary work. Nevertheless the wandering Gosains have done much to foster and maintain the Hindu religion among the people. They are the *gurus* or spiritual preceptors of the middle and lower castes, and though their teaching may be of little advantage, it perhaps quickens and maintains to some extent the religious feelings of their clients. In former times the Gosains travelled over the wildest tracts of country, proselytising the primitive non-Aryan tribes, for whose conversion to Hinduism they are largely responsible. On such journeys they necessarily carried their lives in their hands, and not infrequently lost them.

13. The Gosain caste. The majority of the Gosains are, however, now married and form an ordinary caste. Buchanan states that the ten different orders became exogamous groups, the members of which married with each other, but it is doubtful whether this is the case at present. It is said that all Giri Gosains marry, whether they are mendicants or not, while the Bhārthi order can marry or not as they please. They prohibit any marriage between first cousins, but permit widow remarriage and divorce. They eat the flesh of all clean animals and also of fowls, and drink liquor, and will take cooked food from the higher castes, including Sunārs and Kunbis. Hence they do not rank high socially, and Brāhmans do not take water from them, but their religious character gives them some prestige. Many Gosains have become landholders, obtaining their estates either as charitable grants from clients or through moneylending transactions. In this capacity they do not

[1] Sir E. Maclagan, *Punjab Census Report* (1891), p. 112.

usually turn out well, and are often considered harsh landlords and grasping creditors.

1. Origin of the caste.

Gowāri.[1]—The herdsman or grazier caste of the Marātha country, corresponding to the Ahīrs or Gaolis. The name is derived from *gai* or *gao*, the cow, and means a cowherd. The Gowāris numbered more than 150,000 persons in 1911, of whom nearly 120,000 belonged to the Nāgpur division and nearly 30,000 to Berār. In localities where the Gowāris predominate, Ahīrs or Gaolis, the regular herdsman caste, are found only in small numbers. The honorific title of the Gowāris is Dhare, which is said to mean 'One who keeps cattle.' The Gowāris rank distinctly below the Ahīrs or Gaolis. The legend of their origin is that an Ahīr, who was tending the cows of Krishna, stood in need of a helper. He found a small boy in the forest and took him home and brought him up. He then gave to the boy the work of grazing cows in the jungle, while he himself stayed at home and made milk and butter. This boy was the ancestor of the Gowāri caste. His descendants took to eating fowls and peacocks and drinking liquor, and hence were degraded below the Gaolis. But the latter will allow Gowāris to sit at their feasts and eat, they will carry the corpse of a Gowāri to the grave, and they will act as members of the *panchāyat* in readmitting a Gowāri who has been put out of caste. In the Marātha country any man who touches the corpse of a man of another caste is temporarily excommunicated, and the fact that a Gaoli will do this for a Gowāri demonstrates the close relationship of the castes. The legend, in fact, indicates quite clearly and correctly the origin of the Gowāris. The small boy in the forest was a Gond, and the Gowāri caste is of mixed descent from Ahīrs and Gonds. The Ahīrs or Gaolis of the Marātha country have largely abandoned the work of grazing cattle in the forest, and have taken to the more profitable business of making milk and *ghī*. The herdsman's duties have been relegated to the mixed class of Gowāris, produced from the unions of Ahīrs and Gonds in the forests, and not improbably

[1] This article is based on notes by Mr. Percival, Assistant Conservator of Forests, and Rai Bahādur Hīra Lal.

including a considerable section of pure Gond blood. At present only Gaolis and no other caste are admitted into the Gowāri community, though there is evidence that the rule was not formerly so strict.

2. Subcastes. The Gowāris have three divisions, the Gai Gowāri, Inga, and Māria or Gond Gowāri. The Gai or cow Gowāris are the highest and probably have more Gaoli blood in them. The Inga and Māria or Gond Gowāris are more directly derived from the Gonds. Māria is the name given to a large section of the Gond tribe in Chānda. Both the other two subcastes will take cooked food from the Gai Gowāris and the Gond Gowāris from the Inga, but the Inga subcaste will not take it from the Gond, nor the Gai Gowāris from either of the other two. The Gond Gowāris have been treated as a distinct caste and a separate article is given on them, but at the census Mr. Marten has amalgamated them with the Gowāris. This is probably more correct, as they are locally held to be a branch of the caste. But their customs differ in some points from those of the other Gowāris. They will admit outsiders from any respectable caste and worship the Gond gods,[1] and there seems no harm, therefore, in allowing the separate article on them to remain.

3. Totemism and exogamy. The Gowāris have exogamous sections of the titular and totemistic types, such as Chachania from *chachan*, a bird, Lohār from *loha* iron, Ambadāre a mango-branch, Kohria from the Kohri or Kohli caste, Sarwaina a Gond sept, and Rāwat the name of the Ahīr caste in Chhattīsgarh. Some septs do not permit intermarriage between their members, saying that they are Dūdh-Bhais or foster-brothers, born from the same mother. Thus the Chachania, Kohria, Senwaria, Sendua (vermilion) and Wāgare (tiger) septs cannot intermarry. They say that their fathers were different, but their mothers were related or one and the same. This is apparently a relic of polyandry, and it is possible that in some cases the Gonds may have allowed Ahīrs sojourning in the forest to have access to their wives during the period of their stay. If this was permitted to Ahīrs of different sections coming to the same Gond village in successive years, the offspring might be the ancestors of

[1] For further details see article on Gond Gowāri.

sections who consider themselves to be related to each other in the manner of the Gowāri sections.

Marriage is prohibited within the same section or *kur*, and between sections related to each other as Dūdh-Bhais in the manner explained above. A man can marry his daughter to his sister's son, but cannot take her daughter for his son. The children of two sisters cannot be married.

4. Marriage customs. Girls are usually married after attaining maturity, and a bride-price is paid which is normally two *khandis* (800 lbs.) of grain, Rs. 16 to 20 in cash, and a piece of cloth. The auspicious date of the wedding is calculated by a Mahār Mohturia or soothsayer. Brāhmans are not employed, the ceremony being performed by the *bhānya* or sister's son of either the girl's father or the boy's father. If he is not available, any one whom either the girl's father or the boy's father addresses as *bhānja* or nephew in the village, according to the common custom of addressing each other by terms of relationship, even though he may be no relative and belong to another caste, may be substituted; and if no such person is available a son-in-law of either of the parties. The peculiar importance thus attached to the sister's son as a relation is probably a relic of the matriarchate, when a man's sister's son was his heir. The substitution of a son-in-law who might inherit in the absence of a sister's son perhaps strengthens this view. The wedding is held mainly according to the Marātha ritual.[1] The procession goes to the girl's house, and the bridegroom is wrapped in a blanket and carries a spear, in the absence of which the wedding cannot be held. A spear is also essential among the Gonds. The ancestors of the caste are invited to the wedding by beating a drum and calling on them to attend. The original ancestors are said to be Kode Kodwan, the names of two Gond gods, Bāghoba (the tiger-god), and Meghnāth, son of Rāwan, the demon king of Ceylon, after whom the Gonds are called Rāwanvansi, or descendants of Rāwan. The wedding costs about Rs. 50, all of which is spent by the boy's father. The girl's father only gives a feast to the caste out of the amount which he receives as bride-price. Divorce and the remarriage of widows are permitted.

[1] See article on Kunbi.

5. Funeral rites.

The dead are either buried or burnt, burial being more common. The corpse is laid with head to the south and feet to the north. On returning from the funeral they go and drink at the liquor-shop, and then kill a cock on the spot where the deceased died, and offer some meat to his spirit, placing it outside the house. The caste-fellows sit and wait until a crow comes and pecks at the food, when they think that the deceased has enjoyed it, and begin to eat themselves. If no crow comes before night the food may be given to a cow, and the party can then begin to eat. When the next wedding is held in the family, the deceased is brought down from the skies and enshrined among the deified ancestors.

6. Religion.

The principal deities of the Gowāris are the Kode Kodwan or deified ancestors. They are worshipped at the annual festivals, and also at weddings. When a man or woman dies without children their spirits are known as Dhal, and are worshipped in the families to which they belonged. A male Dhal is represented by a stick of bamboo with one cross-piece at the top, and a female Dhal by a stick with two others crossing each other lashed to it at the top. These sticks are worshipped at the Diwāli festival, and carried in procession. Dudhera is a godling worshipped for the protection of cattle. He is represented by a clay horse placed near a white ant-hill. If a cow stops giving milk her udder is smoked with the burning wood of a tree called *sānwal*, and this is supposed to drive away the spirits who drink the milk from the udder. All Gowāris revere the *haryal*, or green pigeon. They say that it gives a sound like a Gowāri calling his cows, and that it is a kinsman. They would on no account kill this bird. They say that the cows will go to a tree from which green pigeons are cooing, and that on one occasion when a thief was driving away their cows a green pigeon cooed from a tree, and the cows turned round and came back again. This is like the story of the sacred geese at Rome, who gave warning of the attack of the Goths.

7. Caste rules and the *panchāyat*.

The head of the caste committee is known as Shendia, from *shendi*, a scalp-lock or pig-tail, perhaps because he is at the top of the caste as the scalp-lock is at the top of the head. The Shendia is elected, and holds office for life. He has to readmit offenders into caste by being the first to eat and drink with them, thus taking their sins on himself. On such occasions it is necessary to have a little opium, which is mixed with sugar and water, and distributed to all members of the caste. If the quantity is insufficient for every one to drink, the man responsible for preparing it is fined, and this mixture, especially the opium, is indispensable on all such occasions. The custom indicates that a sacred or sacrificial character is attributed to the opium, as the drinking of the mixture together is the sign of the readmission of a temporary outcaste into the community. After this has been drunk he becomes a member of the caste, even though he may not give the penalty feast for some time afterwards. The Ahīrs and Sunārs of the Marātha country have the same rite of purification by the common drinking of opium and water. A caste penalty is incurred for the removal of *bitāl* or impurity arising from the usual offences, and among others for touching the corpse of a man of any other caste, or of a buffalo, horse, cow, cat or dog, for using abusive language to a casteman at any meeting or feast, and for getting up from a caste feast without permission from the headman. For touching the corpse of a prohibited animal and for going to jail a man has to get his head, beard and whiskers shaved. If a woman becomes with child by a man of another caste, she is temporarily expelled, but can be readmitted after the child has been born and she has disposed of it to somebody else. Such children are often made over for a few rupees to Muhammadans, who bring them up as menial servants in their families, or, if they have no child of their own, sometimes adopt them. On readmission a lock of the woman's hair is cut off. In the same case, if no child is born of the *liaison*, the woman is taken back with the simple penalty of a feast. Permanent expulsion is imposed for taking food from, or having an intrigue with a member of an impure caste as Mādgi, Mehtar, Pardhān, Mahār and Māng.

8. Social customs. The Gowāris eat pork, fowls, rats, lizards and peacocks, and abstain only from beef and the flesh of monkeys, crocodiles and jackals. They will take food from a Māna,

Marār or Kohli, and water from a Gond. Kunbis will take water from them, and Gonds, Dhīmars and Dhobis will accept cooked food. All Gowāri men are tattooed with a straight vertical line on the forehead, and many of them have the figures of a peacock, deer or horse on the right shoulder or on both shoulders. A man without the mark on the forehead will scarcely be admitted to be a true Gowāri, and would have to prove his birth before he was allowed to join a caste feast. Women are tattooed with a pattern of straight and crooked lines on the right arm below the elbow, which they call Sīta's arm. They have a vertical line standing on a horizontal one on the forehead, and dots on the temples.

GŪJAR

LIST OF PARAGRAPHS

1. Historical notice of the caste.

Gūjar.—A great historical caste who have given their name to the Gujarāt District and the town of Gujarānwāla in the Punjab, the peninsula of Gujarāt or Kāthiāwār and the tract known as Gūjargarh in Gwālior. In the Central Provinces the Gūjars numbered 56,000 persons in 1911, of whom the great majority belonged to the Hoshangābād and Nimār Districts. In these Provinces the caste is thus practically confined to the Nerbudda Valley, and they appear to have come here from Gwālior probably in the middle of the sixteenth century, to which period the first important influx of Hindus into this area has been ascribed. But some of the Nimār Gūjars are immigrants from Gujarāt. Owing to their distinctive appearance and character and their exploits as cattle-raiders, the origin of the Gūjars has been the subject of much discussion. General Cunningham identified them with the Yueh-chi or Tochāri, the tribe of Indo-Scythians who invaded India in the first century of the Christian era. The king Kadphises I. and his successors belonged to the Kushān section of the Yueh-chi tribe, and their rule extended over north-western India down to Gujarāt in the period 45–225 A.D. Mr. V. A. Smith, however, discards this theory and considers the Gūjars or Gurjaras to have been a branch of the white Huns who invaded India in the fifth and sixth centuries. He writes:[1] "The earliest foreign immigration within the limits of the historical period which can be verified is that of the Sakas in the second century B.C.; and the next is that of the Yueh-chi and Kushāns in the first century A.D. Probably none of the existing Rājpūt clans can carry back their genuine pedigrees so far. The third recorded great irruption of foreign barbarians occurred during the fifth century and the early part of the sixth. There are indications that the immigration from Central Asia continued during the third century, but, if it did, no distinct record of the event has been preserved, and, so far as positive knowledge goes, only three certain irruptions of foreigners on a large scale through the northern and north-western passes can be proved to have taken place within the historical period anterior to the Muhammadan invasions of the tenth and eleventh centuries. The first and second, as above observed, were those of the Sakas and Yueh-chi respectively, and the third was that of the Hūnas or white Huns. It seems to be clearly established that the Hun group of tribes or hordes made their principal permanent settlements in the Punjab and Rājputāna. The most important element in the group after the Huns themselves was that of the Gurjaras, whose name still survives in the spoken form Gūjar as the designation of a widely diffused middle-class caste in north-western India. The prominent position occupied by Gurjara kingdoms in early mediaeval times is a recent discovery. The existence of a small Gurjara principality in Bharōch (Broach), and of a larger state in Rājputāna, has been known to archaeologists for many years, but the recognition of the fact that Bhoja and the other kings of the powerful Kanauj dynasty in the ninth, tenth and eleventh centuries were Gurjaras is of very recent date and is not yet general. Certain misreadings of epigraphic dates obscured the true history of that dynasty, and the correct readings have been established only within the last two or three years. It is now definitely proved that Bhoja (*circ.* A.D. 840–890), his predecessors and successors belonged to the Pratihāra (Parihār) clan of the Gurjara tribe or caste, and, consequently,

[1] *Early History of India*, 3rd ed. pp. 409, 411.

that the well-known clan of Parihār Rājpūts is a branch of the Gurjara or Gūjar stock."[1]

2. The Gūjars and the Khazars.

Sir J. Campbell identified the Gūjars with the Khazar tribe of Central Asia:[2] "What is known of the early history of the Gujaras in India points to their arrival during the last quarter of the fifth or the first quarter of the sixth century (A.D. 470–520). That is the Gujaras seem to have formed part of the great horde of which the Juān-Juān or Avārs, and the Ephthalites, Yetas or White Hūnas were leading elements. The question remains: How far does the arrival of the Gujara in India, during the early sixth century, agree with what is known of the history of the Khazar? The name Khazar appears under the following forms: Among Chinese as Kosa, among Russians as Khwalisses, among Byzantines as Chozars or Chazars, among Armenians as Khazirs and among Arabs as Khozar. Other variations come closer to Gujara. These are Gazar, the form Kazar takes to the north of the sea of Asof; Ghysar, the name for Khazars who have become Jews; and Ghusar, the form of Khazar in use among the Lesghians of the Caucasus. Howarth and the writer in the *Encyclopædia Britannica* follow Klaproth in holding that the Khazars are the same as the White Hūnas. . . .

"Admitting that the Khazar and White Hūna are one, it must also be the case that the Khazars included two distinct elements, a fair or Ak-Khazar, the Akatziroi or Khazaroi of Byzantine historians, and a dark or Kāra Khazar. The Kāra Khazar was short, ugly and as black as an Indian. He was the Ughrian nomad of the steppes, who formed the rank and file of the army. The White Khazar or White Hūna was fair-skinned, black-haired and beautiful, their women (in the ninth and tenth centuries) being sought after in the bazārs of Bāghdād and Byzantium. According to Klaproth, a view adopted by the writer in the *Encyclopædia Britannica*, the White Khazar represented the white race

[1] Mr. Smith ascribes this discovery to Messrs. A. M. T. Jackson (*Bombay Gazetteer*, vol. i. Part I., 1896, p. 467); D. R. Bhandārkar, Gurjaras (*J. Bo. R.A.S.* vol. xx.); and Epigraphic Notes (*ibidem*, vol. xxi.); and Professor Kielhorn's paper on the Gwālior Inscription of Mihira Bhoja in a German journal.

[2] *Bombay Gazetteer, Hindus of Gujarāt*, Appendix B, The Gūjars.

Bemrose, Collo., Derby.

GÜJAR VILLAGE PROPRIETRESS AND HER LAND AGENT.

which, since before Christ, has been settled round the Caspian. As White Hūnas, Ephthalites,[1] White Ughrians and White Bulgars, this white race were the carriers between Europe and East Asia; they were also the bearers of the brunt of the Tartar inroads. A trace both of the beautiful and coarse clans seems to survive in the complimentary Mārwār proverb, 'Handsome as a Hūna,' and in the abusive Gujarāt proverb, 'Yellow and short as a Hūna's beard.' Under its Hindu form Gurjara, Khazar appears to have become the name by which the great bulk of the sixth-century horde was known." Sir J. Campbell was of opinion that the Sesodia or Gahlot Rājpūts, the most illustrious of all the clans, were of Gūjar stock, as well as the Parihār, Chauhān, and Chalukya or Solanki; these last were three of the Agnikula clans or those created from the firepit,[2] and a Solanki dynasty ruled in Gujarāt. He also considered the Nāgar Brāhmans of Gujarāt to be derived from the Gūjars and considerable sections of the Ahīr and Kunbi castes. The Badgūjar (great Gūjar) clan of Rājpūts is no doubt also an aristocratic branch of the caste. In Ajmere it is said that though all Gūjars are not Rājpūts, no Rājpūt becomes a hero unless he is suckled by a Gūjar woman. *Gūjarika dudh, nāhari ka dudh*; or 'Gūjar's milk is tiger's milk.' A Rājpūt who has not been suckled by a Gūjar woman is a *gidar* or jackal.[3]

3. Predatory character of the Gūjars in northern India.

The fact of the White Huns being tall and of fine features, in contrast to the horde which invaded Europe under Attila, accounts for these characteristics being found among the highest Rājpūt clans, who, as has been seen, are probably derived from them. The Gūjar caste generally is now, however, no doubt of mixed and impure blood. They were distinguished in the past as vagrant and predatory marauders, and must have assimilated various foreign elements. Mr. Crooke writes of them:[4] "The Gūjars as a tribe have always been noted for their turbulence and habit of

[1] The Khazars were known to the Chinese as Yetas, the beginning of Yeta-i-li-to, the name of their ruling family, and the nations of the west altered this to Hyatilah and Ephthalite. Campbell, *ibidem.*

[2] See article on Panwār Rājpūt, para. 1.

[3] Campbell, *loc. cit.* p. 495.

[4] *Tribes and Castes*, article Gūjar, para. 12. The description is mainly taken from Elliott's *History of India as told by its own Historians.*

cattle-stealing. Bābar in his Memoirs describes how the commander of the rearguard captured a few Gūjar ruffians who followed the camp, decapitated them and sent their heads to the Emperor. The Gūjars of Pāli and Pāhal became exceedingly audacious while Sher Shāh was fortifying Delhi, and he marched to the hills and expelled them so that not a vestige of their habitations was left. Jahāngīr remarks that the Gūjars live chiefly on milk and curds and seldom cultivate land; and Bābar says: 'Every time I entered Hindustan the Jāts and Gūjars have regularly poured down in prodigious numbers from the hills and wilds to carry off oxen and buffaloes. These were the wretches that really inflicted the chief hardships and were guilty of the chief oppression in the country.' They maintained their old reputation in the Mutiny when they perpetrated numerous outrages and seriously impeded the operations of the British Army before Delhi." In northern India the Gūjars are a pastoral caste. The saying about them is—

Ahīr, Gadaria, Gūjar,
E tinon tâken ujar,

or, 'The Ahīr, Gadaria and Gūjar want waste land'; that is for grazing their flocks. In Kāngra the Gūjars generally keep buffaloes. Here they are described as "A fine, manly race with peculiar and handsome features. They are mild and inoffensive in manner, and in these hills are not distinguished by the bad pre-eminence which attaches to their race in the plains."[1] Sir D. Ibbetson had a very unfavourable opinion of the Gūjars of the plains, of whom he wrote as follows:[2] "The Gūjar is a fine stalwart fellow, of precisely the same physical type as the Jāt; and the theory of aboriginal descent which has been propounded is to my mind conclusively negatived by his cast of countenance. He is of the same social standing as the Jāt, or perhaps slightly inferior; but the two eat and drink in common without any scruple, and the proverb says: 'The Jāt, Gūjar, Ahīr and Gola are all hail fellow well met.' But he is far inferior

[1] Description of the Kāngra Gūjars by Mr. Barnes. Quoted in Ibbetson's *Punjab Census Report* (1881), para. 481.

[2] *Census Report*, para. 481.

in both personal character and repute to the Jāt. He is lazy to a degree, and a wretched cultivator; his women, though not secluded, will not do field-work save of the lightest kind; while his fondness for cattle extends to those of other people. The difference between a Gūjar and a Rājpūt cattle-thief was once explained to me thus by a Jāt: 'The Rajpūt will steal your buffalo. But he will not send his old father to say he knows where it is and will get it back for Rs. 20, and then keep the Rs. 20 and the buffalo too. The Gūjar will.'"

The Gūjars of the Central Provinces have, however, entirely given up the predatory habits of their brethren in northern India and have developed into excellent cultivators and respectable law-abiding citizens. In Hoshangābād they have three subcastes, Lekha, Mundle and Jādam. The Mundle or 'Shaven' are so called because they take off their turbans when they eat and expose their crowns bare of hair, while the Lekha eat with their turbans on. The Mundle are also known as Rewe, from the Rewa or Nerbudda, near which they reside. The Jādam are probably an offshoot from the cultivating caste of Hoshangābād of that name, Jādam being a corruption of Jādubansi, a tribe of Rājpūts. The Badgūjars, who belong to Nimār, consider themselves the highest, deriving their name from *bara* or 'great' Gūjar. As already seen, there is a Badgūjar clan of Rājpūts. The Nimār Badgūjars, however, were formerly engaged in the somewhat humble calling of clearing cotton of its seeds, and on this account they are also known as Ludhāre, the word *lodhna* meaning to work the hand-ginning machine (*charkhi*). It seems possible that the small caste of Lorhas of the Hoshangābād District, whose special avocation is to grow *san*-hemp, may be derived from these Ludhāre Gūjars. The Kekre or Kanwe subcaste are the lowest and are of illegitimate descent. They are known as Kekre or 'Crabs,' but prefer their other name. They will take food from the other subcastes, but these do not return the compliment. Another group in the Sohāgpur Tahsīl of Hoshangābād are the Lilorhia Gūjars. They say that their ancestors were grazing calves when some of them with their herdsmen were stolen by Brahma.

4. Subdivisions.

Then Krishna created fresh cowherds and the Lilorhias were made from the sweat of his forehead (*lilat*). Afterwards Brahma restored the original cowherds, who were known as Murelia, because they were the first players on the *murli* or flute.[1] The Badgūjars or highest branch of the clan are descendants of these Murelias. The caste have also a set of exogamous groups, several of which bear the names of Rājpūt clans, while others are called after villages, titles or nicknames or natural objects. A man is not permitted to marry any one belonging either to his own sept or that of his mother or grandmother.

5. Marriage. At a Gūjar wedding four plough-yokes are laid out to form a square under the marriage booth, with a copper pot full of water in the centre. At the auspicious moment the bride's hand is placed on that of the bridegroom, and the two walk seven times round the pot, the bridegroom leading for the first four rounds and the bride for the last three. Widows are allowed to remarry, and, as girls are rather scarce in the caste, a large price is often paid for the widow to her father or guardian, though this is not willingly admitted. As much as Rs. 3000 is recorded to have been paid. A widow marriage is known as Nātra or Pāt. A woman is forbidden to marry any relative of her first husband. When the marriage of a widow is to take place a fee of Rs. 1-4 must be paid to the village proprietor to obtain his consent. The Gūjars of the Bulandshahr District of the United Provinces furnish, Mr. Crooke says,[2] perhaps the only well-established instance of polyandry among the Hindus of the plains. Owing to the scarcity of women in the caste it was customary for the wife of one brother, usually the eldest, to be occasionally at the disposal of other unmarried brothers living in the house. The custom arose owing to the lack of women caused by the prevalence of female infanticide, and now that this has been stopped it is rapidly dying out, while no trace of it is believed to exist in the Central Provinces.

6. Disposal of the dead. The bodies of unmarried persons are buried, and also

[1] Cf. Krishna's epithet of Murlidhar or the flute-player, and the general association of the flute with herdsmen and shepherds in Greek and Roman mythology.

[2] *Ibidem.*

of those who die of any epidemic disease. Others are cremated. The funeral of an elderly man of good means and family is an occasion for great display. A large feast is given and the Brāhman priests of the caste go about inviting all the Gūjars to attend. Sometimes the number of guests rises to three or four thousand. At the conclusion of the feast one of the hosts claps his hands and all the guests then get up and immediately depart without ceremony or saying farewell. Such an occasion is known as Gūjarwāda, and the Gūjars often spend as much, or more, on a funeral as on a wedding, in the belief that the outlay is of direct benefit to the dead man's spirit. This idea is inculcated and diligently fostered by the family priests and those Brāhmans who receive gifts for the use of the dead, the greed of these cormorants being insatiable.

7. Religion. The household goddess of the caste is known as Kul Devi, the word *kul* meaning family. To her a platform is erected inside the house, and she must be worshipped by the members of the family alone, no stranger being present. Offerings of cocoanuts, rice, turmeric and flowers are made to her, but no animal sacrifices. When a son of the family dies unmarried, an image of him, known as Mujia, is made on a piece of silver, copper or brass, and is worshipped on Mondays and Fridays during the month of Māgh (January). On one of these days also a feast is given to the caste. Each member of the caste has a *guru* or spiritual preceptor, who visits him every second or third year and receives a small present of a cocoanut or a piece of cloth. But he does not seem to perform any duties. The *guru* may belong to any of the religious mendicant castes. A man who is without a *guru* is known as Nugra and is looked down on. To meet him in the morning is considered unlucky and portends misfortune. Sir C. Elliot[1] characterised the Mundle Gūjars as "A very religious race; they never plough on the new moon nor on the 8th of the month, because it is Krishna's birthday. Their religious and social head is the Mahant of the Rāmjidās temple at Hoshangābād." In Nimār many of the Gūjars belong to the Pīrzāda sect,

[1] *Hoshangābād Settlement Report*, para. 16.

which is a kind of reformed creed, based on a mixture of Hinduism and Islām.

8. Character. The Gūjars wear the dress of northern India and their women usually have skirts (*lahenga*) and not *sāris* or body-cloths. Married women have a number of strings of black beads round the neck and widows must change these for red ones. As a rule neither men nor women are tattooed. The men sometimes have their hair long and wear beards and whiskers. The Gūjars are now considered the best cultivators of the Nimār District. They are fond of irrigation and sink unfaced wells to water their land and get a second crop off it. They are generally prosperous and make good landlords. Members of the caste have the custom of lending and borrowing among themselves and not from outsiders, and this no doubt conduces to mutual economy and solvency. Like keen cultivators elsewhere, such as the Panwārs and Kurmis, the Gūjar sets store by having a good house and good cattle. The return from a Mundle Gūjar's wedding, Captain Forsyth wrote,[1] is a sight to be seen. Every Gūjar from far and near has come with his whole family in his best bullock-cart gaily ornamented, and, whatever the road may be, nothing but a smash will prevent a breakneck race homewards at full gallop, cattle which have won in several such races acquiring a much coveted reputation throughout the District.

[1] *Nimār Settlement Report* (1868).

GURAO

LIST OF PARAGRAPHS

Gurao.[1]—A caste of village priests of the temples of Mahādeo in the Marātha Districts. They numbered about 14,000 persons in the Central Provinces and Berār in 1911. The Guraos say that they were formerly Brāhmans and worshippers of Siva, but for some negligence or mistake in his ritual they were cursed by the god and degraded from the status of Brāhmans, though subsequently the god relented and permitted them to worship him and take the offerings made to him. 1. Origin of the caste.

It is related that a certain Brāhman, who was a votary of Siva, had to go on a journey. He left his son behind and strictly enjoined on him to perform the worship of the god at midday. The son had bathed and purified himself for this purpose, when shortly before midday his wife came to him and so importuned him to have conjugal intercourse with her that he was obliged to comply. It was then midday and in his impure condition the son went to the shrine of the god to worship him. But Siva cursed him and said that his descendants should be degraded from the status of Brāhmans, though he afterwards relented so far as to permit of their continuing to act as his priests; and this was the origin of the Guraos. It seems doubtful,

[1] This article is based partly on a paper by Mr. Abdus Subhān Khān, Tahsīldār, Hinganghāt, and Mr. Adūrām Chaudhri of the Gazetteer Office.

however, whether the caste are really of Brāhman origin. They were formerly village priests, and Grant-Duff gives the Gurao as one of the village menials in the Marātha villages. They have the privilege of taking the Naivedya or offerings of cooked food made to the god Mahādeo, which Brāhmans will not accept. They also sell leaf-plates and flowers and *bel* leaves[1] which are offered at the temples of Mahādeo; and on the festival of Shivrātri and during the month of Shrāwan (July) they take round the *bel* leaves which the cultivators require for their offerings and receive presents in return. In Wardha the Guraos get small gifts of grain from the cultivators at seed-time and harvest. They also act as village musicians and blow the conch-shell, beat the drum and play other musical instruments for the morning and evening worship at the temple. They play on the cymbals and drums at the marriages of Brāhmans and other high castes. In the Bombay Presidency[2] some are astrologers and fortune-tellers, and others make the *bāsing* or coronet of flowers which the bridegroom wears. Sometimes they play on the drum or fiddle for their spiritual followers, the dancing-girls or Kalāvants. When a dancing-girl became pregnant she worshipped the Gurao, and he, in return, placed the *missi* or tooth-powder made from myrobalans on her teeth. If this was not done before her child was born, a Kalāvantin was put out of caste. In some localities the Guraos will take food from Kunbis. And further, as will be seen subsequently, the caste have no proper *gotras* or exogamous sections, but in arranging their marriages they simply avoid persons having a common surname. All these considerations point to the fact that the caste is not of Brāhmanical origin but belongs to a lower class of the population. Nevertheless in Wardha they are known as Shaiva Brāhmans and rank above the Kunbis. They may study the Sāma Veda only and not the others, and may repeat the Rudra Gayatri or sacred verse of Siva. Clearly the Brāhmans could not accept the offerings of cooked food made at Siva's shrine; though the larger temples of this deity have Brāhman priests. It seems uncertain whether

[1] The trifoliate leaf of *Aegle Marmelos*.

[2] *Bombay Gazetteer*, vol. xviii. p. 266.

Bemrose. Collo., Derby.

GURAOS WITH FIGURES MADE AT THE HOLI FESTIVAL CALLED GANGOUR.

Siva or Mahādeo was first a village deity and was subsequently exalted to the position of a member of the supreme Hindu Trinity, or whether the opposite process took place and the Guraos obtained their priestly functions on his worship being popularised. But in any case it would appear that they were originally a class of village priests regarded as the servants of the cultivating community, by whose gifts and offerings they were maintained. Grant-Duff in enumerating the village servants says: "Ninth, the Gurao, who is a Sūdra employed to wash the ornaments and attend the idol in the village temples, and on occasions of feasting to prepare the *patraoli* or leaves which the Hindus substitute for plates. They are also trumpeters by profession and in this capacity are much employed in Marātha armies."[1]

2. Internal structure.

The caste has several subdivisions which are principally of a territorial nature, as Warāde from Berār; Jhāde, inhabitants of the forest or rice country; Telanga, of the Telugu country; Dakshne, from the Deccan; Mārwāri, from Mārwār, and so on. Other subcastes are the Ahīr and Jain Guraos, of whom the former are apparently Ahīrs who have adopted the priestly profession, while the Jain Guraos are held in Bombay to be the descendants of Jain temple servants who entered the caste when their own deities were thrown out and their shrines annexed by the votaries of Siva.[2] In Bombay, Mr. Enthoven states "That the Koli and Marātha ministrants at the temples of Siva and other deities often describe themselves as Guraos, but they have not formed themselves into separate castes and are members of the general Koli or Marātha community. They cease to call themselves Guraos when they cease to minister at temples."[3] In the Central Provinces one of the subcastes is known as Vājantri because they act as village musicians. The caste have no regular exogamous sections, but a number of surnames which answer the same purpose. These are of a professional type, as Lokhandes, an iron-dealer; Phulzares, a maker of fireworks; Sontake, a gold-merchant; Gaikwād,

[1] *History of the Marāthas*, vol. i. p. 26, footnote.

[2] *Bombay Gazetteer*, vol. x. p. 119.

[3] *Bombay Ethnographic Survey, Monograph on Gurao.*

a cowherd; Nākade, long-nosed, and so on. They say they all belong to the same *gotra*, Sānkhiāyan, named after Sānkhiāya Rishi, the ancestor of the caste.

3. Marriage and ceremonies of adolescence.

Marriage is avoided between persons having the same surname and those within six degrees of descent from a common ancestor whether male or female. The marriage ceremony generally resembles that of the Brāhmans. Before the wedding the bridegroom's father prepares an image of Siva from rice and til-seed,[1] covers it with a cloth and sends it to the bride's house. In return her mother prepares and sends back a similar image of Gauri, Siva's consort. Girls are married as infants, and when a woman arrives at adolescence the following ritual is observed: She goes to her husband's house and is there secluded for three or four days while her impurity lasts. On its termination she is bathed and clothed in a green dress and yellow *choli* or breast-cloth, and seated in a gaily decked wooden frame. Her lap is filled with wheat and a cocoanut, and her female friends and relatives and father and father-in-law give her presents of sweets and clothes. This is known as the Shāntik ceremony and is practised by the higher castes in the Marātha country. It may continue for as long as sixteen days. Finally, on an auspicious day the bride and bridegroom are given delicate food and dressed in new clothes. The fire sacrifice is offered and they are taken into a room where a bed, the gift of the bride's parents, has been prepared for them, and left to consummate the marriage. This is known as Garbhādhān. Next day the bride's parents give new clothes and a feast to the bridegroom's family; this feast is known as Godai, and after giving it the bride's parents may eat at their daughter's house. A girl seduced by a man of the caste may be properly married to him after her parents have performed *Prāyaschit* or atonement. But if she has a child out of wedlock, he is relegated to the Vidūr or illegitimate group. Even if a girl be seduced by a stranger, provided he be of higher or equal caste, as the Kunbis and Marāthas, she may be taken back into the community.

4. Birth customs.

If a child is born at an unlucky season, they take two winnowing-fans and tie the baby between them with a thread

[1] Sesamum.

wound many times round about. A cow is brought and made to lick the child, which is thus supposed to have been born again from it as a calf, the evil omen of the first birth being removed. The father performs the fire sacrifice, and a human figure is made from cooked rice and worshipped. A burning wick is placed in its stomach and it is taken out and left at cross-roads, this being probably a substitute for the member of the family whose death was presaged by the untimely birth of the child. Similarly if any one dies at the astronomical period known as Panchak, they make five figures of wheat-flour and burn or bury them with the body, as it is thought that otherwise five members of the family would die.

5. The sacred thread.

Boys are invested with the sacred thread at the age of five, seven or nine years, and until that time they are considered to be Sūdras and not members of the caste. From a hundred to three hundred rupees may be spent on the investiture. On the day before the ceremony a Brāhman and his wife are invited to take food, and a yellow thread with a mango leaf is tied round the boy's wrist. The spirits of other boys who died before their thread ceremony was performed and of women of the family who died before their husbands are invited to attend. These are represented by young boys and married women of other families who come to the house and are bathed and anointed with turmeric and oil, and given presents of sugar and new clothes. Next day the initiate is seated on a platform in a shed erected for the purpose and puts on the sacred thread made of cotton and also a strip of the skin of the black-buck with a silk apron and cap. The boy's father takes him on his lap and whispers or, as the Hindus say, blows the Gāyatri *mantra* or sacred text into his ear. A sacrifice is performed, and the friends and fellow-castemen of the family make presents to the boy of copper and silver coin. The amount thus given is not used by the parents, but is spent on the boy's education or on the purchase of an ornament for him. On the conclusion of the ceremony the boy mounts a wooden model of a horse and pretends to set out for Benāres. His paternal uncle then says to him, 'Why are you going away?' And the boy replies, 'Because you have not married me.' His uncle then promises to find a bride for him and he gives up his project. The part played by the maternal uncle in this ceremony is probably a survival of the period of the matriarchate, when a man's property descended to his sister's son. He would thus naturally claim the boy as a husband for his own daughter, and such a marriage apparently became customary and in course of time acquired binding force. And although all recollection of the rule of inheritance through women has long been forgotten, the marriage of a brother's daughter to a sister's son is still considered peculiarly suitable, and the idea that it is the duty of the maternal uncle to find a bride for his nephew appears to be simply a development of this. The above account also gives reason for supposing that the investiture with the sacred thread was originally a ceremony of puberty.

6. Funeral customs. The dead are burnt and the ashes thrown into water or carried to the Ganges. A small piece of gold, two or three small pearls, and some basil leaves are put into the mouth, and flowers, red powder and betel leaves are spread over the corpse. The son or male heir of the deceased walks in front carrying fire in an earthen pot. At a small distance from the burning-ground, when the bearers change places, he picks up a stone, known as the life-stone or *jivkhada*. This is afterwards buried at the burning-*ghāt* until the priest comes to effect the purification of the mourners on the tenth day. It is then dug up, set up and worshipped, and thrown into a well. A man is burnt naked; a woman in a robe and bodice. The heads of widows are not shaved as a rule, but on the tenth day after her husband's death a widow is asked whether she would like her head shaved; if she refuses, the people conclude that she intends to marry again. But if the deceased left no male heir to carry behind his bier the burning wood with which the funeral pyre is to be kindled, then the widow must be shaved before the funeral starts and perform this duty. If there is no male relative and no widow, the pot containing fire is tied to the bier. When the corpse of a woman who has died in child-bed is being carried to the burning-ground various rites are observed to prevent her spirit from becoming a Churel and troubling the living.

Bemrose, Collo., Derby.

GROUP OF GURAO MUSICIANS WITH THEIR INSTRUMENTS.

A lemon charmed by a magician is buried under the corpse and a man follows the body strewing the seeds of *rala*, while nails are driven into the threshold of the house.[1]

The caste has now a fairly high social status and ranks above the Kunbis. They abstain from all flesh and from liquor and will take food only from the hands of a Marātha Brāhman, while Kunbis and other cultivating and serving castes will accept food from their hands. They worship Siva principally on Mondays, this day being sacred to the deity, who carries the moon as an ornament on his head, crowning the matted locks from which the Ganges flows. **7. Social position.**

Of the Jain Guraos Mr. Enthoven quotes the following interesting description from the *Bombay Gazetteer*: "They are mainly servants in village temples which, though dedicated to Brāhmanic gods, have still by their sides broken remains of Jain images. This, and the fact that most of the temple land-grants date from a time when Jainism was the State religion, support the theory that the Jain Guraos are probably Jain temple servants who have come under the influence partly of Lingāyatism and partly of Brāhmanism. A curious survival of their Jainism occurs at Dasahra, Shimga and other leading festivals, when the village deity is taken out of the temple and carried in procession. On these occasions, in front of the village god's palanquin, three, five or seven of the villagers, among whom the Gurao is always the leader, carry each a long, gaily-painted wooden pole resting against their right shoulder. At the top of the pole is fastened a silver mask or hand and round it is draped a rich silk robe. Of these poles, the chief one, carried by the Gurao, is called the Jain's pillar, *Jainācha khāmb*." **8. The Jain Guraos.**

[1] *Bombay Gazetteer*, vol. xix. p. 101.

HALBA

LIST OF PARAGRAPHS

1. Traditions of the caste.

Halba, Halbi.[1]—A caste of cultivators and farmservants whose home is the south of the Raipur District and the Kānker and Bastar States; from here small numbers of them have spread to Bhandāra and parts of Berār. In 1911 they numbered 100,000 persons in the combined Provinces. The Halbas have several stories relating to their own origin. One of these, reported by Mr. Gokul Prasād, is as follows: One of the Uriya Rājas had erected four scarecrows in his field to keep off the birds. One night Mahādeo and Pārvati were walking on the earth and happened to pass that way, and Pārvati saw them and asked what they were. When it was explained to her she thought that as they had excited her interest something should be done for them, and at her request Mahādeo gave them life

[1] This article is compiled principally from a monograph by Munshi Kanhya Lāl, Assistant Master, Raipur High School, and formerly of the Gazetteer Office; and also from papers by Mr. Panda Baijnāth, Superintendent of Bastar State, and Mr. Gokul Prasād, Tahsīldār of Dhamtari. The descriptions of marriage, funeral and birth customs are taken from Munshi Kanhya Lāl's monograph.

Bemrose, Collo., Derby.

PLOUGHING WITH COWS AND BUFFALOES IN CHHATTĪSGARH.

and they became two men and two women. Next morning they presented themselves before the Rāja and told him what had happened. The Rāja said, "Since you have come on earth, you must have a caste. Run after Mahādeo and find out what caste you should belong to." So they ran after the god and inquired of him, and he said that as they had excited his and Pārvati's attention by waving in the wind they should be called Halba, from *halna*, to wave. This story is clearly based on one of those fanciful punning derivations so dear to the Brāhmanical mind, but the legend about being created from scarecrows is found among other agricultural castes of non-Aryan origin, as the Lodhis. The story continues that the reason why the Halbas came to settle in Bastar and Kānker was that they had accompanied one of the Rājas of Jagannāth in Orissa, who was afflicted with leprosy, to the Sihāwa jungles, where he proposed to pass the rest of his life in retirement. On a certain day the Rāja went out hunting with his dogs, one of which was quite white. This dog jumped into a spring of water and came out with his white skin changed to copper red. The Rāja, observing this miracle, bathed in the spring himself and was cured of his leprosy. He then wished to return to Orissa, but the Halbas induced him to remain in his adopted country, and he became the ancestor of the Rājas of Kānker. The Halbas are still the household servants of the Kānker family, and when a fresh chief succeeds, one of them, who has the title of Kapardār, takes him to the temple and invests him with the *Durbār kī poshak* or royal robes, affixing also the *tīka* or badge of office on his forehead with turmeric, rice and sandalwood, and rubbing his body over with ottar of roses. Until lately the Kapardār's family had a considerable grant of rent-free land, but this has now been taken away. A Halba is or was also the priest of the temple at Sihāwa, which is said to have been built by the first Rāja over the spring where he was healed of his leprosy. The Halbas are also connected with the Rājas of Bastar, and a suggestion has been made[1] that they originally belonged to the Telugu country and came with the Rājas of Bastar from Warangal in the Deccan. Mr. Gilder derives

[1] By the Rev. G. K. Gilder of the Methodist Episcopal Mission of Raipur.

the name from an old Canarese word *Halbar* or *Halbaru*, meaning 'old ones or ancients' or 'primitive inhabitants.' The Halba dialect, however, contains no traces of Canarese, and on the question of their entering Bastar with the Rājas, Rai Bahādur Panda Baijnāth, Diwān of Bastar, writes as follows: In the following saying relating to the coming of the Bastar Rājas, which is often repeated, the Halba's name does not occur:

Chalkibans Rāja	*Dibdibi bāja.*
Kosaria Rāwat	*Pita Bhatra.*
Peng Parja	*Rāja Muria.*
Tendu khuti	*Pania lava.*

Which may be rendered: "The Rāja was of the Chalki race.[1] The drum was called Dibdibi. Kosaria Rāwat, Pita Bhatra, Peng Parja and Rāja Muria,[2] these four castes came with the Rāja. The tribute paid (to the Rāja) was a comb of *tendu* wood and a *lava* quail." This doggerel rhyme is believed to recall the circumstances of the immigration of the Bastar Rājas. So the Halbas did not perhaps come with the Rāja, but they were his guards for a long time. In the Dasahra ceremony a Halba carried the royal Chhatra or Umbrella, and the Rāja walked under the protection of another Halba's naked sword. A Halba's widows were not sold and his intestate property was not taken over by the Rāja.

2. Halba landowners in Bastar and Bhandāra.

Thus the Halbas occupy a comparatively honourable position in Bastar. They are the highest local caste with the exception of the Brāhmans, the Dhākars or illegitimate descendants of Brāhmans, and a few Rājpūt families. The reason for this is no doubt that they have become landholders in the State, a position which it would not be difficult for them to acquire when their only rivals were the Gonds. They are moderately good cultivators, and in Dhamtari can hold their own with Hindus, so that they could well surpass the Gond. Traditions also remain in Bastar of a Halba revolt. It is said that during Rāja

[1] Chalki is said to have been a Brāhman who gave shelter to the pregnant fugitive widow of a Rāja; and her child was the ancestor of the Bastar dynasty. But the name may also be taken from the Chalukya Rājpūt clan.

[2] The Rāwats or Ahīrs are graziers, and the Bhatra, Parja and Muria are primitive tribes allied to the Gonds.

Daryao Deo's reign, about 125 years back, the Halbas rebelled and many were thrown down a waterfall ninety feet high, one only of these escaping with his life. The eyes of some were also put out as a punishment for the oppression they had exercised, and a stone inscription at Donger records the oath of fealty taken by the Halbas before the image of Danteshwari, the tutelary deity of Bastar, after their insurrection was put down in Samvat 1836 or A.D. 1779. The Halbas were thus a caste of considerable influence, since they could attempt to subvert the ruling dynasty. In Bhandāra again the caste have quite a different story, and say that they came from the United Provinces or, according to another version, the Makrai State, where they were of the status of Rājpūts and wore the sacred thread. There a girl of their family, of great beauty, was asked in marriage by a Muhammadan king. The father could not refuse the king, but would not give his daughter in marriage to one not of his own caste. So he fled south and took asylum with the Gond Rāja of Chānda, from whom the Halba zamīndārs subsequently received their estates. It seems unnecessary to attach any importance to this story; the tale of the beautiful daughter is most hackneyed, and the whole has probably been devised by the Brāhmans to give the Halba zamīndārs of Bhandāra a more respectable ancestry than they could claim if they admitted having come from Bastar, certainly no home of Rājpūts. But if this supposition is correct it is interesting to note how a legend may show a caste as originating in some place with which it never had any connection whatever; and it seems a necessary conclusion that no importance can be attached to such traditions without corroborating evidence.

3. Internal structure: subcastes.

The caste have local divisions known as Bastarha, Chhattīsgarhia and Marethia, according as they live in Bastar, Chhattīsgarh, or Bhandāra and the other Marātha Districts. The last two groups, however, intermarry, so only the Bastar Halbas really form a separate subcaste. But the caste is also everywhere divided into two groups of pure and mixed Halbas. These are known in Bastar and Chhattīsgarh as Purāit or Nekha, and Surāit or Nāyak, respectively, and in Bhandāra as Barpangat and Khālpangat or those of good and bad stock. The Surāits or Khālpangats are said to be of mixed origin, born from Halba fathers and women of other castes. But in past times unions of Halba mothers and men of other castes were perhaps not less frequent. These two sets of groups do not intermarry. A Surāit Halba will take food from a Purāit, but the Purāits do not return the compliment; though in some localities they will accept food which does not contain salt. The two divisions will take water from each other and exchange leaf-pipes. In Bhandāra the Barpangat or pure Halbas have now further split into two groups, the zamīndāri families having constituted themselves into a separate subdivision; they practise hypergamy with the others, taking daughters from them in marriage but not giving their daughters to them. This is simply of a piece with their claim to be Rājpūts, hypergamy being a custom of northern India.

4. Exogamous sections. The exogamous sections of the caste afford further evidence of their mixed origin. Many of the names recorded are those of other castes, as Baretha (a washerman), Bhoyar (Bhoi or bearer), Rāwat (herdsman), Barhai (carpenter), Mālia (Māli or gardener), Dhākar (Vidūr or illegitimate Brāhman), Bhandāri (barber), Pardhān (Gond), Mānkar (title of various tribes), Sahara (Saonr), Kanderi (turner), Agri (Agarwāla Bania), Baghel (a sept of Rājpūts), Elmia (from Velama, Telugu cultivators), and Chalki and Ponwār (Chalukya and Panwār Rājpūts). It may be concluded that these groups are descended from ancestors of the caste after which they are named. There are also a number of territorial and titular names of the usual type, and many totemistic names, as Ghorapatia (a horse), Kawaliha (lotus), Aurila (tamarind), Lendia (a tree), Gohi (a lizard), Manjur (a peacock), Bhringrāj (a blackbird) and so on. In Bastar they revere the animal or plant after which their sept is named and will not kill or injure it. If a man accidentally kills his *devak* or sacred animal he will tear off a small piece of his cloth and throw it away to make a shroud for the corpse. A few of them will break their earthen pots as if a relative had died in their house, but this is not general. In Bastar the totemistic groups are named *barags*, and many men also belong to a *thok*, having some titular name which they use as a surname. Nowadays

marriage is avoided by persons having the same *thok* or surname as well as between those of the same *barag*.

5. Theory of the origin of the caste.

In view of the information available the most probable theory of the origin of the Halbas is that they were a mixed caste, born of irregular alliances between the Uriya Rājas and their retainers with the women of their household servants and between the different servants themselves. Mr. Gokul Prasād points out that many of the names of Halba sections are those of the *haguas* or household menials of the Uriya chiefs. The Halbas, according to their own story, came here in attendance on one of the chiefs, and are still employed as household servants in Kānker and Bastar. They are clearly a caste of mixed origin as they still admit women of other castes married by Halba men into the community, and one of their two subcastes in each locality consists of families of impure descent. The Dhākars of Bastar are the illegitimate offspring of Brāhmans with women of the country who have grown into a caste, and Mr. Panda Baijnāth quotes a proverb, saying that 'The Halbas and Dhākars form two portions of a bedsheet.' Instances of other castes similarly formed are the Audhelias of Bilāspur, who are said to be the offspring of Daharia Rājpūts by their kept women, and the Bargāhs, descended from the nurses of Rājpūt families. The name Halba might be derived from *hal*, a plough, and be a variant for *harwāha*, the common term for a farmservant in the northern Districts. This derivation they give themselves in one of their stories, saying that their first ancestor was created from a sod of earth on the plough of Balarām or Haladhara, the brother of Krishna; and it has also the support of Sir G. Grierson. The caste includes no doubt a number of Gonds, Rāwats (herdsmen) and others, and it may be partly occupational, consisting of persons employed as farmservants by the Hindu settlers. The farmservant in Chhattīsgarh has a very definite position, his engagement being permanent and his wages consisting always in a fourth share of the produce, which is divided among them when several are employed. The caste have a peculiar dialect of their own, which Dr. Grierson describes as follows:[1]

[1] *Linguistic Survey*, vol. vii. p. 331, and a note kindly furnished by Sir G. Grierson at the time of the census.

"Linguistic evidence also points to the fact that the Halbas are an aboriginal tribe, who have adopted Hinduism and an Aryan language. Their dialect is a curious mixture of Uriya, Chhattīsgarhi and Marāthi, the proportions varying according to the locality. In Bhandāra it is nearly all Marāthi, but in Bastar it is much more mixed and has some forms which look like Telugu." If the home of the Halbas was in the debateable land between Chhattīsgarh and the Uriya country to the east and south of the Mahānadi, their dialect might, as Mr. Hira Lāl points out, have originated here. They themselves give the ruined but once important city of Sihāwa on the banks of the Mahānadi in this tract as that of their first settlement; and Uriya is spoken to the east of Sihāwa and Marāthi to the west, while Chhattīsgarhi is the language of the locality itself and of the country extending north and south. Subsequently the Halbas served as soldiers in the armies of the Ratanpur kings and their position no doubt considerably improved, so that in Bastar they became an important landholding caste. Some of these soldiers may have migrated west and taken service under the Gond kings of Chānda, and their descendants may now be represented by the Bhandāra zamīndārs, who, however, if this theory be correct, have entirely forgotten their origin. Others took up weaving and have become amalgamated with the Koshti caste in Bhandāra and Berār.

6. Marriage. Girls are not usually married until they are above ten years old, or nearly adult as age goes in India; but there is no rule on the subject. Many girls reach twenty without entering wedlock. If the parents are too poor to pay for their daughter's marriage the neighbours will subscribe. In Bastar, however, the Uriya custom prevails, and an unmarried girl in whom the signs of puberty appear is put out of caste. In such a case her father marries her to a mahua tree. The strictness of the rule on this subject among the Uriyas is probably due to the strength of Brāhmanical influence, the priestly caste possessing more power and property in Sambalpur and Orissa than in almost any part of India. If a death occurs in the family of the bridegroom just before the date fixed for the wedding, and the ceremonies of purification cannot be completed prior to

it, the bride is formally wedded to an *achar*[1] or mahua tree;[2] the marriage crown is tied on to the tree, and the bride walks round it seven times. After the bridegroom's purification the couple are taken to the same tree, and here the forehead of the bridegroom is marked with turmeric paste and rice. The couple sit one on each side of the tree, and the Tikāwan ceremony or presentation of gifts by the relatives and friends is performed, and the marriage is considered to be complete. If an unmarried girl goes wrong with an outsider of low caste she is expelled from the community; but if with a member of a caste from whom a Halba can take water she may be readmitted to caste, provided she has not eaten food cooked in an earthen pot from the hands of her seducer; but not if she has done so. If there be a child of the seducer she must wait until it be weaned and either taken by the putative father or given away to a Chamār or Gond. The girl can then be given in marriage to any Halba as a widow. Women of other castes married by Halbas are admitted into the community. This happens most frequently in the case of women of the Rāwat (herdsman) caste.

7. Importance of the sister's son.

A match which is commonly arranged where practicable is that of a brother's daughter to a sister's son. And a man always shows a special regard and respect for his sister's son, touching his feet as to a superior, while, whenever he desires to make a gift as an offering of thanks or atonement or as a meritorious action, the sister's son is the recipient. At his death he usually leaves a substantial legacy, such as one or two buffaloes, to his sister's son, the remainder of the property going to his own family. This recognition of a special relationship is probably a survival of the matriarchate, when property descended through women, and a sister's son would be his uncle's heir. Thus a man would naturally desire to marry his daughter to his nephew in order that she might participate in his property, and hence arose the custom of making this match, which is still the most favoured among the Halbas and Gonds, though

[1] *Buchanania latifolia.*

[2] *Bassia latifolia.* Both these trees are valued because the fruit of the first and the flowers of the second afford food.

the reasons which led to it have been forgotten for several centuries.

8. The wedding ceremony.

Matches are usually arranged on the initiative of the boy's father through a mutual friend who resides in the girl's village, and is known as the Mahālia or matchmaker. When the contract is concluded the boy's father sends a present of fixed quantities of grain to the girl, which are in the nature of a bride-price, and subsequently on an auspicious day selected by the family priest he and his friends proceed to the girl's village. The girl meets them, standing at the entrance of the principal house, dressed in the new clothes sent on behalf of the bridegroom, and holding out her cloth for the reception of presents. The boy's father goes up to her and smooths her hair with his hand, chucks her under the chin with his right hand, and makes a noise with his lips as if he were kissing her. He then touches her feet, places a rupee on the skirt of her cloth, and retires. The other members of his party follow his example, giving small presents of copper, and afterwards the women of the girl's party treat the bridegroom in the same manner, but they actually kiss him (*chūmna*). Betrothals can be held only in the five months from Māgh (January) to Jeth (May), while marriages may be celebrated during the eight dry months. The auspicious date is selected by the Joshi or caste-priest, who is chosen by the community for his personal qualities. If the names of the couple do not point to an auspicious union the bridegroom's name may be changed either temporarily or permanently. The Joshi takes two pieces of cloth, which should be torn from the scarf of the boy's father, and ties up in each of them some rice, areca nuts, turmeric and *dūb* grass (*Cynodon dactylon*). One of these is marked with red lead, and is intended for the bride, and the other, which is left plain, is for the bridegroom. At the wedding some of this rice with pulse is placed with a twig of mahua in a hole in the marriage-shed and addressed: 'You are the goddess Lachhmi; you have come to assist in the marriage.'

The Halbas, like the other lower castes of Chhattīsgarh, have two forms of wedding, known as the 'Small' and 'Large,' the former being held at the bridegroom's house with curtailed ceremonies, and being much cheaper than the latter or Hindu marriage proper, which is held at the bride's house. The 'small' wedding is more popular among the Halbas, and for this the bride, accompanied by some of her girl and boy friends, arrives at the bridegroom's village in the evening, her parents following her only on the third day. On entering the lands of the village her party begin singing obscene songs filled with abuse of the bridegroom's parents and relatives. Nobody goes to receive or welcome them, and on reaching the bridegroom's house they enter it without ceremony and sit down in the room where the family gods are kept. All this time they continue singing, and the musicians keep up a deafening din in accompaniment. Subsequently the bride's party are shown to their lodging, known as the *Dulhi-kuria* or bride's apartments, and here the bridegroom's father visits her and washes her big toes first with milk and then with water. The practice of washing the feet of guests, which strikes strangely on our minds when we meet it in Scripture, was obviously a welcome attention when travellers went bare-footed, or at most wore sandals, and arrived at their journey's end with the feet soiled and bruised by the rigours of the way. Another of the bridegroom's friends pretends to act as a barber, and shaves all the bride's men friends with a piece of straw as if it were a razor. For the marriage ceremony proper the bride and bridegroom stand facing each other by the marriage hut with a sheet held between them; the Joshi or caste-priest takes two lamps and mingles their flames, and the cloth between the couple being pulled down the bridegroom drags the bride over to him. If the wedding is held on a Sunday, Tuesday or Saturday the bridegroom stands facing the east, and if on a Monday, Thursday or Friday, to the north. After this the cloths of the couple are tied together, or the end of the bridegroom's scarf is tucked in the bride's waistcloth, and they go round the marriage-post seven times, the bride following the bridegroom throughout. A plough-yoke is then brought and placed close by the marriage-post and the couple take their seats on it, the bride sitting on the left of the bridegroom. The bundles of rice consecrated by the Joshi are given to them and they throw it over each other. The bridegroom takes some red lead and smears the bride's face with it, making a line from the end of her nose up across her forehead and along the parting of her hair. He says her name aloud and covers her head with her cloth. This signifies that she is a married woman, as in Chhattīsgarh unmarried girls go about with the head bare. After this the mother and father of the bride come and wash the feet of the couple with milk and water. This ceremony is known as Dharam Tīka, and after its completion the bride's parents will take food in the bridegroom's house, which they abstain from doing from the date of the betrothal up to this washing of the feet. It is on this account that they do not accompany the bride but only follow her on the third day, but the reason for the rule is by no means clear. On the following day more ceremonies are performed, and the friends of the couple touch their foreheads with rice and make presents to them of cowries. Last of all the bride's parents come and give them cattle and other articles according to their means. These gifts are known as Tikāwan and remain the separate property of the bride which she can dispose of as she pleases. The ceremonies usually extend over four days, the wedding itself taking place on the third. The bride's party then go home, leaving her with her husband, and after a week or so they return and take the couple to the bride's house for the ceremony known as Pinar Dhawai or getting their yellow wedding clothes washed. The bridegroom stays here two or three weeks, and during this time he must work at building or repairing the walls of his father-in-law's house. The custom of serving for a wife still obtains among the Halbas, and the above rule may perhaps indicate that it was once more general. At the end of the bridegroom's visit his father-in-law gives him a new cloth and pair of shoes and sends him back to his parents' house with his wife. The expenses of the wedding average about fifty rupees for the bridegroom's family and from five to thirty rupees for the bride's family.

9. Going-away ceremony.

After the wedding if the bride is grown up she lives with her husband at once; but if she is a child she goes back to her parents until her adolescence, when the ceremony of Pathoni or 'Going away' is performed. On this occasion some people from the bridegroom's home go to fetch her and their number must be even, so that when she returns with them the party may be an odd one, which is lucky. They take a new cloth for the bride and stay the night at her house; next morning the bride's parents put some rice, pulse, oil and a comb in a basket for her, and she sets out with the party, wearing her new cloth. But when she gets outside the village this is taken off her and placed in the basket, which she has to carry on her head as far as her husband's house. As she enters his village the people stretch a rope across the way and prevent her passage until her father-in-law gives them a present. On arriving at his house her feet are washed by her mother-in-law, and she is then made to cook the food brought in her basket. After a fortnight she again goes back to her parents' house and stays with them for another year, before finally taking up her abode with her husband. It has been remarked that this return of a married woman to her parents' house for such lengthened periods is likely to be a pregnant source of immorality, and the advantage of the custom has been questioned; the explanation may perhaps be that it is an outcome of the joint family system by which young married couples live with the bridegroom's parents, and that the object is to accustom the girl gradually to the habits of a fresh household and the yoke, necessarily irksome, of her mother-in-law. The proverb with reference to a young wife, 'If your husband loves you your mother-in-law can do nothing,' indicates how formidable this may be in the event of any cooling of marital affection; and it is well known that if she does not please her husband's family a young wife may be treated as little better than a slave. To throw a young girl, therefore, into a family of complete strangers is probably too severe a trial, and this is the reason of the goings and returnings of the bride after her wedding between her husband's home and her own.

10. Widow-marriage and divorce.

The remarriage of a widow must be held during the bright fortnight of the month, and on any odd day of the fortnight excluding the first. The couple are seated together on a yoke in a part of the courtyard cleaned with cowdung, and their clothes are tied together, while the husband rubs vermilion on his wife's hair. A bachelor should not take a widow in marriage, and if he does so he must at the same time also wed a maiden with the regular ceremony, as otherwise he is likely after death to become a *masān* or evil spirit. In order to avoid this contingency a bachelor who espouses a widow in Kānker is first wedded to a spear. Turmeric and oil are rubbed on his body and on the spear, and he walks round it seven times. Divorce is freely permitted in Chhattīsgarh at the instance of either party and for the most trivial reasons, as a mere allegation of disagreement; but if a husband puts away his wife when she has not been unfaithful to him he must give her something for her support. In some localities no ceremony is performed at all, but a wife or husband who tires of wedlock simply leaves the other as the case may be. In Bastar a wife cannot divorce her husband. A divorced woman does not break her glass bangles until she marries again, when new ones are given to her by her second husband.

11. Religion. A large proportion of the Halbas of Chhattīsgarh belong to the Kabīrpanthi sect. These are known as Kabīrhas and abjure the consumption of flesh and alcoholic liquor; while the others who indulge in these articles are known as Sakatha or Sakta, that is, a worshipper of Devi or Durga. These latter, however, also revere all the village godlings of Chhattīsgarh.

12. Disposal of the dead. The dead are always buried by the Kabīrpanthis and usually by other Halbas, cremation being reserved by the latter as a special mark of respect for elders and heads of families. A dead body is wrapped in a new white cloth and laid on an inverted cot. The Kabīrpanthis lay plantain leaves at the sides of the cot and over the body to cover it. One of the mourners carries a burning cowdung cake with the party. Before burial the thread which every male wears round his waist is broken, the clothes are taken off the corpse and given to a sweeper, and the body is wrapped in the shroud and laid in the grave, salt being sprinkled under and over it. If the dead body should be touched by any person of another caste, the deceased's family has to pay a fine or give a penal caste-feast. After the interment the mourners bathe and return to the deceased's house in their wet clothes.

Before entering it they wash their feet in water, which is kept for that purpose at the door, and chew the leaves of the *nīm* tree (*Melia indica*). They smoke their *chongis* or leaf-pipes and console the deceased's family and then return home, washing their feet again and changing their clothes at their own houses. On the third day, known as *Tīj Nahān*, the male members of the family with the relatives and mourners walk in Indian file to a river or tank, where they are all shaved by the barber, the sons of the dead man or woman having the entire head and face cleared of hair, while in the case of other relatives, the scalp-lock and moustache may be left, and the mourning friends are only shaved as on ordinary occasions. For his services the barber receives a cow or a substantial cash present, which he divides with the washerman. The latter subsequently washes all clothes worn at the funeral and on this occasion. On the Akti festival, or commencement of the agricultural year, libations of water and offerings of urad[1] cakes are made to the spirits of ancestors. A feast is given to women in honour of all departed female ancestors on the ninth day of the Pitripaksh or mourning fortnight of Kunwār (September), and feasts for male ancestors may be held on the same day of the fortnight as that on which they died at any other time of the year.[2] Such observances are practised only by the well-to-do. Nothing is done for persons who die before their marriage or without children, unless they trouble some member of the family and appear in a dream to demand that these honours be paid to them. During an epidemic of cholera all funeral and mourning ceremonies are suspended, and a general purification of the village takes place on its conclusion.

13. Propitiating the spirits of those who have died a violent death.

If a person has been killed by a tiger, the people go out, and if any remains of the body are found, these are burnt on the spot. The Baiga is then invoked to bring back the spirit of the deceased, a most essential precaution as will shortly be seen. In order to do this he suspends a copper ring on a long thread above a vessel of water and then burns butter and sugar on the fire, muttering incanta-

[1] A black pulse.

[2] The Hindus number the days of each lunar fortnight separately.

tions, while the people sing songs and call on the spirit of the dead man to return. The thread swings to and fro, and at length the copper ring falls into the pot, and this is taken as a sign that the spirit has come and entered the vessel. The mouth of this is immediately covered and it is buried or kept in some secure place. The people believe that unless the dead man's spirit is secured it will accompany the tiger and lure solitary travellers to destruction. This is done by calling out and offering them tobacco to smoke, and when they proceed in the direction of the voice the tiger springs out and kills them. And they think that a tiger directed in this manner grows fiercer and fiercer with every person whom it kills. When somebody has been killed by a tiger the relatives will not even remove the ornaments from the corpse, for they think that these would constitute a link by which its spirit would cause the tiger to track them down. The malevolence thus attributed to persons killed by tigers is explained by their bitter wrath at having encountered such an untimely death and consequent desire to entice others to the same.

14. Impurity of women.

During the monthly period of menstruation women are spoken of as '*Mund maili*' or having the head dirty, and are considered to be impure for four or five days, for which time they sleep on the ground and not on cots. In Kānker they are secluded in a separate room, and forbidden to cook or to touch the clothes or persons of other members of the family. They must not walk on a ploughed field, nor will the men of their family drive the plough or sow seed during the time of their impurity. On the fifth day they wash their heads with earth and boil their clothes in water mixed with wood ashes. Cloth stained with the menstrual blood is usually buried underground; if it is burnt it is supposed that the woman to whom it belonged will become barren, and if a barren woman should swallow the ashes of the cloth the fertility of its owner would be transferred to her.

15. Childbirth.

When pregnant women experience longings for strange kinds of food, it is believed that these really come from the child in the womb and must be satisfied if its development is not to be retarded. Consequently in the fifth month of a wife's first pregnancy, or shortly before delivery, her mother takes to her various kinds of rich food and feeds her with them. It is a common custom also for pregnant women, driven by perverted appetite, to eat earth of a clayey texture, or the ordinary black cotton soil, or dried clay scraped off the walls of houses, or the ashes of burnt cowdung cakes. This is done by low-caste women in most parts of the Province, and if carried to excess leads to severe intestinal derangement which may prove fatal. A pregnant woman must not cross a river or eat anything with a knife, and she must observe various precautions against the machinations of witches. At the time of delivery the woman sits on the ground and is attended by a midwife, who may be a Chamār, Mahār or Gānda by caste. The navel cord is burnt in the lying-in room, but the after-birth, known as Phul, is usually buried in a rubbish pit outside the house. The portion of the cord attached to the child's body is also burnt when it falls off, but in the northern Districts it is preserved and used as a cure for the child if it suffers from sore eyes. If a woman who has borne only girl children can obtain the dried navel-string of a male child and swallow it, they believe that she will have a son, and that the mother of the boy will henceforth bear only daughters. This is the reason why the cord is carefully secreted and not simply thrown away. In Bastar on the sixth or naming day the female relatives and friends of the family are invited to take food at the house. The father touches the feet of the child with blades of *dūb* grass (*Cynodon dactylon*) steeped first in milk or melted butter, then in sandal-paste, and finally in water, and each time passes the blade over his head as a mark of respect. The blades of grass are afterwards thrown over the roof of the house, so that they may not be trampled under foot. The women guests then bring leaf-cups containing rice and a few copper coins, which they offer to the mother, the younger ones bowing before her with a prayer that the child may grow as old as the speaker. All the women kiss the child, and the elder ones the mother also. The offerings of rice and coins are taken by the midwife.

The names of the Halbas are of the ordinary type 16. Names.

found in Chhattīsgarh, but at present they often add the termination Sinha or Singh in imitation of the Rājpūts. Two names are sometimes given, one for daily use and the other for comparison with that of the girl when the marriage is to be arranged. As already seen, either the bride's or bridegroom's name may be changed to make their union auspicious. When a daughter-in-law comes into her husband's house she is usually not called by her own name, but by some nickname or that of her home, as Jabalpurwāli, Raipurwāli (she who comes from Jabalpur or Raipur), and so on. Sometimes men of the caste are addressed by the name of the clan or section and not by their own. A woman must not utter the names of her husband, his parents or brothers, nor of the sons of his elder brother and his sisters. But for these last as well as for her own son-in-law she may invent fictitious names. These rules she observes to show her respect for her husband's relatives. A child must not be called by name at night, because if an owl hears the name and repeats it the child will probably die. The owl is everywhere regarded as a bird of the most evil omen. Its hoot is unlucky, and a house in which its nest is built will be destroyed or deserted. If it perches on the roof of a house and hoots, some one of the family will probably fall ill, or if a member of the household is already ill, he or she will probably die.

17. Social status.

The social customs of the caste present some differences. In Bastar, where they have a fairly high status, the Purāit Halbas abstain from liquor, though they will eat the flesh of clean animals and of the wild pig. The Halbas of Raipur on the other hand, who are usually farmservants, will eat fowls, pigs and rats, and abstain only from beef and the leavings of others. In Bastar, Sunārs, Kurmis and castes of similar position will take water from the hands of a Halba, and Kosaria Rāwats will eat all kinds of food with them. In Chhattīsgarh the Halbas will accept water from Telis, Kahārs and other like castes, and will also allow any of them to become a Halba. In Chhattīsgarh they will take even food cooked with water from the hands of a man of these castes, provided that they are not in their own villages. These differences of custom are probably due to the varying social status of the caste. In Bastar they hold land and behave accordingly, while in Chhattīsgarh they are only labourers. They do not employ Brāhmans for ceremonial purposes but have their own caste priest, known as Joshi, while among the Kabīrpanthis the local Mahant or Bairāgi of the sect takes his place.

18. Caste *panchāyat.*

They have a caste *panchāyat* or committee, the headman of which is known as Kursha; he has jurisdiction over ten or twenty villages, and is usually chosen from the Kotwār, Chanap or Nāik sections. It is the duty of the men of these sections to scatter the *sonpāni* or 'water of gold'[1] as an act of purification over persons who have been temporarily put out of caste for social offences. They are also the first to eat food with such offenders on readmission to social intercourse, and thereby take the sins of these persons upon their own heads. In order to counteract the effect of this the purifier usually asks three or four other men to eat with him at his own house, and passes on a part of his burden to them. For such duties he receives a payment of money varying from four annas to a rupee and a half. Among the offences punished with temporary exclusion from caste are those of rearing the lac insect and tasar silk cocoons, probably because such work involves the killing of the insects and caterpillars which produce the dye and silk. In Bastar a man loses his caste if he is beaten with a shoe except by a Government servant, and is not readmitted to it. If a man seduces a married woman and is beaten with a shoe by her husband he is also finally expelled from caste. But happily, Mr. Panda Baijnāth remarks, shoes are very scarce in the State, and hence such cases do not often arise. They never yoke cows to the plough as other castes do in Bastar, nor do they tie up two cows with the same rope.

19. Dress.

The dress of the Halbas, as of other Chhattīsgarh castes, is scanty, and most of them have only a short cloth about the loins and another round the shoulders. They dispense with both shoes and head-cloth, but every man must have a thread tied round his waist. To this thread in former times, Colonel Dalton remarks, the apron of leaves was not

[1] It is simply water in which gold has been dipped.

improbably suspended. The women do not wear nose-rings, spangles on the forehead or rings on the toes; but girl children have the left nostril pierced, and this must always be done on the full moon day of the month of Pūs (December). A copper ring is inserted in the nostril and worn for a few months, but must be removed before the girl's marriage. A married woman has a cloth over her head, and smears vermilion on the parting of her hair and also on her forehead. An unmarried girl may have the copper ring already mentioned, and may place a dab of vermilion on her forehead, but must not smear it on the parting of her hair. She goes bare-headed till marriage, as is the custom in Chhattīsgarh. A widow should not have vermilion on her face at all, nor should she use glass bangles or ornaments about the ankles. She may have a string of glass beads about her neck. A woman's cloth is usually white with a broad red border all round it. The Gonds and Halbas tie the cloth round the waist and carry the slack end from the left side behind up the back and over the head and right shoulder; while women of higher castes take the cloth from the right side over the head and left shoulder.

20. Tattooing. Girls are tattooed before marriage, usually at the age of four or five years, with dots on the left nostril and centre of the chin, and three dots in a line on the right shoulder. A girl is again tattooed after marriage, but before leaving for her husband's house. On this occasion four pairs of parallel lines are made on the leg above the ankle, in front, behind, and on the sides. As a rule, the legs are not otherwise tattooed, nor the trunk of the body. Groups of dots, triangles and lines are made on the arms, and on the left arm is pricked a zigzag line known as the *sikri* or chain, the pattern of which is distinctive. Teli and Gahra (Ahīr) women also have the *sikri*, but in a slightly different form. The tattooing is done by a woman of the Dewar caste, and she receives some corn and the cloth worn by the girl at the time of the operation. If a child is slow in learning to walk they tattoo it on the loins above the hips, and believe that this is efficacious. Men who suffer from rheumatism also get the affected joints tattooed, and are said to experience much relief. The tattooing acts no

doubt as a blister, and may produce a temporarily beneficial effect. It may be compared to the bee-sting cure for rheumatism now advocated in England. Tattooing is believed to enhance the beauty of women, and it is also said that the tattoo marks are the only ornament which will accompany the soul to the other world. From this belief it seems clear that they expect to have the same body in the after-life.

21. Occupation.

Nearly all the Halbas are now engaged in agriculture as tenants and labourers. Seven zamīndāri estates are held by members of the caste, six in Bhandāra and one in Chānda, and they also have some villages in the south of the Raipur and Drūg Districts. It is probable that they obtained this property in reward for military service, at the period when they were employed in the armies of the Ratanpur kings and of the Gond dynasty of Chānda. In the forest tracts of Dhamtari they are considered the best cultivators next to the Telis, and they show themselves quite able to hold their own in the open country, where their villages are usually prosperous. In Bastar they still practise shifting cultivation, sowing their crops on burnt-out patches of forest. Though hunting is not now one of their regular occupations, Mr. Gokul Prasād describes them as catching game by the following method: Six or seven men go out together at night, tying round their feet *ghunghunias* or two small hollow balls of brass with stones inside which tinkle as they move, such as are worn by postal runners. They move in Indian file, the first man carrying a lantern and the others walking behind him in its shadow. They walk with measured tread, and the *ghunghunias* give out a rhythmical harmonious sound. Hares and other small animals are attracted by the sound, and at the same time half-blinded by the light, so that they do not see the line of men. They approach, and are knocked over or caught by the men following the leader.

Halwai.—The occupational caste of confectioners, numbering about 3000 persons in the Central Provinces and Berār in 1911. The Halwai takes his name from *halwa*, a sweet made of flour, clarified butter and sugar, coloured with saffron and flavoured with almonds, raisins and pistachio-nuts.[1] The caste gives no account of its origin in northern India, but it is clearly a functional group composed of members of respectable middle-class castes who adopted the profession of sweetmeat-making. The Halwais are also called Mithaihas, or preparers of sweets, and in the Uriya country are known as Guria from *gur* or unrefined sugar. The caste has several subdivisions with territorial names, generally derived from places in northern India, as Kanaujia from Kanauj, and Jaunpuria from Jaunpur; others are Kāndu, a grain-parcher, and Dobisya, meaning two score. One of the Guria subdivisions is named Haldia from *haldi*, turmeric, and members of this subcaste are employed to prepare the *mahāprasād* or cooked rice which is served at the temple of Jagannāth and which is eaten by all castes together without scruple. The Gurias have exogamous divisions or *bargas*, the names of which are generally functional, as Darbān, door-keeper; Sarāf, treasurer; Bhitarya, one who looks to household affairs, and others. Marriage within the *barga* is forbidden, but the union of first cousins is not prohibited. Marriage may be infant or adult. A girl who has a *liaison* with a man of the caste may be wedded to him by the form used for the remarriage of a widow, but if she goes wrong with an outsider she is finally expelled. Widow-marriage is allowed, and divorce may be effected for misconduct on the part of the wife.

The social standing of the Halwai is respectable. "His art," says Mr. Nesfield,[2] "implies rather an advanced state of culture, and hence his rank in the social scale is a high one. There is no caste in India which considers itself too pure to eat what a confectioner has made. In marriage banquets it is he who supplies a large part of the feast, and at all times and seasons the sweetmeat is a favourite food to a Hindu requiring a temporary refreshment. There is a kind of bread called *puri*, consisting of wheaten dough fried in melted butter, which is taken as a substitute for the *chapāti* or wheaten pancake by travellers and others who happen to be unable to have their bread cooked at their own fire, and is made by the Halwais."

[1] Crooke, ii. 481.

[2] *Brief View*, p. 31.

Bemrose, Collo., Derby.

HALWAI OR CONFECTIONER'S SHOP.

The real reason why the Halwai occupies a good position perhaps simply results from the necessity that other castes should be able to take cakes from him. Among the higher castes food cooked with water should not be eaten except at the hearth after this has been specially cleansed and spread with cowdung, and those who are to eat have bathed and otherwise purified themselves. But as the need continuously arises for travellers and others to take a meal abroad where they cannot cook it for themselves, sweetmeats and cakes made without water are permitted to be eaten in this way, and the Halwai, as the purveyor of these, has been given the position of a pure caste from whose hands a Brāhman can take water. In a similar manner, water may be taken from the hands of the Dhīmar who is a household servant, the Kahār or palanquin-bearer, the Barai or betel-leaf seller, and the Bharbhūnja or rice-parcher, although some of these castes have a very low origin and occupy the humble position of menial servants.

The Halwai's shop is one of the most familiar in an Indian bazār, and in towns a whole row of them may be seen together, this arrangement being doubtless adopted for the social convenience of the caste-fellows, though it might be expected to decrease the custom that they receive. His wares consist of trays full of white and yellow-coloured sweetmeats and cakes of flour and sugar, very unappetising to a European eye, though Hindu boys show no lack of appreciation of them. The Hindus are very fond of sweet things, which is perhaps a common trait of an uneducated palate. Hindu children will say that such sweets as chocolate almonds are too bitter, and their favourite drink, sherbet, is simply a mixture of sugar and water with some flavouring, and seems scarcely calculated to quench the thirst produced by an Indian hot weather. Similarly their tea is so sweetened with sugar and spices as to be distasteful to a European.

The ingredients of a Halwai's sweets are wheat and gram-flour, milk and country sugar. Those called *batāshas* consist merely of syrup of sugar boiled with a little flour, which is taken out in spoonfuls and allowed to cool. They are very easy to make and are commonly distributed to schoolboys on any occasion of importance, and are something like a meringue in composition. The kind called *barafi* or ice is made from thick boiled milk mixed with sugar, and is more expensive and considered more of a treat than *batāshas*. *Laddus* are made from gram-flour which is mixed with water and dropped into boiling butter, when it hardens into lumps. These are taken out and dipped in syrup of sugar and allowed to cool. *Pheni* is a thin strip of dough of fine wheat-flour fried in butter and then dipped in syrup of sugar. Other sweets are made from the flour of *singāra* or water-nut and from *chironji*, the kernel of the *achār*[1] nut, coated with sugar. Of ordinary sweets the cheaper kinds cost 8 annas a seer of 2 lb. and the more expensive ones 10 or 12 annas. Sweets prepared by Bengali confectioners are considered the best of all. The Halwai sits on a board in his shop surrounded by wooden trays of the different kinds of sweets. These are often covered with crowds of flies and in some places with a variety of formidable-looking hornets. The latter do not appear to be vicious, however, and when he wishes to take sweets off a tray the Halwai whisks them off with a palm-leaf brush. Only if one of them gets into his cloth, or he unguardedly pushes his hand down into a heap of sweets and encounters a hornet, he may receive a sting of which the mark remains for some time. The better-class confectioners now imitate English sweets, and at fairs when they retail boiled grain and *ghī* they provide spoons and little basins for their customers.

1. Derivation and historical notice.

Hatkar, Hatgar.[2]—A small caste of Berār, numbering about 14,000 persons in 1911. They are found principally in the Pusad tāluk of Yeotmāl District, their villages being placed like a line of outposts along the Hyderābād border. The Hatkars are a branch of the Dhangar or shepherd caste, and in some localities they are considered as a subcaste of Dhangars. The derivation of the name Hatkar is obscure, but the Hatkars appear to be those Dhangars who first took to military service under Sivaji and hence became a

[1] *Buchanania latifolia.*

[2] Based principally on the account of the Hatkars on p. 200 of Sir A. Lyall's *Berār Gazetteer*, with some notes taken by Mr. Hīra Lāl in Buldāna.

distinct group. "Undisciplined, often unarmed, men of the Māwals or mountain valleys above the Ghauts who were called Māwallees, and of those below the mountains towards the sea, called Hetkurees, joined the young leader."[1] The Hatkars were thus the soldiers of the Konkan in Sivaji's army. The *Ain-i-Akbari* states that the Hatkars were driven westward across the Wardha by the Gonds. At this time (A.D. 1600) they were holding the country round Bāsim by force of arms, and are described as a refractory and perfidious race.[2] "The Hatkars of Berār are all Bargi or Bangi Dhangars, the shepherds with the spears. They say that formerly when going on any expedition they took only a blanket seven cubits long and a bear-spear. They would appear to have been all footmen. The Nāiks or village headman of Bāsim were principally Hatkars. The duty of a Nāik was to maintain order and stop robbery; but in time they became law-breakers and their men the dacoits of the country. Some of them were very powerful, and in 1818 Nowsāji Nāik's troops gave battle to the Nizām's regular forces under Major Pitman before Umarkhar. He was beaten and sent to Hyderābād, where he died, and the power of the Nāiks was broken by Major Sutherland. He hanged so many that the Nāiks pronounce his name to this day with awe. To some of the Nāiks he gave money and told them to settle down in certain villages. Others who also came, expecting money, were at once hanged."[3] But it would appear that only those leaders were hanged who did not come in before a certain fixed date.

2. The Gauli Hatkar's reverence for cattle.

The Hatkars are also called Bangi Dhangars, and in Berār rank above other Dhangars because they took to soldiering and obtained grants of land, just as the Marāthas rank above the Kunbis. Another group have given up sheep-tending and keep cattle, which is a more respectable occupation on account of the sanctity of cattle, and these call themselves Gauli Hatkars. These Gauli Hatkars have given up drinking liquor and eating fowls. They will not touch or sell the milk of buffaloes and cows before sunset on Mondays, the day on which they worship Krishna. If

[1] Colonel Meadows Taylor, *Tara*, p. 404.
[2] *Ain-i-Akbari*, quoted in *Berār Gazetteer*, p. 200. [3] *Berār Gazetteer*.

any one is in need of milk on that day they will let him milk the animal himself, but will take no price for the milk. On a Monday also they will not give fire from their house to any member of a low caste, such as a Mahār. On the day of Diwāli they worship their cows, tying a bunch of wool to the animal's forehead and putting rice on it; they make a mud image of Govardhan, the mountain held up by Krishna as an umbrella to protect the people from the rain, and then let the cows trample it to pieces with their hoofs. If a bullock dies with the rope halter through its nose, the owner is put out of caste; this rule also obtains among the Ahīrs and Gaulis, and is perhaps responsible for the objection felt in some localities to putting string through the nostrils of plough- and cart-bullocks, though it is the only means of obtaining any control over them.

3. Funeral rites.

Formerly the Hatkars burned the corpses only of men who died in battle or the chase or subsequently of their wounds, cremation being reserved for this honourable end. Others were buried sitting cross-legged, and a small piece of gold was placed in the mouth of the corpse. Now they either burn or bury the dead according to their means. Most of them at the time they were soldiers never allowed the hair on their face to be cut.

4. Exogamous groups.

The Hatkars of Berār are said to be divided into three exogamous clans who apparently marry with each other, their names being Poli, Gurdi and Muski. In the Central Provinces they have a set of exogamous sections with titular names of a somewhat curious nature; among them are Hakkya, said to be so called because their ancestor was absent when his cow gave birth to a calf; Wakmar, one who left the Pangat or caste feast while his fellows were eating; and Polya, one who did not take off his turban at the feast.

Hijra, Khasua.[1]—The class of eunuchs, who form a separate community, recruited by the admission of persons born with this deformity or reduced to the like condition by amputation. In Saugor it is said that the Khasuas are natural and the Hijras artificial eunuchs, and the Khasuas

[1] Partly based on a paper by Munshi Kanhaya Lāl of the Gazetteer Office.

deny that they admit Hijras into their society. They may be either Hindus or Muhammadans by birth, but all become Muhammadans. Children born in the condition of eunuchs are usually made over to the Khasuas by their parents. The caste are beggars, and also sing and dance at weddings and at the births of male children, and obtain presents of grain from the cultivators at seedtime and harvest. They wear female clothes and ornaments and assume the names of women. They are admitted to mosques, but have to stand behind the women, and in Saugor they have their own mosque. They observe Muhammadan rites and festivals generally, and are permitted to smoke from the huqqas of other Muhammadans. They are governed by a caste *panchāyat* or committee, which imposes fines but does not expel any member from the community. Each Khasua has a beat or locality reserved to him for begging and no other may infringe on it, violations of this rule being punished by the committee. Sometimes a well-to-do Khasua adopts an orphan and celebrates the child's marriage with as much expense and display as he can afford, and the Kāzi officiates at the ceremony.

The Hijras form apparently a separate group, and the following account of them is mainly taken from the *Bombay Gazetteer*.[1] In Gujarāt they are the emasculated male votaries of the goddess Bouchera or Behechra, a sister of Devi. She is the spirit of a martyred Chāran or Bhāt woman. Some Chāran women were travelling from Sulkhunpur in Gujarāt when they were attacked and plundered by Kolis. One of the women, of the name of Bouchera, snatched a sword from a boy who attended her and with it cut off both her breasts. She immediately perished, and was deified and worshipped as a form of Devi in the Chunwāl.[2] The Hijras usually mutilate themselves in the performance of a religious vow, sometimes taken by the mother as a means of obtaining children, and in rare cases by the boy himself to obtain recovery by the favour of the goddess from a dangerous illness.[3] Hence it is clear that

[1] *Muhammadans of Gujarāt*, by Khān Bahādur Fazalullah Lutfullah Faridi, pp. 21, 22.

[2] *Râsmāla*, ii. p. 90.

[3] Faridi, *ibidem*.

they worship Boucheraji on the ground that she obtained divine honours by self-mutilation and should enable her votaries to do the same. But the real reason for the Chāran woman cutting off her breasts was no doubt that her ghost might haunt and destroy the Koli robbers, in accordance with the usual practice of the Chārans.[1] As a further fulfilment of their vow the Hijras pull out the hair of their beards and moustaches, bore their ears and noses for female ornaments, and affect female speech and manners. The meaning of the vow would appear to be that the mother sacrifices her great blessing of a boy child and transforms him after a fashion into a girl, at the same time devoting him to the service of the goddess. Similarly, as a much milder form of the same idea, a mother whose sons have died will sometimes bore the nose of a later-born son and put a small nose-ring in it to make believe he is a girl. But in this case the aim is also partly to cheat the goddess or the evil spirits who cause the death of children, and make them think the boy is a girl and therefore not worth taking.

The rite of mutilation is described by Mr. Farīdi as follows: "The initiation takes place at the temple of the goddess Behechra about 60 miles from Ahmadābād, where the neophyte repairs under the guardianship or adoption of some older member of the brotherhood. The lad is called the daughter of the old Hijra his guardian. The emasculation is a secret rite and takes place under the direction of the chief Hijra priest of Behechra. It is said that the operation and initiation are held in a house with closed doors, where all the Hijras meet in holiday dress. A special dish of fried pastry is cooked, and the neophyte is bathed, dressed in red female attire, decked with flower-garlands and seated on a stool in the middle of the room, while the others sing to the accompaniment of a small drum and copper cymbals. Another room is prepared for the operation, soft ashes being spread on the floor and piled in a heap in the centre. When the time for the operation approaches, the neophyte is led to the room and is made to lie on his back on the ash-heap. The operator approaches

[1] See article on Bhāt.

chewing betel-leaf. The hands and legs of the neophyte are firmly held by some one of the fraternity, and the operator, carelessly standing near with an unconcerned air, when he finds the attention of his patient otherwise occupied, with great dexterity and with one stroke completely cuts off the genital organs. He spits betel and areca juice on the wound and staunches the bleeding with a handful of the ashes of the *babūl*.[1] The operation is dangerous and not uncommonly fatal." Another method is to hold the organs in a cleft bamboo and slice them off. The Hijras are beggars like the Khasuas, and sometimes become very importunate. Soon after the birth of a child in Gujarāt the hated Hijras or eunuchs crowd round the house for gifts. If the demand of one of them is refused the whole rank and file of the local fraternity besiege the house with indecent clamour and gesture. Their claim to alms rests, as with other religious mendicants, in the sacred character which attaches to them. In Bombay there is also a belief that the god Hanumān cries out once in twelve years, and that those men who hear him are transformed into eunuchs.[2] Some of them make money by allowing spectators to look at the mutilated part of their body, and also by the practice of pederasty.

Homosexual practices are believed to be distinctly rare among Hindus, and not common among Muhammadans of the Central Provinces. For this the early age of marriage may probably be considered a principal cause. The Hindu sacred books, however, do not attach severe penalties to this offence. "According to the Laws of Manu, a twice-born man who commits an unnatural offence with a male, or has intercourse with a female in a cart drawn by oxen, in water or in the daytime, shall bathe, dressed in his clothes; and all these are reckoned as minor offences."[3] In his *Origin and Development of the Moral Ideas* Dr. Westermarck shows that, apart from the genuine cases of sexual perversion, as to the frequency of which opinions differ, homosexual love frequently arises in three conditions

[1] *Acacia arabica.*

[2] The late Mr. A. M. T. Jackson's notes, *Ind. Ant.*, August 1912, p. 56.

[3] *Laws of Manu*, xi. p. 175, quoted in *The Origin and Development of the Moral Ideas*, ii. p. 476.

of society. These are, when women are actually scarce, as among the Australian aborigines and other primitive races; when the men are frequently engaged in war or in predatory expeditions and are separated from their wives for long periods, a condition which accounts for its prevalence among the Sikhs and Pathāns; and lastly, when women are secluded and uneducated and hence their society affords little intellectual pleasure to men. This was the case in ancient Greece where women received no education and had no place at the public spectacles which were the chief means of culture;[1] and the same reason probably accounts for the frequency of the vice among the Persians and modern Egyptians. "So also it seems that the ignorance and dulness of Muhammadan women, which is a result of their total lack of education and their secluded life, is a cause of homosexual practices; Moors are sometimes heard to defend pederasty on the plea that the company of boys, who have always news to tell, is so much more entertaining than the company of women."[2]

The Christian Church in this as in other respects has set a very high standard of sexual morality. Unnatural crimes were regarded with peculiar horror in the Middle Ages, and the punishments for them in English law were burying and burning alive, though these were probably seldom or never enforced.[3] The attitude of the Church, which was reflected in the civil law, was partly inherited from the Jews of the Old Testament, and reinforced by similar conditions in mediaeval society. In both cases this crime was especially associated with the heathen and heretics, as shown in Dr. Westermarck's interesting account:[4]

"According to Genesis, unnatural vice was the sin of a people who were not the Lord's people, and the Levitical legislation represents Canaanitish abominations as the chief reason why the Canaanites were exterminated. Now we know that sodomy entered as an element in their religion. Besides *kedēshōth*, or female prostitutes, there were *kedēshīm* or male prostitutes, attached to their temples. The word

1 Westermarck, *The Origin and Development of the Moral Ideas*, ii. p. 470.

2 *Ibidem*, ii. p. 471.

3 *Ibidem*, ii. pp. 481, 482.

4 *Ibidem*, ii. pp. 487-489.

kādēsh, translated 'Sodomite,' properly denotes a man dedicated to a deity; and it appears that such men were consecrated to the mother of the gods, the famous Dea Syria, whose priests or devotees they were considered to be. The male devotees of this and other goddesses were probably in a position analogous to that occupied by the female devotees of certain gods, who also, as we have seen, have developed into libertines; and the sodomitic acts committed with these temple prostitutes may, like the connections with priestesses, have had in view to transfer blessings to the worshippers. In Morocco supernatural benefits are expected not only from heterosexual, but also from homosexual intercourse with a holy person. The *kedēshīm* are frequently alluded to in the Old Testament, especially in the period of the monarchy, when rites of foreign origin made their way into both Israel and Judah. And it is natural that the Yāhveh worshipper should regard their practices with the utmost horror as forming part of an idolatrous cult.

"The Hebrew conception of homosexual love to some extent affected Muhammadanism, and passed into Christianity. The notion that it is a form of sacrilege was here strengthened by the habits of the Gentiles. St. Paul found the abominations of Sodom prevalent among nations who had 'changed the truth of God into a lie, and worshipped and served the creature more than the creator.' During the Middle Ages heretics were accused of unnatural vice as a matter of course. Indeed, so closely was sodomy associated with heresy that the same name was applied to both. In *La Coutume de Touraine-Anjou* the word *hérite*, which is the ancient form of *hérétique*, seems to be used in the sense of 'sodomite'; and the French *bougre* (from the Latin *Bulgarus*, Bulgarian), as also its English synonym, was originally a name given to a sect of heretics who came from Bulgaria in the eleventh century and was afterwards applied to other heretics, but at the same time it became the regular expression for a person guilty of unnatural intercourse. In mediaeval laws sodomy was also repeatedly mentioned together with heresy, and the punishment was the same for both. It thus remained a religious offence of the first order. It was not only a 'vitium nefandum et super omnia detestandum,' but it was one of the four 'clamantia peccata,' or crying sins, a 'crime de Majestie, vers le Roy celestre.' Very naturally, therefore, it has come to be regarded with somewhat greater leniency by law and public opinion in proportion as they have emancipated themselves from theological doctrines. And the fresh light which the scientific study of the sexual impulse has lately thrown upon the subject of homosexuality must also necessarily influence the moral ideas relating to it, in so far as no scrutinising judge can fail to take into account the pressure which a powerful non-volitional desire exercises upon an agent's will."

Holia.[1]—A low caste of drummers and leather-workers who claim to be degraded Golars or Telugu Ahīrs, under which caste most of the Holias seem to have returned themselves in 1901.[2] The Holias relate the following story of their origin. Once upon a time two brothers, Golar by caste, set out in search of service, having with them a bullock. On the way the elder brother went to worship his tutelary deity Holiāri Deva; but while he was doing so the bullock accidentally died, and the ceremony could not be proceeded with until the carcase was removed. Neither a Chamār nor anybody else could be got to do this, so at length the younger brother was prevailed upon by the elder one to take away the body. When he returned, the elder brother would not touch him, saying that he had lost his caste. The younger brother resigned himself to his fate and called himself Holu, after the god whom he had been worshipping at the time he lost his caste. His descendants were named Holias. But he prayed to the god to avenge him for the treachery of his brother, and from that moment misfortunes commenced to shower upon the Golar until he repented and made what reparation he could; and in memory of this, whenever a Golar dies, the Holias are feasted by the other Golars to the present day. The story indicates a connection between the

[1] This article is compiled from a paper by Mr. Bābu Rao, Deputy Inspector of Schools, Seoni District.

[2] In this year only 33 Holias were returned as against more than 4000 in 1891; but, on the other hand, in 1901 the number of Golars was double that of the previous census.

castes, and it is highly probable that the Holias are a degraded class of Golars who took to the trade of tanning and leather-working. When a Holia goes to a Golar's house he must be asked to come in and sit down or the Golar will be put out of caste; and when a Golar dies the house must be purified by a Holia. The caste is a very numerous one in Madras. Here the Holia is superior only to the Mādiga or Chamār.[1] In the Central Provinces they are held to be impure and to rank below the Mahārs, and they live on the outskirts of the village. Their caste customs resemble generally those of the Golars. They believe their traditional occupation to be the playing of leathern drums, and they still follow this trade, and also make slippers and leather thongs for agricultural purposes. But they must not make or mend shoes on pain of excommunication from caste. They are of middle stature, dark in colour, and very dirty in their person and habits. Like the Golars, the Holias speak a dialect of Canarese, which is known as Golari, Holia or Komtau. Mr. Thurston gives the following interesting particulars about the Holias:[2] "If a man of another caste enters the house of a Mysore Holia, the owner takes care to tear the intruder's cloth, and turn him out. This will avert any evil which might have befallen him. It is said that Brāhmans consider great luck will wait upon them if they can manage to pass through a Holia village unmolested. Should a Brāhman attempt to enter their quarters, the Holias turn him out, and slipper him, in former times it is said to death."

Injhwār.[3]—A caste of agricultural labourers and fisher- 1. Origin of the caste.
men found in the Marātha tract of the Wainganga Valley, comprised in the Bhandāra and Bālāghāt Districts. In 1901 they numbered 8500 persons as against 11,000 in 1891. The name Injhwār is simply a Marāthi corruption of Binjhwār, as *īs* for *bīs* (twenty) and Ithoba for Bithoba or Vithoba. In his Census Report of 1891 Sir Benjamin Robertson remarked that the name was often entered in the census books as Vinjhwār, and in Marāthi *B* and *V* are practically

[1] *Mysore Census Report* (1891), p. 254.

[2] *Ethnographic Notes in Southern India*, p. 258.

[3] This article is principally based on information collected by Mr. Hīra Lāl in Bhandāra.

interchangeable. The Injhwārs are thus a caste formed from the Binjhwārs or highest subdivision of the Baiga tribe of Bālāghāt; they have adopted the social customs of the Marāthi-speaking people among whom they live, and have been formed into a separate caste through a corruption of their name. They still worship Injha or Vindhya Devi, the tutelary deity of the Vindhyan hills, from which the name of the Binjhwārs is derived. The Injhwārs have also some connection with the Gowāri or cowherd caste of the Marātha country. They are sometimes known as Dūdh-Gowāri, and say that this is because an Injhwār woman was a wet-nurse of the first-born Gowāri. The Gowāris themselves, as a low caste of herdsmen frequenting the jungles, would naturally be brought into close connection with both the Baigas and Gonds. Their alliances with the Gonds have produced the distinct caste of Gond-Gowāri, and it is not improbable that one fact operating to separate the Injhwārs from their parent tribe of the Baigas was an admixture of Gowāri blood. But they rank higher than the Gond-Gowāris, who are regarded as impure; this is probably on account of the superior position of the Binjhwārs, who form the aristocracy of the Baiga tribe, and, living in the forests, were never reduced to the menial and servile condition imposed on the Gond residents in Hindu villages. The Injhwārs, however, admit the superiority of the Gowāris by taking food from their hands, a favour which the latter will not reciprocate. Several of the sept or family names of the caste are also taken from the Gonds, and this shows an admixture of Gond blood; the Injhwārs are thus probably a mixed group of Gonds, Gowāris, and Binjhwārs or Baigas.

2. Subdivisions. The Injhwārs have four subcastes, three of the territorial and one of the occupational class. These are the Lānjiwār, or those living round Lānji in Bālāghāt; the Korre, or those of the Korai hill tract in Seoni; the Chāndewār or Marātha Injhwārs who belong to Chānda, and are distinguished by holding their weddings only in the evening after the Marātha custom, while other Injhwārs will perform the ceremony at any time of day; and the Sonjharias, or those who have taken to washing for gold in the beds of streams. Of their sept or family names some, as already stated, are taken from

the Gonds, as Mesrām, Tekām, Marai, Ukya.[1] Three names, Bhoyar, Kawara and Kohrya (from Kohli), are the names of other castes or tribes, and indicate that members of these became Injhwārs and founded families; and others are of the territorial, titular and totemistic types. Among them may be mentioned the Pīthvālyās, from *pīth*, flour; all families of this sept should steal a little rice from somebody else's field as soon as it is ripe, husband and wife making a joint expedition for the purpose. They must not speak a word to each other from the time they start until they have brought back the rice, pounded and cooked it, offered it to the god and made their meal. The Paunpats, named after the lotus, will not touch the flowers or leaves of the lotus plants, or even drink water from a tank in which the lotus grows. The Dobokria Rāwats are so named because they make an offering of two goats to their gods. Some of the septs are subdivided. Thus the Sonwāni or gold-water sept, whose members readmit social culprits, is divided into the Paunpat or lotus Sonwānis; the Gurhiwāl, who revere a brass vessel tied to a bamboo on the first day of the year; the Sati Sonwāni, who worship the spirit of a *sati* woman ancestor; and the Mūngphātia Sonwānis, whose token is the broken *mung* pulse. At present these subsepts cannot intermarry, the union of any two Sonwānis being forbidden, but it seems likely that intermarriage may be permitted in the course of time.

3. Marriage and other customs.

The social customs of the Injhwārs resemble those of the lower Marātha castes.[2] Marriage is forbidden between members of the same sept and first cousins, and a man should also not take a wife from the sept of his brother or sister-in-law. This rule prevents the marriage of two brothers to two sisters, to which there is of course no objection on the ground of affinity. Girls are usually not married until they are grown up; but in places where they have been much subjected to Hindu influences, the Injhwārs will sometimes wed an adult girl to a basil plant in order to avoid the stigma of keeping her in the house unmarried. The boy's father goes to make a proposal of marriage, and the girl's father, if he approves it, intimates his consent by washing

[1] A corruption of Uika.

[2] See the articles Mahār and Kunbi.

his visitor's feet. A bride-price of about Rs. 20 is usually paid, which is increased somewhat if the bridegroom is a widower, and decreased if the bride has been seduced before marriage. The marriage is performed by throwing coloured rice over the couple. Divorce and the remarriage of widows are permitted. A bachelor who marries a widow must first go through the ceremony with an *arka* or swallow-wort plant, this being considered his real marriage. The Injhwārs usually bury the dead, and in accordance with Dravidian custom place the corpse in the grave with the feet to the north. When the body is that of a young girl, the face is left exposed as it is carried to the grave. The regular ceremonies are performed for the welfare of the deceased's soul, and they try to ascertain its fate in the next incarnation by spreading flour on the ground overnight and looking in the morning for anything resembling the footmark of a human being, animal or bird. On the festival of Akhātīj and in the month of Kārtik (October) they offer libations to the dead, setting out a large pitcher of water for a male and a small one for a female. On the former they paint five lines of sandalwood to represent a man's caste-mark, and on the latter five splashes of *kunku* or the red powder which women rub on their foreheads. A burning lamp is placed before the pitchers, and they feed a male Māli or gardener as representative of a dead man and a female for a woman.

4. Occupation and social status.

The Injhwārs are generally labourers and cultivators, while the Sonjharias wash for gold. The women of the Marātha or Chāndewār subcaste serve as midwives. Their social status is low, and in the forest tracts they will eat snakes and crocodiles, and in fact almost anything except beef. They will admit members of the Brāhman, Dhīmar (waterman), Māli and Gowāri castes into the community on payment of a premium of five to fifteen rupees and a dinner to the caste-fellows. The candidate for admission, whether male or female, must have his head shaved clean. Both men and women can obtain pardon for a *liaison* with an outsider belonging to any except the most impure castes by giving a feast to the community. To be beaten with a shoe involves temporary excommunication from caste, unless the striker be a Government official, when no penalty is inflicted. If a man kills a cat, he is required to have an image of it made in silver, which, after being worshipped, is presented to a temple or thrown into a river.

Jādam.[1]—A branch of the well-known Yādu or Yādava sept of Rājpūts which has now developed into a caste in the Nerbudda valley. Colonel Tod describes the Yādu as the most illustrious of all the tribes of India, this name having been borne by the descendants of Buddha, progenitor of the Lunar race. The Yādavas were the herdsmen of Mathura, and Krishna was born in this tribe. His son was Bhārat, from whom the classical name of Bhāratavārsha for India is held to be derived. It is related that when Krishna was about to ascend to heaven, he reflected that the Yādavas had multiplied exceedingly and would probably cause trouble to the world after he had left it. So he decided to reduce their numbers, and one day he persuaded one of his companions to dress up as a pregnant woman in jest, and they took him to the hermitage of the saint Durvāsa and asked the saint to what the woman would give birth. Durvāsa, who was of a very irascible temper, divined that he was being trifled with, and replied that a rice-pestle would be born by which the Yādavas would be destroyed. On the return of the party they found to their astonishment that a pestle had actually, as it were, been born from the man. So they were alarmed at the words of the saint and tried to destroy the pestle by rubbing it on a stone. But as the sawdust of the pestle fell on the ground there sprang up from it the shoots of the Gondla or Elephant grass, which grows taller than the head of a man on horseback. And some time afterwards a quarrel arose among the Yādavas, and they tore up the stalks of this grass and slew each other with it. Only one woman escaped, whose son was afterwards the King of Mathura and the ancestor of the existing tribe. Another body, however, with whom was Krishna, fled to Gujarāt, and on the coast there built the great temple of Dwārka, in the place known as Jagat Khant.

[1] This article is partly based on a paper by Bihāri Lāl, Patwāri, of Hoshangābād.

or the World's End. The story has some resemblance to that of the sowing of the dragon's teeth by Cadmus at Thebes. The principal branches of the Yādavas are the Yāduvansi chiefs of Karauli, in Rājputāna, and the Bhatti chiefs of Jaisalmer. The Jādams of Hoshangābād say that they immigrated from Karauli State about 700 years ago, having come to the country on a foray for plunder and afterwards settled here. They have now developed into a caste, marrying among themselves. In Hoshangābād the caste has two subdivisions, the Kachhotia who belong principally to the Sohāgpur tahsil, and the Adhodias who live in Seoni and Harda. These two groups are endogamous and do not marry with each other. The Kachhotia are the offspring of irregular unions and are looked down upon by the others. They say that they have fifty-two exogamous groups or sections, but this number is used locally as an expression of indefinite magnitude. All the sections appear to be named after villages where their ancestors once lived, but the preference for totemism has led some of the groups to connect their names with natural objects. Thus the designation of the Semaria section may be held to be derived from a village of that name, both on account of its form, and because the other known section-names are taken from villages. But the Semaria Jādams have adopted the *semar* or cotton-tree as their totem and pay reverence to this.[1]

Infant-marriage is favoured in the caste, and polygamy is also prevalent. This is often the case among the agricultural castes, where a man will marry several wives in order to obtain their assistance in his cultivation, a wife being a more industrious and reliable worker than a hired servant. No penalty is, however, imposed for allowing a girl to reach adolescence before marriage, and this not infrequently happens. If a girl becomes with child through a man of the caste she is united to him by a simple rite known as *gunda*, in which she merely gives him a ring or throws a garland of flowers over his neck. A caste feast is

[1] Semaria is a common name of villages, and is of course as such derived from the *semar* tree, but the argument is that the Jādams took the name from the village and not from the tree. Totem is perhaps rather a strong word for the kind of veneration paid; the vernacular term used in Bombay is *devak*.

also exacted, and the couple are then considered to be married. The remarriage of widows is permitted, but it is known by the opprobrious name of *Kukar-gauna* or 'dog-marriage,' signifying that it is held to be little or no better than a simple illicit connection. Divorce is also somewhat common in the caste, notwithstanding that the person who occupies the position of co-respondent must repay to the husband the expenses incurred by him on the marriage ceremony. Some women are known to have had ten or twelve husbands.

The Jādams are proprietors, tenants and labourers, and are reckoned to be efficient cultivators; they plough with their own hands and allow their women to work in the fields. They will also eat food cooked with water in the field, which is against the practice of the higher castes. They eat flesh, including that of the wild pig, and fish, but abstain from liquor, and will take food cooked with water only from Jijhotia or Sanādhya Brāhmans who are their family priests. A Brāhman will take water from the hands of a Jādam in a metal, but not in an earthen, vessel. Boys are invested with the sacred thread at the time of their wedding, a common practice among the higher agricultural castes, and one pointing to the hypothesis suggested in the article on Gurao that the investiture with the sacred thread was in its origin a rite of puberty. The women wear a peculiar dress know as *sawang*, consisting of a small skirt of about six feet of cloth and a long body-cloth wrapped round the waist and over the shoulders. They also have larger spangles on the forehead than other women. The women of the caste are emancipated to an unusual degree, and it is stated that they commonly accompany their husbands to market for shopping, to prevent them from being cheated. Dr. Hunter describes the Jādam as a brave soldier, but a bad agriculturist; but in the Central Provinces his courage is rated less highly, and a proverb quoted about him is: '*Patta khatka, Jādam satka*,' or 'The Jādam trembles at the rustle of a leaf.'

Jādua-, Jāduah-Brāhman.[1]—This is the name of a

[1] This article is based on an account of the Jāduas by Mr. A. Knyvett, Superintendent of Police, Patna, and kindly communicated by Mr. C. W. C.

class of swindlers, who make money by pretending to turn other metals into gold or finding buried treasure. They are believed to have originated from the caste of Bhadris or Jyotishis, the astrologers of western India. The Jyotishi or Joshi astrologers are probably an offshoot of the Brāhman caste. The name Jādua is derived from *jādu*, magic. The Bhadris or Jyotishis were in former times, Mr. Knyvett writes, attached to the courts of all important rājas in western India, where they told fortunes and prophesied future events from their computations of the stars, often obtaining great influence and being consulted as oracles. Readers of *Quentin Durward* will not need to be reminded that an exactly similar state of things obtained in Europe. And both the European and Indian astrologers were continually searching for the philosopher's stone and endeavouring by the practice of alchemy to discover the secret of changing silver and other metals into gold. It is easy to understand how the more dishonest members of the community would come to make a livelihood by the pretence of being possessed of this power. The Jāduas belong principally to Bihār, and Mr. Knyvett's account of them is based on inquiries in that Province. But it is probable that, like the Bhadris, travelling parties of Jāduas occasionally visit the Central Provinces. Their method of procedure is somewhat as follows. They start out in parties of three or four and make inquiries for the whereabouts of some likely dupe, in the shape of an ignorant and superstitious person possessed of property. Sometimes they settle temporarily in a village and open a small grain-shop in order to facilitate their search. When the victim has been selected one of them proceeds to his village in the disguise of a Sādhu or anchorite, being usually accompanied by another as his *chela* or disciple. Soon afterwards the others come, one of them perhaps posing as a considerable landholder, and go about inquiring if a very holy Brāhman has been seen. They go to the house of their intended dupe, who naturally asks why they are seeking the Brāhman; they reply that

Plowden, Deputy Inspector-General of Police, Bengal, through Mr. G. W. Gayer, in charge of the Central Provinces Criminal Investigation Department.

they have come to do homage to him as he had turned their silver and brass ornaments into gold. The dupe at once goes with them in search of the Brāhman, and is greatly impressed by seeing the landholder worship him with profound respect and make him presents of cloth, money and cattle. He at once falls into the trap and says that he too has a quantity of silver which he would like to have turned into gold. The Brāhman pretends reluctance, but eventually yields to the dupe's entreaties and allows himself to be led to the latter's house, where with his *chela* he takes up his quarters in an inner room, dark and with a mud floor. A variety of tricks are now resorted to, to impress the dupe with the magic powers of the swindlers. Sometimes he is directed to place a rupee on his forehead and go to the door and look at the sun for five minutes, being assured that when he returns the Brāhman will have disappeared by magic. Having looked at the sun for five minutes he can naturally see nothing on returning to a dark room and expresses wonder at the Brāhman's disappearance and gradual reappearance as his eyes get accustomed to the darkness. Or if the trick to be practised is the production of buried treasure, a rupee may be buried in the ground and after various incantations two rupees are produced from the same spot by sleight of hand. Or by some trickery the victim is shown the mouth of an earthen vessel containing silver or gold coins in a hole dug in the ground. He is told that the treasure cannot be obtained until more treasure has been added to it and religious rites have been performed. Sometimes the victim is made to visit a secluded spot, where he is informed that after repeating certain incantations Sivaji will appear before him. A confederate, dressed in tinsel and paint, appears before the victim posing as Sivaji, and informs him that there is treasure buried in his house, and it is only necessary to follow the instructions of the holy Brāhman in order to obtain it. The silver ornaments, all that can be collected, are then made over to the Brāhman, who pretends to tie them in a cloth or place them in an earthen pot and bury them in the floor of the room. If buried treasure is to be found the Brāhman explains that it is first necessary to bury more treasure in order to obtain it, and if the ornaments are to be turned into gold they are buried for the purpose of transmutation. During the process the victim is induced on some pretence to leave the room or cover himself with a sheet, when a bundle containing mud or stones is substituted for the treasure. The Brāhman calls for *ghī*, oil and incense, and lights a fire over the place where the ornaments are supposed to be buried, bidding his victim watch over it for some hours or days until his return. The Brāhman and his disciple, with the silver concealed about them, then leave the house, join their confederates and make their escape. The duped villager patiently watches the fire until he becomes tired of waiting for the Brāhman's return, when he digs up the earth and finds nothing in the cloth but stones and rubbish.

Jangam, Jangama.—A Sivite order of wandering religious mendicants. The Jangams are the priests or *gurus* of the Sivite sect of Lingāyats. They numbered 3500 persons in the Central Provinces and Berār in 1911, and frequent the Marātha country. The Jangam is said to be so called because he wears a movable emblem of Siva (*jana gama*, to come and go) in contradistinction to the Sthāwar or fixed emblems found in temples. The Jangams discard many of the modern phases of Hinduism. They reject the poems in honour of Vishnu, Rāma and Krishna, such as the Bhāgavad Gīta and Rāmāyana; they also deny the authority of Brāhmans, the efficacy of pilgrimage and self-mortification, and the restrictions of caste; while they revere principally the Vedas and the teaching of the great Sivite reformer Shankar Achārya.[1] Like other religious orders, the Jangams have now become a caste, and are divided into two groups of celibate and married members. The Gharbāris (married members) celebrate their weddings in the usual Marātha fashion, except that they perform no *hom* or fire sacrifice. They permit the remarriage of widows. The Jangams wear ochre-coloured or *badāmi* clothes and long necklaces of seeds called *rudrāksha*[2] beads, which resemble a nutmeg in size, in colour and nearly in shape;

1 Sherring, *Castes and Tribes*, iii. p. 123.
2 The nut of *Eleocarpus lanceolatus*.

they besmear their forehead, arms and various other parts of the body with cowdung ashes. They wear the *lingam* or phallic sign of Siva either about the neck or loins in a little casket of gold, silver, copper or brass. As the *lingam* is supposed to represent the god and to be eternal, they are buried and not burnt after death, because the *lingam* must be buried with them and must not be destroyed in the fire. If any Jangam loses the *lingam* he or she must not eat or drink until it has been replaced by the *guru* or spiritual preceptor. It must be worshipped thrice a day, and ashes and *bel*[1] leaves are offered to it, besides food when the owner is about to partake of this himself. The Jangams worship no deity other than Siva or Mahādeo, and their great festival is the Shivrātri. Some of them make pilgrimages to Pachmarhi, to the Mahādeo hills. Most of them subsist by begging and singing songs in praise of Mahādeo. Grant-Duff gives the Jangam as one of the twenty-four village servants in a Marātha village, perhaps as the priest of the local shrine of Siva, or as the caste priest of the Lingāyats, who are numerous in some Districts of Bombay. He carries a wallet over the shoulder and a conch-shell and bell in the hand. On approaching the door of a house he rings his bell to bring out the occupant, and having received alms proceeds on his way, blowing his conch-shell, which is supposed to be a propitious act for the alms-giver, and to ensure his safe passage to heaven. The wallet is meant to hold the grain given to him, and on returning home he never empties it completely, but leaves a little grain in it as its own share. The Jangams are strict vegetarians, and take food only from the hands of Lingāyats. They bless their food before eating it and always finish it completely, and afterwards wash the dish with water and drink down the water. When a child is born, the priest is sent for and his feet are washed with water in a brass tray. The water is then rubbed over the bodies of those present, and a few drops sprinkled on the walls of the house as a ceremony of purification. The priest's great toes are then washed in a cup of water, and he dips the *lingam* he wears into this, and then sips a few drops of the water, each person present

[1] *Aegle marmelos.*

doing the same. This is called *karuna* or sanctification. He then dips a new *lingam* into the holy water, and ties it round the child's neck for a minute or two, afterwards handing it to the mother to be kept till the child is old enough to wear it. The dead are buried in a sitting posture, the *lingam* being placed in the palm of the hand. On the third day a clay image of Mahādeo is carried to the grave, and food and flowers are offered to it, as well as any intoxicants to which the deceased person may have been addicted. The following notice of the Jangams more than a century ago may be quoted from the Abbé Dubois, though the custom described does not, so far as is known, prevail at present, at least in the Central Provinces:[1] "The *gurus* or priests of Siva, who are known in the Western Provinces by the name of Jangams, are for the most part celibates. They have a custom which is peculiar to themselves, and curious enough to be worth remarking. When a *guru* travels about his district he lodges with some member of the sect, and the members contend among themselves for the honour of receiving him. When he has selected the house he wishes to stay in, the master and all the other male inmates are obliged, out of respect for him, to leave it and go and stay elsewhere. The holy man remains there day and night with only the women of the house, whom he keeps to wait on him and cook for him, without creating any scandal or exciting the jealousy of the husbands. All the same, some scandal-mongers have remarked that the Jangams always take care to choose a house where the women are young." The Jangams are not given to austerities, and go about well clad.

[1] *Hindu Manners, Customs, and Ceremonies*, 1897 ed. p. 118.

JĀT

LIST OF PARAGRAPHS

1. Theories of the origin of the caste.

Jāt.[1]—The representative cultivating caste of the Punjab, corresponding to the Kurmi of Hindustān, the Kunbi of the Deccan, and the Kāpu of Telingāna. In the Central Provinces 10,000 Jāts were returned in 1911, of whom 5000 belonged to Hoshangābād and the bulk of the remainder to Narsinghpur, Saugor and Jubbulpore. The origin of the Jāt caste has been the subject of much discussion. Sir D. Ibbetson stated some of the theories as follows:[2] "Suffice it to say that both General Cunningham and Major Tod agree in considering the Jāts to be of Indo-Scythian stock. The former identifies them with the Zanthii of Strabo and the Jatii of Pliny and Ptolemy; and holds that they probably entered the Punjab from their home on the Oxus very shortly after the Meds or Mands, who also were Indo-Scythians, and who moved into the Punjab about a century before Christ. . . . Major Tod classes the Jāts as

[1] This article is partly based on information contributed by Mr. Debendra Nāth Dutt, Pleader, Narsinghpur; Mr. Ganga Singh, Extra Assistant Commissioner, Hoshangābād; and Mr. Adurām Chaudhri of the Gazetteer Office. The correct pronunciation of the caste name is Jat, but in the Central Provinces it is always called Jāt.

[2] *Punjab Census Report* (1881), para. 421.

one of the great Rājpūt tribes, and extends his identification with the Getae to both races; but here General Cunningham differs, holding the Rājpūts to belong to the original Aryan stock, and the Jāts to a later wave of immigrants from the north-west, probably of Scythian race." It is highly probable that the Jāts may date their settlement in the Punjab from one of the three Scythian inroads mentioned by Mr. V. A. Smith,[1] but I do not know that there is as yet considered to be adequate evidence to identify them with any particular one.

The following curious passage from the Mahābhārata would appear to refer to the Jāts:[2]

"An old and excellent Brāhman reviling the countries Bāhīka and Madra in the dwelling of Dhritarāshtra, related facts long known, and thus described those nations. External to the Himāvan, and beyond the Ganges, beyond the Sārasvati and Yamuna rivers and Kurukshetra, between five rivers, and the Sindhu as the sixth, are situated the Bāhīkas, devoid of ritual or observance, and therefore to be shunned. Their figtree is named Govardhana (*i.e.* the place of cow-killing); their market-place is Subhadram (the place of vending liquor: at least so say the commentators), and these give titles to the doorway of the royal palace. A business of great importance compelled me to dwell amongst the Bāhīkas, and their customs are therefore well known to me. The chief city is called Shākāla, and the river Apaga. The people are also named Jarttikas; and their customs are shameful. They drink spirits made from sugar and grain, and eat meat seasoned with garlic; and live on flesh and wine: their women intoxicated appear in public places, with no other garb than garlands and perfumes, dancing and singing, and vociferating indecencies in tones more harsh than those of the camel or the ass; they indulge in promiscuous intercourse and are under no restraint. They clothe themselves in skins and blankets, and sound the cymbal and drum and conch, and cry aloud with hoarse voices: 'We will hasten to delight, in thick forests and in

[1] *Early History of India.*

[2] Mahābhārata, viii. 2026, *et seq.*, translated by Professor H. H. Wilson, and quoted in vol. i. pp. 260, 262 of Dr. J. Wilson's *Indian Caste.*

pleasant places; we will feast and sport; and gathering on the highways spring upon the travellers, and spoil and scourge them!' In Shākāla, a female demon (a Rākshasi) on the fourteenth day of the dark fortnight sings aloud: 'I will feast on the flesh of kine, and quaff the inebriating spirit attended by fair and graceful females.' The Sūdra-like Bāhīkas have no institutes nor sacrifices; and neither deities, manes, nor Brāhmans accept their offerings. They eat out of wooden or earthen plates, nor heed their being smeared with wine or viands, or licked by dogs, and they use equally in its various preparations the milk of ewes, of camels and of asses. Who that has drunk milk in the city Yugandhara can hope to enter Svarga? Bāhi and Hīka were the names of two fiends in the Vipāsha river; the Bāhīkas are their descendants and not of the creation of Brahma. Some say the Arattas are the name of the people and Bāhīka of the waters. The Vedas are not known there, nor oblation, nor sacrifice, and the gods will not partake of their food. The Prasthalas (perhaps borderers), Madras, Gandharas, Arattas, Khashas, Vasas, Atisindhus (or those beyond the Indus), Sauvīras, are all equally infamous. There one who is by birth a Brāhman, becomes a Kshatriya, or a Vaishya, or a Sūdra, or a Barber, and having been a barber becomes a Brāhman again. A virtuous woman was once violated by Aratta ruffians, and she cursed the race, and their women have ever since been unchaste. On this account their heirs are their sisters' children, not their own. All countries have their laws and gods: the Yavanas are wise, and pre-eminently brave; the Mlechchas observe their own ritual, but the Madrakas are worthless. Madra is the ordure of the earth: it is the region of inebriety, unchastity, robbery, and murder: fie on the Panchanada people! fie on the Aratta race!"

In the above account the country referred to is clearly the Punjab, from the mention of the five rivers and the Indus. The people are called Bāhīka or Jarttika, and would therefore seem to be the Jāts. And the account would appear to refer to a period when they were newly settled in the Punjab and had not come under Hindu influence. But at the same time the Aryans or Hindus had passed through the Punjab and were settled in Hindustān. And it would therefore seem to be a necessary inference that the Jāts were comparatively late immigrants, and were one of the tribes who invaded India between the second century B.C. and the fifth century A.D. as suggested above.

2. Sir D. Ibbetson's description of the caste.

Sir D. Ibbetson held that the Jāts and Rājpūts must be, to some extent at least, of the same blood. Though the Jāts are represented in the Central Provinces only by a small body of immigrants it will be permissible to quote the following passages from his admirable and classical account of the caste:[1]

"It may be that the original Rājpūt and the original Jāt entered India at different periods in its history, though to my mind the term Rājpūt is an occupational rather than an ethnological expression. But if they do originally represent two separate waves of immigration, it is at least exceedingly probable, both from their almost identical physique and facial character and from the close communion which has always existed between them, that they belong to one and the same ethnic stock; while, whether this be so or not, it is almost certain that they have been for many centuries and still are so intermingled and so blended into one people that it is practically impossible to distinguish them as separate wholes. It is indeed more than probable that the process of fusion has not ended here, and that the people who thus in the main resulted from the blending of the Jāt and the Rājpūt, if these two were ever distinct, is by no means free from foreign elements. . . .

3. Are the Jāts and Rājpūts distinct?

"But whether Jāts and Rājpūts were or were not originally distinct, and whatever aboriginal elements may have been affiliated to their society, I think that the two now form a common stock, the distinction between Jāt and Rājpūt being social rather than ethnic. I believe that those families of that common stock whom the tide of fortune has raised to political importance have become Rājpūts almost by mere virtue of their rise; and that their descendants have retained the title and its privileges on the condition, strictly enforced, of observing the rules by which the higher are distinguished from the lower castes in the Hindu scale of precedence; of

[1] *Ibidem*, paras. 422-424.

preserving their purity of blood by refusing to marry with families of inferior social rank, of rigidly abstaining from widow-marriage, and of refraining from degrading occupations. Those who transgressed these rules have fallen from their high position and ceased to be Rājpūts; while such families as, attaining a dominant position in their territory, began to affect social exclusiveness and to observe the rules, have become not only Rājas but also Rājpūts or sons of Rājas. For the last seven centuries at least the process of elevation has been almost at a standstill. Under the Delhi Emperors king-making was practically impossible. Under the Sikhs the Rājpūt was overshadowed by the Jāt, who resented his assumption of superiority and his refusal to join him on equal terms in the ranks of the Khālsa, deliberately persecuted him wherever and whenever he had the power, and preferred his title of Jāt Sikh to that of the proudest Rājpūt. On the frontier the dominance of Pathāns and Biloches and the general prevalence of Muhammadan feelings and ideas placed recent Indian origin at a discount, and led the leading families who belonged to neither of these two races to claim connection not with the Kshatriyas of the Sanskrit classics but with the Mughal conquerors of India or the Qureshi cousins of the Prophet; in so much that even admittedly Rājpūt tribes of famous ancestry, such as the Khokha, have begun to follow the example. But in the hills, where Rājpūt dynasties, with genealogies perhaps more ancient and unbroken than can be shown by any other royal families in the world, retained their independence till yesterday, and where many of them still enjoy as great social authority as ever, the twin processes of degradation from and elevation to Rājpūt rank are still to be seen in operation. The Rāja is there the fountain not only of honour but also of caste, which is the same thing in India. . . .

4. The position of the Jāt in the Punjab.

"The Jāt is in every respect the most important of the Punjab peoples. In point of numbers he surpasses the Rājpūt, who comes next to him, in the proportion of nearly three to one; while the two together constitute twenty-seven per cent of the whole population of the Province. Politically he ruled the Punjab till the Khālsa yielded to our arms.

Ethnologically he is the peculiar and most prominent product of the plain of the five rivers. And from an economical and administrative point of view he is the husbandman, the peasant, the revenue-payer *par excellence* of the Province. His manners do not bear the impress of generations of wild freedom which marks the races of our frontier mountains. But he is more honest, more industrious, more sturdy, and no less manly than they. Sturdy independence indeed and patient, vigorous labour are his strongest characteristics. The Jāt is of all Punjab races the most impatient of tribal or communal control, and the one which asserts the freedom of the individual most strongly. In tracts where, as in Rohtak, the Jāt tribes have the field to themselves, and are compelled, in default of rival castes as enemies, to fall back upon each other for somebody to quarrel with, the tribal ties are strong. But as a rule a Jāt is a man who does what seems right in his own eyes and sometimes what seems wrong also, and will not be said nay by any man. I do not mean, however, that he is turbulent; as a rule he is very far from being so. He is independent and he is self-willed; but he is reasonable, peaceably inclined if left alone, and not difficult to manage. He is usually content to cultivate his fields and pay his revenue in peace and quietness if people will let him do so; though when he does go wrong he takes to anything from gambling to murder, with perhaps a preference for stealing other people's wives and cattle. As usual the proverbial wisdom of the villages describes him very fairly though perhaps somewhat too severely: 'The soil, fodder, clothes, hemp, grass-fibre, and silk, these six are best beaten; and the seventh is the Jāt.' 'A Jāt, a Bhāt, a caterpillar, and a widow woman; these four are best hungry. If they eat their fill they do harm.' 'The Jāt, like a wound, is better when bound.' In agriculture the Jāt is pre-eminent. The market-gardening castes, the Arāin, the Māli, the Saini are perhaps more skilful cultivators on a small scale; but they cannot rival the Jāt as landowners and yeoman cultivators. The Jāt calls himself zamīndār or 'husbandman' as often as Jāt, and his women and children alike work with him in the fields: 'The Jāt's baby has a plough-handle for a plaything.' 'The Jāt stood on his corn heap and said to the king's elephant-drivers, Will you sell those little donkeys?' Socially the Jāt occupies a position which is shared by the Ror, the Gūjar, and the Ahīr, all four eating and smoking together. He is, of course, far below the Rājpūt, from the simple fact that he practises widow-marriage. The Jāt father is made to say in the rhyming proverbs of the countryside, 'Come, my daughter, and be married; if this husband dies there are plenty more.' But among the widow-marrying castes he stands first. The Bania with his sacred thread, his strict Hinduism, and his twice-born standing, looks down on the Jāt as a Sūdra. But the Jāt looks down upon the Bania as a cowardly, spiritless money-grubber, and society in general agrees with the Jāt. The Khatri, who is far superior to the Bania in manliness and vigour, probably takes precedence of the Jāt. But among the races or tribes of purely Hindu origin, I think that the Jāt stands next after the Brāhman, the Rājpūt, and the Khatri."

5. Social status of the Jāts.

The above account clearly indicates the social position of the Jāt. His is the highest caste except the aristocracy consisting of the Brāhmans and Rājpūts, the Khatris who are derived from the Rājpūts, and the Banias who are recognised as ranking not much below the Rājpūts. The derivation of some of the Rājpūt clans from the Jāts seems highly probable, and is confirmed by other instances of aristocratic selection in such castes as the Marāthas and Kunbis, the Rāj-Gonds and Gonds, and so on. If, however, the Rājpūts are a Jāt aristocracy, it is clear that the Jāts were not the Sūdras, who are described as wholly debased and impure in the Hindu classics; and the present application of the term Sūdra to them is a misnomer arising from modern errors in classification by the Hindus themselves. The Jāts, if Sir D. Ibbetson's account be accepted, must have been the main body of the invading host, whether Aryan or Scythian, of whom the Rājpūts were the leaders. They settled on the land and formed village communities, and the status of the Jāt at present appears to be that of a member of the village community and part-holder of its land. A slightly undue importance may perhaps have been given in the above passage to the practice of widow-marriage as determining the position of a great caste like the Jāts. Some Rājpūts, Kāyasths and Banias permit widow-marriage, and considerable sections of all these castes, and Brāhmans also, permit the practice of keeping widows, which, though not called a marriage, does not differ very widely from it. The Jāt probably finds his women too valuable as assistants in cultivation to make a pretence at the abolition of widow-marriage in order to improve his social status as some other castes do. The Jāt, of course, ranks as what is commonly called a pure caste, in that Brāhmans take water to drink from him. But his status does not depend on this, because Brāhmans take water from such menials as barbers, Kahārs or bearers, Bāris or household servants, and so on, who rank far below the Jāt, and also from the Mālis and other gardening castes who are appreciably below him. The Jāt is equal to the Gūjar and Ahīr so far as social purity is concerned, but still above them, because they are graziers and vagrants, while he is a settled cultivator. It is from this fact that his status is perhaps mainly derived; and his leading characteristics, his independence, self-sufficiency, doggedness, and industry, are those generally recognised as typical of the peasant proprietor. But the Jāt, in the Punjab at any rate, has also a higher status than the principal cultivating castes of other provinces, the Kurmi and the Kunbi. And this may perhaps be explained by his purer foreign descent, and also by the fact that both as Jāt and as Sikh his caste has been a military and dominant one in history and has furnished princes and heads of states.

6. Brāhmanical legend of origin.

The Jāts themselves relate the following Brāhmanical legend of their origin. On one occasion when Himāchal or Daksha Rāja, the father-in-law of Mahādeo, was performing a great sacrifice, he invited all the gods to be present except his son-in-law Mahādeo (Siva). The latter's wife Pārvati was, however, very anxious to go, so she asked Mahādeo to let her attend, even though she had not been invited. Mahādeo was unwilling to do this, but finally consented. But Daksha treated Pārvati with great want of respect at the sacrifice, so she came home and told Mahādeo about him. When Mahādeo heard this he was filled with wrath, and untying his matted hair (*jata*) dashed it on the ground, when two powerful beings arose from it. He sent them to destroy Daksha's sacrifice and they went and destroyed it, and from these were descended the race of the Jāts, and they take their name from the matted locks (*jata*) of the lord Mahādeo. Another saying of the caste is that "The ancestor of the Rājpūts was Kashyap[1] and of the Jāts Siva. In the beginning these were the only two races of India."

7. The Jāts in the Central Provinces.

No detailed description of the Jāts need be attempted here, but some information which has been obtained on their customs in this Province may be recorded. They entered the Hoshangābād District, Sir C. Elliot states,[2] in the eighteenth century, and came originally from Bharatpur (Bhurtpur), but halted in Mārwār on the way. "They are the best cultivators in the District after the Pardeshi Kurmis, and though they confine themselves to ordinary crops they are very laborious, and the tilth of their fields is pleasant to look on." For the purposes of marriage the caste is divided into exogamous sections in the usual manner. The bulk of the section-names cannot be explained, being probably corrupted forms of the names of villages, but it is noticeable that several pairs of them are considered to be related so that their members cannot intermarry. Thus no marriages can take place between the Golia and Gwalwa, the Choyala and Sārana, the Bhukar and Bhāri, and the Lathial and Lālar sections, as each pair is considered to be descended from a common ancestor.

8. Marriage customs.

A man may not take a wife either from his own section or that of his mother or his grandmother, nor from those of the husbands of his father's sisters. For a Jāt wedding a square enclosure is marked out with pegs, and a thread is wound seven times round the pegs touching the ground, and covered over with rice or wheat so that it may not be burnt. The enclosure is known as Chaonri, and inside it the *hom* or fire sacrifice is performed with butter,

[1] Kashyap was a Rīshi or saint, but he may probably have developed into an eponymous hero from Kachhap, a tortoise.

[2] *Hoshangābād Settlement Report*, p. 62.

barley, sesamum, sugar and saffron placed on the top of a heap of wheat-flour. After the sacrifice the bride and bridegroom walk seven times round the Chaonri with their right hands inwards. After this tufts of cotton are thrown over the bodies of the bridegroom and bride and they have to pick it off each other, the one who finishes first being considered the winner. This is apparently a symbolical imitation of the agricultural operation of cotton-picking. The remarriage of widows is permitted, the ceremony being usually performed on a Saturday. A bachelor who is to marry a widow must first walk seven times round a pīpal tree. Contrary to the usual custom, a widow is forbidden to espouse her deceased husband's younger brother or any of his relations within three degrees of consanguinity.

9. Funeral rites.

The dead are burnt, with the exception of children under seven whose bodies are buried. After the death of a married man his widow walks round his body seven times with her left hand inwards, or in the reverse direction to the perambulation of the Chaonri at marriage. This ceremony is therefore, as it were, a sort of undoing of the marriage. The women wear lac or ivory bangles, and the widow breaks a few of these when the corpse of her husband is lifted up to be carried outside the house. She breaks the remaining ones on the twelfth day after the death and throws them on the *chūlha* or earthen hearth.

10. The Paida ceremony.

An important occasion for display among the Jāts is known as the Paida ceremony. This is sometimes performed by wealthy families when the head of the household or his wife dies or a daughter is married. They get a long pole of teakwood and plant it in the ground so that it stands some forty feet high. Before being raised the pole is worshipped with offerings of milk; a cart-wheel is tied to the upper end and it is then pulled erect with ropes, and if any difficulty is experienced the celebrant believes himself to be in fault and gives away some cows in charity. On the axle of the cart-wheel is secured a brass pot called *kaseri*, containing wheat and money, with a cloth tied over the mouth. The pole is left standing for three days, and during this time the celebrant feasts the Bhāts or genealogists of the caste and all the caste-fellows from his own and the surrounding villages. If the occasion of the ceremony be a death, male and female calves are taken and their marriage is performed; oil and turmeric are rubbed on their bodies, and they are led seven times round the high pole. The heifer is then given to a Brāhman, and the male, being first branded on one flank with a figure of a trident and on the other with a representation of the sun and moon, is set at liberty for life, and no Hindu will injure it. This last practice is, however, falling into desuetude, owing to the injury which such animals inflict on the crops. A Jāt who performs the Paida ceremony obtains great consideration in the community, and his opinion is given weight in caste disputes. A similar liberality is observed in other ways by wealthy men; thus one rich proprietor in Hoshangābād, whose son was to be married, gave a feast to all the residents of every village through which the wedding procession passed on its way to the bride's house. Another presented each of his wedding guests with new cloth to the value of ten or twelve rupees, and as in the case of a prominent family the number of guests may be a thousand or more, the cost of such liberality can be easily realised. Similarly Colonel Tod states that on the occasion of their weddings the Jāts of Bikaner even blocked up the highways to obtain visitors, whose numbers formed the measure of the liberality and munificence of the donor of the fête. Indeed, the desire for the social distinction which accrues to generous hosts on such occasions has proved to be the undoing of many a once notable family.

11. Customs at birth.

If a woman is barren, she is taken to the meeting of the boundaries of three villages and bathed there. On the birth of a boy a brass dish is hammered to announce the event, but on that of a girl only a winnowing-fan. The navel-string is buried in the lying-in room. When the newborn child is a few days old, it is taken out of doors and made to bow to the sun. When a man proposes to adopt a son the caste-fellows are invited, and in their presence the boy is seated in his lap, while music is played and songs are sung by the women. Each of the guests then comes up and presents the boy with a cocoanut, while sugar is distributed and a feast is afterwards given.

12. Religion. The favourite deity of the caste is Siva or Mahādeo, whom they consider to be their ultimate ancestor. On the festival of Shivrātri (Siva's night) they observe a total fast, and pass the whole day and night singing songs in honour of the god, while offerings of *bel*[1] leaves, flowers, rice and sandalwood are made on the following morning. In Hoshangābād the caste have two minor deities, Rāmji Deo and Bairam Deo, who are presumably the spirits of defunct warriors. These are worshipped on the eleventh day of every month, and many Jāts wear an impression of their images on a piece of gold or silver round the neck. On the Dasahra festival the caste worship their swords and horses in memory of their soldier ancestors, and they revere their implements of husbandry on the Akshaya Tritiya of Baisākh (June), the commencement of the agricultural year, while each cultivator does the same on the days that he completes the sowing of his rain crops and winter crops.

13. Social customs. The caste employ Brāhmans for the performance of their ceremonies, and also as their *gurus* or spiritual preceptors. They eat flesh and drink liquor in the Central Provinces, but in Hoshangābād they do not consume either birds or fish; and when they eat mutton or the flesh of the wild pig, they do this only outside the house, in order not to offend their women, who will not eat flesh. In Hoshangābād the Jāts, like other immigrants from Mārwār, commonly wear their hair long and keep the face unshaven, and this gives them rather a wild and *farouche* appearance among the neatly shorn Hindus of the Nerbudda Valley.[2] They are of light complexion, the difference in shade between the Jāts and ordinary residents in the locality being apparent to the casual observer. Their women are fond of the hollow anklets known as *bora*, which contain small balls or pebbles, and tinkle as they walk. Girls are tattooed before marriage, and while the operation is being carried out the women of the caste collect and sing songs to divert the sufferer's attention from the pain. The men have *pagris* or turbans made of many little strings of twisted cloth, which come down over the ears. If a man kills a cow or a squirrel, he must stay outside the village for five weeks and nobody looks upon his

[1] *Aegle marmelos.*

[2] *Hoshangābād Settlement Report, loc. cit.*

face. After this he should go and bathe in the Ganges, but if he is too poor the Nerbudda may be substituted for it with the permission of the caste committee. The penalty for killing a cat is almost as severe, but to slay a dog involves no sin. If a man who has committed a murder escapes conviction but his guilt is known to the caste, it is absolutely incumbent on him to go and bathe in the Ganges and be purified there, having his head and face shaved. After this he may be readmitted to caste intercourse. The caste observe some curious rules or taboos: they never drink the milk of a black cow; their women do not have their noses bored for nose-rings, but if a woman loses several children she will have the nose bored of the next one which is born; women never wear glass bangles, but have them made of ivory or lac and clay; they never wear the *bāzuband* or armlet with bars crossed on hinges which can be pulled in or out, but instead of it the *kara* or rigid bangle; and the caste never keep a basil plant in the house for worship, though they may revere it outside the house. As the basil is the emblem of Vishnu, and the Jāts consider themselves to be descended from Siva, they would naturally not be inclined to pay any special respect to the plant.

14. Occupation.

The Jāts are good cultivators, and at the thirty years' settlement (1865) several members of the caste held considerable estates; but a number of these have now been lost, owing probably to extravagance of living. In Saugor the Jāts are commonly employed as masons or navvies.

JHĀDI TELENGA

LIST OF PARAGRAPHS

1. General notice.

Jhādi Telenga.[1]—A small caste in the Bastar State who appear to be a mixture of Gonds and the lower Telugu castes, the name meaning 'The jungly Telugus.' Those living in the open country are called Māndar Telengas. In the census of 1901 these Telengas were wrongly classified under the Balji or Balija caste. They numbered about 5000 persons. The caste have three divisions according to their comparative purity of descent, which are named Purāit, Surāit and Pohni. The son of a Purāit by a woman of different caste will be a Surāit, and the son of a Surāit by such a woman will be a Pohni. Such alliances are now, however, infrequent, and most of the Telengas in Bastar belong to the Purāit or legitimate group. A Pohni will take cooked food from the two higher groups and a Surāit from a Purāit. The last will take water from the two lower groups, but not food.

2. Exogamous divisions.

For the purposes of marriage the caste is divided into the usual exogamous septs, and these are further arranged in two groups. The first group contains the following septs: Kudmulwādu, from *kudmul*, a preparation of rice; Kolmulwādu, from *kolmul*, a treasure-pit; Lingawādu, from the *linga* emblem; and Nāgulwādu, a ploughman. The second group contains the following septs: Kodamajjiwādu,

[1] This article is entirely based on an account of the caste furnished by Rai Bahādur Panda Baijnāth, Superintendent, Bastar State.

a hunter and trapper of animals; Wargaiwādu, one who makes ropes from wood-fibre; Paspulwādu, one who prepares turmeric; Pankiwādu, one who distributes cooked food; Bhandāriwādu, a rich man; and one or two others. The rule is that no man or woman of a sept belonging to the first group should marry in any other sept of that group, but always from some sept of the other. This, therefore, appears to be a relic of the classificatory system of marriage, which obtains among the Australian aborigines. The rule is now, however, sometimes violated. The caste say that their ancestors came from Warangal with the ruling family of Bastar.

3. Admission of outsiders.

They will admit Brāhmans, Rājpūts and Halbas into the community. If a man of any of these castes has a child by a Telenga woman, this child will be considered to belong to the same group of the Jhādi Telengas as its mother. If a man of lower caste, such as Rāwat, Dhākar, Jangam, Kumhār or Kalār has such a child it will be admitted into the next lower group than that to which the mother belonged. Thus the child of a Purāit woman by one of these castes will become a Surāit. A Telenga woman having a child by a Gond, Sunār, Lohār or Mehra man is put out of caste.

4. Marriage.

A girl cannot be properly married unless the ceremony is performed before she arrives at puberty. After this she can only be married by an abridged rite, which consists of rubbing her with oil and turmeric, investing her with glass bangles and a new cloth, and giving a feast to the caste. In such a case the bridegroom first goes through a sham marriage with the branch of a mahua tree. The boy's father looks out for a girl, and the most suitable match is considered to be his sister's daughter. Before giving away his daughter he must ask his wife's brother and his own sister whether they want her for one of their sons. When setting out to make a proposal they take the omens from a bird called Usi. The best omen is to hear this bird's call on both sides of them as they go into the jungle. When asking for the girl the envoys say to her father, 'You have got rice and pulse; give them to us for our friend's son.' The wedding should be held on a Monday or Thursday, and the bridegroom should arrive at the bride's village on a Sunday, Tuesday, Wednesday or Friday. The sacred post in the centre of the marriage-shed must be of the mahua[1] tree, which is no doubt held sacred by these people, as by the Gonds, because spirituous liquor is made from its fruit. A widow must mourn her husband for a month, and can then marry again. But she may not marry her late husband's brother, nor his first cousin, nor any member of her father's sept. Divorce is allowed, but no man will divorce his wife unless she leaves him of her own accord or is known to be intriguing with a man of lower caste.

5. Religion. Each sept has a deity of its own who is usually some local god symbolised by a wooden post or a stone. Instances of these are Kondrāj of Santoshpur represented by a wooden pillar carved into circular form at the top; Chikat Rāj of Bijāpur by two bamboos six feet in length leaning against a wall; Kaunam Rāj of Gongla by a stone image, and at fairs by a bamboo with peacock's feathers tied at the top. They offer incense, rice and a fowl to their ancestors in their own houses in Chait (March) at the new year, and at the festival of the new rice in Bhādon (August). At the sowing festival they go out hunting, and those who return empty-handed think they will have ill-luck. Each tenant also worships the earth-goddess, whose image is then decorated with flowers and vermilion. He brings a goat, and rice is placed before it at her shrine. If the animal eats the sacrifice is held to be accepted, but if not it is returned to the owner, and it is thought that some misfortune will befall him. The heads of all the goats offered are taken by the priest and the bodies returned to the worshippers to be consumed at a feast. Each village has also its tutelary god, having a hut to himself. Inside this a post of mahua wood is fixed in the ground and roughly squared, and a peg is driven into it at the top. The god is represented by another bamboo peg about two inches long, which is first worshipped in front of the post and then suspended from it in a receptacle. In each village the smallpox goddess is also present in the form of a stone, either with or without a hut over it. A Jangam or devotee of the Lingāyat sect is usually the caste priest, and at a funeral he follows the

[1] *Bassia latifolia.*

corpse ringing his bell. If a man is put out of caste through getting maggots in a wound or being beaten by a shoe, he must be purified by the Jangam. The latter rubs some ashes on his own body and places them in the offender's mouth, and gives him to drink some water from his own *lota* in place of water from a sacred river. For this the offender pays a fee of five rupees and a calf to the Jangam and must also give a feast to the caste. The dead are either buried or burnt, the head being placed to the east. The eldest son has his head and face shaved on the death of the father of the family, and the youngest on that of the mother.

6. Names.

A child is named on the seventh or eighth day after birth by the old women. If it is much given to crying they consider the name unsuitable and change it, repeating those of deceased relatives. When the child stops crying at the mention of a particular name, they consider that the relative mentioned has been born again in the child and name it after him. Often the name of the sept is combined with the personal name as Lingam-Lachha, Lingam-Kachchi, Pānki-Samāya, Pānki-Ganglu, Pānki-Buchcham, Nāgul-Sama, Nāgul-Mutta.

7. Magical devices.

When a man wishes to destroy an enemy he makes an image of him with earth and offers a pig and goat to the family god, praying for the enemy's destruction. Then the operator takes a frog or a tree-lizard which has been kept ready and breaks all its limbs, thinking that the limbs of his enemy will similarly be broken and that the man will die. Or he takes some grains of *kossa*, a small millet, and proceeds to a *sāj*[1] or mahua tree. A pigeon is offered to the tree and to the family god, and both are asked to destroy the foe. The man then ascends the tree, and muttering incantations throws the grains in the direction of his enemy thinking that they will enter his body and destroy him. To counteract these devices a man who thinks himself bewitched calls in the aid of a wizard, who sucks out of his body the grains or other evil things which have been caused to enter it as shown above. Occasionally a man will promise a human sacrifice to his god. For this he must get

[1] *Boswellia serrata.*

some hair or a piece of cloth belonging to somebody else and wash it in water in the name of the god, who may then kill the owner of the hair or cloth and thus obtain the sacrifice. Or the sacrificer may pick a quarrel and assault the other person so as to draw blood from him. He picks up a drop or two of the blood and offers it to the deity with the same end in view.

8. Occupation. The caste are cultivators and farmservants, and are, as a rule, very poor, living from hand to mouth. They practise shifting cultivation and are too lazy to grow the more valuable crops. They eat grain twice a day during the four months from October to January only, and at other times eke out their scanty provision with edible roots and leaves, and hunt and fish in the forest like the Muria and Māria Gonds.

JOGI

[*Bibliography*: Sir E. Maclagan's *Punjab Census Report* (1891); Mr. Crooke's *Tribes and Castes*, articles Jogi, Kānphata and Aghorpanthi; Mr. Kitts' *Berār Census Report* (1881); Professor Oman's *Mystics, Ascetics and Saints of India* (London: T. Fisher Unwin).]

LIST OF PARAGRAPHS

Jogi, Yogi.—The well-known order of religious mendicants and devotees of Siva. The Jogi or Yogi, properly so called, is a follower of the Yoga system of philosophy founded by Pātanjali, the main characteristics of which are a belief in the power of man over nature by means of austerities and the occult influences of the will. The idea is that one who has obtained complete control over himself, and entirely subdued all fleshly desires, acquires such potency of mind and will that he can influence the forces of nature at his pleasure. The Yoga philosophy has indeed so much substratum of truth that a man who has complete control of himself has the strongest will, and hence the most power to influence others, and an exaggerated idea of this power is no doubt fostered by the display of mesmeric control and similar phenomena. The fact that the influence which can be exerted over other human beings through their minds in no way extends to the physical phenomena of inanimate nature is obvious to us, but was by no means so to the uneducated 1. The Yoga philosophy.

Hindus, who have no clear conceptions of the terms mental and physical, animate and inanimate, nor of the ideas connoted by them. To them all nature was animate, and all its phenomena the results of the actions of sentient beings, and hence it was not difficult for them to suppose that men could influence the proceedings of such beings. And it is a matter of common knowledge that savage peoples believe their magicians to be capable of producing rain and fine weather, and even of controlling the course of the sun.[1] The Hindu sacred books indeed contain numerous instances of ascetics who by their austerities acquired such powers as to compel the highest gods themselves to obedience.

2. Abstraction of the senses or auto-hypnotism.

The term Yoga is held to mean unity or communion with God, and the Yogi by virtue of his painful discipline and mental and physical exercises considered himself divine. "The adept acquires the knowledge of everything past and future, remote or hidden; he divines the thoughts of others, gains the strength of an elephant, the courage of a lion, and the swiftness of the wind; flies into the air, floats in the water, and dives into the earth, contemplates all worlds at one glance and performs many strange things."[2]

The following excellent instance of the pretensions of the Yogis is given by Professor Oman:[3] "Wolff went also with Mr. Wilson to see one of the celebrated Yogis who was lying in the sun in the street, the nails of whose hands were grown into his cheeks and a bird's nest upon his head. Wolff asked him, 'How can one obtain the knowledge of God?' He replied, 'Do not ask me questions; you may look at me, for I am God.'

"It is certainly not easy at the present day," Professor Oman states,[4] "for the western mind to enter into the spirit of the so-called Yoga philosophy; but the student of religious opinions is aware that in the early centuries of our era the Gnostics, Manichæans and Neo-Platonists derived their peculiar tenets and practices from the *Yoga-vidya* of India, and that at a later date the *Sufi* philosophy of Persia drew its most remarkable ideas from the same source.[5] The

[1] This has been fully demonstrated by Sir J. G. Frazer in *The Golden Bough*.

[2] Colebrooke's *Essays*.

[3] Quoting from Dr. George Smith's *Life of Dr. Wilson*, p. 74.

[4] *Ibidem*, pp. 13-15.

[5] Weber's *Indian Literature*, p. 239.

Bemrose. Collo., Derby.

JOGI MENDICANTS OF THE KANPHATA SECT

great historian of the Roman Empire refers to the subject in the following passage: "The Fakīrs of India and the monks of the Oriental Church, were alike persuaded that in total abstraction of the faculties of the mind and body, the pure spirit may ascend to the enjoyment and vision of the Deity. The opinion and practice of the monasteries of Mount Athos will be best represented in the words of an abbot, who flourished in the eleventh century: 'When thou art alone in thy cell,' says the ascetic teacher, 'Shut thy door, and seat thyself in a corner, raise thy mind above all things vain and transitory, recline thy beard and chin on thy breast, turn thine eyes and thy thoughts towards the middle of the belly, the region of the navel, and search the place of the heart, the seat of the soul. At first all will be dark and comfortless; but if you persevere day and night, you will feel an ineffable joy; and no sooner has the soul discovered the place of the heart, than it is involved in a mystic and ethereal light.' This light, the production of a distempered fancy, the creature of an empty stomach and an empty brain, was adored by the Quietists as the pure and perfect essence of God Himself."[1]

"Without entering into unnecessary details, many of which are simply disgusting, I shall quote, as samples, a few of the rules of practice required to be followed by the would-be Yogi in order to induce a state of Samādhi—hypnotism or trance—which is the condition or state in which the Yogi is to enjoy the promised privileges of Yoga. The extracts are from a treatise on the Yoga philosophy by Assistant Surgeon Nobin Chander Pāl."[2]

"Place the left foot upon the right thigh, and the right foot upon the left thigh; hold with the right hand the right great toe and with the left hand the left great toe (the hands coming from behind the back and crossing each other); rest the chin on the interclavicular space, and fix the sight on the tip of the nose.

. . . .

"Inspire through the left nostril, fill the stomach with the inspired air by the act of deglutition, suspend the

[1] Gibbon's *Decline and Fall of the Roman Empire*, chap. lxiii.
[2] Republished in the *Theosophist*.

breath, and expire through the right nostril. Next inspire through the right nostril, swallow the inspired air, suspend the breath, and finally expire through the left nostril.

. . . . . .

"Be seated in a tranquil posture, and fix your sight on the tip of the nose for the space of ten minutes.

"Close the ears with the middle fingers, incline the head a little to the right side and listen with each ear attentively to the sound produced by the other ear, for the space of ten minutes.

"Pronounce inaudibly twelve thousand times the mystic syllable Om, and meditate upon it daily after deep inspirations.

"After a few forcible inspirations swallow the tongue, and thereby suspend the breath and deglutate the saliva for two hours.

"Listen to the sounds within the right ear abstractedly for two hours, with the left ear.

. . . . . .

"Repeat the mystic syllable Om 20,736,000 times in silence and meditate upon it.

"Suspend the respiratory movements for the period of twelve days, and you will be in a state of Samādhi."

Another account of a similar procedure is given by Buchanan:[1] "Those who pretend to be eminent saints perform the ceremony called Yoga, described in the Tantras. In the accomplishment of this, by shutting what are called the nine passages (*dwāra*, lit. doors) of the body, the votary is supposed to distribute the breath into the different parts of the body, and thus to obtain the beatific vision of various gods. It is only persons who abstain from the indulgence of concupiscence that can pretend to perform this ceremony, which during the whole time that the breath can be held in the proper place excites an ecstasy equal to whatever woman can bestow on man."

3. Breathing through either nostril.

It is clear that the effect of some of the above practices is designed to produce a state of mind resembling the hypnotic trance. The Yogis attach much importance to the effect of breathing through one or the other nostril, and this

[1] *Eastern India*, ii. p. 756.

is also the case with Hindus generally, as various rules concerning it are prescribed for the daily prayers of Brāhmans. To have both nostrils free and be breathing through them at the same time is not good, and one should not begin any business in this condition. If one is breathing only through the right nostril and the left is closed, the condition is propitious for the following actions: To eat and drink, as digestion will be quick; to fight; to bathe; to study and read; to ride on a horse; to work at one's livelihood. A sick man should take medicine when he is breathing through his right nostril. To be breathing only through the left nostril is propitious for the following undertakings: To lay the foundations of a house and to take up residence in a new house; to put on new clothes; to sow seed; to do service or found a village; to make any purchase. The Jogis practise the art of breathing in this manner by stopping up their right and left nostril alternately with cotton-wool and breathing only through the other. If a man comes to a Brāhman to ask him whether some business or undertaking will succeed, the Brāhman breathes through his nostrils on to his hand; if the breath comes through the right nostril the omen is favourable and the answer yes; if through the left nostril the omen is unfavourable and the answer no.

4. Self-torture of the Jogis.

The following account of the austerities of the Jogis during the Mughal period is given by Bernier:[1] "Among the vast number and endless variety of Fakīrs or Dervishes, and holy men or Gentile hypocrites of the Indies, many live in a sort of convent, governed by superiors, where vows of chastity, poverty, and submission are made. So strange is the life led by these votaries that I doubt whether my description of it will be credited. I allude particularly to the people called 'Jogis,' a name which signifies 'United to God.' Numbers are seen day and night, seated or lying on ashes, entirely naked; frequently under the large trees near *talābs* or tanks of water, or in the galleries round the Deuras or idol temples. Some have hair hanging down to the calf of the leg, twisted and entangled into knots, like the coats of our shaggy dogs. I have seen several who hold one, and some who hold both arms perpetually lifted above the head,

[1] *Travels in the Mughal Empire*, Constable's edition, p. 316.

the nails of their hands being twisted and longer than half my little finger, with which I measured them. Their arms are as small and thin as the arms of persons who die in a decline, because in so forced and unnatural a position they receive not sufficient nourishment, nor can they be lowered so as to supply the mouth with food, the muscles having become contracted, and the articulations dry and stiff. Novices wait upon these fanatics and pay them the utmost respect, as persons endowed with extraordinary sanctity. No fury in the infernal regions can be conceived more horrible than the Jogis, with their naked and black skin, long hair, spindle arms, long twisted nails, and fixed in the posture which I have mentioned.

"I have often met, generally in the territory of some Rāja, bands of these naked Fakīrs, hideous to behold. Some have their arms lifted up in the manner just described; the frightful hair of others either hung loosely or was tied and twisted round their heads; some carried a club like the Hercules, others had a dry and rough tiger-skin thrown over their shoulders. In this trim I have seen them shamelessly walk stark naked through a large town, men, women, and girls looking at them without any more emotion than may be created when a hermit passes through our streets. Females would often bring them alms with much devotion, doubtless believing that they were holy personages, more chaste and discreet than other men.

"Several of these Fakīrs undertake long pilgrimages not only naked but laden with heavy iron chains, such as are put about the legs of elephants. I have seen others who, in consequence of a particular vow, stood upright during seven or eight days without once sitting or lying down, and without any other support than might be afforded by leaning forward against a cord for a few hours in the night; their legs in the meantime were swollen to the size of their thighs. Others, again, I have observed standing steadily, whole hours together, upon their hands, the head down and the feet in the air. I might proceed to enumerate various other positions in which these unhappy men place their body, many of them so difficult and painful that they could not be imitated by our tumblers; and all this, let it be recollected, is performed from an assumed feeling of piety, of which there is not so much as the shadow in any part of the Indies."

The forest ascetics were credited with prophetic powers, and were resorted to by Hindu princes to obtain omens and oracles on the brink of any important undertaking. This custom is noticed by Colonel Tod in the following passage describing the foundation of Jodhpur:[1] "Like the Druids of the cells, the *vana-perist* Jogis, from the glades of the forest (*vana*) or recess in the rocks (*gopha*), issue their oracles to those whom chance or design may conduct to their solitary dwellings. It is not surprising that the mandates of such beings prove compulsory on the superstitious Rājpūt; we do not mean those squalid ascetics who wander about India and are objects disgusting to the eye, but the genuine Jogi, he who, as the term imports, mortifies the flesh, till the wants of humanity are restricted merely to what suffices to unite matter with spirit, who had studied and comprehended the mystic works and pored over the systems of philosophy, until the full influence of *Maia* (illusion) has perhaps unsettled his understanding; or whom the rules of his sect have condemned to penance and solitude; a penance so severe that we remain astonished at the perversity of reason which can submit to it. We have seen one of these objects, self-condemned never to lie down during forty years, and there remained but three to complete the term. He had travelled much, was intelligent and learned, but, far from having contracted the moroseness of the recluse, there was a benignity of mien and a suavity and simplicity of manner in him quite enchanting. He talked of his penance with no vainglory and of its approaching term without any sensation. The resting position of this Druid (*vana-perist*) was by means of a rope suspended from the bough of a tree in the manner of a swing, having a cross-bar, on which he reclined. The first years of this penance, he says, were dreadfully painful; swollen limbs affected him to that degree that he expected death, but this impression had long since worn off. To these, the Druids of India, the prince and the chieftain would resort for instruction. Such was the ascetic who re-

5. Resort to them for oracles.

[1] *Rājasthān*, ii. p. 19.

commended Joda to erect his castle of Jodhpur on the 'Hill of Strife' (Jodagīr), a projecting elevation of the same range on which Mundore was placed, and about four miles south of it."

6. Divisions of the order. About 15,000 Jogis were returned from the Central Provinces in 1911. They are said to be divided into twelve Panths or orders, each of which venerates one of the twelve disciples of Gorakhnāth. But, as a rule, they do not know the names of the Panths. Their main divisions are the Kanphata and Aughar Jogis. The Kanphatas,[1] as the name denotes, pierce their ears and wear in them large rings (*mundra*), generally of wood, stone or glass; the ears of a novice are pierced by the Guru, who gets a fee of Rs. 1-4. The earring must thereafter always be worn, and should it be broken must be replaced temporarily by a model in cloth before food is taken. If after the ring has been inserted the ear tears apart, they say that the man has become useless, and in former times he was buried alive. Now he is put out of caste, and no tomb is erected over him when he dies. It is said that a man cannot become a Kanphata all at once, but must first serve an apprenticeship of twelve years as an Aughar, and then if his Guru is satisfied he will be initiated as a Kanphata. The elect among the Kanphatas are known as Darshani. These do not go about begging, but remain in the forest in a cave or other abode, and the other Jogis go there and pay their respects; this is called *darshan*, the term used for visiting a temple and worshipping the idol. These men only have cooked food when their disciples bring it to them, otherwise they live on fruits and roots. The Aughars do not pierce their ears, but have a string of black sheep's wool round the neck to which is suspended a wooden whistle called *nadh*; this is blown morning and evening and before meals.[2] The names of the Kanphatas end in Nāth and those of the Aughars in Dās.

7. Hair and clothes. When a novice is initiated all the hair of his head is shaved, including the scalp-lock. If the Ganges is at hand the Guru throws the hair into the Ganges, giving a great feast to celebrate the occasion; otherwise he keeps the hair in his wallet until he and his disciple reach the Ganges and

[1] Maclagan, *l.c.* p. 115. [2] *Ibidem*, *l.c.*

Bemrose, Collo., Derby.

JOGI MUSICIANS WITH SĀRANGI OR FIDDLE.

then throws it into the river and gives the feast. After this the Jogi lets all his hair grow until he comes to some great shrine, when he shaves it off clean and gives it as an offering to the god. The Jogis wear clothes coloured with red ochre like the Jangams, Sanniāsis and all the Sivite orders. The reddish colour perhaps symbolises blood and may denote that the wearers still sacrifice flesh and consume it. The Vaishnavite orders usually wear white clothes, and hence the Jogis call themselves Lāl Pādris (red priests), and they call the Vaishnava mendicants Sīta Pādris, apparently because Sīta is the consort of Rāma, the incarnation of Vishnu. When a Jogi is initiated the Guru gives him a single bead of *rudrāksha* wood which he wears on a string round his neck. He is not branded, but afterwards, if he visits the temple of Dwārka in Gujarāt, he is branded with the mark of the conch-shell on the arm; or if he goes on pilgrimage to the shrine of Badri-Nārāyan in the Himālayas he is branded on the chest. Copper bangles are brought from Badri-Nārāyan and iron ones from the shrine of Kedārnāth. A necklace of small white stones, like juāri-seeds, is obtained from the temple of Hinglāj in the territories of the Jām of Lāsbela in Beluchistān. During his twelve years' period as a Brahmachari or acolyte, a Jogi will make either one or three *parikramas* of the Nerbudda; that is, he walks from the mouth at Broach to the source at Amarkantak on one side of the river and back again on the other side, the journey usually occupying about three years. During each journey he lets his hair grow and at the end of it makes an offering of all except the *choti* or scalp-lock to the river. Even as a full Jogi he still retains the scalp-lock, and this is not finally shaved off until he turns into a Sanniāsi or forest recluse. Other Jogis, however, do not merely keep the scalp-lock but let their hair grow, plaiting it with ropes of black wool over their heads into what is called the *jata*, that is an imitation of Siva's matted locks.[1]

8. Burial.

The Jogis are buried sitting cross-legged with the face to the north in a tomb which has a recess like those of Muhammadans. A gourd full of milk and some bread in a wallet, a crutch and one or two earthen vessels are placed in

[1] Maclagan, *l.c.*

the grave for the sustenance of the soul. Salt is put on the body and a ball of wheat-flour is laid on the breast of the corpse and then deposited on the top of the grave.

9. Festivals. The Jogis worship Siva, and their principal festival is the Shivrātri, when they stay awake all night and sing songs in honour of Gorakhnāth, the founder of their order. On the Nāg-Panchmi day they venerate the cobra and they take about snakes and exhibit them.

10. Caste sub-divisions. A large proportion of the Jogis have now developed into a caste, and these marry and have families. They are divided into subcastes according to the different professions they have adopted. Thus the Barwa or Gārpagāri Jogis ward off hailstorms from the standing crops; the Manihāri are pedlars and travel about to bazārs selling various small articles; the Rītha Bikanāth prepare and sell soap-nut for washing clothes; the Patbīna make hempen thread and gunny-bags for carrying grain on bullocks; and the Ladaimār hunt jackals and sell and eat their flesh. These Jogis rank as a low Hindu caste of the menial group. No good Hindu caste will take food or water from them, while they will accept cooked food from members of any caste of respectable position, as Kurmis, Kunbis or Mālis. A person belonging to any such caste can also be admitted into the Jogi community. Their social customs resemble those of the cultivating castes of the locality. They permit widow-marriage and divorce and employ Brāhmans for their ceremonies, with the exception of the Kanphatas, who have priests of their own order.

11. Begging. Begging is the traditional occupation of the Jogis, but they have now adopted many others. The Kanphatas beg and sell a woollen string amulet (*ganda*), which is put round the necks of children to protect them from the evil eye. They beg only from Hindus and use the cry '*Alakh*,' 'The invisible one.'[1] The Nandia Jogis lead about with them a deformed ox, an animal with five legs or some other malformation. He is decorated with ochre-coloured rags and cowrie shells. They call him Nandi or the bull on which Mahādeo rides, and receive gifts of grain from pious Hindus, half of which they put into their wallet and give the other

[1] Crooke's *Tribes and Castes*, art. Kanphata.

half to the animal. They usually carry on a more profitable business than other classes of beggars. The ox is trained to give a blessing to the benevolent by shaking its head and raising its leg when its master receives a gift.[1] Some of the Jogis of this class carry about with them a brush of peacock's feathers which they wave over the heads of children afflicted with the evil eye or of sick persons, muttering texts. This performance is known as *jhārna* (sweeping), and is the commonest method of casting out evil spirits.

Many Jogis have also adopted secular occupations, as has already been seen. Of these the principal are the Manihāri Jogis or pedlars, who retail small hand-mirrors, spangles, dyeing-powders, coral beads and imitation jewellery, pens, pencils, and other small articles of stationery. They also bring pearls and coral from Bombay and sell them in the villages. The Gārpagāris, who protect the crops from hailstorms, have now become a distinct caste and are the subject of a separate article. Others make a living by juggling and conjuring, and in Saugor some Jogis perform the three-card trick in the village markets, employing a confederate who advises customers to pick out the wrong card. They also play the English game of Sandown, which is known as 'Animur,' from the practice of calling out 'Any more' as a warning to backers to place their money on the board before beginning to turn the fish. **12. Other occupations.**

These people also deal in ornaments of base metal and practise other swindles. One of their tricks is to drop a ring or ornament of counterfeit gold on the road. Then they watch until a stranger picks it up and one of them goes up to him and says, "I saw you pick up that gold ring, it belongs to so-and-so, but if you will make it worth my while I will say nothing about it." The finder is thus often deluded into giving him some hush-money and the Jogis decamp with this, having incurred no risk in connection with the spurious metal. They also pretend to be able to convert silver and other metals into gold. They ingratiate themselves with the women, sometimes of a number of households in one village or town, giving at first small quantities of gold in exchange for silver, and binding them to **13. Swindling practices.**

[1] Crooke's *Tribes and Castes*, art. Jogi.

secrecy. Then each is told to give them all the ornaments which she desires to be converted on the same night, and having collected as much as possible from their dupes the Jogis make off before morning. A very favourite device some years back was to personate some missing member of a family who had gone on a pilgrimage. Up to within a comparatively recent period a large proportion of the pilgrims who set out annually from all over India to visit the famous shrines at Benāres, Jagannāth and other places perished by the way from privation or disease, or were robbed and murdered, and never heard of again by their families. Many households in every town and village were thus in the position of having an absent member of whose fate they were uncertain. Taking advantage of this, and having obtained all the information he could pick up among the neighbours, the Jogi would suddenly appear in the character of the returned wanderer, and was often successful in keeping up the imposture for years.[1]

14. Proverbs about Jogis.

The Jogi is a familiar figure in the life of the people and there are various sayings about him:[2] *Jogi Jogi laren, khopron ka dām*, or 'When Jogis fight skulls are smashed,' that is, the skulls which some of them use as begging-cups, not their own skulls, and with the implication that they have nothing else to break; *Jogi jugat jāni nahīn, kapre range, to kya hua*, 'If the Jogi does not know his magic, what is the use of his dyeing his clothes?' *Jogi ka larka khelega, to sānp se*, or, 'If a snake-charmer's son plays, he plays with a snake.'

[1] Sleeman, *Report on the Badhaks*, pp. 332, 333.

[2] These proverbs are taken from Temple and Fallon's *Hindustāni Proverbs*.

JOSHI

LIST OF PARAGRAPHS

1. The village priest and astrologer.

Joshi, Jyotishi, Bhadri, Parsai.—The caste of village priests and astrologers. They numbered about 6000 persons in 1911, being distributed over all Districts. The Joshis are nearly all Brāhmans, but have now developed into a separate caste and marry among themselves. Their social customs resemble those of Brāhmans, and need not be described in detail. The Joshi officiates at weddings in the village, selects auspicious names for children according to the *nakshatra* or constellation of the moon under which they were born, and points out the auspicious time or *mahūrat* for all such ceremonies and for the commencement of agricultural operations. He is also sometimes in charge of the village temples. He is supported by the contributions from the villagers, and often has a plot of land rent-free from the proprietor. The social position of the Joshis is not very good, and, though Brāhmans, they are considered to rank somewhat below the cultivating castes, the Kurmis and Kunbis, by whose patronage they are supported.[1]

The Bhadris are a class of Joshis who wander about and live by begging, telling fortunes and giving omens. They avert the evil influences of the planet Saturn and accept the gifts offered to this end, which are always black, as black blankets, charcoal, *tilli* or sesamum oil, the *urad* pulse,[2] and iron. People born on Saturday or being otherwise connected with the planet are especially subject to his malign influence. The Joshi ascertains who these unfortunate persons are from their horoscopes, and neutralises the evil influence of the planet by the acceptance of the gifts already mentioned, while he sometimes also receives a buffalo or a cow. He computes by astrological calculations the depth at which water will be found when a cultivator wishes to dig a well. He also practises palmistry, classifying the whorls of the fingers into two patterns, called the Shank or conch-shell and Chakra or discus of Vishnu. The Shank is considered to be unfortunate and the Chakra fortunate. The lines on the balls of the toes and on the forehead are similarly classified. When anything has been lost or stolen the Joshi can tell from the daily *nakshatra* or mansion of the moon in which the loss or theft occurred whether the property has gone to the north, south, east or west, and within what interval it is likely to be found. The people have not nowadays much faith in his prophetic powers, and they say, "If clouds come on Friday, and the sky is black on Saturday, then the Joshi foretells that it will rain on Sunday." The Joshi's calculations are all based on the *rāshis* or signs of the zodiac through which the sun passes during the year, and the *nakshatras* or those which mark the monthly revolutions of the moon. These are given in all Hindu almanacs, and most Joshis simply work from the almanac, being quite ignorant of astronomy. Since the measurement of the sun's apparent path on the ecliptic, and the moon's orbit mapped out by the constellations are of some interest, and govern the arrangement of the Hindu calendar, it has been thought desirable to give some account of them. And in order to make this in-

[1] *Bombay Gazetteer*, vol. xxi. p. 184.

[2] *Phaseolus radiatus*.

telligible it is desirable first to recapitulate some elementary facts of astronomy.

The universe may be conceived for the purpose of understanding the sun's path among the stars as if it were a huge ball, of which looking from the earth's surface we see part of the inside with the stars marked on it, as on the inside of a dome. This imaginary inside of a ball is called the celestial sphere, and the ancients believed that it actually existed, and also, in order to account for the varying distances of the stars, supposed that there were several of them, one inside the other, and each with a number of stars fixed to it. The sun and earth may be conceived as smaller solid balls suspended inside this large one. Then looking from the surface of the earth we see the sun outlined against the inner surface of the imaginary celestial sphere. And as the earth travels round the sun in its orbit, the appearance to us is that the sun moves over the surface of the celestial sphere. The following figure will make this clear.[1] **2. The apparent path of the sun. The ecliptic or zodiac.**

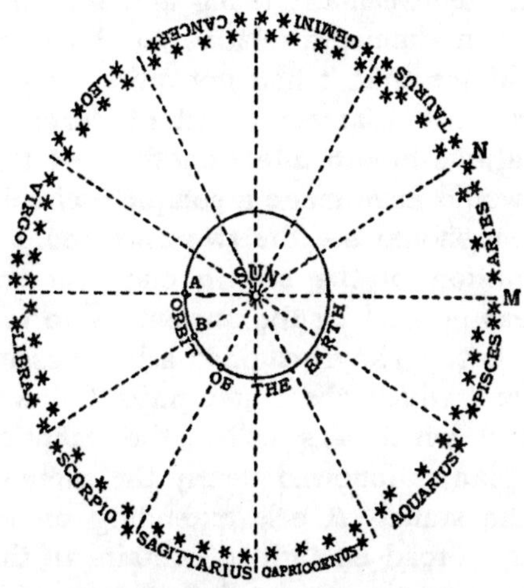

FIG. 1.—The Orbit of the Earth and the Zodiac.

Thus when the earth is at A in its orbit the sun will appear to be at M, and as the earth travels from A to B the sun will appear to move from M to N on the line of the ecliptic. It will be seen that as the earth in a year makes a

[1] Newcomb's *Astronomy for Everybody*, p. 33.

complete circuit round the sun, the sun will appear to have made a complete circuit among the stars, and have come back to its original position. This apparent movement is annual, and has nothing to do with the sun's apparent diurnal course over the sky, which is caused by the earth's daily rotation on its axis. The sun's annual path among the stars naturally cannot be observed during the day. Professor Newcomb says: "But the fact of the motion will be made very clear if, day after day, we watch some particular fixed star in the west. We shall find that it sets earlier and earlier every day; in other words, it is getting continually nearer and nearer the sun. More exactly, since the real direction of the star is unchanged, the sun seems to be approaching the star.

"If we could see the stars in the daytime all round the sun, the case would be yet clearer. We should see that if the sun and a star were together in the morning, the sun would, during the day, gradually work past the star in an easterly direction. Between the rising and setting it would move nearly its own diameter, relative to the star. Next morning we should see that it had got quite away from the star, being nearly two diameters distant from it. This motion would continue month after month. At the end of the year the sun would have made a complete circuit relative to the star, and we should see the two once more together. This apparent motion of the sun in one year round the celestial sphere was noticed by the ancients, who took much trouble to map it out. They imagined a line passing round the celestial sphere, which the sun always followed in its annual course, and which was called the ecliptic. They noticed that the planets followed nearly the same course as the sun among the stars. A belt extending on each side of the ecliptic, and broad enough to contain all the known planets, as well as the sun, was called the *zodiac*. It was divided into twelve signs, each marked by a constellation. The sun went through each sign in a month, and through all twelve signs in a year. Thus arose the familiar signs of the zodiac, which bore the same names as the constellations among which they are situated. This is not the case at present, owing to the precession of the equinoxes." It was by observing the paths of the sun and moon round the celestial sphere along the zodiac that the ancients came to be able to measure the solar and lunar months and years.

3. Inclination of the ecliptic to the equator.

As is well known, the celestial sphere is imagined to be spanned by an imaginary line called the celestial equator, which is in the same plane as the earth's equator, and as it were, a vast concentric circle. The points in the celestial sphere opposite the north and south terrestrial poles are called the north and south celestial poles, and the celestial equator is midway between these. Owing to the special form of the earth the north celestial pole is visible to us in the northern hemisphere, and marked very nearly by the pole-star, its height above the horizon being equal to the latitude of the place where the observer stands. Owing to the daily rotation of the earth the whole celestial sphere seems to revolve daily on the axis of the north and south celestial poles, carrying the sun, moon and stars with it. To this the apparent daily course of the sun and moon is due. Their course seems to us oblique, as we are north of the equator.

If the earth's axis were set vertically to the plane of its orbit round the sun, then it would follow that the plane of the equator would pass through the centre of the sun, and that the line drawn by the sun in its apparent revolution against the background of the celestial sphere would be in the same plane. That is, the sun would seem to move round a circle in the heavens in the same plane as the earth's equator, or round the celestial equator. But the earth's axis is inclined at $23\frac{1}{2}°$ to the plane of its orbit, and therefore the apparent path traced by the sun in the celestial sphere, which is the same path as the earth would really follow to an observer on the surface of the sun, is inclined at $23\frac{1}{2}°$ to the celestial equator. This is the ecliptic, and is really the line of the plane of the earth's orbit extended to cut the celestial sphere.

4. The orbits of the moon and planets.

All the planets move round the sun in orbits whose planes are slightly inclined to that of the earth, the plane of Mercury having the greatest inclination of 6°. The plane of the moon's orbit round the earth is also inclined at 5° 9′

to the ecliptic. The orbits of the moon and all the planets must necessarily intersect the plane of the earth's orbit on the ecliptic at two points, and these are called the nodes of the moon and each planet respectively. In consequence of the inclination being so slight, though the course of the moon and planets is not actually on the ecliptic, they are all so close to it that they are included in the belt of the zodiac. Thus the moon and all the planets follow almost the same apparent course on the zodiac or belt round the ecliptic in the changes of position resulting from their own and the earth's orbital movements with reference to what are called the fixed stars.

5. The signs of the zodiac. As the sun completes his circuit of the ecliptic or zodiac in the course of a year, it followed that if his course could be measured and divided into periods, these periods would form divisions of time for the year. This was what the ancients did, and it is probable that the measurement and division of time was the primary object of the science of astronomy, as apart from the natural curiosity to ascertain the movements of the sun, moon and planets, when they were looked upon as divine beings controlling the world. They divided the zodiac or the path of the sun into twelve parts, and gave to each part the name of the principal constellation situated on, or adjacent to, that section of the line of the ecliptic. When they had done this and observed the dates of the sun's entry into each sign or *rāshi*, as it is called in Hindi, they had divided the year into twelve solar months. The following are the Hindu names and meanings of the signs of the zodiac :

1. Aries.	The ram.	Mesha.
2. Taurus.	The bull.	Vrisha.
3. Gemini.	The twins.	Mithuna.
4. Cancer.	The crab.	Karkati.
5. Leo.	The lion.	Sinha.
6. Virgo.	The virgin.	Kanya.
7. Libra.	The balance.	Tūla.
8. Scorpio.	The scorpion.	Vrischika.
9. Sagittarius.	The archer.	Dhanus or Chapa.
10. Capricornus.	The goat.	Makara (said to mean a sea-monster).
11. Aquarius.	The water-bearer.	Kūmbha (a water-pot).
12. Pisces.	The fishes.	Mina.

The signs of the zodiac were nearly the same among the Greeks, Egyptians, Persians, Babylonians and Indians. They are supposed to have originated in Chaldea or Babylonia, and the fact that the constellations are indicated by nearly the same symbols renders their common origin probable. It seems likely that the existing Hindu zodiac may have been adopted from the Greeks.

6. The Sankrānts.

The solar year begins with the entrance of the sun into Mesha or Aries.[1] The day on which the sun passes into a new sign is called Sankrānt, and is to some extent observed as a holy day. But the Til Sankrānt or entry of the sun into Makara or Capricorn, which falls about the 15th January, is a special festival, because it marks approximately the commencement of the sun's northern progress and the lengthening of the days, as Christmas roughly does with us. On this day every Hindu who is able bathes in a sacred river at the hour indicated by the Joshis of the sun's entrance into the sign. Presents of til or sesamum are given to the Joshi, owing to which the day is called Til Sankrānt. People also sometimes give presents to each other.

7. The *nakshatras* or constellations of the moon's path.

The Sankrānts do not mark the commencement of the Hindu months, which are still lunar and are adjusted to the solar year by intercalation. It is probable that long before they were able to measure the sun's progress along the ecliptic the ancients had observed that of the moon, which it was much easier to do, as she is seen among the stars at night. Similarly there is little reason to doubt that the first division of time was the lunar month, which can be remarked by every one. Ancient astronomers measured the progress of the moon's path along the ecliptic and divided it into twenty-seven sections, each of which represented roughly a day's march. Each section was dis-

[1] Owing to the precession of the equinoxes, the sidereal year is not the same as the solar year, being about 20 minutes longer. That is, the sun passes a particular star a second time in a period of 365 days 6 hours and 9 minutes, while it passes the equatorial point in 365 days 5 hours 48 minutes 49 seconds, this latter period being the solar year. The difference is due to slight changes in the direction of the earth's axis, which change the position of the celestial equator and of the equinoctial point where the sun crosses it. It is not clear how the Hindus get over this difficulty, but the point does not affect the general account.

tinguished by a group of stars either on the ecliptic or so near it, either in the northern or southern hemisphere, as to be occultated by the moon or capable of being in conjunction with it or the planets. These constellations are called *nakshatras*. Naturally, some of these constellations are the same as those subsequently chosen to mark the sun's path or the signs of the zodiac. In some cases a zodiacal constellation is divided into two *nakshatras*. Like the signs, the *nakshatras* were held to represent animals or natural objects. The following is a list of them with their corresponding stars, and the object which each was supposed to represent:[1]

Nakshatra.	Constellation.	Object.	Corresponding zodiacal sign.
1. Aswini.	β and γ Arietis.	A horse's head.	Aries.
2. Bharani.	35, 39 and 41 Arietis.	Pudendum muliebre.	Aries.
3. Krittika.	Pleiades.	A knife.	Part of Taurus.
4. Rohini.	α, γ, δ, ϵ, θ Tauri (Aldebaran).	A wheeled carriage or a temple.	Taurus.
5. Mrigasiras.	λ, ϕ_1, ϕ_2, Orionis (Orion's head).	A deer's head.	
6. Ardra.	Betelgeux or α Orionis (one of Orion's arms).	A gem.	
7. Punarvasu.	Gemini or Castor and Pollux.	A house.	Gemini.
8. Pushya.	γ, δ and θ Cancri.	An arrow.	Cancer.
9. Aslesha.	δ, ϵ, η, ρ and σ Hydrae.	A wheel.	
10. Magha.	α, γ, ϵ, ζ, η and μ Leonis.	A house.	Leo.
11. Pūrva Phālguni.	δ and θ Leonis.	A couch.	Leo.
12. Uttara Phālguni.	β and 93 Leonis.	A bed.	Leo.
13. Hasta.	α, β, γ, δ and ϵ Corvi.	A hand.	
14. Chitra.	Spica (α Virginis).	A pearl.	Virgo.
15. Swāti.	Arcturus (α Boötis).	A coral bead.	

[1] The stars corresponding to the *nakshatras* and their symbols are mainly taken from Mr. L. D. Barnett's *Antiquities of India*, pp. 190, 191, compared with the list in Mr. W. Brennand's *Hindu Astronomy*, pp. 40, 42.

Nakshatra.	Constellation.	Object.	Corresponding zodiacal sign.
16. Visacha.	α, β, γ and ι Librae.	A garland.	Libra.
17. Anurādha.	β, δ and π Scorpionis.	A sacrifice or offering.	Scorpio.
18. Jyestha.	α, σ and τ Scorpionis.	An earring.	Scorpio.
19. Mula.	$\epsilon, \zeta, \eta, \theta, \iota, \kappa, \lambda, \mu, \upsilon$, Scorpionis.	A lion's tail.	Scorpio.
20. Pūrva Ashādha.	δ and ϵ Sagittarii.	A couch or an elephant's tusk.	Sagittarius.
21. Uttara Ashādha.	ζ and σ Sagittarii.	An elephant's tusk or the *singāra* nut.	Sagittarius.
22. Sravana.	α, β and γ Aquilae.	The footprint of Vishnu.	
23. Dhanishtha.	α, β, γ and δ Delphinis.	A drum.	
24. Sata-bhishaj.	λ Aquarii.	A circular jewel or a circle.	Aquarius.
25. Pūrva Bhadrapada.	α and β Pegasi.	A two-faced image.	
26. Uttara Bhadrapada.	γ Pegasi and α Andromedae.	A two-faced image or a couch.	
27. Revati.	ζ Piscium.	A tabor.	Pisces.

8. The revolution of the moon.

All the zodiacal constellations are thus included in the *nakshatras* except Capricorn, for which Aquila and Delphinis are substituted. These, as well as Hydra, are a considerable distance from the ecliptic, but may perhaps be nearer the moon's path, which, as already seen, slightly diverges from it. But this point has not been ascertained by me. The moon completes the circuit of the heavens in its orbit round the earth in a little less than a lunar month or 27 days 8 hours. As twenty-seven *nakshatras* were demarcated, it seems clear that a *nakshatra* was meant to represent the distance travelled by the moon in a day. Subsequently a twenty-eighth small *nakshatra* was formed called Abhijit, out of Uttarāshādha and Sravana, and this may have been meant to represent the fractional part of the day. The days of the lunar month have each, as a matter of fact, a *nakshatra* allotted to them, which is recorded in all Hindu almanacs, and enters largely into the Joshi's astrological calculations. It may have been the case that prior to the naming of the days of the week, the days of the lunar month were distinguished by the names of their *nakshatras*, but this could only have been among the learned. For though there was a *nakshatra* for every day of the moon's path round the ecliptic, the same days in successive months could not have the same *nakshatras* on account of what is called the synodical revolution of the moon. The light of the moon comes from the sun, and we see only that part of it which is illuminated by the sun. When the moon is between the earth and the sun, the light hemisphere is invisible to us, and there is no moon. When the moon is on the opposite side of the earth to the sun we see the whole of the illuminated hemisphere, and it is full moon. Thus in the time between one new moon and the next, the moon must proceed from its position between the earth and the sun to the same position again, and to do this it has to go somewhat more than once round the ecliptic, as is shown by the following figure.[1]

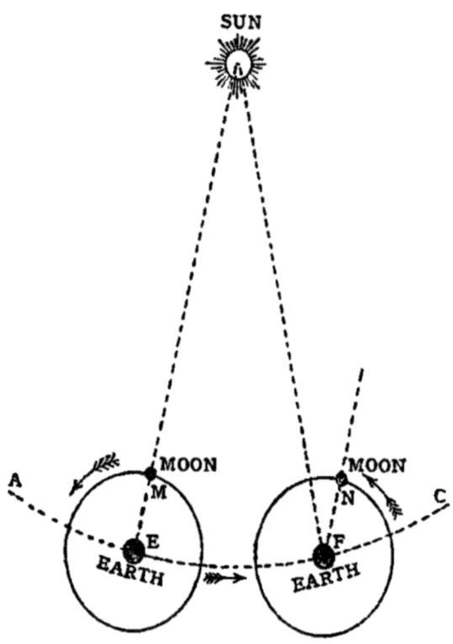

FIG. 2.—Revolution of the Moon round the Earth.

9. The days of the week. As during the moon's circuit of the earth, the earth is also travelling on its orbit, the moon will not be between the earth and the sun again on completion of its

[1] Taken from Professor Newcomb's *Astronomy for Everybody*.

orbit, but will have to traverse the further arc shown in the figure to come between the earth and the sun. When the moon has completed the circle of the ecliptic from the position ME, its position relative to the earth has become as NF and it has not yet come between the earth and the sun. Hence while the moon completes the circuit of the ecliptic[1] in 27 days 8 hours, the time from one new moon to another is 29 days 13 hours. Hence the *nakshatras* will not fall on the same days in successive lunar months, and would not be suitable as names for the days. It seems that, recognising this, the ancient astronomers had to find other names. They had the lunar fortnights of 14 or 15 days from new to full and full to new moon. Hence apparently they hit on the plan of dividing these into half and regulating the influence which the sun, moon and planets were believed to exercise over events in the world by allotting one day to each of them. They knew of five planets besides the sun and moon, and by giving a day to each of them the seven-day week was formed. The term planet signifies a wanderer, and it thus perhaps seemed suitable that they should give their names to the days which would revolve endlessly in a cycle, as they themselves did in the heavens. The names of the days are:

Etwār or Raviwār.	Sunday.	(Ravi—the sun.)
Somwār.	Monday.	(Soma—the moon.)
Mangalwār.	Tuesday.	(Mangal or Bhauma—Mars.)
Budhwār.	Wednesday.	(Buddha—Mercury.)
Brihaspatwār or Guru.	Thursday.	(Brihaspat or Guru—Jupiter.)
Shukurwār.	Friday.	(Shukra—Venus.)
Saniwār or Sanīchara.	Saturday.	(Sani—Saturn.)

The termination *vāra* means a day. The weekdays were similarly named in Rome and other countries speaking Aryan languages, and they are readily recognised in French. In English three days are named after the sun, moon and Saturn, but four, Tuesday, Wednesday, Thursday and Friday, are called after Scandinavian deities, the last three being Woden or Odin, Thor and Freya. I do not know whether these were identified with the planets. It is supposed that the Hindus obtained the seven-day week from the Greeks.[2]

[1] The moon's orbit is really an ellipse like that of the earth and all the planets.

[2] Barnett, *op. cit.* p. 190.

10. The lunar year. Four seven-day weeks were within a day and a fraction of the lunar month, which was the nearest that could be got. The first method of measuring the year would be by twelve lunar months, which would bring it back nearly to the same period. But as the lunar month is 29 days 13 hours, twelve months would be 354 days 12 hours, or nearly eleven days less than the tropical solar year. Hence if the lunar year was retained the months would move back round the year by about eleven days annually. This is what actually happens in the Muhammadan calendar where the twelve lunar months have been retained and the Muharram and other festivals come earlier every year by about eleven days.

11. Intercalary months. In order to reconcile the lunar and solar years the Hindus hit upon an ingenious device. It was ordained that any month in which the sun did not enter a new sign of the zodiac would not count and would be followed by another month of the same name. Thus in the month of Chait the sun must enter the sign Mesha or Aries. If he does not enter it during the lunar month there will be an intercalary Chait, followed by the proper month of the same name during which the sun will enter Mesha.[1] Such an intercalary month is called Adhika. An intercalary month, obtained by having two successive lunar months of the same name, occurs approximately once in three years, and by this means the reckoning by twelve lunar months is adjusted to the solar year. On the other hand, the sun very occasionally passes two Sankrānts or enters into two fresh signs during the lunar month. This is rendered possible by the fact that the time occupied by the sun in passing through different signs of the zodiac varies to some extent. It is said that the zodiac was divided into twelve equal signs of 30° each or 1° for each day, as at this period it was considered that the year was 360 days.[2] Possibly in adjusting the signs to 365 odd days some alterations may have been made in their length, or errors discovered. At any rate, whatever may be the reason, the length of the sun's periods in the signs, or of the solar months, varies from

[1] *The Indian Calendar*, by Messrs. Sewell and Dikshit, pp. 11 and 25.

[2] Brennand's *Hindu Astronomy*, p. 100.

31 days 14 hours to 29 days 8 hours. Three of the months are less than the lunar month, and hence it is possible that two Sankrānts or passages of the sun into a fresh sign may occasionally occur in the same lunar month. When this happens, following the same rule as before, the month to which the second Sankrānt properly belongs, that is the one following that in which two Sankrānts occur, is called a Kshaya or eliminated month and is omitted from the calendar. Intercalary months occur generally in the 3rd, 5th, 8th, 11th, 14th, 16th and 18th years of a cycle of nineteen years, or seven times in nineteen years. It is found that in each successive cycle only one or two months are changed, so that the same month remains intercalary for several cycles of nineteen years and then gives way generally to one of the months preceding and rarely to the following month. Suppressed months occur at intervals varying from 19 to 141 years, and in a year when a suppressed month occurs there must always be one intercalary month and not infrequently there are two.[1]

This method of adjusting the solar and lunar years, though clumsy, is so far scientific that the solar and lunar years are made to agree without any artificial intercalation of days. It has, however, the great disadvantages of the frequent intercalary month, and also of the fact that the lunar months begin on different dates in the English solar calendar, varying by nearly twenty days.

12. Superstitions about numbers.

It seems not improbable that the unlucky character of the number thirteen may have arisen from its being the number of the intercalary month. Though the special superstition against sitting down thirteen to a meal is, no doubt, associated particularly with the Last Supper, the number is generally unlucky as a date and in other connections. And this is not only the case in Europe, but the Hindus, Persians and Pārsis also consider thirteen an unlucky number; and the Muhammadans account for a similar superstition by saying that Muhammad was ill for the first thirteen days of the month Safar. Twelve, as being the number of the months in the lunar and solar years, is an auspicious number; thirteen would be one extra, and as being the intercalary

[1] *The Indian Calendar*, Sewell and Dikshit, p. 28 and Table I.

month would be here this year and missing next year. Hence it might be supposed that one of thirteen persons met together would be gone at their next meeting like the month. Similarly, the auspicious character of the number seven may be due to its being the total of the sun, moon and five planets, and of the days of the week named after them. And the number three may have been invested with mystic significance as representing the sun, moon and earth. In the Hindu Trinity Vishnu and Siva are the sun and moon, and Brahma, who created the earth, and has since remained quiescent, may have been the personified representative of the earth itself.

13. The Hindu months.

The names of the Hindu months were selected from among those of the *nakshatras*, every second or third being taken and the most important constellations apparently chosen. The following statement shows the current names for the months, the *nakshatras* from which they are derived, and the constellations they represent:

Month.	Nakshatra.	Constellation.
1. Chait.	Chitra.	Virgo.
2. Baisākh.	Visacha.	Libra.
3. Jeth.	Jyestha.	Scorpio.
4. Asārh.	Pūrva Ashādha. Uttara Ashādha.	Sagittarius.
5. Shrāwan.	Sravana.	Aquila.
6. Bhādon.	Pūrva (E) Bhadrapada. Uttara (N) Bhadrapada.	Pegasus.
7. Kunwār or Aswīn.	Aswini.	Aries.
8. Kārtik.	Krittika.	Pleiades (Part of Taurus).
9. Aghan or Māgashīr.	Mrigasiras.	Orion.
10. Pūs.	Pushya.	Cancer.
11. Māgh.	Magha.	Leo.
12. Phāgun.	Pūrva (E) Phālguni. Uttara (N) Phālguni.	Leo.

Thus if the Pleiades are reckoned as part of Taurus,[1] eight zodiacal signs give their names to months as well as Orion, Pegasus and Aquila, while two months are included in Leo. It appears that in former times the year began with Pūs or December, as the month Mārgashīr was also called Aghan or Agrahana, or 'That which went before,' that is

[1] This seems to have been done by some ancient Indian astronomers.

the month before the new year. But the renewal of vegetation in the spring has exercised a very powerful effect on the primitive mind, being marked by the Holi festival in India, corresponding to the Carnival in Europe. The vernal equinox was thus perhaps selected as the most important

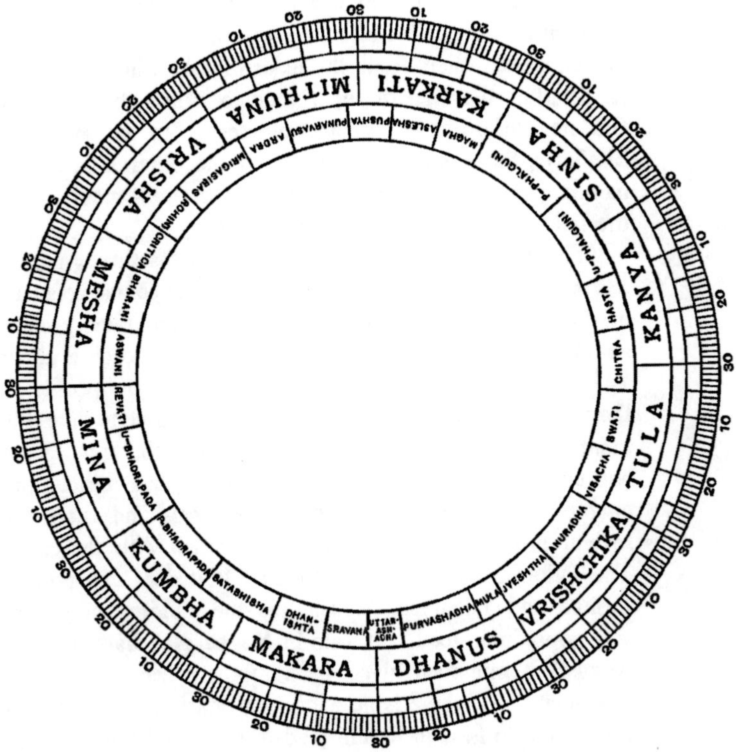

FIG. 3.—The Hindu Ecliptic showing the relative position of Zodiacal Signs and *Nakshatras*.

occasion and the best date for beginning the new year, which now commences in northern India with the new moon of Chait, immediately following the Holi festival, when the sun is in the sign of Mesha or Aries. At first the months appear to have travelled round the year, but subsequently they were fixed by ordaining that the month of Chait should begin with the new moon during the course of which the sun entered the sign Aries.[1] The constellation Chitra, from

[1] *The Indian Calendar*, p. 29.

which the sign is named, is nearly opposite to this in the zodiac, as shown by the above figure.[1]

Consequently, the full moon, being nearly opposite the sun on the ecliptic, would be in the sign Chitra or near it. In southern India the months begin with the full moon, but in northern India with the new moon; it seems possible that the months were called after the *nakshatra*, of the full moon to distinguish them from the solar months which would be called after the sign of the zodiac in which the sun was. But no authoritative explanation seems to be available. Similarly, the *nakshatras* after which the other months are named, fall nearly opposite to them at the new moon, while the full moon would be in or near them.

14. The solar *nakshatras*.

The periods during which the sun passes through each *nakshatra* are also recorded, and they are of course constant in date like the solar months. As there are twenty-seven *nakshatras*, the average time spent by the sun in each is about $13\frac{1}{2}$ days. These periods are well known to the people as they have the advantage of not varying in date like the lunar months, while over most of India the solar months are not used. The commencement of the various agricultural operations is dated by the solar *nakshatras*, and there are several proverbs about them in connection with the crops. The following are some examples: "If it does not rain in Pushya and Punarvasu Nakshatras the children of Nimār will go without food." 'Rain in Magha Nakshatra (end of August) is like food given by a mother,' because it is so beneficial. "If there is no wind in Mrigasiras (beginning of June), and no heat in Rohini (end of May), sell your plough-cattle and go and look for work." 'If it rains during Uttara (end of September) dogs will turn up their noses at grain,' because the harvest will be so abundant. "If it rains during Aslesha (first half of August) the wheat-stalks will be as stout as drum-sticks" (because the land will be well ploughed). 'If rain falls in Chitra or Swāti Nakshatras (October) there won't be enough cotton for lamp-wicks.'

15. Lunar fortnights and days.

The lunar month was divided into two fortnights called *paksha* or wing. The period of the waxing moon was known as *sukla* or *sudi paksha*, that is the light fortnight,

[1] Taken from Brennand's *Hindu Astronomy*, p. 39.

and that of the waning moon as *krishna* or *budi paksha*, that is the dark fortnight.

Each lunar month was also divided into thirty equal periods, called *tithis* or lunar days. Since there are less than thirty days in the lunar month, a *tithi* does not correspond to an ordinary day, but begins and ends at odd hours of the day. Nevertheless the *tithis* are printed in all almanacs, and are used for the calculation of auspicious moments.[1]

16. Divisions of the day.

The day is divided for ordinary purposes of measuring time into eight *pahars* or watches, four of the day and four of the night; and into sixty *gharis* or periods of twenty-four minutes each. The *pahars*, however, are not of equal length. At the equinox the first and fourth *pahar* of the day and night each contain eight *gharis*, and the two middle ones seven *gharis*. In summer the first and fourth *pahars* of the day contain nine *gharis* each, and the two middle ones eight each, while the first and fourth *pahars* of the night contain seven and the two middle ones six each. Thus in summer the four day *pahars* contain 13 hours 36 minutes and the night ones 10 hours 24 minutes. And in winter the exact opposite is the case, the night *pahars* being lengthened and the day ones shortened in precisely the same manner. No more unsatisfactory measure of time could well be devised. The termination of the second watch or *do pahar* always corresponds with midday and midnight respectively.

The apparatus with which the hours were measured and announced consisted of a shallow metal pan, named from its office, *ghariāl*, and suspended so as to be easily struck with a wooden mallet by the *ghariāli*. He measured the passing of a *ghari* by an empty thin brass cup or *katori*, perforated at the bottom, and placed on the surface of a large vessel filled with water, where nothing could disturb it; the water came through the small hole in the bottom of the cup and filled it, causing it to sink in the period of one *ghari*. At the expiration of each *ghari* the *ghariāl* struck its number from one to nine with a mallet on a brass plate, and at the end of each *pahar* he struck a *gujar* or eight strokes to announce the fact, followed by one to four hollow-sounding

[1] Barnett, *Antiquities of India*, p. 193.

strokes to indicate the number of the *pahar*. This custom is still preserved in the method by which the police-guards of the public offices announce the hours on a gong and subsequently strike four, eight and twelve strokes to proclaim these hours of the day and night by our clock. Only rich men could afford to maintain a *gharīāl*, as four persons were required to attend to it during the day and four at night.[1]

17. The Joshi's calculations.

The Joshi calculates auspicious[2] seasons by a consideration of the sun's zodiacal sign, the moon's *nakshatra* or daily mansion, and other rules. From the monthly zodiacal signs and daily *nakshatras* in which children are born, as recorded in their horoscopes, he calculates whether their marriage will be auspicious. Thus the zodiacal signs are supposed to be divided among the four castes, Pisces, Cancer and Scorpio belonging to the Brāhman; Aries, Leo and Sagittarius to the Kshatriya; Taurus, Virgo and Capricorn to the Vaishya; and Gemini, Libra and Aquarius to the Sūdra. If the boy and girl were born under any of the three signs of the same caste it is a happy conjunction. If the boy's sign was of a caste superior to the girl's, it is suitable, but if the girl's sign is of a superior caste to the boy's it is an omen that she will rule the household; and though the marriage may take place, certain ceremonies should be performed to obviate this effect. There is also a division of the zodiacal signs according to their nature. Thus Virgo, Libra, Gemini, Aquarius and half of Sagittarius are considered to be of the nature of man, or formed by him; Aries, Taurus, half of Sagittarius and half of Capricorn are of the nature of animals; Cancer, Pisces and half of Capricorn are of a watery nature; Leo is of the desert or wild nature; and Scorpio is of the nature of insects. If the boy and girl were both born under signs of the same nature their marriage will be auspicious, but if they were born under signs of different

[1] The above particulars regarding the measurement of time by the *gharīāl* are taken from 'An Account of the Hindustāni Horometry' in *Asiatic Researches*, vol. v. p. 81, by John Gilchrist, Esq. The account appears to be to some extent controversial, and it is possible that the arrangement of the *gharis* may have varied in different localities.

[2] The information contained in this paragraph is taken from Captain Mackintosh's *Report on the Rāmosis*, chap. iii. (India Office Library Tracts), in which a large variety of rules are given.

natures, they will share only half the blessings and comforts of the marriage state, and may be visited by strife, enmity, misery or distress. As Leo and Scorpio are looked upon as being enemies, evil consequences are much dreaded from the marriage of a couple born under these signs. There are also numerous rules regarding the *nakshatras* or mansions of the moon and days of the week under which the boy and girl were born, but these need not be reproduced. If on the day of the wedding the sun or any of the planets passes from one zodiacal sign to another, the wedding must be delayed for a certain number of *gharis* or periods of twenty-four minutes, the number varying for each planet. The hours of the day are severally appointed to the seven planets and the twelve zodiacal signs, and the period of ascendancy of a sign is known as *lagan*; this name is also given to the paper specifying the day and hour which have been calculated as auspicious for the wedding. It is stated that no weddings should be celebrated during the period of occultation of the planets Jupiter and Venus, nor on the day before new moon, nor the Sankrānt or day on which the sun passes from one zodiacal sign to another, nor in the Singhast year, when the planet Jupiter is in the constellation Leo. This takes place once in twelve years. Marriages are usually prohibited during the four months of the rainy season, and sometimes also in Pūs, Jeth or other months.

18. Personal names.

The Joshi names children according to the moon's daily *nakshatra* under which they were born, each *nakshatra* having a letter or certain syllables allotted to it with which the name must begin. Thus Magha has the syllables Ma, Mi, Mu and Me, with which the name should begin, as Mansāram, Mithu Lāl, Mukund Singh, Meghnāth; Purwa Phālguni has Mo and Te, as Moji Lāl and Tegi Lāl; Punarvasu has Ke, Ko, Ha and Hi, as Kesho Rao, Koshal Prasād, Hardyāl and Hīra Lāl, and so on. The primitive idea connecting a name with the thing or person to which it belongs is that the name is actually a concrete part of the person or object, containing part of his life, just as the hair, nails and all the body are believed to contain part of the life, which is not at first localised in any part of the body nor conceived of as separate from it. The primitive mind could conceive no abstract idea, that is nothing that could not be seen or heard, and it could not think of a name as an abstract appellation. The name was thought of as part of that to which it was applied. Thus, if one knew a man's name, it was thought that one could use it to injure him, just as if one had a piece of his hair or nails he could be injured through them because they all contained part of his life; and if a part of the life was injured or destroyed the remainder would also suffer injury, just as the whole body might perish if a limb was cut off. For this reason savages often conceal their real names, so as to prevent an enemy from obtaining power to injure them through its knowledge. By a development of the same belief it was thought that the names of gods and saints contained part of the divine life and potency of the god or saint to whom they were applied. And even separated from the original owner the name retained that virtue which it had acquired in association; hence the power assigned to the names of gods and superhuman beings when used in spells and incantations. Similarly, if the name of a god or saint was given to a child it was thought that some part of the nature and virtue of the god might be conferred on the child. Thus Hindu children are most commonly named after gods and goddesses under the influence of this idea; and though the belief may now have decayed the practice continues. Similarly the common Muhammadan names are epithets of Allah or god or of the Prophet and his relations. Jewish children are named after the Jewish patriarchs. In European countries the most common male names are those of the Apostles, as John, Peter, James, Paul, Simon, Andrew and Thomas; and the names of the Evangelists were, until recently, also given. The most common girl's name in several European countries is Mary, and a generation or two ago other Biblical names, as Sarah, Hannah, Ruth, Rachel, and so on, were very usually given to girls. In England the names next in favour for boys and girls are those of kings and queens, and the same idea perhaps originally underlay the application of these names. The following are some of the best-known Hindu names, taken from those of gods:—

Names of Vishnu.

Nārāyan. Probably 'The abode of mortals,' or else 'He who dwelt on the waters (before creation)'; now applied to the sun.

Wāman. The dwarf, one of Vishnu's incarnations.

Janārdan. Said to mean protector of the people.

Narsingh. The man-lion, one of Vishnu's incarnations.

Hari. Yellow or gold-colour or green. Perhaps applied to the sun.

Parashrām. From Parasurāma or Rāma with the axe, one of the incarnations of Vishnu.

Gadadhar. Wielder of the club or *gada*.

Jagannāth. Lord of the world.

Dīnkar. The sun, or he who makes the days (*dīn karna*).

Bhagwān. The fortunate or illustrious.

Anant. The infinite or eternal.

Madhosūdan. Destroyer of the demon Madho (Madho means honey or wine).

Pāndurang. Yellow-coloured.

Names of Rāma, or Vishnu's Great Incarnation as King Rāma of Ayodhia.

Rāmchandra, the moon of Rāma, and Rāmbaksh, the gift of Rāma, are the commonest Hindu male names.

Atmārām. Soul of Rāma.

Sitārām. Rāma and Sita his wife.

Rāmcharan. The footprint of Rāma.

Sakhārām. The friend of Rāma.

Sewārām. Servant of Rāma.

Names of Krishna.

Krishna and its diminutive Kishen are very common names.

Kanhaiya. A synonym for Krishna.

Dāmodar. Because his mother tied him with a rope to a large tree to keep him quiet and he pulled up the tree, roots and all.

Bālkishen. The boy Krishna.

Ghansiām. The dark-coloured or black one (like dark clouds); probably referring to the belief that Krishna belonged to the non-Aryan races.

Madan Mohan. The enchanter of love.

Manohar. The heart-stealer.

Yeshwant. The glorious.

Kesho. Having long, fine hair. A name of Krishna. Also the destroyer of the demon Keshi, who was covered with hair. It would appear that the epithet was first applied to Krishna himself and afterwards to a demon whom he was supposed to have destroyed.

Balwant. Strong. An epithet of Krishna, used in conjunction with other names.

Mādhava. Honey-sweet or belonging to the spring, vernal.

Girdhāri. He who held up the mountain. Krishna held up the mountain Govardhan, balancing the peak on his finger to protect the people from the destructive rains sent by Indra.

Shiāmsundar. The dark and beautiful one.

Nandkishore, Nandkumār. Child of Nand the cowherd, Krishna's foster-father.

Names of Siva.

Sadāsheo. Siva the everlasting.

Mahādeo. The great god.

Trimbak. The three-eyed one (?).

Gangādhar. The holder of the Ganges, because it flows from Siva's hair.

Kāshināth. The lord of Benāres.

Kedārnāth. The lord of cedars (referring to the pine-forests of the Himalayas).

Nīlkanth. The blue-jay sacred to Siva. Name of Siva because his throat is bluish-black either from swallowing poison at the time of the churning of the ocean or from drinking large quantities of *bhāng*.

Shankar. He who gives happiness.

Vishwanāth. Lord of the universe.

Sheo Prasād. Gift of Siva.

Names of Ganpati or Ganesh.

Ganpati is itself a very common name.
Vidhyādhar. The lord of learning.
Vināyak. The remover of difficulties.
Ganesh Prasād. Gift of Ganesh. A child born on the fourth day of any month will often be given this name, as Ganesh was born on the 4th Bhādon (August).

Names of Hanumān.

Hanumān itself is a very common name.
Māroti, son of Mārut the god of the wind.
Mahāvīra or Mahābīr. The strong one.

Other common sacred names are: Amrit, the divine nectar, and Moreshwar, lord of the peacock, perhaps an epithet of the god Ḳartikeya. Men are also often named after jewels, as: Hīra Lāl, diamond; Panna Lāl, emerald; Ratan Lāl, a jewel; Kundan Lāl, fine gold. A child born on the day of full moon may be called Pūran Chand, which means full moon. There are of course many other male names, but those here given are the commonest. Children are also frequently named after the day or month in which they were born.

Common terminations of male names are: Charan, footprint; Dās, slave; Prasād, food offered to a god; Lāl, dear; Datta, gift, commonly used by Maithil Brāhmans; Dīn or Baksh, which also means gift; Nāth, lord of; and Dulāre, dear to. These are combined with the names of gods, as: Ḳālicharan, footprint of Kāli; Rām Prasād or Kishen Prasād, an offering to Rāma or Krishna; Bishen Lāl, dear to Vishnu; Ganesh Datta, a gift from Ganesh; Ganga Dīn, a gift from the Ganges; Sheo Dulāre, dear to Ṡiva; Vishwanāth, lord of the universe. Boys are sometimes given the names of goddesses with such terminations, as Lachmi or Jānki Prasād, an offering to these goddesses. A child born on the 8th of light Chait (April) will be called Durga Prasād, as this day is sacred to the goddess Durga or Devi. 19. Terminations of names.

Women are also frequently named after goddesses, as:

20. Women's names. Pārvati, the consort of Siva; Sīta, the wife of Rāma; Jānki, apparently another name for Sīta; Lakshmi, the consort of Vishnu, and the goddess of wealth; Sāraswati, the goddess of wisdom; Rādha, the beloved of Krishna; Dasoda, the foster-mother of Krishna; Dewāki, who is supposed to have been the real mother of Krishna; Durga, another name for Siva's consort; Devi, the same as Durga and the earth-goddess; Rukhmini, the bright or shining one, a consort of Vishnu; and Tulsi, the basil-plant, sacred to Vishnu.

Women are also named after the sacred rivers, as: Ganga, Jamni or Yamuni (Jumna); Gomti, the river on which Lucknow stands; Godha or Gautam, after the Godāvari river; and Bhāgirathi, another name for the Ganges. The river Nerbudda is commonly found as a man's name, especially in places situated on its banks. Other names of women are: Sona, gold; Puna, born at the full moon; Manohra, enchanting; Kamala, the lotus; Indumati, a moonlight night; Sumati, well-minded; Sushila, well-intentioned; Srimati, wealthy; Amrita, nectar; Phulwa, a flower; Imlia, the tamarind; Malta, jasmine; and so on.

If a girl is born after four sons she will be called Pancho or fifth, and one born in the unlucky Mul Nakshatra is called Mulia. When a girl is married and goes to her husband's house her name is always changed there. If two girls have been married into the household, they may be called Bari Bohu and Choti Bohu, or the elder and younger daughters-in-law; or a girl may be called after the place from which she comes, as Jabalpurwāli, Raipurwāli, and so on.

21. Special names and bad names. The higher castes have two names, one given by the Joshi, which is called *rāshi-ka-nām* or the ceremonial name, *rāshi* meaning the Nakshatra or moon's daily mansion under which the child was born. This is kept secret and only used in marriage and other ceremonies, though the practice is now tending to decay. The other is the *chaltu* or current name, and may either be a second ordinary name, such as those already given, or it may be taken from some peculiarity of the child. Names of the latter class are: Bhūra, brown; Putro, a doll, given to a pretty child; Dukāli, born in

famine-time; Mahinga, dear or expensive; Chhota, little; Bābu, equivalent to little prince or noble; Pāpa, father; Kakku, born in the cucumber season; Lada, pet; Pattu, a somersault; Judāwan, cooling, and so on. Bad names are also given to avert ill-luck and remove the enmity of the spirits hostile to children, if the mother's previous babies have been lost. Instances of these are Raisa, short in stature; Lūla, having a maimed arm; Ghasīta, dragged along on a board; Damru, bought for a farthing; Khairāti, alms; Dukhi, pain; Kubra, hunch-back; Gudri, rag; Kāna, one-eyed; Birla, thin or lean; Bisāhu, bought or purchased; and Bulāki and Chedi, having a pierced nostril; these names are given to a boy whose nostril has been pierced to make him resemble a girl and thus decrease his value.[1] Further instances of such names have been given in other articles.

Julāha, Momin.—A low Muhammadan caste of weavers resident mainly in Saugor and Burhānpur. They numbered about 4000 persons in 1911. In Nāgpur District the Muhammadan weavers generally call themselves Momin, a word meaning 'orthodox.' In northern India and Bengal Julāhas are very numerous and the bulk of them are probably converted Hindus. Mr. (Sir Denzil) Ibbetson remarks: "We find Koli-Julāhas, Chamār-Julāhas, Morhi-Julāhas, Ramdāsi-Julāhas, and so forth; and it is probable that after a few generations these men will drop the prefix which denotes their low origin and become Julāhas pure and simple."[2] The Julāhas claim Adam as the founder of their craft, inasmuch as when Satan made him realise his nakedness he taught the art of weaving to his sons. And they say that their ancestors came from Arabia. In Nimār the Julāhas or Momins assert that they do not permit outsiders to be admitted as members of the caste, but the accuracy of this is doubtful, while in Saugor any Muhammadan who wishes to do so may become a Julāha. They follow the Muhammadan laws of marriage and inheritance. Unions between relatives are favoured, but a man may not marry

[1] Some of these names and also some of the women's names have been taken from Colonel Temple's *Proper Names of the Punjābis.*

[2] *Punjāb Ethnography*, para. 612.

his sister, niece, aunt or foster-sister. The Julāha or Momin women observe no *purda*, and are said to be almost unique among Muhammadans in this respect.

"The Musalmān[1] weaver or Julāha," Sir G. Grierson writes, "is the proverbial fool of Hindu stories and proverbs. He swims in the moonlight across fields of flowering linseed, thinking the blue colour to be caused by water. He hears his family priest reading the Korān, and bursts into tears to the gratification of the reader. When pressed to tell what part affected him most, he says it was not that, but that the wagging beard of the old gentleman so much reminded him of a favourite goat of his which had died. When forming one of a company of twelve he tries to count them and finding himself missing wants to perform his own funeral obsequies. He finds the rear peg of a plough and wants to set up farming on the strength of it. He gets into a boat at night and forgets to pull up the anchor. After rowing till dawn he finds himself where he started, and concludes that the only explanation is that his native village could not bear to lose him and has followed him. If there are eight weavers and nine huqqas, they fight for the odd one. Once on a time a crow carried off to the roof of the house some bread which a weaver had given his child. Before giving the child any more he took the precaution of removing the ladder. Like the English fool he always gets unmerited blows. For instance, he once went to see a ram-fight and got butted himself, as the saying runs:

Karigah chhor tamāsa jay
Nahak chot Julāha khay.

'He left his loom to see the fun and for no reason got a bruising.' Another story (told by Fallon) is that being told by a soothsayer that it was written in his fate that his nose would be cut off with an axe, the weaver was incredulous and taking up an axe, kept flourishing it, saying—

Yon karba ta gor kātbon
Yon karba ta hāth kātbon
Aur yon karba tab nā——

---

1 This passage is taken from Sir G. Grierson's *Peasant Life in Bihār*, p. 64.

'If I do *so* I cut off my leg, if I do *so* I cut off my hand, but unless I do *so* my no——,' and his nose was off. Another proverb *Julāha jānathi jo katai*, 'Does a weaver know how to cut barley,' refers to a story (in Fallon) that a weaver unable to pay his debt was set to cut barley by his creditor, who thought to repay himself in this way. But instead of reaping, the stupid fellow kept trying to untwist the tangled barley stems. Other proverbs at his expense are: 'The Julāha went out to cut the grass at sunset, when even the crows were going home.' 'The Julāha's brains are in his backside.' His wife bears an equally bad character, as in the proverb: 'A wilful Julāhin will pull her own father's beard.'"

Kachera,[1] **Kachāra** (from *kānch*, glass).—The functional caste of makers of glass bangles. The Kacheras numbered 2800 persons in the Central Provinces in 1911, of whom 1800 were found in the Jubbulpore District. The caste say that in former times glass bangles were made only by Turk or Muhammadan Kacheras. The present name of Turkāri is probably derived from Turk. But when Gauri Pārvati was to be married to Mahādeo, she refused to wear the bangles made by a Turkāri. So Mahādeo constructed a *vedi* or furnace, and from this sprang the first Hindu Kachera, who was employed to make bangles for Pārvati. A later variant of the legend, having a sufficiently obvious deduction, is that Mahādeo did not create a man, but caught hold of a Kshatriya who happened to be present and ordered him to make the bangles. His descendants followed the new profession and thus came to be known as Kacheras. It is a possible conclusion from the story that the art of making glass bangles was introduced by the Muhammadans and, as suggested in the article on Lakhera, it may be the case that Hindu women formerly wore ornaments made of lac. 1. Origin of the caste.

The exogamous sections of the Kacheras show that the caste is of very mixed origin. Several of them are named 2. Exogamous groups.

[1] This article is based on a paper by Mr. Pancham Lāl, naib-tahsildar, Murwāra, with extracts from the *Central Provinces Monograph on Pottery and Glassware*, by Mr. Jowers, and some information collected by Mr. Hira Lāl.

after other castes, as Bharia (forest tribe), Gadaria (shepherd), Sunār, Naua (Nai), Thakurel (Thākur or Rājpūt), Kachhwāha and Chauhān (septs of Rājpūts), and Kuria or Kori (weaver), and indicate that members of these castes took to the profession of bangle-making and became Kacheras. It may be surmised that, in the first instance perhaps, when the objection to using the product of the Muhammadan workman arose, if the theory of the prior use of lac bangles be correct, members of different castes took to supplying bangles for their own community, and from these in the course of time the Kachera caste was developed. Other names of sections worth mentioning are Jharrāha, one who frets or worries; Kharrāha, a choleric person; Dukesha, one who carries a begging-bowl; Thuthel, a maimed man, and Khajha, one suffering from the itch.

3. Social customs. The exogamous sections are known as *baink.* The marriage of persons belonging to the same section and of first cousins is forbidden. Girls are generally married at an early age, as there is a scarcity of women in the caste, and they are snapped up as soon as available. As a natural consequence a considerable bride-price is paid, and the desire of the Kachera to make a profit by the marriage of his daughter is ridiculed in the following saying, supposed to be his prayer: "O God, give me a daughter. In exchange for her I shall get a pair of bullocks and a potful of rupees, and I shall be rich for the rest of my life. As her dowry I shall give her a sickle, a hoe and a spinning-machine, and these will suffice for my daughter to earn her livelihood." The usual sum paid for a girl is Rs. 50. The marriage ceremony is performed by walking round the sacred pole, and after it the couple try their strength against each other, the bride trying to push a stone pestle on to a slab with her foot and the groom pushing it off with his. At the end of the wedding an omen is taken, a silver ornament known as *dhāl*[1] which women wear in the ear being fixed on to a wall and milk poured over it. If the ornament is displaced by the stream of milk and falls down, it is considered that the union will be a happy one. The proceeding perhaps symbolises roughly the birth of a child. The marriage of

1 *Dhāl* means a shield, and the ornament is of this shape.

widows is permitted, and in consequence of the scarcity of women the widow is usually married to her late husband's younger brother, if there be one, even though he may be only a child. Divorce is permitted. *Liaisons* within the caste are usually overlooked, but a woman going wrong with an outsider is expelled from the community. The Kacheras commonly burn the dead. They employ Brāhmans for ceremonial purposes, but their social status is low and no high caste will take water from them. They eat flesh and fish, and some of them drink liquor, while others have given it up. They have a caste committee or *panchāyat* for the punishment of social offences, which is headed by officials known as Mālik and Dīwān. Their favourite deity is Devi, and in her honour they sow the Jawaras or pots of wheat corresponding to the gardens of Adonis during the nine days prior to the Rāmnaomi and Dasahra festivals in March and September. Some of them carry their devotion so far as to grow the plants of wheat on their bodies, sitting in one posture for nine days and almost giving up food and drink. At the Diwāli festival they worship the furnace in which glass bangles are made.

4. Occupation.

The traditional occupation of the caste is the manufacture of glass bangles. They import the glass in lumps from northern India and melt it in their furnace, after which the colouring matter is applied and the ring is turned on a slab of stone. Nearly all Hindu married women have glass bangles, which are broken or removed if their husbands die. But the rule is not universal, and some castes do not wear them at all. Mārwāri women have bangles of ivory, and Dhangar (shepherd) women of cocoanut-shell. Women of several castes who engage in labour have glass bangles only on the left wrist and metal ones on the right, as the former are too fragile. Low-caste women sometimes wear the flat, black bangles known as *khagga* on the upper arm. In many castes the glass bangles are also broken after the birth of a child. Bangles of many colours are made, but Hindus usually prefer black or indigo-blue. Among Hindus of good caste a girl may wear green bangles while she is unmarried; at her wedding black bangles are put on her wrists, and thereafter she may have them of black, blue, red or yellow, but not green. Muhammadans usually wear black or dark-green bangles. A Hindu woman has the same number of bangles on each wrist, not less than five and more if she likes. She will never leave her arms entirely without bangles, as she thinks this would cause her to become a widow. Consequently when a new set are purchased one or two of the old ones are kept on each arm. Similarly among castes who wear lac bangles like Banjāras, five should be worn, and these cover the greater part of the space between the wrist and the elbow. The men of the caste usually stay at home and make the bangles, and the women travel about to the different village markets, carrying their wares on little ponies if they can afford them. It is necessary that the seller of bangles should be a woman, as she has to assist her customers to work them on to their wrists, and also display her goods to high-caste women behind the *purda* in their homes.

The Kacheras' bangles are very cheap, from two to fourteen being obtainable for a pice (farthing), according to quality. Many are also broken, and the seller has to bear the loss of all those broken when the purchaser is putting them on, which may amount to 30 per cent. And though an improvement on the old lac bangles, the colours are very dull, and bracelets of better and more transparent glass imported from Austria now find a large sale and tend to oust the indigenous product. The Kachera, therefore, is, as a rule, far from prosperous. The incessant bending over the furnace tends to undermine his constitution and often ruins his eyesight. There is in fact a Hindi saying to the effect that, "When the Kachera has a son the rejoicings are held in the Kundera's (turner's) house. For he will go blind and then he will find nothing else to do but turn the Kundera's lathe."

KĀCHHI

LIST OF PARAGRAPHS

Kāchhi.—An important cultivating caste of the northern Districts, who grow vegetables and irrigated crops requiring intensive cultivation. The distinction between the Kāchhis and Mālis of the Hindustāni Districts is that the former grow regular irrigated crops, while the latter confine their operations to vegetables and flower-gardens; whereas the Māli or Marār of the Marātha country is both a cultivator and a gardener. The Kāchhis numbered about 120,000 persons in 1911, and resided mainly in the Saugor, Damoh, Jubbulpore and Narsinghpur Districts. The word Kāchhi may be derived from *kachhār*, the name given to the alluvial land lying on river banks, which they greatly affect for growing their vegetables. Another derivation is from *kāchhni*, a term used for the process of collecting the opium from the capsules of the poppy.[1] The caste are probably an offshoot of the Kurmis. Owing to the resemblance of names they claim a connection with the Kachhwāha sept of Rājpūts, but this is not at all probable. 1. General notice.

The caste is divided into a number of subcastes, most of which take their names from special plants which they grow. Thus the Hardia Kāchhis grow *haldi* or turmeric; the Alias cultivate the *āl* or Indian madder, from which the well-known red dye is obtained; the Phūlias are flower-gardeners; the Jirias take their name from *jira* or cumin; the Murai or Murao Kāchhis are called after the *muli* or radish; the Pirias 2. Subdivisions.

[1] Crooke's *Tribes and Castes*, article Kāchhi.

take their name from the *piria* or basket in which they carry earth; the Sanias grow *san* or hemp; the Mor Kāchhis are those who prepare the *maur* or marriage-crown for weddings; and the Līlia subcaste are called after the indigo plant (*līl* or *nīl*). In some localities they have a subcaste called Kāchhwāhi, who are considered to have a connection with the Rājpūts and to rank higher than the others.

3. Marriage customs. The social customs of the Kāchhis resemble those of the Kurmis. The descendants of the same parents do not intermarry for three generations. A man may have two sisters to wife at the same time. In the Damoh District, on the arrival of the bridegroom's party, the bride is brought into the marriage-shed, and is there stripped to the waist while she holds a leaf-cup in her hand; this is probably done so that the bridegroom may see that the bride is free from any bodily defect. Girls are usually married before they are ten years old, and if the parents are too poor to arrange a match for their daughter, the caste-fellows often raise a subscription when she attains this age and get her married. The bridegroom should always be older than the bride, and the difference is generally from five to ten years. The bridegroom wears a loin-cloth and long coat reaching to the ground, both of which are stained yellow with turmeric; the bride wears a red cloth or one in which red is the main colour. The girl's father gives her a dowry of a cow or jewels, or at least two rupees; while the boy's father pays all the expenses of the wedding with the exception of one feast. The bridegroom gives the bride a present of three shoulder-cloths and three skirts, and one of these is worn by her at the wedding; this is the old northern method of dress, but married women do not usually adhere to it and have adopted the common *sāri* or single body-cloth. The principal ceremony is the *bhānwar* or walking round the sacred post. While the bride and bridegroom are engaged in this the parents and elderly relatives shut themselves into the house and weep. During the first four rounds of the post the bride walks in front bowing her head and the bridegroom places his right hand on her back; while during the last three the bridegroom walks in front holding the bride by her third finger. After this the bride is hidden somewhere in the house and the

bridegroom has to search for her. Sometimes the bride's younger sister is dressed up in her clothes and the bridegroom catches her in mistake for his wife, whereupon the old women laugh and say to him, 'Do you want her also?' If finally he fails to find the bride he must give her some ornament.

After the wedding the bridegroom's marriage-crown is hung to the roof in a basket. And on the sixth day of the following month of Bhādon (August), he again dresses himself in his wedding clothes, and taking his marriage-crown on a dish, proceeds to the nearest stream or river accompanied by his friends. Here he throws the crown into the water, and the wedding coat is washed clean of the turmeric and unsewn and made up into ordinary clothes. This ceremony is known as *moschatt* and is common to Hindu castes generally. Widows are permitted to marry again, and the most usual match is with the younger brother of the deceased husband. Divorce is allowed at the instance either of the husband or wife, and may be effected by a simple declaration before the caste committee.

4. Child-birth.

After a birth neither the mother nor child are given anything to eat the first day; and on the second they bring a young calf and give a little of its urine to the child, and to the mother a little sugar and the half of a cocoanut. In the evening of this day they buy all kinds of hot spices and herbs from a Bania and make a cake with them and give it to the mother to eat. On the second day the child begins to drink its mother's milk. The navel-string is cut and buried in the room on the first day, and over it a fire is kept burning continuously during the period of impurity. The small piece which falls from the child's body is buried beneath the mother's bed. The period of impurity after the birth of a girl lasts for four days and five days for a boy. On the sixth day the mother is given rice to eat. Twelve days after a child is born the barber's wife cuts its nails for the first time and throws the clippings away.

5. Ear-piercing.

The ears of boys and girls are pierced when they are four or five years old; until this is done they are not considered as members of the caste and may take food from any one. The ear is always pierced by a Sunār (goldsmith), who travels about the country in the pursuit of this calling.

A brass pin is left in the ear for fifteen days, and is then removed and a strip of wood is substituted for it in a boy's ear and a peacock's feather in that of a girl to enlarge the hole. Girls do not have their nostrils pierced nor wear nose-rings, as the Kāchhis are a comparatively low caste. They are tattooed before or after marriage with patterns of a scorpion, a peacock, a *discus*, and with dots on the chin and cheek-bones. During the period of her monthly impurity a girl is secluded in the house and does not eat flesh or fish. When the time is finished she goes to the river and bathes and dresses her hair with earth, which is a necessary ceremony of purification.

6. Disposal of the dead. The bodies of children under five and of persons dying from smallpox, snake-bite or cholera are buried, and those of others are cremated. In Chhindwāra they do not wash or anoint the corpses of the dead, but sprinkle on them a little turmeric and water. On the day of the funeral or cremation the bereaved family is supplied with food by friends. The principal deity of the Kāchhis is Bhainsāsur, who is regarded as the keeper of the vegetable garden and is represented by a stone placed under a tree in any part of it. He is worshipped once a year after the Holi festival with offerings of vermilion, areca-nuts and cocoanuts, and libations of liquor. The Kāchhis raise all kinds of vegetables and garden crops, the principal being chillies, turmeric, tobacco, garlic, onions, yams and other vegetables. They are diligent and laborious, and show much skill in irrigating and manuring their crops.

1. Historical notice. **Kadera, Kandera, Golandāz, Bāndar, Hawāidār.**[1]— A small occupational caste of makers of fireworks. The Kaderas numbered 2200 persons in 1911, and were most numerous in the Narsinghpur District. They consider themselves to have come from Bundelkhand, where the caste is also found, but it is in greatest strength in the Gwalior State. In former times Kaderas were employed to manufacture gunpowder and missiles of iron, and serve cannon in the Indian armies. The term Golandāz or 'ball-thrower' was also applied to native artillerymen. The Bāndar or 'rocket-throwers' were a separate class, who fired rockets containing

[1] Partly based on a paper by Munshi Kanhya Lāl of the Gazetteer office.

missiles, the name being derived from *vān*, an arrow. With them may be classed the Deg-andāz or 'mortar-throwers,' who used thick earthenware pots filled with powder and having fuses attached, somewhat resembling the modern bomb —missiles which inflicted dreadful wounds.[1] Mr. Irvine writes of the Mughal artillery as follows: "The fire was never very rapid. Orme speaks of the artillery firing once in a quarter of an hour. In 1721 the usual rate of fire of heavy guns was once every three hours. Artillery which fired once in two *gharis* or forty-four minutes was praised for its rapidity of action. The guns were usually posted behind the clay walls of houses; or they might take up a commanding position on the top of a brick-kiln; or a temporary entrenchment might be formed out of the earthen bank and ditch which usually surround a grove of mango-trees." Hawāidār is a term for a maker of fireworks, while the name Kandera itself may perhaps be derived from *kand*, an arrow.

2. Subdivisions. In Narsinghpur the Kaderas have three subcastes, Rājpūt or Dāngiwāra, Dhunka, and Matwāla. The first claim to be Rājpūts, but the alternative name of Dāngiwāra indicates that they are a mixed group, perhaps partly of Rājpūt descent like the Dāngis of Saugor. It is by no means unlikely that the lower classes of Rājpūts should have been employed in the avocations of the Kaderas. The term Dhunka signifies a cotton-cleaner, and some of the Kaderas may have taken up this calling, when they could no longer find employment in the native armies. Matwāla means a drinker of country liquor, in which members of this group indulge. But with the exception of the Rājpūt Kaderas in Narsinghpur, other members of the caste also drink it.

3. Social customs. They celebrate their marriages by walking round the sacred post. Divorce and the remarriage of widows are permitted. They have a caste committee, with a headman called Chaudhri or Mehtar, and an inferior officer known as Diwān. When a man has been put out of caste the Chaudhri first takes food with him on readmission, and for this is entitled to a fee of a rupee and a turban, while the

[1] Irvine, *Army of the Mughals*, pp. 158, 159.

Diwān receives a smaller cloth. These offices are hereditary. The Kaderas have no *purda* system, and a wife may speak freely to her father-in-law. They bury the milk-teeth of children below the *ghinochi*, or stand for water-pots, with the idea probably of preventing heat and inflammation in the gums. A child's *jhāla* or birth-hair is usually cut for the first time on the occasion of some marriage in the family, and is thrown into the Nerbudda or buried at a temple. Names are given by the Brāhman on the day of birth or soon afterwards, and a second pet name is commonly used in the family. If a child sees a lamp on the *chhati* or sixth day after its birth they think that it will squint.

4. Religion and occupation.

The caste employ Brāhmans for religious ceremonies, but their social position is low, and they rank with castes from whom a Brāhman cannot take water. On the tenth day of Jeth (May) they worship Lukmān Hakīm, a personage whom they believe to have been the inventor of gunpowder. He is popularly identified with Solomon, and is revered with Muhammadan rites in the shop and not in the house. A Fakīr is called in who sacrifices a goat, and makes an offering of the head, which becomes his perquisite; sugar-cakes and sweet rice are also offered and given away to children, and the flesh of the goat is eaten by the family of the worshipper. Since the worship is paid only in the shop it would appear that Lukmān Hakīm is considered a deity foreign to the domestic religion, and is revered as having invented the substance which enables the caste to make their livelihood; and since he is clearly a Muhammadan deity, and is venerated according to the ritual of this religion by the Kaderas, who are otherwise Hindus, a recognition seems to be implied that as far at least as the Kaderas are concerned the introduction of gunpowder into India is attributed to the Muhammadans. It is not stated whether or not the month of May was selected of set purpose for the worship of the inventor of gunpowder, but it is at any rate a most appropriate season in India. At present the Kadera makes his own gunpowder and manufactures fireworks, and in this capacity he is also known as Atashbāz. The ingredients for gunpowder in Narsinghpur are a pound of saltpetre, two ounces of sulphur, and four ounces of charcoal of a light wood, such as *sāleh*[1] or the stalks of *arhar*.[2] Water is sprinkled on the charcoal and the ingredients are pounded together in a mortar, a dangerous proceeding which is apt to cause occasional vacancies in the family circle. Arsenic and potash are also used for different fireworks, and sesamum oil is added to prevent smoke. Fireworks form a very popular spectacle in India, and can be obtained of excellent quality even in small towns. Bharbhūnjas or grain-parchers now also deal in them.

Kahār,[3] **Bhoi.**—The caste of palanquin-bearers and watermen of northern India. No scientific distinction can be made between the Kahārs and Dhīmars, both names being applied to the same people. In northern India the term Kahār is generally used, and Mr. Crooke has an article on Kahār, but none on Dhīmar. In the Central Provinces the latter is the more common name for the caste, and in 1911 23,000 Kahārs were returned as against nearly 300,000 Dhīmars. Berār had also 27,000 Kahārs. The social customs of the caste are described in the article on Dhīmar, but a short separate notice is given to the Kahārs on account of their special social interest. Some Kahārs refuse to clean household cooking-vessels and hence occupy a slightly higher social position than the Dhīmars generally. Mr. Crooke derives the name of the caste from the Sanskrit Skandha-kāra, or 'One who carries things on his shoulder.' The Brāhmanical genealogists represent the Kahār as descended from a Brāhman father and a Chandāl or sweeper mother, and this is typical of the position occupied by the caste, who, though probably derived from the primitive non-Aryan tribes, have received a special position on account of their employment as household servants, so that all classes may take water and cooked food at their hands. As one of Mr. Crooke's correspondents remarks: "This caste is so low that they clean the vessels of almost all castes except menials like the Chamār and Dhobi, and at the same time so high that, except Kanaujia Brāhmans, all other castes eat

1. Origin and statistics.

[1] *Boswellia serrata.*
[2] *Sesamum indicum.*
[3] This article is compiled from papers by Mr. Sarat Chandra Sanyāl, Sessions Judge, Nāgpur, and Mr. Abdul Samād, Tahsīldār, Sohāgpur.

pakki and drink water at their hands." Sir D. Ibbetson says of the Kahār: "He is a true village menial, receiving customary dues and performing customary service. His social standing is in one respect high; for all will drink water at his hands. But he is still a servant, though the highest of his class." This comparatively high degree of social purity appears to have been conferred on the Kahārs and Dhīmars from motives of convenience, as it would be intolerable to have a palanquin-bearer or indoor servant from whom one could not take a drink of water.

2. The *doli* or palanquin.

The proper occupation of the Kahār is that of *doli* or litter-bearer. When carts could not travel owing to the absence of roads this was the regular mode of conveyance of those who could afford it and did not ride. Buchanan remarks: "Few or none except some chief native officers of Government keep bearers in constant pay; but men of large estates give farms at low rents to their bearers, who are ready at a call and receive food when employed."[1] A superior kind of litter used by rich women had a domed roof supported on eight pillars with side-boards like venetian blinds; and was carried on two poles secured to the sides beneath the roof. This is perhaps the progenitor of the modern Calcutta *ghāri* or four-wheeler, just as the body of the hansom-cab was modelled on the old sedan-chair. It was called Kharkhariya in imitation of the rattling of the blinds when in motion.[2] The *pālki* or ordinary litter consisted of a couch slung under a long bamboo, which formed an arch over it. Over the arch was suspended a tilt made of cloth, which served to screen the passenger from sun and rain. A third kind was the Chaupala or square box open at the sides and slung on a bamboo; the passenger sat doubled up inside this. If as was sometimes the case the Chaupala was hung considerably beneath the bamboo the passenger was miserably draggled by dust and mud. Nowadays regular litters are so little used that they are not to be found in villages; but when required because one cannot ride or for travelling at night they are readily improvised by slinging a native wooden cot from two poles by strings of bamboo-fibre. Most of the Kahārs and Dhīmars have forgotten how to carry a litter, and proceed very

[1] *Eastern India*, ii. 426. [2] *Ibidem*, iii. pp. 119, 120.

slowly with frequent stops to change shoulders or substitute other bearers. But the Kols of Mandla still retain the art, and will do more than four miles an hour for several hours if eight men are allowed. Under native governments the privilege of riding in a palanquin was a mark of distinction; and a rule was enforced that no native could thus enter into the area of the forts in Madras and Bombay without the permission of the Governor; such permission being recorded in the order book at the gates of the fort and usually granted only to a few who were lame or otherwise incapacitated. When General Medows assumed the office of Governor of Bombay in 1788 some Parsis waited on him and begged for the removal of this restriction; to which the Governor replied, "So long as you do not force me to ride in this machine he may who likes it"; and so the rule was abrogated.[1] A passage from Hobson-Jobson, however, shows that the Portuguese were much stricter in this respect: "In 1591 a proclamation of the Viceroy, Matthias d'Alboquerque, ordered: 'That no person of what quality or condition soever, shall go in a *palanquy* without my express licence, save they be over sixty years of age, to be first proved before the Auditor-General of Police . . . and those who contravene this shall pay a penalty of 200 cruzados, and persons of mean estate the half, the *palanquys* and their belongings to be forfeited, and the *bois* or *mouços* who carry such *palanquys* shall be condemned to His Majesty's galleys.'"[2] The meaning of the last sentence appears to be that the bearers were considered as slaves, and were forfeited to the king's service as a punishment to their owner. As the unauthorised use of this conveyance was so severely punished it would appear that riding in a palanquin must have been a privilege of nobility. Similarly to ride on a horse was looked upon in something of the same light; and when a person of inferior consequence met a superior or a Government officer while riding, he had to dismount from his horse as a mark of respect until the other had passed. This last custom still obtains to some extent, though it is rapidly disappearing.

As a means of conveyance the litter would be held sacred

[1] Moor, *Hindu Infanticide*, p. 91.

[2] Yule and Burnell's *Hobson-Jobson*, Crooke's edition, *s.v.* Boy.

by primitive people, and Mr. Crooke gives an instance of the regard paid to it: "At the Holi festival eight days before Diwāli in the western Districts the house is plastered with cowdung and figures of a litter (*dolī*) and bearers are made on the walls with four or five colours, and to them offerings of incense, lights and flowers are given."[1] Even after passable roads were made tongas or carts drawn by trotting-bullocks were slow in coming into general use owing to the objection felt by the Hindus to harnessing the sacred ox.

3. Female bearers.

At royal courts women were employed to carry the litters of the king and the royal ladies into the inner precincts of the palace, the male bearers relinquishing their charge outside. "Another class of attendants at the palace peculiar to Lucknow were the female bearers. Their occupation was to carry the palanquins and various covered conveyances of the king and his ladies into the inner courts of the harem. These female bearers were also under military discipline. They had their officers, commissioned and non-commissioned. The head of them, a great masculine woman of pleasing countenance, was an especial favourite of the king. The *badinage* which was exchanged between them was of the freest possible character—not fit for ears polite, of course; but the extraordinary point in it was that no one hearing it or witnessing such scenes could have supposed it possible that a king and a slave stood before him as the two chief disputants."[2] Similarly female sepoys were employed to guard the harem, dressed in ordinary uniform and regularly drilled and taught to shoot.[3] A battalion of female troops for guarding the zenāna is still maintained in Hyderābād.[4]

4. Indoor servants.

From being a palanquin-bearer the Kahār became the regular indoor servant of Hindu households. Originally of low caste, and derived from the non-Aryan tribes, they did not object to eat the leavings of food of their masters, a relation which is naturally very convenient, if not essential, in poor Hindu houses. Sir H. Risley notes, however, that in Bengal a Kahār engaged in personal service with a Brāhman,

[1] *Tribes and Castes of the N.W.P.*, art. Kahār.

[2] *Private Life of an Eastern King*, p. 207.

[3] *Ibidem*, pp. 200, 202.

[4] Stevens, *In India*, p. 313.

Rājpūt, Bābhan, Kāyasth or Agarwāl, will only eat his master's leavings so long as he is himself unmarried.[1] It seems that the marriage feast may be considered as the sacrificial meal conferring full membership of the caste, after which the rules against taking food from other castes must be strictly observed. Slaves were commonly employed as indoor servants, and hence the term Kahār came to be almost synonymous with a slave. "In the eighteenth century the title Kahār was at Patna the distinctive appellation of a Hindu slave, as Maulazādah was of a Muhammadan, and the tradition in 1774 was that the Kahār slavery took its rise when the Muhammadans first invaded northern India."[2]

As the Kahār was the common indoor servant in Hindu houses so apparently he came to be employed in the same capacity by the English. But he was of too high a caste to serve the food of a European, which would have involved touching the cooked flesh of the cow, and thus lost him his comparatively good status and social purity among the Hindus. Hence arose the anomaly of a body servant who would not touch his master's food, and confined himself to the duties of a valet; while the name of bearer given to this servant indicates clearly that he is the successor of the old-time Kahār or palanquin-bearer. The Uriya bearers of Bengal were well known as excellent servants and most faithful; but in time the inconvenience of their refusal to wait at table has led to their being replaced by low-caste Madrasis and by Muhammadans. The word 'boy' as applied to Indian servants is no doubt of English origin, as it is also used in China and the West Indies; but the South Indian term *boyi* or Hindi *bhoi* for a palanquin-bearer also appears to have been corrupted into boy and to have made this designation more common. The following instances of the use of the word 'boy' from Hobson-Johnson[3] may be quoted in conclusion: "The real Indian ladies lie on a sofa, and if they drop their handkerchief they just lower their voices and say 'Boy,' in a very gentle tone" (*Letters from Madras* in 1826). 'Yes, Sahib, I Christian Boy. Plenty poojah do. Sunday time never no work do' (Trevelyan, *The Dawk Bungalow*,

1 *Tribes and Castes of Bengal*, art. Kahār.

2 *Tribes and Castes of Bengal*, *ibidem*.

3 *S.v.* Boy.

in 1866). The Hindu term Bhoi or bearer is now commonly applied to the Gonds, and is considered by them as an honorific name or title. The hypothesis thus appears to be confirmed that the Kahār caste of palanquin-bearers was constituted from the non-Aryan tribes, who were practically in the position of slaves to the Hindus, as were the Chamārs and Mahārs, the village drudges and labourers. But when the palanquin-bearer developed into an indoor servant, his social status was gradually raised from motives of convenience, until he grew to be considered as ceremonially pure, and able to give his master water and prepare food for cooking. Thus the Kahārs or Dhīmars came to rank considerably above the primitive tribes from whom they took their origin, their ceremonial purity being equal to that of the Hindu cultivating castes, while the degrading status of slavery which had at first attached to them gradually fell into abeyance. And thus one can understand why the Gonds should consider the name of Bhoi or bearer as a designation of honour.

1. Origin and traditions.

Kaikāri, Kaikādi (also called **Bargandi** by outsiders).[1]— A disreputable wandering tribe, whose ostensible profession is to make baskets. They are found in Nimār and the Marātha Districts, and number some 2000 persons in the Central Provinces. The Kaikāris here, as elsewhere, claim to have come from Telingāna or the Deccan, but there is no caste of this name in the Madras Presidency. They may not improbably be the caste there known as Korva or Yerūkala, whose occupations are similar. Mr. Kitts[2] has stated that the Kaikāris are known as Korāvars in Arcot and as Korvas in the Carnatic. The Kaikāris speak a gipsy language, which according to the specimen given by Hislop[3] contains Tamil and Telugu words. One derivation of Kaikāri is from the Tamil *kai*, hand, and *kude*, basket, and if this is correct it is in favour of their identification with the Korvas, who always carry their tattooing and other implements in a basket in the hand.[4] The Kaikāris of the

[1] This article is partly compiled from papers by Mr. G. Falconer Taylor, Forest Divisional Officer, and by Kanhyā Lāl, Clerk in the Gazetteer office.

[2] *Berār Census Report* (1881), p. 141.

[3] *Hislop papers.* Vocabulary.

[4] *North Arcot Manual*, p. 247.

Central Provinces say that their original ancestor was one Kānoba Ramjān who handed a twig to his sons and told them to earn their livelihood by it. Since then they have subsisted by making baskets from the stalks of the cotton-plant, the leaves of the date-palm and grass. They themselves derive their name from *Kai*, standing for Kānoba Ramjān and *kādi*, a twig, an etymology which may be dismissed with that given in the *Berār Census Report*[1] that they are the remnants of the Kaikeyas, who before the Christian era dwelt north of the Jalandhar Doāb. Two subcastes exist in Nimār, the Marāthas and the Phirasti or wandering Kaikāris, the former no doubt representing recruits from Marātha castes, not improbably from the Kunbis. The Marātha Kaikāris look down on the Phirastis as the latter take cooked food from a number of castes including the Telis, while the Marāthas refuse to do this. In the Nāgpur country there are several divisions which profess to be endogamous, as the Kāmāthis or those selling toys made of palm-leaves, the Bhāmtis or those who steal from bazārs, the Kunbis or cultivators, the Tokriwālas or makers and sellers of baskets and the Boriwālas or those who carry bricks, gravel and stone. Kunbi and Bhāmti are the names of other castes, and Kāmāthi is a general term applied in the Marātha country to Telugu immigrants; the names thus show that the Kaikāris, like other vagrant groups, are largely recruited from persons expelled from their own caste for social offences. These groups cannot really be endogamous as yet, but as in the case of several other wandering tribes they probably have a tendency to become so. In Berār[2] an entirely different set of 12½ subcastes is recorded, several of which are territorial, and two, the Pungis or blowers of gourds, and the Wājantris or village musicians, are occupational. In Nimār as in Khāndesh[3] the Kaikāris have only two exogamous clans, Jādon and Gaikwār, who must marry with each other. In the southern Districts there are a number of exogamous divisions, as Jādon, Māne, Kūmre, Jeshti, Kāde, Dāne and others. Jādon is a well-known Rājpūt sept, and the Kaikāris do not explain

[1] 1881, p. 141. [2] *Ibidem.*
[3] *Bombay Gazetteer* (Campbell), vol. xii. p. 120.

how they came by the name, but claim to have fought as soldiers under several kings, during which occasions the name may have been adopted from some Rājpūt leader in accordance with the common practice of imitation. Māne and Gaikwār are family names of the Marātha caste. The names and varied nomenclature of the subdivisions show that the Kaikāris, as at present constituted, are a very mixed caste, though they may not improbably have been originally connected with the Korvas of Madras.

2. Marriage. Marriage within the same *gotra* or section is prohibited, but with one or two exceptions there are no other restrictions on intermarriage between relatives. A sister's son may marry a brother's daughter, but not vice versa. A man may not marry his wife's elder sister either during his wife's lifetime or after her death, and he may marry her younger sister, but not the younger but one. Girls are generally married between 8 and 12 years of age. If a girl cannot get a partner nothing is done, but when the marriage of a boy has not been arranged, a sham rite is performed with an *akao* plant (swallow-wort) or with a silver ring, all the ceremonies of a regular marriage being gone through. The tree is subsequently carefully reared, or the ring worn on the finger. Should the tree die or the ring be lost, funeral obsequies are performed for it as for a member of the family. A bride-price is paid which may vary from Rs. 20 to Rs. 100. In the southern Districts the following custom is in vogue at weddings. After the ceremony the bridegroom pretends to be angry and goes out of the *mandap* or shed, on which the bride runs after him, and throwing a piece of cloth round his neck, drags him back again. Her father then gives him some money or ornaments to pacify him. After this the same performance is gone through with the bride. The bride is taken to her husband's house, but is soon brought back by her relatives. On her second departure the husband himself does not go to fetch her, and she is brought home by his father and other relations, her own family presenting her with new clothes on this occasion. Widow-marriage is permitted, and the widow is expected to marry the next younger brother of the deceased husband. She may not marry any except the next younger, and if

Bemrose, Collo., Derby.

KAIKĀRIS MAKING BASKETS.

another should take her he is expelled from the caste until the connection is severed. If she marries somebody else he must repay to her late husband's brother a half of the expenses incurred on the first marriage. In the southern Districts she may not marry a brother of her husband's at all. A widow cannot be married in her late husband's house, but is taken to her parents' house and married from there. In Nimār her family do not take anything, but in the south they are paid a small sum. Here also the marriage is performed at the second husband's house; the woman carries to it a new earthen pitcher filled with water, and, placing it on the *chauk* or pattern of lines traced with flour in the courtyard, touches the feet of the Panch or caste committee, after which her skirt is tied to her husband's cloth. The pair are seated on a blanket and new bangles are placed on the woman's wrist, widows officiating at the ceremony. The couple then leave the village and pass the night outside it, returning next morning, when the woman manages to enter the house without being perceived by a married woman or unmarried girl. A bachelor marrying a widow must first go through the ceremony with a ring or *akao* plant, as already described, this being his real marriage; if he omits the rite his daughters by the widow will not be considered as members of the caste, though his sons will be admitted. Polygamy is allowed, but the consent of the first wife must be obtained to the taking of a second, and she may require a written promise of good treatment after the second marriage. A second wife is usually only taken if the first is barren, and if she has children her parents usually interfere to dissuade the husband, while other parents are always averse to giving their daughter in marriage to a man under such circumstances. Divorce is permitted for the usual reasons, a deed being drawn up and attested by the *panchāyat*, to whom the husband pays a fine of Rs. 8 or Rs. 10.

3. Religion.

The tutelary god of the Kaikāris is the *Nāg* or cobra, who is worshipped at marriages and on the day of Nāg-Panchmi. Every family has in the house a platform dedicated to Khandoba, the Marātha god of war. They also worship Marīmāta, to whom flowers are offered at festivals, and a little *ghī* is poured out in her honour by way of incense. When the juāri harvest is gathered, *dalias* or cakes of boiled juāri and a ewe are offered to Marīmāta. They do not revere the Hindu sacred trees, the pīpal and banyan, nor the basil plant, and will readily cut them down. They both burn and bury the dead. The Jādons burn all married persons, but if they cannot afford firewood they touch the corpse with a burning cinder and then bury it. The Gaikwārs always bury their dead, the corpse being laid naked on its back with the feet pointing to the south. On returning from the burial-ground each relative of the deceased gives one *roti* or wheaten cake to the bereaved family, and they eat, sharing the cakes with the *panchāyat.* Bread is also presented on the second day, and on the third the family begin to cook again. Mourning lasts for ten days, and on the last day the house is cleaned and the earthen pots thrown out; the clothes of the family are washed and the males are shaved. Ten balls of rice cooked in milk are offered to the soul of the dead person and a feast is given to the caste. After a birth the mother remains impure for five weeks. For the first five days both the mother and child are bathed daily. The navel cord and after-birth are buried by the midwife in a rubbish heap. When the milk teeth fall out they are placed in a ball of the dung of an ass and thrown on to the roof of the house. It is considered that the rats or mice, who have very good and sharp teeth, will take them and give the child good teeth in exchange. Women are impure for five days during the menstrual period. When a girl attains maturity a ceremony called *god-bharni* is performed. The neighbours are invited and songs are sung and the girl is seated in the *chauk* or pattern of lines traced with flour. She is given new clothes and bangles by her father, or her father-in-law if she is married, and rice and plantains, cocoanuts and other fruits are tied up in her skirt. This is no doubt done so that the girl may in like manner be fruitful, the cocoanuts perhaps being meant to represent human heads, as they usually do.

The Kaikāris eat flesh, including pork and fowls, but not beef. In Nimār the animals which they eat must have their throats cut by a Muhammadan with the proper formula, otherwise it is considered as murder to slaughter them. Both men and women drink liquor. They take food cooked with water from Kunbis and Mālis and take water from the same castes, but not from Dhīmars, Nais or Kahārs. No caste will take food from a Kaikāri. Their touch is considered to defile a Brāhman, Bania, Kalār and other castes, but not a Kunbi. They are not allowed to enter temples but may live inside the village. Their status is thus very low. They have a caste *panchāyat* or committee, and punishments are imposed for the usual offences. Permanent exclusion from caste is rarely or never inflicted, and even a woman who has gone wrong with an outsider may be readmitted after a peculiar ceremony of purification. The delinquent is taken to a river, tank or well, and is there shaved clean. Her tongue is branded with a ring or other article of gold, and she is then seated under a wooden shed having two doors. She goes in by one door and sits in the shed, which is set on fire. She must remain seated until the whole shed is burning and is then allowed to escape by the other door. A young boy of the caste is finally asked to eat from her hand, and thus purified she is readmitted to social intercourse. Fire is the great purifier, and this ceremony probably symbolises the immolation of the delinquent and her new birth. A similar ordeal is practised among the Korvas of Bombay, and this fact may be taken as affording further evidence of the identity of the two castes.[1] The morals of the caste are, however, by no means good, and some of them are said to live by prostituting their women. The dog is held especially sacred as with all worshippers of Khandoba, and to swear by a dog is Khandoba's oath and is considered the most binding. The Kaikāris are of dark colour and have repulsive features. They do not bathe or change their clothes for days together. They are also quarrelsome, and in Bombay the word Kaikārin is a proverbial term for a dirty shrew. Women are profusely tattooed, because tattooing is considered to be a record of the virtuous acts performed in this world and must be displayed to the deity after death. If no marks

4. Social customs and position.

[1] *Bombay Gazetteer* (Campbell), vol. xxi. p. 172.

of tattooing are found the soul is sent to hell and punished for having acquired no piety.

5. Occupation. Basket-making is the traditional occupation of the Kaikāris and is still followed by them. They do not however make baskets from bamboos, but from cotton-stalks, palm-leaves and grass. In the south they are principally employed as carriers of stone, lime, bricks and gravel. Like most wandering castes they have a bad character. In Berār the Rān Kaikāris are said to be the most criminal class.[1] They act under a chief who is elected for life, and wander about in the cold weather, usually carrying their property on donkeys. Their ostensible occupations are to make baskets and mend grinding mills. A notice of them in Lawrence's *Settlement Report* of Bhandāra (1867) stated that they were then professional thieves, openly avowing their dependence on predatory occupations for subsistence, and being particularly dexterous at digging through the walls of houses and secret pilfering.

1. Origin. **Kalanga.**—A cultivating caste of Chhattīsgarh numbering 1800 persons in 1911. In Sambalpur they live principally in the Phuljhar zamīndāri on the border, between Chhattīsgarh and the Uriya track. The Kalangas appear to be a Dravidian tribe who took up military service and therefore adopted a territorial name, Kalanga being probably derived from Kalinga, the name of the sea-board of the Telugu country. The Kalangas may be a branch of the great Kalingi tribe of Madras. They have mixed much with the Kawars, and in Phuljhar say that they have three branches, the Kalingia, Kawar and Chero Kalangas; Kawar and Chero are names for the same tribe, and the last two branches are thus probably a mixture of Kalingis and Kawars, while the first comprises the original Kalingis. The Kalangas themselves, like the Kawars, say that they are the descendants of the Kauravas of the Mahābhārata, and that they came from northern India with the Rājas of Patna, whom they still serve. But their features indicate their Dravidian descent as also their social customs, especially that of killing a cock with the bare hands on

[1] *Berār Census Report* (1881), p. 141.

the birth of a child, and anointing the infant's forehead with its blood. They have not retained their Telugu language, however, and like the Kawars now speak a dialect of Chhattīsgarhi at home, while many also know Uriya.

2. Subdivisions.

The Kalangas have no real endogamous divisions but a large number of exogamous groups or *bargas*, the names of which are derived from animals, plants, or material objects, nicknames, occupations or titles. Instances of the totemistic groups are Barha the wild boar, Magar the crocodile, Bichhi the scorpion, Saria a variety of rice, Chhati a mushroom, Khumri a leaf umbrella, and several others. The members of the group revere the animal, plant or other object from which it takes its name and would refuse to injure it or use it for food. They salute the object whenever they see it. Instances of other group names are Mānjhi a headman, Behra a cook, Gunda dusty, Kapāt a shutter, Bhundi a hole, Chīka muddy, Bhīl a tribe, Rendia quarrelsome, and Bersia a Thug or strangler. Some of the nicknames or titles are curious, as for instance Kapāt, a shutter, which stands for gate-keeper, and Bhundi, a hole, which indicates a defective person. Some of the group names are those of other castes, and this probably indicates the admission of families of other castes among the Kalangas. One of the groups is called Kusundi, the meaning of which is not known, but whenever any one of the caste gets maggots in a wound and is temporarily expelled, it is a member of the Kusundi group, if one is available, who gives him water on his readmission into caste. This is a dangerous service, because it renders the performer liable to the burden of the other's sin, and when no Kusundi is present five or seven men of other groups combine in doing it so as to reduce the risk to a fraction. But why this function of a scapegoat should be imposed upon the Kusundi group, or whether it possesses any peculiar sanctity which protects it from danger, cannot be explained.

3. Marriage.

Marriage within the same *barga* or group is prohibited and also the union of first cousins. Marriage is usually adult and matches are arranged between the parents of the parties. A considerable quantity of grain with five pieces of cloth and Rs. 5 are given to the father of the bride. A marriage-shed is erected and a post of the mahua tree fixed inside it. Three days before the wedding a Gānda goes to the shed with some pomp and worships the village gods there. In the ceremony the bridegroom and bride proceed separately seven times round the post, this rite being performed for three days running. During the four days of the wedding the fathers of the bride and bridegroom each give one meal to the whole caste on two days, while the other meal on all four days is given to the wedding party by the members of the caste resident in the village. This may be a survival of the time when all members of the village community were held to be related. Widow-marriage is allowed, but the widow must obtain the consent of the caste people before taking a second husband, and a feast must be given to them. If the widow has no children and there are no relatives to succeed to her late husband's property, it is expended on feeding the caste people. Divorce is permitted and is effected by breaking the woman's bangles in front of the caste *panchāyat.* In memory perhaps of their former military profession the Kalangas worship the sword on the 15th day of Shrāwan and the 9th day of Kunwār. Offerings are made to the dead in the latter month, but not to persons who have died a violent death. The spirits of these must be laid lest they should trouble the living, and this is done in the following manner: a handful of rice is placed at the threshold of the house, and a ring is suspended by at hread so as to touch the rice. A goat is then brought up, and when it eats the rice, the spirit of the dead person is considered to have entered into the goat, which is thereupon killed and eaten by the family so as to dispose of him once for all. If the goat will not eat the rice it is made to do so. The spirit of a man who has been killed by a tiger must, however, be laid by the Sulia or sorcerer of the caste, who goes through the formula of pretending to be a tiger and of mauling another sorcerer.

4. Social position.

The Kalangas are at present cultivators and many of them are farmservants. They do not now admit outsiders into the caste, but they will receive the children begotten on any woman by a Kalanga man. They take food cooked without water from a Guria, but *katchi* food from nobody. Only the lowest castes will take food from them. They drink liquor and eat fowls and rats, but not beef or pork. A man who gets his ear torn is temporarily excluded from caste, and this penalty is also imposed for the other usual offences. A woman committing adultery with a man of another caste is permanently expelled. The Kalangas are somewhat tall in stature. Their features are Dravidian, and in their dress and ornaments they follow the Chhattīsgarhi style.

KALĀR

LIST OF PARAGRAPHS

1. Strength of the caste. **Kalār, Kalwār:**[1]—The occupational caste of distillers and sellers of fermented liquor. In 1911 the Kalārs numbered nearly 200,000 persons in the Central Provinces and Berār, or rather more than one per cent of the population; so they are a somewhat important caste numerically. The name is derived from the Sanskrit Kalyapāla, a distiller of liquor.

2. Internal structure. The caste has a number of subdivisions, of which the bulk are of the territorial type, as Mālvi or the immigrants from Mālwa, Lād those coming from south Gujarāt, Daharia belonging to Dāhar or the Jubbulpore country, Jaiswār and Kanaujia coming from Oudh. The Rai Kalārs are an aristocratic subcaste, the word Rai signifying the highest or ruling group like Rāj. But the Byāhut or 'Married' are perhaps really the most select, and are so called because they forbid the remarriage of widows, their women being thus married once for all. In Bengal they also decline to

[1] Some information for this article has been supplied by Bābu Lāl, Excise Sub-Inspector, Mr. Adurām Chaudhri, Tahsīldār, and Sundar Lāl Richaria, Sub-Inspector of Police.

distil or sell liquor.[1] The Chauske Kalārs are said to be so called because they prohibit the marriage of persons having a common ancestor up to the fourth generation. The name of the Seohāre or Sivahāre subcaste is perhaps a corruption of Somhāre or dealers in *Soma*, the sacred fermented liquor of the Vedas; or it may mean the worshippers of the god Siva. The Seohāre Kalārs say that they are connected with the Agarwāla Banias, their common ancestors having been the brothers Seoru and Agru. These brothers on one occasion purchased a quantity of mahua[2] flowers; the price afterwards falling heavily. Agru sold his stock at a discount and cut the loss; but Seoru, unwilling to suffer it, distilled liquor from his flowers and sold the liquor, thus recouping himself for his expenditure. But in consequence of his action he was degraded from the Bania caste and his descendants became Kalārs. The Jaiswār, Kanaujia and Seohāre divisions are also found in northern India, and the Byāhut both there and in Bengal. Mr. Crooke states that the caste may be an offshoot from the Bania or other Vaishya tribes; and a slight physical resemblance may perhaps be traced between Kalārs and Banias. It may be noticed also that some of the Kalārs are Jains, a religion to which scarcely any others except Banias adhere. Another hypothesis, however, is that since the Kalārs have become prosperous and wealthy they devised a story connecting them with the Bania caste in order to improve their social position.

3. Dandsena Kalārs in Chhattisgarh.

In Chhattīsgarh the principal division of the Kalārs is that of the Dandsenas or 'Stick-carriers,' and in explanation of the name they relate the following story: "A Kalār boy was formerly the Mahāprasād or bosom friend of the son of the Rājpūt king of Balod.[3] But the Rāja's son fell in love with the Kalār boy's sister and entertained evil intentions towards her. Then the Kalār boy went and complained to the Rāja, who was his Phūlbāba,[4] the father of his friend, saying, 'A dog is always coming into my house and defiling it, what am I to do?' The Rāja replied that he must kill the dog. Then the boy asked whether he would be punished

[1] *Tribes and Castes of Bengal*, art. Kalār.

[2] *Bassia latifolia*, the tree from whose flowers fermented liquor is made.

[3] The headquarters of the Sanjāri tahsīl in Drūg District.

[4] Phūlbāba, lit. 'flower-father.'

for killing him, and the Rāja said, No. So the next day as the Rājpūt boy was entering his house to get at his sister, the Kalār boy killed him, though he was his dearest friend. Then the Rājpūts attacked the Kalārs, but they were led only by the queen, as the king had said that the Kalār boy might kill the dog. But the Rājpūts were being defeated and so the Rāja intervened, and the Kalārs then ceased fighting as the Rāja had broken his word. But they left Balod, saying that they would drink no more of its waters, which they have not done to this day."[1] And the Kalārs are called Dandsena, because in this fight sticks were their only weapons.

4. Social customs.

The marriage customs of the caste follow the ordinary Hindu ritual prevalent in the locality and are not of special interest. Before a Kalār wedding procession starts a ceremony known as marrying the well is performed. The mother or aunt of the bridegroom goes to the well and sits in the mouth with her legs hanging down inside it and asks what the bridegroom will give her. He then goes round the well seven times, and a stick of *kāns*[2] grass is thrown into it at each turn. Afterwards he promises the woman some handsome present and she returns to the house. Another explanation of the story is that the woman pretends to be overcome with grief at the bridegroom's departure and threatens to throw herself into the well unless he will give her something. The well-to-do marry their daughters at an early age, but no stigma attaches to those who have to postpone the ceremony. A bride-price is not customary, but if the girl's parents are poor they sometimes receive help from those of the boy in order to carry out the wedding. Matches are usually arranged at the caste feasts, and a Brāhman officiates at the ceremony. Divorce is recognised and widows are allowed to marry again except by the Byāhut subcaste. The Kalārs worship the ordinary Hindu deities, and those who sell liquor revere an earthen jar filled with wine at the Holi festival. The educated are usually Vaishnavas by sect, and as already stated a few of them belong to the Jain religion. The social status of the Kalārs is equiva-

[1] This story is only transplanted, a similar one being related by Colonel Tod in the Annals of the Bundi State (*Rājasthān*, ii. p. 441).

[2] *Saccharum spontaneum*.

lent to that of the village menials, ranking below the good cultivating castes. Brāhmans do not take water from their hands. But in Mandla, where the Kalārs are important and prosperous, certain Sarwaria Brāhmans who were their household priests took water from them, thus recognising them as socially pure. This has led to a split among the local Sarwaria Brāhmans, the families who did not take water from the Kalārs refusing to intermarry with those who did so.

While the highest castes of Hindus eschew spirituous liquor the cultivating and middle classes are divided, some drinking it and others not; and to the menial and labouring classes, and especially to the forest tribes, it is the principal luxury of their lives. Unfortunately they have not learnt to indulge in moderation and nearly always drink to excess if they have the means, while the intoxicating effect of even a moderate quantity is quickly perceptible in their behaviour.

In the Central Provinces the liquor drunk is nearly all distilled from the flowers of the mahua tree (*Bassia latifolia*), though elsewhere it is often made from cane sugar. The smell of the fermented mahua and the refuse water lying about make the village liquor-shop an unattractive place. But the trade has greatly profited the Kalārs by the influence which it has given them over the lower classes. "With the control of the liquor-supply in their hands," Mr. Montgomerie writes, "they also controlled the Gonds, and have played a more important part in the past history of the Chhindwāra District than their numbers would indicate."[1] The Kalār and Teli (oil-presser) are usually about on the same standing; they are the creditors of the poorer tenants and labourers, as the Bania is of the landowners and substantial cultivators. These two of the village trades are not suited to the method of payment by annual contributions of grain, and must from an early period have been conducted by single transactions of barter. Hence the Kalār and Teli learnt to keep accounts and to appreciate the importance of the margin of profit. This knowledge and the system of dealing on credit with the exaction of interest have stood

[1] *Settlement Report*, p. 26.

them in good stead and they have prospered at the expense of their fellow-villagers. The Kalārs have acquired substantial property in several Districts, especially in those mainly populated by Gonds, as Mandla, Betūl and Chhindwāra. In British Districts of the Central Provinces they own 750 villages, or about 4 per cent of the total. In former times when salt was highly taxed and expensive the Gonds had no salt. The Kalārs imported rock-salt and sold it to the Gonds in large pieces. These were hung up in the Gond houses just as they are in stables, and after a meal every one would go up to the lump of salt and lick it as ponies do. When the Gonds began to wear cloth instead of leaves and beads the Kalārs retailed them thin strips of cloth just sufficient for decency, and for the cloth and salt a large proportion of the Gond's harvest went to the Kalār. When a Gond has threshed his grain the Kalār takes round liquor to the threshing-floor and receives a present of grain much in excess of its value. Thus the Gond has sold his birthright for a mess of pottage and the Kalār has taken his heritage. Only a small proportion of the caste are still supported by the liquor traffic, and a third of the whole are agriculturists. Others have engaged in the timber trade, purchasing teak timber from the Gonds in exchange for liquor, a form of commerce which has naturally redounded to their great advantage. A few are educated and have risen to good positions in Government service. Sir D. Ibbetson describes them as 'Notorious for enterprise, energy and obstinacy. Death may budge, but a Kalār won't.' The Sikh Kalārs, who usually call themselves Ahluwālia, contain many men who have attained to high positions under Government, especially as soldiers, and the general testimony is that they make brave soldiers.[1] One of the ruling chiefs of the Punjab belongs to this caste. Until quite recently the manufacture of liquor, except in the large towns, was conducted in small pot-stills, of which there was one for a circle of perhaps two dozen villages with subordinate shops. The right of manufacture and vend in each separate one of these stills was sold annually by auction at the District headquarters, and the Kalārs assembled to bid for it. And here instances of their

[1] Mr. (Sir E.) Maclagan's *Punjab Census Report* (1891).

dogged perseverance could often be noticed; when a man would bid up for a licence to a sum far in excess of the profits which he could hope to acquire from it, rather than allow himself to be deprived of a still which he desired to retain.

Though alcoholic liquor is now eschewed by the higher castes of Hindus and forbidden by their religion, this has by no means always been the case. In Vedic times the liquor known as Soma was held in so much esteem by the Aryans that it was deified and worshipped as one of their principal gods. Dr. Hopkins summarises[1] the attributes of the divine wine, Soma, as follows, from passages in the Rig-Veda: "This offering of the juice of the Soma-plant in India was performed thrice daily. It is said in the Rig-Veda that Soma grows upon the mountain Mūjawat, that its or his father is Parjanya, the rain-god, and that the waters are his sisters. From this mountain, or from the sky, accounts differ, Soma was brought by a hawk. He is himself represented in other places as a bird; and as a divinity he shares in the praise given to Indra. It was he who helped Indra to slay Vritra, the demon that keeps back the rain. Indra, intoxicated by Soma, does his great deeds, and indeed all the gods depend on Soma for immortality. Divine, a weapon-bearing god, he often simply takes the place of Indra and other gods in Vedic eulogy. It is the god Soma himself who slays Vritra, Soma who overthrows cities, Soma who begets the gods, creates the sun, upholds the sky, prolongs life, sees all things, and is the one best friend of god and man, the divine drop (*īndu*), the friend of Indra. As a god he is associated not only with Indra but also with Agni, Rudra and Pushān. A few passages in the later portion of the Rig-Veda show that Soma already was identified with the moon before the end of this period. After this the lunar yellow god was regularly regarded as the visible and divine Soma of heaven represented on earth by the plant." Mr. Hopkins discards the view advanced by some commentators that it is the moon and not the beverage to which the Vedic hymns and worship are addressed, and there is no reason to doubt that he is right.

5. Liquor held divine in Vedic times.

[1] *Religions of India*, p. 113.

The *soma* plant has been thought to be the *Asclepias acida*,[1] a plant growing in Persia and called *hom* in Persian. The early Persians believed that the *hom* plant gave great energy to body and mind.[2] An angel is believed to preside over the plant, and the Hom Yast is devoted to its praises. Twigs of it are beaten in water in the smaller *Agiari* or fire-temple, and this water is considered sacred, and is given to newborn children to drink.[3] Dr. Hopkins states, however, that the *hom* or *Asclepias acida* was not the original *soma*, as it does not grow in the Punjab region, but must have been a later substitute. Afterwards again another kind of liquor, *sura*, became the popular drink, and *soma*, which was now not so agreeable, was reserved as the priests' (gods') drink, a sacrosanct beverage not for the vulgar, and not esteemed by the priests except as it kept up the rite.[4]

Soma is said to have been prepared from the juice of the creeper already mentioned, which was diluted with water, mixed with barley meal, clarified butter and the flour of wild rice, and fermented in a jar for nine days.[5] *Sura* was simply arrack prepared from rice-flour, or rice-beer.

6. Subsequent prohibition of alcohol.

Though in the cold regions of Central Asia the cheering and warming liquor had been held divine, in the hot plains of India the evil effects of alcohol were apparently soon realised. "Even more bold is the scorn of the gods in Hymn x. 119 of the Rig-Veda, which introduces Indra in his merriest humour, ready to give away everything, ready to destroy the earth and all that it contains, boasting of his greatness in ridiculous fashion—all this because, as the refrain tells us, he is in an advanced state of intoxication caused by excessive appreciation of the *soma* offered to him. Another Hymn (vii. 103) sings of the frogs, comparing their voices to the noise of a Brāhmanical school and their hopping round the tank to the behaviour of drunken priests celebrating a nocturnal offering of *soma*."[6] It seems clear, therefore, that the evil effects of drunkenness were early realised,

[1] Apparently also called *Sarcostemma viminalis*.

[2] *Bombay Gazetteer*, *Parsis of Gujarāt*, by Messrs. Nasarvanji Girvai and Behrāmji Patel, p. 228, footnote.

[3] *Ibidem*.

[4] Hopkins, *loc. cit.* p. 213.

[5] Rājendra Lāl Mitra, *Indo-Aryans*, ii. p. 419.

[6] Deussen, *Outlines of Indian Philosophy*, p. 12.

and led to a religious prohibition of alcohol. Dr. Rājendra Lāl Mitra writes:[1] "But the fact remains unquestioned that from an early period the Hindus have denounced in their sacred writings the use of wine as sinful, and two of their greatest law-givers, Manu and Yajnavalkya, held that the only expiation meet for a Brāhman who had polluted himself by drinking spirit was suicide by a draught of spirit or water or cow's urine or milk, in a boiling state taken in a burning hot metal pot. Angira, Vasishtha and Paithūrasi restricted the drink to boiling spirits alone. Dewala went a step farther and prescribed a draught of molten silver, copper or lead as the most appropriate. . . . Manu likewise provides for the judicial cognisance of such offences by Brāhmans, and ordains excommunication, and branding on the forehead the figure of a bottle as the most appropriate punishment."

7. Spirits habitually drunk in ancient times.

Nevertheless the consumption of alcohol was common in classical times. Bhāradwāja, a great sage, offered wine to Bhārata and his soldiers when they spent a night under his roof.[2] When Sīta crossed the Ganges on her way to the southern wilderness she begged the river for a safe passage, saying, "Be merciful to me, O Goddess, and I shall on my return home worship thee with a thousand jars of arrack and dishes of well-dressed flesh meat." When crossing the Jumna she said, "Be auspicious, O Goddess; I am crossing thee. When my husband has accomplished his vow I shall worship thee with a thousand head of cattle and a hundred jars of arrack." Similarly the companions of Krishna, the Yādavas, destroyed each other when they were overcome by drink; and many other instances are given by Dr. Rājendra Lāl Mitra. The Purānas abound in descriptions of wine and drinking, and though the object of many of them is to condemn the use of wine the inference is clear that there was a widespread malady which they proposed to overcome.[3] Pulastya, an ancient sage and author of one of the original Smritis, enumerates twelve different kinds of liquor, besides the *soma* beer which is not usually reckoned under the head of *madya* or wine, and his successors have added

[1] *Indo-Aryans*, i. p. 393.
[2] *Ibidem*, p. 396.
[3] *Ibidem*, p. 402.

largely to the list. The twelve principal liquors of this sage are those of the jack fruit, the grape, honey or mead, date-liquor, palm-liquor or toddy, sugarcane-liquor, mahua-liquor, rum and those made from long-pepper, soap-berries and cocoanuts.[1] All these drinks were not merely fermented, but distilled and flavoured with different kinds of spices, fruits and herbs; they were thus varieties of spirits or liqueurs. It is probable that without the use of glass bottles and corks it would be very difficult to keep fermented wine for any length of time in the Indian climate. But spirits drunk neat as they were would produce more markedly evil results in a hot country, and would strengthen and accelerate the reaction against alcoholic liquor, which has gone so far that probably a substantial majority at least of the inhabitants of India are total abstainers. To this good result the adoption of Buddhism as stated by Dr. Mitra no doubt largely contributed. This was for some centuries the state religion, and was a strong force in aid of temperance as well as of abstention from flesh. The Sivite revival reacted in favour of liquor drinking as well as of the consumption of drugs. But the prohibition of alcohol has again been a leading tenet of practically all the Vaishnava reforming sects.

8. Drunkenness and divine inspiration.

The intoxication of alcohol is considered by primitive people as a form of divine inspiration or possession like epileptic fits and insanity. This is apparently the explanation of the Vedic liquor, Soma, being deified as one of the greatest gods. In later Hindu mythology, Varuni, the goddess of wine, was produced when the gods churned the ocean with the mountain Mandara as a churning-stick on the back of the tortoise, Vishnu, and the serpent as a rope, for the purpose of restoring to man the comforts lost during the great flood.[2] Varuni was considered to be the consort of Varūna, the Vedic Neptune.

Similarly the Bacchantes in their drunken frenzy were considered to be possessed by the wine-god Dionysus. "The Aztecs regarded *pulque* or the wine of the country as bad, on account of the wild deeds which men did under its

[1] *Indo-Aryans*, i. p. 411.

[2] Garrett's *Classical Dictionary*, *s.v.* Varuni and Vishnu.

influence. But these wild deeds were believed to be the acts, not of the drunken man, but of the wine-god by whom he was possessed and inspired; and so seriously was this theory of inspiration held that if any one spoke ill of or insulted a tipsy man, he was liable to be punished for disrespect to the wine-god incarnate in his votary."[1] Sir James Frazer thinks that the grape-juice was also considered to be the blood of the vine. At one time the arrack or rice-beer liquor was also considered by the Hindus as holy and purifying. Siva says to his consort: "Oh, sweet-speaking goddess, the salvation of Brāhmans depends on drinking wine. . . . No one becomes a Brāhman by repeating the Gāyatri, the mother of the Vedas; he is called a Brāhman only when he has knowledge of Brahma. The ambrosia of the gods is their Brahma, and on earth it is arrack, and because one attains the character of a god (*suratva*) therefore is arrack called *sura*."[2] The Sākta Tantras insist upon the use of wine as an element of devotion. The Kaulas, who are the most ardent followers of the Sākta Tantras, celebrate their rites at midnight in a closed room, when they sit in a circle round a jar of country arrack, one or more young women of a lewd character being in the company; they drink, drink and drink until they fall down on the ground in utter helplessness, then rising again they drink in the hope of never having a second birth.[3] "I knew a highly respectable widow lady, connected with one of the most distinguished families in Calcutta, who belonged to the Kaula sect, and had survived the 75th anniversary of her birthday, who never said her prayers (and she did so regularly every morning and evening) without touching the point of her tongue with a tooth-pick dipped in a phial of arrack, and sprinkling a few drops of the liquor on the flowers which she offered to her god. I doubt very much if she had ever drunk a wine-glassful of arrack at once in all her life, and certain it is that she never had any idea of the pleasures of drinking; but as a faithful Kaula she felt herself in duty bound to observe the mandates of her religion with the

1 *The Golden Bough*, 2nd edition, i. pp. 359, 360.

2 *Indo-Aryans*, pp. 408, 409.

3 *Ibidem*, pp. 404, 405.

greatest scrupulousness."[1] In this case it seems clear that the liquor was considered to have a purifying effect, which was perhaps especially requisite for the offerings of a widow.

9. Sanctity of liquor among the Gonds and other castes.

Similarly the Gonds and Baigas revere the mahua tree and consider the liquor distilled from its flowers as sacred and purificatory. At a Gond wedding the sacred post round which the couple go is made of the wood of the mahua tree. The Bhatras of Bastar also use the mahua for the wedding post, and the Sonkars of Chhattīsgarh a forked branch of the tree. Minor caste offences are expiated among the Gonds by a fine of liquor, and by drinking it the culprit is purified. At a Gond funeral one man may be seen walking with a bottle or two of liquor slung to his side; this is drunk by all the party on the spot after the burial or burning of the corpse as a means of purification. Among the Korwas and other tribes the Baiga or priest protects the village from ghosts by sprinkling a line of liquor all round the boundary, over which the ghosts cannot pass. Similarly during epidemics of cholera liquor is largely used in the rites of the Baigas for averting the disease and is offered to the goddess. At their weddings the Mahārs drink together ceremoniously, a pot of liquor being placed on a folded cloth and all the guests sitting round it in a circle. An elder man then lays a new piece of cloth on the pot and worships it. He takes a cup of the liquor himself and hands round a cupful to every person present. At the Hareli or festival of the new green vegetation in July the Gonds take the branches of four kinds of trees and place them at the corners of their fields and also inside the house over the door. They pour *ghī* (butter) on the fire as incense and an offering to the deities. Then they go to the meeting-place of the village and there they all take a bottle or two of liquor each and drink together, having first thrown a little on the ground as an offering. Then they invite each other to their houses to take food. The Baigas do not observe Hareli, but on any moonlight night in Shrāwan (July) they will go to the field where they have sown grain and root up a few plants and bring them to the house, and, laying them on a clean place, pour *ghī* and a little liquor over them. Then they take the corn plants back

[1] *Indo-Aryans*, pp. 405, 406.

to the field and replace them. For these rites and for offerings to the deities of disease the Gonds say that the liquor should be distilled at home by the person who offers the sacrifice and not purchased from the Government contractor. This is a reason or at any rate an excuse for the continuance of the practice of illicit distillation. Hindus generally make a libation to Devi before drinking liquor. They pour a little into their hand and sprinkle it in a circle on the ground, invoking the goddess. The palm-tree is also held sacred on account of the *tāri* or toddy obtained from it. "The shreds of the holy palm-tree, holy because liquor-yielding, are worn by some of the early Konkan tribes and by some of the Konkan village gods. The strip of palm-leaf is the origin of the shape of one of the favourite Hindu gold bracelet patterns."[1]

10. Drugs also considered divine.

The abstinence from liquor enjoined by modern Hinduism to the higher castes of Hindus has unfortunately not extended to the harmful drugs, opium, and gānja[2] or Indian hemp with its preparations. On the contrary gānja is regularly consumed by Hindu ascetics, whether devotees of Siva or Vishnu, though it is more favoured by the Sivite Jogis. The blue throat of Siva or Mahādeo is said to be due to the enormous draughts of *bhāng*[3] which he was accustomed to swallow. The veneration attached to these drugs may probably be explained by the delusion that the pleasant dreams and visions obtained under their influence are excursions of the spirit into paradise. It is a common belief among primitive people that during sleep the soul leaves the body and that dreams are the actual experiences of the soul when travelling over the world apart from the body.[4] The principal aim of Hindu asceticism is also the complete conquest of all sensation and movement in the body, so that while it is immobile the spirit freed from the trammels of the body and from all worldly cares and concerns may, as it is imagined, enter into communion with and be absorbed in the deity. Hence the physical inertia and abnormal mental exaltation produced by these drugs would be an ideal con-

1 *Bombay Gazetteer*, *Poona*, p. 549.

2 *Cannabis sativa.*

3 A liquor made from the flowers of the hemp plant, commonly drunk in the hot weather.

4 See Mr. E. Clodd's *Myths and Dreams*, under Dreams.

dition to the Hindu ascetic; the body is lulled to immobility and it is natural that he should imagine that the delightful fantasies of his drugged brain are beatific visions of heaven. Gānja and bhāng are now considered sacred as being consumed by Mahādeo, and are offered to him. Before smoking gānja a Hindu will say, 'May it reach you, Shankar,'[1] that is, the smoke of the gānja, like the sweet savour of a sacrifice; and before drinking bhāng he will pour a little on the ground and say 'Jai Shankar.'[2] Similarly when cholera visits a village and various articles of dress with food and liquor are offered to the cholera goddess, Marhai Māta, smokers of gānja and *madak*[3] will offer a little of their drugs. Hindu ascetics who smoke gānja are accustomed to mix with it some seeds of the *dhatura* (*Datura alba*), which have a powerful stupefying effect. In large quantities these seeds are a common narcotic poison, being administered to travellers and others by criminals. This tree is sacred to Siva, and the purple and white flowers are offered on his altars, and probably for this reason it is often found growing in villages so that the poisonous seeds are readily available. Its sanctity apparently arises from the narcotic effects produced by the seeds.

The conclusion of hostilities and ratification of peace after a Bhīl fight was marked by the solemn administration of opium to all present by the Jogi or Gammaiti priests.[4] This incident recalls the pipe of peace of the North American Indians, among whom a similar divine virtue was no doubt ascribed to tobacco. In ancient Greece the priestesses of Apollo consumed the leaves of the laurel to produce the prophetic ecstasy; the tree was therefore held sacred and associated with Apollo and afterwards developed into a goddess in the shape of Daphne pursued by Apollo and transformed into a laurel.[5] The laurel was also considered to have a purifying or expiatory effect like alcoholic liquor in India. Wreaths of laurel were worn by such heroes as Apollo and Cadmus before engaging in battle to cleanse themselves from the pollution of bloodshed, and

[1] A name of Siva or Mahādeo.

[2] 'Victory to Shankar.'

[3] A preparation of opium for smoking.

[4] T. H. Hendley, *Account of the Bhils*, *J.A.S.B.* xliv., 1875, p. 360.

[5] M. Salomon Reinach in *Orphéus*, p. 120.

hence the laurel-wreath afterwards became the crown of victory.[1]

In India *bhāng* was regularly drunk by the Rājpūts before going into battle, to excite their courage and render them insensible to pain. The effects produced were probably held to be caused by divine agency. Herodotus says that the Scythians had a custom of burning the seeds of the hemp plant in religious ceremonies and that they became intoxicated with the fumes.[2] Gānja is the *hashīsh* of the Old Man of the Mountain and of Monte Cristo. The term *hashshāsh*, meaning 'a smoker or eater of hemp,' was first applied to Arab warriors in Syria at the time of the Crusades; from its plural *hashshāsheen* our word assassin is derived.[3]

11. Opium and gānja. The sacred or divine character attributed to the Indian drugs in spite of their pernicious effects has thus probably prevented any organised effort for their prohibition. Buchanan notes that "No more blame follows the use of opium and gānja than in Europe that of wine; yet smoking tobacco is considered impure by the highest castes."[4] It is said, however, that a Brāhman should abstain from drugs until he is in the last or ascetic stage of life. In India opium is both eaten and smoked. It is administered to children almost from the time of their birth, partly perhaps because its effects are supposed to be beneficial and also to prevent them from crying and keep them quiet while their parents are at work. One of the favourite methods of killing female children was to place a fatal dose of opium on the nipple of the mother's breast. Many children continue to receive small quantities of opium till they are several years old, sometimes eight or nine, when it is gradually abandoned. It can scarcely be doubted that the effect of the drug must be to impair their health and enfeeble their vitality. The effect of eating opium on adults is much less pernicious than when the habit of smoking it is acquired. *Madak* or opium prepared for smoking may not now be sold, but people make it for themselves, heating the opium in a little brass cup over a fire with an infusion of tamarind leaves. It is then made

1 Sir James Frazer in *Attis, Adonis, Osiris*, ii. p. 241.

2 Book IV., chap. lxxv., quoted in Lane's *Modern Egyptians*, p. 347.

3 Lane, *Modern Egyptians*, p. 348.

4 *Eastern India*, iii. p. 163.

into little balls and put into the pipe. Opium-smokers are gregarious and partake of the drug together. As the fumes mount to their brains, their intellects become enlivened, their tongues unloosed and the conversation ranges over all subjects in heaven and earth. This factitious excitement must no doubt be a powerful attraction to people whose lives are as dull as that of the average Hindu. And thus they become *madakis* or confirmed opium-smokers and are of no more use in life. Dhīmars or fishermen consume opium and gānja largely under the impression that these drugs prevent them from taking cold. Gānja is smoked and is usually mixed with tobacco. It is much less injurious than opium in the same form, except when taken in large quantities, and is also slower in acquiring a complete hold over its votaries. Many cultivators buy a little gānja at the weekly bazār and have one pipeful each as a treat. Sweepers are greatly addicted to gānja, and their patron saint Lālbeg was frequently in a comatose condition from over-indulgence in the drug. Ahīrs or herdsmen also smoke it to while away the long days in the forests. But the habitual consumers of either kind of drug are now only a small fraction of the population, while English education and the more strenuous conditions of modern life have effected a substantial decline in their numbers, at least among the higher classes. At the same time a progressive increase is being effected by Government in the retail price of the drugs, and the number of vend licences has been very greatly reduced.

The prohibition of wine to Muhammadans is held to include drugs, but it is not known how far the rule is strictly observed. But addiction to drugs is at any rate uncommon among Muhammadans.

12. Tobacco. No kind of sanctity attaches to tobacco and, as has been seen, certain classes of Brāhmans are forbidden to smoke though they may chew the leaves. Tobacco is prohibited by the Sikhs, the Satnāmis and some other Vaishnava sects. The explanation of this attitude is simple if, as is supposed, tobacco was first introduced into India by the Portuguese in the fifteenth century.[1] In this case as a new and foreign product it could have no sacred character, only those things

[1] Sir G. Watt's *Commercial Products of India*, *s.v.* Nicotiana.

being held sacred and the gifts of the gods whose origin is lost in antiquity. In a note on the subject[1] Mr. Ganpat Rai shows that several references to smoking and also to the huqqa are found in ancient Sanskrit literature; but it does not seem clear that the plant smoked was tobacco and, on the other hand, the similarity of the vernacular to the English name[2] is strong evidence in favour of its foreign origin.

13. Customs in connection with drinking. The country liquor, consisting of spirits distilled from the flowers of the mahua tree, is an indispensable adjunct to marriage and other ceremonial feasts among the lower castes of Hindus and the non-Aryan tribes. It is usually drunk before the meal out of brass vessels, cocoanut-shells or leaf-cups, water being afterwards taken with the food itself. If an offender has to give a penalty feast for readmission to caste but the whole burden of the expense is beyond his means, other persons who may have committed minor offences and owe something to the caste on that account are called upon to provide the liquor. Similarly at the funeral feast the heir and chief mourner may provide the food and more distant relatives the liquor. The Gonds never take food while drinking, and as a rule one man does not drink alone. Three or four of them go to the liquor-shop together and each in turn buys a whole bottle of liquor which they share with each other, each bottle being paid for by one of the company and not jointly. And if a friend from another village turns up and is invited to drink he is not allowed to pay anything. In towns there will be in the vicinity of the liquor-shop retailers of little roasted balls of meat on sticks and cakes of gram-flour fried in salt and chillies. These the customers eat, presumably to stimulate their thirst or as a palliative to the effects of the spirit. Illicit distillation is still habitual among the Gonds of Mandla, who have been accustomed to make their own liquor from time immemorial. In the rains, when travelling is difficult and the excise officers cannot descend on them without notice, they make the liquor in their houses. In the open season they go to

[1] *Ind. Ant.*, January 1911, p. 39.

[2] Tobacco is no doubt a derivative from some American word, and Platts derives the Hindi *tanbāku* or *tambāku* from tobacco. The fact that *tanbāku* is also Persian for tobacco militates against the Sanskrit derivation suggested by Mr. Ganpat Rai and others, and tends to demonstrate its American importation.

the forest and find some spot secluded behind rocks and also near water. When the fermented mahua is ready they put up the distilling vat in the middle of the day so that the smoke may be less perceptible, and one of them will climb a tree and keep watch for the approach of the Excise Sub-Inspector and his myrmidons while the other distils.

KAMĀR[1]

LIST OF PARAGRAPHS

Kamār.—A small Dravidian tribe exclusively found in the Raipur District and adjoining States. They numbered about 7000 persons in 1911, and live principally in the Khariār and Bindrānawāgarh zamīndāris of Raipur. In Bengal and Chota Nāgpur the term Kamār is merely occupational, implying a worker in iron, and similarly Kammala in the Telugu country is a designation given to the five artisan castes. Though the name is probably the same the Kamārs of the Central Provinces are a purely aboriginal tribe and there is little doubt that they are an offshoot of the Gonds, nor have they any traditions of ever having been metal-workers. They claim to be autochthonous like most of the primitive tribes. They tell a long story of their former ascendancy, saying that a Kamār was the original ruler of Bindrānawāgarh. But a number of Kamārs one day killed the *bhimrāj* bird which had been tamed and taught hawking by a foreigner from Delhi. He demanded satisfaction, and when it was refused went to

1. Origin and traditions.

[1] This article is based on papers drawn up by Mr. Hīra Lāl, Extra Assistant Commissioner, Pyāre Lāl Misra, Ethnographic Clerk, and a very full account of the tribe by Mr. Ganpati Giri, Manager of Bindrānawāgarh, which has furnished the greater part of the article, especially the paragraphs on birth, religion and social customs.

Delhi and brought man-eating soldiers from there, who ate up all the Kamārs except one pregnant woman. She took refuge in a Brāhman's hut in Patna and there had a son, whom she exposed on a dung-heap for fear of scandal, as she was a widow at the time. Hence the boy was called Kachra-Dhurwa or rubbish and dust. This name may be a token of the belief of the Kamārs that they were born from the earth as insects generate in dung and decaying organisms. Similarly one great subtribe of the Gonds are called Dhur or dust Gonds. Kachra-Dhurwa was endowed with divine strength and severed the head of a goat made of iron with a stick of bamboo. On growing up he collected his fellow-tribesmen and slaughtered all the cannibal soldiers, regaining his ancestral seat in Bindrānawāgarh. It is noticeable that the Kamārs call the cannibal soldiers Aghori, the name of a sect of ascetics who eat human flesh. They still point to various heaps of lime-encrusted fossils in Bindrānawāgarh as the bones of the cannibal soldiers. The state of the Kamārs is so primitive that it does not seem possible that they could ever have been workers in iron, but they may perhaps, like the Agarias, be a group of the Gonds who formerly quarried iron and thus obtained their distinctive name.

2. Sub-divisions and marriage.

They have two subdivisions, the Bundhrajia and Mākadia. The latter are so called because they eat monkeys and are looked down on by the others. They have only a few *gots* or septs, all of which have the same names as those of Gond septs. The meaning of the names has now been forgotten. Their ceremonies also resemble those of the Gonds, and there can be little doubt that they are an offshoot of that tribe. Marriage within the sept is prohibited, but is permitted between the children of brothers and sisters or of two sisters. Those who are well-to-do marry their children at about ten years old, but among the bulk of the caste adult-marriage is in fashion, and the youths and maidens are sometimes allowed to make their own choice. At the betrothal the boy and girl are made to stand together so that the caste *panchāyat* or elders may see the suitability of the match, and a little wine is sprinkled in the name of the gods. The marriage ceremony is a simple one, the marriage-post being erected at the boy's house. The party go to the girl's house to fetch her, and there is a feast, followed by a night of singing and dancing. They then return to the boy's house and the couple go round the sacred pole and throw rice over each other seven times. All the guests also throw rice over the couple with the object, it is said, of scaring off the spirits who are always present on this occasion, and protecting the bride and bridegroom from harm. But perhaps the rice is really meant to give fertility to the match. The wife remains with her husband for four days and then they return to the house of her parents, where the wedding clothes stained yellow with turmeric must be washed. After this they again proceed to the bridegroom's house and live together. Polygamy and widow-marriage are allowed, the ceremony in the marriage of a widow consisting simply in putting bangles on her wrists and giving her a piece of new cloth. The Kamārs never divorce their wives, however loose their conduct may be, as they say that a lawful wife is above all suspicion. They also consider it sinful to divorce a wife. The *liaison* of an unmarried girl is passed over even with a man outside the caste, unless he is of a very low caste, such as a Gānda.

3. The sister's son.

As among some of the other primitive tribes, a man stands in a special relation to his sister's children. The marriage of his children with his sister's children is considered as the most suitable union. If a man's sister is poor he will arrange for the wedding of her children. He will never beat his sister's children, however much they may deserve it, and he will not permit his sister's son or daughter to eat from the dish from which he eats. This special connection between a maternal uncle and his nephew is held to be a survival of the matriarchate, when a man stood in the place a father now occupies to his sister's children, the real father having nothing to do with them.

4. Menstruation.

During the period of her monthly impurity a woman is secluded for eight days. She may not prepare food nor draw water nor worship the gods, but she may sweep the house and do outdoor work. She sleeps on the ground and every morning spreads fresh cowdung over the place where she has slept. The Kamārs think that a man who touched a woman in this condition would be destroyed by the household god. When a woman in his household is impure in this manner a man will bathe before going into the forest lest he should pollute the forest gods.

5. Birth customs.

A woman is impure for six days after a birth until the performance of the Chathi or sixth-day ceremony, when the child's head is shaved and the mother and child are bathed and their bodies rubbed with oil and turmeric. After this a woman can go about her work in the house, but she may not cook food nor draw water for two and a half months after the birth of a male child, nor for three months after that of a female one. Till the performance of the Chathi ceremony the husband is also impure, and he may not worship the gods or go hunting or shooting or even go for any distance into the forest. If a child is born within six months of the death of any person in the family, they think that the dead relative has been reborn in the child and give the child the same name, apparently without distinction of sex. If a mother's milk runs dry and she cannot suckle her child they give her fresh fish and salt to eat, and think that this will cause the milk to flow. The idea of eating the fish is probably that being a denizen of the liquid element it will produce liquid in the mother's body, but it is not clear whether the salt has any special meaning.

6. Death and inheritance.

The dead are buried with the head to the north, and mourning is nominally observed for three days. But they have no rules of abstinence, and do not even bathe to purify themselves as almost all castes do. Sons inherit equally, and daughters do not share with sons. But if there are no sons, then an unmarried daughter or one married to a Lamsena, or man who has served for her, and living in the house, takes the whole property for her lifetime, after which it reverts to her father's family. Widows, Mr. Ganpati Giri states, only inherit in the absence of male heirs.

7. Religious beliefs.

They worship Dūlha Deo and Devi, and have a firm belief in magic. They tell a curious story about the origin of the world, which recalls that of the Flood. They say that in the beginning God created a man and a woman to whom two children of opposite sex were born in their old age. Mahādeo, however, sent a deluge over the world in order to drown a jackal who had angered him. The old couple heard that there was going to be a deluge, so they shut up their children in a hollow piece of wood with provision of food to last them until it should subside. They then closed up the trunk, and the deluge came and lasted for twelve years, the old couple and all other living things on the earth being drowned, but the trunk floated on the face of the waters. After twelve years Mahādeo created two birds and sent them to see whether his enemy the jackal had been drowned. The birds flew over all the corners of the world, but saw nothing except a log of wood floating on the surface of the water, on which they perched. After a short time they heard low and feeble voices coming from inside the log. They heard the children saying to each other that they only had provision for three days left. So the birds flew away and told Mahādeo, who then caused the flood to subside, and taking out the children from the log of wood, heard their story. He thereupon brought them up, and they were married, and Mahādeo gave the name of a different caste to every child who was born to them, and from them all the inhabitants of the world are descended. The fact that the Kamārs should think their deity capable of destroying the whole world by a deluge, in order to drown a jackal which had offended him, indicates how completely they are wanting in any exalted conception of morality. They are said to have no definite ideas of a future life nor any belief in a resurrection of the body. But they believe in future punishment in the case of a thief, who, they say, will be reborn as a bullock in the house of the man whose property he has stolen, or will in some other fashion expiate his crime. They think that the sun and moon are beings in human shape, and that darkness is caused by the sun going to sleep. They also think that a railway train is a live and sentient being, and that the whistle of the engine is its cry, and they propitiate the train with offerings lest it should do them some injury. When a man purposes to go out hunting, Mr. Ganpati Giri states, he consults the village priest, who tells him whether he will fail or succeed. If the prediction is unfavourable he promises a fowl or a goat to his family god in order to obtain his assistance, and then confidently expects success. When an animal has been killed and brought home, the hunter cuts off the head, and after washing it with turmeric powder and water makes an offering of it to the forest god. Ceremonial fishing expeditions are sometimes held, in which all the men and women of the village participate, and on such occasions the favour of the water-goddess is first invoked with an offering of five chickens and various feminine adornments, such as vermilion, lamp-black for the eyes, small glass bangles and a knot of ribbons made of cotton or silk, after which a large catch of fish is anticipated. The men refrain from visiting their wives on the day before they start for a hunting or fishing expedition.

8. Veneration of iron and liquor.

The tribe have a special veneration for iron, which they now say is the emblem of Durga Māta or the goddess of smallpox. On their chief festivals of Hareli and Dasahra all iron implements are washed and placed together in the house, where they are worshipped with offerings of rice, flowers and incense ; nor may any iron tool be brought into use on this day. On the day appointed for the worship of Dūlha Deo, the bridegroom god, or other important deities, and on the Dasahra festival, they will not permit fire or anything else to be taken out of the house. Before drinking liquor they will pour a few drops on the ground, making a libation first to mother-earth, then to their family and other important gods, and lastly to their ancestors.

9. Social customs and caste penalties.

The Kamārs will eat with all except the very lowest castes, and do not refuse any kind of food. The Bundhrajias, however, abstain from the flesh of snakes, crocodiles and monkeys, and on this account claim to be superior to the Mākadias who eat these animals. Temporary exclusion from caste is imposed for the usual offences, and in serious cases, such as adultery with a woman of impure caste or taking food from her, the penalty is severe. The offender puts a straw and a piece of iron between his teeth, and stands before the elders with one leg lifted in his clasped hands. He promises never to repeat the offence nor permit his children to do so, and falls prostrate at the feet of each elder, imploring his forgiveness. He supplies the elders with rice, pulse, salt and vegetables for two days, and on the third day he and his family prepare a feast with one or more goats and two rupees' worth of liquor. The elders eat of this in his house, and readmit him to social intercourse.

10. Tattooing. The women are tattooed either before or after marriage, the usual figures being a peacock on the shoulders, a scorpion on the back of the hand, and dots representing flies on the fingers. On their arms and legs they have circular lines of dots representing the ornaments usually worn, and they say that if they are destitute in the other world they will be able to sell these. This indicates that the more civilised of them, at any rate, now believe in a future life. They also have circular dotted lines round the knees which they say will help them to climb to heaven. Like the Gonds the men scarify their bodies by burning the outer skin of the forearm in three or four places with a small piece of burning cloth.

11. Hair. The men shave the whole head on the death of a father or other venerable relative, but otherwise they never cut their hair, and let it grow long, twisting it into a bunch at the back of the head. They shave off or eradicate the hair of the face and pubes, but that on other parts of the body is allowed to remain. The hair of the head is considered to be sacred.

12. Occupation and manner of life. The tribe wear only the narrowest possible strip of cloth round the loins, and another strip on the head, one end of which is often allowed to hang down over the ear. Formerly they lived by *dahya* cultivation, burning down patches of forest and scattering seed on the ground fertilised by the ashes, and they greatly resent the prohibition of this destructive method. They have now taken to making baskets and other articles from the wood of the bamboo. They are of dirty habits, and seldom wash themselves. Forty years ago their manner of life was even ruder than at present, as shown in the following notice[1] of them by Mr. Ball in 1876:

"Proceeding along the bed of the valley I came upon two colonies of a wild race of people called Kamārs by their neighbours. They were regular Troglodytes in their habits, dwelling in caves and existing chiefly on roots and fish. It is singular to observe how little the people of these wild races do to protect themselves from the inclemency of the weather.

[1] *Jungle Life in India*, p. 588.

In one of these caves the sole protection from the air was a lean-to of loosely placed branches. The people seemed to be very timid, hiding themselves on our approach. I did not therefore like to attempt an examination of their dwellings. After some calling on our part one man was induced to make his appearance. He was a most wretched-looking, leprous object, having lost several fingers and toes. He could give no very definite explanation as to his means of subsistence. All he could say was that he lived 'by picking up odds and ends here and there.' However, he seemed to be able to afford himself the solace of tobacco. A few cocks and hens at one of the caves, and a goat at the other, were the only domestic animals which I saw."

13. Their skill with bows and arrows.

The tribe are of small stature. They are very fond of hunting, and are expert at using their bows and arrows, with which they have killed even bison. Mr. W. E. Ley, C.S., relates the following particulars of a recent murder by a Kamār in Raipur: Two Hindus went to a Kamār's house in the jungle to dun him for a debt. He could not pay the debt, but invited them to take food in his house. At the meal the creditor's companion said the food was bad, and a quarrel thereupon ensuing, slapped the Kamār in the face. The latter started up, snatched up his bow and arrow and axe, and ran away into the jungle. The Hindus then set out for home, and as they were afraid of being attacked by the Kamār, they took his brother with them as a protection. Nevertheless the Kamār shot one of them through the side, the arrow passing through the arm and penetrating the lung. He then shot the other through the chest, and running in, mutilated his body in a shocking manner. When charged with the murders he confessed them freely, saying that he was a wild man of the woods and knew no better.

KANJAR

[*Bibliography*: Mr. J. C. Nesfield's *The Kanjars of Upper India*, *Calcutta Review*, vol. lxxvii., 1883; Mr. Crooke's *Castes and Tribes*, art. Kanjar; Major Gunthorpe's *Criminal Tribes*; Mr. Kitts' *Berār Census Report* (1881); Mr. Gayer's *Lectures on Criminal Tribes of the Central Provinces.*]

LIST OF PARAGRAPHS

1. Derivation of the Kanjars from the Doms.

Kanjar.—A name applied somewhat loosely to various small communities of a gipsy character who wander about the country. In 1911 about 1000 Kūchbandhia Kanjars were returned in the Province. In Berār the Kanjars seem to be practically identical with the Sānsias; Major Gunthorpe[1] gives Kanjar and Sānsia as alternative names of the same caste of criminals, and this is also done by Mr. Kennedy in Bombay.[2] Mr. Kitts writes of them:[3] "The Deccani and Mārwāri Kanjars were originally Bhāts (bards) of the Jāt tribe; and as they generally give themselves out to be Bhāts are probably not included at all among the Kanjars returned at the census. They are a vagrant people, living in tents and addicted to crime. The women are good-looking; some are noted for their obscene songs, filthy alike in word and gesture; while others, whose husbands play on the *sārangi*, lead a life of immorality. The men are often skilful acrobats." And in another passage:[4] "The Sānsia family or the 'Long Firm' of India includes two principal divisions represented

1 *Criminal Tribes*, p. 78.
2 *Criminal Classes.*
3 *Berār Census Report* (1881), p. 140.
4 Page 139.

in Berār by the Kanjars and Kolhātis respectively. They will eat, drink and smoke together, and occasionally join in committing dacoity. They eat all kinds of meat and drink all liquors; they are lax of morals and loose of life." Now in northern India the business of acting as bards to the Jāts and begging from them is the traditional function of the Sānsias; and we may therefore conclude that so far as Berār and the Marātha Districts are concerned the Kanjars are identical with the Sānsias, while the Kolhātis mentioned by Mr. Kitts are the same people as the Berias, as shown in the article on Kolhāti, and the Berias themselves are another branch of the Sānsias.[1] There seems some reason to suppose that these four closely allied groups, the Kanjar or Sānsia, and the Kolhāti or Beria, may have their origin from the great Dom caste of menials and scavengers in Hindustān and Bengal. In the Punjab the Doms are the regular bards and genealogists of the lower castes, being known also as Mirāsi: "The two words are used throughout the Province as absolutely synonymous. The word Mirāsi is derived from the Arabic *mirās* or inheritance; and the Mirāsi is to the inferior agricultural castes and the outcaste tribes what the Bhāt is to the Rājpūts."[2] In the article on Sānsia it is shown that the primary calling of the Sānsias was to act as bards and genealogists of the Jāts; and this common occupation is to some extent in favour of the original identity of the two castes Dom and Sānsia, though Sir D. Ibbetson was not of this opinion.[3] In the United Provinces Mr. Crooke gives the Jallād or executioners as one of the main divisions of the Kanjars;[4] and the Jallāds of Umballa are said to be the descendants of a Kanjar family who were attached to the Delhi Court as executioners.[5] But the Jallād or *sūpwāla* is also a name of the Doms. "The term Jallād, which is an Arabic name for 'A public flogger,' is more especially applied to those Doms who are employed in cities to kill ownerless dogs and to act as public executioners."[6] Mr. Gayer states that as the result of special inquiries made by an experienced police-officer it would appear that these Jallād Kanjars are really Doms.[7]

[1] See art. Beria, para. 1.

[2] Ibbetson, *Punjab Census Report* (1881), para. 527.

[3] *Ibidem.*

[4] Art. Kanjar, para. 3.

[5] Ibbetson.

[6] Crooke, art. Dom, para. 21.

[7] *Lectures*, p. 59.

Bemrose, Collo., Derby.

KANJARS MAKING ROPES.

In Gujarāt the Mīrs or Mirāsis are also known as Dom after the tribe of that name; they were originally of two classes, one the descendants of Gujarāt Bhāts or bards, the other from northern India, partly of Bhāt descent and partly connected with the Doms.[1] And the Sānsias and Berias in Bombay when accompanied by their families usually pass themselves off as Gujarāti Bhāts, that is, bards of the Jāt caste from Mārwār or of the Kolis from Gujarāt.[2] Major Gunthorpe states that the Kolhātis or Berias of Berār appear to be the same as the Domras of Bengal;[3] and Mr. Kitts that the Khām Kolhātis are the Domarus of Telingāna.[4] In writing of the Kanjar bards Sherring also says: "These are the Kanjars of Gondwāna, the Sānsis of northern India; they are the most desperate of all dacoits and wander about the country as though belonging to the Gujarāti Domtaris or showmen." The above evidence seems sufficient to establish a *prima facie* case in favour of the Dom origin of these gipsy castes. It may be noticed further that the Jallād Kanjars of the United Provinces are also known as Sūpwāla or makers of sieves and winnowing-fans, a calling which belongs specially to the Doms, Bhangis, and other sweeper castes. Both Doms and Bhangis have divisions known as Bānsphor or 'breaker of bamboos,' a name which has the same signification as Sūpwāla. Again, the deity of the criminal Doms of Bengal is known as Sānsari Mai.[5]

2. The Kanjars and the Gipsies.

The Kanjars and Berias are the typical gipsy castes of India, and have been supposed to be the parents of the European gipsies. On this point Mr. Nesfield writes: "The commonly received legend is that multitudes of Kanjars were driven out of India by the oppressions of Tamerlane, and it is inferred that the gipsies of Europe are their direct descendants by blood, because they speak like them a form of the Hindi language."[6] Sir G. Grierson states:[7] "According to the Shāh-nāma, the Persian monarch Bahrām Gaur received in the fifth century from an Indian

1 *Bombay Gazetteer, Muhammadans of Gujarāt*, p. 83.

2 Kennedy, *Criminal Tribes of Bombay*, p. 257.

3 *Criminal Tribes*, p. 46.

4 *Berār Census Report* (1881), p. 140.

5 *Tribes and Castes of Bengal*, art. Dom.

6 Nesfield, *l.c.* p. 393.

7 *Ind. Ant.* xvi. p. 37.

king 12,000 musicians who were known as Lūris, and the Lūris or Lūlis, that is gipsies, of modern Persia are the descendants of these." These people were also called Lutt, and hence it was supposed that they were the Indian Jāts. Sir G. Grierson, however, shows it to be highly improbable that the Jāts, one of the highest castes of cultivators, could ever have furnished a huge band of professional singers and dancers. He on the contrary derives the gipsies from the Dom tribe:[1] "Mr. Leland has made a happy suggestion that the original gipsies may have been Doms of India. He points out that Romany is almost letter for letter the same as Domni (डोमनी), the plural of Dom. Domni is the plural form in the Bhojpuri dialect of the Bihāri language. It was originally a genitive plural; so that Romany-Rye, 'A gipsy gentleman,' may be well compared with the Bhojpuri Domni Rai, 'A king of the Doms.' The Bhojpuri-speaking Doms are a famous race, and they have many points of resemblance with the gipsies of Europe. Thus they are darker in complexion than the surrounding Bihāris, are great thieves, live by hunting, dancing and telling fortunes, their women have a reputation for making love-philtres and medicines to procure abortion, they keep fowls (which no orthodox Hindu will do), and are said to eat carrion. They are also great musicians and horsemen. The gipsy grammar is closely connected with Bhojpuri, and the following mongrel, half-gipsy, half-English rhyme will show the extraordinary similarity of the two vocabularies:[2]

Gipsy.	The Rye (squire) he mores (hunts) adrey the wesh (wood)
Bhojpuri.	*Rai* *mare* *andal* *besh* (Pers. بیش)
Gipsy.	The kaun-engro (ear-fellow, hare) and chiriclo (bird).
Bhojpuri.	*Kānwāla* *chirin*
Gipsy.	You sovs (sleep) with leste (him) drey (within) the wesh (wood)
Bhojpuri.	*soe* *andal* *besh*
Gipsy.	And rigs (carry) for leste (him) the gono (sack, game-bag).
Bhojpuri.	*gon*

---

[1] *Ind. Ant.* xv. p. 15.

[2] In Sir G. Grierson's account the Bhojpuri version is printed in the Nāgari character; but this cannot be reproduced. It is possible that one or two mistakes have been made in transliteration.

Gipsy. } Oprey (above) the rukh (tree) adrey (within) the wesh (wood)
Bhojpuri. } *Upri* *rukh* *andal* *besh*

Gipsy. } Are chiriclo (male-bird) and chiricli (female-bird).
Bhojpuri. } *chirin* *chirin*

Gipsy. } Tuley (below) the rukh (tree) adrey (within) the wesh (wood)
Bhojpuri. } *Tule* *rukh* *andal* *besh*

Gipsy. } Are pireno (lover) and pireni (lady-love).
Bhojpuri. } *pyara* *pyāri*

In the above it must be remembered that the verbal terminations of the gipsy text are English and not gipsy."

Sir G. Grierson also adds (in the passage first quoted): "I may note here a word which lends a singular confirmation to the theory. It is the gipsy term for bread, which is *mānrō* or *manro.* This is usually connected either with the Gaudian *mānr* 'rice-gruel' or with *manrua*, the millet (*Eleusine coracana*). Neither of these agrees with the idea of bread, but in the Magadhi dialect of Bihāri, spoken south of the Ganges in the native land of these Maghiya Doms, there is a peculiar word *mānda* or *mānra* which means wheat, whence the transition to the gipsy *mānrō*, bread, is eminently natural."

The above argument renders it probable that the gipsies are derived from the Doms; and as Mr. Nesfield gives it as a common legend that they originated from the Kanjars, this is perhaps another connecting link between the Doms and Kanjars. The word gipsy is probably an abbreviation of 'Egyptian,' the country assigned as the home of the gipsies in mediaeval times. It has already been seen that the Doms are the bards and minstrels of the lower castes in the Punjab, and that the Kanjars and Sānsias, originally identical or very closely connected, were in particular the bards of the Jāts. It is a possible speculation that they may have been mixed up with the lower classes of Jāts or have taken their name, and that this has led to the confusion between the Jāts and gipsies. Some support is afforded to this suggestion by the fact that the Kanjars of Jubbulpore say that they have three divisions, the Jāt, Multāni and Kūchbandia. The Jāt Kanjars are, no doubt, those who acted as bards to the Jāts, and hence took the name; and if the ancestors of these people emigrated from India they may have given themselves out as Jāt.

3. The Thugs derived from the Kanjars.

In the article on Thug it is suggested that a large, if not the principal, section of the Thugs were derived from the Kanjars. At the Thug marriages an old matron would sometimes repeat, "Here's to the spirits of those who once led bears and monkeys; to those who drove bullocks and marked with the *godini* (tattooing-needle); and those who made baskets for the head." And these are the occupations of the Kanjars and Berias. The Goyandas of Jubbulpore, descendants of Thug approvers, are considered to be a class of gipsy Muhammadans, akin to or identical with the Kanjars, of whom the Multāni subdivision are also Muhammadans. Like the Kanjar women the Goyandas make articles of net and string. There is also a colony of Berias in Jubbulpore, and these are admittedly the descendants of Thugs who were located there. If the above argument is well founded, we are led to the interesting conclusion that four of the most important vagrant and criminal castes of India, as well as the Mirāsis or low-class Hindu bards, the gipsies, and a large section of the Thugs, are all derived from the great Dom caste.

4. The Doms.

The Doms appear to be one of the chief aboriginal tribes of northern India, who were reduced to servitude like the Mahārs and Chamārs. Sir H. M. Elliot considered them to be "One of the original tribes of India. Tradition fixes their residence to the north of the Ghāgra, touching the Bhars on the east in the vicinity of the Rohini. Several old forts testify to their former importance, and still retain the names of their founders, as, for instance, Domdiha and Domingarh in the Gorakhpur district. Rāmgarh and Sahukot on the Rohini are also Dom forts."[1] Sir G. Grierson quotes Dr. Fleet as follows: "In a south Indian inscription a king Rudradeva is said to have subdued a certain Domma, whose strength evidently lay in his cavalry. No clue is given as to who this Domma was, but he may have been the leader of some aboriginal tribe which had not then lost all its power"; and suggests that this Domma may have been a leader of the Doms, who would then be shown to have been dominant in southern India. As already seen there is a Domāru caste of Telingāna, with whom Mr. Kitts

[1] Quoted in Mr. Crooke's article on Dom.

identified the Berias or Kolhātis. In northern India the Doms were reduced to a more degraded condition than the other pre-Aryan tribes as they furnished a large section of the sweeper caste. As has been seen also they were employed as public executioners like the Māngs. This brief mention of the Doms has been made in view of the interest attaching to them on account of the above suggestions, and because there will be no separate article on the caste.

5. The criminal Kanjars.

In Berār two main divisions of the Kanjars may be recognised, the Kūnchbandhia or those who make weavers' brooms and are comparatively honest, and the other or criminal Kanjars.[1] The criminal Kanjars may again be divided into the Mārwāri and Deccani groups. They were probably once the same, but the Deccanis, owing to their settlement in the south, have adopted some Marātha or Gujarāti fashions, and speak the Marāthi language; their women wear the *angia* or Marātha breast-cloth fastening behind, and have a gold ornament shaped like a flower in the nose;[2] while the Mārwāri Kanjars have no breast-cloth and may not wear gold ornaments at all. The Deccani Kanjars are fond of stealing donkeys, their habit being either to mix their own herds with those of the village and drive them all off together, or, if they catch the donkeys unattended, to secrete them in some water-course, tying their legs together, and if they remain undiscovered to remove them at nightfall. The animals are at once driven away for a long distance before any attempt is made to dispose of them. The Mārwāri Kanjars consider it derogatory to keep donkeys and therefore do not steal these animals. They are pre-eminently cattle-lifters and sheep-stealers, and their encampments may be recognised by the numbers of bullocks and cows about them. Their women wear the short Mārwāri petticoat reaching half-way between the knees and ankles. Their hair is plaited over the forehead and cowrie shells and brass ornaments like buttons are often attached in it. Bead necklaces are much worn by the women and bead and horse-hair necklets by the men. A peculiarity about the

[1] Gayer, *Lectures*, p. 59.

[2] Gunthorpe, p. 81. Mr. Kennedy says: "Sānsia and Beria women have a clove (*lavang*) in the left nostril; the Sānsias, but not the Berias, wear a *bullāq* or pendant in the fleshy part of the nose."

women is that they are confirmed snuff-takers and consume great quantities of the weed in this form. The women go into the towns and villages and give exhibitions of singing and dancing; and picking up any information they can acquire about the location of property, impart this to the men. Sometimes they take service, and a case was known in Jubbulpore of Kanjar women hiring themselves out as pankha-pullers, with the result that the houses in which they were employed were subsequently robbed.[1] It is said, however, that they do not regularly break into houses, but confine themselves to lurking theft. I have thought it desirable to record here the above particulars of the criminal Kanjars, taken from Major Gunthorpe's account; for, though the caste is, as already stated, identical with the Sānsias, their customs in Berār differ considerably from those of the Sānsias of Central India, who are treated of in the article on that caste.

6. The Kūnchband Kanjars. We come, finally, to the Kūnchband Kanjars, the most representative section of the caste, who as a body are not criminals, or at any rate less so than the others. The name Kūnchband or Kūchband, by which they are sometimes known, is derived from their trade of making brushes (*kūnch*) of the roots of *khas-khas* grass, which are used by weavers for cleaning the threads entangled on the looms. This has given rise to the proverb '*Kori ka bigāri Kūnchbandhia*' or 'The Kūnchbandhia must look to the Kori (weaver) as his patron'; the point being that the Kori is himself no better than a casual labourer, and a man who is dependent on him must be in a poor way indeed. The Kūnchbandhias are also known in northern India as Sankat or Patharkat, because they make and sharpen the household grinding-stones, this being the calling of the Tākankār Pārdhis in the Marātha Districts, and as Goher because they catch and eat the *goh*, the large lizard or iguana.[2] Other divisions are the Dhobibans or washerman's race, the Lakarhār or wood-cutters, and the Untwār or camelmen.

7. Marriage and religion. In the Central Provinces there are other divisions, as the Jāt and Multāni Kanjars. They say they have two exogamous divisions, Kalkha and Malha, and a member of either of these must take a wife from the other division.

[1] Gayer, *l.c.* p. 61.

[2] Crooke, *l.c.* para. 3.

Both the Kalkhas and Malhas are further divided into *kuls* or sections, but the influence of these on marriage is not clear. At a Kanjar marriage, Mr. Crooke states, the *gadela* or spade with which they dig out the *khas-khas* grass and kill wolves or vermin, is placed in the marriage pavilion during the ceremony. The bridegroom swears that he will not drive away nor divorce his wife, and sometimes a *mehar* or dowry is also fixed for the bride. The father-in-law usually, however, remits a part or the whole of this subsequently, when the bridegroom goes to take food at his house on festival occasions. Mr. Nesfield states that the principal deity of the Kanjars is the man-god Māna, who was not only the teacher and guide, but also the founder and ancestor of the tribe. He is buried, as some Kanjars relate, at Kara in the Allahābād District, not far from the Ganges and facing the old city of Mānikpur on the opposite bank. Māna is worshipped with special ceremony in the rainy season, when the tribe is less migratory than in the dry months of the year. On such occasions, if sufficient notice is circulated, several encampments unite temporarily to pay honour to their common ancestor. The worshippers collect near a tree under which they sacrifice a pig, a goat, a sheep, or a fowl, and make an offering of roasted flesh and spirituous liquor. Formerly, it is said, they used to sacrifice a child, having first made it insensible with fermented palm-juice or toddy.[1] They dance round the tree in honour of Māna, and sing the customary songs in commemoration of his wisdom and deeds of valour.

8. Social customs.

The dead are usually buried, both male and female corpses being laid on their faces with the feet pointing to the south. Kanjars who become Muhammadans may be readmitted to the community after the following ceremony. A pit is dug and the convert sits in it and each Kanjar throws a little curds on to his body. He then goes and bathes in a river, his tongue is touched or branded with heated gold and he gives a feast to the community. A Kanjar woman who has lived in concubinage with a Brāhman, Rājpūt, Agarwāl Bania, Kurmi, Ahīr or Lodhi may be taken back

[1] In a footnote Mr. Nesfield states: "The Kanjar who communicated these facts said that the child used to open out its neck to the knife as if it desired to be sacrificed to the deity."

into the caste after the same ceremony; but not one who has lived with a Kāyasth, Sunār or Lohār or any lower caste. A Kanjar is not put out of caste for being imprisoned, nor for being beaten by an outsider, nor for selling shoes. If a man touches his daughter-in-law even accidentally he is fined the sum of Rs. 2-8.

9. Industrial arts.

The following account of the industries of the vagrant Kanjars was written by Mr. Nesfield in 1883. In the Central Provinces many of them are now more civilised, and some are employed in Government service. Their women also make and retail string-net purses, balls and other articles.

"Among the arts of the Kanjar are making mats of the *sirki* reed, baskets of wattled cane, fans of palm-leaves and rattles of plaited straw: these last are now sold to Hindu children as toys, though originally they may have been used by the Kanjars themselves (if we are to trust to the analogy of other backward races) as sacred and mysterious implements. From the stalks of the *munj* grass and from the roots of the *palās*[1] tree they make ropes which are sold or bartered to villagers in exchange for grain and milk. They prepare the skins of which drums are made and sell them to Hindu musicians; though, probably, as in the case of the rattle, the drum was originally used by the Kanjars themselves and worshipped as a fetish; for even the Aryan tribes, who are said to have been far more advanced than the indigenous races, sang hymns in honour of the drum or *dundubhi* as if it were something sacred. They make plates of broad leaves which are ingeniously stitched together by their stalks; and plates of this kind are very widely used by the inferior Indian castes and by confectioners and sellers of sweetmeats. The mats of *sirki* reed with which they cover their own movable leaf huts are models of neatness and simplicity and many of these are sold to cart-drivers. The toddy or juice of the palm tree, which they extract and ferment by methods of their own and partly for their own use, finds a ready sale among low-caste Hindus in villages and market towns. They are among the chief stone-cutters in Upper India, especially in the manufacture of the grinding-

[1] *Butea frondosa.*

mill which is very widely used. This consists of two circular stones of equal diameter; the upper one, which is the thicker and heavier, revolves on a wooden pivot fixed in the centre of the lower one and is propelled by two women, each holding the same handle. But it is also not less frequent for one woman to grind alone." It is perhaps not realised what this business of grinding her own grain instead of buying flour means to the Indian woman. She rises before daybreak to commence the work, and it takes her perhaps two or three hours to complete the day's provision. Grain-grinding for hire is an occupation pursued by poor women. The *pisanhāri*, as she is called, receives an anna (penny) for grinding 16 lbs. of grain, and can get through 30 lbs. a day. In several localities temples are shown supposed to have been built by some pious *pisanhāri* from her earnings. "The Kanjars," Mr. Nesfield continues, "also gather the white wool-like fibre which grows in the pods of the *semal* or Indian cotton tree and twist it into thread for the use of weavers.[1] In the manufacture of brushes for the cleaning of cotton-yarn the Kanjars enjoy almost a complete monopoly. In these brushes a stiff mass of horsehair is attached to a wooden handle by sinews and strips of hide; and the workmanship is remarkably neat and durable.[2] Another complete or almost complete monopoly enjoyed by Kanjars is the collection and sale of sweet-scented roots of the *khas-khas* grass, which are afterward made up by the Chhaparbands and others into door-screens, and through being continually watered cool the hot air which passes through them. The roots of this wild grass, which grows in most abundance on the outskirts of forests or near the banks of rivers, are dug out of the earth by an instrument called *khunti*. This has a handle three feet long, and a blade about a foot long resembling that of a knife. The same implement serves as a dagger or short spear for killing wolves or jackals, as a tool for carving a secret entrance through the clay wall of a villager's hut in which a burglary is meditated, as a spade or hoe for digging

[1] It is not, I think, used for weaving now, but only for stuffing quilts and cushions.

[2] But elsewhere Mr. Nesfield says that the brushes are made from the *khas-khas* grass, and this is, I think, the case in the Central Provinces.

snakes, field-rats, and lizards out of their holes, and edible roots out of the earth, and as a hatchet for chopping wood."

Kāpewār,[1] **Munurwār.**—A great cultivating caste of the Telugu country, where they are known as Kāpu or Reddi, and correspond to the Kurmi in Hindustān and the Kunbi in the Marātha Districts. In the Central Provinces about 18,000 persons of the caste were enumerated in the Chānda District and Berār in 1911. The term Kāpu means a watchman, and Reddi is considered to be a corruption of Rāthor or Rāshtrakūta, meaning a king, or more properly the headman of a village. Kāpewār is simply the plural form of Kāpu, and Munurwār, in reality the name of a subcaste of Kāpewārs, is used as a synonym for the main caste in Chānda. They are divided into various occupational subcastes, as the Upparwars or earth-diggers, from *uppar*, earth; the Gone, who make *gonas* or hemp gunny-bags; the Elmas, who are household servants; the Gollewārs, who sell milk; and the Gamadis or masons. The Kunte or lame Kāpewārs, the lowest group, say that their ancestor was born lame; they are also called Bhiksha Kunte or lame beggars and serve as the bards of the caste besides begging from them. They are considered to be of illegitimate origin. No detailed account of the caste need be given here, but one or two interesting customs reported from Chānda may be noted. Girls must be married before they are ten years old, and in default of this the parents are temporarily put out of caste and have to pay a penalty for readmission. But if they take the girl to some sacred place on the Godāvari river and marry her there the penalty is avoided. Contrary to the usual custom the bride goes to the bridegroom's house to be married. On the fourth night of the marriage ceremony the bridegroom takes with him all the parts of a plough as if he was going out to the field, and walks up the marriage-shed to the further end followed by the bride, who carries on her head some cooked food tied up in a cloth. The skirts of the couple are knotted together. On reaching the end of the shed the

1 This article is compiled principally from a note by Mr. Paiku, Inspector of Police, Chānda.

bridegroom makes five drills in the ground with a bullock-goad and sows cotton and juāri seeds mixed together. Then the cooked food is eaten by all who are present, the bridal couple commencing first, and the seed is irrigated by washing their hands over it. This performance is a symbolical portrayal of the future life of the couple, which will be spent in cultivation. In Chānda a number of Kāpewārs are stone-masons, and are considered the most proficient workers at this trade in the locality. Major Lucie Smith, the author of the *Chānda Settlement Report* of 1869, thought that the ancestors of the caste had been originally brought to Chānda to build the fine walls with ramparts and bastions which stretch for a length of six or seven miles round the town. The caste are sometimes known as Telugu Kunbis. Men may be distinguished by the single dot which is always tattooed on the forehead during their infancy. Men of the Gowāri caste have a similar mark.

Karan,[1] Karnam, Mahanti.—The indigenous writer caste of Orissa. In 1901 a total of 5000 Karans were enumerated in Sambalpur and the Uriya States, but the bulk of these have since passed under the jurisdiction of Bihār and Orissa, and only about 1000 remain in the Central Provinces. The total numbers of the caste in India exceed a quarter of a million. The poet Kālidās in his Rāghuvansa describes Karans as the offspring of a Vaishya father and a Sūdra mother. The caste fulfils the same functions in Orissa as the Kāyasths elsewhere, and it is said that their original ancestors were brought from northern India by Yayāti Kesari, king of Orissa (A.D. 447–526), to supply the demand for writers and clerks. The original of the word Karan is said to be the Hindi *karāni, kirān*, which Wilson derives from Sanskrit *karan*, 'a doer.' The word *karāni* was at one time applied by natives to the junior members of the Civil Service—'Writers,' as they were designated. And the 'Writers' Buildings' of Calcutta were known as *karāni ki-barīk*. From this term a corruption 'Cranny' came into use, and was applied in Bengal to a clerk writing English,

[1] This article is based principally on a paper by Nand Kishore, Bohidār, Sambalpur.

and thence to the East Indians or half-castes from whom English copyists were subsequently recruited.[1] The derivation of Mahanti is obscure, unless it be from *maha*, great, or from Mahant, the head of a monastery. The caste prefer the name of Karan, because that of Mahanti is often appropriated by affluent Chasas and others who wish to get a rise in rank. In fact a proverb says: *Jār nahīn Jāti, tāku bolanti Mahanti*, or 'He who has no caste calls himself a Mahanti.' The Karans, like the Kāyasths, claim Chitragupta as their first ancestor, but most of them repudiate any connection with the Kāyasths, though they are of the same calling. The Karans of Sambalpur have two subcastes, the Jhādua or those of the *jhādi* or jungle and the Utkali or Uriyas. The former are said to be the earlier immigrants and are looked down on by the latter, who do not intermarry with them. Their exogamous divisions or *gotras* are of the type called eponymous, being named after well-known Rishis or saints like those of the Brāhmans. Instances of such names are Bhāradwāj, Parāsar, Vālmik and Vasishtha. Some of the names, however, are in a manner totemistic, as Nāgas, the cobra; Kounchhas, the tortoise; Bachās, a calf, and so on. These animals are revered by the members of the *gotra* named after them, but as they are of semi-divine nature, the practice may be distinguished from true totemism. In some cases, however, members of the Bhāradwāj *gotra* venerate the blue-jay, and of the Parāsar *gotra*, a pigeon. Marriage is regulated according to the table of prohibited degrees in vogue among the higher castes. Girls are commonly married before they are ten years old, but no penalty attaches to the postponement of the ceremony to a later age. The binding portion of the marriage is Hastabandhan or the tying of the hands of the couple together with *kusha* grass,[2] and when this has been done the marriage cannot be annulled. The bride goes to her husband's house for a few days and then returns home until she attains maturity. Divorce and remarriage of widows are prohibited, and an unfaithful wife is finally expelled from the caste. The Karans worship the usual Hindu gods and call themselves Smārths. Some belong to the local Parmārth and Kumbhīpatia sects, the former of

[1] *Hobson-Jobson*, art. Cranny.

[2] *Eragrostis cynosuroides*.

which practises obscene rites. They burn their dead, excepting the bodies of infants, and perform the *shrāddh* ceremony. The caste have a high social position in Sambalpur, and Brāhmans will sometimes take food cooked without water from them. They wear the sacred thread. They eat fish and the flesh of clean animals but do not drink liquor. Bhandāris or barbers will take *katcha* food from a Karan. They are generally engaged in service as clerks, accountants, schoolmasters or patwāris. Their usual titles are Patnāik or Bohidār. The Karans are considered to be of extravagant habits, and one proverb about them is—

Mahanti jāti, udhār paile kinanti hāthi,

or, 'The Mahānti if he can get a loan will at once buy an elephant.' Their shrewdness in business transactions and tendency to overreach the less intelligent cultivating castes have made them unpopular like the Kāyasths, and another proverb says—

Patarkata, Tankarkata, Pāniota, Gaudini mai
E chāri jāti ku vishwās nai,

or, 'Trust not the palm-leaf writer (Karan), the weaver, the liquor-distiller nor the milk-seller.'

KASAI

LIST OF PARAGRAPHS

1. General notice of the caste.

Kasai, Kassāb.—The caste of Muhammadan butchers, of whom about 4000 persons were returned from the Central Provinces and Berār in 1911. During the last decade the numbers of the caste have very greatly increased owing to the rise of the cattle-slaughtering industry. Two kinds of Kasais may be distinguished, the Gai Kasai or cow-killers and the Bakar Kasai or mutton butchers. The latter, however, are usually Hindus and have been formed into a separate caste, being known as Khatīk. Like other Muhammadans who have adopted professions of a not too reputable nature, the Kasais have become a caste, partly because the ordinary Muhammadan declines to intermarry with them, and partly no doubt in imitation of the Hindu social system. The Kasais are one of the lowest of the Muhammadan castes, and will admit into their community even low-caste Hindu converts. They celebrate their weddings by the *nikāh* form, but until recently many Hindu rites were added to it. The Kāzi is employed to conduct the marriage, but if his services are not available a member of the caste may officiate instead. Polygamy is permitted to the number of four wives. A man may divorce his wife simply for disobedience, but if a woman wishes to divorce her husband she must forego the Meher or dowry promised at the time of the wedding. The Kasai women, perhaps owing to their meat diet, are noticeably strong and well nourished, and there is a saying to the effect that, 'The butcher's daughter will bear children when she is ten years old.' The deities of the Kasais are a number of Muhammadan saints, who are known as Aulia or Favourites of God. The caste bury the dead, and on the third day they read the Kalma over some parched grain and distribute this to the caste-fellows, who eat it in the name of the deceased man, invoking a blessing upon him. On the ninth day after the death they distribute food to Muhammadan Fakīrs or beggars, and on the twentieth and fortieth days two more feasts are given to the caste and a third on the anniversary of the death. Owing to what is considered the degrading nature of his occupation, the social position of the Kasai is very low, and there is a saying—

Na dekha ho bāgh, to dekh belai;
Na dekha ho Thag, to dekh Kasai,

or, 'If you have not seen a tiger, look at a cat; and if you have not seen a Thug, look at a butcher.' Many Hindus have a superstition that leprosy is developed by the continual eating of beef.

2. The cattle-slaughtering industry.

In recent years an extensive industry in the slaughter of cattle has sprung up all over the Province. Worn-out animals are now eagerly bought up and killed; their hides are dried and exported, and the meat is cured and sent to Madras and Burma, a substantial profit being obtained from its sale. The blood, horns and hoofs are other products which yield a return. The religious scruples of the Hindus have given way to the temptation of obtaining what is to them a substantial sum for a valueless animal, and, with the exception perhaps of Brāhmans and Banias, all castes now dispose of their useless cattle to the butchers. At first this was done by stealth, and efforts were made to impose severe penalties on anybody guilty of the crime of being accessory to the death of the sacred kine, while it is said that the emissaries of the butchers were sent to the markets disguised as Brāhmans or religious mendicants, and pretended that they wished to buy cattle in order to preserve their lives as a meritorious act. But such attempts at restriction have generally proved fruitless, and the trade is now openly practised and acquiesced in by public opinion. In spite of many complaints of the shortage of plough cattle caused by the large numbers of animals slaughtered, the results of this traffic are probably almost wholly advantageous; for the villages no longer contain a horde of worn-out and decrepit animals to deprive the valuable plough and milch cattle of a share of the too scanty pasturage. Kasais themselves are generally prosperous.

3. Muhammadan rite of *zibah* or *halāl.* When killing an animal the butcher lays it on the ground with its feet to the west and head stretched towards the north and then cuts its throat saying:

> In the name of God;
> God is great.

This method of killing an animal is known as *zibah.* The Muhammadan belief that an animal is not fit for food unless its throat has been cut so that the blood flows on to the ground is thus explained in Professor Robertson Smith's *Religion of the Semites*[1]: "In heathen Canaan all the animals belonged to the god of the country; but it was lawful to kill them if payment was made to the god by pouring out their life or blood on the ground." The Arabs are of the same Semitic stock, and this may be partly the underlying idea of their rite of *zibah.* It seems doubtful, however, whether the explanation suffices to explain its continuance for so long a period among the Muhammadans who have long ceased to reverence any earth-deity, and in a foreign country where the soil cannot be sacred to them; and a short summary of Dr. Robertson Smith's luminous explanation of the underlying principle of animal sacrifice in early times seems requisite to its full understanding.

[1] (London, A. & C. Black.)

Primitive man did not recognise any difference of intelligence and self-consciousness between himself and the lower animals and even plants, but believed them all to be possessed of consciousness and volition as he was. He knew of no natural laws of the constitution of matter and the action of forces, and therefore thought that all natural phenomena, the sun, moon and stars, the wind and rain, were similarly appearances, manifestations or acts of volition of beings conscious like himself. This is what is meant by animism. Among several races the community was divided into totem-clans, and each clan held sacred some animal or bird, which was considered as a kinsman. All the members of the clan were kin to each other through the tie formed by their eating their totem animal, which in the hunting stage was probably their chief means of subsistence, and from which they consequently thought that they derived their common life.[1] In process of time the animals which were domesticated, such as the horse, the sheep, the cow and the camel, acquired a special sanctity, and became, in fact, the principal deities of the community, such as the calf-god Apis, the cow-goddess Isis-Hathor, and the ram-god Amen in Egypt, Hera, probably a cow-goddess, and Dionysus, who may be the deified bull or goat (or a combination of them) in Greece, and so on. 4. Animism.

It is easy to see how these domestic animals would overshadow all others in importance when the tribe had arrived at the pastoral or agricultural stage; thus in the former the camel, horse, goat or sheep, and in the latter pre-eminently the bull and cow, as the animals which afforded subsistence to the whole tribe, would become their 5. Animal-gods. The domestic animals.

1 This definition of totemism is more or less in accord with that held by the late Professor Robertson Smith, but is not generally accepted. The exhaustive collection of totemic beliefs and customs contained in Sir J. G. Frazer's *Totemism and Exogamy* affords, however, substantial evidence in favour of it among tribes still in the hunting stage in Australia, North America and Africa. The Indian form of totemism is, in the writer's opinion, a later one, arising when the totem animal has ceased to be the main source of life, and when the clan come to think that they are descended from their totem animal and that the spirits of their ancestors pass into the totem animal. When this belief arises, they cease eating the totem as a mark of veneration and respect, and abstain from killing or injuring it. Finally the totem comes to be little more than a clan-name or family name, which serves the purpose of preventing marriage between persons related through males, who believe themselves to be descended from a common ancestor.

greatest gods. It must be presumed that men forgot that their ancestors had tamed these animals, and looked on them as divine helpers who of their own free will had come to give mankind their aid in gaining a subsistence. Those who have observed the reverence paid to the cow and bull in India will have no difficulty in realising this point of view. Many other instances can be obtained. Thus in the Vedic religion of the Aryans the Ashvins, from *ashva*, a horse, were the divine horsemen of the dawn or of the sun. The principal sacrifice was that of the horse, considered, perhaps, as the representative of the sun or carrier of celestial fire. In a hymn the horse is said to be sprung from the gods. In Greece Phaethon was the charioteer of the horses of the sun. Mars, as the Roman god of war, may perhaps have been the deified horse, as suggested later. The chieftains of the Anglo-Saxon invaders of England, Hengist and Horsa, were held to be descended from the god Odin, to whom horses were sacrificed ; Hengist means a stallion and Horsa a horse, the word having survived in modern English. Other mythical kings in Bede's chronicle have names derived from that of the horse (*vicg.*).[1] The camel does not seem to have become an anthropomorphic god, but the Arabs venerated it and refrained from killing it except as a sacrifice, when it was offered to the Morning-Star and partaken of sacramentally by the worshippers as will be seen subsequently. The ox as the tiller of the ground, with the cow as milk-giver and mother of the ox, are especially venerated by races in the early agricultural stage. Egyptian and Greek instances have already been given. In modern Egypt, as in India, bulls are let loose and held sacred. "Sometimes a peasant vows that he will sacrifice, for the sake of a saint, a calf which he possesses, as soon as it is full grown and fatted. It is let loose, by consent of all his neighbours, to pasture where it will, even in fields of young wheat; and at last, after it has been sacrificed, a public feast is made with its meat. Many a large bull is thus given away."[2] Dionysus Zagreus was a young bull devoured by the Titans, whom Zeus raised again

[1] *Orphéus* (Heinemann), p. 197.
[2] Lane, *Modern Egyptians*, p. 248.

to a glorious life.[1] The Babylonians had a bull-god, Ninit.[2] Brazen images of bulls were placed in Babylonian temples. The Pārsis hold the bull sacred, and a child is made to drink a bull's urine as a rite of purification. After a funeral the mourners free themselves from the impurity caused by contact with the dead in a similar manner.[3] The monotheistic religion of Persia, Mitraism, which was an outcome of the faith of Zoroaster, and being introduced by the Emperors Commodus and Julian into the Roman world contended for some time with Christianity, was apparently sun-worship, Mitra being the sun-god of the ancient Aryans and Iranians; M. Reinach says: "Mitra is born from a rock; he makes water flow from the rock by striking it with an arrow, makes an alliance with the sun, and enters into a struggle with a bull, whom he conquers and sacrifices. The sacrifice of the bull appears to indicate that the worship of Mitra in its most ancient form was that of a sacred bull, conjoined to or representing the sun, which was sacrificed as a god, and its flesh and blood eaten in a sacrificial meal. Mitra, the slayer of the bull, figures in a double rôle as one finds in all the religions which have passed from totemism to anthropomorphism."[4] In Scandinavia the god Odin and his brothers were the grandsons of a divine cow, born from the melting ice in the region of snow and darkness.[5] In Rome a white bull was sacrificed to the Feriae Latinae, apparently the spirit of the Latin holy days, and distributed among all the towns of Latium.[6] Altars of the ancient Celts or Gauls have been found in France carved with the image of a bull.[7] In Palestine there is the familiar instance of the golden calf. In the open court of Solomon's temple stood the brazen sea on twelve oxen, and figures of lions, oxen and cherubim covered the portable tanks.[8] The veneration of the bull survived into Christian England in the Middle Ages. "At St. Edmundsbury a white bull, which enjoyed full ease and plenty in the fields, and was never yoked to the plough nor employed in any service, was

[1] *Orphéus*, p. 47.
[2] *Ibidem*, p. 50.
[3] *B.G. Parsis of Gujarāt*, pp. 232, 241.
[4] *Orphéus*, pp. 101, 102.
[5] *Ibidem*, p. 204.
[6] *Ibidem*, p. 144.
[7] *Ibidem*, p. 169.
[8] D. M. Flinders-Petrie, *Egypt and Israel*, p. 61.

led in procession in the chief streets of the town to the principal gate of the monastery, attended by all the monks singing and a shouting crowd.[1] "Such remedies as cowdung and cow's urine have been used on the continent of Europe by peasant physicians down to our times";[2] and the belief in their efficacy must apparently have arisen from the sanctity attaching to the animal. In India Siva rides upon the bull Nandi, and when the Kunbis were too weak from famine to plough the fields, he had Nandi castrated and harnessed to the plough, thus teaching them to use oxen for ploughing; the image of Nandi is always carved in stone in front of Siva, and there seems little reason to doubt that in his beneficent aspect of Mahādeo the god was originally the deified bull. Bulls were let loose in his honour and allowed to graze where they would, and formerly a good Hindu would not even sell a bull, though this rule has fallen into abeyance. The sacred cow, Kāmdhenu, was the giver of all wealth in Hindu mythology, and Lakshmi, the goddess of wealth, is considered to have been the deified cow. Hindus are purified from grave offences by drinking the five products of the sacred cow, milk, curds, butter, dung and urine; and the floors of Hindu houses are daily plastered with cowdung to the same end.

6. Other animals.

Of the exaltation of minor animals into anthropomorphic gods and goddesses only a few instances need be given. As is shown by Sir J. G. Frazer, Demeter and Proserpine probably both represent the deified pig.[3] "The Greek drama has arisen from the celebrations of Dionysus. In the beginning the people sacrificed a goat totem-god, that is to say, Dionysus himself; they wept for his death and then celebrated his resurrection with transports of joy."[4] And again M. Reinach states: "There are more than mere vestiges of totemism in ancient Greece. We may take first the attendant animals of the gods, the eagle of Zeus, the owl of Athena, the fawn of Artemis, the dolphin of Poseidon, the dove of Aphrodite and so on; the sacred animal can develop into the companion of the god, but also into his enemy or

[1] Gomme, *Folk-lore as a Historical Science*, p. 161.

[2] Haug's *Essays on the Parsis*, p. 286.

[3] *Golden Bough*, ii. pp. 299-301. See article on Kumhār.

[4] *Orphéus*, p. 139.

victim; thus Apollo Sauroctonos is, as the epithet shows, a killer of lizards; but in the beginning it was the lizard itself which was divine. We have seen that the boar before becoming the slayer of Adonis had been Adonis himself."[1]

In early Rome "The wolf was the animal most venerated. Its association with Mars, as the sacrifice most pleasing to him, leaves no doubt as to the primitive nature of the god. It was a wolf which acted as guide to the Samnites in their search for a place to settle in, and these Samnites called themselves Hirpi or Hirpini, that is to say, wolves. Romulus and Remus, sons of the wolf Mars and the she-wolf Silvia (the forest-dweller), are suckled by a she-wolf."[2] It seems possible that Mars as the deified wolf was at first an agricultural deity, the wolf being worshipped by the shepherd and farmer because he was their principal enemy, as the sāmbhar stag and the wild buffalo are similarly venerated by Indian cultivators. At a later period, in becoming the god of war, he may have represented the deified horse as well. Races of war-horses were held at his festivals on 14th March and 27th February, and a great race on the Ides of October when the winner was solemnly slain.[3] "In Egypt the baboon was regarded as the emblem of Tahuti, the god of wisdom; the serious expression and human ways of the large baboons are an obvious cause for their being regarded as the wisest of animals. Tahuti is represented as a baboon from the earliest dynasty down to late times; and four baboons were sacred in his temple at Heliopolis."[4] "The hippopotamus was the goddess Ta-urt, 'the great one,' the patroness of pregnancy, who is never shown in any other form. Rarely this animal appears as the emblem of the god Set. The jackal haunted the cemeteries on the edge of the desert, and so came to be taken as the guardian of the dead and identified with Anubis, the god of departing souls. The vulture was the emblem of maternity as being supposed to care especially for her young. Hence she is identified with Mut, the mother-goddess of Thebes. The cobra serpent was sacred from the earliest times to the

[1] *Orphéus*, pp. 119, 120.

[2] *Ibidem*, p. 144.

[3] *Religions, Ancient and Modern, Ancient Rome*, Cyril Bailey, p. 86.

[4] *Religions, Ancient and Modern, Ancient Egypt*, Professor Flinders-Petrie, p. 22.

present day. It was never identified with any of the great deities, but three goddesses appear in serpent form."[1]

7. Animals worshipped in India.

Finally, in India we have Hanumān, originally the deified ape, about whose identity there can be no doubt as he still retains his monkey's tail in all sculpture. Bhairon, the watchman of Mahādeo's temples, rides on a black dog, and was perhaps originally the watch-dog, or in his more terrible character of the devourer of human beings, the wolf. Ganesh or Ganpati has the head of an elephant and rides on a rat and appears to have derived his divine attributes from both these animals, as will be explained elsewhere;[2] Kartikeya, the god of war, rides on a peacock, and as the peacock is sacred, he may originally have been that bird, perhaps because its plumes were a favourite war emblem. Among his epithets are Sarabhu, born in the thicket, Dwāda-sakara and Dwādasāksha, twelve-handed and twelve-eyed. He was fostered by the maidens who make the Pleiades, and his epithet of twelve-eyed may be taken from the eyes in the peacock's feathers.[3] But, like the Greek gods, the Hindu gods have now long become anthropomorphic, and only vestiges remain of their animal associations. Enough has been said to show that most of the pantheons are largely occupied by deified animals and birds.

8. The sacrificial meal.

The original sacrifice was that in which the community of kinsmen ate together the flesh of their divine or totem animal-god and drank its blood. In early religion the tribal god was the ancestor and relative of the tribe. He protected and fostered the tribe in its public concerns, but took no special care of individuals; the only offences of which he took cognisance were those against the tribe as a whole, such as shedding a kinsman's blood. At periodical intervals the tribe renewed their kinship with the god and each other by eating his flesh together at a sacrificial meal by which they acquired his divine attributes; and every tribesman was not only invited, but bound, to participate. "According to antique ideas those who eat and drink together are by this very act tied to one another by a bond of friendship

[1] *Religions, Ancient and Modern, Ancient Egypt*, Professor Flinders-Petrie, pp. 24, 26.

[2] *Vide* article on Bania.

[3] *Dowson's and Garrett's Classical Dictionaries*, art. Kartikeya.

and mutual obligation. Hence when we find that in ancient religions all the ordinary functions of worship are summed up in the sacrificial meal, and that the ordinary intercourse between gods and men has no other form, we are to remember that the act of eating and drinking together is the solemn and stated expression of the fact that all who share the meal are brethren, and that the duties of friendship and brotherhood are implicitly acknowledged in their common act.[1] The one thing directly expressed in the sacrificial meal is that the god and his worshippers are *commensals*, but every other point in their mutual relations is included in what this involves. Those who sit at meat together are united for all social effects; those who do not eat together are aliens to one another, without fellowship in religion and without reciprocal social duties. The extent to which this view prevailed among the ancient Semites, and still prevails among the Arabs, may be brought out most clearly by reference to the law of hospitality. Among the Arabs every stranger whom one meets in the desert is a natural enemy, and has no protection against violence except his own strong hand or the fear that his tribe will avenge him if his blood be spilt. But if I have eaten the smallest morsel of food with a man I have nothing further to fear from him; 'there is salt between us,' and he is bound not only to do me no harm, but to help and defend me as if I were his brother. So far was this principle carried by the old Arabs that Zaid-al-Khail, a famous warrior in the days of Muhammad, refused to slay a vagabond who carried off his camels, because the thief had surreptitiously drunk from his father's milk-bowl before committing the theft."[2] It is in this idea that the feeling of hospitality originally arose. Those who ate together the sacred food consisting of the body of the god were brothers, and bound to assist each other and do each other no harm; and the obligation extended in a modified form to all food partaken of together, more especially as with some races, as the ancient Romans and the Hindus, all the regular household meals are sacred; they may only be partaken of after purifying the body, and a portion of the food at each meal is offered to the gods.

[1] *Religion of the Semites*, p. 265. [2] *Ibidem*, pp. 269, 270.

"There was a sworn alliance between the Lihyān and the Mostalic—they were wont to eat and drink together. This phrase of an Arab narrator supplies exactly what is wanted to define the significance of the sacrificial meal. The god and his worshippers are wont to eat and drink together, and by this token their fellowship is declared and sealed."[1]

9. Primitive basis of kinship.

The primitive idea of kinship rested on this participation in the sacrificial meal, and not on blood-relationship. "In ancient times the fundamental obligations of kinship had nothing to do with degrees of relationship, but rested with absolute and identical force on every member of the clan. To know that a man's life was sacred to me and that every blood-feud that touched him involved me also, it was not necessary for me to count cousinship with him by reckoning up to our common ancestor; it was enough that we belonged to the same clan and bore the same clan-name. What was my clan was determined by customary law, which was not the same in all stages of society; in the earliest Semitic communities a man was of his mother's clan, in later times he belonged to the clan of his father. But the essential idea of kinship was independent of the particular form of the law. A kin was a group of persons whose lives were so bound up together, in what must be called a physical unity, that they could be treated as parts of one common life. The members of one kindred looked on themselves as one living whole, a single animated mass of blood, flesh, and bones, of which no member could be touched without all the members suffering. This point of view is expressed in the Semitic tongues in many familiar forms of speech. In case of homicide Arabian tribesmen do not say, 'The blood of M or N has been spilt,' naming the man; they say, 'Our blood has been spilt.' In Hebrew the phrase by which one claims kinship is, 'I am your bone and your flesh.' Both in Hebrew and in Arabic 'flesh' is synonymous with 'clan' or kindred group."[2] Similarly in India a Hindu speaks of any member of his subcaste or clan as his *bhai* or brother.

"Indeed, in a religion based on kinship, where the god and his worshippers are of one stock, the principle of sanctity

[1] *Religion of the Semites*, pp. 270, 271.
[2] *Ibidem*, pp. 273, 274.

and that of kinship are identical. The sanctity of a kinsman's life and the sanctity of the godhead are not two things but one; for ultimately the only thing which is sacred is the common tribal life or the common blood which is identified with the life. Whatever being partakes in this life is holy, and its holiness may be described indifferently as participation in the divine life and nature, or as participation in the kindred blood."[1]

"At a later period the conception is found current that any food which two men partake of together, so that the same substance enters into their flesh and blood, is enough to establish some sacred unity of life between them; but in ancient times this significance seems to be always attached to participation in the flesh of a sacrosanct victim, and the solemn mystery of its death is justified by the consideration that only in this way can the sacred cement be procured which creates or keeps alive a living bond of union between the worshippers and their god. This cement is nothing less than the actual life of the sacred and kindred animal, which is conceived as residing in its flesh, but especially in its blood, and so, in the sacred meal, is actually distributed among all the participants, each of whom incorporated a particle of it with his own individual life."[2] 10. The bond of food.

It thus appears that the sacrifice of the divine animal which was the god of the tribe or clan, and the eating of its flesh and drinking of its blood together, was the only tangible bond or obligation on which such law and morality as existed in primitive society was based. Those who participated in this sacrifice were brothers and forbidden to shed each other's blood, because in so doing they would have spilt the blood of the god impiously and unlawfully; the only lawful occasion on which it could be shed being by participation of all the clan or kinsmen in the sacrificial meal. All other persons outside the clan were strangers or enemies, and no rights or obligations existed in connection with them; the only restraint on killing them being the fear that their kinsmen would take blood-revenge, not solely on the murderer, but on any member of his clan. A man's life was protected only by this readiness of his clansmen to avenge him; if he 11. The blood-feud.

[1] *Religion of the Semites*, p. 289. [2] *Ibidem*, p. 313.

slew a fellow-kinsman, thus shedding the blood of the god which flowed in the veins of every member, or committed any other great impiety against the god, he was outlawed, and henceforth there was no protection for his life except such as he could afford himself by his own strength. This reflection puts the importance of the blood-feud in primitive society in a clear light. It was at that time really a beneficent institution, being the only protection for human life; and its survival among such backward races as the Pathāns and Corsicans, long after the State has undertaken the protection and avenging of life and the blood-feud has become almost wholly useless and evil, is more easily understood.

12. Taking food together and hospitality. The original idea of the sacrificial meal was that the kinsmen in concert partook of the body of the god, thereby renewing their kinship with him and with each other. By analogy, however, the tie thus formed was extended to the whole practice of eating together. It has been seen how a stranger who partook of food with an Arab became sacred and as a kinsman to his host and all the latter's clan for such time as any part of the food might remain in his system, a period which was conventionally taken as about three days. "The Old Testament records many cases where a covenant was sealed by the parties eating and drinking together. In most of these the meal is sacrificial, and the deity is taken in as a third party to the covenant. But in Joshua i. 14 the Israelites enter into alliance with the Gibeonites by taking of their victuals without consulting Jehovah. A formal league confirmed by an oath follows, but by accepting the proffered food the Israelites are already committed to the alliance."[1] From the belief in the strength and sanctity of the tie formed by eating together the obligation of hospitality appears to be derived. And this is one of the few moral ideas which are more binding in primitive than in civilised society.

13. The Roman *sacra*. "A good example of the clan sacrifice, in which a whole kinship periodically joins, is afforded by the Roman *sacra gentilicia*. As in primitive society no man can belong to more than one kindred, so among the Romans no one could share in the *sacra* of two *gentes*—to do so was to confound

[1] *Religion of the Semites*, p. 271.

the ritual and contaminate the purity of the *gens*. The *sacra* consisted in common anniversary sacrifices, in which the clansmen honoured the gods of the clan, and after them the whole kin, living and dead, were brought together in the service." [1]

14. The Hindu caste-feasts.

The intense importance thus attached to eating in common on ceremonial occasions has a very familiar ring to any one possessing some acquaintance with the Indian caste-system. The resemblance of the *gotra* or clan and the sub-caste to the Greek *phratry* and *phule* and the Roman *gens* and *curia* or tribe has been pointed out by M. Emile Senart in *Les Castes dans l'Inde*. The origin of the subcaste or group, whose members eat together and intermarry, cannot be discussed here. But it seems probable that the real bond which unites it is the capacity of its members to join in the ceremonial feasts at marriages, funerals, and the readmission of members temporarily excluded, which are of a type closely resembling and seemingly derived from the sacrificial meal. Before a wedding the ancestors of the family are formally invited, and when the wedding-cakes are made they are offered to the ancestors and then partaken of by all relatives of the family as in the Roman *sacra*. In this case grain would take the place of flesh as the sacrificial food among a people who no longer eat the flesh of animals. Thus Sir J. G. Frazer states: "At the close of the rice harvest in the East Indian island of Buro each clan (*fenna*) meets at a common sacramental meal, to which every member of the clan is bound to contribute a little of the new rice. This meal is called 'eating the soul of the rice,' a name which clearly indicates the sacramental character of the repast. Some of the rice is also set apart and offered to the spirits." [2] Grain cooked with water is sacred food among the Hindus. The bride and bridegroom worship Gauri, perhaps a corn-goddess, and her son Ganesh, the god of prosperity and full granaries. It has been suggested that yellow is the propitious Hindu colour for weddings, because it is the colour of the corn.[3] At the wedding feast all the guests sit knee to knee touching each other as a sign of their brotherhood. Sometimes the bride eats with the men in token of her inclusion in the

[1] *Religion of the Semites*, p. 275.
[2] *Golden Bough*, ii. p. 321.
[3] *Vide* art. Kumhār.

brotherhood. In most castes the feast cannot begin until all the guests have come, and every member of the subcaste who is not under the ban of exclusion must be invited. If any considerable number of the guests wilfully abstain from attending it is an insult to the host and an implication that his own position is doubtful. Other points of resemblance between the caste feast and the sacrificial meal will be discussed elsewhere.

15. Sacrifice of the camel. The sacrifice of the camel in Arabia, about the period of the fourth century, is thus described: "The camel chosen as the victim is bound upon a rude altar of stones piled together, and when the leader of the band has thrice led the worshippers round the altar in a solemn procession accompanied with chants, he inflicts the first wound while the last words of the hymn are still upon the lips of the congregation, and in all haste drinks of the blood that gushes forth. Forthwith the whole company fall on the victim with their swords, hacking off pieces of the quivering flesh and devouring them raw, with such wild haste that in the short interval between the rise of the day-star, which marked the hour for the service to begin, and the disappearance of its rays before the rising sun, the entire camel, body and bones, skin, blood and entrails, is wholly devoured."[1]

In this case the camel was offered as a sacrifice to Venus or the Morning Star, and it had to be devoured while the star was visible. But it is clear that the camel itself had been originally revered, because except for the sacrifice it was unlawful for the Arabs to kill the camel otherwise than as a last resort to save themselves from starvation. "The ordinary sustenance of the Saracens was derived from pillage or from hunting and from the milk of their herds. Only when these supplies failed they fell back on the flesh of their camels, one of which was slain for each clan or for each group which habitually pitched their tents together—always a fraction of a clan—and the flesh was hastily devoured by the kinsmen in dog-like fashion, half raw and merely softened over the fire."[2] In Bhopāl it is stated that a camel is still sacrificed annually in perpetuation of the ancient rite. Hindus who keep camels revere them like

[1] *Religion of the Semites*, p. 338. [2] *Ibidem*, p. 281.

other domestic animals. When one of my tent-camels had broken its leg by a fall and had to be killed, I asked the camelman, to whom the animal belonged, to shoot it; but he positively refused, saying, 'How shall I kill him who gives me my bread'; and a Muhammadan orderly finally shot it.

16. The joint sacrifice.

The camel was devoured raw almost before the life had left the body, so that its divine life and blood might be absorbed by the worshippers. The obligation to devour the whole body perhaps rested on the belief that its slaughter otherwise than as a sacrifice was impious, and if any part of the body was left unconsumed the clan would incur the guilt of murder. Afterwards, when more civilised stomachs revolted against the practice of devouring the whole body, the bones were buried or burnt, and it is suggested that our word bonfire comes from bone-fire.[1] Primitive usage required the presence of every clansman, so that each might participate in shedding the sacred blood. Neither the blood of the god nor of any of the kinsmen might be spilt by private violence, but only by consent of the kindred and the kindred god. Similarly in shedding the blood of a member of the kin all the others were required to share the responsibility, and this was the ancient Hebrew form of execution where the culprit was stoned by the whole congregation.[2]

17. Animal sacrifices in Greece.

M. Salomon Reinach gives the following explanation of Greek myths in connection with the sacrificial meal: "The primitive sacrifice of the god, usually accompanied by the eating of the god in fellowship, was preserved in their religious rites, and when its meaning had been forgotten numerous legends were invented to account for it. In order to understand their origin it is necessary to remember that the primitive worshippers masqueraded as the god and took his name. As the object of the totem sacrifice is to make the participants like the god and confer his divinity on them, the faithful endeavoured to increase the resemblance by taking the name of the god and covering themselves with the skins of animals of his species. Thus the Athenian damsels celebrating the worship of the bear Artemis dressed themselves in bear-skins and called themselves bears; the

[1] Dr. Jevons, *Introduction to the History of Religion*, p. 150.

[2] *Religion of the Semites*, p. 285.

Maenads who sacrificed the doe Penthea were clad in doe-skins. Even in the later rites the devotees of Bacchus called themselves Bacchantes. A whole series of legends can be interpreted as semi-rationalistic explanations of the sacrificial meal. Actaeon was really a great stag sacrificed by women devotees who called themselves the great hind and the little hinds; he became the rash hunter who surprised Artemis at her bath, and was transformed into a stag and devoured by his own dogs. The dogs are a euphemism; in the early legend they were the human devotees of the sacred stag who tore him to pieces and devoured him with their bare teeth. These feasts of raw flesh survived in the secret religious cults of Greece long after uncooked meat had ceased to be consumed in ordinary life. Orpheus (*ophreus*, the haughty), who appears in art with the skin of a fox on his head, was originally a sacred fox devoured by the women of the fox totem-clan; these women call themselves Bassarides in the legend, and *bassareus* is one of the old names of the fox. Zagreus is a son of Zeus and Persephone who transformed himself into a bull to escape from the Titans, excited against him by Hera; the Titans, worshippers of the divine bull, killed and ate him; Zagreus was invoked in his worship as the 'good bull,' and when Zagreus by the grace of Zeus was reborn as Dionysus, the young god carried on his forehead the horns which bore witness to his animal nature. Hippolytus in the fable is the son of Theseus who repels the advances of Phaedra, his stepmother, and was killed by his runaway horses because Theseus, deceived by Phaedra, invoked the anger of a god upon him. But Hippolytus in Greek means 'One torn to pieces by horses.' Hippolytus is himself a horse whom the worshippers of the horse, calling themselves horses and disguised as such, tore to pieces and devoured. Phaethon (The Shining One) is a son of Apollo, who demands leave to drive the chariot of the sun, drives it badly, nearly burns up the world, and finally falls and perishes in the sea. This legend is the product of an old rite at Rhodes, the island of the sun, where every year a white horse and a burning chariot were thrown into the sea to help the sun, fatigued by his labours."[1]

[1] *Orphéus*, pp. 123, 125.

M. Reinach points out that the Passover of the Israelites was in its origin a similar sacrifice. A lamb or kid, the first-fruit of the flocks, was eaten entire without the bones being broken, the blood smeared on the doorway being an offering to the god. The story connecting this sacrifice with the death of the first-born in Egypt was of later origin, devised to account for it when the real meaning had been forgotten.[1] The name Rachel[2] means a ewe, and it would appear that the children of Israel in the pastoral stage had the sheep for their totem deity and supposed themselves to be descended from it, as the Jāts consider themselves to be descended from Siva, probably in his form of Mahādeo, the deified bull. As held in Canaan, the festival may have been a relic of the former migratory life of the Israelites when they tended flocks and regarded the sheep, or goat, as their most important domestic animal. It may have been in memory of this wandering life that the festival was accompanied by the eating of unleavened bread, and the sacrifice was consumed with loins girded up and staffs in their hands, as if in readiness for a journey. The Banjāras retain in their marriage and other customs various reminiscences of their former migratory life, as shown in the article on that caste. The Gadarias of the Central Provinces worship a goddess called Dishai Devi, who is represented by a stone platform just outside the sheep-pen. She has thus probably developed from the deified sheep or goat, which itself was formerly worshipped. On the eighth day of the fasts in Chait and Kunwār the Gadarias offer the goddess a virgin she-goat. They wash the goat's feet in water and rub turmeric on its feet and head. It is given rice to eat and brought before the goddess, and water is poured over its body; when the goat begins to shiver they think that the goddess has accepted the offering, and cut its throat with a sickle or knife. Then the animal is roasted whole and eaten in the veranda of the house, nothing being thrown away but the bones. Only men may join in this sacrifice, and not women.

18. The Passover.

[1] In following the explanation of the Passover given by Professor Robertson Smith and M. Reinach, it is necessary with great diffidence to dissent from the hypothesis of Sir J. G. Frazer that the lamb was a substitute for the previous sacrifice by the Israelites of their first-born sons.

[2] *Orphéus*, p. 272; *Religion of the Semites*, p. 311.

19. Sanctity of domestic animals.

Thus it was a more or less general rule among several races that the domestic animals were deified and held sacred, and were slain only at a sacrifice. It followed that it was sinful to kill these animals on any other occasion. It has already been seen that the Arabs forbore to kill their worn-out camels for food except when driven to it by hunger as a last resort. "That it was once a capital offence to kill an ox, both in Attica and the Peloponnesus, is attested by Varro. So far as Athens is concerned, this statement seems to be drawn from the legend that was told in connection with the annual sacrifice at the Diipolia, where the victim was a bull and its death was followed by a solemn inquiry as to who was responsible for the act. In this trial everyone who had anything to do with the slaughter was called as a party; the maidens who drew water to sharpen the axe and knife threw the blame on the sharpeners, they put it on the man who handed the axe, he on the man who struck down the victim, and he again on the one who cut its throat, who finally fixed the responsibility on the knife, which was accordingly found guilty of murder and cast into the sea."[1] "At Tenedos the priest who offered a bull-calf to Dionysus *anthroporraistes* was attacked with stones and had to flee for his life; and at Corinth, in the annual sacrifice of a goat to Hera Acraea, care was taken to shift the responsibility of the death off the shoulders of the community by employing hirelings as ministers. Even they did no more than hide the knife in such a way that the goat, scraping with its feet, procured its own death."[2] "Agatharchides, describing the Troglodytes of East Africa, a primitive pastoral people in the polyandrous state of society, tells us that their whole sustenance was derived from their flocks and herds. When pasture abounded, after the rainy season, they lived on milk mingled with blood (drawn apparently, as in Arabia, from the living animal), and in the dry season they had recourse to the flesh of aged or weakly beasts. Further, 'they gave the name of parent to no human being, but only to the ox and cow, the ram and ewe, from whom they had their nourishment.' Among the Caffres the cattle kraal is sacred; women may not enter it, and to defile it is a

[1] *Religion of the Semites*, p. 304.

[2] *Ibidem*, pp. 305, 306.

capital offence."[1] Among the Egyptians also cows were never killed.[2]

Gradually, however, as the reverence for animals declined and the true level of their intelligence compared to that of man came to be better appreciated, the sanctity attaching to their lives no doubt grew weaker. Then it would become permissible to kill a domestic animal privately and otherwise than by a joint sacrifice of the clan; but the old custom of justifying the slaughter by offering it to the god would still remain. "At this stage,[3] at least among the Hebrews, the original sanctity of the life of domestic animals is still recognised in a modified form, inasmuch as it is held unlawful to use their flesh for food except in a sacrificial meal. But this rule is not strict enough to prevent flesh from becoming a familiar luxury. Sacrifices are multiplied on trivial occasions of religious gladness or social festivity, and the rite of eating at the sanctuary loses the character of an exceptional sacrament, and means no more than that men are invited to feast and be merry at the table of their god, or that no feast is complete in which the god has not his share."[4] This is the stage reached by the Hebrews in the time of Samuel, as described by Professor Robertson Smith, and it bears much resemblance to that of the lower Hindu castes and the Gonds at the present time. They too, when they can afford to kill a goat or a pig, cows being prohibited in deference to Hindu susceptibility, take it to the shrine of some village deity and offer it there prior to feasting on it with their friends. At intervals of a year or more many of the lower castes sacrifice a goat to Dūlha Deo, the bridegroom-god, and Thākur Deo, the corn-god, and eat the body as a sacrificial meal within the house, burying the bones and other remnants beneath the floor of the house.[5] Among the Kāfirs of the Hindu Kush, when a man wishes to become a Jast, apparently a revered elder or senator, he must give a series of feasts to the whole community, so expensive that many men utterly ruin themselves in becoming Jast. The initiatory proceedings are sacrifices of bulls and male goats to Gīsh, the

20. Sacrificial slaughter for food.

[1] *Religion of the Semites*, pp. 296, 297.

[2] *Golden Bough*, ii. p. 313.

[3] When the blood of the animal was poured out before the god as his share.

[4] *Religion of the Semites*, p. 246.

[5] *Vide* article on Dhanwār.

war-god, at the village shrine. The animals are examined with jealous eyes by the spectators, to see that they come up to the prescribed standard of excellence. After the sacrifice the meat is divided among the people, who carry it to their homes. These special sacrifices at the shrine recur at intervals; but the great slaughterings are at the feast-giver's own house, where he entertains sometimes the Jast exclusively and sometimes the whole tribe, as already mentioned.[1] Even in the latter case, however, after a big distribution at the giver's house one or two goats are offered to the war-god at his shrine; and while the animals are being killed at the house offerings are made on a sacrificial fire, and as each goat is slain a handful of its blood is taken and thrown on the fire.[2] The Kāfirs would therefore appear to be in the stage when it is still usual to kill domestic animals as a sacrifice to the god, but no longer obligatory.

21. Animal fights. Finally animals are recognised for what they are, all sanctity ceases to attach to them, and they are killed for food in an ordinary manner. Possibly, however, such customs as roasting an ox whole, and the sports of bull-baiting and bull-fighting, may be relics of the ancient sacrifice. Formerly the buffaloes sacrificed at the shrine of the goddess Rankini or Kāli in Dalbhūm zamīndāri of Chota Nāgpur were made to fight. "Two male buffaloes are driven into a small enclosure and on a raised stage adjoining and overlooking it the Rāja and his suite take up their position. After some ceremonies the Rāja and his family priest discharge arrows at the buffaloes, others follow their example, and the tormented and enraged beasts fall to and gore each other whilst arrow after arrow is discharged. When the animals are past doing very much mischief, the people rush in and hack at them with battle-axes till they are dead."[3]

22. The sacrificial method of killing. Muhammadans however cannot eat the flesh of an animal unless its throat is cut and the blood allowed to flow before it dies. At the time of cutting the throat a sacred text or invocation must be repeated. It has been seen that in former times the blood of the animal was offered to the god and scattered on the altar or collected in a pit at its

[1] Sir G. Robertson, *Kāfirs of the Hindu Kush*, pp. 450, 451.

[2] *Ibidem*, p. 460.

[3] Dalton, *Ethnology of Bengal*, p. 176.

foot. It may be suggested that the method of killing which still survives was that formerly practised in offering the sacrifice, and that the necessity of allowing the blood to flow is a relic of the blood offering. When it no longer became necessary to sacrifice every animal at a shrine the sacrificial method of slaughter and the invocation to the god might be retained as removing the impiety of the act. At present it is said that unless an animal's blood flows it is a *murda* or corpse, and hence not suitable for food. But this idea may have grown up to account for the custom when its original meaning had been forgotten. The Gonds, when sacrificing a fowl, hold it over the sacred post or stone, which represents the god, and let the blood drop upon it. And when sacrificing a pig they first cut its tongue and let the blood fall upon the symbol of the god. In Chhattīsgarh, when a Hindu is ill he makes a vow of the affected limb to the god; then on recovering he goes to the temple, and cutting this limb, lets the blood fall on to the symbol of the god as an offering. Similarly the Sikhs are forbidden to eat flesh unless the animal has been killed by *jatka* or cutting off the head with one stroke, and the same rule is observed by some of the lower Hindu castes. In Hindu sacrifices it is often customary that the head of the animal should be made over to the officiating priest as his share, and so in killing the animal he would naturally cut off its head. The above rule may therefore be of the same character as the rite of *halāl* among the Muhammadans, and here also the sacrificial method of killing an animal may be retained to legalise its slaughter after the sacrifice itself has fallen into desuetude. In Berār some time ago the Mullah or Muhammadan priest was a village servant and the Hindus paid him dues. In return he was accustomed to kill the goats and sheep which they wished to sacrifice at temples, or in their fields to propitiate the deities presiding over them. He also killed animals for the Khatīk or mutton-butcher and the latter exposed them for sale. The Mullah was entitled to the heart of the animal killed as his perquisite and a fee of two pice. Some of the Marāthas were unmindful of the ceremony, but in general they professed not to eat flesh unless the sacred verse had been pronounced either by the Mullah or some Muhammadan capable of rendering it *halāl* or lawful to be eaten.[1] Hence it would appear that the Hindus, unprovided by their own religion with any sacrificial mode of legalising the slaughter of animals, adopted the ritual of a foreign faith in order to make animal sacrifices acceptable to their own deities. The belief that it is sinful to kill a domestic animal except with some religious sanction is thus clearly shown in full force.

23. Animal sacrifices in Indian ritual.

Among high-caste Hindus also sacrifices, including the killing of cows, were at one time legal. This is shown by several legends,[2] and is also a historical fact. One of Asoka's royal edicts prohibited at the capital the celebration of animal sacrifices and merry-makings involving the use of meat, but in the provinces apparently they continued to be lawful.[3] This indicates that prior to the rise of Buddhism such sacrifices had been customary, and also that when a feast was to be given, involving the consumption of meat, the animal was offered as a sacrifice. It is noteworthy that Asoka's rules do not forbid the slaughter of cows.[4] In ancient times also the most important royal sacrifice was that of the horse. The development of religious belief and practice in connection with the killing of domestic animals has thus proceeded on exactly opposite lines in India as compared with most of the world. Domestic animals have become more instead of less sacred and several of them cannot be killed at all. The reason usually given to account for this is the belief in the transmigration of souls, leading to the conclusion that the bodies of animals might be tenanted by human souls. Probably also Buddhism left powerful traces of its influence on the Hindu view of the

[1] Grant-Duff, *History of the Marāthas*, vol. i. p. 27. Mr. Hīra Lāl notes that owing to the predominance of Muhammadans in Berār the practice of slaughtering all animals by the method of *halāl* and the regular employment of the Mullah to pronounce the sacred text before slaughter may have grown up for their convenience. And, as in other instances, the Hindus may have simply imitated the Muhammadans in regarding this method of slaughter as necessary. This however scarcely seems to impair the force of the argument if the Hindus actually refused to eat animals not killed by *halāl*; they must in that case have attached some religious significance or virtue to the rite, and the most probable significance is perhaps that stated in the text. As Mr. Hīra Lāl points out, the Hindu sacred books provide an elaborate ritual for the sacrifice of animals, but this may have fallen into abeyance with the decline in the custom of eating meat.

[2] *Vide* article on Mochi.

[3] V. A. Smith, *Asoka*, p. 56.

[4] *Ibidem*, p. 58.

sanctity of animal life even after it had ceased to be the state religion. Perhaps the Brāhmans desired to make their faith more popular and took advantage of the favourite reverence of all cultivators for the cow to exalt her into one of their most powerful deities, and at the same time to extend the local cult of Krishna, the divine cowherd, thus following exactly the contrary course to that taken by Moses with the golden calf. Generally the growth of political and national feeling has mainly operated to limit the influence of the priesthood, and the spread of education and development of reasoned criticism and discussion have softened the strictness of religious observance and ritual. Both these factors have been almost entirely wanting in Hindu society, and this perhaps explains the continued sanctity attaching to the lives of domestic animals as well as the unabated power of the caste system.

Kasār, Kasera, Kansari, Bharewa.[1]—The professional caste of makers and sellers of brass and copper vessels. In 1911 the Kasārs numbered 20,000 persons in the Central Provinces and Berār, and were distributed over all Districts, except in the Jubbulpore division, where they are scarcely found outside Mandla. Their place in the other Districts of this division is taken by the Tameras. In Mandla the Kasārs are represented by the inferior Bharewa group. The name of the caste is derived from *kānsa*, a term now applied to bell-metal. The kindred caste of Tameras take their name from *tāmba*, copper, but both castes work in this metal indifferently, and in Saugor, Damoh and Jubbulpore no distinction exists between the Kasārs and Tameras, the same caste being known by both names. A similar confusion exists in northern India in the use of the corresponding terms Kasera and Thathera.[2] In Wardha the Kasārs are no longer artificers, but only dealers, employing Panchāls to make the vessels which they retail in their shops. And the same is the case with the Marātha and Deshkar subcastes in Nāgpur. The Kasārs are a respectable caste, ranking next to the Sunārs among the urban craftsmen.

1. Distribution and origin of the caste.

[1] This article is compiled from papers by Mr. Rājarām Gangādhar, Tahsīldār, Arvi; Mr. Sadāsheo Jairām, Sanskrit Professor, Hislop College; and Mr. Deodatta Nāmdār, Manager, Court of Wards, Chauri.

[2] Crooke's *Tribes and Castes*, art. Thathera.

According to a legend given by Mr. Sadāsheo Jairām they trace their origin from Dharampāl, the son of Sahasra Arjun or Arjun of the Thousand Arms. Arjun was the greatgrandson of Ekshvaku, who was born in the forests of Kalinga, from the union of a mare and a snake. On this account the Kasārs of the Marātha country say that they all belong to the Ahihaya clan (*Ahi*, a snake; and *Haya*, a mare). Arjun was killed by Parasurāma during the slaughter of the Kshatriyas and Dharampāl's mother escaped with three other pregnant women. According to another version all the four women were the wives of the king of the Somvansi Rājpūts who stole the sacred cow Kāmdhenu. Their four sons on growing up wished to avenge their father and prayed to the Goddess Kāli for weapons. But unfortunately in their prayer, instead of saying *bān*, arrow, they said *vān*, which means pot, and hence brass pots were given to them instead of arrows. They set out to sell the pots, but got involved in a quarrel with a Rāja, who killed three of them, but was defeated by the fourth, to whom he afterwards gave his daughter and half his kingdom; and this hero became the ancestor of the Kasārs. In some localities the Kasārs say that Dharampāl, the Rājpūt founder of their caste, was the ancestor of the Haihaya Rājpūt kings of Ratanpur; and it is noticeable that the Thatheras of the United Provinces state that their original home was a place called Ratanpur, in the Deccan.[1] Both Ratanpur and Mandla, which are very old towns, have important brass and bell-metal industries, their bell-metal wares being especially well known on account of the brilliant polish which is imparted to them. And the story of the Kasārs may well indicate, as suggested by Mr. Hīra Lāl, that Ratanpur was a very early centre of the brass-working industry, from which it has spread to other localities in this part of India.

2. Internal structure. The caste have a number of subdivisions, mainly of a territorial nature. Among these are the Marātha Kasārs; the Deshkar, who also belong to the Marātha country; the Pardeshi or foreigners, the Jhāde or residents of the forest country of the Central Provinces, and the Audhia or

[1] Crooke's art. Thathera.

Bemrose, Collo., Derby.

A GROUP OF KASĀRS OR BRASS-WORKERS.

Ajudhiabāsi who are immigrants from Oudh. Another subdivision, the Bharewas, are of a distinctly lower status than the body of the caste, and have non-Aryan customs, such as the eating of pork. They make the heavy brass ornaments which the Gonds and other tribes wear on their legs, and are probably an occupational offshoot from one of these tribes. In Chānda some of the Bharewas serve as grooms and are looked down upon by the others. They have totemistic septs, named after animals and plants, some of which are Gond words; and among them the bride goes to the bridegroom's house to be married, which is a Gond custom. The Bharewas may more properly be considered as a separate caste of lower status. As previously stated, the Marātha and Deshkar subcastes of the Marātha country no longer make vessels, but only keep them for sale. One subcaste, the Otāris, make vessels from moulds, while the remainder cut and hammer into shape the imported sheets of brass. Lastly comes a group comprising those members of the caste who are of doubtful or illegitimate descent, and these are known either as Tākle ('Thrown out' in Marāthi), Bidur, 'Bastard,' or Laondi Bachcha, 'Issue of a kept wife.' In the Marātha country the Kasārs, as already seen, say that they all belong to one *gotra*, the Ahihaya. They have, however, collections of families distinguished by different surnames, and persons having the same surname are forbidden to marry. In the northern Districts they have the usual collection of exogamous septs, usually named after villages.

3. Social customs.

The marriages of first cousins are generally forbidden, as well as of members of the same sept. Divorce and the remarriage of widows are permitted. Devi or Bhawāni is the principal deity of the caste, as of so many Hindus. At her festival of Māndo Amāwas or the day of the new moon of Phāgun (February), every Kasār must return to the community of which he is a member and celebrate the feast with them. And in default of this he will be expelled from caste until the next Amāwas of Phāgun comes round. They close their shops and worship the implements of their trade on this day and also on the Pola day. The Kasārs, as already stated, rank next to the Sunārs among the artisan castes, and the Audhia Sunārs, who make ornaments of bell-metal, form a connecting link between the two groups. The social status of the Kasārs varies in different localities. In some places Brāhmans take water from them but not in others. Some Kasārs now invest boys with the sacred thread at their weddings, and thereafter it is regularly worn.

4. Occupation. The caste make eating and drinking vessels, ornaments and ornamental figures from brass, copper and bell-metal. Brass is the metal most in favour for utensils, and it is usually imported in sheets from Bombay, but in places it is manufactured from a mixture of three parts of copper and two of zinc. This is considered the best brass, though it is not so hard as the inferior kinds, in which the proportion of zinc is increased. Ornaments of a grey colour, intended to resemble silver, are made from a mixture of four parts of copper with five of zinc. Bell-metal is an alloy of copper and tin, and in Chānda is made of four parts of copper to one part tin or tinfoil, the tin being the more expensive metal. Bells of fairly good size and excellent tone are moulded from this amalgam, and plates or saucers in which anything acid in the way of food is to be kept are also made of it, since acids do not corrode this metal as they do brass and copper. But bell-metal vessels are fragile and sometimes break when dropped. They cannot also be heated in the fire to clean them, and therefore cannot be lent to persons outside the family; while brass vessels may be lent to friends of other castes, and on being received back pollution is removed by heating them in the fire or placing hot ashes in them. Brāhmans make a small fire of grass for this purpose and pass the vessels through the flame. Copper cooking-pots are commonly used by Muhammadans but not by Hindus, as they have to be coated with tin; the Hindus consider that tin is an inferior metal whose application to copper degrades the latter. Pots made of brass with a copper rim are called 'Ganga Jamni' after the confluence of the dark water of the Jumna with the muddy stream of the Ganges, whose union they are supposed to symbolise. Small figures of the deities or idols are also made of brass, but some Kasārs will not attempt this work, because they are afraid of the displeasure of the god in case the figure should not be well or symmetrically shaped.

KASBI

LIST OF PARAGRAPHS

Kasbi,[1] Tawāif, Devadāsi.—The caste of dancing-girls and prostitutes. The name Kasbi is derived from the Arabic *kasab*, prostitution, and signifies rather a profession than a caste. In India practically all female dancers and singers are prostitutes, the Hindus being still in that stage of the development of intersexual relations when it is considered impossible that a woman should perform before the public and yet retain her modesty. It is not so long that this idea has been abandoned by Western nations, and the fashion of employing women actors is perhaps not more than two or three centuries old in England. The gradual disappearance of the distinctive influence of sex in the public and social conduct of women is presumably a sign of advancing civilisation, and is greatest in the West, the old standards retaining more and more vitality as we proceed Eastward. Among the Anglo-Saxon races women are almost entirely emancipated from any handicap due to their sex, and direct their lives with the same freedom and independence as men. Among the Latin races many people still object to girls walking out alone in towns, and in Italy the number of women to be seen in the streets is so small that it must be considered improper for a young and respectable woman to go about alone. Here also survives the *mariage de*

1. General notice.

[1] A part of the information contained in this article is furnished by Mr. Adurām Chaudhri of the Gazetteer Office.

convenance or arrangement of matches by the parents; the underlying reason for this custom, which also partly accounts for the institution of infant-marriage, appears to be that it is not considered safe to permit a young girl to frequent the society of unmarried men with sufficient freedom to be able to make her own choice. And, finally, on arrival in Egypt and Turkey we find the seclusion of women still practised, and only now beginning to weaken before the influence of Western ideas. But again in the lowest scale of civilisation, among the Gonds and other primitive tribes, women are found to enjoy great freedom of social intercourse. This is partly no doubt because their lives are too hard and rude to permit of any seclusion of women, but also partly because they do not yet consider it an obligatory feature of the institution of marriage that a girl should enter upon it in the condition of a virgin.

2. Girls dedicated to temples.

In the Deccan girls dedicated to temples are called Devadāsis or 'Hand-maidens of the gods.' They are thus described by Marco Polo: "In this country," he says, "there are certain abbeys in which are gods and goddesses, and here fathers and mothers often consecrate their daughters to the service of the deity. When the priests desire to feast their god they send for those damsels, who serve the god with meats and other goods, and then sing and dance before him for about as long as a great baron would be eating his dinner. Then they say that the god has devoured the essence of the food, and fall to and eat it themselves."[1] Mr. Francis writes of the Devadāsis as follows:[1] "It is one of the many inconsistences of the Hindu religion that though their profession is repeatedly and vehemently condemned by the Shāstras it has always received the countenance of the church. The rise of the caste and its euphemistic name seem both of them to date from the ninth and tenth centuries of our era, during which much activity prevailed in southern India in the matter of building temples and elaborating the services held in them. The dancing-girls' duties then as now were to fan the idol with *chamaras*

[1] *Madras Census Report* (1901), p. 151, quoting from *South Indian Inscriptions*, Buchanan's *Mysore, Canara and Malabar*, and Elliot's *History of India*.

Bemrose, Collo., Derby.

DANCING GIRLS AND MUSICIANS.

or Thibetan ox-tails, to hold the sacred light called Kumbarti and to sing and dance before the god when he was carried in procession. Inscriptions show that in A.D. 1004 the great temple of the Chola king Rajarāja at Tanjore had attached to it 400 women of the temple who lived in free quarters in the surrounding streets, and were given a grant of land from the endowment. Other temples had similar arrangements. At the beginning of last century there were a hundred dancing-girls attached to the temple at Conjeeveram, and at Madura, Conjeeveram and Tanjore there are still numbers of them who receive allowances from the endowments of the big temples at those places. In former days the profession was countenanced not only by the church but by the state. Abdur Razāk, a Turkish ambassador to the court of Vijayanagar in the fifteenth century, describes women of this class as living in state-controlled institutions, the revenue of which went towards the upkeep of the police."

The dedication of girls to temples and religious prostitution was by no means confined to India but is a common feature of ancient civilisation. The subject has been mentioned by Dr. Westermarck in *The Origin and Development of the Moral Ideas*, and fully discussed by Sir James Frazer in *Attis, Adonis, Osiris*. The best known and most peculiar instance is that of the temple of Istar in Babylonia. "Herodotus says that every woman born in that country was obliged once in her life to go and sit down in the precinct of Aphrodite and there consort with a stranger. A woman who had once taken her seat was not allowed to return home till one of the strangers threw a silver coin into her lap and took her with him beyond the holy ground. The silver coin could not be refused because, since once thrown, it was sacred. The woman went with the first man who threw her money, rejecting no one. When she had gone with him and so satisfied the goddess, she returned home, and from that time forth no gift, however great, would prevail with her. In the Canaanitish cults there were women called *kedēshōth*, who were consecrated to the deity with whose temple they were associated, and who at the same time acted as prostitutes."[1] Other instances are given from

[1] *Origin and Development of the Moral Ideas*, ii. pp. 444, 445.

Africa, Egypt and ancient Greece. The principal explanation of these practices was that the act of intercourse, according to the principle of sympathetic magic, produced fertility, usually of the crops, though in the Babylonian case, Dr. Westermarck thinks, of the woman herself. Several instances have been recorded of people who perform the sexual act as a preliminary or accompaniment to sowing the crops,[1] and there seems little doubt that this explanation is correct. A secondary idea of religious prostitution may have been to afford to the god the same sexual pleasures as delighted an earthly king. Thus the Skanda Purāna relates that Kārtikeya, the Hindu god of war, was sent by his father to frustrate the sacrifice of Daksha, and at the instigation of the latter was delayed on his way by beautiful damsels, who entertained him with song and dance. Hence it is the practice still for dancing-girls who serve in the pagodas to be betrothed and married to him, after which they may prostitute themselves but cannot marry a man.[2] Similarly the Murlis or dancing-girls in Marātha temples are married to Khandoba, the Marātha god of war. Sometimes the practice of prostitution might begin by the priests of the temple as representatives of the god having intercourse with the women. This is stated to have been the custom at the temple of Jagannāth in Orissa, where the officiating Brāhmans had adulterous connection with the women who danced and sang before the god.[3]

3. Music and dancing.

Both music and dancing, like others of the arts, probably originated as part of a religious or magical service or ritual, and hence would come to be practised by the women attached to temples. And it would soon be realised what potent attractions these arts possessed when displayed by women, and in course of time they would be valued as accomplishments in themselves, and either acquired independently by other courtesans or divorced from a sole application to religious ritual. In this manner music, singing and dancing may have grown to be considered as the regular attractions of the courtesan and hence immoral in themselves, and not

[1] *The Golden Bough*, vol. ii. p. 205 *et seq.*

[2] Garrett's *Classical Dictionary of the Hindus*, p. 322.

[3] Westermarck, *ibidem*, quoting Ward's *Hindus*, p. 134.

suitable for display by respectable women. The Emperor Shāh Jahān is said to have delighted in the performances of the Tawāif or Muhammadan singing and dancing girls, who at that time lived in bands and occupied mansions as large as palaces.[1] Aurāngzeb ordered them all to be married or banished from his dominions, but they did not submit without a protest; and one morning as the Emperor was going to the mosque he saw a vast crowd of mourners marching in file behind a bier, and filling the air with screams and lamentations. He asked what it meant, and was told that they were going to bury Music; their mother had been executed, and they were weeping over her loss. 'Bury her deep,' the Emperor cried, 'she must never rise again.'

4. Education of courtesans.

The possession of these attractions naturally gave the courtesān an advantage over ordinary women who lacked them, and her society was much sought after, as shown in the following description of a native court:[2] "Nor is the courtesan excluded, she of the smart saying, famed for the much-valued cleverness which is gained in 'the world,' who when the learned fail is ever ready to cut the Gordian knot of solemn question with the sharp blade of her repartee, for—The sight of foreign lands; the possession of a Pandit for a friend; a *courtesan*; access to the royal court; patient study of the Shāstras; the roots of cleverness are these five." Mr. Crooke also remarks on the tolerance extended to this class of women: "The curious point about Indian prostitutes is the tolerance with which they are received into even respectable houses, and the absence of that strong social disfavour in which this class is held in European countries. This feeling has prevailed for a lengthened period. We read in the Buddhist histories of Ambapāta, the famous courtesan, and the price of her favours fixed at two thousand *masurans*. The same feeling appears in the folk-tales and early records of Indian courts."[3] It may be remarked, however, that the social ostracism of such women has not always been the rule in Europe, while as regards

[1] Wheeler's *History of India*, vol. iv. part ii. pp. 324, 325.

[2] Forbes, *Rāsmāla*, i. p. 247.

[3] Crooke's *Tribes and Castes*, art. Tawāif.

conjugal morality Indian society would probably appear to great advantage beside that of Europe in the Middle Ages. But when the courtesan is alone possessed of the feminine accomplishments, and also sees much of society and can converse with point and intelligence on public affairs, her company must necessarily be more attractive than that of the women of the family, secluded and uneducated, and able to talk about nothing but the petty details of household management. Education so far as women were concerned was to a large extent confined to courtesans, who were taught all the feminine attainments on account of the large return to be obtained in the practice of their profession. This is well brought out in the following passage from a Hindu work in which the mother speaks:[1] "Worthy Sir, this daughter of mine would make it appear that I am to blame, but indeed I have done my duty, and have carefully prepared her for that profession for which by birth she was intended. From earliest childhood I have bestowed the greatest care upon her, doing everything in my power to promote her health and beauty. As soon as she was old enough I had her carefully instructed in the arts of dancing, acting, playing on musical instruments, singing, painting, preparing perfumes and flowers, in writing and conversation, and even to some extent in grammar, logic and philosophy. She was taught to play various games with skill and dexterity, how to dress well and show herself off to the greatest advantage in public; yet after all the time, trouble and money which I have spent upon her, just when I was beginning to reap the fruit of my labours, the ungrateful girl has fallen in love with a stranger, a young Brāhman without property, and wishes to marry him and give up her profession (of a prostitute), notwithstanding all my entreaties and representations of the poverty and distress to which all her family will be reduced if she persists in her purpose; and because I oppose this marriage, she declares that she will renounce the world and become a devotee." Similarly the education of another dancing-girl is thus described:[2]

[1] Extract from the *Dasa Kumara Charita* or Adventures of the Ten Youths, in *A Group of Hindu Stories*, p. 72.

[2] S. M. Edwardes, *By-ways of Bombay*, p. 31.

Bemrose, Collo., Derby.

GIRL IN FULL DRESS AND ORNAMENTS.

"Gauhar Jān did her duty by the child according to her lights. She engaged the best 'Gawayyas' to teach her music, the best 'Kathaks' to teach her dancing, the best 'Ustāds' to teach her elocution and deportment, and the best of Munshis to ground her in Urdu and Persian *belles lettres*; so that when Imtiazān reached her fifteenth year her accomplishments were noised abroad in the bazār." It is still said to be the custom for the Hindus in large towns, as among the Greeks of the time of Pericles, to frequent the society of courtesans for the charm of their witty and pointed conversation. Betel-nut is provided at such receptions, and at the time of departure each person is expected to deposit a rupee in the tray. Of course it is in no way meant to assert that the custom is at all generally prevalent among educated men, as this would be quite untrue.

The association of all feminine charms and intellectual attainments with public women led to the belief that they were incompatible with feminine modesty; and this was even extended to certain ornamental articles of clothing such as shoes. The Abbé Dubois remarks:[1] "The courtesans are the only women in India who enjoy the privilege of learning to read, to dance and to sing. A well-bred respectable woman would for this reason blush to acquire any one of these accomplishments." Buchanan says:[2] "The higher classes of Hindu women consider every approach to wearing shoes as quite indecent; so that their use is confined to Muhammadans, camp trulls and Europeans, and most of the Muhammadans have adopted the Hindu notion on this subject; women of low rank wear sandals." And again:[3] "A woman who appears clean in public on ordinary occasions may pretty confidently be taken for a prostitute; such care of her person would indeed be considered by her husband as totally incompatible with modesty." And as regards accomplishments:[4] "It is considered very disgraceful for a modest woman to sing or play on any musical instrument; the only time when such a practice is permitted is among the Muhammadans at the Muharram, when women are

[1] *Hindu Manners, Customs and Ceremonies*, p. 93.

[2] *Eastern India*, i. p. 119.

[3] *Ibidem*, iii. p. 107.

[4] *Ibidem*, ii. p. 930.

allowed to join in the praises of Fātima and her son." And a current saying is: "A woman who sings in the house as she goes about her work and one who is fond of music can never be a Sati"; a term which is here used as an equivalent for a virtuous woman. Buchanan wrote a hundred years ago, and things have no doubt improved since his time, but this feeling appears to be principally responsible for much of the prejudice against female education, which has hitherto been so strong even among the literate classes of Hindus; and is only now beginning to break down as the highly cultivated young men of the present day have learned to appreciate and demand a greater measure of intelligence from their wives.

5. Caste customs. Among the better class of Kasbis a certain caste feeling and organisation exists. When a girl attains adolescence her mother makes a bargain with some rich man to be her first consort. Oil and turmeric are rubbed on her body for five days as in the case of a bride. A feast is given to the caste and the girl is married to a dagger, walking seven times round the sacred post with it. Her human consort then marks her forehead with vermilion and covers her head with her head-cloth seven times. In the evening she goes to live with him for as long as he likes to maintain her, and afterwards takes up the practice of her profession. In this case it is necessary that the man should be an outsider and not a member of the Kasbi caste, because the quasi-marriage is the formal commencement on the part of the woman of her hereditary trade. As already seen, the feeling of shame and degradation attaching to this profession in Europe appears to be somewhat attenuated in India, and it is counterbalanced by that acquiescence in and attachment to the caste-calling which is the principal feature of Hindu society. And no doubt the life of the dancing-girl has, at any rate during youth, its attractions as compared with that of a respectable married woman. Tavernier tells the story [1] of a Shāh of Persia who, desiring to punish a dancing-girl for having boxed the ears of one of her companions within his hearing (it being clearly not the effect of the operation on the patient which annoyed his majesty) made an order that

[1] *Persian Travels*, book iii. chap. xvii.

she should be married. And a more curious instance still is the following from a recent review:[1] "The natives of India are by instinct and custom the most conservative race in the world. When I was stationed at Aurangābād—fifty years ago it is true, but that is but a week in regard to this question—a case occurred within my own knowledge which shows the strength of hereditary feeling. An elderly wealthy native adopted two baby girls, whose mother and family had died during a local famine. The children grew up with his own girls and were in all respects satisfactory, and apparently quite happy until they arrived at the usual age for marriage. They then asked to see their papa by adoption, and said to him, 'We are very grateful to you for your care of us, but we are now grown up. We are told our mother was a Kasbi (prostitute), and we must insist on our rights, go out into the world, and do as our mother did.'"

6. First pregnancy. In the fifth or seventh month of the first pregnancy of a Kasbi woman 108 fried wafers of flour and sugar, known as *gūjahs*, are prepared, and are eaten by her as well as distributed to friends and relatives who are invited to the house. After this they in return prepare similar wafers and send them to the pregnant woman. Some little time before the birth the mother washes her head with gram flour, puts on new clothes and jewels, and invites all her friends to the house, feasting them with rice boiled in milk, cakes and sweetmeats.

7. Different classes of women. Though the better-class Kasbis appear to have a sort of caste union, this is naturally quite indefinite, inasmuch as marriage, at present the essential bond of caste-organisation, is absent. The sons of Kasbis take up any profession that they choose; and many of them marry and live respectably with their wives. Others become musicians and assist at the performances of the dancing-girls, as the Bhadua who beats the cymbals and sings in chorus and also acts as a pimp, and the Sārangia, one who performs on the *sārangi* or fiddle. The girls themselves are of different classes, as the Kasbi or Gāyan who are Hindus, the Tawāif who are Muhammadans, and the Bogam or Telugu dancing-girls. Gond women are

[1] From a review of *A German Staff Officer in India*, written by Sir Evelyn Wood in the *Saturday Review*, 5th February 1910.

known as Deogarhni, and are supposed to have come from Deogarh in Chhindwāra, formerly the headquarters of a Gond dynasty. The Sārangias or fiddlers are now a separate caste. In the northern Districts the dancing-girls are usually women of the Beria caste and are known as Berni. After the spring harvest the village headman hires one or two of these girls, who dance and do acrobatic feats by torchlight. They will continue all through the night, stimulated by draughts of liquor, and it is said that one woman will drink two or three bottles of the country spirit. The young men of the village beat the drum to accompany her dancing, and take turns to see how long they can go on doing so without breaking down. After the performance each cultivator gives the woman one or two pice (farthings) and the headman gives her a rupee. Such a celebration is known as Rai, and is distinctive of Bundelkhand.

In Bengal this class of women often become religious mendicants and join the Vaishnava or Bairāgi community, as stated by Sir H. Risley:[1] "The mendicant members of the Vaishnava community are of evil repute, their ranks being recruited by those who have no relatives, by widows, by individuals too idle or depraved to lead a steady working life, and by prostitutes. Vaishnavi, or Baishtabi according to the vulgar pronunciation, has come to mean a courtesan. A few undoubtedly join from sincere and worthy motives, but their numbers are too small to produce any appreciable effect on the behaviour of their comrades. The habits of these beggars are very unsettled. They wander from village to village and from one *akhāra* (monastery) to another, fleecing the frugal and industrious peasantry on the plea of religion, and singing songs in praise of Hari beneath the village tree or shrine. Members of both sexes smoke Indian hemp (*gānja*), and although living as brothers and sisters are notorious for licentiousness. There is every reason for suspecting that infanticide is common, as children are never seen. In the course of their wanderings they entice away unmarried girls, widows, and even married women on the pretence of visiting Sri Kshetra (Jagannāth)

[1] *Tribes and Castes of Bengal*, art. Vaishnava. The notice, as stated, refers only to the lowest section of Bairāgis.

Brindāban or Benares, for which reason they are shunned by all respectable natives, who gladly give charity to be rid of them."

In large towns prostitutes belong to all castes. An old list obtained by Rai Bahādur Hīra Lāl of registered prostitutes in Jubbulpore showed the following numbers of different castes: Barai six, Dhīmar four, and Nai, Khangār, Kāchhi, Gond, Teli, Brāhman, Rājpūt and Bania three each. Each woman usually has one or two girls in training if she can obtain them, with a view to support herself by their earnings in the same method of livelihood when her own attractions have waned. Fatherless and orphan girls run a risk of falling into this mode of life, partly because their marriages cannot conveniently be arranged, and also from the absence of strict paternal supervision. For it is to be feared that a girl who is allowed to run about at her will in the bazār has little chance of retaining her chastity even up to the period of her arrival at adolescence. This is no doubt one of the principal considerations in favour of early marriage. The caste-people often subscribe for the marriage of a girl who is left without support, and it is said that in former times an unmarried orphan girl might go and sit *dharna*, or starving herself, at the king's gate until he arranged for her wedding. Formerly the practice of obtaining young girls was carried on to a much greater extent than at present. Malcolm remarks:[1] "Slavery in Mālwa and the adjoining provinces is chiefly limited to females; but there is perhaps no part of India where there are so many slaves of this sex. The dancing-girls are all purchased, when young, by the Nakins or heads of the different sets or companies, who often lay out large sums in these speculations, obtaining advances from the bankers on interest like other classes." But the attractions of the profession and the numbers of those who engage in it have now largely declined.

8. Dancing and singing.

The better class of Kasbi women, when seen in public, are conspicuous by their wealth of jewellery and their shoes of patent leather or other good material. Women of other castes do not commonly wear shoes in the streets. The

[1] *Memoir of Central India.*

Kasbis are always well and completely clothed, and it has been noticed elsewhere that the Indian courtesan is more modestly dressed than most women. No doubt in this matter she knows her business. A well-to-do dancing-girl has a dress of coloured muslin or gauze trimmed with tinsel lace, with a short waist, long straight sleeves, and skirts which reach a little below the knee, a shawl falling from the head over the shoulders and wrapped round the body, and a pair of tight satin trousers, reaching to the ankles. The feet are bare, and strings of small bells are tied round them. They usually dance and sing to the accompaniment of the *tabla*, *sārangi* and *majīra*. The *tabla* or drum is made of two half-bowls—one brass or clay for the bass, and the other of wood for the treble. They are covered with goat-skin and played together. The *sārangi* is a fiddle. The *majīra* (cymbals) consist of two metallic cups slung together and used for beating time. Before a dancing-girl begins her performance she often invokes the aid of Sāraswati, the goddess of music. She then pulls her ear as a sign of remembrance of Tānsen, India's greatest musician, and a confession to his spirit of the imperfection of her own sense of music. The movements of the feet are accompanied by a continual opening and closing of henna-dyed hands; and at intervals the girl kneels at the feet of one or other of the audience. On the festival of Basant Panchmi or the commencement of spring these girls worship their dancing-dress and musical instruments with offerings of rice, flowers and a cocoanut.

1. General notice.

Katia, Katwa, Katua.—An occupational caste of cotton-spinners and village watchmen belonging to the Satpūra Districts and the Nerbudda valley. In 1911 they numbered 41,000 persons and were returned mainly from the Hoshangābād, Seoni and Chhindwāra Districts. The caste is almost confined to the Central Provinces. The name is derived from the Hindi *kātna*, to spin thread, and the Katias are an occupational group probably recruited from the Mahārs and Koris. They have a tradition, Mr. Crooke states,[1] that they were originally Bais Rājpūts, whose

[1] *Tribes and Castes of the N.-W. P.*, art. Katwa.

ancestors, having been imprisoned for resistance to authority, were released on the promise that they would follow a woman's occupation of spinning thread. In the Central Provinces they are sometimes called Renhta Rājpūts or Knights of the Spinning Wheel. The tradition of Rājpūt descent need not of course be taken seriously. The drudgery of spinning thread was naturally imposed on any widow in the household, and hence the saying, 'It is always moving, like a widow's spinning-wheel.'[1]

2. Subcastes and exogamous groups.

The Katias have several subcastes, with names generally derived from places in the Central Provinces, as Pathāri from a village in the Chhindwāra District, Mandilwār from Mandla, Gadhewāl from Garha, near Jubbulpore, and so on. The Dulbuha group consist of those who were formerly palanquin-bearers (from *doli*, a litter). They have also more than fifty exogamous septs, with names of the usual low-caste type, derived from places, animals or plants, or natural objects. Some of the septs are subdivided. Thus the Nāgotia sept, named after the cobra, is split up into the Nāgotia, Dirat[2] Nāg, Bhārowar[3] Nāg, Kosam Karia and Hazāri[4] Nāg groups. It is said that the different groups do not intermarry; but it is probable that they do, as otherwise there seems to be no object in the subdivision. The Kosam Karias worship a cobra at their weddings, but not the others. The Singhotia sept, from *singh*, a horn, is divided into the Bakaria (goat) and Ghāgar-bharia (one who fills an earthen vessel) subsepts. The Bakarias offer goats to their gods; and the Ghāgar-bharias on the Akti[5] festival, just before the breaking of the rains, fill an earthen vessel and worship it, and consider it sacred for that day. Next day it is brought into ordinary use. The Dongaria sept, from *dongar*, a hill, revere the *chheola* tree.[6] They choose any tree of this species outside the village, and say that it is placed on a hill, and go and worship it once a year. In this case it would appear that a hill was first venerated as an animate being and the ancestor of the sept. When hills were no longer so regarded, a *chheola* tree growing on a hill

[1] Temple and Fallon's *Hindustāni Proverbs*.

[2] Perhaps a leather strap or belt.

[3] A revolution or circuit.

[4] A thousand.

[5] The third Baisākh (June).

[6] *Butea frondosa*.

was substituted; and now the tree only is revered, probably a good deal for form's sake, and so far as the hill is concerned, the mere pretence that it is growing on a hill is sufficient.

3. Marriage customs. A man must not take a wife from his own sept nor from that of his mother or grandmother. Girls are commonly married between eight and twelve years of age; and a customary payment of Rs. 9 is made to the father of the bride, double this amount being given by a widower. An unmarried girl seduced by a man of the caste is united to him by the ceremony used for a widow, and a fine is imposed on her parents; if she goes wrong with an outsider she is expelled from the community. In the marriage ceremony the customary ritual of the northern Districts is followed,[1] and the binding portion of it consists in the bride and bridegroom walking seven times around the *bhānwar* or sacred pole. While she does this it is essential that the bride should wear a string of black beads round her neck and brass anklets on her feet. After the ceremony the bride's mother and other women dance before the company. Whether the bride be a child or young woman she always returns home after a stay of a few days at her husband's house, and at her subsequent final departure the Gauna or going-away ceremony is performed. If the bridegroom dies after the wedding and before the Gauna, his younger brother or cousin or anybody else may come and take away the bride after performing this ceremony, and she will be considered as fully married to him. She is known as a Gonhyai wife, as distinguished from a Byāhta or one married in the ordinary manner, and a Karta or widow married a second time. But the children of all three inherit equally. A widow may marry again, and take any one she pleases for her second husband. Widow-marriages must not be celebrated in the rainy months of Shrāwan, Bhādon and Kunwār. No music is allowed at them, and the husband must present a fee of a rupee and a cocoanut to the mālguzār (proprietor) of the village and four annas to the kotwār or watchman. A bachelor who is to marry a widow first goes through a formal ceremony with a cotton plant. Divorce is permitted for mutual disagreement.

[1] A description of the ceremony is given in the article on Kurmi.

The couple stand before the caste committee and each takes a stick, breaks it in two halves, and throws them apart, saying, "I have no further connection with my husband (or wife), and I break my marriage with him (or her) as I break this stick."

The dead may be either buried or burnt, as convenient, and mourning is always observed for three days. Before the corpse is removed a new earthen pot filled with rice is placed on the bier. The chief mourner raises it, and addressing the deceased informs him that after a certain period he will be united to the sainted dead, and until that day his spirit should abide happily in the pot and not trouble his family. The mouth of the pot is then covered, and after the funeral the mourners take it home with them. When the day appointed for the final ceremony has come, a miniature platform is made from sticks tied together, and garlands and offerings of cakes are hung on to it. A small heap of rice is made on the platform, and just above it a clove is suspended from a thread. Songs are sung, and the principal relative opens the pot in which the spirit of the deceased has been enclosed. The spirit is called upon to join the sacred company of the dead, and the party continue to sing and to adjure it with all their force. The thread from which the clove is suspended begins to swing backwards and forwards over the rice; and a pig and two or three chickens are crushed to death as offerings to the soul of the deceased. Finally the clove touches the rice, and it is believed that the spirit of the dead man has departed to join the sainted dead. The Katias consider that after this he requires nothing more from the living, and so they do not make the annual offerings to the souls of the departed. 4. Funeral rites.

The caste sometimes employ a Brāhman for the marriage ceremony; but generally his services are limited to fixing an auspicious date, and the functions of a priest are undertaken by members of the family. They invite a Brāhman to give a name to a boy, and call him by this name. They think that if they changed the name they would not be able to get a wife for the child. They will eat any kind of flesh, including pork and fowls, but they are not considered to be impure. They are generally illiterate, and dirty in appearance. Unmarried girls wear glass bangles on both hands, but married 5. Social rules.

women wear metal bracelets on the right hand and glass on the left. Girls are twice tattooed : first in childhood, and a second time after marriage. The proper avocations of the Katias were the spinning of cotton thread and the weaving of the finer kinds of cloth ; but most of them have had to abandon their ancestral calling from want of custom, and they are now either village watchmen or cultivators and labourers. A few of them own villages. The Katias think themselves rather knowing ; but this opinion is not shared by their neighbours, who say ironically of them, " A Katia is eight times as wise as an ordinary man, and a Kāyasth thirteen times. Any one who pretends to be wiser than these must be an idiot."

KAWAR[1]

LIST OF PARAGRAPHS

1. Tribal legend.

Kawar, Kanwar, Kaur (honorific title, Sirdār).—A primitive tribe living in the hills of the Chhattīsgarh Districts north of the Mahānadi. The hill-country comprised in the northern zamīndāri estates of Bilāspur and the adjoining Feudatory States of Jashpur, Udaipur, Sargūja, Chāng Bhakār and Korea is the home of the Kawars, and is sometimes known after them as the Kamrān. Eight of the Bilāspur zamīndārs are of the Kawar tribe. The total numbers of the tribe are nearly 200,000, practically all of whom belong to the Central Provinces. In Bilāspur the name is always pronounced with a nasal as Kanwar. The Kawars trace their origin from the Kauravas of the Mahābhārata, who were defeated by the Pāndavaş at the great battle of Hastināpur. They say that only two pregnant women survived and fled to the hills of Central India, where they took refuge in the houses of a Rāwat (grazier) and a Dhobi (washerman) respectively, and the boy and girl children who were born to them became the ancestors of the Kawar tribe. Consequently, the Kawars will take food from the hands of Rāwats, especially those of the Kauria subcaste, who are in all probability descended from Kawars. And when a Kawar

[1] This article is based almost entirely on a monograph contributed by Mr. Hīra Lāl.

is put out of caste for having maggots in a wound, a Dhobi is always employed to readmit him to social intercourse. These facts show that the tribe have some close ancestral connection with the Rāwats and Dhobis, though the legend of descent from the Kauravas is, of course, a myth based on the similarity of the names. The tribe have lost their own language, if they ever had one, and now speak a corrupt form of the Chhattīsgarhi dialect of Hindi. It is probable that they belong to the Dravidian tribal family.

2. Tribal sub-divisions.

The Kawars have the following eight endogamous divisions: Tanwar, Kamalbansi, Paikara, Dūdh-Kawar, Rathia, Chānti, Cherwa and Rautia. The Tanwar group, also known as Umrao, is that to which the zamīndārs belong, and they now claim to be Tomara Rājpūts, and wear the sacred thread. They prohibit widow-remarriage, and do not eat fowls or drink liquor; but they have not yet induced Brāhmans to take water from them or Rājpūts to accept their daughters in marriage. The name Tanwar is not improbably simply a corruption of Kawar, and they are also altering their sept names to make them resemble those of eponymous Brāhmanical *gotras*. Thus Dhangur, the name of a sept, has been altered to Dhananjaya, and Sarvaria to Sāndilya. Telāsi is the name of a sept to which four zamīndārs belong, and is on this account sometimes returned as their caste by other Kawars, who consider it as a distinction. The zamīndāri families have now, however, changed the name Telāsi to Kairava. The Paikaras are the most numerous subtribe, being three-fifths of the total. They derive their name from Pāik, a foot-soldier, and formerly followed this occupation, being employed in the armies of the Haihaivansi Rājas of Ratanpur. They still worship a two-edged sword, known as the Jhagra Khand, or 'Sword of Strife,' on the day of Dasahra. The Kamalbansi, or 'Stock of the Lotus,' may be so called as being the oldest subdivision; for the lotus is sometimes considered the root of all things, on account of the belief that Brahma, the creator of the world, was himself born from this flower. In Bilāspur the Kamalbansis are considered to rank next after the Tanwars or zamīndārs' group. Colonel Dalton states that the term Dūdh or 'Milk' Kawar has the signification of 'Cream of the Kawars,' and he considered this subcaste to be the highest. The Rathias are a territorial group, being immigrants from Rāth, a wild tract of the Raigarh State. The Rautias are probably the descendants of Kawar fathers and mothers of the Rāwat (herdsman) caste. The traditional connection of the Kawars with a Rāwat has already been mentioned, and even now if a Kawar marries a Rāwat girl she will be admitted into the tribe, and the children will become full Kawars. Similarly, the Rāwats have a Kauria subcaste, who are also probably the offspring of mixed marriages; and if a Kawar girl is seduced by a Kauria Rāwat, she is not expelled from the tribe, as she would be for a *liaison* with any other man who was not a Kawar. This connection is no doubt due to the fact that until recently the Kawars and Rāwats, who are themselves a very mixed caste, were accustomed to intermarry. At the census persons returned as Rautia were included in the Kol tribe, which has a subdivision of that name. But Mr. Hīra Lāl's inquiries establish the fact that in Chhattīsgarh they are undoubtedly Kawars. The Cherwas are probably another hybrid group descended from connections formed by Kawars with girls of the Chero tribe of Chota Nāgpur. The Chānti, who derive their name from the ant, are considered to be the lowest group, as that insect is the most insignificant of living things. Of the above subcastes the Tanwars are naturally the highest, while the Chānti, Cherwa and Rautia, who keep pigs, are considered as the lowest. The others occupy an intermediate position. None of the subcastes will eat together, except at the houses of their zamīndārs, from whom they will all take food. But the Kawars of the Chhuri estate no longer attend the feasts of their zamīndār, for the following curious reason. One of the latter's village *thekādārs* or farmers had got the hide taken off a dead buffalo so as to keep it for his own use, instead of making the body over to a Chamār (tanner). The caste-fellows saw no harm in this act, but it offended the zamīndār's more orthodox Hindu conscience. Soon afterwards, at some marriage-feast of his family, when the Kawars of his zamīndāri attended in accordance with the usual custom, he remarked, 'Here come our Chamārs,' or words to that effect. The Chhuri Kawars were insulted, and the more so because the

Pendra zamīndār and other outsiders were present. So they declined to take food any longer from their zamīndār. They continued to accept it, however, from the other zamīndārs, until their master of Chhuri represented to them that this would result in a slur being put upon his standing among his fellows. So they have now given up taking food from any zamīndār.

3. Exogamous groups. The tribe have a large number of exogamous septs, which are generally totemistic or named after plants and animals. The names of 117 septs have been recorded, and there are probably even more. The following list gives a selection of the names:

Sept	Meaning	Sept	Meaning
Andīl	Born from an egg.	Hundār	A wolf.
Bāgh	Tiger.	Jānta	Grinding-mill.
Bichhi	Scorpion.	Kothi	A store-house.
Bilwa	Wild cat.	Khumari	A leaf-umbrella.
Bokra	Goat.	Lodha	A wild dog.
Chandrama	Moon.	Māma	Maternal uncle.
Chanwar	A whisk.	Mahādeo	The deity.
Chīta	Leopard.	Nūnmutaria	A packet of salt.
Chuva	A well.	Sendur	Vermilion.
Champa	A sweet-scented flower.	Sua	A parrot.
Dhenki	A pounding-lever.	Telāsi	Oily.
Darpan	A mirror.	Thath Murra	Pressed in a sugar-cane press.
Gobīra	A dung insect.		

Generally it may be said that every common animal or bird and even articles of food or dress and household implements have given their names to a sept. In the Paikara subcaste a figure of the plant or animal after which the sept is named is made by each party at the time of marriage. Thus a bridegroom of the Bāgh or tiger sept prepares a small image of a tiger with flour and bakes it in oil; this he shows to the bride's family to represent, as it were, his pedigree, or prove his legitimacy; while she on her part, assuming that she is, say, of the Bilwa or cat sept, will bring a similar image of a cat with her in proof of her origin. The Andīl sept make a representation of a hen sitting on eggs. They do not worship the totem animal or plant, but when they learn of the death of one of the species, they throw away an earthen cooking-pot as a sign of mourning. They generally think themselves descended from the totem animal or plant, but when the sept is called after some inanimate object, such as a grinding-mill or pounding-lever, they repudiate the idea of descent from it, and are at a loss to account for the origin of the name. Those whose septs are named after plants or animals usually abstain from injuring or cutting them, but where this rule would cause too much inconvenience it is transgressed : thus the members of the Karsāyal or deer sept find it too hard for them to abjure the flesh of that animal, nor can those of the Bokra sept abstain from eating goats. In some cases new septs have been formed by a conjunction of the names of two others, as Bāgh-Daharia, Gauriya-Sonwāni, and so on. These may possibly be analogous to the use of double names in English, a family of one sept when it has contracted a marriage with another of better position adding the latter's name to its own as a slight distinction. But it may also simply arise from the constant tendency to increase the number of septs in order to remove difficulties from the arrangement of matches.

4. Betrothal and marriage.

Marriage within the same sept is prohibited and also between the children of brothers and sisters. A man may not marry his wife's elder sister but he can take her younger one in her lifetime. Marriage is usually adult and, contrary to the Hindu rule, the proposal for a match always comes from the boy's father, as a man would think it undignified to try and find a husband for his daughter. The Kawar says, 'Shall my daughter leap over the wall to get a husband.' In consequence of this girls not infrequently remain unmarried until a comparatively late age, especially in the zamīndāri families where the provision of a husband of suitable rank may be difficult. Having selected a bride for his son the boy's father sends some friends to her village, and they address a friend of the girl's family, saying, "So-and-so (giving his name and village) would like to have a cup of *pej* (boiled rice-water) from you ; what do you say ?" The proposal is communicated to the girl's family, and if they approve of it they commence preparing the rice-water, which is partaken of by the parties and their friends. If the bride's people do not begin cooking the *pej*, it is understood that the proposal is rejected. The ceremony of betrothal comes next, when the boy's party go to the girl's house with a present of bangles, clothes, and fried cakes of rice and *urad* carried by a Kaurai Rāwat. They also take with them the bride-price, known as Suk, which is made up of cash, husked or unhusked rice, pulses and oil. It is a fixed amount, but differs for each subcaste, and the average value is about Rs. 25. To this is added three or four goats to be consumed at the wedding. If a widower marries a girl, a larger bride-price is exacted. The wedding follows, and in many respects conforms to the ordinary Hindu ritual, but Brāhmans are not employed. The bridegroom's party is accompanied by tomtom-players on its way to the wedding, and as each village is approached plenty of noise is made, so that the residents may come out and admire the dresses, a great part of whose merit consists in their antiquity, while the wearer delights in recounting to any who will listen the history of his garb and of his distinguished ancestors who have worn it. The marriage is performed by walking round the sacred pole, six times on one day and once on the following day. After the marriage the bride's parents wash the feet of the couple in milk, and then drink it in atonement for the sin committed in bringing their daughter into the world. The couple then return home to the bridegroom's house, where all the ceremonies are repeated, as it is said that otherwise his courtyard would remain unmarried. On the following day the couple go and bathe in a tank, where each throws five pots full of water over the other. And on their return the bridegroom shoots arrows at seven straw images of deer over his wife's shoulder, and after each shot she puts a little sugar in his mouth. This is a common ceremony among the forest tribes, and symbolises the idea that the man will support himself and his wife by hunting. On the fourth day the bride returns to her father's house. She visits her husband for two or three months in the following month of Asārh (June-July), but again goes home to play what is known as 'The game of Gauri,' Gauri being the name of Siva's consort. The young men and girls of the village assemble round her in the evening, and the girls sing songs while the men play on drums. An obscene representation of Gauri is made, and some of them pretend to be possessed by the deity, while the men beat the girls with ropes of grass. After she has enjoyed this amusement with her mates for some three months, the bride finally goes to her husband's house.

5. Other customs connected with marriage.

The wedding expenses come to about seventy rupees on the bridegroom's part in an ordinary marriage, while the bride's family spend the amount of the bride-price and a few rupees more. If the parties are poor the ceremony can be curtailed so far as to provide food for only five guests. It is permissible for two families to effect an exchange of girls in lieu of payment of the bride-price, this practice being known as Gunrāwat. Or a prospective bridegroom may give his services for three or four years instead of a price. The system of serving for a wife is known as Gharjiān, and is generally resorted to by widows having daughters. A girl going wrong with a Kawar or with a Kaurai Rāwat before marriage may be pardoned with the exaction of a feast from her parents. For a *liaison* with any other outsider she is finally expelled, and the exception of the Kaurai Rāwats shows that they are recognised as in reality Kawars. Widow-remarriage is permitted except in the Tanwar subcaste. New bangles and clothes are given to the widow, and the pair then stand under the eaves of the house; the bridegroom touches the woman's ear or puts a rolled mango-leaf into it, and she becomes his wife. If a widower marries a girl for his third wife it is considered unlucky for her. An earthen image of a woman is therefore made, and he goes through the marriage ceremony with it; he then throws the image to the ground so that it is broken, when it is considered to be dead and its funeral ceremony is performed. After this the widower may marry the girl, who becomes his fourth wife. Such cases are naturally very rare. If a widow marries her deceased husband's younger brother, which is considered the most suitable match, the children by her first husband rank equally with those of the second. If she marries outside the family her children and property remain with her first husband's relatives.

Dalton[1] records that the Kawars of Sargūja had adopted

[1] *Ethnology*, p. 158.

the practice of *sati*: "I found that the Kawars of Sargūja encouraged widows to become Satis and greatly venerated those who did so. Sati shrines are not uncommon in the Tributary Mahāls. Between Partābpur and Jhilmili in Sargūja I encamped in a grove sacred to a Kauraini Sati. Several generations have elapsed since the self-sacrifice that led to her canonisation, but she is now the principal object of worship in the village and neighbourhood, and I was informed that every year a *fowl* was sacrificed to her, and every third year a black goat. The Hindus with me were intensely amused at the idea of offering fowls to a Sati!" Polygamy is permitted, but is not common. Members of the Tanwar subtribe, when they have occasion to do so, will take the daughters of Kawars of other groups for wives, though they will not give their daughters to them. Such marriages are generally made clandestinely, and it has become doubtful as to whether some families are true Tanwars. The zamīndārs have therefore introduced a rule that no family can be recognised as a Tanwar for purposes of marriage unless it has a certificate to that effect signed by the zamīndār. Some of the zamīndārs charge considerable sums for these certificates, and all cannot afford them; but in that case they are usually unable to get husbands for their daughters, who remain unwed. Divorce is permitted for serious disagreement or bad conduct on the part of the wife.

6. Childbirth.

During childbirth the mother sits on the ground with her legs apart, and her back against the wall or supported by another woman. The umbilical cord is cut by the midwife: if the parents wish the boy to become eloquent she buries it in the village Council-place; or if they wish him to be a good trader, in the market; or if they desire him to be pious, before some shrine; in the case of a girl the cord is usually buried in a dung-heap, which is regarded as an emblem of fertility. As is usual in Chhattīsgarh, the mother receives no food or water for three days after the birth of a child. On the fifth day she is given regular food and on that day the house is purified. Five months after birth the lips of the child are touched with rice and milk and it is named. When twins are born a metal vessel is broken to sever the connection between them, as it is believed that otherwise they must die at the same time. If a boy is born after three girls he is called *titura*, and a girl after three boys, *tituri*. There is a saying that 'A *titura* child either fills the storehouse or empties it'; that is, his parents either become rich or penniless. To avert ill-luck in this case oil and salt are thrown away, and the mother gives one of her bangles to the midwife.

7. Disposal of the dead.

The dead are usually buried, though well-to-do families have adopted cremation. The corpse is laid on its side in the grave, with head to the north and face to the east. A little *til*, cotton, *urad* and rice are thrown on the grave to serve as seed-grain for the dead man's cultivation in the other world. A dish, a drinking vessel and a cooking-pot are placed on the grave with the same idea, but are afterwards taken away by the Dhobi (washerman). They observe mourning for ten days for a man, nine days for a woman, and three days for children under three years old. During the period of mourning the chief mourner keeps a knife beside him, so that the iron may ward off the attacks of evil spirits, to which he is believed to be peculiarly exposed. The ordinary rules of abstinence and retirement are observed during mourning. In the case of cremation the ceremonies are very elaborate and generally resemble those of the Hindus. When the corpse is half burnt, all the men present throw five pieces of wood on to the pyre, and a number of pieces are carried in a winnowing fan to the dead man's house, where they are touched by the women and then brought back and thrown on to the fire. After the funeral the mourners bathe and return home walking one behind the other in Indian file. When they come to a cross-road, the foremost man picks up a pebble with his left foot, and it is passed from hand to hand down the line of men until the hindmost throws it away. This is supposed to sever their connection with the spirit of the deceased and prevent it from following them home. On the third day they return to the cremation ground to collect the ashes and bones. A Brāhman is called who cooks a preparation of milk and rice at the head of the corpse, boils *urad* pulse at its feet, and bakes eight wheaten *chapātis* at the sides. This food is placed in leaf-cups at two corners of the ground. The mourners sprinkle cow's urine and milk over the bones, and picking them up with a *palās* (*Butea frondosa*) stick, wash them in milk and deposit them in a new earthen pot until such time as they can be carried to the Ganges. The bodies of men dying of smallpox must never be burnt, because that would be equivalent to destroying the goddess, incarnate in the body. The corpses of cholera patients are buried in order to dispose of them at once, and are sometimes exhumed subsequently within a period of six months and cremated. In such a case the Kawars spread a layer of unhusked rice in the grave, and address a prayer to the earth-goddess stating that the body has been placed with her on deposit, and asking that she will give it back intact when they call upon her for it. They believe that in such cases the process of decay is arrested for six months.

8. Laying spirits.

When a man has been killed by a tiger they have a ceremony called 'Breaking the string,' or the connection which they believe the animal establishes with a family on having tasted its blood. Otherwise they think that the tiger would gradually kill off all the remaining members of the family of his victim, and when he had finished with them would proceed to other families in the same village. This curious belief is no doubt confirmed by the tiger's habit of frequenting the locality of a village from which it has once obtained a victim, in the natural expectation that others may be forthcoming from the same source. In this ceremony the village Baiga or medicine-man is painted with red ochre and soot to represent the tiger, and proceeds to the place where the victim was carried off. Having picked up some of the blood-stained earth in his mouth, he tries to run away to the jungle, but the spectators hold him back until he spits out the earth. This represents the tiger being forced to give up his victim. The Baiga then ties a string round all the members of the dead man's family standing together; he places some grain before a fowl saying, 'If my charm has worked, eat of this'; and as soon as the fowl has eaten some grain the Baiga states that his efforts have been successful and the attraction of the man-eater has been broken; he then breaks the string and all the party return to the village. A similar ceremony is performed when a man has died of snake-bite.

9. Religion. The religion of the Kawars is entirely of an animistic character. They have a vague idea of a supreme deity whom they call Bhagwān and identify with the sun. They bow to him in reverence, but do no more as he does not interfere with men's concerns. They also have a host of local and tribal deities, of whom the principal is the Jhagra Khand or two-edged sword, already mentioned. The tiger is deified as Bagharra Deo and worshipped in every village for the protection of cattle from wild animals. They are also in great fear of a mythical snake with a red crest on its head, the mere sight of which is believed to cause death. It lives in deep pools in the forest which are known as *Shesh Kund*, and when it moves the grass along its track takes fire. If a man crosses its track his colour turns to black and he suffers excruciating pains which end in death, unless he is relieved by the Baiga. In one village where the snake was said to have recently appeared, the proprietor was so afraid of it that he never went out to his field without first offering a chicken. They have various local deities, of which the Mandwa Rāni or goddess of the Mandwa hill in Korba zamīndāri may be noticed as an example. She is a mild-hearted maiden who puts people right when they have gone astray in the forest, or provides them with food for the night and guides them to the water-springs on her hill. Recently a wayfarer had lost his path when she appeared and, guiding him into it, gave him a basket of brinjāls.[1] As the traveller proceeded he felt his burden growing heavier and heavier on his head, and finally on inspecting it found that the goddess had played a little joke on him and the brinjāls had turned into stones. The Kawars implicitly believe this story. Rivers are tenanted by a set of goddesses called the Sat Bahini or seven sisters. They delight in playing near waterfalls, holding up the water and suddenly letting it drop. Trees are believed to be harmless sentient beings, except when occasionally possessed by evil spirits, such as the ghosts of man-eating tigers. Sometimes a tree catches hold of a cow's tail as the

[1] Fruit of the egg-plant.

animal passes by and winds it up over a branch, and many cattle have lost their tails in this way. Every tank in which the lotus grows is tenanted by Purainha, the godling who tends this plant. The sword, the gun, the axe, the spear have each a special deity, and, in fact, in the Bangawān, the tract where the wilder Kawars dwell, it is believed that every article of household furniture is the residence of a spirit, and that if any one steals or injures it without the owner's leave, the spirit will bring some misfortune on him in revenge. Theft is said to be unknown among them, partly on this account and partly, perhaps, because no one has much property worth stealing. Instances of deified human beings are Kolin Sati, a Kol concubine of a zamīndār of Pendra who died during pregnancy, and Sārangarhni, a Ghasia woman who was believed to have been the mistress of a Rāja of Sārangarh and was murdered. Both are now Kawar deities. Thākur Deo is the deity of agriculture, and is worshipped by the whole village in concert at the commencement of the rains. Rice is brought by each cultivator and offered to the god, a little being sown at his shrine and the remainder taken home and mixed with the seed-grain to give it fertility. Two bachelors carry water round the village and sprinkle it on the brass plates of the cultivators or the roofs of their houses in imitation of rain.

10. Magic and witchcraft.

The belief in witchcraft is universal and every village has its *tonhi* or witch, to whom epidemic diseases, sudden illnesses and other calamities are ascribed. The witch is nearly always some unpopular old woman, and several instances are known of the murder of these unfortunate creatures, after their crimes had been proclaimed by the Baiga or medicine-man. In the famine of 1900 an old woman from another village came and joined one of the famine-kitchens. A few days afterwards the village watchman got ill, and when the Baiga was called in he said the old woman was a witch who had vowed the lives of twenty children to her goddess, and had joined the kitchen to kill them. The woman was threatened with a beating with castor-oil plants if she did not leave the village, and as the kitchen officer refused to supply her with food, she had to go. The Baiga takes action to stop and keep off epidemics by the methods common in Chhattīsgarh villages. When a woman asks him to procure her offspring, the Baiga sits *dharna* in front of Devi's shrine and fasts until the goddess, wearied by his importunity, descends on him and causes him to prophesy the birth of a child. They have the usual belief in imitative and sympathetic magic. If a person is wounded by an axe he throws it first into fire and then into cold water. By the first operation he thinks to dry up the wound and prevent its festering, and by the second to keep it cool. Thin and lean children are weighed in a balance against moist cowdung with the idea that they will swell out as the dung dries up. In order to make a bullock's hump grow, a large grain-measure is placed over it. If cattle go astray an iron implement is placed in a pitcher of water, and it is believed that this will keep wild animals off the cattle, though the connection of ideas is obscure. To cure intermittent fever a man walks through a narrow passage between two houses. If the children in a family die, the Baiga takes the parents outside the village and breaks the stem of some plant in their presence. After this they never again touch that particular plant, and it is believed that their children will not die. Tuesday is considered the best day for weddings, Thursday and Monday for beginning field-work and Saturday for worshipping the gods. To have bats in one's granary is considered to be fortunate, and there is a large harmless snake which, they say, produces fertility when it makes its home in a field. If a crow caws on the house-top they consider that the arrival of a guest is portended. A snake or a cat crossing the road in front and a man sneezing are bad omens.

The dress of the Kawars presents no special features calling for remark. Women wear pewter ornaments on the feet, and silver or pewter rings on the neck. They decorate the ears with silver pendants, but as a rule do not wear nose-rings. Women are tattooed on the breast with a figure of Krishna, on the arms with that of a deer, and on the legs with miscellaneous patterns. The operation is carried out immediately after marriage in accordance with the usual custom in Chhattīsgarh. 11. Dress.

The tribe consider military service to be their tradi-

12. Occupation and social rules. tional occupation, but the bulk of them are now cultivators and labourers. Many of them are farmers of villages in the zamīndāris. Rautias weave ropes and make sleeping-cots, but the other Kawars consider such work to be degrading. They have the ordinary Hindu rules of inheritance, but a son claiming partition in his father's lifetime is entitled to two bullocks and nothing more. When the property is divided on the death of the father, the eldest son receives an allowance known as *jithai* over and above his share, this being a common custom in the Chhattīsgarh country where the Kawars reside. The tribe do not admit outsiders with the exception of Kaurai Rāwat girls married to Kawars. They have a tribal *panchāyat* or committee, the head of which is known as Pardhān. Its proceedings are generally very deliberate, and this has led to the saying: "The Ganda's *panchāyat* always ends in a quarrel; the Gond's *panchāyat* cares only for the feast; and the Kawar's *panchāyat* takes a year to make up its mind." But when the Kawars have decided, they act with vigour. They require numerous goats as fines for the caste feast, and these, with fried *urad*, form the regular provision. Liquor, however, is only sparingly consumed. Temporary exclusion from caste is imposed for the usual offences, which include going to jail, getting the ears split, or getting maggots in a wound. The last is the most serious offence, and when the culprit is readmitted to social intercourse the Dhobi (washerman) is employed to eat with him first from five different plates, thus taking upon himself any risk of contagion from the impurity which may still remain. The Kawar eats flesh, fowls and pork, but abjures beef, crocodiles, monkeys and reptiles. From birds he selects the parrot, dove, pigeon, quail and partridge as fit for food. He will not eat meat sold in market because he considers it *halāli* or killed in the Muhammadan fashion, and therefore impure. He also refuses a particular species of fish called *rechha*, which is black and fleshy and has been nicknamed 'The Telī's bullock.' The higher subtribes have now given up eating pork and the Tanwars abstain from fowls also. The Kawars will take food only from a Gond or a Kaurai Rāwat, and Gonds will also take food from them. In appearance and

manners they greatly resemble the Gonds, from whom they are hardly distinguished by the Hindus. Dalton [1] described them as "A dark, coarse-featured, broad-nosed, wide-mouthed and thick-lipped race, decidedly ugly, but taller and better set up than most of the other tribes. I have also found them a clean, well-to-do, industrious people, living in comfortable, carefully-constructed and healthily-kept houses and well dressed."

Of their method of dancing Ball [2] writes as follows: "In the evening some of the villagers—Kaurs they were I believe—entertained us with a dance, which was very different from anything seen among the Santāls or Kols. A number of men performed a kind of ladies' chain, striking together as they passed one another's pronged sticks which they carried in their hands. By foot, hand and voice the time given by a tom-tom is most admirably kept."

[1] *Ethnology*, pp. 136, 137. [2] *Jungle Life in India*, pp. 315, 316.

KĀYASTH

LIST OF PARAGRAPHS

1. General notice and legend of origin.

Kāyasth,[1] Kaith, Lāla.—The caste of writers and village accountants. The Kāyasths numbered 34,000 persons in 1911 and were found over the whole Province, but they are most numerous in the Saugor, Damoh, Jubbulpore and Narsinghpur Districts. In the Marātha country their place is to some extent taken by the Prabhus, the Marātha writer caste, and also by the Vidūrs. No probable derivation of the name Kāyasth appears to have been suggested. The earliest reference to Kāyasths appears in an inscription in Mālwa dated A.D. 738–739. The inscription is of a Maurya king, and the term Kāyasth is used there as a proper noun to mean a writer. Another dated A.D. 987 is written by a Kāyasth named Kānchana. An inscription on the Delhi Siwālik pillar dated A.D. 1164 is stated to have been written by a Kāyasth named Sispati, the son of Māhava, by the king's command. The inscription adds that the Kāyasth was of Gauda (Bengal) descent, and the term Kāyasth is

[1] This article is based partly on papers by Mūnshi Kanhya Lāl of the Gazetteer office, Mr. Sundar Lāl, Extra Assistant Commissioner, Saugor, and Mr. J. N. Sil, Pleader, Seoni.

here used in the sense of a member of the Kāyasth caste and not simply meaning a writer as in the Mālwa inscription.[1] From the above account it seems possible that the caste was of comparatively late origin. According to their own legend the first progenitor of the Kāyasths was Chitragupta, who was created by Brahma from his own body and given to Yama the king of the dead, to record the good and evil actions of all beings, and produce the result when they arrived in the kingdom of the dead. Chitragupta was called Kāyastha, from *kaya stha*, existing in or incorporate in the body, because he was in the body of Brahma. Chitragupta was born of a dark complexion, and having a pen and ink-pot in his hand. He married two wives, the elder being the granddaughter of the sun, who bore him four sons, while the younger was the daughter of a Brāhman Rishi, and by her he had eight sons. These sons were married to princesses of the Nāga or snake race; the Nāgas are supposed to have been the early nomad invaders from Central Asia, or Scythians. The twelve sons were entrusted with the government of different parts of India and the twelve subcastes of Kāyasths are named after these localities.

2. The origin of the caste.

There has been much discussion on the origin of the Kāyasth caste, which now occupies a high social position owing to the ability and industry of its members and their attainment of good positions in the public services. All indications, however, point to the fact that the caste has obtained within a comparatively recent period a great rise in social status, and formerly ranked much lower than it does now. Dr. Bhattachārya states:[2] "The Kāyasths of Bengal are described in some of the Hindu sacred books as Kshatriyas, but the majority of the Kāyasth clans do not wear the sacred thread, and admit their status as Sūdra also by the observance of mourning for thirty days. But whether Kshatriya or Sūdra, they belong to the upper layer of Hindu society, and though the higher classes of Brāhmans neither perform their religious ceremonies nor enlist them among their disciples, yet the gifts of the Kāyasths are usually accepted by the great Pandits of the

[1] *Hindus of Gujarāt*, p. 59, quoting from *Ind. Ant.* vi. 192-193.
[2] *Hindu Castes and Sects*, p. 175.

country without hesitation." There is no doubt that a hundred years ago the Kāyasths of Bengal and Bihār were commonly looked upon as Sūdras. Dr. Buchanan, an excellent observer, states this several times. In Bihār he says that the Kāyasths are the chief caste who are looked upon by all as pure Sūdras and do not reject the appellation.[1] And again that "Pandits in Gorakhpur insist that Kāyasths are mere Sūdras, but on account of their influence included among gentry (*Ashrāf*). All who have been long settled in the district live pure and endeavour to elevate themselves; but this has failed of success as kindred from other countries who still drink liquor and eat meat come and sit on the same mat with them."[2] Again he calls the Kāyasths the highest Sūdras next to Vaidyas.[3] And "In Bihār the penmen (Kāyasthas) are placed next to the Kshatris and by the Brāhmans are considered as illegitimate, to whom the rank of Sūdras has been given, and in general they do not presume to be angry at this decision, which in Bengal would be highly offensive.[4] Colebrooke remarks of the caste: "Karana, from a Vaishya by a woman of the Sūdra class, is an attendant on princes or secretary. The appellation of Kāyastha is in general considered as synonymous with Karana; and accordingly the Karana tribe commonly assumes the name of Kāyastha; but the Kāyasthas of Bengal have pretensions to be considered as true Sūdras, which the Jātimāla seems to authorise, for the origin of the Kāyastha is there mentioned before the subject of mixed castes is introduced, immediately after describing the Gopa as a true Sūdra."[5] Similarly Colonel Dalton says: "I believe that in the present day the Kāyasths arrogate to themselves the position of first among commoners, or first of the Sūdras, but their origin is involved in some mystery. Intelligent Kāyasths make no pretension to be other than Sūdras."[6] In his Census Report of the United Provinces Mr. R. Burn discusses the subject as follows:[7] "On the authority of these Purānic accounts, and in view of the fact that the Kāyasths observe certain of the

[1] *Eastern India*, i. p. 162.
[2] *Ibidem*, ii. p. 466.
[3] *Ibidem*, ii. p. 736.
[4] *Ibidem*, ii. p. 122.
[5] *Essays*, vol. ii. p. 182.
[6] *Ethnology of Bengal*, pp. 312, 313.
[7] *United Provinces Census Report* (1901), pp. 222-223.

Sanskārs in the same method as is prescribed for Kshatriyas, the Pandits of several places have given formal opinions that the Kāyasths are Kshatriyas. On the other hand, there is not the slightest doubt that the Kāyasths are commonly regarded either as a mixed caste, with some relationship to two if not three of the twice-born castes, or as Sūdras. This is openly stated in some of the reports, and not a single Hindu who was not a Kāyasth of the many I have personally asked about the matter would admit privately that the Kāyasths are twice-born, and the same opinion was expressed by Muhammadans, who were in a position to gauge the ordinary ideas held by Hindus, and are entirely free from prejudice in the matter. One of the most highly respected orthodox Brāhmans in the Provinces wrote to me confirming this opinion, and at the same time asked that his name might not be published in connection with it. The matter has been very minutely examined in a paper sent up by a member of the Benāres committee who came to the conclusion that while the Kāyasths have been declared to be Kshatriyas in the Purānas, by Pandits, and in several judgments of subordinate courts, and to be Sūdras by Manu and various commentators on him, by public opinion, and in a judgment of the High Court of Calcutta, they are really of Brāhmanical origin. He holds that those who to-day follow literary occupations are the descendants of Chitragupta by his Brāhman and Kshatriya wives, that the so-called Unaya Kāyasths are descended from Vaishya mothers, and the tailors and cobblers from Sūdra mothers. It is possible to trace to some extent points which have affected public opinion on this question. The Kāyasths themselves admit that in the past their reputation as hard drinkers was not altogether unmerited, but they deserve the highest credit for the improvements which have been effected in this regard. There is also a widespread belief that the existing general observance by Kāyasths of the ceremonies prescribed for the twice-born castes, especially in the matter of wearing the sacred thread, is comparatively recent. It is almost superfluous to add that notwithstanding the theoretical views held as to their origin and position, Kāyasths undoubtedely rank high in the social scale. All European writers have borne testimony to their excellence and success in many walks of life, and even before the commencement of British power many Kāyasths occupied high social positions and enjoyed the confidence of their rulers."

3. The rise of the Kāyasths under foreign rulers.

It appears then a legitimate conclusion from the evidence that the claim of the Kāyasths to be Kshatriyas is comparatively recent, and that a century ago they occupied a very much lower social position than they do now. We do not find them playing any prominent part in the early or mediæval Hindu kingdoms. There is considerable reason for supposing that their rise to importance took place under the foreign or non-Hindu governments in India. Thus a prominent Kāyasth gentleman says of his own caste:[1] "The people of this caste were the first to learn Persian, the language of the Muhammadan invaders of India, and to obtain the posts of accountants and revenue collectors under Muhammadan kings. Their chief occupation is Government service, and if one of the caste adopts any other profession he is degraded in the estimation of his caste-fellows." Malcolm states:[2] "When the Muhammadans invaded Hindustān and conquered its Rājpūt princes, we may conclude that the Brāhmans of that country who possessed knowledge or distinction fled from their intolerance and violence; but the conquerors found in the Kāyastha or Kaith tribe more pliable and better instruments for the conduct of the details of their new Government. This tribe had few religious scruples, as they stand low in the scale of Hindus. They were, according to their own records, which there is no reason to question, qualified by their previous employment in all affairs of state; and to render themselves completely useful had only to add the language of their new masters to those with which they were already acquainted. The Muhammadans carried these Hindus into their southern conquests, and they spread over the countries of Central India and the Deccan; and some families who are Kānungos[3] of

[1] Lāla Jwāla Prasād, Extra Assistant Commissioner, in Sir E. A Maclagan's *Punjab Census Report* for 1891.

[2] *Memoir of Central India*, vol. ii. pp. 165-166.

[3] The Kānungo maintains the statistical registers of land-revenue, rent, cultivation, cropping, etc., for the District as a whole which are compiled from those prepared by the patwāris for each village.

districts and patwaris of villages trace their settlement in this country from the earliest Muhammadan conquest." Similarly the *Bombay Gazetteer* states that under the arrangements made by the Emperor Akbar, the work of collecting the revenues of the twenty-eight Districts subordinate to Surat was entrusted to Kāyasths.[1] And the Māthur Kāyasths of Gujarāt came from Mathura in the train of the Mughal viceroys as their clerks and interpreters.[2] Under the Muhammadans and for some time after the introduction of English rule, a knowledge of Persian was required in a Government clerk, and in this language most of the Kāyasths were proficient, and some were excellent clerks.[3] Kāyasths attained very high positions under the Muhammadan kings of Bengal and were in charge of the revenue department under the Nawābs of Murshīdābād; while Rai Durlao Rām, prime minister of Ali Verdi Khān, was a Kāyasth. The governors of Bihār in the period between the battle of Plassey and the removal of the exchequer to Calcutta were also Kāyasths.[4] The Bhatnāgar Kāyasths, it is said, came to Bengal at the time of the Muhammadan conquest.[5] Under the Muhammadan kings of Oudh, too, numerous Kāyasths occupied posts of high trust.[6] Similarly the Kāyasths entered the service of the Gond kings of the Central Provinces. It is said that when the Gond ruler Bakht Buland of Deogarh in Chhindwāra went to Delhi, he brought a number of Kāyasths back with him and introduced them into the administration. One of these was appointed Bakshi or paymaster to the army of Bakht Buland. His descendant is a leading landholder in the Seoni District with an estate of eighty-four villages. Another Kāyasth landholder of Jubbulpore and

1 *Hindus of Gujarāt*, p. 60.

2 *Ibidem*, p. 64.

3 *Ibidem*, p. 61.

4 Bhattachārya, *Hindu Castes and Sects*, p. 177. It is true that Dr. Bhattachārya states that the Kāyasths were also largely employed under the Hindu kings of Bengal, but he gives no authority for this. The Gaur Kāyasths also claim that the Sena kings of Bengal were of their caste, but considering that these kings were looked on as spiritual heads of the country and one of them laid down rules for the structure and intermarriage of the Brāhman caste, it is practically impossible that they could have been Kāyasths. The Muhammadan conquest of Bengal took place at an early period, and very little detail is known about the preceding Hindu dynasties.

5 Risley, *Tribes and Castes of Bengal*, art. Bihār Kāyasth.

6 Sherring, *Tribes and Castes*, vol. iii. pp. 253-254.

Mandla occupied some similar position in the service of the Gond kings of Garha-Mandla.

Finally in the English administration the Kāyasths at first monopolised the ministerial service. In the United Provinces, Bengal and Bihār, it is stated that the number of Kāyasths may perhaps even now exceed that of all other castes taken together.[1] And in Gujarāt the Kāyasths have lost in recent years the monopoly they once enjoyed as Government clerks.[2] The Mathura Kāyasths of Gujarāt are said to be declining in prosperity on account of the present keen competition for Government service,[3] of which it would thus appear they formerly had as large a share as they desired. The Prabhus, the writer-caste of western India corresponding to the Kāyasths, were from the time of the earliest European settlements much trusted by English merchants, and when the British first became supreme in Gujarāt they had almost a monopoly of the Government service as English writers. To such an extent was this the case that the word Prabhu or Purvu was the general term for a clerk who could write English, whether he was a Brāhman, Sunār, Prabhu, Portuguese or of English descent.[4] Similarly the word Cranny was a name applied to a clerk writing English, and thence vulgarly applied in general to the East Indians or half-caste class from among whom English copyists were afterwards chiefly recruited. The original is the Hindi *karāni*, *kirani*, which Wilson derives from the Sanskrit *karan*, a doer. Karana is also the name of the Orissa writer-caste, who are writers and accountants. It is probable that the name is derived from this caste, that is the Uriya Kāyasths, who may have been chiefly employed as clerks before any considerable Eurasian community had come into existence. Writers' Buildings at Calcutta were recently still known to the natives as Karāni ki Barīk, and this supports the derivation from the Karans or Uriya Kāyasths, the case thus being an exact parallel to that of the Prabhus in Bombay.[5]

From the above argument it seems legitimate to deduce

1 Bhattachārya, *Hindu Castes and Tribes*, p. 177.

2 *Hindus of Gujarāt*, p. 81.

3 *Ibidem*, p. 67.

4 *Ibidem*, p. 68, and Mackintosh, *Report in the Rāmosis*, India Office Tracts, p. 77.

5 *Hobson-Jobson*, *s.v.* Cranny.

4. The original profession of the Kāyasths.

that the Kāyasths formerly occupied a lower position in Hindu society. The Brāhmans were no doubt jealous of them and, as Dr. Bhattachārya states, would not let them learn Sanskrit.[1] But when India became subject to foreign rulers the Kāyasths readily entered their service, learning the language of their new employers in order to increase their efficiency. Thus they first learnt Persian and then English, and both by Muhammadans and English were employed largely, if not at first almost exclusively, as clerks in the public offices. It must be remembered that there were at this time practically only two other literate castes among Hindus, the Brāhmans and the Banias. The Brāhmans naturally would be for long reluctant to lower their dignity by taking service under foreign masters, whom they regarded as outcaste and impure; while the Banias down to within the last twenty years or so have never cared for education beyond the degree necessary for managing their business. Thus the Kāyasths had at first almost a monopoly of public employment under foreign Governments. It has been seen also that it is only within about the last century that the status of the Kāyasths has greatly risen, and it is a legitimate deduction that the improvement dates from the period when they began to earn distinction and importance under these governments. But they were always a literate caste, and the conclusion is that in former times they discharged duties to which literacy was essential in a comparatively humble sphere. "The earliest reference to the Kāyasths as a distinct caste," Sir H. Risley states, "occurs in Yājnavalkya, who describes them as writers and village accountants, very exacting in their demands from the cultivators." The profession of patwāri or village accountant appears to have been that formerly appertaining to the Kāyasth caste, and it is one which they still largely follow. In Bengal it is now stated that Kāyasths of good position object to marry their daughters in the families of those who have served as patwāris or village accountants. Patwāris, one of them said to Sir H. Risley, however rich they may be, are considered as socially lower than other Kāyasths, *e.g.* Kānungo, Akhauri, Pānde or Bakshi. Thus it appears that the old patwāri

[1] *Hobson-Jobson*, p. 167.

Kāyasths are looked down upon by those who have improved their position in more important branches of Government service. Kānungo, as explained, is a sort of head of the patwāris; and Bakshi, a post already noticed as held by a Kāyasth in the Central Provinces, is the Muhammadan office of paymaster.

Similarly Mr. Crooke states that while the higher members of the caste stand well in general repute, the village Lāla (or Kāyasth), who is very often an accountant, is in evil odour for his astuteness and chicanery. In Central India, as already seen, they are Kānungos of Districts and patwāris of villages; and here again Malcolm states that these officials were the oldest settlers, and that the later comers, who held more important posts, did not intermarry with them.[1] In Gujarāt the work of collecting the revenue in the Surat tract was entrusted to Kāyasths. Till 1868, in the English villages, and up to the present time in the Baroda villages, the subdivisional accountants were mostly Kāyasths.[2] In the Central Provinces the bulk of the patwāris in the northern Districts and a large proportion in other Districts outside the Marātha country are Kāyasths. If the Kāyasths were originally patwāris or village accountants, their former low status is fully explained. The village accountant would be a village servant, though an important one, and would be supported like the other village artisans by contributions of grain from the cultivators. This is the manner in which patwāris of the Central Provinces were formerly paid. His status would technically be lower than that of the cultivators, and he might be considered as a Sūdra or a mixed caste.

5. The caste an offshoot from Brāhmans.

As regards the origin of the Kāyasths, the most probable hypothesis would seem to be that they were an offshoot of Brāhmans of irregular descent. The reason for this is that the Kāyasths must have learnt reading and writing from some outside source, and the Brāhmans were the only class who could teach it them. The Brāhmans were not disposed to spread the benefits of education, which was the main source of their power, with undue liberality, and when another literate class was required for the performance of

1 *Memoir of Central India, loc. cit.*

2 *Hindus of Gujarāt*, p. 60.

duties which they disdained to discharge themselves, it would be natural that they should prefer to educate people closely connected with them and having claims on their support. In this connection the tradition recorded by Sir H. Risley may be noted to the effect that the ancestors of the Bengal Kāyasths were five of the caste who came from Kanauj in attendance on five Brāhmans who had been summoned by the king of Bengal to perform for him certain Vedic ceremonies.[1] It may be noted also that the Vidūrs, another caste admittedly of irregular descent from Brāhmans, occupy the position of patwāris and village accountants in the Marātha districts. The names of their subcastes indicate generally that the home of the Kāyasths is the country of Hindustān, the United Provinces, and part of Bengal. This is also the place of origin of the northern Brāhmans, as shown by the names of their most important groups. The Rājpūts and Banias on the other hand belong mainly to Rājputāna, Gujarāt and Bundelkhand, and in most of this area the Kāyasths are immigrants. It has been seen that they came to Mālwa and Gujarāt with the Muhammadans; the number of Kāyasths returned from Rājputāna at the census was quite small, and it is doubtful whether the Kāyasths are so much as mentioned in Tod's *Rājasthān*. The hypothesis therefore of their being derived either from the Rājpūts or Banias appears to be untenable. In the Punjab also the Kāyasths are found only in small numbers and are immigrants. As stated by Sir H. Risley, both the physical type of the Kāyasths and their remarkable intellectual attainments indicate that they possess Aryan blood; similarly Mr. Sherring remarks: "He nevertheless exhibits a family likeness to the Brāhman; you may not know where to place him or how to designate him; but on looking at him and conversing with him you feel quite sure that you are in the presence of a Hindu of no mean order of intellect."[2] No doubt there was formerly much mixture of blood in the

[1] *Tribes and Castes of Bengal*, art. Bengal Kāyasth. The Kāyasths deny the story that the five Kāyasths were servants of the five Brāhmans, and say that they were Kshatriyas sent on a mission from the king of Kanauj to the king of Bengal. This, however, is improbable in view of the evidence already given as to the historical status of the Kāyasths.

[2] *Tribes and Castes*, *ibidem*.

caste; some time ago the Kāyasths were rather noted for keeping women of other castes, and Sir H. Risley gives instances of outsiders being admitted into the caste. Dr. Bhattachārya states[1] that, "There are many Kāyasths in eastern Bengal who are called Ghulāms or slaves. Some of them are still attached as domestic servants to the families of the local Brāhmans, Vaidyas and aristocratic Kāyasths. Some of the Ghulāms have in recent times become rich landholders, and it is said that one of them has got the title of Rai Bahādur from Government. The marriage of a Ghulām generally takes place in his own class, but instances of Ghulāms marrying into aristocratic Kāyasth families are at present not very rare."

Further, the Dakshina Rārhi Kāyasths affect the greatest veneration for the Brāhmans and profess to believe in the legend that traces their descent from the five menial servants who accompanied the five Brāhmans invited by king Adisur. The Uttara Rārhi Kāyasths or those of northern Burdwān, on the other hand, do not profess the same veneration for Brāhmans as the southerners, and deny the authenticity of the legend. It was this class which held some of the highest offices under the Muhammadan rulers of Bengal, and several leading zamīndārs or landholders at present belong to it.[2] It was probably in this capacity of village accountant that the Kāyasth incurred the traditional hostility of one or two of the lower castes which still subsists in legend.[3] The influence which the patwāri possesses at present, even under the most vigorous and careful supervision and with the liability to severe punishment for any abuse of his position, is a sufficient indication of what his power must have been when supervision and control were almost nominal. On this point Sir Henry Maine remarks in his description of the village community: "There is always a village accountant, an important personage among an unlettered population; so important indeed, and so conspicuous that, according to the reports current in India, the earliest English functionaries engaged in settlements of land were occasionally led, by their assumption that there

[1] *Hindu Castes and Sects*, p. 155.
[2] *Ibidem*, pp. 375, 380.
[3] See articles on Ghasia and Dhobi.

must be a single proprietor somewhere, to mistake the accountant for the owner of the village, and to record him as such in the official register.[1] In Bihār Sir H. Risley shows that Kāyasths have obtained proprietary right in a large area.

6. The success of the Kāyasths and their present position.

It may be hoped that the leading members of the Kāyasth caste will not take offence, because in the discussion of the origin of their caste, one of the most interesting problems of Indian ethnology, it has been necessary to put forward a hypothesis other than that which they hold themselves. It would be as unreasonable for a Kāyasth to feel aggrieved at the suggestion that centuries ago their ancestors were to some extent the offspring of mixed unions as for an Englishman to be insulted by the statement that the English are of mixed descent from Saxons, Danes and Normans. If the Kāyasths formerly had a comparatively humble status in Hindu society, then it is the more creditable to the whole community that they should have succeeded in raising themselves by their native industry and ability without adventitious advantages to the high position in which by general admission the caste now stands. At present the Kāyasths are certainly the highest caste after Brāhman, Rājpūt and Bania, and probably in Hindustān, Bengal and the Central Provinces they may be accounted as practically equal to Rājpūts and Banias. Of the Bengal Kāyasths Dr. Bhattachārya wrote:[2] "They generally prove equal to any position in which they are placed. They have been successful not only as clerks but in the very highest executive and judicial offices that have yet been thrown open to the natives of this country. The names of the Kāyastha judges, Dwārka Nāth Mitra, Ramesh Chandra Mitra and Chandra Mādhava Ghose are well known and respected by all. In the executive services the Kāyasths have attained the same kind of success. One of them, Mr. R. C. Dutt, is now the Commissioner of one of the most important divisions of Bengal. Another, named Kālika Dās Datta, has been for several years employed as Prime Minister of the Kuch Bihār State, giving signal proofs of

[1] *Village Communities*, p. 125.
[2] *Hindu Castes and Sects*, *ibidem*, p. 177.

his ability as an administrator by the success with which he has been managing the affairs of the principality in his charge." In the Central Provinces, too, Kāyasth gentlemen hold the most important positions in the administrative, judicial and public works departments, as well as being strongly represented in the Provincial and subordinate executive services. And in many Districts Kāyasths form the backbone of the ministerial staff of the public offices, a class whose patient laboriousness and devotion to duty, with only the most remote prospects of advancement to encourage them to persevere, deserve high commendation.

7. Sub-castes.

The northern India Kāyasths are divided into the following twelve subcastes, which are mainly of a territorial character:

(*a*) Srivāstab.
(*b*) Saksena.
(*c*) Bhatnāgar.
(*d*) Ambastha or Amisht.
(*e*) Ashthāna or Aithāna.
(*f*) Bālmīk or Vālmīki.
(*g*) Māthur.
(*h*) Kulsreshtha.
(*i*) Sūryadhwaja.
(*k*) Karan.
(*l*) Gaur.
(*m*) Nigum.

(*a*) The Srivāstab subcaste take their name from the old town of Sravāsti, now Sahet-Mahet, in the north of the United Provinces. They are by far the most numerous subcaste both there and here. In these Provinces nearly all the Kāyasths are Srivāstabs except a few Saksenas. They are divided into two sections, Khare and Dūsre, which correspond to the Bīsa and Dasa groups of the Banias. The Khare are those of pure descent, and the Dūsre the offspring of remarried widows or other irregular alliances.

(*b*) The Saksena are named from the old town of Sankisa, in the Farukhābād District. They also have the Khare and Dūsre groups, and a third section called Kharua, which is said to mean pure, and is perhaps the most aristocratic. A number of Saksena Kāyasths are resident in Seoni District, where their ancestors were settled by Bakht Buland, the Gond Rāja of Deogarh in Chhīndwāra. These constituted hitherto a separate endogamous group, marrying among themselves, but since the opening of the railway negotiations have been initiated with the Saksenas of northern India, with the result that intermarriage is to be resumed between the two sections.

(*c*) The Bhatnāgar take their name from the old town of Bhātner, near Bikaner. They are divided into the Vaishya or Kadīm, of pure descent, and the Gaur, who are apparently the offspring of intermarriage with the Gaur subcaste.

(*d*) Ambastha or Amisht. These are said to have settled on the Girnār hill, and to take their name from their worship of the goddess Ambāji or Amba Devi. Mr. Crooke suggests that they may be connected with the old Ambastha caste who were noted for their skill in medicine. The practice of surgery is the occupation of some Kāyasths.[1] It is also supposed that the names may come from the Ameth pargana of Oudh. The Ambastha Kāyasths are chiefly found in south Bihār, where they are numerous and influential.[2]

(*e*) Ashthāna or Aithāna. This is an Oudh subcaste. They have two groups, the Pūrabi or eastern, who are found in Jaunpur and its neighbourhood, and the Pachhauri or western, who live in or about Lucknow.

(*f*) Bālmīk or Vālmīki. These are a subcaste of western India. Bālmīk or Vālmīk was the traditional author of the Rāmāyana, but they do not trace their descent from him. The name may have some territorial meaning. The Vālmīki are divided into three endogamous groups according as they live in Bombay, Cutch or Surat.

(*g*) The Māthur subcaste are named after Mathura or Muttra. They are also split into the local groups Dihlawi of Delhi, Katchi of Cutch and Lachauli of Jodhpur.

(*h*) The Kulsreshtha or 'well-born' Kāyasths belong chiefly to the districts of Agra and Etah. They are divided into the Bārakhhera, or those of twelve villages, and the Chha Khera of six villages.

(*i*) The Sūryadhwaja subcaste belong to Ballia, Ghāzipur and Bijnor. Their origin is obscure. They profess excessive purity, and call themselves Sakadwīpi or Scythian Brāhmans.

[1] *Tribes and Castes*, art. Kāyasth.

[2] *Bhattachārya*, *loc. cit.*, p. 188.

(*k*) The Karan subcaste belong to Bihār, and have two local divisions, the Gayawāle from Gāya, and the Tirhūtia from Tirhūt.

(*l*) The Gaur Kāyasths, like the Gaur Brāhmans and Rājpūts, apparently take their name from Gaur or Lakhnauti, the old kingdom of Bengal. They have the Khare and Dūsre subdivisions, and also three local groups named after Bengal, Delhi and Budaun.

(*m*) The Nigum subcaste, whose name is apparently the same as that of the Nikumbh Rājpūts, are divided into two endogamous groups, the Kadīm or old, and the Unāya, or those coming from Unao. Sometimes the Unāya are considered as a separate thirteenth subcaste of mixed descent.

8. Exogamy. Educated Kāyasths now follow the standard rule of exogamy, which prohibits marriage between persons within five degrees of affinity on the female side and seven on the male. That is, persons having a common grandparent on the female side cannot intermarry, while for those related through males the prohibition extends a generation further back. This is believed to be the meaning of the rule but it is not quite clear. In Damoh the Srivāstab Kāyasths still retain exogamous sections which are all named after places in the United Provinces, as Hamīrpur ki baink (section), Lucknowbar, Kāshi ki Pānde (a wise man of Benāres), Partābpūria, Cawnpore-bar, Sultānpuria and so on. They say that the ancestors of these sections were families who came from the above places in northern India, and settled in Damoh; here they came to be known by the places from which they had immigrated, and so founded new exogamous sections. A man cannot marry in his own section, or that of his mother or grandmother. In the Central Provinces a man may marry two sisters, but in northern India this is prohibited.

9. Marriage customs. Marriage may be infant or adult, and, as in many places husbands are difficult to find, girls occasionally remain unmarried till nearly twenty, and may also be mated to boys younger than themselves. In northern India a substantial bridegroom-price is paid, which increases for a well-educated boy, but this custom is not so well established in the Central

Provinces. However, in Damoh it is said that a sum of Rs. 200 is paid to the bridegroom's family. The marriage ceremony is performed according to the proper ritual for the highest or Brahma form of marriage recognised by Manu with Vedic texts. When the bridegroom arrives at the bride's house he is given sherbet to drink. It is said that he then stands on a pestle, and the bride's mother throws wheat-flour balls to the four points of the compass, and shows the bridegroom a miniature plough, a grinding pestle, a churning-staff and an arrow, and pulls his nose. The bridegroom's struggles to prevent his mother-in-law pulling his nose are the cause of much merriment, while the two parties afterwards have a fight for the footstool on which he stands.[1] An image of a cow in flour is then brought, and the bridegroom pierces its nostrils with a little stick of gold. Kāyasths do not pierce the nostrils of bullocks themselves, but these rites perhaps recall their dependence on agriculture in their capacity of village accountants.

After the wedding the bridegroom's father takes various kinds of fruit, as almonds, dates and raisins, and fills the bride's lap with them four times, finally adding a cocoanut and a rupee. This is a ceremony to induce fertility, and the cocoanut perhaps represents a child.

10. Marriage songs.

The following are some specimens of songs sung at weddings. The first is about Rāma's departure from Ajodhia when he went to the forests:

Now Hari (Rāma) has driven his chariot forth to the jungle.
His father and mother are weeping.
Kaushilya[2] stood up and said, 'Now, whom shall I call my diamond and my ruby?'
Dasrath went to the tower of his palace to see his son;
As Rāma's chariot set forth under the shade of the trees, he wished that he might die.
Bharat ran after his brother with naked feet.
He said, 'Oh brother, you are going to the forest, to whom do you give the kingdom of Oudh?'
Rāma said, 'When fourteen years have passed away I shall come back from the jungles. Till then I give the kingdom to you.'

The following is a love dialogue:

[1] *Hindus of Gujarāt*, p. 72.
[2] Dasrath and Kaushilya were the father and mother of Rāma.

Make a beautiful garden for me to see my king.
In that garden what flowers shall I set?
Lemons, oranges, pomegranates, figs.
In that garden what music shall there be?
A tambourine, a fiddle, a guitar and a dancing girl.
In that garden what attendants shall there be?
A writer, a supervisor, a secretary for writing letters.[1]

The next is a love-song by a woman:

How has your countenance changed, my lord?
Why speak you not to your slave?
If I were a deer in the forest and you a famous warrior, would you not shoot me with your gun?
If I were a fish in the water and you the son of a fisherman, would you not catch me with your drag-net?
If I were a cuckoo in the garden and you the gardener's son, would you not trap me with your liming-stick?

The last is a dialogue between Rādha and Krishna. Rādha with her maidens was bathing in the river when Krishna stole all their clothes and climbed up a tree with them. Girdhāri is a name of Krishna:

R. You and I cannot be friends, Girdhāri; I am wearing a silk-embroidered cloth and you a black blanket.
You are the son of old Nānd, the shepherd, and I am a princess of Mathura.
You have taken my clothes and climbed up a *kadamb* tree. I am naked in the river.
K. I will not give you your clothes till you come out of the water.
R. If I come out of the water the people will laugh and clap at me.
All my companions seeing your beauty say, 'You have vanquished us; we are overcome.'

11. Social rules.

Polygamy is permitted but is seldom resorted to, except for the sake of offspring. Neither widow-marriage nor divorce are recognised, and either a girl or married woman is expelled from the caste if detected in a *liaison.* A man may keep a woman of another caste if he does not eat from her hand nor permit her to eat in the *chauk* or purified place where he and his family take their meals. The practice of keeping women was formerly common but has now been largely suppressed. Women of all castes were kept except Brāhmans and Kāyasths. Illegitimate children were known as Dogle or Surāit and called Kāyasths, ranking as

[1] These are the occupations of the Kāyasths.

an inferior group of the caste. And it is not unlikely that in the past the descendants of such irregular unions have been admitted to the Dūsre or lower branch of the different subcastes.

During the seventh month of a woman's pregnancy a dinner is given to the caste-fellows and songs are sung. After this occasion the woman must not go outside her own village, nor can she go to draw water from a well or to bathe in a tank. She can only go into the street or to another house in her own village. 12. Birth customs.

On the sixth day after a birth a dinner is given to the caste and songs are sung. The women bring small silver coins or rupees and place them in the mother's lap. The occasion of the first appearance of the signs of maturity in a girl is not observed at all if she is in her father's house. But if she has gone to her father-in-law's house, she is dressed in new clothes, her hair after being washed is tied up, and she is seated in the *chauk* or purified space, while the women come and sing songs.

The Kāyasths venerate the ordinary Hindu deities. They worship Chitragupta, their divine ancestor, at weddings and at the Holi and Diwāli festivals. Twice a year they venerate the pen and ink, the implements of their profession, to which they owe their great success. The patwāris in Hoshangābād formerly received small fees, known as *diwāt pūja*, from the cultivators for worshipping the ink-bottle on their behalf, presumably owing to the idea that, if neglected, it might make a malicious mistake in the record of their rights. 13. Religion.

The dead are burnt, and the proper offerings are made on the anniversaries, according to the prescribed Hindu ritual. Kāyasth names usually end in Prasād, Singh, Baksh, Sewak, and Lāla in the Central Provinces. Lāla, which is a term of endearment, is often employed as a synonym for the caste. Dāda or uncle is a respectful term of address for Kāyasths. Two names are usually given to a boy, one for ceremonial and the other for ordinary use. 14. Social customs.

The Kāyasths will take food cooked with water from Brāhmans, and that cooked without water (*pakki*) from Rājpūts and Banias. Some Hindustāni Brāhmans, as well as Khatris and certain classes of Banias, will take *pakki* food from Kāyasths. Kāyasths of different subcastes will sometimes also take it from each other. They will give the huqqa with the reed in to members of their own subcaste, and without the reed to any Kāyasth. The caste eat the flesh of goats, sheep, fish, and birds. They were formerly somewhat notorious for drinking freely, but a great reform has been effected in this respect by the community itself through the agency of their caste conference, and many are now total abstainers.

15. Occupation. The occupations of the Kāyasths have been treated in discussing the origin of the caste. They set the greatest store by their profession of writing and say that the son of a Kāyasth should be either literate or dead. The following is the definition of a Lekhak or writer, a term said to be used for the Kāyasths in Purānic literature:

"In all courts of justice he who is acquainted with the languages of all countries and conversant with all the Shāstras, who can arrange his letters in writing in even and parallel lines, who is possessed of presence of mind, who knows the art of how and what to speak in order to carry out an object in view, who is well versed in all the Shāstras, who can express much thought in short and pithy sentences, who is apt to understand the mind of one when one begins to speak, who knows the different divisions of countries and of time,[1] who is not a slave to his passions, and who is faithful to the king deserves the name and rank of a Lekhak or writer."[2]

1. General notice. **Kewat, Khewat, Kaibartta.**[3]—A caste of fishermen, boatmen, grain-parchers, and cultivators, chiefly found in the Chhattīsgarh Districts of Drūg, Raipur, and Bilāspur. They numbered 170,000 persons in 1911. The Kewats or Kaibarttas, as they are called in Bengal, are the modern representatives of the Kaivartas, a caste mentioned in Hindu classical literature. Sir H. Risley explains the

[1] Geography and Astronomy.

[2] Quoted from the Matsapūrān in a criticism by Babu Krishna Nāg Verma.

[3] This article is based on papers by Mr. Mahfuz Ali, tahsīldār, Rājnandgaon, Mr. Jowāhir Singh, Settlement Superintendent, Sambalpur, and Mr. Adurām Chaudhri of the Gazetteer Office.

origin of the name as follows:[1] "Concerning the origin of the name Kaibartta there has been considerable difference of opinion. Some derive it from *ka*, water, and *vartta*, livelihood; but Lassen says that the use of *ka* in this sense is extremely unusual in early Sanskrit, and that the true derivation is Kivarta, a corruption of Kimvarta, meaning a person following a low or degrading occupation. This, he adds, would be in keeping with the pedigree assigned to the caste in Manu, where the Kaivarta, also known as Mārgava or Dāsa, is said to have been begotten by a Nishāda father and an Ayogavi mother, and to subsist by his labour in boats. On the other hand, the Brāhma-Vaivarta Purāna gives the Kaibartta a Kshatriya father and a Vaishya mother, a far more distinguished parentage; for the Ayogavi having been born from a Sūdra father and a Vaishya mother is classed as *pratiloma*, begotten against the hair, or in the inverse order of the precedence of the castes." The Kewats are a mixed caste. Mr. Crooke says that they merge on one side into the Mallāhs and on the other into the Binds. In the Central Provinces their two principal subdivisions are the Laria and Uriya, or the residents of the Chhattīsgarh and Sambalpur plains respectively. The Larias are further split up into the Larias proper, the Kosbonwas, who grow *kosa* or tasar silk cocoons, and the Binjhwārs and Dhuris (grain-parchers). The Binjhwārs are a Hinduised group of the Baiga tribe, and in Bhandāra they have become a separate Hindu caste, dropping the first letter of the name, and being known as Injhwār. The Binjhwār Kewats are a group of the same nature. The Dhuris are grain-parchers, and there is a separate Dhuri caste; but as grain-parching is also a traditional occupation of the Kewats, the Dhuris may be an offshoot from them. The Kewats are so closely connected with the Dhīmars that it is difficult to make any distinction; in Chhattīsgarh it is said that the Dhīmars will not act as ferrymen, while the Kewats will not grow or sell *singāra* or water-nut. The Dhīmars worship their fishing-nets on the Akti day, which the Kewats will not do. Both the Kewats and Dhīmars are almost certainly derived from the primitive tribes. The Kewats say that formerly the

[1] *Tribes and Castes of Bengal*, art. Kaibartta.

Hindus would not take water from them; but on one occasion during his exile Rāma came to them and asked them to ferry him across a river; before doing so they washed his feet and drank the water, and since that time the Hindus have considered them pure and take water from their hands. This story has no doubt been invented to explain the fact that Brāhmans will take water from the non-Aryan Kewats, the custom having in reality been adopted as a convenience on account of their employment as palanquin-bearers and indoor servants. But in Saugor, where they are not employed as servants, and also grow *san*-hemp, their position is distinctly lower and no high caste will take water from them.

2. Exogamous divisions and marriage.

The caste have also a number of exogamous groups, generally named after plants or animals, or bearing some nickname given to the reputed founder. Instances of the first class are Tūma, a gourd, Karsāyal, a deer, Bhalwa, a bear, Ghughu, an owl, and so on. Members of such a sept abstain from injuring the animal after which the sept is named or eating its flesh; those of the Tūma sept worship a gourd with offerings of milk and a cocoanut at the Holi festival. Instances of titular names are Garhtod, one who destroyed a fort, Jhagarha quarrelsome, Dehri priest, Kāla black, and so on. One sept is named Rāwat, its founder having probably belonged to the grazier caste. Members of this sept must not visit the temple of Mahādeo at Rājim during the annual fair, but give no explanation of the prohibition. Others are the Ahira, also from the Ahīr (herdsman) caste; the Rautele, which is the name of a subdivision of Kols and other tribes; and the Sonwāni or 'gold water' sept, which is often found among the primitive tribes. In some localities these three have now developed into separate subcastes, marrying among themselves; and if any of their members become Kabīrpanthis, the others refuse to eat and intermarry with them. The marriage of members of the same sept is prohibited, and also the union of first cousins. Girls are generally married under ten years of age, but if a suitable husband cannot be found for a daughter, the parents will make her over to any member of the caste who offers himself on condition that he bears the expenses of the marriage. In Sambalpur she is married to a flower. Sir H. Risley notes[1] the curious fact that in Bihār it is deemed less material that the bridegroom should be older than the bride than that he should be taller. "This point is of the first importance, and is ascertained by actual measurement. If the boy is shorter than the girl, or if his height is exactly the same as hers, it is believed that the union of the two would bring ill-luck, and the match is at once broken off." The marriage is celebrated in the customary manner by walking round the sacred pole, after which the bridegroom marks the forehead of the bride seven times with vermilion, parts her hair with a comb, and then draws her cloth over her head. The last act signifies that the bride has become a married woman, as a girl never covers her head. In Bengal[2] a drop of blood is drawn from the fingers of the bride and bridegroom and mixed with rice, and each eats the rice containing the blood of the other. The anointing with vermilion is probably a substitute for this. Widow-remarriage and divorce are permitted. In Sambalpur a girl who is left a widow under ten years of age is remarried with full rites as a virgin.

3. Social customs.

The Kewats worship the ordinary Hindu deities and believe that a special goddess, Chaurāsi Devi, dwells in their boats and keeps them from sinking. She is propitiated at the beginning of the rains and in times of flood, and an image of her is painted on their boats. They bury the dead, laying the corpse with the feet to the south, while some clothes, cotton, til and salt are placed in the grave, apparently as a provision for the dead man's soul. They worship their ancestors at intervals on a Monday or a Saturday with an offering of a fowl. As is usual in Chhattīsgarh, their rules as to food are very lax, and they will eat both fowls and pork. Nevertheless Brāhmans will take water at their hands and eat the rice and gram which they have parched. The caste consider fishing to have been their original occupation, and tell a story to the effect that their ancestors saved the deity in their boat on the occasion of the Deluge, and in return were given the power of catching three or four times

1 *Tribes and Castes of Bengal*, art. Kewat.
2 *Tribes and Castes of Bengal*, *ibidem*.

as many fish as ordinary persons in the same space of time. Some of them parch gram and rice, and others act as coolies and *banghy*-bearers.[1] Kewats are usually in poor circumstances, but they boast that the town of Bilāspur is named after Bilāsa Keotin, a woman of their caste. She was married, but was sought after by the king of the country, so she held out her cloth to the sun, calling on him to set it on fire, and was burnt alive, preserving her virtue. Her husband burnt himself with her, and the pair ascended to heaven.

[1] A curved stick carried across the shoulders, from which are suspended two panniers.

KHAIRWĀR

[*Authorities*: Colonel Dalton's *Ethnology of Bengal*; Sir H. Risley's *Tribes and Castes of Bengal*; Mr. Crooke's *Tribes and Castes of the N.-W.P. and Oudh.*]

LIST OF PARAGRAPHS

Khairwār, Kharwār, Khaira, Khairwa.[1]—A primitive tribe of the Chota Nāgpur plateau and Bihār. Nearly 20,000 Khairwārs are now under the jurisdiction of the Central Provinces, of whom two-thirds belong to the recently acquired Sargūja State, and the remainder to the adjoining States and the Bilāspur District. A few hundred Khairwārs or Khairwas are also returned from the Damoh District in the Bundelkhand country. Colonel Dalton considers the Khairwārs to be closely connected with the Cheros. He relates that the Cheros, once dominant in Gorakhpur and Shāhābād, were expelled from these tracts many centuries ago by the Gorkhas and other tribes, and came into Palāmau. "It is said that the Palāmau population then consisted of Kharwārs, Gonds, Mārs, Korwas, Parheyas and Kisāns. Of these the Kharwārs were the people of most consideration. The Cheros conciliated them and allowed them to remain in peaceful possession of the hill tracts bordering on Sargūja; all the Cheros of note who assisted in the expedition obtained military service grants of land, which they still retain. 'It is

1. Historical notice of the tribe.

[1] This article is based on Mr. Crooke's and Colonel Dalton's accounts, and some notes taken by Mr. Hīra Lāl at Raigarh.

popularly asserted that at the commencement of the Chero rule in Palāmau they numbered twelve thousand families and the Kharwārs eighteen thousand, and if an individual of one or the other is asked to what tribe he belongs, he will say not that he is a Chero or a Kharwār, but that he belongs to the twelve thousand or the eighteen thousand, as the case may be. Intermarriages between Chero and Kharwār families have taken place. A relative of the Palāmau Rāja married a sister of Maninăth Singh, Rāja of Rāmgarh, and this is among themselves an admission of identity of origin, as both claiming to be Rājpūts they could not intermarry till it was proved to the satisfaction of the family priest that the parties belonged to the same class. . . . The Rājas of Rāmgarh and Jashpur are members of this tribe, who have nearly succeeded in obliterating their Turanian traits by successive intermarriages with Aryan families. The Jashpur Rāja is wedded to a lady of pure Rājpūt blood, and by liberal dowries has succeeded in obtaining a similar union for three of his daughters. It is a costly ambition, but there is no doubt that the liberal infusion of fresh blood greatly improves the Kharwār physique."[1] This passage demonstrates the existence of a close connection between the Cheros and Khairwārs. Elsewhere Colonel Dalton connects the Santāls with the Khairwārs as follows:[2] "A wild goose coming from the great ocean alighted at Ahiri Pipri and there laid two eggs. From these two eggs a male and female were produced, who were the parents of the Santāl race. From Ahiri Pipri our (Santāl) ancestors migrated to Hara Dutti, and there they greatly increased and multiplied and were called Kharwār." This also affords some reason for supposing that the Khairwārs are an offshoot of the Cheros and Santāls. Mr. Crooke remarks, "That in Mīrzāpur the people themselves derive their name either from their occupation as makers of catechu (*khair*) or on account of their emigration from some place called Khairāgarh, regarding which there is a great difference of opinion. If the Santāl tradition is to be accepted, Khairāgarh is the place of that name in the Hazāribāgh District; but the Mīrzāpur tradition seems to point to some locality in the south or

[1] *Ethnology of Bengal*, pp. 128, 129. [2] *Ibidem*, pp. 209, 210.

west, in which case Khairāgarh may be identified with the most important of the Chhattīsgarh Feudatory States, or with the pargana of that name in the Allahābād District."[1] According to their own traditions in Chota Nāgpur, Sir H. Risley states that,[2] "The Kharwārs declare their original seat to have been the fort of Rohtās, so called as having been the chosen abode of Rohitāswa, son of Harīschandra, of the family of the Sun. From this ancient house they also claim descent, calling themselves Sūrajvansis, and wearing the *Janeo* or caste thread distinguishing the Rājpūts. A less flattering tradition makes them out to be the offspring of a marriage between a Kshatriya man and a Bhar woman contracted in the days of King Ben, when distinctions of caste were abolished and men might marry whom they would." A somewhat similar story of themselves is told by the tribe in the Bāmra State. Here they say that their original ancestors were the Sun and a daughter of Lakshmi, the goddess of wealth, who lived in the town of Sara. She was very beautiful and the Sun desired her, and began blowing into a conch-shell to express his passion. While the girl was gaping at the sight and sound, a drop of the spittle fell into her mouth and impregnated her. Subsequently a son was born from her arm and a daughter from her thigh, who were known as Bhujbalrai and Janghrai.[3] Bhujbalrai was given great strength by the Sun, and he fought with the people of the country, and became king of Rāthgarh. But in consequence of this he and his family grew proud, and Lakshmi determined to test them whether they were worthy of the riches she had given them. So she came in the guise of a beggar to the door, but was driven away without alms. On this she cursed them, and said that their descendants, the Khairwārs, should always be poor, and should eke out a scanty subsistence from the forests. And in consequence the Khairwārs have ever since been engaged in boiling wood for catechu. Mr. Hira Lāl identifies the Rāthgarh of this story with the tract of Rāth in the north of the Raigarh

1 *Tribes and Castes*, art. Kharwār.

2 *Tribes and Castes of Bengal.*

3 From *bhuj*, an arm, and *jangh*, a thigh. These are Hindi words, and the whole story is obviously a Brāhmanical legend. Balrai seems a corruption of Balarām, the brother of Krishna.

State and the town of Sara, where Lakshmi's daughter lived and her children were born, with Saria in Sārangarh.

2. Its origin. On the information available as to the past history of the tribe it seems probable that the Khairwārs may, as suggested by Sir H. Risley, be an offshoot from some other group. The most probable derivation of the name seems to be from the *khair* or catechu tree (*Acacia catechu*); and it may be supposed that it was the adoption as a calling of the making of catechu which led to their differentiation. Mr. Crooke derives their name either from the *khair* tree or a place called Khairāgarh; but this latter name almost certainly means 'The fort of the *khair* trees.' The Khairwās or Khairwārs of the Kaimur hills, who are identified by Colonel Dalton and in the India Census of 1901 with the Khairwārs of Chota Nāgpur, are certainly named after the tree; they are generally recognised as being Gonds who have taken to the business of boiling catechu, and are hence distinguished, being a little looked down upon by other Gonds. Mr. Crooke describes them in Mīrzāpur as "Admittedly a compound of various jungle tribes who have taken to this special occupation; while according to another account they are the offspring of the Saharias or Saonrs, with whom their sept names are said to be identical." He also identifies them with the Kathkāris of Bombay, whose name means 'makers of *katha* or prepared catechu.' The Khairwārs of Chota Nāgpur have everywhere a subdivision which makes catechu, this being known as Khairchūra in the Central Provinces, Khairi in Bengal and Khairaha in the United Provinces. This group is looked down upon by the other Khairwārs, who consider their occupation to be disreputable and do not marry with them. Possibly the preparation of catechu, like basket- and mat-making, is despised as being a profession practised by primitive dwellers in forests, and so those Khairwārs who have become more civilised are now anxious to disclaim it. Sir H. Risley has several times pointed out the indeterminate nature of the constitution of the Chota Nāgpur tribes, between several of whom intermarriage is common. And it seems certain that the tribes as we know them now must have been differentiated from one or more common stocks much in the same fashion

as castes, though rather by the influence of local settlement than by differences of occupation, and at a much earlier date. And on the above facts it seems likely that the Khairwārs of Chota Nāgpur are an occupational offshoot of the Cheros and Santāls, as those of the Kaimur hills are of the Gonds and Savars.

3. Tribal sub-divisions.

Colonel Dalton states that the tribe had four subdivisions, Bhogta, Mahto, Rāwat and Mānjhi. Of these Mahto simply means a village headman, and is used as a title by many castes and tribes; Rāwat is a term meaning chief, and is in common use as a title; and Mānjhi too is a title, being specially applied to boatmen, and also means a village headman among the Santāls. These divisions, too, afford some reason for considering the tribe to be a mixed group. Other occupational subtribes are recorded by Sir H. Risley, and are found in the Central Provinces, but these apparently have grown up since Colonel Dalton's time.

The most important group in Bengal are the Bhogtas, who are found, says Colonel Dalton, "In the hills of Palāmau, skirting Sargūja, in Tori and Bhanwar Pahār of Chota Nāgpur and other places. They have always had an indifferent reputation. The head of the clan in Palāmau was a notorious freebooter, who, after having been outlawed and successfully evaded every attempt to capture him, obtained a *jāgīr*[1] on his surrendering and promising to keep the peace. He kept to his engagement and died in fair repute, but his two sons could not resist the opportunity afforded by the disturbances of 1857–58. After giving much trouble they were captured; one was hanged, the other transported for life and the estate was confiscated." Mr. Crooke notes that the Khairwārs since adopting Hinduism performed human sacrifices to Kāli. Some of our people who fell into their hands during the Mutiny were so dealt with.[2]

In the Central Provinces there is a group known as Sūrajvansi or Descendants of the Sun, or Janeodhāri, 'Those who wear the sacred thread.' This is the aristocratic division of the caste, to which the chiefs and zamīndārs belong, and according to the usual practice they have consolidated their

[1] Estate held on feudal tenure.

[2] *Religion and Folklore of Northern India*, vol. ii. p. 170.

higher position by marrying only among themselves. Other groups are the Duālbandhi, who say that they are so called because they make a livelihood by building the earthen *diwāls* or walls for houses and yards; but in Mīrzāpur they derive the name from *duāl*, a leather belt which is supposed to have been the uniform of their forefathers when serving as soldiers.[1] The Pātbandhi or silk-makers, according to their own story, are thus named because their ancestors were once very rich and wore silk; but a more probable hypothesis is that they were rearers of tasar silk cocoons. The Beldār or Matkora work as navvies, and are also known as Kawarvansi or 'Descendants of the Kawars,' another tribe of the locality; and last come the Khairchūra, who take their name from the *khair* tree and are catechu-makers.

4. Exogamous septs.

The tribe have a large number of exogamous groups named after plants and animals. Members of the mouse, tortoise, parrot, pig, monkey, vulture, banyan tree and date-palm septs worship their totem animal or tree, and when they find the dead body of the animal they throw away an earthen cooking-pot to purify themselves, as is done when a member of the family dies. Those of the *Dhān* (rice), *Non* (salt), *Dila* (plough) and *Dhenki* (rice pounding-lever) septs cannot dispense with the use of these objects, but make a preliminary obeisance before employing them. Those of the *Kānsi* sept sprinkle water mixed with *kāns*[2] grass over the bride and bridegroom at the marriage ceremony, and those of the *Chandan* or sandalwood sept apply sandal-paste to their foreheads. They cannot clearly explain the meaning of these observances, but some of them have a vague idea that they are descended from the totem object.

5. Marriage.

Marriage is either infant or adult, and in the latter case a girl is not disposed of without her consent. A bride-price varying from five to ten rupees is paid, and in the case of a girl given to a widower the amount is doubled. The Hindu ceremonial has been adopted for the wedding, and an auspicious day is fixed by a Brāhman. In Bengal Sir H. Risley notes that "Remnants of non-Aryan usage may be discerned in the marriage ceremony itself. Both parties must first go through the form of marriage to a mango tree or at least a branch of

[1] Crooke, *Tribes and Castes*.

[2] *Saccharum spontaneum*.

the tree; and must exchange blood mixed with *sindur*, though in the final and binding act *sindur* alone is smeared by the bridegroom upon the bride's forehead and the parting of her hair." As has been pointed out by Mr. Crooke, the custom of smearing vermilion on the bride's forehead is a substitute for an earlier anointing with blood; just as the original idea underlying the offering of a cocoanut was that of substitution for a human head. In some cases blood alone is still used. Thus Sir H. Risley notes that among the Birhors the marriage rite is performed by drawing blood from the little fingers of the bride and bridegroom and smearing it on each of them.[1] The blood-covenant by which a bride was admitted to her husband's sept by being smeared with his blood is believed to have been a common rite among primitive tribes.

6. Disposal of the dead.

As a rule, the tribe bury the dead, though the Hindu custom of cremation is coming into fashion among the well-to-do. Before the interment they carry the corpse seven times round the grave, and it is buried with the feet pointing to the north. They observe mourning for ten days and abstain from animal food and liquor during that period. A curious custom is reported from the Bilāspur District, where it is said that children cut a small piece of flesh from the finger of a dead parent and swallow it, considering this as a requital for the labour of the mother in having carried the child for nine months in her womb. So in return they carry a piece of her flesh in their bodies. But the correct explanation as given by Sir J. G. Frazer is that they do it to prevent themselves from being haunted by the ghosts of their parents. "Thus Orestes,[2] after he had gone mad from murdering his mother, recovered his wits by biting off one of his own fingers; since his victim was his own mother it might be supposed that the tasting of his own blood was the same as hers; and the furies of his murdered mother, which had appeared black to him before, appeared white as soon as he had mutilated himself in this way. The Indians of Guiana believe that an

[1] *Tribes and Castes*, art. Birhor.

[2] The above instances are reproduced from Sir J. G. Frazer's *Psyche's Task* (London, 1909). These cases are all of homicide, but it seems likely that the action of the Khairwārs may be based on the same motives, as the fear of ghosts is strong among these tribes.

avenger of blood who has slain his man must go mad unless he tastes the blood of his victim, the notion apparently being that the ghost drives him crazy. A similar custom was observed by the Maoris in battle. When a warrior had slain his foe in combat, he tasted his blood, believing that this preserved him from the avenging spirit (*atua*) of his victim; for they imagined that 'the moment a slayer had tasted the blood of the slain, the dead man became a part of his being and placed him under the protection of the *atua* or guardian-spirit of the deceased.' Some of the North American Indians also drank the blood of their enemies in battle. Strange as it may seem, this truly savage superstition exists apparently in Italy to this day. There is a widespread opinion in Calabria that if a murderer is to escape he must suck his victim's blood from the reeking blade of the dagger with which he did the deed."

7. Religion. The religion of the tribe is of the usual animistic type. Colonel Dalton notes that they have, like the Kols, a village priest, known as Pahan or Baiga. He is always one of the impure tribes, a Bhuiya, a Kharwār or a Korwa, and he offers a great triennial sacrifice of a buffalo in the sacred grove, or on a rock near the village. The fact that the Khairwārs employed members of the Korwa and Bhuiya tribes as their village priests may be taken to indicate that the latter are the earlier residents of the country, and are on this account employed by the Khairwārs as later arrivals for the conciliation of the indigenous deities. Colonel Dalton states that the Khairwārs made no prayers to any of the Hindu gods, but when in great trouble they appealed to the sun. In the Central Provinces the main body of the tribe, and particularly those who belong to the landholding class, profess the Hindu religion.

8. Inheritance. The Khairwārs have now also adopted the Hindu rule of inheritance, and have abandoned the tribal custom which Sir H. Risley records as existing in Bengal. "Here the eldest son of the senior wife, even if younger than one of the sons of the second wife, inherits the entire property, subject to the obligation of providing for all other legitimate children. If the inheritance consists of land, the heir is expected to create separate maintenance grants in favour of his younger

brothers. Daughters can never inherit, but are entitled to live in the ancestral home till they are married."[1]

The Khairwas or Khairwārs of the Kaimur hills are derived, as already seen, from the Gonds and Savars, and therefore are ethnologically a distinct group from those of the Chota Nāgpur plateau, who have been described above. But as nearly every caste is made up of diverse ethnological elements held together by the tie of a common occupation, it does not seem worth while to treat these groups separately. Colonel Dalton, who also identifies them with the main tribe, records an interesting notice of them at an earlier period:[2] **9. The Khairwas of Damoh.**

"There is in the seventh volume of the Asiatic Researches a notice of the Kharwārs of the Kaimur hills in the Mīrzāpur District, to the north of the Son river, by Captain J. P. Blunt, who in his journey from Chunār to Ellora in A.D. 1794, met with them and describes them as a very primitive tribe. He visited one of their villages consisting of half a dozen poor huts, and though proceeding with the utmost caution, unattended, to prevent alarm, the inhabitants fled at his approach. The women were seen, assisted by the men, carrying off their children and moving with speed to hide themselves in the woods. It was observed that they were nearly naked, and the only articles of domestic use found in the deserted huts were a few gourds for water-vessels, some bows and arrows, and some fowls as wild as their masters. With great difficulty, by the employment of Kols as mediators, some of the men were induced to return. They were nearly naked, but armed with bows and arrows and a hatchet."

In Damoh the Khairwārs are said to come from Panna State. During the working season they live in temporary sheds in the forest, and migrate from place to place as the supply of trees is exhausted. Having cut down a tree they strip off the bark and cut the inner and tender wood into small pieces, which are boiled for two or three days until a thick black paste is obtained. From this the water is allowed to drain off, and the residue is made into cakes and dried in the sun. It is eaten in small pieces with betel-leaf and areca-nut. Duty is levied by the Forest Department at the

[1] Risley, *loc. cit.*

[2] *Ethnology of Bengal*, pp. 128, 129.

rate of a rupee per *handi* or pot in which boiling is carried on. In Bombay various superstitious observances are connected with the manufacture of catechu; and Mr. Crooke quoted the following description of them from the *Bombay Gazetteer*:[1] "Every year on the day after the Holi the *chūlha* ceremony takes place. In a trench seven feet long by three, and about three deep, *khair* logs are carefully stacked and closely packed till they stand in a heap about three feet above ground. The pile is then set on fire and allowed to burn to the level of the ground. The village sweeper breaks a cocoanut, kills a couple of fowls and sprinkles a little liquor near the pile. Then, after washing their feet, the sweeper and the village headman walk barefoot hurriedly across the fire. After this strangers come to fulfil vows, and giving one anna and a half cocoanut to the sweeper, and the other half cocoanut to the headman, wash their feet, and turning to the left, walk over the pile. The fire seems to cause none of them any pain." The following description of the Kathkāris as hunters of monkeys is also taken by Mr. Crooke from the *Bombay Gazetteer*:[2] "The Kathkāris represent themselves as descended from the monkeys of Rāma. Now that their legitimate occupation of preparing catechu (*kath*) has been interfered with, they subsist almost entirely by hunting, and habitually kill and eat monkeys, shooting them with bows and arrows. In order to approach within range they are obliged to have recourse to stratagems, as the monkeys at once recognise them in their ordinary costume. The ruse usually adopted is for one of the best shots to put on a woman's robe (*sāri*), under the ample folds of which he conceals his murderous weapons. Approaching the tree in which the monkeys are seated, the sportsman affects the utmost unconcern, and busies himself with the innocent occupation of picking up twigs and leaves, and thus disarming suspicion he is enabled to get a sufficiently close shot to render success a certainty."

Khandait, Khandayat.—The military caste of Orissa, the word Khandait meaning 'swordsman,' and being derived

[1] Crooke's *Tribes and Castes*, art. Khairwa. Quoting from *Bombay Gazetteer*, x. 48 and iii. 310.

[2] *Loc. cit.*

from the Uriya *khanda*, a sword. Sir H. Risley remarks of the Khandaits:[1] "The caste is for the most part, if not entirely, composed of Bhuiyas, whose true affinities have been disguised under a functional name, while their customs, their religion and in some cases even their complexion and features have been modified by long contact with Hindus of relatively pure Aryan descent. The ancient Rājas of Orissa kept up large armies and partitioned the land on strictly military tenures. These armies consisted of various castes and races, the upper ranks being officered by men of good Aryan descent, while the lower ones were recruited from the low castes alike of the hills and the plains. In the social system of Orissa, the *Sresta* or 'best' Khandaits rank next to the Rājpūts, who have not the intimate connection with the land which has helped to raise the Khandaits to their present position." The Khandaits are thus like the Marāthas, and the small body of Paiks in the northern Districts, a caste formed from military service; and though recruited for the most part originally from the Dravidian tribes, they have obtained a considerable rise in status owing to their occupation and the opportunity which has been afforded to many of them to become landholders. The best Khandaits now aspire to Rājpūt rank, while the bulk of them have the position of cultivators, from whom Brāhmans will take water, or a much higher one than they are entitled to by descent. In[2] the Central Provinces the Khandaits have no subcastes, and only two *gotras* or clans, named after the Kachhap or tortoise and the Nāgas or cobra respectively. These divisions appear, however, to be nominal, and do not regulate marriage, as to which the only rule observed is that persons whose descent can be traced from the same parent should not marry each other. Early marriage is usual, and if a girl arrives at adolescence without a husband having been found for her, she goes through the ceremony of wedlock with an arrow. Polygamy is permitted, but a person resorting to it is looked down on and nicknamed Maipkhia or wife-eater. The essential portion of the marriage ceremony is the *bandan* or

[1] *Tribes and Castes of Bengal*, art. Khandait. In 1911, after the transfer of Sambalpur, only 18 Khandaits remained in the Central Provinces.

[2] The following particulars are from a paper by Mr. Kāshināth Bohidār, Assistant Settlement Superintendent, Sonpur.

tying of the hands of the bride and bridegroom together with *kusha* grass. The bridegroom must lift up the bride and walk seven times round the marriage altar carrying her. Widow-marriage and divorce are permitted in the Central Provinces, and Brāhmans are employed for religious and ceremonial purposes.

KHANGĀR

LIST OF PARAGRAPHS

1. Origin and traditions.

Khangār,[1] called also *Kotwāl*, *Jemādār* or *Darbānia* (gatekeeper).—A low caste of village watchmen and field-labourers belonging to Bundelkhand, and found in the Saugor, Damoh, Narsinghpur and Jubbulpore Districts. They numbered nearly 13,000 in 1911. The Khangārs are also numerous in the United Provinces. Hindu ingenuity has evolved various explanations of the word Khangār, such as '*khand*,' a pit, and '*gar*,' maker, digger, because the Khangār digs holes in other people's houses for the purposes of theft. The caste is, however, almost certainly of non-Aryan origin, and there is little doubt also that Bundelkhand was its original home. It may be noted that the Munda tribe have a division called Khangār with which the caste may have some connection. The Khangārs themselves relate the following story of their origin. Their ancestors were formerly the rulers of the fort and territory of Kurār in Bundelkhand, when a Bundela Rājpūt came and settled there. The Bundela had a very pretty daughter whom the Khangār Rāja demanded in marriage. The Bundela did not wish to give his daughter to the Khangār, but could not refuse the Rāja outright, so he said that he would consent if all the Khangārs would agree to adopt Bundela practices. This the Khangārs readily agreed to do, and the Bundela thereupon invited them all to a wedding feast, and having

[1] Compiled principally from a paper by Kanhyā Lāl, clerk in the Gazetteer Office.

summoned his companions and plied the Khangārs with liquor until they were dead drunk, cut them all to pieces. One pregnant woman only escaped by hiding in a field of *kusum* or safflower,[1] and on this account the Khangārs still venerate the *kusum* and will not wear cloths dyed with saffron. She fled to the house of a Muhammadan eunuch or Fakīr, who gave her shelter and afterwards placed her with a Dāngi landowner. The Bundelas followed her up and came to the house of the Dāngi, who denied that the Khangār woman was with him. The Bundelas then asked him to make all the women in his house eat together to prove that none of them was the Khangārin, on which the Dāngi five times distributed the *maihar*, a sacrificial cake which is only given to relations, to all the women of the household including the Khangārin, and thus convinced the Bundelas that she was not in the house. The woman who was thus saved became the ancestor of the whole Khangār caste, and in memory of this act the Khangārs and Nadia Dāngis are still each bidden to eat the *maihar* cake at the weddings of the other, or at least so it is said; while the Fakīrs, in honour of this great occasion when one of their number acted as giver rather than receiver, do not beg for alms at the wedding of a Khangār, but on the contrary bring presents. The basis of the story, that the Khangārs were the indigenous inhabitants of Bundelkhand and were driven out and slaughtered by the immigrant Bundelas, may not improbably be historically correct. It is also said that no Khangār is even now allowed to enter the fort of Kurār, and that the spirit of the murdered chief still haunts it; so that if a bed is placed there in the evening with a tooth-stick, the tooth-stick will be split in the morning as after use, and the bed will appear as if it had been slept in.[2]

2. Caste sub-divisions.

The caste has four subdivisions, named Rai, Mirdha or Nakīb, Karbal and Dahāt. The Rai or royal Khangārs are the highest group and practise hypergamy with families of the Mirdha and Karbal groups, taking daughters from them in marriage but not giving their daughters to them.

[1] *Carthamus tinctorius.*

[2] In the Ethnographic Appendices to the *India Census Report* of 1901 a slightly different version of the story is given by Captain Luard. The Dāngis, it must be remembered, are a high caste ranking just below Rājpūts.

The Mirdhas or Nakībs are so called because they act as mace-bearers and form the bodyguard of princes. Very few, if any, are to be found in the Central Provinces. The Karbal are supposed to be especially valorous. The Dahāts have developed into a separate caste called Dahait, and are looked down on by all the other divisions as they keep pigs. The caste is also divided into numerous exogamous septs, all of which are totemistic; and the members of the sept usually show veneration to the object from which the sept takes its name. Some of the names of septs are as follows: Bachhiyā from *bachhrā* a calf; Barha from *barāh* a pig, this sept worshipping the pig; Belgotia from the *bel* tree; Chandan from the sandalwood tree; Chirai from *chiriya* a bird, this sept revering sparrows; Ghurgotia from *ghora* a horse (members of this sept touch the feet of a horse before mounting it and do not ride on a horse in wedding processions); Guae from the iguana; Hanumān from the monkey god; Hāthi from the elephant; Kasgotia from *kānsa* bell-metal (members of this sept do not use vessels of bell-metal on ceremonial occasions nor sell them); Mahiyar from *maihar* fried cakes (members of this sept do not use *ghī* at their weddings and may not sell *ghī* by weight though they may sell it by measure); *San* after *san*-hemp (members of this sept place pieces of hemp near their family god); Sāndgotia from *sānd* a bullock; Tāmbagotia from *tāmba* copper; and Vishnu from the god of that name, whom the sept worship. The names of 31 septs in all are reported and there are probably others. The fact that two or three septs are named after Hindu deities may be noticed as peculiar.

3. Marriage.

The marriage of members of the same sept is prohibited and also that of first cousins. Girls are usually married at about ten years of age, the parents of the girl having to undertake the duty of finding a husband. The ceremonial in vogue in the northern Districts is followed throughout, an astrologer being consulted to ascertain that the horoscopes of the pair are favourable, and a Brāhman employed to draw up the *lagan* or auspicious paper fixing the date of the marriage. The bridegroom is dressed in a yellow gown and over-cloth, with trousers of red chintz, red shoes, and a marriage-crown of date-palm leaves. He has the silver ornaments usually worn by women on his neck, as the *khangwāri* or silver ring, and the *hamel* or necklace of rupees. In order to avert the evil eye he carries a dagger or nutcracker, and a smudge of lampblack is made on his forehead to disfigure him and thus avert the evil eye, which it is thought would otherwise be too probably attracted by his exquisitely beautiful appearance in his wedding garments. The binding portion of the ceremony is the *bhānwar* or walking round the sacred post of the *munga* tree (*Moringa pterygosperma*). This is done six times by the couple, the bridegroom leading, and they then make a seventh turn round the *bedi* or sacrificial fire. If the bride is a child this seventh round is omitted at the marriage and performed at the *Dusarta* or going-away ceremony. After the marriage the *haldi* ceremony takes place, the father of the bridegroom being dressed in women's clothes; he then dances with the mother of the bride, while they throw turmeric mixed with water over each other. Widow-marriage is allowed, and the widow may marry anybody in the caste; the ceremony consists in the placing of bangles on her wrist, and is always performed at night, a Wednesday being usually selected. A feast must afterwards be given to the caste-fellows. Divorce is also permitted, and may be effected at the instance of either party in the presence of the caste *panchāyat* or committee. When a husband divorces his wife he must give a feast.

4. Religion. The Khangārs worship the usual Hindu deities and especially venerate Dūlha Deo, a favourite household godling in the northern Districts. Pachgara Deo is a deity who seems to have been created to commemorate the occasion when the Dāngi distributed the marriage cakes five times to the fugitive ancestress of the caste. His cult is now on the decline, but some still consider him the most important deity of all, and it is said that no Khangār will tell an untruth after having sworn by this god. Children dying unmarried and persons dying of leprosy or smallpox are buried, while others are buried or burnt according as the family can afford the more expensive rite of cremation or not. As among other castes a corpse must not be burnt between sunset and

sunrise, as it is believed that this would cause the soul to be born blind in the next birth. Nor must the corpse be wrapped in stitched clothes, as in that case the child in which it is reincarnated would be born with its arms and legs entangled. The corpse is laid on its back and some *ghī*, til, barley cakes and sandalwood, if available, are placed on the body. The soul of the deceased is believed to haunt the house for three days, and each night a lamp and a little water in an earthen pot are placed ready for it. When cremation takes place the ashes are collected on the third day and the burning ground is cleaned with cowdung and sprinkled with milk, mustard and salt, in order that a cow may lick over the place and the soul of the deceased may thus find more easy admission into *Baikunth* or heaven. Well-to-do persons take the bones of the dead to the Ganges, a few from the different parts of the body being selected and tied round the bearer's neck. Mourning is usually only observed for three days.

5. Social status.

The Khangārs do not admit outsiders into the caste, except children born of a Khangār father and a mother belonging to one of the highest castes. A woman going wrong with a man of another caste is finally expelled, but *liaisons* within the caste may be atoned for by the usual penalty of a feast. The caste eat flesh and drink liquor but abjure fowls, pork and beef. They will take food cooked without water from Banias, Sunārs and Tameras, but *katchi roti* only from the Brāhmans who act as their priests. Such Brāhmans are received on terms of equality by others of the caste. Khangārs bathe daily, and their women take off their outer cloth to eat food, because this is not washed every day. Food cooked with water must be consumed in the *chauka* or place where it is prepared, and not carried outside the house. Men of the caste often have the suffix Singh after their names in imitation of the Rājpūts. Although their social observances are thus in some respects strict, the status of the caste is low, and Brāhmans do not take water from them.

6. Occupation.

The Khangārs say that their ancestors were soldiers, but at present they are generally tenants, field-labourers and village watchmen. They were formerly noted thieves, and several proverbs remain in testimony to this. "The Khangār is strong only when he possesses a *khunta* (a pointed iron rod to break through the wall of a house)." 'The Sunār and the Khangār only flourish together'; because the Sunār acts as a receiver of the property stolen by the Khangār. They are said to have had different ways of breaking into a house, those who got through the roof being called *chhappartor*, while others who dug through the side walls were known as *khonpāphor*. They have now, however, generally relinquished their criminal practices and settled down to live as respectable citizens.

KHARIA

LIST OF PARAGRAPHS

Kharia.[1]—A primitive Kolarian tribe, of which about 900 persons were returned from the Central Provinces in 1911. They belong to the Bilāspur District and the Jashpur and Raigarh States. The Kharias are one of the most backward of the Kolarian tribes, and appear to be allied to the Mundas and Savars. Colonel Dalton says of them: "In the Chota Nāgpur estate they are found in large communities, and the Kharias belonging to these communities are far more civilised than those who live apart. Their best settlements lie near the southern Koel river, which stream they venerate as the Santāls do the Dāmudar, and into it they throw the ashes of their dead." Chota Nāgpur is the home of the Kharias, and their total strength is over a lakh. They are found elsewhere only in Assam, where they have probably migrated to the tea-gardens. 1. General notice.

The Kharia legend of origin resembles that of the Mundas, and tends to show that they are an elder branch of that tribe. They say that a child was born to a woman in the jungle, and she left it to fetch a basket in which to carry it home. On her return she saw a cobra spreading its hood 2. Legend of origin.

[1] This article is mainly based on notes taken by Rai Bahādur Hira Lāl at Raigarh, with extracts from Colonel Dalton's and Sir H. Risley's accounts of the tribe.

over the child to protect it from the sun. On this account the child was called Nāgvansi (of the race of the cobra), and became the ancestor of the Nāgvansi Rājas of Chota Nāgpur. The Kharias say this child had an elder brother, and the two brothers set out on a journey, the younger riding a horse and the elder carrying a *kāwar* or banghy with their luggage. When they came to Chota Nāgpur the younger was made king, on which the elder brother also asked for a share of the inheritance. The people then put two caskets before him and asked him to choose one. One of the caskets contained silver and the other only some earth. The elder brother chose that which contained earth, and on this he was told that the fate of himself and his descendants would be to till the soil, and carry banghys as he had been doing. The Kharias say that they are descended from the elder brother, while the younger was the ancestor of the Nāgvansi Rājas, who are really Mundas. They say that they can never enter the house of the Nāgvansi Rājas because they stand in the relation of elder brother-in-law to the Rānis, who are consequently prohibited from looking on the face of a Kharia. This story is exactly like that of the Parjas in connection with the Rājas of Bastar. And as the Parjas are probably an older branch of the Gonds, who were reduced to subjection by the subsequent Rāj-Gond immigrants under the ancestors of the Bastar Rājas, so it seems a reasonable hypothesis that the Kharias stood in a similar relationship to the Mundas or Kols. This theory derives some support from the fact that, according to Sir H. Risley, the Mundas will take daughters in marriage from the Kharias, but will not give their daughters to them, and the Kharias speak of the Mundas as their elder brethren.[1] Mr. Hīra Lal suggests that the name Khaṛia is derived from *kharkhari*, a palanquin or litter, and that the original name Kharkharia has been contracted into Kharia. He states that in the Uriya country Oraons, who carry litters, are also called Kharias. This derivation is in accordance with the tradition of the Kharias that their first ancestor carried a banghy, and with the fact that the Kols are the best professional *dhoolie*-bearers.

[1] *Tribes and Castes of Bengal*, art. Kharia.

In Raigarh the Kharias have only two subtribes, the Dūdh, or milk Kharias, and the Delki. Of these the Delki are said to be of mixed origin. They take food from Brāhmans, and explain that they do so because an ancestress went wrong with a Brāhman. It seems likely that they may be descended from the offspring of immigrant Hindus in Chota Nāgpur with Kharia women, like similar subdivisions in other tribes. The Delkis look down on the Dūdh Kharias, saying that the latter eat the flesh of tigers and monkeys, from which the Delkis abstain. In Bengal the tribe have two other divisions, the Erenga and Munda Kharias. 3. Subcastes.

The tribe is divided, like others, into totemistic exogamous septs, which pay reverence to their totems. Thus members of the Kulu (tortoise), Kiro (tiger), Nāg (cobra), Kankul (leopard) and Kuto (crocodile) septs abstain from killing their totem animal, fold their hands in obeisance when they meet it, and taking up some dust from the animal's track place it on their heads as a mark of veneration. Certain septs cannot wholly abstain from the consumption of their sept totem, so they make a compromise. Thus members of the Baa, or rice sept, cannot help eating rice, but they will not eat the scum which gathers over the rice as it is being boiled. Those of the Bilum or salt sept must not take up a little salt on one finger and suck it, but must always use two or more fingers for conveying salt to the mouth, presumably as a mark of respect. Members of the Suren or stone sept will not make ovens with stones but only with clods of earth. The tribe do not now think they are actually descended from their totems, but tell stories accounting for the connection. Thus the Katang Kondai or bamboo sept say that a girl in the family of their ancestors went to cut bamboos and never came back. Her parents went to search for her and heard a voice calling out from the bamboos, but could not find their daughter. Then they understood that the bamboo was of their own family and must not be cut by them. The supposition is apparently that the girl was transformed into a bamboo. 4. Exogamy and totemism.

Marriage between members of the same sept is forbidden, but the rule is not always observed. A brother's daughter 5. Marriage.

may marry a sister's son, but not vice versa. Marriage is always adult, and overtures come from the boy's father. The customary bride-price is twelve bullocks, but many families cannot afford this, and resort is then made to a fiction. The boy's party make twelve models of bullocks in earth, and placing each in a leaf-plate send them to the girl's party, who throw away two, saying that one has been eaten by a tiger, and the other has fallen into a pit and died. The remaining ten are returned to the bridegroom's party, who throw away two, saying that they have been sold to provide liquor for the Panch. For two of the eight now left real animals are substituted, and for the other six one rupee each, and the two cattle and six rupees are sent back to the bride's party as the real bride-price. Poor families, however, give four rupees instead of the two cattle, and ten rupees is among them considered as the proper price, though even this is reduced on occasion. The marriage party goes from the bride's to the bridegroom's house, and consists of women only. The men do not go, as they say that on one occasion all the men of a Kharia wedding procession were turned into stones, and they fear to undergo a similar fate. The real reason may probably be that the journey of the bride is a symbolic reminiscence of the time when she was carried off by force, and hence it would be derogatory for the men to accompany her. The bridegroom comes out to meet the bride riding on the shoulders of his brother-in-law or paternal aunt's husband, who is known as Dherha. He touches the bride, and both of them perform a dance. At the wedding the bridegroom stands on a plough-yoke, and the bride on a grinding-slab, and the Dherha walks seven times round them sprinkling water on them from a mango-leaf. The couple are shut up alone for the night, and next morning the girl goes to the river to wash her husband's clothes. On her return a fowl is killed, and the couple drink two drops of its blood in water mixed with turmeric, as a symbol of the mixing of their own blood. A goat is killed, and they step in its blood and enter their houses. The caste-people say to them, "Whenever a Kharia comes to your house, give him a cup of water and tobacco and food if you have it," and the wedding is over.

After a girl is married her own mother will not eat food cooked by her, as no two Kharias will take food together unless they are of the same sept. When a married daughter goes back to the house of her parents she cooks her food separately, and does not enter their cook-room ; if she did all the earthen pots would be defiled and would have to be thrown away. A similar taboo marks the relations of a woman towards her husband's elder brother, who is known as Kura Sasur. She must not enter his house nor sit on a cot or stool before him, nor touch him, nor cook food for him. If she touches him a fine of a fowl with liquor is imposed by the caste, and for his touching her a goat and liquor. This idea may perhaps have been established as a check on the custom of fraternal polyandry, when the idea of the eldest brother taking the father's place as head of the joint family became prevalent. **6. Taboos as to food.**

Widow-marriage is permitted at the price of a feast to the caste, and the payment of a small sum to the woman's family. A widow must leave her children with her first husband's family if required to do so. If she takes them with her they become entitled to inherit her second husband's property, but receive only a half-share as against a full share taken by his children. Divorce is permitted by mutual agreement or for adultery of the woman. But the practice is not looked upon with favour, and a divorced man or woman rarely succeeds in obtaining another mate. **7. Widow-marriage and divorce.**

The principal deity of the Kharias is a hero called Banda. They say that an Oraon had vowed to give his daughter to the man who would clear the *kāns*[1] grass off a hillock. Several men tried, and at last Banda did it by cutting out the roots. He then demanded the girl's hand, but the Oraon refused, thinking that Banda had cleared the grass by magic. Then Banda went away and the girl died, and on learning of this Banda went and dug her out of her grave, when she came to life and they were married. Since then Banda has been worshipped. The tribe also venerate their ploughs and axes, and on the day of Dasahra they make offerings to the sun. **8. Religion.**

[1] *Saccharum spontaneum.* This grass infests cultivated fields and is very difficult to eradicate.

9. Funeral rites.

The tribe bury the dead, placing the head to the north. When the corpse is taken out of the house two grains of rice are thrown to each point of the compass to invite the ancestors of the family to the funeral. And on the way, where two roads meet, the corpse is set down and a little rice and cotton-seed sprinkled on the ground as a guiding-mark to the ancestors. Before burial the corpse is anointed with turmeric and oil, and carried seven times round the grave, probably as a symbol of marriage to it. Each relative puts a piece of cloth in the grave, and the dead man's cooking and drinking-pots, his axe, stick, pipe and other belongings, and a basketful of rice are buried with him. The mourners set three plants of *orai* or *khas-khas* grass on the grave over the dead man's head, middle and feet, and then they go to a tank and bathe, chewing the roots of this grass. It would appear that the *orai* grass may be an agent of purification or means of severance from the dead man's ghost, like the leaves of the sacred *nīm*[1] tree.

10. Bringing back the souls of the dead.

On the third day they bathe and are shaved, and catch a fish, which is divided among all the relatives, however small it may be, and eaten raw with salt, turmeric and garlic. It seems likely that this fish may be considered to represent the dead man's spirit, and is eaten in order to avoid being haunted by his ghost or for some other object, and the fish may be eaten as a substitute for the dead man's body, itself consumed in former times. On the tenth night after the death the soul is called back, a lighted wick being set in a vessel at the cross-roads where the rice and cotton had been sprinkled. They call on the dead man, and when the flame of the lamp wavers in the wind they break the vessel holding the lamp, saying that his soul has come and joined them, and go home. On the following Dasahra festival, when ancestors are worshipped, the spirit of the deceased is mingled with the ancestors. A cock and hen are fed and let loose, and the headman of the sept calls on the soul to come and join the ancestors and give his protection to the family. When a man is killed by a tiger the remains are collected and burnt on the spot. A goat is sacrificed and eaten by the caste, and thereafter, when a wedding takes place in that man's family,

[1] *Melia indica.*

a goat is offered to his spirit. The Kharias believe that the spirits of the dead are reborn in children, and on the Bārhi day, a month after the child's birth, they ascertain which ancestor has been reborn by the usual method of divination with grains of rice in water.

11. Social customs. The strict taboos practised by the tribe as regards food have already been mentioned. Men will take food from one another, but not women. Men will also accept food cooked without water from Brāhmans, Rājputs and Bhuiyas. The Kharias will eat almost any kind of flesh, including crocodile, rat, pig, tiger and bear; they have now generally abandoned beef in deference to Hindu prejudice, and also monkeys, though they formerly ate these animals, the Topno sept especially being noted on this account.

12. Caste rules and organisation. Temporary expulsion from caste is imposed for the usual offences, and also for getting shaved or having clothes washed by a barber or washerman other than a member of the caste. This rule seems to arise either from an ultra-strict desire for social purity or from a hostile reaction against the Hindus for the low estimation in which the Kharias are held. Again it is a caste offence to carry the palanquin of a Kāyasth, a Muhammadan, a Koshta (weaver) or a Nai (barber), or to carry the *tāzias* or representations of the tomb of Husain in the Muharram procession. The caste have a headman who has the title of Pardhān, with an assistant called Negi and a messenger who is known as Gānda. The headman must always be of the Samer sept, the Negi of the Suren sept, and the Gānda of the Bartha or messenger sept. The headman's duty is to give water for the first time to caste offenders on readmission, the Negi must make all arrangements for the caste feast, and the Gānda goes and summons the tribesmen. In addition to the penalty feast a cash fine is imposed on an erring member; of this rather more than half is given to the assembled tribesmen for the purpose of buying *murra* or fried grain on their way home on the following morning. The remaining sum is divided between the three officers, the Pardhān and Negi getting two shares each and the Gānda one share. But the division is only approximate, as the Kharias are unable to do the necessary calculation for an odd number of rupees. The men have their hair tied in a knot on the right side of the head, and women on the left. The women are tattooed, but not the men.

Colonel Dalton writes of the tribal dances:[1] "The nuptial dances of the Kharias are very wild, and the gestures of the dancers and the songs all bear more directly than delicately on what is evidently considered the main object of the festivities, the public recognition of the consummation of the marriage. The bride and bridegroom are carried through the dances seated on the hips of two of their companions. Dancing is an amusement to which the Kharias, like all Kolarians, are passionately devoted. The only noticeable difference in their style is that in the energy, vivacity and warmth of their movements they excel all their brethren."

13. Occupation and character. The Kharias say that their original occupation is to carry *dhoolies* or litters, and this, as well as the social rules prohibiting them from carrying those of certain castes, is in favour of the derivation of the name from *kharkhari*, a litter. They are also cultivators, and collect forest produce. They are a wild and backward tribe, as shown in the following extracts from an account by Mr. Ball:[2] "The first Kharias I met with were encamped in the jungle at the foot of some hills. The hut was rudely made of a few *sāl* branches, its occupants being one man, an old and two young women, besides three or four children. At the time of my visit they were taking their morning meal; and as they regarded my presence with the utmost indifference, without even turning round or ceasing from their occupations, I remained for some time watching them. They had evidently recently captured some small animal, but what it was, as they had already eaten the skin, I could not ascertain. As I looked on, the old woman distributed to the others, on plates of *sāl* leaves, what appeared to be the entrails of the animal, and wrapping up her own portion between a couple of leaves threw it on the fire in order to give it a very primitive cooking. With regard to their ordinary food the Kharias chiefly depend on the jungle for a supply of fruits, leaves and roots.

"The Kharias never make iron themselves, but are altogether dependent on the neighbouring bazārs for their

[1] *Ethnology of Bengal.* [2] *Jungle Life in India*, p. 89.

supplies. Had they at any period possessed a knowledge of the art of making iron, conservative of their customs as such races are, it is scarcely likely that they would have forgotten it. It is therefore not unreasonable to suppose that there was a period prior to the advent of the Hindus when iron was quite unknown to them—when, owing to the absence of cultivation in the plains, they were even more dependent on the supply of jungle food than they are at present. In those times their axes and their implements for grubbing up roots were in all probability made of stone, and their arrows had tips of the same material.

"In their persons the Kharias are very dirty, seldom if ever washing themselves. Their features are decidedly of a low character, not unlike the Bhumij, but there seemed to me to be an absence of any strongly-marked type in their faces or build, such as enables one to know a Santāl and even a Kurmi at a glance."

Of the Kharia dialect Sir George Grierson states that it is closely allied to Savara, and has also some similarity to Korku and Juāng:[1] "Kharia grammar has all the characteristics of a language which is gradually dying out and being superseded by dialects of quite different families. The vocabulary is strongly Aryanised, and Aryan principles have pervaded the grammatical structure. Kharia is no longer a typical Munda language. It is like a palimpsest, the original writing on which can only be recognised with some difficulty."[2] An account of the Kharia dialect has been published in Mr. G. B. Banerjee's *Introduction to the Kharia Language* (Calcutta, 1894). 14. Language.

Khatīk.—A functional caste of Hindu mutton-butchers and vegetable sellers. They numbered nearly 13,000 persons in the Central Provinces and Berār in 1911, and are, as might be expected, principally returned from the Districts with a considerable urban population, Amraoti, Jubbulpore, Nāgpur and Saugor. The name is derived from the Sanskrit Khattika,[3] a butcher or hunter. In northern

[1] *Linguistic Survey*, vol. iv. *Munda and Dravidian Languages*, p. 22.

[2] *Ibidem*, p. 129.

[3] Mr. Crooke's *Tribes and Castes*, art. Khatīk.

India Mr. Crooke states that the caste are engaged in keeping and selling pigs and retailing vegetables and fruits, and does not specially mention that they slaughter animals, though in Agra one of their subcastes is named Būchar, a corruption of the English word butcher. In the Punjab Sir D. Ibbetson[1] says of them that, "They form a connecting link between the scavengers and the leather-workers, though they occupy a social position distinctly inferior to that of the latter. They are great keepers of pigs and poultry, which a Chamār would not keep.[2] At the same time many of them tan and dye leather and indeed are not seldom confused with the Chamrāng. The Khatīk is said sometimes to keep sheep and goats and twist their hair into waist-bands for sale." Sir H. Risley again describes the Khatīks of Bihār as a cultivating and vegetable-selling caste.[3] The differences in the principal occupations ascribed to the caste are thus somewhat remarkable. In the Central Provinces the Khatīks are primarily slaughterers of sheep and goats and mutton-butchers, though they also keep pigs, and some of them, who object to this trade, make their livelihood by selling vegetables. Both in the United Provinces and Punjab the Khatīks are considered to be connected with the Pāsis and probably an offshoot of that caste. In the Central Provinces they are said to be an inferior branch of the Gadaria or shepherd caste. The Gadarias state that their old sheep were formerly allowed to die. Then they appointed some poor men of the community to kill them and sell the flesh, dividing the profits with the owner, and thus the Khatīk caste arose. The Khatīks accept cooked food from the Gadarias, but the latter do not reciprocate.

The Khatīks are both Hindu and Muhammadan by religion, the latter being also known as Gai-Khatīk or cow-killer; but these may more suitably be classed with the Kasais or Muhammadan butchers. In the Marātha Districts the Hindu Khatīks are divided into two subcastes, the Berāria or those from Berār, and the Jhādi or those of the forest country of the Wainganga valley. These will take

[1] *Census Report* (1881), para. 502.

[2] This statement does not apply to the Chamārs of the Central Provinces.

[3] *Tribes and Castes of Bengal*, art. Khatīk.

food together, but do not intermarry. They have the usual set of exogamous clans or septs, many of which are of a totemistic nature, being named after plants, animals or natural objects. In Jubbulpore, owing to their habit of keeping pigs and the dirty state of their dwellings, one of their divisions is named Lendha, which signifies the excrement of swine. Here the sept is called *bān*, while in Wardha it is known as *kul* or *ādnām*. Marriage within the sept is forbidden. When arranging a match they consider it essential that the boy should be taller than the girl, but do not insist on his being older. A bride-price is sometimes paid, especially if the parents of the girl are poor, but the practice is considered derogatory. In such a case the father is thought to sell his daughter and he is called Bād or Bhānd. Marriages commonly take place on the fifth, seventh or ninth day after the Holi festival, or on the festival of Badsāvitri, the third day of Baisākh (light fortnight). When the bridegroom leaves the house to set out for the wedding his mother or aunt waves a pestle and churning-stick round him, puts a piece of betel-vine in his mouth and gives him her breast to suck. He then steps on a little earthen lamp-saucer placed over an egg and breaks them, and leaves the house without looking back. These rites are common to many castes, but their exact significance is obscure. The pestle and churning-stick and egg may perhaps be emblems of fertility. At the wedding the fathers of the couple split some wood into shreds, and, placing it in a little pit with cotton, set a light to it. If it is all burnt up the ceremony has been properly performed, but if any is left, the people laugh and say that the corpses of the family's ancestors were not wholly consumed on the pyre. To effect a divorce the husband and wife break a stick in the presence of the caste *panchāyat* or committee, and if a divorced woman or one who has deserted her husband marries again, the first husband has to give a feast to the caste on the tenth day after the wedding; this is perhaps in the nature of a funeral feast to signify that she is dead to him. The remarriage of widows is permitted. A girl who is seduced by a member of the caste, even though she may be delivered of a child, may be married to him by the maimed rites used for widows. But she cannot take part in auspicious ceremonies, and her feet are not washed by married women like those of a proper bride. Even if a girl be seduced by an outsider, except a Hindu of the impure castes or a Muhammadan, she may be taken back into the community and her child will be recognised as a member of it. But they say that if a Khatīk keeps a woman of another caste he will be excommunicated until he has put her away, and his children will be known as Akre or bastard Khatīks, these being numerous in Berār. The caste burn or bury the dead as their means permit, and on the third day they place on the pyre some sugar, cakes, liquor, sweets and fruit for the use of the dead man's soul.

The occupation of the Khatīk is of course horrible to Hindu ideas, and the social position of the caste is very low. In some localities they are considered impure, and high-caste Hindus who do not eat meat will wash themselves if forced to touch a Khatīk. Elsewhere they rank just above the impure castes, but do not enter Hindu temples. These Khatīks slaughter sheep and goats and sell the flesh, but they do not cure the skins, which are generally exported to Madras. The Hindu Khatīks often refuse to slaughter animals themselves and employ a Muhammadan to do so by the rite of *halāl*. The blood is sometimes sold to Gonds, who cook and eat it mixed with grain. Other members of the caste are engaged in cultivation, or retail vegetables and grain.

1. Rājpūt origin.

Khatri.—A prominent mercantile caste of the Punjab, whose members to the number of about 5000 have settled in the Central Provinces and Berār, being distributed over most Districts. The Khatris claim to be derived from the Rājpūt caste, and say that their name is a corruption of Kshatriya. At the census of 1901 Sir Herbert Risley approved of their demand on the evidence laid before him by the leading representatives of the caste. This view is assented to by Mr. Crooke and Mr. Nesfield. In Gujarāt also the caste are known as Brahma-Kshatris, and their Rājpūt origin is considered probable, while their appearance bears out the claim to be derived either from the Aryans or some later immigrants from Central Asia: "They are a handsome fair-skinned class, some of them with blue or grey eyes, in make and appearance like Vānias (Banias), only larger and more vigorous."[1] Mr. Crooke states that, "their women have a reputation for their beauty and fair complexion. The proverb runs, 'A Khatri woman would be fair without fine clothes or ornaments,' and, 'Only an albino is fairer than a Khatri woman.'"[2] Their legend of origin is as follows: "When Parasurāma the Brāhman was slaying the Kshatriyas in revenge for the theft of the sacred cow Kāmdhenu and for the murder of his father, a pregnant Kshatriya woman took refuge in the hut of a Sāraswat Brāhman. When Parasurāma came up he asked the Brāhman who the woman was, and he said she was his daughter. Parasurāma then told him to eat with her in order to prove it, and the Brāhman ate out of the same leaf-plate as the woman. The child to whom she subsequently gave birth was the ancestor of the Khatris, and in memory of this Sāraswat Brāhmans will eat with Khatris to the present day." The Sāraswat Brāhman priests of the Khatris do as a matter of fact take *katcha* food or that cooked with water from them, and smoke from their huqqas, and this is another strong argument in favour of their origin either from Brāhmans or Rājpūts.

The classical account of the Khatris is that given in Sir George Campbell's *Ethnology of India*, and it may be reproduced here as in other descriptions of the caste:

2. Sir George Campbell's account of the Khatris.

"Trade is their main occupation; but in fact they have broader and more distinguishing features. Besides monopolising the trade of the Punjab and the greater part of Afghānistān, and doing a good deal beyond those limits, they are in the Punjab the chief civil administrators, and have almost all literate work in their hands. So far as the Sikhs have a priesthood, they are, moreover, the priests or *gurus* of the Sikhs. Both Nānak and Govind were, and the Sodis and Bedis of the present day are, Khatris. Thus then they are in fact in the Punjab, so far as a more

[1] *Bombay Gazetteer, Hindus of Gujarāt*, pp. 55, 56.
[2] *Tribes and Castes*, art. Khatri.

energetic race will permit them, all that Mahratta Brāhmins are in the Mahratta country, besides engrossing the trade which the Mahratta Brāhmins have not. They are not usually military in their character, but are quite capable of using the sword when necessary. Diwān Sāwan Mal, Governor of Multan, and his notorious successor Mūlraj, and very many of Ranjīt Singh's chief functionaries were Khatris.

"Even under Mahomedan rulers in the west they have risen to high administrative posts. There is a record of a Khatri Diwān of Badakshān or Kurdāz; and, I believe, of a Khatri Governor of Peshāwar under the Afghans. The Emperor Akbar's famous minister, Todarmal, was a Khatri; and a relative of that man of undoubted energy, the great commissariat contractor of Agra, Joti Pershād, lately informed me that he also is a Khatri. Altogether, there can be no doubt that these Khatris are one of the most acute, energetic and remarkable races in India, though in fact, except locally in the Punjab, they are not much known to Europeans. The Khatris are staunch Hindus, and it is somewhat singular that, while giving a religion and priests to the Sikhs, they themselves are comparatively seldom Sikhs. The Khatris are a very fine, fair, handsome race, and, as may be gathered from what I have already said, they are very generally educated.

"There is a large subordinate class of Khatris, somewhat lower, but of equal mercantile energy, called Rors or Roras. The proper Khatris of higher grade will often deny all connection with them, or at least only admit that they have some sort of bastard kindred with Khatris, but I think there can be no doubt that they are ethnologically the same, and they are certainly mixed up with Khatris in their avocations. I shall treat the whole kindred as generically Khatris.

"Speaking of the Khatris then thus broadly, they have, as I have said, the whole trade of the Punjab and of most of Afghānistān. No village can get on without the Khatri who keeps the accounts, does the banking business, and buys and sells the grain. They seem, too, to get on with the people better than most traders and usurers of this kind. In Afghānistān, among a rough and alien people, the Khatris are as a rule confined to the position of humble dealers, shopkeepers and moneylenders; but in that capacity the Pathāns seem to look on them as a kind of valuable animal, and a Pathān will steal another man's Khatri, not only for the sake of ransom, as is frequently done on the frontier of Peshāwar and Hazāra, but also as he might steal a milch-cow, or as Jews might, I dare say, be carried off in the Middle Ages with a view to render them profitable.

"I do not know the exact limits of Khatri occupation to the West, but certainly in all Eastern Afghānistān they seem to be just as much a part of the established community as they are in the Punjab. They find their way far into Central Asia, but the further they get the more depressed and humiliating is their position. In Turkistan, Vambéry speaks of them with great contempt, as yellow-faced Hindus of a cowardly and sneaking character. Under Turcoman rule they could hardly be otherwise. They are the only Hindus known in Central Asia. In the Punjab they are so numerous that they cannot all be rich and mercantile; and many of them hold land, cultivate, take service, and follow various avocations."

3. Higher and lower groups.

The Khatris have a very complicated system of sub-divisions, which it is not necessary to detail here in view of their small strength in the Province. As a rule they marry only one wife, though a second may be taken for the purpose of getting offspring. But parents are very reluctant to give their daughters to a man who is already married. The re-marriage of widows is forbidden and divorce also is not recognised, but an unfaithful wife may be turned out of the house and expelled from the caste. Though they practise monogamy, however, the Khatris place no restrictions on the keeping of concubines, and from the offspring of such women inferior branches of the caste have grown up. In Gujarāt these are known as the Dasa and Pancha groups, and they may not eat or intermarry with proper Khatris.[1] The name Khatri seems there to be restricted to these inferior groups, while the caste proper is called Brahma-Kshatri. There is also a marked distinction in their occupation, for, while the Brahma-Kshatris are hereditary District

[1] *Bombay Gazetteer, Hindus of Gujarāt*, p. 55.

officials, pleaders, bankers and Government servants, the Khatris are engaged in weaving, and formerly prepared the fine cotton cloth of Surat and Broach, while they also make gold and silver thread, and the lace used for embroidery.[1] As a class they are said to be thriftless and idle, and at least the Khatris of Surat to be excessively fond of strong drink. The Khatris of Nimār in the Central Provinces are also weavers, and it seems not unlikely that they may be a branch of these Gujarāt Khatris of the inferior class, and that the well-known gold and silver lace and embroidery industry of Burhānpur may have been introduced by them from Surat. The Khatris of Narsinghpur are dyers, and may not improbably be connected with the Nimār weavers. The other Khatris scattered here and there over the Provinces may belong to the higher branch of the caste.

4. Marriage and funeral customs.

In conclusion some extracts may be given from the interesting account of the marriage and funeral customs of the Brahma-Kshatris in Gujarāt:[2] "On the wedding-day shortly before the marriage hour the bridegroom, his face covered with flower-garlands and wearing a long tunic and a yellow silk waistcloth, escorted by the women of his family, goes to the bride's house on horseback in procession. . . . Before the bridegroom's party arrive the bride, dressed in a head-cloth, bodice, a red robe, and loose yellow Muhammadan trousers, is seated in a closed palanquin or *balai* set in front of the house. The bridegroom on dismounting walks seven times round the palanquin, the bride's brother at each turn giving him a cut with an oleander twig, and the women of the family throwing showers of cake from the windows. He retires, and while mounting his horse, and before he is in the saddle, the bride's father comes out, and, giving him a present, leads him into the marriage-hall. . . . The girl keeps her eyes closed throughout the whole day, not opening them until the bridegroom is ushered into the marriage-booth, so that the first object she sees is her intended husband. On the first Monday, Thursday or Friday after the marriage the bride is hid either in her own or in a neighbour's house. The bridegroom comes in state,

[1] *Bombay Gazetteer, Hindus of Gujarāt*, p. 189.

[2] *Ibidem*, pp. 58, 59.

and with the point of his sword touches the outer doors of seven houses, and then begins to search for his wife. The time is one of much fun and merriment, the women of the house bantering and taunting the bridegroom, especially when he is long in finding his wife's hiding-place. When she is found the bridegroom leads the bride to the marriage-hall, and they sit there combing each other's hair."

In connection with their funeral ceremonies Mr. Bhīmbhai Kirpārām gives the following particulars of the custom of beating the breasts:[1] "Contrary to the Gujarāt practice of beating only the breast, the Brahma-Kshatri women beat the forehead, breast and knees. For thirteen days after a death women weep and beat their breasts thrice a day, at morning, noon and evening. Afterwards they weep and beat their breasts every evening till a year has passed, not even excepting Sundays, Tuesdays or Hindu holidays. During this year of mourning the female relations of the deceased used to eat nothing but millet-bread and pulse; but this custom is gradually being given up."

Khojāh.[2]—A small Muhammadan sect of traders belonging to Gujarāt, who retain some Hindu practices. They reside in Wardha, Nāgpur and the Berār Districts, and numbered about 500 persons in 1911 as against 300 in 1901. The Khojāhs are Muhammadans of the Shia sect, and their ancestors were converted Hindus of the Lohāna trading caste of Sind, who are probably akin to the Khatris. As shown in the article on Cutchi, the Cutchi or Meman traders are also converted Lohānas. The name Khojāh is a corruption of the Turkish Khwājah, Lord, and this is supposed to be a Muhammadan equivalent for the title Thākur or Thakkar applied to the Lohānas. The Khojāhs belong to the Nazārian branch of the Egyptian Ismailia sect, and the founder of this sect in Persia was Hasan Sabāh, who lived at the beginning of the eleventh century and founded the order of the Fidawis or devotees, who were the Assassins of the Crusades. Hasan subsequently threw off

1 *Hindus of Gujarāt*, pp. 58, 59.

2 This article consists mainly of extracts from Mr. F. L. Farīdi's full account of the Khojāhs in the *Bombay Gazetteer*, *Muhammadans of Gujarāt*.

his allegiance to the Egyptian Caliph and made himself the head of his own sect with the title of Shaikh-ul-Jabal or Lord. He was known to the Crusaders as the 'Old Man of the Mountain.' His third successor Hasan (A.D. 1163) declared himself to be the unrevealed Imām and preached that no action of a believer in him could be a sin. It is through this Hasan that His Highness the Aga Khān traces his descent from Ali. Subsequently emissaries of the sect came to India, and one Pīr Sadr-ud-dīn converted the Lohānas. According to one account this man was a Hindu slave of Imām Hasan. Sadr-ud-dīn preached that his master Hasan was the Nishkalanki or tenth incarnation of Vishnu. The Adam of the Semitic story of the creation was identified with the Hindu deity Vishnu, the Prophet Muhammad with Siva, and the first five Imāms of Ismailia with the five Pāndava brothers. By this means the new faith was made more acceptable to the Lohānas. In 1845 Aga Shāh Hasan Ali, the Ismailia unrevealed Imām, came and settled in India, and his successor is His Highness the Aga Khān.

The Khojāhs retain some Hindu customs. Boys have their ears bored and a lock of hair is left on a child's head to be shaved and offered at some shrine. Circumcision and the wearing of a beard are optional. They do not have mosques, but meet to pray at a lodge called the Jama'at Khāna. They repeat the names of their Pīrs or saints on a rosary made of 101 beads of clay from Karbala, the scene of the death of Hasan and Husain. At their marriages, deaths and on every new-moon day, contributions are levied which are sent to His Highness the Aga Khān. "A remarkable feature at a Khojāh's death," Mr. Farīdi states, "is the *samarchhanta* or Holy Drop. The Jama'at officer asks the dying Khojāh whether he wishes for the Holy Drop, and if the latter agrees he must bequeath Rs. 5 to Rs. 500 to the Jama'at. The officer dilutes a cake of Karbala clay in water and moistens the lips of the dying man with it, sprinkling the remainder over his face, neck and chest. The touch of the Holy Drop is believed to save the departing soul from the temptation of the Arch-Fiend, and to remove the death-agony as completely as among the Sunnis does the recital at a death-bed of the chapter of the Korān known as the Sūrah-i-Yā-sīn. If the dead man is old and grey-haired the hair after death is dyed with henna. A garland of cakes of Karbala clay is tied round the neck of the corpse. If the body is to be buried locally two small circular patches of silk cloth cut from the covering of Husain's tomb, called *chashmah* or spectacles, are laid over the eyes. Those Khojāhs who can afford it have their bodies placed in air-tight coffins and transported to the field of Karbala in Persia to be buried there. The bodies are taken by steamer to Bāghdād, and thence by camel to Karbala.

"The Khojāhs are keen and enterprising traders, and are great travellers by land and sea, visiting and settling in distant countries for purposes of trade. They have business connections with Ceylon, Burma, Singapore, China and Japan, and with ports of the Persian Gulf, Arabia and East Africa. Khojāh boys go as apprentices in foreign Khojāh firms on salaries of Rs. 200 to Rs. 2000 a year with board and lodging."

KHOND[1]

[The principal authorities on the Khonds are Sir H. Risley's *Tribes and Castes of Bengal*, Major-General Campbell's *Wild Tribes of Khondistān*, and Major MacPherson's *Report on the Khonds of the Districts of Ganjām and Cuttack* (Reprint, Madras Scottish United Press, 1863). When the inquiries leading up to these volumes were undertaken, the Central Provinces contained a large body of the tribe, but the bulk of these have passed to Bihār and Orissa with the transfer of the Kālāhandi and Patna States and the Sambalpur District. Nevertheless, as information of interest had been collected, it has been thought desirable to reproduce it, and Sir James Frazer's description of the human sacrifices formerly in vogue has been added. Much of the original information contained in this article was furnished by Mr. Panda Baijnāth, Extra Assistant Commissioner, when Dīwān of Patna State. Papers were also contributed by Rai Sāhib Dīnbandhu Patnāik, Dīwān of Sonpur, Mr. Miān Bhai, Extra Assistant Commissioner, Sambalpur, and Mr. Chāru Chandra Ghose, Deputy Inspector of Schools, Kālāhandi.]

LIST OF PARAGRAPHS

1. Traditions of the tribe.

Khond, Kandh.[1]—A Dravidian tribe found in the Uriya-speaking tract of the Sambalpur District and the adjoining Feudatory States of Patna and Kālāhandi, which up to 1905 were included in the Central Provinces, but now belong to Bihār and Orissa. The Province formerly contained 168,000 Khonds, but the number has been reduced to about 10,000, residing mainly in the Khariār zamīndāri to the south-east of the Raipur District and the Sārangarh State. The tract inhabited by the Khonds was known generally as the Kondhān. The tribe call themselves Kuiloka, or

[1] Kandh is the Uriya spelling, and Kond or Khond that of the Telugus.

Kuienju, which may possibly be derived from *ko* or *kū*, a Telugu word for a mountain.[1] Their own traditions as to their origin are of little historical value, but they were almost certainly at one time the rulers of the country in which they now reside. It was the custom until recently for the Rāja of Kālāhandi to sit on the lap of a Khond on his accession while he received the oaths of fealty. The man who held the Rāja was the eldest member of a particular family, residing in the village of Gugsai Patna, and had the title of Patnaji. The coronation of a new Rāja took place in this village, to which all the chiefs repaired. The Patnaji would be seated on a large rock, richly dressed, with a cloth over his knees on which the Rāja sat. The Dīwān or minister then tied the turban of state on the Rāja's head, while all the other chiefs present held the ends of the cloth. The ceremony fell into abeyance when Raghu Kesari Deo was made Rāja on the deposition of his predecessor for misconduct, as the Patnaji refused to install a second Rāja, while one previously consecrated by him was still living. The Rāja was also accustomed to marry a Khond girl as one of his wives, though latterly he did not allow her to live in the palace. These customs have lately been abandoned; they may probably be interpreted as a recognition that the Rājas of Kālāhandi derived their rights from the Khonds. Many of the zamīndāri estates of Kālāhandi and Sonpur are still held by members of the tribe.

2. Tribal divisions. There is no strict endogamy within the Khond tribe. It has two main divisions: the Kutia Khonds who are hillmen and retain their primitive tribal customs, and the plain-dwelling Khonds who have acquired a tincture of Hinduism. The Kutia or hill Khonds are said to be so called because they break the skulls of animals when they kill them for food; the word *kutia* meaning one who breaks or smashes. The plain-dwelling Khonds have a number of subdivisions which are supposed to be endogamous, though the rule is not strictly observed. Among these the Rāj Khonds are the highest, and are usually landed proprietors. A man, however, is not considered to be a Rāj Khond unless he

[1] *Linguistic Survey of India.*

possesses some land, and if a Rāj Khond takes a bride from another group he descends to it. A similar rule applies among some of the other groups, a man being relegated to his wife's division when he marries into one which is lower than his own. The Dal Khonds may probably have been soldiers, the word *dal* meaning an army. They are also known as Adi Kandh or the superior Khonds, and as Bālūsudia or 'Shaven.' At present they usually hold the honourable position of village priest, and have to a certain extent adopted Hindu usages, refusing to eat fowls or buffaloes, and offering the leaves of the *tulsi* (basil) to their deities. The Kandhanas are so called because they grow turmeric, which is considered rather a low thing to do, and the Pākhia because they eat the flesh of the *por* or buffalo. The Gauria are graziers, and the Nāgla or naked ones apparently take their name from their paucity of clothing. The Utār or Satbhuiyān are a degraded group, probably of illegitimate descent; for the other Khonds will take daughters from them, but will not give their daughters to them.

3. Exogamous septs.

Traditionally the Khonds have thirty-two exogamous septs, but the number has now increased. All the members of one sept live in the same locality about some central village. Thus the Tūpa sept are collected round the village of Teplagarh in the Patna State, the Loa sept round Sindhekala, the Borga sept round Bangomunda, and so on. The names of the septs are derived either from the names of villages or from titles or nicknames. Each sept is further divided into a number of subsepts whose names are of a totemistic nature, being derived from animals, plants or natural objects. Instances of these are Bachhās calf, Chhatra umbrella, Hikoka horse, Kelka the kingfisher, Konjaka the monkey, Mandinga an earthen pot, and so on. It is a very curious fact that while the names of the septs appear to belong to the Khond language, those of the subsepts are all Uriya words, and this affords some ground for the supposition that they are more recent than the septs, an opinion to which Sir H. Risley inclines. On the other hand, the fact that the subsepts have totemistic names appears difficult of explanation under this hypothesis.

Members of the subsept regard the animal or plant after which it is named as sacred. Those of the Kadam group will not stand under the tree of that name. Those of the Narsingha[1] sept will not kill a tiger or eat the meat of any animal wounded or killed by this animal. The same subsept will be found in several different septs, and a man may not marry a woman belonging either to the same sept or subsept as his own. But kinship through females is disregarded, and he may take his maternal uncle's daughter to wife, and in Kālāhandi is not debarred from wedding his mother's sister.[2]

4. Marriage.

Marriage is adult and a large price, varying from 12 to 20 head of cattle, was formerly demanded for the bride. This has now, however, been reduced in some localities to two or three animals and a rupee each in lieu of the others, or cattle may be entirely dispensed with and some grain given. If a man cannot afford to purchase a bride he may serve his father-in-law for seven years as the condition of obtaining her. A proposal for marriage is made by placing a brass cup and three arrows at the door of the girl's father. He will remove these once to show his reluctance, and they will be again replaced. If he removes them a second time, it signifies his definite refusal of the match, but if he allows them to remain, the bridegroom's friends go to him and say, 'We have noticed a beautiful flower in passing through your village and desire to pluck it.' The wedding procession goes from the bride's to the bridegroom's house as among the Gonds; this custom, as remarked by Mr. Bell, is not improbably a survival of marriage by capture, when the husband carried off his wife and married her at his own house. At the marriage the bride and bridegroom come out, each sitting on the shoulders of one of their relatives. The bridegroom pulls the bride to his side, when a piece of cloth is thrown over them, and they are tied together with a string of new yarn wound round them seven times. A cock is sacrificed, and the cheeks of the couple are singed with burnt bread. They pass the night in a veranda, and

[1] Narsingha means a man-lion and is one of Vishnu's incarnations; this subsept would seem, therefore, to have been formed since the Khonds adopted Hinduism.

[2] In Orissa, however, relationship through females is a bar to marriage, as recorded in Sir H. Risley's article.

next day are taken to a tank, the bridegroom being armed with a bow and arrows. He shoots one through each of seven cowdung cakes, the bride after each shot washing his forehead and giving him a green twig for a tooth-brush and some sweets. This is symbolical of their future course of life, when the husband will procure food by hunting, while the wife will wait on him and prepare his food. Sexual intercourse before marriage between a man and girl of the tribe is condoned so long as they are not within the prohibited degrees of relationship, and in Kālāhandi such *liaisons* are a matter of ordinary occurrence. If a girl is seduced by one man and subsequently married to another, the first lover usually pays the husband a sum of seven to twelve rupees as compensation. In Sambalpur a girl may choose her own husband, and the couple commonly form an intimacy while engaged in agricultural work. Such unions are known as *Udhlia* or 'Love in the fields.' If the parents raise any objection to the match the couple elope and return as man and wife, when they have to give a feast to the caste, and if the girl was previously betrothed to another man the husband must pay him compensation. In the last case the union is called *Paisa moli* or marriage by purchase. A trace of fraternal polyandry survives in the custom by which the younger brothers are allowed access to the elder brother's wife till the time of their own marriage. Widow-marriage and divorce are recognised.

5. Customs at birth.

For one day after a child has been born the mother is allowed no food. On the sixth day she herself shaves the child's head and bites his nails short with her teeth, after which she takes a bow and arrows and stands with the child facing successively to the four points of the compass. The idea of this is to make the child a skilful hunter when he grows up. Children are named in their fifth or sixth year. Names are sometimes given after some personal peculiarity, as Lammudia, long-headed, or Khanja, one having six fingers; or after some circumstance of the birth, as Ghosian, in compliment to the Ghasia (grass-cutter) woman who acts as midwife; Jugi, because some holy mendicant (Yogi) was halting in the village when the child was born; or a child may be named after the day of the week or month on which it was born. The tribe believe that the souls of the departed are born again as children, and boys have on occasion been named Majhiān Budhi or the old head-woman, whom they suppose to have been born again with a change of sex. Major Macpherson observed the same belief:[1] "To determine the best name for the child, the priest drops grains of rice into a cup of water, naming with each grain a deceased ancestor. He pronounces, from the movements of the seed in the fluid, and from observations made on the person of the infant, which of his progenitors has reappeared in him, and the child generally, but not uniformly, receives the name of that ancestor." When the children are named, they are made to ride a goat or a pig, as a mark of respect, it is said, to the ancestor who has been reborn in them. Names usually recur after the third generation.

6. Disposal of the dead. The dead are buried as a rule, but the practice of cremating the bodies of adults is increasing. When a body is buried a rupee or a copper coin is tied in the sheet, so that the deceased may not go penniless to the other world. Sometimes the dead man's clothes and bows and arrows are buried with him. On the tenth day the soul is brought back. Outside the village, where two roads meet, rice is offered to a cock, and if it eats, this is a sign that the soul has come. The soul is then asked to ride on a bowstick covered with cloth, and is brought to the house and placed in a corner with those of other relatives. The souls are fed annually with rice on the harvest and Dasahra festivals. In Sambalpur a ball of powdered rice is placed under a tree with a lamp near it, and the first insect that settles on the ball is taken to be the soul, and is brought home and worshipped. The souls of infants who die before the umbilical cord has dropped are not brought back, because they are considered to have scarcely come into existence; and Sir E. Gait records that one of the causes of female infanticide was the belief that the souls of girl-children thus killed would not be born again, and hence the number of future female births would decrease. This belief partially conflicts with that of the change of sex on rebirth mentioned above; but the two might very well exist together. The

[1] *Report on the Khonds*, p. 56.

souls of women who die during pregnancy or after a miscarriage, or during the monthly period of impurity are also not brought back, no doubt because they are held to be malignant spirits.

7. Occupation. The Khond traditionally despises all occupations except those of husbandry, hunting and war. "In Orissa," Sir H. Risley states, "they claim full rights of property in the soil in virtue of having cleared the jungle and prepared the land for cultivation. In some villages individual ownership is unknown, and the land is cultivated on a system of temporary occupation subject to periodical redistribution under the orders of the headman or *mālik*." Like the other forest tribes they are improvident and fond of drink.

Macpherson [1] described the Khonds as faithful to friends, devoted to their chiefs, resolute, brave, hospitable and laborious; but these high qualities meet with no recognition among the Uriya Hindus, who regard their stupidity as the salient attribute of the Khonds and have various tales in derision of them, like those told of the weavers. They consider the Khonds as only a little superior to the impure Doms (musicians and sweepers), and say, '*Kandh ghare Domna Mantri*,' or 'In a Kandh house the Dom is Prime Minister.' This is paralleled by the similar relation between the Gonds and Pardhāns. The arms of the Khonds were a light, long-handled sword with a blade very curiously carved, the bow and arrow and the sling—no shields being used. The axe also was used with both hands, to strike and guard, its handle being partly defended by brass plates and wire for the latter purpose. The following description of a battle between rival Khond clans was recorded by Major Macpherson as having been given to him by an eye-witness, and may be reproduced for its intrinsic interest; the fight was between the hostile tribes of Bora Mūta and Bora Des in the Gumsur territory:

8. A Khond combat. "At about 12 o'clock in the day the people of Bora Des began to advance in a mass across the Sālki river, the boundary between the Districts, into the plain of Kurmīngia, where a much smaller force was arrayed to oppose them. The combatants were protected from the neck to the loins

[1] *Report*, p. 59.

by skins, and cloth was wound round their legs down to the heel, but the arms were quite bare. Round the heads of many, too, cloth was wound, and for distinction the people of Bora Mūta wore peacock's feathers in their hair, while those of Bora Des had cock's tail plumes. They advanced with horns blowing, and the gongs beat when they passed a village. The women followed behind carrying pots of water and food for refreshments, and the old men who were past bearing arms were there, giving advice and encouragement. As the adverse parties approached, showers of stones, handed by the women, flew from slings from either side, and when they came within range arrows came in flights and many fell back wounded. At length single combats sprang up betwixt individuals who advanced before the rest, and when the first man fell all rushed to dip their axes in his blood, and hacked the body to pieces. The first man who himself unwounded slew his opponent, struck off the latter's right arm and rushed with it to the priest in the rear, who bore it off as an offering to Loha Pennu (the Iron God or the God of Arms) in his grove. The right arms of the rest who fell were cut off in like manner and heaped in the rear beside the women, and to them the wounded were carried for care, and the fatigued men constantly retired for water. The conflict was at length general. All were engaged hand-to-hand, and now fought fiercely, now paused by common consent for a moment's breathing. In the end the men of Bora Des, although superior in numbers, began to give way, and before four o'clock they were driven across the Sālki, leaving sixty men dead on the field, while the killed on the side of the Bora Mūta did not exceed thirty. And from the entire ignorance of the Khonds of the simplest healing processes, at least an equal number of the wounded died after the battle. The right hands of the slain were hung up by both parties on the trees of the villages and the dead were carried off to be burned. The people of Bora Des the next morning flung a piece of bloody cloth on the field of battle, a challenge to renew the conflict which was quickly accepted, and so the contest was kept up for three days." The above account could, of course, find no place in a description of the Khonds of this generation, but has been thought worthy of quotation, as detailed descriptions of the manner of fighting of these tribes, now weaned from war by the British Government, are so rarely to be found.

9. Social customs. The Khonds will admit into the community a male orphan child of any superior caste, including the Binjhwārs and Gonds. A virgin of any age of one of these castes will also be admitted. A Gond man who takes a Khond girl to wife can become a Khond by giving a feast. As might be expected the tribe are closely connected with the Gaurs or Uriya shepherds, whose business leads them to frequent the forests. Either a man or woman of the Gaurs can be taken into the community on marrying a Khond, and if a Khond girl marries a Gaur her children, though not herself, can become members of that caste. The Khonds will eat all kinds of animals, including rats, snakes and lizards, but with the exception of the Kutia Khonds they have now given up beef. In Kālāhandi social delinquencies are punished by a fine of so many field-mice, which the Khond considers a great delicacy. The catching of twenty to forty field-mice to liquidate the fine imposes on the culprit a large amount of trouble and labour, and when his task is completed his friends and neighbours fry the mice and have a feast with plenty of liquor, but he himself is not allowed to participate. Khond women are profusely tattooed with figures of trees, flowers, fishes, crocodiles, lizards and scorpions on the calf of the leg and the arms, hands and chest, but seldom on the face. This is done for purposes of ornament. Husband and wife do not mention each other's names, and a woman may not speak the names of any of her husband's younger brothers, as, if left a widow, she might subsequently have to marry one of them. A paternal or maternal aunt may not name her nephew, nor a man his younger brother's wife.

10. Festivals. The tribe have three principal festivals, known as the Semi Jātra, the Māhul Jātra and the Chāwal Dhūba Jātra. The Semi Jātra is held on the tenth day of the waning moon of Aghan (November) when the new *semi* or country beans are roasted, a goat or fowl is sacrificed, and some milk or water is offered to the earth god. From this day the tribe commence eating the new crop of beans. Similarly the Māhul Jātra is held on the tenth of the waning

moon of Chait (March), and until this date a Khond may eat boiled mahua flowers, but not roasted ones. The principal festival is the Dasahra or Chāwal Dhūba (boiled rice) on the tenth day of the waning moon of Kunwār (September), which, in the case of the Khonds, marks the rice-harvest. The new rice is washed and boiled and offered to the earth god with the same accompaniment as in the case of the Semi Jātra, and until this date the Khond may not clean the new rice by washing it before being boiled, though he apparently may partake of it so long as it is not washed or cleaned, this rule and that regarding the mahua flowers being so made as concessions to convenience.

The Khond pantheon consists of eighty-four gods, of whom Dharni Deota, the earth god, is the chief. In former times the earth goddess was apparently female and was known as Tāri Pennu or Bera Pennu. To her were offered the terrible human sacrifices presently to be described. There is nothing surprising in the change of sex of the divine being, for which parallels are forthcoming. Thus in Chhattīsgarh the deity of the earth, who also received human sacrifices, is either Thākur Deo, a god, or Thakurāni Mai, a goddess. Deota is an Aryan term, and the proper Khond name for a god is Pennu. The earth god is usually accompanied by Bhātbarsi Deota, the god of hunting. Dharni Deota is represented by a rectangular peg of wood driven into the ground, while Bhātbarsi has a place at his feet in the shape of a piece of conglomerate stone covered with circular granules. Once in four or five years a buffalo is offered to the earth god, in lieu of the human sacrifice which was formerly in vogue. The animal is predestined for sacrifice from its birth, and is allowed to wander loose and graze on the crops at its will. The stone representing Bhātbarsi is examined periodically, and when the granules on it appear to have increased, it is decided that the time has come for the sacrifice. In Kālāhandi a lamb is sacrificed every year, and strips of its flesh distributed to all the villagers, who bury it in their fields as a divine agent of fertilisation, in the same way as the flesh of the human victim was formerly buried. The Khond worships his bow and arrows before he goes out hunting, and believes that every hill and valley has its

11. Religion.

separate deity, who must be propitiated with the promise of a sacrifice before his territory is entered, or he will hide the animals within it from the hunter, and enable them to escape when wounded. These deities are closely related to each other, and it is important when arranging for an expedition to know the connection between them all; this information can be obtained from any one on whom the divine afflatus from time to time descends.

12. Human sacrifice. The following account of the well-known system of human sacrifice, formerly in vogue among the Khonds, is contained in Sir James Frazer's *Golden Bough*, having been compiled by him from the accounts of Major Macpherson and Major-General John Campbell, two of the officers deputed to suppress it:

"The best known case of human sacrifices systematically offered to ensure good crops is supplied by the Khonds or Kandhs, another Dravidian race in Bengal. Our knowledge of them is derived from the accounts written by British officers who, forty or fifty years ago, were engaged in putting them down. The sacrifices were offered to the Earth-Goddess, Tāri Pennu or Bera Pennu, and were believed to ensure good crops and immunity from all disease and accidents. In particular they were considered necessary in the cultivation of turmeric, the Khonds arguing that the turmeric could not have a deep red colour without the shedding of blood. The victim or Meriāh was acceptable to the goddess only if he had been purchased, or had been born a victim—that is the son of a victim father—or had been devoted as a child by his father or guardian. Khonds in distress often sold their children for victims, 'considering the beatification of their souls certain, and their death, for the benefit of mankind, the most honourable possible.' A man of the Panua (Pān) tribe was once seen to load a Khond with curses, and finally to spit in his face, because the Khond had sold for a victim his own child, whom the Panua had wished to marry. A party of Khonds, who saw this, immediately pressed forward to comfort the seller of his child, saying, 'Your child has died that all the world may live, and the Earth-Goddess herself will wipe that spittle from your face.' The victims were often kept for years before they were sacrificed. Being regarded as consecrated beings, they were treated with extreme affection, mingled with deference, and were welcomed wherever they went. A Meriāh youth, on attaining maturity, was generally given a wife, who was herself usually a Meriāh or victim, and with her he received a portion of land and farm-stock. Their offspring were also victims. Human sacrifices were offered to the Earth-Goddess by tribes, branches of tribes, or villages, both at periodical festivals and on extraordinary occasions. The periodical sacrifices were generally so arranged by tribes and divisions of tribes that each head of a family was enabled, at least once a year, to procure a shred of flesh for his fields, generally about the time when his chief crop was laid down. The mode of performing these tribal sacrifices was as follows. Ten or twelve days before the sacrifice, the victim was devoted by cutting off his hair, which, until then, had been kept unshorn. Crowds of men and women assembled to witness the sacrifice; none might be excluded, since the sacrifice was declared to be for all mankind. It was preceded by several days of wild revelry and gross debauchery. On the day before the sacrifice the victim, dressed in a new garment, was led forth from the village in solemn procession, with music and dancing, to the Meriāh grove, a clump of high forest trees standing a little way from the village and untouched by the axe. Here they tied him to a post, which was sometimes placed between two plants of the *sankissār* shrub. He was then anointed with oil, ghee and turmeric, and adorned with flowers; and 'a species of reverence, which it is not easy to distinguish from adoration,' was paid to him throughout the day. A great struggle now arose to obtain the smallest relic from his person; a particle of the turmeric paste with which he was smeared, or a drop of his spittle, was esteemed of sovereign virtue, especially by the women. The crowd danced round the post to music, and addressing the Earth said, 'O God, we offer this sacrifice to you; give us good crops, seasons, and health.'

"On the last morning the orgies, which had been scarcely interrupted during the night, were resumed and coutinued till noon, when they ceased, and the assembly proceeded to consummate the sacrifice. The victim was again anointed with oil, and each person touched the anointed part, and wiped the oil on his own head. In some places they took the victim in procession round the village, from door to door, where some plucked hair from his head, and others begged for a drop of his spittle, with which they anointed their heads. As the victim might not be bound nor make any show of resistance, the bones of his arms and, if necessary, his legs were broken; but often this precaution was rendered unnecessary by stupefying him with opium. The mode of putting him to death varied in different places. One of the commonest modes seems to have been strangulation, or squeezing to death. The branch of a green tree was cleft several feet down the middle; the victim's neck (in other places, his chest) was inserted in the cleft, which the priest, aided by his assistants, strove with all his force to close. Then he wounded the victim slightly with his axe, whereupon the crowd rushed at the wretch and cut the flesh from the bones, leaving the head and bowels untouched. Sometimes he was cut up alive. In Chinna Kimedy he was dragged along the fields, surrounded by the crowd, who, avoiding his head and intestines, hacked the flesh from his body with their knives till he died. Another very common mode of sacrifice in the same district was to fasten the victim to the proboscis of a wooden elephant, which revolved on a stout post, and, as it whirled round, the crowd cut the flesh from the victim while life remained. In some villages Major Campbell found as many as fourteen of these wooden elephants, which had been used at sacrifices.[1] In one district the victim was put to death slowly by fire. A low stage was formed, sloping on either side like a roof; upon it they laid the victim, his limbs wound round with cords to confine his struggles. Fires were then lighted and hot brands applied, to make him roll up and down the

[1] Sir H. Risley notes that the elephant represented the earth-goddess herself, who was here conceived in elephant form. In the hill tracts of Gumsur she was represented in peacock form, and the post to which the victim was bound bore the effigy of a peacock. Macpherson also records that when the Khonds attacked the victim they shouted, 'No sin rests on us; we have bought you with a price.'

slopes of the stage as long as possible; for the more tears he shed the more abundant would be the supply of rain. Next day the body was cut to pieces.

"The flesh cut from the victim was instantly taken home by the persons who had been deputed by each village to bring it. To secure its rapid arrival it was sometimes forwarded by relays of men, and conveyed with postal fleetness fifty or sixty miles. In each village all who stayed at home fasted rigidly until the flesh arrived. The bearer deposited it in the place of public assembly, where it was received by the priest and the heads of families. The priest divided it into two portions, one of which he offered to the Earth-Goddess by burying it in a hole in the ground with his back turned, and without looking. Then each man added a little earth to bury it, and the priest poured water on the spot from a hill gourd. The other portion of flesh he divided into as many shares as there were heads of houses present. Each head of a house rolled his shred of flesh in leaves and buried it in his favourite field, placing it in the earth behind his back without looking. In some places each man carried his portion of flesh to the stream which watered his fields, and there hung it on a pole. For three days thereafter no house was swept; and, in one district, strict silence was observed, no fire might be given out, no wood cut, and no strangers received. The remains of the human victim (namely, the head, bowels and bones) were watched by strong parties the night after the sacrifice, and next morning they were burned along with a whole sheep, on a funeral pile. The ashes were scattered over the fields, laid as paste over the houses and granaries, or mixed with the new corn to preserve it from insects. Sometimes, however, the head and bones were buried, not burnt. After the suppression of the human sacrifices, inferior victims were substituted in some places; for instance, in the capital of Chinna Kimedy a goat took the place of a human victim.

"In these Khond sacrifices the Meriāhs are represented by our authorities as victims offered to propitiate the Earth-Goddess. But from the treatment of the victims both before and after death it appears that the custom cannot be explained as merely a propitiatory sacrifice. A part of the flesh certainly was offered to the Earth-Goddess, but the rest of the flesh was buried by each householder in his fields, and the ashes of the other parts of the body were scattered over the fields, laid as paste on the granaries, or mixed with the new corn. These latter customs imply that to the body of the Meriāh there was ascribed a direct or intrinsic power of making the crops to grow, quite independent of the indirect efficacy which it might have as an offering to secure the good-will of the deity. In other words, the flesh and ashes of the victim were believed to be endowed with a magical or physical power of fertilising the land. The same intrinsic power was ascribed to the blood and tears of the Meriāh, his blood causing the redness of the turmeric, and his tears producing rain; for it can hardly be doubted that, originally at least, the tears were supposed to bring down the rain, not merely to prognosticate it. Similarly the custom of pouring water on the buried flesh of the Meriāh was no doubt a rain-charm. Again, magical power as an attribute of the Meriāh appears in the sovereign virtue believed to reside in anything that came from his person, as his hair or spittle. The ascription of such power to the Meriāh indicates that he was much more than a mere man sacrificed to propitiate a deity. Once more, the extreme reverence paid him points to the same conclusion. Major Campbell speaks of the Meriāh as 'being regarded as something more than mortal,' and Major Macpherson says: 'A species of reverence, which it is not easy to distinguish from adoration, is paid to him.' In short, the Meriāh appears to have been regarded as divine. As such, he may originally have represented the Earth-Goddess, or perhaps a deity of vegetation, though in later times he came to be regarded rather as a victim offered to a deity than as himself an incarnate god. This later view of the Meriāh as a victim rather than a divinity may perhaps have received undue emphasis from the European writers who have described the Khond religion. Habituated to the later idea of sacrifice as an offering made to a god for the purpose of conciliating his favour, European observers are apt to interpret all religious slaughter in this sense, and to suppose that wherever such slaughter takes place, there must necessarily be a deity to whom the carnage is believed by the slayers to be acceptable. Thus their preconceived ideas unconsciously colour and warp their descriptions of savage rites."[1]

In his *Ethnographic Notes in Southern India* Mr. Thurston states:[2] "The last recorded Meriāh sacrifice in the Ganjam Māliāhs occurred in 1852, and there are still Khonds alive who were present at it. Twenty-five descendants of persons who were reserved for sacrifice, but were rescued by Government officers, returned themselves as Meriāh at the Census of 1901. The Khonds have now substituted a buffalo for a human being. The animal is hewn to pieces while alive, and the villagers rush home to their villages to bury the flesh in the soil, and so secure prosperous crops. The sacrifice is not unaccompanied by risk to the performers, as the buffalo, before dying, frequently kills one or more of its tormentors. It was stated by the officers of the Māliāh Agency that there was reason to believe that the Rāja of Jaipur (Madras), when he was installed at his father's decease in 1860–61, sacrificed a girl thirteen years of age at the shrine of the Goddess Durga in the town of Jaipur. The last attempted human sacrifice (which was nearly successful) in the Vizagāpatam District, among the Kutia Khonds, was, I believe, in 1880. But the memory of the abandoned practice is kept green by one of the Khond songs, for a translation of which we are indebted to Mr. J. E. Friend-Pereira:[3] 13. Last human sacrifices.

At the time of the great Kiābon (Campbell) Sāhib's coming, the country was in darkness; it was enveloped in mist.
Having sent pāiks to collect the people of the land, they, having surrounded them, caught the Meriāh sacrificers.
Having caught the Meriāh sacrificers, they brought them; and again they went and seized the evil councillors.
Having seen the chains and shackles, the people were afraid; murder and bloodshed were quelled.
Then the land became beautiful; and a certain Mokodella (Macpherson) Sāhib came.
He destroyed the lairs of the tigers and bears in the hills and rocks, and taught wisdom to the people.

---

[1] *Golden Bough*, 2nd ed. vol. ii. p. 241 *sq*.

[2] Pages 517-519. Published 1906.

[3] *Journal, A. S. of Bengal*, 1898.

After the lapse of a month he built bungalows and schools; and he advised them to learn reading and law.
They learnt wisdom and reading; they acquired silver and gold. Then all the people became wealthy.

14. Khond rising in 1882.

In 1882 an armed rising of the Khonds of the Kālāhandi State occurred as a result of agrarian trouble. The Feudatory Chief had encouraged the settlement in the State of members of the Kolta caste who are excellent cultivators and keenly acquisitive of land. They soon got the Khonds heavily indebted to them for loans of food and seed-grain, and began to oust them from their villages. The Khonds, recognising with some justice that this process was likely to end in their total expropriation from the soil, concerted a conspiracy, and in May 1882 rose and murdered the Koltas of a number of villages. The signal for the outbreak was given by passing a knotted string from village to village; other signals were a bent arrow and a branch of a *mahua* tree. When the Khond leaders were assembled an axe was thrown on to the ground and each of them grasping it in turn swore to join in the rising and support his fellows. The taint of cruelty in the tribe is shown by the fact that the Kutia Khonds, on being requested to join in the rising, replied that if plunder was the only object they would not do so, but if the Koltas were to be murdered they agreed. Some of the murdered Koltas were anointed with turmeric and offered at temples, the Khonds calling them their goats, and in one case a Kolta is believed to have been made a Meriāh sacrifice to the earth god. The Khonds appeared before the police, who were protecting a body of refugees at the village of Norla, with the hair and scalps of their murdered victims tied to their bows. To the Political Officer, who was sent to suppress the rising, the Khonds complained that the Koltas had degraded them from the position of lords of the soil to that of servants, and justified their plundering of the Koltas on the ground that they were merely taking back the produce of their own land, which the Koltas had stolen from them. They said that if they were not to have back their land Government might either drive them out of the country or exterminate them, and that Koltas and Khonds could no more live together than tigers and goats. Another grievance was that a new Rāja of Kālāhandi had been installed without their consent having been obtained. The Political Officer, Mr. Berry, hanged seven of the Khond ringleaders and effected a settlement of their grievances. Peace was restored and has not since been broken. At a later date in the same year, 1882, and independently of the rising, a Khond landholder was convicted and executed for having offered a five-year-old girl as a Meriāh sacrifice.

The Khond or Kandh language, called Kui by the Khonds themselves, is spoken by rather more than half of the total body of the tribe. It is much more nearly related to Telugu than is Gondi and has no written character.[1] 15. Language.

Kir.[2]—A cultivating caste found principally in the Hoshangābād District. They numbered about 7000 persons in 1911. The Kīrs claim to have come from the Jaipur State, and this is borne out by the fact that they still retain a dialect of Mārwāri, though they have been living among the Hindi-speaking population of Hoshangābād for several generations. According to their traditions they immigrated into the Central Provinces when Rāja Mān was ruling at Jaipur. He was a contemporary of Akbar's and died in A.D. 1615.[3] This story tallies with Colonel Sleeman's statement that the first important influx of Hindus into the Nerbudda valley took place in the time of Akbar.[4] The Kīrs are akin to the Kirārs, and at the India Census of 1901 were amalgamated with them. Like the Kirārs they claim to be descended from the mythical Rāja Karan of Jaipur. Their story is that on a summer day Mahādeo and Pārvati created a melon-garden, and Mahādeo made a man and a woman out of a piece of *kusha* grass (*Eragrostis cynosuroides*) to tend the garden. From these the Kīrs are descended. The name may possibly be a corruption of *karar*, a river-bank. 1. Origin and traditions.

The Kīrs have no endogamous divisions. For the purpose of marriage the caste is divided into 12½ *gotras* or sections. A man must not marry within his own *gotra* or in 2. Marriage.

[1] Sir G. A. Grierson's *Linguistic Survey*, *Munda and Dravidian Languages*.

[2] This article is compiled principally from a paper by Pandit Sakhāram, Revenue Inspector, Hoshangābād District.

[3] Tod's *Rājasthān*, vol. ii. p. 327.

[4] Elliott's *Hoshangābād Settlement Report*, p. 60.

that to which his mother belonged. The names of the 12 *gotras* are as follows: Namchuria, Daima, Bania, Bāman, Nāyar, Jāt, Huwād, Gādri, Lohāria, Hekdya, Mochi and Māli, while the half-*gotra* contains the Bhāts or genealogists of the caste, who are not allowed to marry with the other subdivisions and have now formed one of their own. Of the twelve names of *gotras* at least seven—Bāman (Brāhman), Bania, Māli, Mochi, Gādri (Gadaria), Lohāria and Jāt—are derived from other castes, and this fact is sufficient to show that the origin of the Kīrs is occupational, and that they are made up of recruits from different castes. Infant-marriage is customary, but no penalty is incurred if a girl remains unmarried after puberty. Only the poorest members of the caste, however, fail to marry their daughters at an early age. For the marriage of girls who are left unprovided for, a subscription is raised among the caste-fellows in accordance with the usual Hindu practice, the giving of money for this purpose being considered to be an especially pious act. At the time of the betrothal a bride-price called *chāri*, varying between Rs. 14 and Rs. 20, is paid by the boy's father, and the deed of betrothal, called *lagan*, is then drawn up in the presence of the caste *panchāyat* who are regaled with liquor purchased out of the bride-price. A peculiarity of the marriage ceremony is that the bridegroom is taken to the bride's house riding on a buffalo. This custom is noteworthy, since other Hindus will not usually ride on a buffalo, as being the animal on which Yama, the god of death, rides. After the marriage the bride returns to the bridegroom's house with the wedding party and stays there for eight days, during which period she worships the family gods of her father-in-law's house. The cost of the marriage is usually Rs. 60 for the boy's party and Rs. 40 for the girl's. But a widower on his remarriage has to spend double this sum. The ceremonies called Gauna and Rauna are both performed after the marriage. The former generally takes place within a year, the bride being dressed in special new clothes called *bes*, and sent with ceremony to her husband's house on an auspicious day fixed by a Brāhman. She remains there for two months and the marriage is consummated, when she returns to her father's house. Four months afterwards the bridegroom again goes to fetch her and takes her away permanently, this being the Rauna ceremony. No social stigma attaches to polygamy, and divorce is allowed on the usual grounds. Widow-marriage is permitted, the ceremony consisting in giving new clothes and ornaments to the widow and feeding the Panch for a day.

3. Religion.

The caste worships especially Bhairon and Devi, and each section of it reveres a special incarnation of Devi, and the Bhairon of some particular village. Thus, for instance, the Namchurias worship the goddess Pārvati and the Bhairon of Jaria Gowāra; the Bania, Nāyar, Hekdya and Mochi septs worship Chāmunda Māta and the Bhairon of Jaipur, and so on. Members of the caste get triangular, rectangular or round pieces of silver impressed with the images of these gods, and wear them suspended by a thread from their necks. A similar respect is paid to the Ahut or the spirit of a relative who has met with a violent death or died without progeny or as a bachelor, the spirits of such persons being always prone to trouble their living relatives. In order to appease them songs are sung in their praise on important festivals, the members of the family staying awake the whole night, and wearing their images on a silver piece round the neck. When they eat and drink they first touch the food with the image by way of offering it to the dead, so that their spirits may be appeased and refrain from harassing the living. Kīrs revere and worship the cow and the pīpal tree. No Kīr may sell a cow to a butcher. A man who is about to die makes a present of a cow to a Brāhman or a temple in order that by catching hold of the tail of this cow he may be able to cross the horrible river Vaitarni, the Styx of Hinduism, which bars the passage to the nether regions. The Kīrs believe in magic, and some members of the caste profess to cure snake-bite. The poison-curer, when sent for, has a small space cleared and plastered with cowdung, on which he draws lines with wheat flour. A new earthen pot is then brought and placed over the drawing. On the pot the operator draws a figure of Hanumān in vermilion, and another figure on the nearest wall facing the pot. A brass plate is put over the pot and the person who has been bitten by the snake is brought near it. The snake-charmer then begins to name various gods and goddesses and to play upon the plate, which emits, it is said, a very melancholy sound. This performance is called *bharni* and is supposed to charm all beings, even gods and serpents. The snake who has inflicted the bite is then believed to appear in an invisible form to listen to the *bharni*, and to enter into the sufferer. The sufferer is questioned, being supposed to be possessed by the snake, and asked why the bite was inflicted and how the snake can be appeased. The replies are thought to be given by the snake, who explains that he was trampled on, or something to that effect, and asks that milk or some sweet-smelling article be placed at his hole. The offering is promised, and the snake is asked not to kill the sufferer, to which he agrees. The snake usually gives the history of his former human birth, stating his name and village and the cause of his transmigration into the body of a serpent. The Kīrs believe that human beings who commit offences are re-born as snakes, and they think that snakes live for a thousand years. After giving this information the snake departs, and the person who has been bitten is supposed to recover. The chief festivals of the Kīrs are Diwāli and Sitala Athāin. They worship their ancestors at Diwāli, making offerings of cooked food, *kusha* grass and lamps made of dough at the river-side. The head of the family sprinkles water and throws the *kusha* grass into the river, lights the wicks placed in the lamps and burns a little food in them, calling on the names of his ancestors. The rest of the food he takes home and distributes to his caste-fellows. Sitala Athāin is observed on the seventh day of the dark fortnight of Chait. Devi is worshipped at night with offerings of milk and whey, and on the next day no food is cooked, the remains of that of the previous day being eaten cold, and the whole day is devoted to singing the praises of the goddess.

4. Birth and death ceremonies.

The Kīrs usually burn their dead, but children under twelve are buried. The ashes and bones are either sent to the Ganges or consigned to the nearest river or lake. Children have only one name, which is given on the seventh day after birth by a Brāhman. During the birth ceremony the husband's younger brother catches hold of the skirt of the child's mother, who on this pays him a few pice and pulls away her cloth. If this custom has any meaning it is apparently in symbolical memory of polyandry, the women bribing her husband's younger brother so that he may not claim the child as his own.

5. Food, dress and occupation.

The Kīrs do not take food from any caste except the Dadhāria Brāhmans, who are Mārwāris, and act as their family priests. Brāhmans and other high castes will drink water brought in a brass vessel by a Kīr. The Kīrs eat no meat except goats' flesh and fish, but are much addicted to liquor, which is always conspicuous at their feasts and festivals. They have a caste *panchāyat*, which deals with the ordinary offences. Temporary excommunication is removed by the offender giving three feasts, on which an amount varying with his social position and means must be expended. The first of these is eaten on a river-bank, the second in a garden, and the third, which confers complete readmission to caste intercourse, in the offender's house. The Kīrs live along river-banks, where they grow melons in the sand and castor and vegetables in alluvial soil. They are considered very skilful at raising these crops, and fully appreciate the use of manure. For their own consumption they usually grow *bājra* and *arhar*, being, like all Mārwāris, very fond of *bājra*. The members of the caste are easily distinguished by their dress, the men wearing a white *mirzai* or short coat, a *dhoti* reaching to the knees, and a head-cloth placed in a crooked position on the head, so as to leave the hair of the scalp uncovered. They wear necklaces of black wooden beads, besides the images of Bhairon and Devi. The women wear Jaipur *chunris* or over-cloths and *ghānghras* or skirts. They have red lac bangles on their wrists and arms above the elbow, and ornaments called *ramjhul* on their legs. The women have a gait like that of men. The speech of the Kīrs sounds like Mārwāri, and they are peculiar in their preference for riding on buffaloes.

Kirār[1] or Kirād.

1. Origin and traditions.

Kirār[1] or Kirād.—A cultivating caste found in the

[1] Compiled from papers by Mr. Mūlchand, Deputy Inspector of Schools, Betūl; Mr. Shams-ul-Husain, Tahsīldār, Sohāgpur; Mr. Kalyān Chand, Manager, Court of Wards, Betūl; and Kanhya Lāl, clerk in the Gazetteer Office.

Narsinghpur, Hoshangābād, Betūl, Seoni, Chhindwāra and Nāgpur Districts. They numbered 48,000 persons in 1911. The Kirārs claim to be Dhākar or bastard Rājpūts, and in 1891 more than half of them returned themselves under this designation. About a thousand persons who were returned as Dhākar Rājpūts from Hoshangābād in 1901 are probably Kirārs. The caste say that they immigrated from Gwalior, and this statement seems to be correct, as about 66,000 of them are found in that State. They claim to have left Gwalior as early as Samvat 1525 or A.D. 1468, when Alru and Dalru, the leaders of the migration into the Central Provinces, abandoned their native village, Doderi Kheda in Gwalior, and settled in Chāndon, a village in the Sohāgpur tahsīl of Hoshangābād. But according to the story related to Mr. (Sir Charles) Elliott, the migration took place in A.D. 1650 or at the beginning of Aurāngzeb's reign.[1] He quotes the names of the leaders as Alrāwat and Dalrāwat, and says that the migration took place from the Dholpur country, but this is probably a mistake, as none of the caste are now found in Dholpur. Elliott stated that he could find no traces of any cultivating caste having settled in Hoshangābād as far back as Akbar's time, though Sir W. Sleeman was of opinion that the first great migration into the Nerbudda valley took place in that reign. The truth is probably that the valley began to be regularly colonised by Hindus during the years that Aurāngzeb spent at Burhānpur and in the Deccan, and the immigration of the Kirārs may most reasonably be attributed to this period. The Kirārs, Gūjars, and Rāghuvansis apparently entered the Central Provinces together, and the fact that they still smoke from the same huqqa and take water from each other's drinking vessels may be a reminiscence of this bond of fellowship. All these castes claim, and probably with truth, to be degraded Rājpūts. The Kirārs' version is that they took to widow-marriage and were consequently degraded. According to another story they were driven from their native place by a Muhammadan invasion. Mr. J. D. Cunningham says that the word *Kirār* in Central India literally means dalesmen or foresters, but during the lapse

[1] *Hoshangābād Settlement Report* (1867), p. 60.

of centuries has become the name of a caste.[1] Another derivation is from Kirār, a corn-chandler, an occupation which they may originally have followed in combination with agriculture. In the Punjab the name Kirār appears to be given to all the western or Punjabi traders as distinct from a Bania of Hindustān, and is so used even in the Kāngra hills, but the Arora, who is the trader *par excellence* of the south-west of the Punjab, is the person to whom the term is most commonly applied.[2] As a curiosity of folk-etymology it may be stated that some derive the caste-name from the fact that a holy sage's wife, who was about to be delivered of a child, was being pursued by a Rākshas or demon, and fell over the steep bank (*karār*) of a river and was thereupon delivered. The child was consequently called Karār and became the ancestor of the Kirār caste. The name may in fact be derived from the habit which the Kirārs have in some localities of cultivating on the banks of rivers, like the Kīrs, who are probably a branch of the same caste.

2. Marriage.

In the Central Provinces the Kirārs have no regular subcastes. In Chhindwāra a subdivision is in course of formation from the illegitimate offspring of male Kirārs, who are known as Vidūr or Saoneria. The Dhākar Kirārs do not marry or eat with Saonerias. The section-names of the Kirārs are not eponymous, as might be anticipated from their claim to Rājpūt descent, but they are generally territorial. Instances are Bankhedi, from Bankhedi, a village in Hoshangābād; Garhya, from Garha, near Jubbulpore; and Teharia, from Tehri, a State in Bundelkhand. Other section-names are Chaudharia, from Chaudhari, headman; Khandait or swordsman, and Bānda, or tailless. Some *gotras* are derived from the names of other castes or subcastes, or of Rājpūt septs, as Lohāria, from Lohār (blacksmith); Chauria, a subcaste of Kurmīs; Lilorhia, a subcaste of Gūjars; and Solankī and Chauhān, the names of Rājpūt septs. These names may probably be taken to indicate the mixed origin of the caste, and record the admission of families from other castes. A man cannot

[1] *History of the Sikhs*, p. 15, footnote.
[2] *Ibbetson's Census Report* (1881), p. 297.

marry in his own *gotra* nor in the families of his grandmother, paternal uncle or maternal aunt to three degrees of consanguinity. Boys and girls are usually married between the ages of five and twelve. Marriages take place so long as the planet Venus or Shukra is visible at nights, *i.e.* between the months of Aghan (November) and Asārh (June). The proposal for marriage proceeds from the boy's father, who ascertains the wishes of the girl's father through a barber. If the latter is willing, the Sagai or betrothal ceremony is performed at the girl's house. The boy's father proceeds there with a rupee, two pice and a cocoanut-core, which he presents to the girl, taking her into his lap. The fathers of the boy and girl embrace, and this seals the compact of betrothal. The date of the marriage is usually fixed in consultation with a Brāhman, who computes an auspicious day from the ceremonial names of the couple. But if it is desired to perform the marriage at once, it may take place on Akhātīj, or the third day of the bright fortnight of Baisākh (April-May), which is always auspicious. The *lagan* or paper containing the date of the marriage is drawn up ceremonially by a Brāhman of the girl's house, and he also writes another, giving the names of the relatives who are selected to officiate at the ceremony. The first ceremony at the marriage is that of Māngar Māti, or bringing earth for ovens, the earth being worshipped by a burnt offering of butter and sugar, and then dug up by the Sawāsin or girl's attendant for the marriage, and carried home by several women in baskets. This is done in the morning, and in the evening the boy and girl in their respective houses are anointed with oil and turmeric, a little being first thrown on the ground for the family gods. This ceremony is repeated every evening for some three to fifteen days. The *mandwa* or marriage-shed is then erected at both houses, under which the ceremony of *tel* or touching the feet, knees, shoulders and forehead of the boy and the girl with oil is performed. Next day the *khām* or marriage-post is placed in the *mandwa*, a little rice, turmeric and two pice being put in the hole in which it is fixed, and the shed is covered with leaves. The bridegroom, clad in a blanket and with date-leaves tied on his head, is taken out for the *binaiki* or the marriage procession on horseback. Before mounting, he bows to Māta or Devi, Mahābīr, Hardaul Lāla, and Patel Deo, the spirit of the deceased mālguzār of the village. He is taken round to the houses of friends and relatives, who present him with a few pice. On his return he bathes and puts on the marriage dress, which consists of a red or yellow *jāma* or gown, a pair of trousers, a pagrī, a *maur* or marriage crown and a cloth about his waist. A few women's ornaments are put on his neck, and he is furnished with a *katār* or dagger, and in its absence a nutcracker or knife. He then comes out of the house and the *parchhan* ceremony is performed, the boy's mother putting her nipple in his mouth and giving him a little *ghī* and sugar to eat as a symbol of the termination of his infancy. The Barāt or marriage procession then sets out for the girl's village, being met on its outskirts by the bride's father, and the forehead of the bridegroom is marked with sandalwood paste. The bridegroom touches the Mandwa with his hand or throws a bamboo fan over it and returns with his followers to the Janwāsa or lodging given to the Barāt. Next morning the ceremony of Chadhao or decorating the bride is performed, and the bridegroom's party give her the clothes and ornaments which they have brought for her, these being first offered to an image of Ganesh made of cowdung. The bride is then mounted on a horse provided by the bridegroom's party and goes round to the houses of the friends of the family, accompanied by music and the women of her party, and receives small presents. The *Bhānwar* ceremony is performed during the night, the couple being seated near the marriage-post with their backs to the house. A ball of kneaded flour is put in the girl's right hand, which is then placed on the right hand of the bridegroom, and the bride's brother pours water over their hands. The bride's maternal uncle and aunt, with the skirts of their clothes tied together, step forward and wash the feet of the couple and give them presents. The other relatives follow suit, and this completes the ceremony of Paon Pakhurai or Daija, that is giving the dowry. The couple then go round the marriage-post seven times, the girl leading for the first four rounds and the boy for the last three. This is the *Bhānwar* ceremony or binding portion of the marriage, and the polar star is called on to make it inviolable. The bridegroom's party are then feasted, the women meantime singing obscene songs. The bride goes back to the bridegroom's house and stays there for a few days, after which she returns to her parents' house and does not leave it again until the *gauna* ceremony is performed. On this occasion the bridegroom's party go to the girl's house with a present of sweets and clothes which they present to her parents, and they then take away the girl. Even after this she is again sent back to her parents' house, and the bridegroom comes a second time to fetch her, on which occasion the parents of the bride have to make a present in return for the sweets and clothes previously given to them. The marriage expenses are said to average between Rs. 50 and Rs. 100, but the extravagance of Kirārs is notorious. Sir R. Craddock says[1] that they are much given to display, the richer members of the caste being heavily weighted with jewellery, while a well-to-do Kirār will think nothing of spending Rs. 1000 on his house, or if he is a landowner Rs. 5000. Extravagance ruins a great many of the Kirār community. This statement, however, perhaps applies to those of the Nāgpur District rather than to their comrades of the Nerbudda valley and Satpūra highlands. The remarriage of widows is permitted, and the widow may marry either her husband's younger brother or any other member of the caste at her choice. The ceremony takes place at night, the woman being brought to her husband's house by the back door and given a new cloth and bangles. Turmeric is then applied to her body, and the clothes of the couple are tied together. When a bachelor marries a widow, he must first be married to an *akau* plant (swallow-wort). Divorce may be effected for infidelity on the part of the wife or for serious disagreement. A divorced woman may marry again. Polygamy is allowed, and in Chhindwāra is said to be restricted to three wives, all living within the District, but elsewhere no such limitation is enforced. A man seldom, however, takes more than one wife, except for the sake of children.

3. Religion. They worship the ordinary Hindu gods and especially

1 *Nāgpur Settlement Report*, p. 24.

Devi, to whom they offer female kids. During the months of Baisākh and Jeth (April-June) those living in Betūl and Chhindwāra make a pilgrimage to the Nāg Deo or cobra god, who is supposed to have his seat somewhere on the border of the two Districts. Every third year they also take their cattle outside the village, and turning their faces in the direction of the Nāg Deo sprinkle a little water and kill goats and fowls. They worship the Patel Deo or spirit of the deceased mālguzār of the village only on the occasion of marriages. They consider the service of the village headman to be their traditional occupation besides agriculture, and they therefore probably pay this special compliment to the spirit of their employer. They worship their implements of husbandry on some convenient day, which must be a Wednesday or a Sunday, after they have sown the spring crops. Those who grow sugarcane offer a goat or a cocoanut to the crop before it is cut, and a similar offering is made to the stock of grain after harvest, so that its bulk may not decrease. They observe the ordinary festivals, and like other Hindus cease to observe one on which a death has occurred in the family, until some happy event such as the birth of a child, or even of a calf, supervenes on the same day. Unmarried children under seven and persons dying of smallpox, snake-bite or cholera are buried, and others are either buried or burnt according to the convenience of the family. Males are placed on the pyre or in the grave on their faces and females on their backs, with their feet pointing to the south in each case. In some places the corpse is buried stark naked, and in others with a piece of cloth wrapped round it, and two pice are usually placed in the grave to buy the site. When a corpse is burnt the head is touched with a bamboo before it is laid on the funeral pyre, by way of breaking it in and allowing the soul to escape if it has not already done so. For three days the mourners place food, water and tobacco in cups for the disembodied soul. Mourning is observed for children for three days and for adults from seven to ten days. During this period the mourners refrain from luxurious food such as flesh, turmeric, vegetables, milk and sweets; they do not wear shoes, nor change their clothes, and males are not shaved until the last day of mourning. Balls of rice are then offered to the dead, and the caste people are feasted. Oblations of water are offered to ancestors in the month of Kunwār (September-October).

4. Social customs. The caste do not admit outsiders. In the matter of food they eat flesh and fish, but abstain from liquor and from eating fowls, except in the Marātha country. They will take *pakka* food or that cooked without water from Gūjars, Rāghuvansis and Lodhis. In the Nāgpur country, where the difference between *katcha* and *pakka* food is not usually observed, they will not take it from any but Marātha Brāhmans. Ahīrs and Dhīmars are said to eat with them, and the northern Brāhmans will take water from them. They have a caste *panchāyat* or committee with a hereditary president called Sethia, whose business it is to eat first when admitting a person who has been put out of caste. Killing a cat or a squirrel, selling a cow to a butcher, growing hemp or selling shoes are offences which entail temporary excommunication from caste. A woman who commits adultery with a man of another caste is permanently excluded. The Kirārs are tall in stature and well and stoutly built. They have regular features and are generally of a fair colour. They are regarded as quarrelsome and untruthful, and as tyrannical landlords. As agriculturists they are supposed to be of encroaching tendencies, and the proverbial prayer attributed to them is, "O God, give me two bullocks, and I shall plough up the common way." Another proverb quoted in Mr. Standen's *Betūl Settlement Report*, in illustration of their avarice, is "If you put a rupee between two Kirārs, they become like *mast* buffaloes in Kunwār." The men always wear turbans, while the women may be distinguished in the Marātha country by their adherence to the dress of the northern Districts. Girls are tattooed on the back of their hands before they begin to live with their husbands. A woman may not name her husband's elder brother or even touch his clothes or the vessels in which he has eaten food. They are not distinguished for cleanliness.

5. Occupation. Agriculture and the service of the village headman are the traditional occupations of Kirārs. In Nāgpur they are considered to be very good cultivators, but they have no

special reputation in the northern Districts. About a thousand of them are landowners, and the large majority are tenants. They grow garden crops and sugarcane, but abstain from the cultivation of hemp.

Kohli.—A small caste of cultivators found in the Marāthi-speaking tracts of the Wainganga Valley, comprised in the Bhandāra and Chānda Districts. They numbered about 26,000 persons in 1911. The Kohlis are a notable caste as being the builders of the great irrigation reservoirs or tanks, for which the Wainganga Valley is celebrated. The water is used for irrigating rice and sugarcane, the latter being the favourite crop of the Kohlis. The origin of the caste is somewhat doubtful. The name closely resembles that of the Koiri caste of market-gardeners in northern India; and the terms Kohiri and Kohli are used there as variations of the caste name Koiri. The caste themselves have a tradition that they were brought to Bhandāra from Benāres by one of the Gond kings of Chānda on his return from a visit to that place;[1] and the Kohlis of Bhandāra say that their first settlement in the Central Provinces was at Lānji, which lies north of Bhandāra in Bālāghāt. But on the other hand all that is known of their language, customs, and sept or family names points to a purely Marātha origin, the caste being in all these respects closely analogous to the Kunbis. The Settlement Officer of Chānda, Colonel Lucie Smith, stated that they thought their forefathers came from the south. They tie their head-cloths in a similar fashion to the Gāndlis, who are oilmen from the Telugu country. If they belonged to the south of India they might be an offshoot from the well-known Koli tribe of Bombay, and this hypothesis appears the more probable. As a general rule castes from northern India settling in the Marātha country have not completely abandoned their ancestral language and customs even after a residence of several centuries. In the case of such castes as the Panwārs and Bhoyars their foreign extraction can be detected at once; and if the Kohlis had come from Hindustān the rule would probably hold good with them. On

1. General notice.

[1] Mr. Lawrence's *Bhandāra Settlement Report* (1867), p. 46.

the other hand the Kolis have in some parts of Bombay now taken to cultivation and closely resemble the Kunbis. In Satāra it is said[1] that they associate and occasionally eat with Kunbis, and their social and religious customs resemble those of the Kunbi caste. They are quiet, orderly, settled and hard-working. Besides fishing they work ferries along the Krishna, are employed in villages as water-carriers, and grow melons in river-beds with much skill. The Kolis of Bombay are presumably the same tribe as the Kols of Chota Nāgpur, and they probably migrated to Gujarāt along the Vindhyan plateau, where they are found in considerable numbers, and over the hills of Rājputāna and Central India. The Kols are one of the most adaptive of all the non-Aryan tribes, and when they reached the sea they may have become fishermen and boatmen, and practised these callings also in rivers. From plying on rivers they might take to cultivating melons and garden-crops on the stretches of silt left uncovered in their beds in the dry season, which is the common custom of the boating and fishing castes. And from this, as seen in Satāra, some of them attained to regular cultivation and, modelling themselves on the Kunbis, came to have nearly the same status. They may thus have migrated to Chānda and Bhandāra with the Kunbis, as their language and customs would indicate, and retaining their preference for irrigated and garden-crops have become expert growers of sugarcane. The description which has been received of the Kohlis of Bhandāra would be rather favourable than otherwise to the hypothesis of their ultimate origin from the Kol tribe, allowing for their having acquired the Marātha language and customs from a lengthened residence in Bombay. It has been mentioned above that the Kohlis have a legend of their ancestors having come from Benāres, but this story appears to be not infrequently devised as a means of obtaining increased social estimation, Benāres being the principal centre of orthodox Hinduism. Thus the Dāngris, a small caste of vegetable- and melon-growers who are certainly an offshoot of the Kunbis, and therefore of Marātha extraction, have the same story. As regards the tradition

[1] *Bombay Gazetteer*, *Satāra*, p. 106.

Bemrose, Collo., Derby.

OLD TYPE OF SUGARCANE MILL.

of the Bhandāra Kohlis that their first settlement was at Lānji, this may well have been the case even though they came from the south, as Lānji was an important place and a centre of administration under the Marāthas. It is probable, however, that they first came to Chānda and from here spread north to Lānji, as, if they had entered Bhandāra through Wardha and Nāgpur, some of them would probably have remained in these Districts.

2. Marriage and other customs.

The Kohlis have no subcastes. They are divided into the usual exogamous groups or septs with the object of preventing marriages between relations, and these have Marāthi names of the territorial or titular type. Among them may be mentioned Handifode (one who breaks a cooking vessel), Sahre (from *shahar*, a town), Nāgpure (from Nāgpur), Shende (from *shend*, cowdung), Parwate (from *parwat*, mountain), Hatwāde (an obstinate man), Mungus-māre (one who killed a mongoose), Pustode (one who broke a bullock's tail), and so on. Marriage within the sept is prohibited. A brother's daughter may be married to his sister's son, but not vice versa. Girls are usually wedded before arriving at adolescence, more especially as there is a great demand for brides. Like other castes engaged in spade cultivation, the Kohlis marry two or more wives when they can afford it, a wife being a more willing servant than a hired labourer, apart from the other advantages. If his wives do not get on together, the Kohli gives them separate huts in his courtyard, where each lives and cooks her meals for herself. He will also allot them separate tasks, assigning to one the care of his household affairs, to another the watching of his sugarcane plot, and so on. If he does this successfully the wives are kept well at work and have not time to quarrel. It is said that whenever a Kohli has a bountiful harvest he looks out for another wife. This naturally leads to a scarcity of women and the payment of a substantial bride-price. The recognised amount is Rs. 30, but this is only formal, and from Rs. 50 to Rs. 150 may be given according to the attractions of the girl, the largest sum being paid for a woman of full age who can go and live with her husband at once. As a consequence of this state of things poor men are sometimes unable to get wives at all. Though they pay highly for their wives the Kohlis are averse to extravagant expenditure on weddings, and all marriages in a village are generally celebrated on the same day once a year, the number of guests at each being thus necessarily restricted. The officiating Brāhman ascends the roof of a house and, after beating a brass dish to warn the parties, repeats the marriage texts as the sun goes down. At this moment all the couples place garlands of flowers on each other's shoulders, each bridegroom ties the *mangal-sūtram* or necklace of black beads round his bride's neck, and the weddings are completed. The bride's brother winds a thread round the marriage crowns of the couple and is given two rupees for untying it. The services of a Brāhman are not indispensable, and an elder of the caste may officiate as priest. Next day the barber and washerman take the bridegroom and bride in their arms and dance, holding them, to the accompaniment of music, while the women throw red rose-powder over the couple. At their weddings the Kohlis make models in wood of a Chamār's *rāmpi* or knife and *khurpa* or scraper, this custom perhaps indicating some connection with the Chamārs; or it may have arisen simply on account of the important assistance rendered by the Chamār to the cultivation of sugarcane, in supplying the *mot* or leather bag for raising water from the well. After the wedding is over a string of hemp from a cot is tied round the necks of the pair, and their maternal uncles then run and offer it at the shrine of Marai Māta, the goddess of cholera. Widows with any remains of youth or personal attractions always marry again, the ceremony being held at midnight according to the customary ritual of the Marātha Districts.[1] Sometimes the husband does not attend at all, and the widow is united to a sword or dagger as representing him. Otherwise the widow may be conducted to her new husband's house by five other widows, and in this case they halt at a stream by the way and the bangles and beads are broken from off her neck and wrists. On account, perhaps, of the utility of their wives, and the social temptations which beset them from being continually abroad at work, the Kohlis are lenient to

[1] See article on Kunbi.

conjugal offences, and a woman going wrong even with an outsider will be taken back by her husband and only a trifling punishment imposed by the caste. A Kohli can also keep a woman of any other caste, except of those regarded as impure, without incurring any censure. Divorce is very seldom resorted to and involves severe penalties to both parties. As among the Panwārs, a wife retains any property she may bring to her husband and her wedding gifts at her own disposal, this separate portion being known as *khamora.* The caste burn their dead when they can afford it, placing the head of the corpse to the north on the pyre. The bodies of those who have died from cholera or small-pox are buried. Like the Panwārs it is the custom of the Kohlis on bathing after a funeral to have a meal of cakes and sugar on the river-bank, a practice which is looked down on by orthodox Hindus. After a month or so the deceased person is considered to be united to the ancestors, and when he was the head of the family his successor is inducted to the position by the presentation of a new head-cloth and a silver bangle. The bereaved family are then formally escorted to the weekly market and are considered to have resumed their regular social relations. The Kohlis revere the ordinary Hindu deities, and on the day of Dasahra they worship their axe, sickle and ploughshare by washing them and making an offering of rice, flowers and turmeric. The axe is no doubt included because it serves to cut the wood for fencing the sugarcane garden.

3. The Kohlis as tank-builders.

The Kohlis were the builders of the great tanks of the Bhandāra District. The most important of these are Nawegaon with an area of five square miles and a circumference of seventeen, and Seoni, over seven miles round, while smaller tanks are counted by thousands. Though the largest are the work of the Kohlis, many of the others have been constructed by the Panwārs of this tract, who have also much aptitude for irrigation. Built as they were without technical engineering knowledge, the tanks form an enduring monument to the native ability and industry of these enterprising cultivators. "Working," Mr. Danks remarks,[1] "without instruments, unable even to take a level, finding out their mistakes by the

[1] *Bhandāra District Gazetteer*, para. 90.

destruction of the works they had built, ever repairing, reconstructing, altering, they have raised in every village a testimony to their wisdom, their industry and their perseverance." Although Nawegaon tank has a water area of seven square miles, the combined length of the two artificial embankments is only 760 yards, and this demonstrates the great skill with which the site has been selected. At some of the tanks men are stationed day and night during the rainy season to see if the embankment is anywhere weakened by the action of the water, and in that case to give the alarm to the village by beating a drum. The Nawegaon tank is said to have been built at the commencement of the eighteenth century by one Kolu Patel Kohli. As might be expected, Kolu Patel has been deified as Kolāsur Deo, and his shrine is on one of the peaks surrounding the tank. Seven other peaks are known as the Sāt Bahini or 'Seven Sisters,' and it is said that these deities assisted Kolu in building the tank, by coming and working on the embankment at night when the labourers had left. Some whitish-yellow stones on Kolāsur's hill are said to be the baskets of the Seven Sisters in which they carried earth. "The Kohli," Mr. Napier states,[1] "sacrifices all to his sugarcane, his one ambition and his one extravagance being to build a large reservoir which will contain water for the irrigation of his sugarcane during the long, hot months." Each rates the other according to the size of his tank and the strength of its embankment. Under the Gond kings a man who built a tank received a grant of the fields lying below it either free of revenue or on a very light assessment. Such grants were known as Tukm, and were probably a considerable incentive to tank-building. Unfortunately sugarcane, formerly a most profitable crop, has been undersold by the canal- and tank-irrigated product of northern India, and at present scarcely repays cultivation.

4. Agricultural customs.

The Kohli villages are managed on a somewhat patriarchal system, and the dealings between proprietors and cultivators are regulated by their own custom without much regard to the rules imposed by Government. Mr. Napier says of them:[2] "The Kohlis are very good landlords as a general rule; but in their dealings with their tenants and their

[1] *Bhandāra Settlement Report.* [2] *Ibidem.*

labourers follow their own customs, while the provisions of the Tenancy Act often remain in abeyance. They admit no tenant right in land capable of being irrigated for sugar-cane, and change the tenants as they please; and in many villages a large number of the labourers are practically serfs, being fed, clothed and married by their employers, for whom they and their children work all their lives without any fixed wages. These customs are acquiesced in by all parties, and, so far as I could learn, there was no discontent. They have a splendid caste discipline, and their quarrels are settled expeditiously by their *panchāyats* or committees without reference to courts of law."

5. General characteristics.

In appearance and character the Kohlis cannot be said to show much trace of distinction. The men wear a short white *bandi* or coat, and a small head-cloth only three feet long. This is often scarcely more than a handkerchief which tightly covers the crown, and terminates in knots, inelegant and cheap. The women wear glass bangles only on the left hand and brass or silver ones on the right, no doubt because glass ornaments would interfere with their work and get broken. Their cloth is drawn over the left shoulder instead of the right, a custom which they share with Gonds, Kāpewārs and Buruds. In appearance the caste are generally dirty. They are ignorant themselves and do not care that their children should be educated. Their custom of polygamy leads to family quarrels and excessive subdivision of property; thus in one village, Ashti, the proprietary right is divided into 192 shares. On this account they are seldom well-to-do. Their countenances are of a somewhat inferior type and generally dark in colour. In character they are peaceful and amenable, and have the reputation of being very respectful to Government officials, who as a consequence look on them with favour. 'Their heart is good,' a tahsīldār[1] of the Bhandāra District remarked. If a guest comes to a Kohli, the host himself offers to wash his feet, and if the guest be a Brāhman, will insist on doing so. They eat flesh and fowls, but abstain from liquor. In social status they are on a level with the Mālis and a little below the regular cultivating castes.

[1] Subordinate revenue officer.

KOL

[This article is based mainly on Colonel Dalton's classical description of the Mundas and Hos in the *Ethnology of Bengal* and on Sir H. Risley's article on Munda in *The Tribes and Castes of Bengal*. Extracts have also been made from Mr. Sarat Chandra Roy's exhaustive account in *The Mundas and their Country* (Calcutta, 1912). Information on the Mundas and Kols of the Central Provinces has been collected by Mr. Hīra Lāl in Raigarh and by the author in Mandla, and a monograph has been furnished by Mr. B. C. Mazumdār, Pleader, Sambalpur. It should be mentioned that most of the Kols of the Central Provinces have abandoned the old tribal customs and religion described by Colonel Dalton, and are rapidly coming to resemble an ordinary low Hindu caste.]

LIST OF PARAGRAPHS

1. General notice. Strength of the Kols in India.

Kol, Munda, Ho.—A great tribe of Chota Nāgpur, which has given its name to the Kolarian family of tribes and languages. A part of the District of Singhbhūm near Chaibāsa is named the Kolhān as being the special home of the Larka Kols, but they are distributed all over Chota Nāgpur, whence they have spread to the United Provinces, Central Provinces and Central India. It seems probable also that the Koli tribe of Gujarāt may be an offshoot of the Kols, who migrated there by way of Central India. If the total of the Kols, Mundas and Hos or Larka Kols be taken together they number about a million persons in India. The real strength of the tribe is, however, much greater than this. As shown in the article on that tribe, the Santāls are a branch of the Kols, who have broken off from the parent stock and been given a separate designation by the Hindus. They numbered two millions in 1911. The Bhumij (400,000) are also probably a section of the tribe. Sir H. Risley[1] states that they are closely allied to if not identical with the Mundas. In some localities they intermarry with the Mundas and are known as Bhumij Munda.[2] If the Kolis also be taken as an offshoot of the Kol tribe, a further addition of nearly three millions is made to the tribes whose parentage can be traced to this stock. There is little doubt also that other Kolarian tribes, as the Kharias, Khairwars, Korwas and Korkus, whose tribal languages closely approximate to Mundāri, were originally one with the Mundas, but have been separated for so long a period that their direct connection can no longer be proved. The disintegrating causes, which have split up what was originally one into a number of distinct tribes, are probably no more than distance and settlement in different parts of the country, leading to cessation of intermarriage and social intercourse. The tribes have then obtained some variation in the original name or been given separate territorial or occupational designations by the Hindus and their former identity has gradually been forgotten.

2. Names of the tribe.

"The word Kol is probably the Santāli *hār*, a man. This word is used under various forms, such as *har*, *hāra*, *ho* and *koro* by most Munda tribes in order to denote themselves. The change of *r* to *l* is familiar and does not give rise to any difficulty."[3] The word Korku is simply a corruption of Kodaku, young men, and there is every probability that the Hindus, hearing the Kol tribe call themselves *hor* or *horo*, may have corrupted the name to a form more familiar to themselves. An alternative derivation from the

[1] *Tribes and Castes of Bengal*, art. Bhumij.

[2] *The Mundas and their Country*, p. 400.

[3] *Linguistic Survey, Munda and Dravidian Languages*, vol. vi. p. 7.

Sanskrit word *kola*, a pig, is improbable. But it is possible, as suggested by Sir G. Grierson, that after the name had been given, its Sanskrit meaning of pig may have added zest to its employment by the Hindus. The word Munda, Sir H. Risley states, is the common term employed by the Kols for the headman of a village, and has come into general use as an honorific title, as the Santāls call themselves Mānjhi, the Gonds Bhoi, and the Bhangis and other sweepers Mehtar. Munda, like Mehtar, originally a title, has become a popular alternative name for the caste. In Chota Nāgpur those Kols who have partly adopted Hinduism and become to some degree civilised are commonly known as Munda, while the name Ho or Larka Kol is reserved for the branch of the tribe in Singhbhūm who, as stated by Colonel Dalton, "From their jealous isolation for so many years, their independence, their long occupation of one territory, and their contempt for all other classes that come in contact with them, especially the Hindus, probably furnish the best illustration, not of the Mundāris in their present state, but of what, if left to themselves and permanently located, they were likely to become. Even at the present day the exclusiveness of the old Hos is remarkable. They will not allow aliens to hold land near their villages; and indeed if it were left to them no strangers would be permitted to settle in the Kolhān."

It is this branch of the tribe whose members have come several times into contact with British troops, and on account of their bravery and warlike disposition they are called the Larka or fighting Kols. The Mundas on the other hand appear now to be a very mixed group. The list of their subcastes given[1] by Sir H. Risley includes the Khangār, Kharia, Mahali, Oraon and Savar Mundas, all of which are the names of separate tribes, now considered as distinct, though with the exception of the Oraons they were perhaps originally offshoots of the Kols or akin to them; while the Bhuinhār or landholders and Nāgvansi or Mundas of the royal house are apparently the aristocracy of the original tribe. It would appear possible from the list of subtribes already given that the village headmen of other tribes,

[1] *Tribes and Castes of Bengal*, art. Munda.

having adopted the designation of Munda and intermarried with other headmen so as to make a superior group, have in some cases been admitted into the Munda tribe, which may enjoy a higher rank than other tribes as the Rāja of Chota Nāgpur belongs to it; but it is also quite likely that these groups may have simply arisen from the intermarriages of Mundas with other tribes, alliances of this sort being common. The Kols of the Central Provinces probably belong to the Munda tribe of Chota Nāgpur, and not to the Hos or Larka Kols, as the latter would be less likely to emigrate. But quite a separate set of subcastes is found here, which will be given later.

3. Origin of the Kolarian tribes.

The Munda languages have been shown by Sir G. Grierson to have originated from the same source as those spoken in the Indo-Pacific islands and the Malay Peninsula. "The Mundas, the Mon-Khmer, the wild tribes of the Malay Peninsula and the Nicobarese all use forms of speech which can be traced back to a common source though they mutually differ widely from each other."[1] It would appear therefore that the Mundas, the oldest known inhabitants of India, perhaps came originally from the south-east, the islands of the Indian Archipelago and the Malay Peninsula, unless India was their original home and these countries were colonised from it.

Sir E. Gait states: "Geologists tell us that the Indian Peninsula was formerly cut off from the north of Asia by sea, while a land connection existed on the one side with Madagascar and on the other with the Malay Archipelago; and though there is nothing to show that India was then inhabited we know that it was so in palaeolithic times, when communication was probably still easier with the countries to the north-east and south-west than with those beyond the Himalayas."[2] In the south of India, however, no traces of Munda languages remain at present, and it seems therefore necessary to conclude that the Mundas of the Central Provinces and Chota Nāgpur have been separated from the tribes of Malaysia who speak cognate languages for an indefinitely long period, or else that they did not

[1] *Tribes and Castes of Bengal*, p. 15.
[2] Introduction to *The Mundas and their Country*, p. 9.

come through southern India to these countries, but by way of Assam and Bengal or by sea through Orissa. There is good reason to believe from the names of places and from local tradition that the Munda tribes were once spread over Bihār and parts of the Ganges valley; and if the Kolis are an offshoot of the Kols, as is supposed, they also penetrated across Central India to the sea in Gujarāt and the hills of the Western Ghāts. It is presumed that the advance of the Aryans or Hindus drove the Mundas from the open country to the seclusion of the hills and forests. The Munda and Dravidian languages are shown by Sir G. Grierson to be distinct groups without any real connection.

4. The Kolarians and Dravidians.

Though the physical characteristics of the two sets of tribes display no marked points of difference, it has been generally held by ethnologists who know them that they represent two distinct waves of immigration, and the absence of connection between their languages bears out this view. It has always been supposed that the Mundas were in the country of Chota Nāgpur and the Central Provinces first, and that the Dravidians, the Gonds, Khonds and Oraons came afterwards. The grounds for this view are the more advanced culture of the Dravidians; the fact that where the two sets of tribes are in contact those of the Munda group have been ousted from the more open and fertile country, of which according to tradition they were formerly in possession; and the practice of the Gonds and other Dravidian tribes of employing the Baigas, Bhuiyas and other Munda tribes for their village priests, which is an acknowledgment that the latter as the earlier residents have a more familiar acquaintance with the local deities, and can solicit their favour and protection with more prospect of success. Such a belief is the more easily understood when it is remembered that these deities are not infrequently either the human ancestors of the earliest residents or the local animals and plants from which they supposed themselves to be descended.

5. Date of the Dravidian immigration.

The Dravidian languages, Gondi, Kurukh and Khond, are of one family with Tamil, Telugu, Malayalam and Canarese, and their home is the south of India. As stated[1]

[1] Introduction to *The Mundas and their Country*, p. 9.

by Sir E. Gait, there is at present no evidence to show that the Dravidians came to southern India from any other part of the world, and for anything that is known to the contrary the languages may have originated there. The existence of the small Brahui tribe in Baluchistān, who speak a Dravidian language but have no physical resemblance to other Dravidian races, cannot be satisfactorily explained, but as he points out this is no reason for holding that the whole body of speakers of Dravidian languages entered India from the north-west, and, with the exception of this small group of Brahuis, penetrated to the south of India and settled there without leaving any traces of their passage.

The Dravidian languages occupy a large area in Madras, Mysore and Hyderābād, and they extend north into the Central Provinces and Chota Nāgpur, where they die out, practically not being found west and north of this tract. As the languages are more highly developed and the culture of their speakers is far more advanced in the south, it is justifiable to suppose, pending evidence to the contrary, that the south is their home and that they have spread thence as far north as the Central Provinces. The Gonds and Oraons too have stories to the effect that they came from the south. It has hitherto been believed, at least in the Central Provinces, that both the Gonds and Baigas have been settled in this territory for an indefinite period, that is, from prior to any Aryan or Hindu immigration. Mr. H. A. Crump, however, has questioned this assumption. He points out that the Baiga tribe have entirely lost their own language and speak a dialect of Chhattīsgarhi Hindi in Mandla, while half the Gonds still speak Gondi. If the Baigas and Gonds were settled here together before the arrival of any Hindus, how is it that the Baigas do not speak Gondi instead of Hindi? A comparison of the caste and language tables of the census of 1901 shows that several of the Munda tribes have entirely lost their own language, among these being the Binjhwār, Baiga, Bhaina, Bhuiya, Bhumij, Chero and Khairwār, and the Bhīls and Kolis if these are held to be Munda tribes. None of these tribes have adopted a Dravidian language, but all speak corrupt forms of the current Aryan vernaculars derived from Sanskrit. The Mundas and Hos themselves with the Kharias, Santāls and Korkus retain Munda languages. On the other hand a half of the Gonds, nearly all the Oraons and three-fourths of the Khonds still preserve their own Dravidian speech. It would therefore seem that the Munda tribes who speak Aryan vernaculars must have been in close contact with Hindu peoples at the time they lost their own language and not with Gonds or Oraons. In the Central Provinces it is known that Rājpūt dynasties were ruling in Jubbulpore from the sixth to the twelfth century, in Seoni about the sixth century and in Bhāndak near Chānda from an early period as well as at Ratanpur in Chhattīsgarh. From about the twelfth century these disappear and there is a blank till the fourteenth century or later, when Gond kingdoms are found established at Kherla in Betul, at Deogarh in Chhindwāra, at Garha-Mandla [1] including the Jubbulpore country, and at Chānda fourteen miles from Bhāndak. It seems clear then that the Hindu dynasties were subverted by the Gonds after the Muhammadan invasions of northern India had weakened or destroyed the central powers of the Hindus and prevented any assistance being afforded to the outlying settlements. But it seems *prima facie* more likely that the Hindu kingdoms of the Central Provinces should have been destroyed by an invasion of barbarians from without rather than by successful risings of their own subjects once thoroughly subdued. The Haihaya Rājpūt dynasty of Ratanpur was the only one which survived, all the others being supplanted by Gond states. If then the Gond incursion was subsequent to the establishment of the old Hindu kingdoms, its probable date may be placed from the ninth to the thirteenth centuries, the subjugation of the greater part of the Province being no doubt a gradual affair. In favour of this it may be noted that some recollection still exists of the settlement of the Oraons in Chota Nāgpur being later than that of the Mundas, while if it had taken place long before this time all tradition of it would probably have been forgotten. In Chhindwāra the legend still remains that the founder of the Deogarh Gond dynasty, Jātba, slew and supplanted the

[1] Garha is six miles from Jubbulpore.

Gaoli kings Ransur and Ghansur, who were previously ruling on the plateau. And the Bastar Rāj-Gond Rājas have a story that they came from Warangal in the south so late as the fourteenth century, accompanied by the ancestors of some of the existing Bastar tribes. Jadu Rai, the founder of the Gond-Rājpūt dynasty of Garha-Mandla, is supposed to have lived near the Godāvari. A large section of the Gonds of the Central Provinces are known as Rāwanvansi or of the race of Rāwan, the demon king of Ceylon, who was conquered by Rāma. The Oraons also claim to be descended from Rāwan.[1] This name and story must clearly have been given to the tribes by the Hindus, and the explanation appears to be that the Hindus considered the Dravidian Gonds and Oraons to have been the enemy encountered in the Aryan expedition to southern India and Ceylon, which is dimly recorded in the legend of Rāma. On the other hand the Bhuiyas, a Munda tribe, call themselves *Pāwan-ka-put* or Children of the Wind, that is of the race of Hanumān, who was the Son of the Wind; and this name would appear to show, as suggested by Colonel Dalton, that the Munda tribes gave assistance to the Aryan expedition and accompanied it, an alliance which has been preserved in the tale of the exploits of Hanumān and his army of apes. Similarly the name of the Rāmosi caste of Berār is a corruption of Rāmvansi or of the race of Rāma; and the Rāmosis appear to be an offshoot of the Bhīls or Kolis, both of whom are not improbably Munda tribes. A Hindu writer compared the Bhīl auxiliaries in the camp of the famous Chalukya Rājpūt king Sidhrāj of Gujarāt to Hanumān and his apes, on account of their agility.[2] These instances seem to be in favour of the idea that the Munda tribes assisted the Aryans, and if this were the case it would appear to be a legitimate inference that at the same period the Dravidian tribes were still in southern India and not mixed up with the Munda tribes in the Central Provinces and Chota Nāgpur as at present. Though the evidence is perhaps not very strong, the hypothesis, as suggested by Mr. Crump,

1 *The Mundas and their Country*, p. 124.

2 *Rāsmāla*, i. p. 113.

that the settlement of the Gonds in the Central Provinces is comparatively recent and subsequent to the early Rājpūt dynasties, is well worth putting forward.

6. Strength of the Kols in the Central Provinces.

In the Central Provinces the Kols and Mundas numbered 85,000 persons in 1911. The name Kol is in general use except in the Chota Nāgpur States, but it seems probable that the Kols who have immigrated here really belong to the Munda tribe of Chota Nāgpur. About 52,000 Kols, or nearly a third of the total number, reside in the Jubbulpore District, and the remainder are scattered over all Districts and States of the Province.

7. Legend of origin.

The Kol legend of origin is that Sing-Bonga or the Sun created a boy and a girl and put them together in a cave to people the world; but finding them to be too innocent to give hope of progeny he instructed them in the art of making rice-beer, which inflames the passions, and in course of time they had twelve sons and twelve daughters. The divine origin ascribed by the Kols, in common with other peoples, to their favourite liquor may be noticed. The children were divided into pairs, and Sing-Bonga set before them various kinds of food to choose for their sustenance before starting out into the world; and the fate of their descendants depended on their choice. Thus the first and second pairs took the flesh of bullocks and buffaloes, and from them are descended the Kols and Bhumij; one pair took shell-fish and became Bhuiyas, two pairs took pigs and were the ancestors of the Santāls, one pair took vegetables only and originated the Brāhman and Rājpūt castes, and other pairs took goats and fish, from whom the various Sūdra castes are sprung. One pair got nothing, and seeing this the Kol pair gave them of their superfluity and the descendants of these became the Ghasias, who are menials in Kol villages and supported by the cultivators. The Larka Kols attribute their strength and fine physique to the fact that they eat beef. When they first met English soldiers in the beginning of the nineteenth century the Kols were quickly impressed by their wonderful fighting powers, and finding that the English too ate the flesh of bullocks, paid them the high compliment of assigning to them the same pair of ancestors as themselves. The Nāgvansi Rājas of

Chota Nāgpur say that their original ancestor was a snake-god who assumed human form and married a Brāhman's daughter. But, like Lohengrin, the condition of his remaining a man was that he should not disclose his origin, and when he was finally brought to satisfy the incessant curiosity of his wife, he reverted to his first shape, and she burned herself from remorse. Their child was found by some wood-cutters lying in the forest beneath a cobra's extended hood, and was brought up in their family. He subsequently became king, and his seven elder brothers attended him as banghy-bearers when he rode abroad. The Mundas are said to be descended from the seven brothers, and their sign-manual is a *kawar* or banghy.[1] Hence the Rājas of Chota Nāgpur regard the Mundas as their elder brothers, and the Rānis veil their faces when they meet a Munda as to a husband's elder brother. The probable explanation of the story is that the Hos or Mundas, from whom the kings are sprung, were a separate section of the tribe who subdued the older Mundas. In memory of their progenitor the Nāgvansi Rājas wear a turban folded to resemble the coils of a snake with a projection over the brow for its head.[2]

8. Tribal subdivisions. The subcastes of the Kols in the Central Provinces differ entirely from those in Chota Nāgpur. Of the important subcastes here the Rautia and Rautele take their name from Rāwat, a prince, and appear to be a military or landholding group. In Chota Nāgpur the Rautias are a separate caste, holding land. The Rautia Kols practise hypergamy with the Rauteles, taking their daughters in marriage but not giving daughters. They will eat with Rauteles at wedding feasts only and not on any other occasion. The Thākuria, from *thākur*, a lord, are said to be the progeny of Rājput fathers and Kol mothers; and the Kagwaria to be named from *kagwār*, an offering made to ancestors in the month of Kunwār. The Desāha, from *desh*, native country, belong principally to Rewah. In some localities Bharias, Savars and Khairwārs are found who call themselves Kols and appear to be included in the tribe. The Bharias may be an offshoot of the Bhar tribe of

[1] Two baskets slung from a stick across the shoulders.

[2] Dalton, *Ethnology of Bengal*, p. 166.

northern India. It has already been seen that several groups of other tribes have been amalgamated with the Muṇdas of Chota Nāgpur, probably in a great measure from intermarriage, and a similar fusion seems to have occurred in the Central Provinces. Intermarriage between the different subtribes, though nominally prohibited, not infrequently takes place, and a girl forming a *liaison* with a man of another division may be married to him and received into it. The Rautias, however, say that they forbid this practice.

9. Totemism. The Mandla Kols have a number of totemistic septs. The Bargaiyan are really called after a village Bargaon, but they connect their name with the *bar* or banyan tree, and revere it. At their weddings a branch of this tree is laid on the roof of the marriage-shed, and the wedding-cakes are cooked in a fire made of the wood of the banyan tree and served to all the relations of the sept on its leaves. At other times they will not pluck a leaf or a branch from a banyan tree or even go beneath its shade. The Kathotia sept is named after *kathota*, a bowl, but they revere the tiger. Bagheshwar Deo, the tiger-god, resides on a little platform in their verandas. They may not join in a tiger-beat nor sit up for a tiger over a kill. In the latter case they think that the tiger would not come and would be deprived of his food, and all the members of their family would get ill. If a tiger takes one of their cattle, they think there has been some neglect in their worship of him. They say that if one of them meets a tiger in the forest he will fold his hands and say, 'Mahārāj, let me pass,' and the tiger will then get out of his way. If a tiger is killed within the limits of his village a Kathotia Kol will throw away his earthen pots as in mourning for a relative, have his head shaved and feed a few men of his sept. The Katharia sept take their name from *kathri*, a mattress. A member of this sept must never have a mattress in his house nor wear clothes sewn in cross-pieces as mattresses are sewn. The word *kathri* should never be mentioned before him as he thinks some great misfortune would thereby happen to his family, but this belief is falling into abeyance. The name of the Mudia or Mudrundia sept is said to mean shaven head, but they apparently revere the white *kumhra* or gourd, perhaps because it has some

resemblance to a shaven head. They give a white gourd to a woman on the third day after she has borne a child, and her family then do not eat this vegetable for three years. At the expiration of the period the head of the family offers a chicken to Dulha Deo, frying it with the feathers left on the head, and eating the head and feet himself. Women may not join in this sacrifice. The Kumraya sept revere the brown *kumhra* or gourd. They grow this vegetable on the thatch of their house-roof, and from the time of planting it until the fruits have been plucked they do not touch it. The Bhuwar sept are named after *bhu* or *bhumi*, the earth. They must always sleep on the earth and not on cots. Other septs are Nathunia, a nose-ring; Karpatia, a kind of grass; and Binjhwār, from the tribe of that name. From Raigarh a separate group of septs is reported, the names of which further demonstrate the mixed nature of the tribe. Among these are Bandi, a slave; Kawar, Gond, Dhanuhār, Birjhia, all of which are the names of distinct tribes; Sonwāni, gold-water; Keriāri, or bridle; Khūnta, a peg; and Kapāt, a shutter.

10. Marriage customs.

Marriage within the sept is prohibited, but violations of this rule are not infrequent. Outside the sept a man may marry any woman except the sisters of his mother or stepmother. Where, as in some localities, the septs have been forgotten, marriage is forbidden between those relatives to whom the sacramental cakes are distributed at a wedding. Among the Mundas, before a father sets out to seek a bride for his son, he invites three or four relatives, and at midnight taking a bottle of liquor pours a little over the household god as a libation and drinks the rest with them. They go to the girl's village, and addressing her father say that they have come to hunt. He asks them in what jungle they wish to hunt, and they name the *sarna* or sacred grove in which the bones of his ancestors are buried. If the girl's father is satisfied with the match, he then agrees to it. A bride-price of Rs. 10-8 is paid in the Central Provinces. Among the Hos of Chota Nāgpur so large a number of cattle was formerly demanded in exchange for a bride that many girls were never married. Afterwards it was reduced to ten head of cattle, and it was decided that one pair of bullocks, one cow and seven rupees should be equivalent to ten head, while for poor families Rs. 7 was to be the whole price.[1] Among the Mundas of Raigarh the price is three or four bullocks, but poor men may give Rs. 12 or Rs. 18 in substitution. Here weddings may only be held in the three months of Aghan, Māgh and Phāgun,[2] and preferably in Māgh. Their marriage ceremony is very simple, the bridegroom simply smearing vermilion on the bride's forehead, after which water is poured over the heads of the pair. Two pots of liquor are placed beside them during the ceremony. It is also a good marriage if a girl of her own accord goes and lives in a man's house and he shows his acceptance by dabbing vermilion on her. But her offspring are of inferior status to those of a regular marriage. The Kols of Jubbulpore and Mandla have adopted the regular Hindu ceremony.

11. Divorce and widow-marriage.

Divorce and widow-marriage are permitted. In Raigarh the widow is bound to marry her deceased husband's younger brother, but not elsewhere. Among these Mundas, if divorce is effected by mutual consent, the husband must give his wife a pair of loin-cloths and provisions for six months. Polygamy is seldom practised, as women can earn their own living, and if a wife is superseded she will often run away home or set up in a house by herself. In Mandla a divorce can be obtained by either party, the person in fault having to pay a fee of Rs. 1-4 to the *panchāyat*; the woman then breaks her bangles and the divorce is complete.

12. Religion.

At the head of the Munda pantheon, Sir H. Risley states,[3] stands Sing-Bonga or the sun, a beneficent but ineffective deity who concerns himself but little with human affairs. But he may be invoked to avert sickness or calamity, and to this end sacrifices of white goats or white cocks are offered to him. Next to him comes Marang Buru, the mountain god, who resides on the summit of the most prominent hill in the neighbourhood. Animals are sacrificed to him here, and the heads left and appropriated by the priest. He controls the rainfall, and is appealed to in time of drought and when epidemic sickness is abroad. Other

[1] Dalton, p. 152.

[2] November, January and February.

[3] *Tribes and Castes*, art. Munda.

Bemrose, Collo., Derby.

GROUP OF KOL WOMEN.

deities preside over rivers, tanks, wells and springs, and it is believed that when offended they cause people who bathe in the water to be attacked by leprosy and skin diseases. Even the low swampy rice-fields are haunted by separate spirits. Deswāli is the god of the village, and he lives with his wife in the Sarna or sacred grove, a patch of the primeval forest left intact to afford a refuge for the forest gods. Every village has its own Deswāli, who is held responsible for the crops, and receives an offering of a buffalo at the agricultural festival. The Jubbulpore Kols have entirely abandoned their tribal gods and now worship Hindu deities. Devi is their favourite goddess, and they carry her iron tridents about with them wherever they go. Twice in the year, when the baskets of wheat or Gardens of Adonis are sown in the name of Devi, she descends on some of her worshippers, and they become possessed and pierce their cheeks with the trident, sometimes leaving it in the face for hours, with one or two men standing beside to support it. When the trident is taken out a quid of betel is given to the wounded man, and the part is believed to heal up at once. These Kols also employ Brāhmans for their ceremonies. Before sowing their fields they say—

> *Thuiya, Bhuiya,*[1] *Dharti Māta, Thākur Deo, Bhainsa Sur; khūb paida kariye Mahārāj;*

that is, they invoke Mother Earth, Thākur Deo, the corn-god, and Bhainsāsur, the buffalo demon, to give them good crops; and as they say this they throw a handful of grain in the air in the name of each god.

"Among the Hos," Colonel Dalton states, "all disease in men or animals is attributed to one of two causes—the wrath of some evil spirit who has to be appeased, or the spell of some witch or sorcerer who should be destroyed or driven out of the land. In the latter case a *sokha* or witch-finder is employed to ascertain who has cast the spell, and various methods of divination are resorted to. In former times the person denounced and all his family were put to death in the belief that witches breed witches and sorcerers. The taint is in the blood. When, during the Mutiny, 13. Witchcraft.

[1] Thuiya, Bhuiya is a mere jingle.

Singhbhūm District was left for a short time without officers, a terrible raid was made against all who had been suspected for years of dealing with the evil one, and the most atrocious murders were committed. Young men were told off for the duty by the elders; neither age nor sex were spared. When order was restored, these crimes were brought to light, and the actual perpetrators punished; and since then we have not only had no recurrence of witch murders, but the superstition itself is dying out in the Kolhān." Mr. H. C. Streatfeild states that among the Mundas witches used to be hung head downwards from a pīpal tree over a slow fire, the whole village dancing as they were gradually roasted, but whether this ceremony was purely vindictive or had any other significance there is nothing to show.[1]

14. Funeral rites. The Hos of Chota Nāgpur were accustomed to place large slabs of stone as tombstones over their graves, and a collection of these massive gravestones indelibly marks the site of every Ho or Mundāri village, being still found in parts of the country where there have been no Kols for ages. In addition to this slab, a megalithic monument is set up to the deceased in some conspicuous spot outside the village; the pillars vary in height from five or six to fifteen feet, and apparently fragments of rock of the most fantastic shape are most favoured. All the clothes, ornaments and agricultural implements of the dead man were buried with the body. The funeral rites were of a somewhat touching character:[2] "When all is ready, a funeral party collects in front of the deceased's house, three or four men with very deep-toned drums, and a group of about eight young girls. The chief mourner comes forth, carrying the bones exposed on a decorated tray, and behind him the girls form two rows, carrying empty or broken pitchers or battered brass vessels, while the men with drums bring up the rear. The procession advances with a ghostly dancing movement, slow and solemn as a minuet, in time to the beat of the deep-toned drums, not straight forward, but mysteriously gliding—now right, now left, now marking time, all in the same mournful cadence. In this manner the remains are taken to the house of every friend and relative

[1] *J.A.S.B.*, No. 1 of 1903, p. 31.

[2] Dalton, *ibidem*.

of the deceased within a circle of a few miles, and to every house in the village. As the procession approaches each house in the manner described, the inmates all come out, and the tray having been placed on the ground at their door, they kneel over it and mourn. The bones are also thus conveyed to all his favourite haunts, the fields he cultivated, the grove he planted, the tank he excavated, the threshing-floor where he worked with his people, the Akhāra or dancing-arena where he made merry with them, and each spot which is hallowed with reminiscences of the deceased draws forth fresh tears." In Sambalpur[1] the dead body of a Munda is washed in wine before interment, and a mark of vermilion is made on the forehead. The mourners drink wine sitting by the grave. They then bathe, and catch a small fish and roast it on a fire, smearing their hands with oil and warming them at the fire. It would appear that this last rite is a purification of the hands after contact with the dead body, but whether the fish is meant to represent the deceased and the roasting of it is a substitute for the rite of cremation is not clear. During the eight days of mourning the relatives abstain from flesh-meat, but they eat fish. The Kols of Jubbulpore now bury or burn the dead, and observe mourning exactly like ordinary Hindus.

Succession among the Mundas passes to sons only. Failing these, the property goes to the father or brothers if any. At partition the eldest son as a rule gets a slightly larger share than the other sons, a piece of land, and in well-to-do families a yoke of plough cattle, or only a bullock or a goat, and sometimes a bundle of paddy weighing from 10 to 16 maunds.[2] Partition cannot usually be made till the youngest son is of age. Daughters get no share in the inheritance, and are allotted among the sons just like livestock. Thus if a man dies leaving three sons and three daughters and thirty head of cattle, on a division each son would get ten head of cattle and one sister; but should there be only one sister, they wait till she marries and divide the bride-price. A father may, however, in his lifetime make presents of cash or movables to a daughter, **15. Inheritance.**

[1] Mr. B. C. Mazumdār's Monograph.

[2] Roy, *ibidem*, p. 428.

though not of land. It is doubtful whether these rules still obtain among the Hinduised Kols.

16. Physical appearance. "The Mundas," Colonel Dalton states, "are one of the finest of the aboriginal tribes. The men average something like 5 feet 6 inches, and many of them are remarkably well developed and muscular. Their skin is of the darkest brown, almost black in many cases, and their features coarse, with broad flat noses, low foreheads and thick lips, presenting as a rule a by no means prepossessing appearance. The women are often more pleasing, the coarseness of the features being less accentuated or less noticeable on account of the extreme good-nature and happy carelessness that seldom fail to mark their countenance. They are fond of ornament, and a group of men and girls fully decked out for a festival makes a fine show. Every ornament in the shape of bead necklace, silver collar, bracelet, armlet and anklet would seem to have been brought out for the occasion. The head-dress is the crowning point of the turn-out. The long black hair is gathered up in a big coil, most often artificially enlarged, the whole being fastened at the right-hand side of the back of the head just on a level with and touching the right ear. In this knot are fastened all sorts of ornaments of brass and silver, and surmounting it, stuck in every available space, are gay plumes of feathers that nod and wave bravely with the movements of the dance. The ears are distorted almost beyond recognition by huge earrings that pierce the lobe and smaller ones that ornament them all round." In Mandla women are tattooed with the figure of a man or a man on horseback, and on the legs behind also with the figure of a man. They are not tattooed on the face. Men are never tattooed.

17. Dances. "Dancing is the inevitable accompaniment of every gathering, and they have a great variety suitable to the special times and seasons. The motion is slow and graceful, a monotonous sing-song being kept up all through. The steps are in perfect time and the action wonderfully even and regular. This is particularly noticeable in some of the variations of the dances representing the different seasons and the necessary acts of cultivation that each brings with it. In one the dancers bending down make a motion with their

hands as though they were sowing the grain, keeping step with their feet all the time. Then come the reaping of the crop and the binding of the sheaves, all done in perfect time and rhythm, and making with the continuous droning of the voices a quaint and picturesque performance." In the Central Provinces the Kols now dance the Karma dance of the Gonds, but they dance it in more lively fashion. The step consists simply in advancing or withdrawing one foot and bringing the other up or back beside it. The men and women stand opposite each other in two lines, holding hands, and the musicians alternately face each line and advance and retreat with them. Then the lines move round in a circle with the musicians in the centre.

18. Social rules and offences.

Munda boys are allowed to eat food cooked by other castes, except the very lowest, until they are married, and girls until they let their hair grow long, which is usually at the age of six or seven. After this they do not take food as a tribe from any other caste, even a Brāhman, though some subtribes accept it from certain castes as the Telis (oil-pressers) and Sundis or liquor-vendors. In Jubbulpore the Kols take food from Kurmis, Dhīmars and Ahīrs. The Mundas will eat almost all kinds of flesh, including tigers and pigs, while in Raigarh they consider monkey as a delicacy, hunting these animals with dogs. In the Central Provinces they have generally abjured beef, in deference to Hindu prejudice, and sometimes refuse field-mice, to which the Khonds and Gonds are very partial. Neither Kols nor Mundas are, however, considered impure and the barber and washerman will work for them. In Sambalpur a woman is finally expelled from caste for a *liaison* with one of the impure Gāndas, Ghasias or Doms, and a man is expelled for taking food from a woman of these castes, but adultery with her may be expiated by a big feast. Other offences are much the same as among the Hindus. A woman who gets her ear torn through where it is pierced is put out of caste for six months or a year and has to give two feasts on readmission.

19. The caste *panchāyat*.

In Mandla the head of the *panchāyat* is known as Gaontia, a name for a village headman, and he is always of the Bargaiya sept, the office being usually hereditary. When a serious offence is committed the Gaontia fixes a period of six months to a year for the readmission of the culprit, or the latter begs for reinstatement when he has obtained the materials for the penalty feast. A feast for the whole Rautele subcaste will entail 500 seers or nearly 9 cwt. of kodon, costing perhaps Rs. 30, and they say there would not be enough left for a cold breakfast for the offender's family in the morning. When a man has a petition to make to the Gaontia, he folds his turban round his neck, leaving the head bare, takes a piece of grass in his mouth, and with four prominent elders to support him goes to the Gaontia and falls at his feet. The others stand on one leg behind him and the Gaontia asks them for their recommendation. Their reverence for the caste *panchāyat* is shown by their solemn form of oath, 'Sing-Bonga on high and the Panch on earth.'[1] The Kols of Jubbulpore and Mandla are now completely conforming to Hindu usage and employ Brāhmans for their ceremonies. They are most anxious to be considered as good Hindus and ape every high-caste custom they get hold of. On one occasion I was being carried on a litter by Kol coolies and accompanied by a Rājpūt chuprāssie and was talking to the Kols, who eagerly proclaimed their rigid Hindu observances. Finally the chuprāssie said that Brāhmans and Rājpūts must have three separate brushes of date-palm fibre for their houses, one to sweep the cook-room which is especially sacred, one for the rest of the house, and one for the yard. Lying gallantly the Kols said that they also kept three palm brushes for cleaning their houses, and when it was pointed out that there were no date-palms within several miles of their village, they said they sent periodical expeditions to the adjoining District to bring back fibre for brushes.

20. Names. Colonel Dalton notes that the Kols, like the Gonds, give names to their children after officers visiting the village when they are born. Thus Captain, Major, Doctor are common names in the Kolhān. Mr. Mazumdār gives an instance of a Kol servant of the Rāja of Bāmra who greatly admired some English lamp-chimneys sent for by the Rāja and called his daughter 'Chimney.' They do not address any relative or caste-man by his name if he is older than them-

[1] *The Mundas and their Country*, p. 121.

selves, but use the term of relationship to a relative and to others the honorific title of Gaontia.

21. Occupation. The Mundāri language has no words for the village trades nor for the implements of cultivation, and so it may be concluded that prior to their contact with the Hindus the Mundas lived on the fruits and roots of the forests and the pursuit of game and fish. Now, however, they have taken kindly to several kinds of labour. They are much in request on the Assam tea-gardens owing to their good physique and muscular power, and they make the best bearers of *dhoolies* or palanquins. Kol bearers will carry a *dhoolie* four miles an hour as against the best Gond pace of about three, and they shake the occupant less. They also make excellent masons and navvies, and are generally more honest workers than the other jungle tribes. A Munda seldom comes into a criminal court.

22. Language. The Kols of the Central Provinces have practically abandoned their own language, Mundāri being retained only by about 1000 persons in 1911. The Kols and Mundas now speak the Hindu vernacular current in the tracts where they reside. Mundāri, Santāli, Korwa and Bhumij are practically all forms of one language which Sir G. Grierson designates as Kherwāri.[1]

[1] *Linguistic Survey*, vol. iv., *Munda and Dravidian Languages*, p. 27.

KOLĀM

LIST OF PARAGRAPHS

1. General notice of the tribe.

Kolām.[1]—A Dravidian tribe residing principally in the Wūn tāluk of the Yeotmāl District. They number altogether about 25,000 persons, of whom 23,000 belong to Wūn and the remainder to the adjoining tracts of Wardha and Hyderābād. They are not found elsewhere. The tribe are generally considered to be akin to the Gonds[2] on the authority of Mr. Hislop. He wrote of them: "The Kolāms extend all along the Kandi Konda or Pindi Hills on the south of the Wardha river and along the table-land stretching east and north of Mānikgad and thence south to Dāntanpalli, running parallel to the western bank of the Prānhīta. The Kolāms and the common Gonds do not intermarry, but they are present at each other's nuptials and eat from each other's hand. Their dress is similar, but the Kolām women wear fewer ornaments, being generally content with a few black beads of glass round their neck. Among their deities, which are the usual objects of Gond adoration, Bhīmsen is chiefly honoured." Mr. Hislop was, however, not always of this opinion, because he first excluded the Kolāms from the Gond tribes and afterwards included them.[3] In Wardha they are usually distinguished from the Gonds. They have a language of their own, called after them Kolāmi. Sir G.

[1] This article includes some extracts from notes made by Colonel Mackenzie when Commissioner of Berār, and subsequently published in the *Pioneer* newspaper; and information collected for the District Gazetteers in Yeotmāl and Wardha.

[2] *Papers relating to the Aboriginal Tribes of the Central Provinces*, p. 10.

[3] *Ibidem*, Editor's Note.

Bemrose, Collo., Derby.

GROUP OF KOLĀMS.

Grierson[1] describes it as, "A minor dialect of Berār and the Central Provinces which occupies a position like that of Gondi between Canarese, Tamil and Telugu. The so-called Kolāmi, the Bhīli spoken in the Pusad tāluk of Bāsim and the so-called Naiki of Chānda agree in so many particulars that they can almost be considered as one and the same dialect. They are closely related to Gondi. The points in which they differ from that language are, however, of sufficient importance to make it necessary to separate them from that form of speech. The Kolāmi dialect differs widely from the language of the neighbouring Gonds. In some points it agrees with Telugu, in other characteristics with Canarese and connected forms of speech. There are also some interesting points of analogy with the Toda dialect of the Nīlgiris, and the Kolāms must, from a philological point of view, be considered as the remnants of an old Dravidian tribe who have not been involved in the development of the principal Dravidian languages, or of a tribe who have not originally spoken a Dravidian form of speech."

The family names of the tribe also are not Gondi, but resemble those of Marātha castes. Out of fifty sept names recorded, only one, Tekām, is found among the Gonds. "All their songs and ballads," Colonel Mackenzie says, "are borrowed from the Marāthas: even their women when grinding corn sing Marāthi songs." In Wūn their dress and appearance resembles that of the Kunbis, but in some respects they retain very primitive customs. Colonel Mackenzie states that until recently in Berār they had the practice of capturing husbands for women who would otherwise have gone unwedded, this being apparently a survival of the matriarchate. It does not appear that the husbands so captured were ever unphilosophical enough to rebel under the old regime, though British enlightenment has taught them otherwise. Widows and widowers were exempt from capture and debarred from capturing. In view of the connection mentioned by Sir G. Grierson between the Kolāmi dialect and that of the Todas of the Nīlgiri hills who are a small remnant of an ancient tribe and still practise polyandry, Mr. Hīra Lāl suggests that the Kolāms may be connected

[1] *Linguistic Survey*, vol. iv., *Munda and Dravidian Languages*, p. 561.

with the Kolas, a tribe akin to the Todās[1] and as low in the scale of civilisation, who regard the Kolamallai hills as their original home.[2] He further notes that the name of the era by which the calendar is reckoned on the Malabar coast is Kolamba. In view of Sir G. Grierson's statement that the Kolāmi dialect is the same as that of the Nāik Gonds of Chānda it may be noted that the headman of a Kolām village is known as Nāik, and it is possible that the Kolāms may be connected with the so-called Nāik Gonds.

2. Marriage. The Kolāms have no subtribes, but are divided for purposes of marriage into a number of exogamous groups. The names of these are in the Marāthi form, but the tribe do not know their meaning. Marriage between members of the same group is forbidden, and a man may not marry two sisters. Marriage is usually adult, and neither a betrothal nor a marriage can be concluded in the month of Poush (December), because in this month ancestors are worshipped. Colonel Mackenzie states that marriages should be celebrated on Wednesdays and Saturdays at sundown, and Monday is considered a peculiarly inauspicious day. If a betrothal, once contracted, is broken, a fine of five or ten rupees must be paid to the caste-fellows together with a quantity of liquor. Formerly, as stated above, the tribe sometimes captured husbands, and they still have a curious method of seizing a wife when the father cannot procure a mate for his son. The latter attended by his comrades resorts to the jungle where his wife-elect is working in company with her female relations and friends. It is a custom of the tribe that the sexes should, as a rule, work in separate parties. On catching sight of her the bridegroom pursues her, and unless he touches her hand before she gets back to her village, his friends will afford him no assistance. If he can lay hold of the girl a struggle ensues between the two parties for her possession, the girl being sometimes only protected by women, while on other occasions her male relatives hear of the fray and come to her assistance. In the latter case a fight ensues with sticks, in which, however, no combatant may hit another on the head. If the girl is captured the

[1] *India Census Report* (1901), p. 287.

[2] Hunter's *Imperial Gazetteer*, art. Kolamallai hills.

marriage is subsequently performed, and even if she is rescued the matter is often arranged by the payment of a few rupees to the girl's father. Nowadays the whole affair tends to degenerate into a pretence and is often arranged beforehand by the parties. The marriage ceremony resembles that of the Kunbis except that the bridegroom takes the bride on his lap and their clothes are tied together in two places. After the ceremony each of the guests takes a few grains of rice, and after touching the feet, knees and shoulders of the bridal couple with the rice, throws it over his own back. The idea may be to remove any contagion of misfortune or evil spirits who may be hovering about them. A widow can remarry only with her parents' consent, but if she takes a fancy to a man and chooses to enter his house with a pot of water on her head he cannot turn her out. A man cannot marry a widow unless he has been regularly wedded once to a girl, and once having espoused a widow by what is known as the *pāt* ceremony, he cannot again go through a proper marriage. A couple who wish to be divorced must go before the caste *panchāyat* or committee with a pot of liquor. Over this is laid a dry stick and the couple each hold an end of it. The husband then addresses his wife as sister in the presence of the caste-fellows, and the wife her husband as brother; they break the stick and the divorce is complete.

3. Disposal of the dead.

The tribe bury their dead, and observe mourning for one to five days in different localities. The spirits of deceased ancestors are worshipped on any Monday in the month of Poush. The mourner goes and dips his head into a tank or stream, and afterwards sacrifices a fowl on the bank, and gives a meal to the caste-fellows. He then has the hair of his face and head shaved. Sons inherit equally, and if there are no sons the property devolves on daughters.

4. Religion and superstitions.

The Kolāms, Colonel Mackenzie states, recognise no god as a principle of beneficence in the world; their principal deities are Sīta, to whom the first-fruits of the harvest are offered, and Devi who is the guardian of the village, and is propitiated with offerings of goats and fowls to preserve it from harm. She is represented by two stones set up in the centre of the village when it is founded. They worship their implements of agriculture on the last day of Chait (April), applying turmeric and vermilion to them. In May they collect the stumps of juāri from a field, and, burning them to ashes, make an offering of the same articles. They have a curious ceremony for protecting the village from disease. All the men go outside the village and on the boundary at the four points pointing north-east, north-west and opposite place four stones known as *bandi*, burying a fowl beneath each stone. The Nāik or headman then sacrifices a goat and other fowls to Sīta, and placing four men by the stones, proceeds to sprinkle salt all along the boundary line, except across one path on which he lays his stick. He then calls out to the men that the village is closed and that they must enter it only by that path. This rule remains in force throughout the year, and if any stranger enters the village by any other than the appointed route, they consider that he should pay the expenses of drawing the boundary circuit again. But the rule is often applied only to carts, and relaxed in favour of travellers on foot. The line marked with salt is called *bandesh*, and it is believed that wild animals cannot cross it, while they are prevented from coming into the village along the only open road by the stick of the Nāik. Diseases also cannot cross the line. Women during their monthly impurity are made to live in a hut in the fields outside the boundary line. The open road does not lead across the village, but terminates at the *chauri* or meeting-house.

5. Social position. Though the Kolāms retain some very primitive customs, those of Yeotmāl, as already stated, are hardly distinguishable from the Kunbis or Hindu cultivators. Colonel Mackenzie notes that they are held to be lower than the Gonds, because a Kolām will take food from a Gond, but the latter will not return the compliment. They will eat the flesh of rats, tigers, snakes, squirrels and of almost any animals except dogs, donkeys and jackals. In another respect they are on a level with the lowest aborigines, as some of them do not use water to clean their bodies after performing natural functions, but only leaves. Yet they are not considered as impure by the Hindus, are permitted

to enter Hindu temples, and hold themselves to be defiled by the touch of a Mahār or a Māng. A Kolām is forbidden to beg by the rules of the tribe, and he looks down on the Mahārs and Māngs, who are often professional beggars. In Wardha, too, the Kolāms will not collect dead-wood for sale as fuel.

Here their houses contain only a single room with a small store-house, and all the family sleep together without privacy. Consequently there is no opportunity at night for conjugal intimacy, and husband and wife seek the solitude of the forest in the daytime. Colonel Mackenzie states: "All Kolāms are great smokers, but they are not allowed to smoke in their own houses, but only at the *chauri* or meeting-house, where pipes and fire are kept; and this rule is enforced so that the Nāik or headman can keep an eye on all male members of the community; if these do not appear at least once a day, satisfactory reasons are demanded for their absence, and from this rule only the sick and infirm are exempt. The Kolāms have two musical instruments: the *tāpate* or drum, and the *wāss* or flute, the name of which is probably derived from the Sanskrit *wāunsh*, meaning bamboo (of which the instrument is made). In old times all Kolāms could read and write, and it is probably only poverty which prevents them from having all their children educated now." This last statement must, however, be accepted with reserve in the absence of intimation of the evidence on which it is based. At present they are, as a rule, quite illiterate. The Nāik or headman formerly had considerable powers, being entrusted with the distribution of land among the cultivators, and exercising civil and criminal jurisdiction with the assistance of the *panchāyat*. His own land was ploughed for him by the villagers. Even now they seldom enter a court of justice and their disputes are settled by the *panchāyat*. A strong feeling of clannishness exists among them, and the village unites to avenge an injury done to one of its members. Excommunication from caste is imposed for the usual offences, and the ceremony of readmission is as follows: The offender dips his head in a river or stream and the village barber shaves his head and

6. Miscellaneous customs.

moustaches. He then sits beside a lighted pile of wood, being held to be purified by the proximity of the holy element, and afterwards bathes, and drinks some water into which the caste-fellows have dipped their toes. A woman has to undergo the same ceremony and have her head shaved. If an unmarried girl becomes with child by a member of the caste, she is married to him by the simple rite used for widow-remarriage. A Kolām must not swear by a dog or cat, and is expelled from caste for killing either of these two animals. A Kolām does not visit a friend's house in the evening, as he would be suspected in such an event of having designs upon his wife's virtue. The tribe are cultivators and labourers. They have not a very good reputation for honesty, and are said to be addicted to stealing the ripe cotton from the bolls. They never wear shoes, and the soles of their feet become nearly invulnerable and capable of traversing the most thorny ground without injury. They have an excellent knowledge of the medicinal and other uses of all trees, shrubs and herbs.

KOLHĀTI

[*Bibliography*: Mr. Kitts' *Berār Census Report* (1881); Major Gunthorpe's *Criminal Tribes of Bombay, Berar and the Central Provinces* (Times Press, Bombay).]

LIST OF PARAGRAPHS

Kolhāti, Dandewāla, Bānsberia, Kabūtari.[1]—The name by which the Beria caste of Northern and Central India is known in Berār. The Berias themselves, in Central India at any rate, are a branch of the Sānsias, a vagrant and criminal class, whose traditional occupation was that of acting as bards and genealogists to the Jāt caste. The main difference between the Sānsias and Berias is that the latter prostitute their women, or those of them who are not married.[2] The Kolhātis of Berār, who also do this, appear to be a branch of the Beria caste who have settled in the Deccan and now have customs differing in several respects from those of the parent caste. It is therefore desirable to reproduce briefly the main heads of the information given about them in the works cited above. In 1901 the Kolhātis numbered 1300 persons in Berār. In the Central Provinces they were not shown separately, but were included with the Nats. But in 1891 a total of 250 Kolhātis were returned. The word Kolhāti is said to be derived from the long bamboo poles which they use for jumping, known as Kolhāt. The other names, Dandewāla and Bānsberia, meaning those who perform feats with a stick or bamboo, also have reference to this

1. Introductory notice.

[1] Based partly on papers by Mr. Bihāri Lāl, Naib-Tahsīldār, Bilāspur, and Mr. Adurām Chaudhri of the Gazetteer Office.

[2] For further information the articles on Sānsia and Beria may be consulted.

pole. Kabūtari as applied to the women signifies that their dancing resembles the flight of a pigeon (*kabūtar*). They say that once on a time a demon had captured some Kunbis and shut them up in a cavern. But the Kunbis besought Mahādeo to save them, and he created a man and a woman who danced before the demon and so pleased him that he promised them whatever they should ask; and they thus obtained the freedom of the Kunbis. The man and woman were named Kabūtar and Kabūtari on account of their skilful dancing, and were the ancestors of the Kolhātis. The Kolhātis of the Central Provinces appear to differ in several respects from those of Berār, with whom the following article is mainly concerned.

2. Internal structure. The caste has two main divisions in Berār, the Dukar Kolhātis and the Khām or Pāl Kolhātis. The name of the former is derived from *dukar*, hog, because they are accustomed to hunt the wild pig with dogs and spears when these animals become too numerous and damage the crops of the villagers. They also labour for themselves by cultivating land and taking service as village watchmen; and they are daring criminals and commit dacoity, burglary and theft; but they do not steal cattle. The Khām Kolhātis, on the other hand, are a lazy, good-for-nothing class of men, who, beyond making a few combs and shuttles of bone, will set their hands to no kind of labour, but subsist mainly by the immoral pursuits of their women. At every large fair may be seen some of the portable huts of this tribe, made of *rusa* grass,[1] the women decked in jewels and gaudy attire sitting at each door, while the men are lounging lazily at the back. The Dukar Kolhāti women, Mr. Kitts states, also resort to the same mode of life, but take up their abode in villages instead of attending fairs. Among the Dukar Kolhātis the subdivisions have Rājpūt names; and just as a Chauhān Rājpūt may not marry another Chauhān so also a Chauhān Dukar Kolhāti may not marry a person of his own clan. In Bilāspur they are said to have four subcastes, the Marethi or those coming from the Marātha country, the Bānsberia or pole-jumpers, the Suarwāle or hunters of the wild pig, and the Muhammadan Kolhātis, none of whom

[1] *Andropagon Schoenanthus.*

marry or take food with each other. Each group is further subdivided into the Asal and Kamsal (*Kam-asal*), or the pure and mixed Kolhātis, who marry among themselves, outsiders being admitted to the Kamsal or mixed group.

3. Marriage.

The marriage ceremony in Berār[1] consists simply in a feast at which the bride and bridegroom, dressed in new clothes, preside. Much liquor is consumed and the dancing-girls of the tribe dance before them, and the happy couple are considered duly married according to Kolhāti rites. Married women do not perform in public and are no less moral and faithful than those of other castes, while those brought up as dancing-girls do not marry at all. In Bilāspur weddings are arranged through the headman of the village, who receives a fee for his services, and the ceremony includes some of the ordinary Hindu rites. Here a widow is compelled to marry her late husband's younger brother on pain of exclusion from caste. People of almost any caste may become Kolhātis. When an outsider is admitted he must have a sponsor into whose clan he is adopted. A feast is given to the caste, and the applicant catches the right little finger of his sponsor before the assembly. Great numbers of Rājpūts and Muhammadans join them, and on the other hand a large proportion of the fair but frail Kolhātis embrace the Muhammadan faith.[2]

4. Funeral rites.

The bodies of children are buried, and those of the adult dead may be either buried or cremated. Mr. Kitts states that on the third day, if they can afford the ceremony, they bring back the skull and placing it on a bed offer to it powder, dates and betel-leaves; and after a feast lasting for three days it is again buried. According to Major Gunthorpe the proceedings are more elaborate: "Each division of the caste has its own burial-ground in some special spot, to which it is the heart's desire of every Kolhāti to carry, when he can afford it, the bones of his deceased relatives. After the cremation of an adult the bones are collected and buried pending such time as they can be conveyed to the appointed cemetery, if this be at a distance. When the time comes, that is, when means can be found for the removal, the bones

1 Gunthorpe, *loc. cit.*

2 *Ibidem*, p. 49.

are disinterred and placed in two saddle-bags on a donkey, the skull and upper bones in the right bag and the leg and lower bones in the left. The ass is then led to the deceased's house, where the bags of bones are placed under a canopy made ready for their reception. High festival, as for a marriage, is held for three days, and at the end of this time the bags are replaced on the donkey, and with tom-toms beating and dancing-girls of the tribe dancing in front, the animal is led off to the cemetery. On arrival, the bags, with the bones in them, are laid in a circular hole, and over it a stone is placed to mark the spot, and covered with oil and vermilion; and the spirit of the deceased is then considered to be appeased." They believe that the spirits of dead ancestors enter the bodies of the living and work evil to them, unless they are appeased with offerings. The Dukar Kolhātis offer a boar to the spirits of male ancestors and a sow to females. An offering of a boar is also made to Bhagwān (Vishnu), who is the principal deity of the caste and is worshipped with great ceremony every second year.[1]

5. Other customs. Although of low caste the Kolhātis refrain from eating the flesh of the cow and other animals of the same tribe. The wild cat, mongoose, wild and tame pig and jackal are considered as delicacies. The caste have the same ordeals as are described in the article on the Sānsias. As might be expected in a class which makes a living by immoral practices the women considerably outnumber the men. No one is permanently expelled from caste, and temporary exclusion is imposed only for a few offences, such as an intrigue with or being touched by a member of an impure caste. The offender gives a feast, and in the case of a man the moustache is shaved, while a woman has five hairs of her head cut off. The women have names meant to indicate their attractions, as Panna emerald, Munga coral, Mehtāb dazzling, Gulti a flower, Moti a pearl, and Kesar saffron. If a girl is detected in an intrigue with a caste-fellow they are fined seven rupees and must give a feast to the caste, and are then married. When, however, a girl is suspected of unchastity and no man will take the responsibility on himself, she is put to an ordeal. She

[1] Kitts, *loc. cit.*

fasts all night, and next morning is dressed in a white cloth, and water is poured over her head from a new earthen pot. A piece of iron is heated red hot between cowdung cakes, and she must take up this in her hand and walk five steps with it, also applying it to the tip of her tongue. If she is burnt her unchastity is considered to be proved, and the idea is therefore apparently that if she is innocent the deity will intervene to save her.

The Dukar Kolhāti males, Major Gunthorpe states, are a fine manly set of fellows. They hunt the wild boar with dogs, the men armed with spears following on foot. They show much pluck in attacking the boar, and there is hardly a man of years who does not bear scars received in fights with these animals. The villagers send long distances for a gang to come and rid them of the wild pig, which play havoc with the crops, and pay them in grain for doing so. But they are also much addicted to crime, and when they have decided on a dacoity or house-breaking they have a good drinking-bout and start off with their dogs as if to hunt the boar. And if they are successful they bury the spoil, and return with the body of a pig or a hare as evidence of what they have been doing. Stolen property is either buried at some distance from their homes or made over to the safe keeping of men with whom the women of the caste may be living. Such men, who become intimate with the Kolhātis through their women, are often headmen of villages or hold other respectable positions, and are thus enabled to escape suspicion. Boys who are to become acrobats are taught to jump from early youth. The acrobats and dancing-girls go about to fairs and other gatherings and make a platform on a cart, which serves as a stage for their performances. The dancing-girl is assisted by her admirers, who accompany her with music. Some of them are said now to have obtained European instruments, as harmoniums or gramophones. They do not give their performances on Thursdays and Mondays, which are considered to be unlucky days. In Bombay they are said to make a practice of kidnapping girls, preferably of high caste, whom they sell or bring up as prostitutes.[1]

6. Occupation.

[1] *Ind. Ant.* iii. p. 185, *Satāra Gazetteer*, p. 119.

KOLI

LIST OF PARAGRAPHS

1. General notice of the caste.

Koli.—A primitive tribe akin to the Bhīls, who are residents of the western Satpūra hills. They have the honorific title of Nāik. They numbered 36,000 persons in 1911, nearly all of whom belong to Berār, with the exception of some 2000 odd, who live in the Nimār District. These have hitherto been confused with the Kori caste. The Koris or weavers are also known as Koli, but in Nimār they have the designation of Khangār Koli to distinguish them from the tribe of the same name. The Kolis proper are found in the Burhānpur tahsīl, where most villages are said to possess one or two families, and on the southern Satpūra hills adjoining Berār. They are usually village servants, their duties being to wait on Government officers, cleaning their cooking-vessels and collecting carts and provisions. The duties of village watchman or *kotwār* were formerly divided between two officials, and while the Koli did the most respectable part of the work, the Mahār or Balāhi carried baggage, went messages, and made the prescribed reports to the police. In Berār the Kolis acted for a time as guardians of the hill passes. A chain of outposts or watch towers ran along the Satpūra hills to the north of Berār, and these were held by Kolis and Bhīls, whose duties were to restrain the predatory inroads of their own tribesmen, in the same manner as the Khyber Rifles now guard the passes on the North-West Frontier. And again along the Ajanta hills to the south of the Berār valley a tribe of Kolis under their Nāiks had charge of the *ghāts* or gates of the ridge, and acted as a kind of local militia paid by assignments of land in the villages.[1] In Nimār the Kolis, like the Bhīls, made a trade of plunder and dacoity during the unsettled times of the eighteenth century, and the phrase 'Nāhal, Bhīl, Koli' is commonly used in old Marāthi documents to designate the hill-robbers as a class. The priest of a Muhammadan tomb in Burhānpur still exhibits an imperial Parwāna or intimation from Delhi announcing the dispatch of a force for the suppression of the Kolis, dated A.D. 1637. In the Bombay Presidency, so late as 1804, Colonel Walker wrote: "Most Kolis are thieves by profession, and embrace every opportunity of plundering either public or private property."[2] The tribe are important in Bombay, where their numbers amount to more than 1½ million. It is supposed that the common term 'coolie' is a corruption of Koli,[3] because the Kolis were usually employed as porters and carriers in western India, as 'slave' comes from Slav. The tribe have also given their name to Colāba.[4] Various derivations have been given of the meaning of the word Koli,[5] and according to one account the Kolis and Mairs were originally the same tribe and came from Sind, while the Mairs were the same as the Meyds or Mihiras who entered India in the fifth century as one of the branches of the great White Hun horde. "Again, since the settlement of the Mairs in Gujarāt," the writer of the *Gujarāt Gazetteer* continues, "reverses of fortune, especially the depression of the Rājpūts under the yoke of the Muhammadans in the fourteenth century, did much to draw close the bond between the higher and middle grades of the warrior class. Then many Rājpūts sought shelter among the Kolis and married with them, leaving descendants who still claim a Rājpūt descent and bear the names of Rājpūt families. Apart from this, and probably as the result of an original sameness of race, in some parts of Gujarāt and Kāthiawār

[1] Lyall's *Berār Gazetteer*, pp. 103-5.

[2] *Kāthiawār Gazetteer*, p. 140.

[3] Crooke's edition of *Hobson-Jobson*, art. Koli.

[4] *Bombay City Census Report* (1901) (Edwards).

[5] *Gujarāt Gazetteer*, p. 238.

intermarriage goes on between the daughters of Talabda Kolis and the sons of Rājpūts." Thus the Thākur of Talpuri Mahi Kāntha in Bombay calls himself a Prāmara Koli, and explains the term by saying that his ancestor, who was a Prāmara or Panwār Rājpūt, took water at a Koli's house.[1] As regards the origin of the Kolis, however, whom the author of the *Gujarāt Gazetteer* derives from the White Huns, stating them to be immigrants from Sind, another and perhaps more probable theory is that they are simply a western outpost of the great Kol or Munda tribe, to which the Korkus and Nāhals and perhaps the Bhīls may also belong. Mr. Hīra Lāl suggests that it is a common custom in Marāthi to add or alter so as to make names end in *i*. Thus Halbi for Halba, Koshti for Koshta, Patwi for Patwa, Wanjāri for Banjāra, Gowari for Goala; and in the same manner Koli from Kol. This supposition appears a very reasonable one, though there is little direct evidence. The Nimār Kolis have no tradition of their origin beyond the saying—

Siva kī jholi
Us men ka Koli,

or 'The Koli was born from Siva's wallet.'

2. Sub-divisions. In the Central Provinces the tribe have the five sub-divisions of Sūrajvansi, Malhār, Bhilaophod, Singāde, and the Muhammadan Kolis. The Sūrajvansi or 'descendants of the sun' claim to be Rājpūts. The Malhār or Pānbhari sub-tribe are named from their deity Malhāri Deo, while the alternative name of Pānbhari means water-carrier. The Bhilaophod extract the oil from *bhilwa*[2] nuts like the Nāhals, and the Singāde (*sing*, horn, and *gādna*, to bury) are so called because when their buffaloes die they bury the horns in their compounds. As with several other castes in Burhānpur and Berār, a number of Kolis embraced Islām at the time of the Muhammadan domination and form a separate subcaste.

In Berār the principal group is that of the Mahādeo Kolis, whose name may be derived from the Mahādeo or Pachmarhi hills. This would tend to connect them with the Korkus, and through them with the Kols. They are divided

[1] *Golden Book of India, s.v.*
[2] *Semecarpus anacardium*, the marking-nut tree.

into the Bhās or pure and the Akarāmāse or impure Kolis.[1] In Akola most of the Kolis are stated to belong to the Kshatriya group, while other divisions are the Nāiks or soldiers, the begging Kolis, and the Watandārs who are probably hereditary holders of the post of village watchman.[2]

3. Exogamous divisions. The tribe have exogamous septs of the usual nature, but they have forgotten the meaning of the names, and they cannot be explained. In Bombay their family names are the same as the Marātha surnames, and the writer of the *Ahmadnagar Gazetteer*[3] considers that some connection exists between the two classes. A man must not marry a girl of his own sept nor the daughter of his maternal uncle. Girls are usually married at an early age. A Brāhman is employed to conduct the marriage ceremony, which takes place at sunset: a cloth is held between the couple, and as the sun disappears it is removed and they join hands amid the clapping of the assembled guests. Afterwards they march seven times round a stone slab surrounded by four plough-yokes. Among the Rewa Kāntha Kolis the boy's father must not proceed on his journey to find a bride for his son until on leaving his house he sees a small bird called *devi* on his right hand; and consequently he is sometimes kept waiting for weeks, or even for months. When the betrothal is arranged the bridegroom and his father are invited to a feast at the bride's house, and on leaving the father must stumble over the threshold of the girl's door; without this omen no wedding can prosper.[4]

4. Widow-marriage or divorce. The remarriage of widows is permitted, and the ceremony consists simply in tying a knot in the clothes of the couple; in Ahmadābād all they need do is to sit on the ground while the bridegroom's father knocks their heads together.[5] Divorce is allowed for a wife's misconduct, and if she marries her fellow delinquent he must repay to the husband the expenses incurred by him on his wedding. Otherwise the caste committee may inflict a fine of Rs. 100 on him and put him out of caste for twelve years in default of payment, and order one side of his moustache to be shaved. In Gujarāt

[1] Kitts, *Berār Census Report* (1881), p. 131.

[2] *Akola Gazetteer* (Mr. C. Brown), p. 116.

[3] P. 197.

[4] *Hindus of Gujarāt*, *l.c.*

[5] *Indian Antiquary*, vol. iii. p. 236.

a married woman who has an intrigue with another man is called *savāsan*, and it is said that a practice exists, or did exist, for her lover to pay her husband a price for the woman and marry her, though it is held neither respectable nor safe.[1] In Ahmadābād, if one Koli runs away with another's wife, leaving his own wife behind him, the caste committee sometimes order the offender's relatives to supply the bereaved husband with a fresh wife. They produce one or more women, and he selects one and is quite content with her.[2]

5. Religion. The Kolis of Nimār chiefly revere the goddess Bhawāni, and almost every family has a silver image of her. An important shrine of the goddess is situated in Ichhāpur, ten or twelve miles from Burhānpur, and here members of the tribe were accustomed to perform the hook-swinging rite in honour of the goddess. Since this has been forbidden they have an imitation ceremony of swinging a bundle of bamboos covered with cloth in lieu of a human being.

6. Disposal of the dead. The Kolis both bury and burn the dead, but the former practice is more common. They place the body in the grave with head to the south and face to the north. On the third day after the funeral they perform the ceremony called *Kandhe kanchhna* or 'rubbing the shoulder.' The four bearers of the corpse come to the house of the deceased and stand as if they were carrying the bier. His widow smears a little *ghī* (butter) on each man's shoulder and rubs the place with a small cake which she afterwards gives to him. The men go to a river or tank and throw the cakes into it, afterwards bathing in the water. This ceremony is clearly designed to sever the connection established by the contact of the bier with their shoulders, which they imagine might otherwise render them likely to require the use of a bier themselves. On the eleventh day a Brāhman is called in, who seats eleven friends of the deceased in a row and applies sandal-paste to their foreheads. All the women whose husbands are alive then have turmeric rubbed on their foreheads, and a caste feast follows.

7. Social rules. The Kolis eat flesh, including fowls and pork, and drink

[1] *Bombay Gazetteer, Hindus of Gujarāt*, p. 250.

[2] *Indian Antiquary*, vol. iii. p. 236.

liquor. They will not eat beef, but have no special reverence for the cow. They will not remove the carcase of a dead cow or a dead horse. The social status of the tribe is low, but they are not considered as impure, and Gūjars, Kunbis, and even some Rājpūts will take water from them. Children are named on the twelfth day after birth. Their hair is shaved in the month of Māgh following the birth, and on the first day of the next month, Phāgun, a little oil is applied to the child's ear, after which it may be pierced at any time that is convenient.

Kolta,[1] **Kolita, Kulta.**—An agricultural caste of the Sambalpur District and the adjoining Uriya States. In 1901 the Central Provinces contained 127,000 Koltas out of 132,000 in India, but since the transfer of Sambalpur the headquarters of the caste belong to Bihār and Orissa, and only 36,000 remain in the Central Provinces. In Assam more than two lakhs of persons were enumerated under the caste name of Kalita in 1901, but in spite of the resemblance of the name the Kalitas apparently have no connection with the Uriya country, while the Koltas know nothing of a section of their caste in Assam. The Koltas of Sambalpur say that they immigrated from Baud State, which they regard as their ancestral home, and a member of their caste formerly held the position of Dīwan of the State. According to one of their legends their first ancestors were born from the leavings of food of the legendary Rāja Janak of Mithila or Tirhūt, whose daughter Sīta married King Rāma of Ajodhya, the hero of the Rāmāyana. Some Koltas went with Sīta to Ajodhya and were employed as water-bearers in the royal household. When Rāma was banished they accompanied him in his wanderings, and were permitted to settle in the Uriya country at the request of the Raghunathia Brāhmans, who wanted cultivators to till the soil. Another legend is that once upon a time, when Rāma was wandering in the forests of Sambalpur, he met three brothers and asked them to draw water for him. The first

1. Origin and traditions.

[1] This article is largely compiled from an interesting paper submitted by Mr. Parmānand Tiwāri, Extra Assistant Commissioner and Assistant Settlement Officer, Sambalpur.

brought water in a clean brass pot, and was called Sudh (good-mannered). The second made a cup of leaves and drew water from a well with a rope; he was called Dumāl, from *dori-māl*, à coil of rope. The third brought water only in a hollow gourd, and he was named Kolta, from *ku-rīta*, bad-mannered. This story serves to show that the Koltas, Sudhs and Dumāls acknowledge some connection, and in the Sambalpur District they will take food together at festivals. But this degree of intimacy may simply have arisen from their common calling of agriculture, and may be noticed among the cultivating castes elsewhere, as the Kirārs, Gūjars and Rāghuvansis in Hoshangābād. The most probable theory of the origin of the Koltas is that they are an offshoot of the great Chasa caste, the principal cultivating caste of the Uriya country, corresponding to the Kurmis and Kunbis in Hindustān and the Deccan. Several of their family names are identical with those of the Chasas, and there is actually a subcaste of Kolita Chasas. Mr. Hīra Lāl conjectures that the Koltas may be those Chasas who took to growing *kultha* (*Dolichos uniflorus*), a favourite pulse in Sambalpur; just as the Santora Kurmis are so named from their growing *san*-hcmp, and the Alia Banias and Kunbis from the *āl* or Indian madder. This hypothesis derivcs some support from the fact that the Koltas have no subcastes, and the formation of the caste may therefore be supposed to have occurred at a comparatively recent period.

2. Exogamous groups. The Koltas have both family namcs or *gotras* and exogamous sections or *bargas*. The *gotras* are generally named after animals or other objects, as Dīp (lamp), Bachhās (calf), Hasti (elephant), Bhāradwāj (blue-jay), and so on. Members of the Bachhās *gotra* must not yoke a young bullock to the plough for the first time, but must get this done by somebody else. The names of the *bargas* are generally derived from villages or from offices or titles. In one or two cases they show the admission of members of other castes; thus the Rāwat *barga* are the descendants of a Rāwat (herdsman) who was in the service of the Rāja of Sambalpur. The Rāja had brought him up from infancy, and, wishing to make him a Kolta, married him to a Kolta

girl, despite the protests of the caste. The ancestor of the Hinmiya Bhoi *barga* had a mistress of the Khond tribe, who left him some property, and is still worshipped in the family. The number of *gotras* is smaller than that of the *bargas*, and some *gotras*, as the Nāg or cobra, the tortoise and the pīpal tree, are common to many *bargas*. Marriage is forbidden between members of the same *barga*, and between first cousins on the father's side. To have the same *gotra* is no bar to marriage.

3. Marriage. Girls should be wedded before maturity, as among most of the Uriya castes, and if no suitable husband is forthcoming a nominal marriage is sometimes arranged with an old man, and the girl is afterwards disposed of as a widow. The boy's father makes the proposal for the marriage, and if this is accepted the following formal ceremony takes place. He goes to the girl's village, accompanied by some friends, and taking a quantity of *gur* (raw sugar), and staying at some other house, sends a messenger known as Jalangia to the girl's father, intimating that he has a request to make. The girl's father pretends not to know what it is, and replies that if he has anything to say the elders of the village should be called to hear it. These assemble, and the girl's father informs them that a stranger from another village has come to ask something of him, and as he is ignorant of its purport, he has asked them to do him the favour of being present. The boy's father then opens a parable, saying that he was carried down a river in flood, and saved himself by grasping a tree on the bank. The girl's father replies that the roots of a riverside tree are weak, and he fears that the tree itself would go down in the flood. The boy's father replies that in that case he would be content to perish with the tree. Thereupon the caste priest places a nut and some sacred rice cooked at Jagannāth's temple in the hands of the parties, who stand together facing the company, and the girl's father says he has no objection to giving his daughter in marriage, provided that she may not be abandoned if she should subsequently become disfigured. The nut is broken and distributed to all present in ratification of the agreement. After this, other visits and a formal interchange of presents take place prior to the marriage proper. This is performed with the customary ceremonial of the Uriya castes. The marriage altar is made of earth brought from outside the village by seven married women. Branches of the mahua tree are placed on the altar, and after the conclusion of the ceremony are thrown into a tank. The women also take a jar of water to a tank and, emptying it, fill the jar with the tank water. They go round to seven houses, and at each empty and refill the jar with water from the house. The water finally brought back is used for bathing the bride and bridegroom, and is believed to protect them from all supernatural dangers. An image of the family totem made from powdered rice is anointed with oil and turmeric, and worshipped daily while the marriage is in progress. If the boy or girl is the eldest child, the parents go through a mock marriage ceremony which the child is not allowed to see. When the couple are brought into the marriage-shed, they throw seven handfuls of rice mixed with *mung*[1] and salt on each other. The priest ties the hands of the couple with thread spun by virgins, and the relatives then pour water over the knot. The bride's brother comes up and unties the knot, and gives the bridegroom a blow on the back. This is meant to show his anger at being deprived of his sister. He is given a piece of cloth and goes away. Presents are made to the pair, and the women throw rice on them. They are then taken inside the house and set to gamble with cowries. If the bridegroom wins he promises an ornament to the bride. If she wins she promises to serve him. The boy then asks her to sit with him on a bench, and she at first refuses, and agrees when he promises her other presents. Next day the bride's mother singes the cheeks of the bridegroom with betel-leaves heated over a lamp, and throws cowdung and rice over the couple to protect them from evil. The party takes its departure for the bridegroom's village, and on arrival there his sisters hold a cloth over the door of the house and will not let the couple in till they are given a present. The bridegroom then shoots an arrow at an image of a monkey or a deer, made of powdered rice, which

[1] *Phaseolus mungo.*

is brought back, cooked and eaten. The bride goes home in a day or two, and the Bandāpana ceremony is performed when she finally departs to live with her husband on arrival at maturity. The Koltas allow widow-marriage, but the husband has to pay a sum of about Rs. 100 to the caste-people, the bulk of which is expended in feasting. Divorce may be effected in the presence of the caste committee.

4. Religion. The caste worship the goddess Rāmchandi, whose principal shrine is at Sarsara in Baud State. In order to establish a local Rāmchandi, a handful of earth must be brought from her shrine at Sarsara and made into a representation of the goddess. Some consider that Rāmchandi is the personification of Mother Earth, and the Koltas will not swear by the earth. They worship the plough in the month of Shrāwan, washing it with water and milk, and applying sandal-paste with offerings of flowers and food. The Puājiuntia festival is observed in Kunwār for the well-being of a son. On this occasion barren women try to ascertain whether they will get a son. A hole is made in the ground and filled with water, and a living fish is placed in it. The woman sits by the hole holding her cloth spread out, and if the fish in struggling jumps into her cloth, it is held to prognosticate the birth of a son. The caste worship their family gods and totems on the 10th day of Asārh, Bhādon, Kārtik and Māgh, which are called the pure months. They employ Brāhmans for religious ceremonies. Every man has a *guru* who is a Bairāgi, and he must be initiated by his *guru* before he is allowed to marry. The caste both burn and bury the dead. They eat flesh and fish, but generally abstain from liquor and the flesh of unclean animals, though in some places they are known to eat rats and crocodiles, and also the leavings of Brāhmans. Brāhmans will take water from Koltas, and their social standing is equal to that of the good agricultural castes.

5. Occupation. The Koltas are skilful cultivators and have the usual characteristics belonging to the cultivating castes, of frugality, industry, hunger for land, and readiness to resort to any degree of litigation rather than relinquish a supposed right to it. They strongly appreciate the advantages of

irrigation and show considerable public spirit in constructing tanks which will benefit the lands of their tenants as well as their own. Nevertheless they are not popular, probably because they are generally more prosperous than their neighbours. The rising of the Khonds of Kālāhandi in 1882 was caused by their discontent at being ousted from their lands by the Koltas. The Rāja of Kālāhandi had imported a number of Kolta cultivators, and these speedily got the Khond headmen and ryots into their debt, and possessed themselves of all the best land in the Khond villages. In May 1882 the Khonds rose and slaughtered more than 80 Koltas, while 300 more were besieged in the village of Norla, the Khonds appearing with portions of the scalp and hair of the murdered victims hanging to their bows. On the arrival of a body of police which had been summoned from Vizagapatam, they dispersed, and the outbreak was soon afterwards suppressed, seven of the ringleaders being arrested, tried and hanged by the Political Officer. A settlement was made of the grievances of the Khonds and tranquillity was restored.

Komti, Komati.—The Madras caste of traders corresponding to Banias. In 1911 they numbered 11,000 persons in the Central Provinces, principally in the Chānda and Yeotmāl Districts. The Komtis claim to be of the same status as Banias and to belong to the Vaishya division of the Aryans, but this is a very doubtful pretension. Mr. Francis remarks of them:[1] "Three points which show them to be of Dravidian origin are their adherence to the custom of obliging a boy to marry his paternal uncle's daughter, however unattractive she may be, a practice which is condemned by Manu; their use of the Purānic or lower ritual instead of the Vedic rites in their ceremonies; and the fact that none of the 102 *gotras* into which the caste is divided are those of the twice-born, while some at any rate seem to be totemistic as they are the names of trees and plants, and the members of each *gotra* abstain from touching or using the plant or tree after which their *gotra* is called." They are also of noticeably dark complexion. Komati is

[1] *Madras Census Report* (1901), p. 162.

said to be a corruption of Gomati, a tender of cows.[1] The caste have, however, a great reputation for cunning and astuteness, and hence have arisen the popular derivations of *ko-mati*, fox-minded, and *go-mati*, cow-minded. The real meaning of the word is obscure. In Mysore the caste have the title of Setti or Chetty, which is a corruption of the Sanskrit Sreshtha, good, and in the Central Provinces their names often terminate with Appa.

The Komtis have the following story about themselves: Long ago, in the Kaliyuga era, there lived a Rājpūt king of Rājahmundry, who on his travels saw a beautiful Vaishya girl and fell in love with her. Her father refused him, saying that they were of different castes. But the king persisted and would not be denied. On which the maiden determined to sacrifice herself to save her honour, and her clansmen resolved to die with her. So she told the king that she would marry him if he would agree to the *hom* sacrifice being performed at the ceremony. When the fire was kindled the girl threw herself on it and perished, followed by a hundred and two of her kinsmen. But the others were cowardly and fled from the fire. Before she died the girl cursed the king and her caste-fellows who had fled, and they and their families were cut off from the earth. But from those who died the hundred and two clans of the Komtis are descended, and they worship the maiden as Kanika Devī. She is considered to have been an incarnation of Pārvati and is the heroine of the Kānikya Purān. It is also said that she ordained that henceforth all Komtis should be black, so that none of their women might come to harm by being desired for their beauty as she had been. It is said that the caste look out for a specially dark girl as a bride, and think that she will bring luck to her husband and cause him to make money. Another explanation of their dark colour is that they originally lived in Ceylon, and when the island was set on fire by Rāma their faces were blackened in the smoke. The hundred and two clans have each a particular kind of flower or tree which they do not grow, eat, touch or burn, and the explanation they give of this custom is that their ancestors who went into the fire

1 *Mysore Ethnographic Survey*, Komati caste (H. V. Nanjundayya).

were transformed into these trees and plants. The names of the plants revered by each clan in the Central Provinces appear to be the same as in Mysore. They include the brinjal, the mango, the cotton-plant, wheat, linseed and others.

The caste have several subcastes, among which are the Yajna, or those whose ancestors went into the fire; the Patti, who are apparently thread-sellers; the Jaina, or those who follow the Jain faith; and the Vidūrs, a half-caste section, who are the offspring of a Yajna father and a mother of some low caste. There is a scarcity of girls, and a bride-price of Rs. 200 to Rs. 500 is often paid. Perhaps for the same reason the obligation to give a daughter to a sister's son is strictly enforced, and a man who refuses to do this is temporarily put out of caste. The *gotras* of the mothers of the bride and bridegroom should not be the same, and there should be no 'Turning back of the creeper,' as they say, that is, when a girl has married into a family, the latter cannot give a girl in marriage to that girl's family ever afterwards. Before the regular betrothal when a girl has been selected, they appoint a day and the bridegroom's party proceed outside the village to take the omens. If a bad omen occurs, they give up the idea of the match and choose another girl. When the bridegroom has arrived at the bride's village, before the marriage takes place, he performs the Kāshi-Yātra or Going to Benares. He is dressed as for a journey and carries a small handful of rice and other provisions tied up in packages in his upper garment. Thus accoutred, he sets out with a stick and umbrella on a pretended visit to Benares, for the purpose of devoting his life to study. The parents of the bride meet him and beg him to give up the journey, promising him their daughter in marriage.[1] The binding function of the marriage is the tying of the *mangal-sūtram* or piece of gold strung on a thread round the bride's neck by the bridegroom. This gold piece is called *pushti* and must never be taken off. If a woman loses it, she should hide herself from everybody until it is replaced. On the way to her husband's house, the bride should upset with her foot a measure of rice kept

[1] H. V. Nanjundayya, *loc. cit.*

on purpose in the way, perhaps with the idea of showing that there will be so much grain in her household that she can afford to waste it.[1] The Komtis did not eat in kitchens in the famines, but accepted dry rations of food with great reluctance. They wear the sacred thread and have caste-marks on their foreheads. They usually rub powdered turmeric on their face and hands, and this lends an unpleasant greenish tinge to the skin.

Kori.—The Hindu weaving caste of northern India, as distinct from the Julāhas or Momins who are Muhammadans. In 1911 the Koris numbered 35,000 persons, and resided mainly in Jubbulpore, Saugor and Damoh. Mr. Crooke states that their name has been derived from that of the Kol caste, of whom they have by some been assumed to be an offshoot.[2] The Koris themselves trace their origin from Kabīr, the apostle of the weaving castes. He, they say, met a Brāhman girl on the bank of a tank, and, being saluted by her, replied, 'May God give you a son.' She objected that she was a virgin and unmarried, but Kabīr answered that his word could not fail; and a boy was born out of her hand, whom she left on the bank of the tank. He was suckled by a heifer and subsequently adopted by a weaver and was the ancestor of the Koris. Therefore the caste say of themselves: "He was born of an undefiled vessel, and free from passion; he lowered his body and entered the ocean of existence." This legend is a mere perversion of the story of Kabīr himself, designed to give the Koris a distinguished pedigree. In the Central Provinces the caste appears to be almost entirely a functional group, made up of members of other castes who were either expelled from their own community or of their own accord adopted the profession of weaving. The principal subdivision is the Ahirwār, taking its name from the old town of Ahar in the Bulandshahr District. Among the others are Kushta (Koshta), Chadār, Katia, Mehra, Dhīmar and Kotwār, all of which, except the last, are the names of distinct castes; while the Kotwārs represent members of the caste who became village

1. Description of the caste.

[1] H. V. Nanjundayya, *loc. cit.*

[2] *Tribes and Castes of the North-West Provinces*, iii. 316.

watchmen, and considering themselves somewhat superior to the others, have formed a separate subcaste. None of the subcastes will eat together or intermarry, and this fact is in favour of the supposition that they are distinct groups amalgamated into a caste by their common profession of weaving. The caste seem to have a fairly close connection with Chamārs in some localities. A number of Koris belong to the sect of Rohidās, and some of their family names are the same, while a Chamār will often call himself a Kori to conceal his identity. For the purposes of marriage they are divided into a number of *bainks* or septs, the names of which are territorial or totemistic. Among the latter may be mentioned the Kulhariya from *kulhāri*, an axe, and the Barmaiya from the *bar* or banyan tree; members of these septs pay reverence to an axe and a banyan tree respectively at weddings.

2. Marriages. The marriage of persons belonging to the same sept and also that of first cousins is prohibited, while a family will not, if they can help it, marry a daughter into the sept from which a son has taken a wife. The rule of exogamy is thus rather wide in its action, as is often found to be the case among the lowest and most primitive castes. At the betrothal the father of the girl produces a red cloth folded up, and on this the boy's father lays a rupee. This is passed round to five members of the caste who cry, 'So-and-so's daughter and So-and-so's son, *Har bolo* (In the name of Vishnu).' This completes the betrothal, the father of the boy giving three rupees for a feast to the caste-fellows. A girl who is made pregnant by a man of the caste or any higher caste may be disposed of in marriage as a widow, but if the man is of a lower caste than the Koris she is finally expelled. The *lagan* or paper fixing the date of the marriage is written by a Brāhman and must not be shown to the bridegroom in the interval, lest he should grow as thin as the paper bearing his name. While he is being anointed and rubbed with turmeric the bridegroom is wrapped in a black blanket, and his bridal dress consists of a yellow shirt, pyjamas of red cloth, and red shoes, while he carries in his hand a dagger, nut-cracker or knife. As he leaves his house to proceed to the bride's village he steps on two clay lamp-saucers, crushing

them with his foot. When the party arrives the fathers of the bride and bridegroom sit together with a pot full of curds between them and give each other to drink from it as a mark of amity. The binding portion of the marriage consists in walking round the sacred pole and the other ceremonies customary in the northern Districts are performed. The bride does not return with her husband unless she is adult; otherwise the usual *gauna* ceremony is held subsequently. When she arrives at her husband's house she makes prints of her hands smeared with turmeric on the wall before entering it for the first time. The remarriage of widows is freely permitted; the second husband takes the widow to his house after sunset, and here she is washed by the barber's wife and puts on glass bangles again, and new jewellery and clothes, if any are provided. No married woman may see her as she enters the house. The husband must give a feast to the caste-fellows, or at least to the *panchāyat* or committee. Divorce is freely permitted on payment of a fine to the *panchāyat*. When a man takes a second wife a *sot* or silver image of the deceased first wife is hung round her neck when she enters his house, and is worshipped on ceremonial occasions.

3. Customs at birth and death.

A child is named on the day after its birth by some woman of the caste; a Brāhman is asked whether the day is auspicious, and he also chooses the name. If this is the same as that of any living relation or one recently dead, another name is given for ordinary use. A daughter-in-law is usually given a new name when she goes to her husband's house, such as Badi (elder), Manjhli (second son's wife), Bāri (innocent or simple), Jabalpurwāli (belonging to Jubbulpore), and so on. If a woman has borne only female children, the umbilical cord is sometimes put in a small earthen pot and buried at a place where three cross-roads meet, and it is supposed that the birth of a male child will follow. Children whose shaving ceremony has not been performed, and adults dying from snake-bite, cholera, smallpox or leprosy, are buried, while others are burnt. Children are carried to the grave in their parents' arms. On the return of a funeral party, liquor, provided by the relatives of the family, is drunk at the house of the deceased.

4. Religion. The Koris worship the ordinary Hindu deities and especially Devi. They become inspired by this goddess at the Jawara festival and pierce their cheeks with iron needles and tridents. Every family has a household god or Kul-Deo to whom a small platform is erected; offerings other than animal sacrifices are made to him on festivals and on the celebration of a marriage.

5. Occupation and social status. Those of the caste who are Kabīrpanthis abstain from animal food, but the others eat the flesh of most animals except tame pig, and also drink liquor. Their social status is very low, but they are not usually considered as impure. Their women are tattooed on the right arm before marriage, and on the left after arrival at their husband's house. Like several other low castes, they do not wear nose-rings. The principal occupation of the caste is the weaving of coarse country cloth, but as the trade of the hand-weaver is nowadays precarious and unprofitable many of them have forsaken it and taken to cultivation or daily labour. Mr. Nesfield says of them: "The material used by the Kori is the thread supplied by the Dhunia (Bahna); and thus the weaver caste has risen imperceptibly out of that of the cotton-carder, in the same way as the cobbler caste has risen out of the tanner. The art of weaving and plaiting threads is very much the same process as that of plaiting osiers, reeds and grass, and converting them into baskets and mats. This circumstance explains the puzzle why the weaver caste in India stands at such a low social level. He, however, ranks several degrees above the Chamār or tanner; as, among Hindus, herbs and their products (cotton being of course included) are invariably considered pure, while the hides of dead animals are regarded as a pollution." This argument is part of Mr. Nesfield's theory that the rank of each caste depends on the period of civilisation at which its occupation came into being, which is scarcely tenable. The reason why the weavers rank so low may, perhaps, be that the Aryans when they settled in villages in northern India despised all handicrafts as derogatory to their dignity. These were left to the subject tribes, and as a large number of weavers would be required, the industry would necessarily be embraced by the bulk of those who formed the lowest

stratum of the population, and has ever since remained in their hands. If cloth was first woven from the tree-cotton plant growing wild, the business of picking and weaving it would naturally have fallen to the non-Aryan jungle tribes, who afterwards became the impure menial and labouring castes of the villages.

The weaver is the proverbial butt of Hindu ridicule, like the tailor in England. 'One Gadaria will account for ten weavers'; 'Four weavers will spoil any business.' The following story also illustrates their stupidity: Twenty weavers got into a field of *kāns* grass. They thought it was a tank and began swimming. When they got out they said, "Let us all count and see how many we are, in case anybody has been left in the tank." They counted and each left out himself, so that they all made out nineteen. Just then a Sowār came by, and they cried to him, 'Oh, Sir, we were twenty, and one of us has been drowned in this tank.' The Sowār seeing that there was only a field of grass, counted them and found there were twenty; so he said, 'What will you give me if I find the twentieth?' They promised him a piece of cloth, on which the Sowār, taking his whip, lashed each of the weavers across the shoulders, counting as he did so. When he had counted twenty he took the cloth and rode away. Another story is that a weaver bought a buffalo for twenty rupees. His brother then came to him and wanted a share in the buffalo. They did not know how he should be given a share until at last the weaver said, "You go and pay the man who sold me the buffalo twenty rupees; and then you will have given as much as I have and will be half-owner of the buffalo." Which was done. The ridicule attaching to the weaver's occupation is due to its being considered proper for a woman rather than a man, and similar jests were current at the tailor's expense in England. In India the weaver probably takes the tailor's place because woven and not sewn clothes have hitherto been generally worn, as explained in the article on Darzi.

KORKU

LIST OF PARAGRAPHS

1. Distribution and origin.

Korku.[1]—A Munda or a Kolarian tribe akin to the Korwas, with whom they have been identified in the India Census of 1901. They number about 150,000 persons in the Central Provinces and Berār, and belong to the west of the Satpūra plateau, residing only in the Hoshangābād, Nimār, Betūl and Chhindwāra Districts. About 30,000 Korkus dwell in the Berār plain adjoining the Satpūras, and a few thousand belong to Bhopāl. The word Korku means simply 'men' or 'tribesmen,' *koru* being their term for a man and *kū* a plural termination. The tribe have a language of their own, which resembles that of the Kols of Chota Nāgpur. The language of the Korwas, another Munda tribe found in Chota Nāgpur, is also known as Korakū or Korkū, and one of their subcastes has the same name.[2] Some Korkus or Mowāsis are found in Chota Nāgpur, and Colonel Dalton considered them a branch of the Korwas. Another argument may be adduced from the sept names of the Korkus

[1] This article is largely based on a monograph contributed by Mr. H. R. Crosthwaite, Assistant Commissioner, Hoshangābād, and contains also extracts from a monograph by Mr. Ganga Prasād Khatri, Forest Divisional Officer, Betūl, and from the description of the Korkus given by Mr. (Sir Charles) Elliott in the *Hoshangābād Settlement Report* (1867), and by Major Forsyth in the *Nimār Settlement Report* (1868–69).

[2] Risley's *Tribes and Castes of Bengal*, Appendix V. : Korwā.

Bemrose, Collo., Derby.

KORKUS OF THE MELGHĀT HILLS.

which are in many cases identical with those of the Kols and Korwas. There is little reason to doubt then that the Korkus are the same tribe as the Korwas, and both of these may be taken to be offshoots of the great Kol or Munda tribe. The Korkus have come much further west than their kinsmen, and between their residence on the Mahādeo or western Satpūra hills and the Korwas and Kols, there lies a large expanse mainly peopled by the Gonds and other Dravidian tribes, though with a considerable sprinkling of Kols in Mandla, Jubbulpore and Bilāspur. These latter may have immigrated in comparatively recent times, but the Kolis of Bombay may not improbably be another offshoot of the Kols, who with the Korkus came west at a period before the commencement of authentic history.[1] One of the largest subdivisions of the Korkus is termed Mowāsi, and this name is sometimes applied to the whole tribe, while the tract of country where they dwell was formerly known as the Mowās. Numerous derivations of this term have been given, and the one commonly accepted is that it signifies 'The troubled country,' and was applied to the hills at the time when bands of Koli or Korku freebooters, often led by dispossessed Rājpūt chieftains, harried the rich lowlands of Berār from their hill forts on the Satpūras, exacting from the Marāthas, with poetical justice, the payments known as 'Tankha Mowāsi' for the ransom of the settled and peaceful villages of the plains. The fact, however, that the Korkus found in Chota Nāgpur are also known as Mowāsi militates against this supposition, for if the name was applied only to the Korkus of the Satpūra plateau it would hardly have travelled as far east as Chota Nāgpur. Mr. Hislop derived it from the mahua tree. But at any rate Mowāsi meant a robber to Marātha ears, and the forests of Kalībhīt and Melghāt are known as the Mowās.

2. Tribal legends.

According to their own traditions the Korkus like so many other early people were born from the soil. They state that Rāwan, the demon king of Ceylon, observed that the Vindhyan and Satpūra ranges were uninhabited and besought Mahādeo[2] to populate them. Mahādeo despatched his messenger, the crow Kāgeshwar, to find for him an ant-

[1] See also art. Kol.

[2] The local term for the god Siva.

hill made of red earth, and the crow discovered such an ant-hill between the Saolīgarh and Bhānwargarh ranges of Betūl. Mahādeo went to the place, and, taking a handful of red earth, made images in the form of a man and a woman, but immediately two fiery horses sent by Indra rose from the earth and trampled the images to dust. For two days Mahādeo persisted in his attempts, but as often as the images were made they were destroyed in a similar manner. But at length the god made an image of a dog and breathed into it the breath of life, and this dog kept off the horses of Indra. Mahādeo then made again his two images of a man and woman, and giving them human life, called them Mūla and Mūlai with the surname of Pothre, and these two became the ancestors of the Korku tribe. Mahādeo then created various plants for their use, the *mahul*[1] from whose strong and fibrous leaves they could make aprons and head-coverings, the wild plantain whose leaves would afford other clothing, and the mahua, the *chironji*, the *sewan* and *kullu*[2] to provide them with food. Time went on and Mūla and Mūlai had children, and being dissatisfied with their condition as compared with that of their neighbours, besought Mahādeo to visit them once more. When he appeared Mūla asked the god to give him grain to eat such as he had heard of elsewhere on the earth. Mahādeo sent the crow Kāgeshwar to look for grain, and he found it stored in the house of a Māng named Japre who lived at some distance within the hills. Japre on hearing what was required besought the honour of a visit from the god himself. Mahādeo went, and Japre laid before him an offering of 12 *khandis*[3] of grain, 12 goats and 12 buckets of water, and invited Mahādeo to eat and drink. The god was pleased with the offering and unwilling to reject it, but considered that he could not eat food defiled by the touch of the outcaste Māng, so Pārvati created the giant Bhīmsen and bade him eat up the food offered to Mahādeo. When Bhīmsen had finished the offering, however, it occurred to him that he also had been defiled by taking food from a

[1] *Bauhinia Vahlii.*

[2] *Bassia latifolia, Buchanania latifolia, Gmelina arborea* and *Sterculia urens.*

[3] Nearly $3\frac{1}{2}$ tons.

Māng, and in revenge he destroyed Japre's house and covered the site of it with débris and dirt. Japre then complained to Mahādeo of this sorry requital of his offering and prayed to have his house restored to him. Bhīmsen was ordered to do this, and agreed to comply on condition that Mūla should pay to him the same honour and worship as he accorded to Rāwan, the demon king. Mūla promised to do so, and Bhīmsen then sent the crow Kāgeshwar to the tank Daldal, bidding him bring thence the pig Buddu, who being brought was ordered to eat up all the dirt that covered Japre's house. Buddu demurred except on condition that he also should be worshipped by Mūla and his descendants for ever. Mūla agreed to pay worship to him every third year, whereupon Buddu ate up all the dirt, and dying from the effects received the name of Mahābissum, under which he is worshipped to the present day. Mahādeo then took some seed from the Māng and planted it for Mūla's use, and from it sprang the seven grains—*kodon*, *kutki*, *gurgi*, *mandgi*, *barai*, *rāla* and *dhān*[1] which the Korkus principally cultivate. It may be noticed that the story ingeniously accounts for and sheds as it were an orthodox sanction on the custom of the Korkus of worshipping the pig and the local demon Bhīmsen, who is placed on a sort of level with Rāwan, the opponent of Rāma. After recounting the above story Mr. Crosthwaite remarks: "This legend given by the Korkus of their creation bears a curious analogy to our own belief as set forth in the Old Testament. They even give the tradition of a flood, in which a crow plays the part of Noah's dove. There is a most curious similarity between their belief in this respect and that found in such distant and widely separated parts as Otaheite and Siberia. Remembering our own name 'Adam,' which I believe means in Hebrew 'made of red earth,' it is curious to observe the stress that is laid in the legend on the necessity for finding red earth for the making of man." Another story told by the Korkus with the object of providing themselves with Rājpūt ancestry is to the effect that their forefathers dwelt in the city of Dhārānagar, the modern Dhār. It happened one day that

[1] *Paspalum scrobiculatum*, *Panicum psilopodium*, *Coix Lachryma*, *Eleusine coracana*, *Saccharum officianarum Setaria italica*, *Oryza sativa*.

they were out hunting and followed a *sāmbhar* stag, which fled on and on until it finally came to the Mahādeo or Pachmarhi hills and entered a cave. The hunters remained at the mouth waiting for the stag to come out, when a hermit appeared and gave them a handful of rice. This they at once cooked and ate as they were hungry from their long journey, and they found to their surprise that the rice sufficed for the whole party to eat their fill. The hermit then told them that he was the god Mahādeo, and had assumed the form of a stag in order to lead them to these hills, where they were to settle and worship him. They obeyed the command of the god, and a Korku zamīndār is still the hereditary guardian of Mahādeo's shrine at Pachmarhi. This story has of course no historical value, and the Korkus have simply stolen the city of Dhārānagar for their ancestral home from their neighbours the Bhoyars and Panwārs. These castes relate similar stories, which may in their case be founded on fact.

3. Tribal subdivisions.

As is usual among the forest tribes the Korkus formerly had a subdivision called Rāj-Korkū, who were made up of landowning members of the caste and were admitted to rank among those from whom a Brāhman would take water, while in some cases a spurious Rājpūt ancestry was devised for them, as in the story given above. The remainder of the tribe were called Potharia, or those to whom a certain dirty habit is imputed. These main divisions have, however, become more or less obsolete, and have been supplanted by four subcastes with territorial names, Mowāsi, Bāwaria, Rūma and Bondoya. The meaning of the term Mowāsi has already been given, and this subcaste ranks as the highest, probably owing to the gentlemanly calling of armed robbery formerly practised by its members. The Bāwarias are the dwellers in the Bhānwargarh tract of Betūl, the Rūmas those who belong to Bāsim and Gangra in the Amraoti District, and the Bondoyas the residents of the Jītgarh and Pachmarhi tract. These last are also called Bhovadāya and Bhopa, and this name has been corrupted into Bopchi in the Wardha District, a few hundred Bondoya Korkus who live there being known as Bopchi and considered a distinct caste. Except among the Mowāsis, who usually marry in their own subcaste, the rule of endogamy is not strictly observed. The above description refers to Betūl and Nimār, but in Hoshangābād, Mr. Crosthwaite says: "Four-fifths of the Korkus have been so affected by the spread of Brāhmanical influence as to have ceased to differ in any marked way from the Hindu element in the population, and the Korku has become so civilised as to have learnt to be ashamed of being a Korku." Each subcaste has traditionally 36 exogamous septs, but the numbers have now increased. The sept names are generally taken from those of plants and animals. These were no doubt originally totemistic, but the Korkus now say that the names are derived from trees and other articles in or behind which the ancestors of each sept took refuge after being defeated in a great battle. Thus the ancestor of the Atkul sept hid in a gorge, that of the Bhūri Rāna sept behind a dove's nest, that of the Dewda sept behind a rice plant, that of the Jāmbu sept behind a *jāmun* tree,[1] that of the Kāsada sept in the bed of a river, that of the Tākhar sept behind a cucumber plant, that of the Sakum sept behind a teak tree, and so on. Other names are Banku or a forest-dweller; Bhūrswa or Bhoyar, perhaps from the caste of that name; Basam or Baoria, the god of beehives; and Marskola or Mawāsi, which the Korkus take to mean a field flooded by rain. One sept has the name Killībhasam, and its ancestor is said to have eaten the flesh of a heifer half-devoured by a tiger and parched by a forest fire. In Hoshangābād the lĕgend of the battle is not known, and among the names given by Mr. Crosthwaite are Akandi, the benighted one; Tandil, a rat; and Chuthar, the flying black-bug. In a few cases the names of septs are Hindi or Marāthi words, these perhaps affording a trace of the foundation of separate families by members of other castes. No totemistic usages are followed as a rule, but one curious instance may be given. One sept has the name *lobo*, which means a piece of cloth. But the word *lobo* also signifies 'to leak.' If a person says a sentence containing the word *lobo* in either signification before a member of the sept while he is eating, he will throw away the food before him as if it were contaminated and prepare a meal afresh.

[1] *Eugenia jambolana.*

Ten of the septs[1] consider the regular marriage of girls to be inauspicious, and the members of these simply give away their daughters without performing a ceremony.

4. Marriage. Betrothal. Marriage between members of the same sept is prohibited and also the union of first cousins. The preliminaries to a marriage commence with the *bāli-dūdna* or arrangement of the match. The boy's father having selected a suitable bride for his son sends two elders of the caste to propose the match to her father, who as a matter of etiquette invariably declines it, swearing with great oaths that he will not allow his daughter to get married or that he will have a son-in-law who will serve for her. The messengers depart, but return again and again until the father's obduracy is overcome, which may take from six months to two years, while from nine to twelve months is considered a respectable period. When his consent is finally obtained the residents of the girl's village are called to hear it, and the compact is sealed with large potations of liquor. A ceremony of betrothal follows at which the *daij* or dowry is arranged, this signifying among the Korkus the compensation to be paid to the girl's father for the loss of her services. It is computed by a curious system of symbolic higgling. The women of the girl's party take two plates and place on them two heaps containing respectively ten and fifty seeds of a sort used for reckoning. The ten seeds on the first plate represent five rupees for the *panchāyat* and five cloths for the mother, brother, paternal aunt and paternal and maternal uncles of the girl. The heap of fifty seeds indicates that Rs. 50 must be paid to the girl's father. When the plates are received by the boy's party they take away forty-five of the seeds from the larger heap and return the plate, to indicate that they will only pay five rupees to the girl's father. The women add twenty-five seeds and send back the plate again. The men then take away fifteen, thus advancing the bride-price to fifteen rupees. The women again add twenty-five seeds and send back the plate, and the men again take away twenty, and returning the remaining twenty which are taken as the sum agreed upon, in addition to the five cloths and

[1] Makyātotha, Jondhrātotha, Dharsīma, Changri, Lobo, Khambi, Dagde, Kullya, Bursūma and Killībhasam.

Bemrose, Collo.. Derby.

KORKU WOMEN IN FULL DRESS.

five rupees for the *panchāyat.* The total amount paid averages about Rs. 60. Wealthy men sometimes refuse this payment or exchange a bride for a bridegroom. The dowry should be paid before the wedding, and in default of this the bridegroom's father is made not a little uncomfortable at that festival. Should a betrothed girl die before marriage, the dowry does not abate and the parents of the girl have a right to stop her burial until it is paid. But if a father shows himself hard to please and refuses eligible offers, or if a daughter has fallen in love, as sometimes happens, she will leave her home quietly some morning and betake herself to the house of the man of her choice. If her young affections have not been engaged, she may select of her own accord a protector whose circumstances and position make him attractive, and preferably one whose mother is dead. Occasionally a girl will install herself in the house of a man who does not want her, and his position then is truly pitiable. He dare not turn her out as he would be punished by the caste for his want of gallantry, and his only course is to vacate his own house and leave her in possession. After a time his relations represent to her that the man she wants has gone on a journey and will not be back for a long time, and induce her to return to the paternal abode. But such a case is very rare.

5. The marriage ceremony.

The marriage ceremony resembles that of the Hindus but has one or two special features. After the customary cleaning of the house which should be performed on a Tuesday, the bridegroom is carried to the heap of stones which represents Mutua Deo, and there the Bhumka or priest invokes the various sylvan deities, offering to them the blood of chickens. Again when he is dressed for the wedding the boy is given a knife or dagger carrying a pierced lemon on the blade, and he and his parents and relatives proceed to a *ber*[1] or wild plum tree. The boy and his parents sit at the foot of the tree and are tied to it with a thread, while the Bhumka again spills the blood of a fowl on the roots of the tree and invokes the sun and moon, whom the Korkus consider to be their ultimate ancestors. The *ber* fruit may perhaps be selected as symbolising the red orb of the setting

[1] *Zizyphus jujuba.*

sun. The party then dance round the tree. When the wedding procession is formed the following ceremony takes place: A blanket is spread in the yard of the house and the bridegroom and his elder brother's wife are made to stand on it and embrace each other seven times. This may probably be a survival of the modified system of polyandry still practised by the Khonds, under which the younger brothers are allowed access to the elder brother's wife until their own marriage. The ceremony would then typify the cessation of this intercourse at the wedding of the boy. The procession must reach the bride's village on a Monday, a Wednesday or a Friday, a breach of this rule entailing a fine of Rs. 8 on the boy's father. On arrival at the bride's village its progress is barred by a rope stretched across the road by the bride's relatives, who must be given two pice each before it is removed. The bridegroom touches the marriage-shed with a bamboo fan. Next day the couple are seated in the shed and covered with a blanket on to which water is poured to symbolise the fertilising influence of rain. The groom ties a necklace of beads to the girl's neck, and the couple are then lifted up by the relatives and carried three times round the yard of the house, while they throw yellow-coloured rice at each other. Their clothes are tied together and they proceed to make an offering to Mutua Deo. In Hoshangābād, Mr. Crosthwaite states, the marriage ceremony is presided over by the bridegroom's aunt or other collateral female relative. The bride is hidden in her father's house. The aunt then enters carrying the bridegroom and searches for the bride. When the bride is found the brother-in-law of the bridegroom takes her up, and bride and bridegroom are then seated under a sheet. The rings worn on the little finger of the right hand are exchanged under the sheet and the clothes of the couple are knotted together. Then follow the *sapta padi* or seven steps round the post, and the ceremony concludes with a dance, a feast and an orgy of drunkenness. A priest takes no part in a Korku marriage ceremony, which is a purely social affair. If a man has only one daughter, or if he requires an assistant for his cultivation, he often makes his prospective son-in-law serve for his wife for a period varying from five to twelve years, the marriage being then celebrated at the father-in-law's expense. If the boy runs away with the girl before the end of his service, his parents have to pay to the girl's father five rupees for each year of the unexpired term. Marriage is usually adult, girls being wedded between the ages of ten and sixteen and boys at about twenty. Polygamy is freely practised by those who are well enough off to afford it, and instances are known of a man having as many as twelve wives living. A man must not marry his wife's younger sister if she is the widow of a member of his own sept nor his elder brother's widow if she is his wife's elder sister. Widow-marriage is allowed, and divorce may be effected by a simple proclamation of the fact to the *panchāyat* in a caste assembly.

6. Religion.

The Korkus consider themselves as Hindus, and are held to have a better claim to a place in the social structure of Hinduism than most of the other forest tribes, as they worship the sun and moon which are Hindu deities and also Mahādeo. In truth, however, their religion, like that of many low Hindu castes, is almost purely animistic. The sun and moon are their principal deities, the name for these luminaries in their language being Gomaj, which is also the term for god or a god. The head of each family offers a white she-goat and a white fowl to the sun every third year, and the Korkus stand with the face to the sun when beginning to sow, and perform other ceremonies with the face turned to the east. The moon has no special observances, but as she is a female deity she is probably considered to participate in those paid to the sun. These gods are, however, scarcely expected to interest themselves in the happenings of a Korku's daily life, and the local godlings who are believed to regulate these are therefore propitiated with greater fervour. The three most important village deities are Dongar Deo, the god of the hills, who resides on the nearest hill outside the village and is worshipped at Dasahra with offerings of cocoanuts, limes, dates, vermilion and a goat; Mutua Deo, who is represented by a heap of stones within the village and receives a pig for a sacrifice, besides special oblations when disease and sickness are prevalent; and Māta, the goddess of smallpox, to whom cocoanuts and sweetmeats, but no animal sacrifices, are offered.

7. The Bhumka.

The priests of the Korkus are of two kinds—Parihārs and Bhumkas. The Parihār may be any man who is visited with the divine afflatus or selected as a mouthpiece by the deity; that is to say, a man of hysterical disposition or one subject to epileptic fits. He is more a prophet than a priest, and is consulted only on special occasions. Parihārs are also rare, but every village has its Bhumka, who performs the regular sacrifices to the village gods and the special ones entailed by disease or other calamities. On him devolves the dangerous duty of keeping tigers out of the boundaries. When a tiger visits the village the Bhumka repairs to Bāgh Deo[1] and makes an offering to the god, promising to repeat it for so many years on condition that the tiger does not appear for that time. The tiger on his part never fails to fulfil the contract thus silently made, for he is pre-eminently an honourable upright beast, not faithless and treacherous like the leopard whom no contract can bind. Some Bhumkas, however, masters of the most powerful spells, are not obliged to rely on the traditional honour of the tiger, but compel his attendance before Bāgh Deo; and such a Bhumka has been seen as a very Daniel among tigers muttering his incantations over two or three at a time as they crouched before him. Of one Bhumka in Kālibhīt it is related that he had a fine large *sāj* tree, into which, when he uttered his spells, he would drive a nail, and on this the tiger came and ratified the compact with his enormous paw, with which he deeply scored the bark. In this way some have lost their lives, victims of misplaced confidence in their own powers.[2] If a man is sick and it is desired to ascertain what god or spirit of an ancestor has sent the malady, a handful of grain is waved over the sick man and then carried to the Bhumka. He makes a heap of it on the floor, and, sitting over it, swings a lighted lamp suspended by four strings from his fingers. He then repeats slowly the name of the village deities and the sick man's ancestors, pausing between each, and the name at which the lamp stops swinging is that of the offended one. He then inquires in a similar

1 The tiger-god.

2 The above passage is taken from Mr. (Sir Charles) Elliott's *Hoshangābād Settlement Report* written in 1867. Since that time the belief in the magical powers of the Bhumka has somewhat declined.

manner whether the propitiation shall be a pig, a chicken, a goat, a cocoanut and so on. The office of Bhumka is usually, but not necessarily, hereditary, and a new one is frequently chosen by lot, this being also done when a new village is founded. All the villagers then sit in a line before the shrine of Mutua Deo, to whom a black and a white chicken are offered. The Parihār, or, if none be available, the oldest man present, then sets a *pai*[1] rolling before the line of men, and the person before whom it stops is marked out by this intervention of the deity as the new Bhumka. When a new village is to be founded a *pai* measure is filled with grain to a level with the brim, but with no head (this being known as a *mundi* or bald *pai*), and is placed before Mutua Deo in the evening and watched all night. In the morning the grain is poured out and again replaced in the measure; if it now fills this and also leaves enough for a head, and still more if it brims and runs over, it is a sign that the village will be very prosperous and that every cultivator's granaries will run over in the same way. But it is an evil omen if the grain does not fill up to the level of the rim of the measure. The explanation of the difference in bulk may be that the grains increase or decrease slightly in size according as the atmosphere is moist or dry, or perhaps the Bhumka works the oracle. The Bhumka usually receives contributions in grain from all the houses in the village; but occasionally each cultivator gives him a day's ploughing, a day's weeding and a day's wood-cutting free. The Bhumka is also employed in Hindu villages for the service of the village gods. But the belief in the powers of these deities is decaying, and with it the tribute paid to the Bhumka for securing their favour. Whereas formerly he received substantial contributions of grain on the same scale as a village menial, the cultivator will now often put him off with a basketful or even a handful, and say, 'I cannot spare you any more, Bhumka; you must make all the gods content with that.' In curing diseases the Parihār resorts to swindling tricks. He will tell the sick man that a sacrifice is necessary, asking for a goat if the patient can afford one. He will say it

[1] A small measure for grain.

must be of a particular colour, as all black, white or red, so that the sick man's family may have much trouble in finding one, and they naturally think the sacrifice is more efficacious in proportion to the difficulty they experience in arranging for it. If they cannot afford a goat the Parihār tells them to sacrifice a cock, and requires one whose feathers curl backwards, as they occasionally do. If the family is very poor any chicken which has come out of the shell, so long as it has a beak, will do duty for a cock. If a man has a pain in his body the Parihār will suck the place and produce small pieces of bone from his mouth, stained with vermilion to imitate blood, and say that he has extracted them from the patient's body. Perhaps the idea may be that the bones have been caused to enter his body and make him ill by the practice of magic. Formerly the Parihār had to prove his supernatural powers by whipping himself on the back with a rope into which the ends of nails were twisted, and to continue this ordeal for a period long enough to satisfy the villagers that he could not have borne it without some divine assistance. But this salutary custom has fallen into abeyance.

8. Magical practices.

The Korkus have the same belief in the efficacy of imitative and sympathetic magic as other primitive peoples.[1] Thus to injure an enemy, a clay image of him is made and pierced with a knife, in the belief that the real person will suffer in the same manner. If the clay can be taken from a place where his foot has made an impression in walking, or the image wrapped round with his hair, the charm is more efficacious. Or an image may be made with charcoal on some stolen portion of his apparel, and similarly wrapped in his hair; it is then burnt in the belief that the real person will be attacked by fever. Sometimes the image is buried in a place where it is likely that the victim will walk over it, when the same result is hoped for. In order to produce rain, a frog, as the animal delighting in the element of water, is caught and slung on a stick; the boys and girls then carry it from house to house and the householders pour water over it. If it is desired to stop rain a frog is caught and buried alive, this being done by a naked boy. Another

[1] Most of the information in this paragraph is taken from Mr. Ganga Prasād Khatri's Report.

device for producing rain is to yoke two naked women to a plough, who are then driven across a field like bullocks and goaded by a third naked woman. This device may possibly be intended to cause the gods to send rain, by showing how the natural order of the world is upset and reversed by the continued drought. In order to stop rain an unmarried youth collects water in a new earthen pot from the eaves and buries it below the hearth so that the water may disappear by evaporation and the rain may cease in the same manner. Another method is to send a man belonging to the Kāsada sept—*Kāsada* meaning slime—to bring a plough from the field and place it in his house. He also stops bathing or washing for the period for which a break in the rains is required, and the idea is perhaps that as the man whose name and nature are mud or slime is dry so the mud on the earth will dry up; and as the plough is dry, the ploughed fields which have been in contact with it will also become dry. In order to produce a quarrel the quills of a porcupine are smoked with the burnt parings of an enemy's nails and deposited in the eaves of his house. And as the fretful porcupine raises his quills when angry with an enemy, these will have the effect of causing strife among the members of the household. If a person wishes to transfer his sickness to another, he obtains the latter's cloth and draws on it with lamp-black two effigies, one upright and the other upside down. As soon as the owner puts on the cloth, he will fall a victim to the ailment of the person who drew the effigies. In order to obtain children the hair of a woman who has borne several is secured by a barren woman and buried below her bathing-stone, when the quality of fertility will be transferred to her from the owner of the hair. In order to facilitate child-birth a twisted thread is untwined before the eyes of the pregnant woman with the idea that the delivery will thus be made direct and easy; or she is given water to drink in which her husband's left leg, a gun-barrel, a pestle, or a thunder-bolt has been washed; it being supposed that as each of these articles has the quality of direct and powerful propulsion, this quality will be conveyed to the woman and enable her to propel the child from her womb. The Korkus also trust largely to omens. It is inauspicious when starting out on some business to see a black-faced monkey or a hare passing either on the left or right, or a snake crossing in front. A person seeing any of these will usually return and postpone his business to a more favourable occasion. It is a bad omen for a hen to cackle or lay eggs at night. One sneeze is a bad omen, but two neutralise the effect and are favourable. An empty pot is a bad omen and a full one good. To break a pot when commencing any business is fatal, and shows that the work will come to naught. Thursdays and Fridays are favourable days for working, and Mondays and Tuesdays for propitiating one's ancestors. Odd numbers are lucky. In order to lay to rest the spirit of a dead person, who it is feared may trouble the living, five pieces of bamboo are taken as representing the bones of the dead man, and these with five crab's legs, five grains of rice and other articles are put into a basket and thrust into a crab's hole under water. The occasion is made an excuse for much feasting and drinking, and the son or other representative who lays the spirit works himself up into a state of drunken excitement before he enters the water to search for a suitable hole. The fat of a tiger is considered to be an excellent medicine for rheumatism and sprains, and much store is set by it. The tiger's tongue is also supposed to be a very powerful tonic or strengthening medicine for weakly children. It is cooked, pounded up, and a small quantity administered in milk or water. When a tiger has been killed the Gonds and Korkus will singe off his whiskers, as they think this will prevent the tiger's spirit from haunting them. Another idea is that the whiskers if chopped up and mixed in the food of an enemy will poison him. They frequently object to touch a man who has been injured or mauled by a tiger, as they think that to do so would bring down the tiger's vengeance on them. And in some places any Gond or Korku who touches a man mauled by a tiger is put temporarily out of caste and has to be purified and give a feast on readmission.

9. Funeral rites.

The dead are usually buried, two pice being first thrown into the grave to buy the site. The body is laid on its back, naked and with the head pointing to the south.

The earth is mixed with briars and thorns while being filled in so as to keep off hyenas, and stones are placed over the grave. No fixed period of mourning is observed, but after the lapse of some days, the deceased's family or relatives go to the burial-place, taking with them a piece of turmeric. This they cut into strips, and, placing them in a leaf-cup, pour water over them. As the water falls on the tomb, a god is called to witness that this day the dead man's spirit has been sent to live with the ancestors. The pieces of turmeric are then tied in a cloth which, after receiving an oblation of fowl's blood, is suspended from the main beam of the house, this being considered the dwelling-place of the departed. This ceremony, called Pitar Miloni, is the first rite for the admission of the deceased with the spirits of his ancestors, and is preliminary to the final ceremony of Sedoli which may be performed at any time between four months and fifteen years after the death. But until it is complete the spirit of the deceased has not been laid finally to rest and has the power of sending aches and pains to molest the bodies of its living relatives. Each sept has a place in which the Sedoli rites must be performed, and however far the Korku may have wandered from the original centre of his tribe, he must return there to set his father's spirit at rest and enable it to join the ancestral ghosts. When the Sedoli is to be performed an unblemished teak or *salai*[1] tree is selected and wrapped round with a thread, while seven circuits of it are made and a bottle of liquor and two pice are offered as purchase money. It is then cut down and brought home, and from it a smooth stake called *mūnda* is fashioned, 24 to 30 inches high, and squared or pointed at the top, often being arrow-headed. On it are carved representations of the sun and moon, a spider and a human ear, and below these a figure representing the principal person in whose honour the stake is erected, on horseback with weapons in his hand. The proper method is to have one *mūnda* for each ancestor, but poor persons make one do for several and their figures are then carved below. But care must be taken that the total number of figures representing the dead does not exceed that of the

[1] *Boswellia serrata.*

members of the family who have died during the period for which the Sedoli is performed. For in that case another person is likely to die for each extra figure. The little bags of turmeric representing the ancestors are then taken from the main beam of the house and carried with the *mūnda* to the burial-place. There a goat is sacrificed and these articles are besmeared with its blood, after which a feast is held accompanied by singing and dancing. Next day the party again go to the burial-place and plant the *mūnda* in it, placing two pice in the hole beneath it. They then proceed to the riverside, and, making a little ball from the flesh of the sacrificed animal, place it together with the bags of turmeric on a leaf platter, and throw the whole into the river saying, 'Ancestors, find your home.' If the ball sinks at once they consider that the ancestors have been successful, but if any delay takes place, they attribute it to the difficulty experienced by the ancestors in the selection of a home and throw in two pice to assist them. The pith of a bamboo may be substituted for turmeric to represent the bones. The dead are supposed to inhabit a village of their own similar to that in which they dwelt on earth and to lead there a colourless existence devoid alike of pleasure and of pain.

10. Appearance and social customs.

The following description of the Korkus is given by Major Forsyth in the Nimār Settlement Report of 1868–69, with the addition of some remarks made by other observers. The Korkus are well built and muscular. The average Korku has a round face, a nose rather wide but not flat like a negro's, prominent cheek-bones, a scanty moustache and his head shaved after the Hindu fashion. They are slightly taller than the Gond, a shade darker and a good many shades dirtier. In the wilder parts one may come across some quite too awful Korkus, from whom an intervening space of fifty yards is an insufficient protection, though strange to say there are no less than six words in their language which mean 'to wash'; one to wash the whole body, one the limbs, one for the face, one for the mouth, one for the hair and one for the clothes, besides a word for scouring the body with a stone and another word for bathing in a stream. Their habitations on the other hand present quite a contrast to their individual want of cleanliness. They build their villages of a close bamboo wattle-work and with almost Swisslike neatness, a picturesque site being usually chosen, and the plan being one long street with a wide open roadway, or several such parallel with each other. The villages are kept remarkably clean, in striking contrast to the habitations of other aboriginal tribes. The average village contains about twenty huts, and it is the custom to bind these so closely together that forest fires often sweep through a whole village before a hut can be removed to check their course. The average hut is about fifteen feet square with a rather flat roof covered with loose grass over a layer of leaves and pressed down by outside poles. No nails are required as the posts are bound firmly together with bamboo or creeper fibre. The inmates generally sleep on the ground, and a few low stools carved from teak wood serve them for pillows. Every village has a few pigs and fowls running about, both of which are eaten after being sacrificed. The Korku is an adept in the crude process of distillation in which the only apparatus required consists of two *gharas* or earthen pots, a hollow bamboo, some mahua flowers, water and a fire. By this means the Korku manages to produce liquor upon which he can effectually get drunk. They are by no means particular about what they eat. Fowls, pork, fish, crabs and tortoise are all consumed, and beef and rats are eaten in some localities but not in others. The Rūma and Bondoya Korkus eat buffaloes, and the latter add monkeys to an already comprehensive dietary. The lowest caste with whom they are said to eat are Kolis. They do not eat with Gonds. Gonds, Māngs, Basors and a few other low castes take food from them and also, it is said, Bhīls. The Korkus will freely admit members of the higher castes into the community, and a woman incurs no social penalty for a *liaison* with a member of any caste from which a Korku can take food. But if she goes wrong with a low-caste man she is permanently expelled and a fine of Rs. 40 is exacted from the parents before they are readmitted to social intercourse. In the case of adultery with a member of the caste, if the husband does not wish to keep his wife, the offending parties have a lock of hair cut off and give a dinner, and are then considered to be married. But if the husband does not turn his wife away, he, on his wife's account, and the seducer must give a joint dinner to the caste. They have a tribal council or *panchāyat* which inflicts the usual penalties for social offences, while in very serious cases, such as intercourse with a low caste, it causes the offender to be born again. He is placed inside a large earthen pot which is sealed up, and when taken out of this he is said to be born again from his mother's womb. He is then buried in sand and comes out as a fresh incarnation from the earth, placed in a grass hut which is fired, and from within which he runs out as it is burning, immersed in water, and finally has a tuft cut from his scalp-lock and is fined two and a half rupees. The Korkus as a race are very poor, and a poor Korku manages to exist with even less clothing than a poor Gond. A loin-cloth of the scantiest and a wisp of turban coiled on the top of the head and leaving the centre of the skull uncovered form his complete costume for dry weather. Sometimes a large brass chain is worn in the turban or attached to the waist, and to it are suspended a flint and steel and a small dry gourd full of cotton—the implements for obtaining fire. It is also common to wear a large brass ring in one ear. A special habit of the Korku in Nimār, Major Forsyth states, is to carry a small bamboo flute behind the ear like a pen, from which he discourses a not unpleasant strain, chiefly when drunk or engaged in propitiating Bāgh Deo, Devi or any other dread power whom he reverences. The women as a rule wear only a dirty white *sāri* and are loaded with cheap ornaments. Necklaces of beads are worn on the neck, covering the chest, while the arms and legs are weighed down with brass and iron.

11. Character. Like most hill tribes the Korkus are remarkably honest and truthful, slow at calculation and very indignant at being cheated. They are very improvident and great drunkards, and it is the latter habit which has aggravated the obstacles to their improvement.

12. Inheritance. The Korku law of inheritance differs somewhat from that of the Hindus. Among them a grandson does not

inherit the property of his grandfather unless it is openly and clearly granted to him during the latter's lifetime. A married son living separately from his father has no right of succession to the paternal property, but if he is unmarried, he receives half the share of a son who is living with his father. A daughter or a daughter's son does not inherit the father's property unless it is granted to either of them by a deed of gift. The sons and mother share equally.

The Korkus formerly lived principally by hunting, and practised the shifting cultivation in the forests which is now forbidden. Very few of them are landowners, but some large zamīndāri estates in Hoshangābād and Chhindwāra are held by Korku proprietors, who are protected by the prohibition of alienation. Though too improvident and lazy to be good cultivators, they are in great request as farmservants and ploughmen, being too honest to defraud their master of labour or material. A remarkable change has thus taken place from their former character of notorious robbers. They cultivate mainly in the hilly tracts and grow light grains, though some have colonised the waste lands of the upper Tapti valley in Nimār and raise good crops of wheat. They do not as a rule keep cattle other than the few oxen required for cultivating the soil and hauling out timber. Game of all kinds is caught by means of heavy log traps for the larger varieties such as sāmbhar, bear and spotted deer and even leopard; while hares, jungle-fowl and the smaller sort of game are caught under heavy stones held up by nicely adjusted strings. Occasionally, when in search of meat, a whole village will sally out into the forest. The *shikāri* has generally a matchlock concealed in some hiding-place in the jungle, and once he is posted the others beat towards him and any animal that turns up is shot at. In the hot weather the water-hole and the bow and arrow play no small part in helping to fill the Korku larder. Another method of catching birds is to spread the pounded fruit of a certain parasitic airplant on a rock. A thick shining gum exudes which so entangles the feet of the smaller birds as to prevent their escape. Fish dams are built when the water subsides after the rains, and a cylindrical basket six or eight feet in length being

13. Occupation.

adjusted at the outlet, the fish are driven into this from above. During the hot season the fruit of the *ghetu* is thrown into the pools, and this stupefies the fish and causes them to float on the surface of the water, where they are easily caught.

14. Language. The Korkus have a language of their own which belongs to the Kolarian or Munda sub-family. Dr. Grierson says of it: "The Munda, sometimes called the Kolarian family, is probably the older branch of the Dravido-Munda languages. It exhibits the characteristics of an agglutinative language to an extraordinarily complete degree." In the Central Provinces nearly 90 per cent of Korkus were returned as speaking their own language in 1911. Mr. Crosthwaite remarks: "The language is in a state of decay and transition, and Hindi and Marāthi terms have crept into its vocabulary. But very few Gondi words have been adopted. A grammar of the Korku language by Drake has been printed at the Baptist Mission Press, Calcutta."

KORWA

LIST OF PARAGRAPHS

Korwa.[1]—A Kolarian tribe of the Chota Nāgpur plateau. In 1911 about 34,000 Korwas were returned in the Central Provinces, the great bulk of whom belong to the Sargūja and Jashpur States and a few to the Bilāspur District. The Korwas are one of the wildest tribes. Colonel Dalton writes of them:[2] "Mixed up with the Asuras and not greatly differing from them, except that they are more cultivators of the soil than smelters, we first meet the Korwas, a few stragglers of the tribe which under that name take up the dropped links of the Kolarian chain, and carry it on west, over the Sargūja, Jashpur and Palāmau highlands till it reaches another cognate tribe, the Kūrs (Korkus) or Muāsis of Rewah and the Central Provinces, and passes from the Vindhyan to the Satpūra range. 1. General notice.

"In the fertile valleys that skirt and wind among the plateaus other tribes are now found intermixed with the Korwas, but all admit that the latter were first in the field and were at one time masters of the whole; and we have good confirmatory proof of their being the first settlers in the fact that for the propitiation of the local spirits Korwa

[1] This article is based on Colonel Dalton's account of the tribe and on notes by Mr. N. T. Kunte, Jailor, Sargūja, and Mr. Narbad Dhanu Sao, Assistant Manager, Uprora.

[2] *Ethnology of Bengal*, p. 221.

Baigas are always selected. There were in existence within the last twenty years, as highland chiefs and holders of manors, four Korwa notables, two in Sargūja and two in Jashpur; all four estates were valuable, as they comprised substantial villages in the fertile plains held by industrious cultivators, and great tracts of hill country on which were scattered the hamlets of their more savage followers. The Sargūja Korwa chiefs were, however, continually at strife with the Sargūja Rāja, and for various acts of rebellion against the Lord Paramount lost manor after manor till to each but one or two villages remained. The two Jashpur thanes conducted themselves right loyally at the crucial period of the Mutiny and they are now prosperous gentlemen in full enjoyment of their estates, the only Korwa families left that keep up any appearance of respectability. One of them is the hereditary Diwān of Jashpur, lord of the mountain tract of Khūria and Maini, and chief of perhaps two-thirds of the whole tribe of Korwas. The other holds an estate called Kakia comprising twenty-two villages.

2. Physical appearance. "The hill Korwas are the most savage-looking of all the Kolarian tribes. They are frightfully wild and uncouth in their appearance, and have good-humouredly accepted the following singular tradition to account for it. They say that the first human beings that settled in Sargūja, being very much troubled by the depredations of wild beasts on their crops, put up scarecrows in their fields, figures made of bamboos dangling in the air, the most hideous caricatures of humanity that they could devise to frighten the animals. When the great spirit saw the scarecrow he hit on an expedient to save his votaries the trouble of reconstructing them. He animated the dangling figures, thus bringing into existence creatures ugly enough to frighten all the birds and beasts in creation, and they were the ancestors of the wild Korwas."

This legend is not peculiar to the Korwas but is also told by the Halbas, Lodhis and other castes, and is a favourite Brāhmanical device for accounting for the existence of the autochthonous tribes.

"The Korwas," Dalton continues, "are short of stature and dark brown in complexion, strongly built and active, with good muscular development, but, as appeared to me, disproportionately short-legged. The average height of twenty Sargūja Korwas that I measured was 5 feet 3 inches and of their women 4 feet 9 inches only. Notwithstanding the scarecrow tradition the Korwas are, as a rule, better-looking than the Gonds and Oraons. The males, I noticed, were more hirsute than the generality of their cognates, many of them cultivating beards or rather not interfering with their spontaneous growth, for in truth in their toilets there is nothing like cultivation. They are as utterly ungroomed as the wildest animals. The neglected back hair grows in matted tails which fall behind like badly-frayed ropes, or is massed in a *chignon* of gigantic proportions, as preposterous as any that the present tasteless period has produced; sticking out behind sometimes a foot from the back of the head.

"The women appear ground down by the hard work imposed on them, stunted in growth, black, ugly, and wretchedly clad, some having only a few dirty rags tied round their persons, and in other respects untidy and unclean."

It is noticeable that the Korwas have a subtribe called Korāku, and like the Korkus of the Satpūra range they are called Muāsi, a term having the meaning of raider or robber. Mr. Crooke thinks that the Korwas and Korkus are probably branches of the same tribe, but Sir G. Grierson dissents from this opinion. He states that the Korwa dialect is most closely related to Asuri and resembles Mundāri and Santāli. The Korwas have the honorific title of Mānjhi, also used by the Santāls. The Korba zamīndāri in Bilāspur is probably named after the Korwas.

3. Subdivisions.

The principal subdivisions of the tribe are the Diharia or Kisān Korwas, those who live in villages (*dih*) and cultivate, and the Pahāria Korwas of the hills, who are also called Benwaria from their practising *bewar* or shifting cultivation. Two minor groups are the Korāku or young men, from *kora,* a young man, and the Birjias, who are probably the descendants of mixed marriages between Korwas and the tribe of that name, themselves an offshoot of the Baigas. The tribe is also divided into totemistic exogamous septs.

4. Marriage customs.

Marriage within the sept is forbidden, but this appears to be the only restriction. In Korba the Pahāria Korwas are said to marry their own sisters on occasion. The ordinary bride-price is Rs. 12. In Bilāspur there is reported to be no regular marriage feast, but the people dance together round a big earthen drum, called *māndhar*, which is played in the centre. This is bound with strips of leather along the sides and leather faces at the ends to be played on by the hands. They dance in a circle taking hands, men and women being placed alternately. Among the Pahāria Korwas of Sargūja, Mr. Kunte states, the consent of the parents is not required, and boys and girls arrange their own weddings. Men who can afford the bride-price have a number of wives, sometimes as many as eight or ten. After she has had a child each wife lives and cooks her food separately, but gives a part of it to her husband. The women bring roots and herbs from the forest and feed their husbands, so that the man with several wives enjoys a larger share of creature comforts. Among these people adultery is said to be very rare, but if a woman is detected in adultery she is at once made over to the partner of her act and becomes his wife. Divorce and the remarriage of widows are permitted, and a widow usually marries her late husband's younger brother, though she is not obliged to do so. A husband divorcing his wife is obliged to feed the caste for five days.

5. Funeral rites.

The tribe bury the dead, placing the corpse in the grave with the head to the south. A little rice is buried with the corpse. In Bilāspur the dead are buried in the forest, and the graves of old men are covered with branches of the *sāl*[1] tree. Then they go to a little distance and make a fire, and pour *ghī* and incense on it as an offering to the ancestors, and when they hear a noise in the forest they take it to be the voice of the dead man. When a man dies his hut is broken down and they do not live in it again. The bodies of children under five are buried either in the house or under the shade of a banyan tree, probably with the idea that the spirit will come back and be born again. They say that a banyan tree is chosen because it

[1] *Shorea robusta.*

lives longest of all trees and is evergreen, and hence it is supposed that the child's spirit will also live out its proper span instead of being untimely cut off in its next birth.

6. Religion.

The Korwas worship Dūlha Deo, the bridegroom god of the Gonds, and in Sargūja their principal deity is Khuria Rāni, the tutelary goddess of the Khuria plateau. She is a bloodthirsty goddess and requires animal sacrifices; formerly at special sacrifices 30 or 40 buffaloes were slaughtered as well as an unlimited number of goats.[1] Thākur Deo, who is usually considered a corn-god, dwells in a sacred grove, of which no tree or branch may be cut or broken. The penalty for breach of the rules is a goat, but an exception is allowed if an animal has to be pursued and killed in the grove. Thākur Deo protects the village from epidemic disease such as cholera and smallpox. The Korwas have three festivals: the Deothān is observed on the full moon day of Pūs (December), and all their gods are worshipped; the Nawanna or harvest festival falls in Kunwār (September), when the new grain is eaten; and the Faguwa or Holi is the common celebration of the spring and the new vegetation.

7. Social customs.

The Korwas do not admit outsiders into the tribe. They will take food from a Gond or Kawar, but not from a Brāhman. A man is permanently expelled from caste for a *liaison* with a woman of the impure Gānda and Ghasia castes, and a woman for adultery with any person other than a Korwa. Women are tattooed with patterns of dots on the arms, breasts and feet, and a girl must have this operation done before she can be married. Neither men nor women ever cut their hair.

8. Dancing.

Of their appearance at a dance Colonel Dalton states:[2] "Forming a huge circle, or rather coil, they hooked on to each other and wildly danced. In their hands they sternly grasped their weapons, the long stiff bow and arrows with bright, broad, barbed heads and spirally-feathered reed shafts in the left hand, and the gleaming battle-axe in the right. Some of the men accompanied the singing on deep-toned drums and all sang. A few scantily-clad females formed the inner curl of the coil, but in the centre

[1] Dalton, *loc. cit.* p. 229.

[2] *Ethnology of Bengal*, p. 228.

was the Choragus who played on a stringed instrument, promoting by his grotesque motions unbounded hilarity, and keeping up the spirit of the dancers by his unflagging energy. Their matted back hair was either massed into a *chignon*, sticking out from the back of the head like a handle, from which spare arrows depended hanging by the bands, or was divided into clusters of long matted tails, each supporting a spare arrow, which, flinging about as they sprang to the lively movements of the dance, added greatly to the dramatic effect and the wildness of their appearance. The women were very diminutive creatures, on the average a foot shorter than their lords, clothed in scanty rags, and with no ornaments except a few tufts of cotton dyed red taking the place of flowers in the hair, a common practice also with the Santāl girls. Both tribes are fond of the flower of the cockscomb for this purpose, and when that is not procurable, use the red cotton."

They dance the *karma* dance in the autumn, thinking that it will procure them good crops, the dance being a kind of ritual or service and accompanied by songs in praise of the gods. If the rains fail they dance every night in the belief that the gods will be propitiated and send rain.

9. Occupation. Of their occupation Colonel Dalton states: "The Korwas cultivate newly cleared ground, changing their homesteads every two or three years to have command of virgin soil. They sow rice that ripens in the summer, vetches, millets, pumpkins, cucumbers—some of gigantic size—sweet potatoes, yams and chillies. They also grow and prepare arrowroot and have a wild kind which they use and sell. They have as keen a knowledge of what is edible among the spontaneous products of the jungle as have monkeys, and have often to use this knowledge for self-preservation, as they are frequently subjected to failure of crops, while even in favourable seasons some of them do not raise sufficient for the year's consumption ; but the best of this description of food is neither palatable nor wholesome. They brought to me nine different kinds of edible roots, and descanted so earnestly on the delicate flavour and nutritive qualities of some of them, that I was induced to have two or three varieties cooked under their instructions

and served up, but the result was far from pleasant; my civilised stomach indignantly repelled the savage food, and was not pacified till it had made me suffer for some hours from cold sweat, sickness and giddiness."[1]

The Korwas in the Tributary States have other resources than these. They are expert hunters, and to kill a bird flying or an animal running is their greatest delight. They do not care to kill their game without rousing it first. They are also very fond of dacoity and often proceed on expeditions, their victims being usually travellers, or the Ahīrs who bring large herds of cattle to graze in the Sargūja forests. These cattle do much damage to the village crops, and hence the Korwas have a standing feud with the herdsmen. They think nothing of murder, and when asked why he committed a murder, a Korwa will reply, 'I did it for my pleasure'; but they despise both house-breaking and theft as cowardly offences, and are seldom or never guilty of them. The women are also of an adventurous disposition and often accompany their husbands on raids. Before starting they take the omens. They throw some rice before a chicken, and if the bird picks up large solid grains first they think that a substantial booty is intended, but if it chooses the thin and withered grains that the expedition will have poor results. One of their bad omens is that a child should begin to cry before the expedition starts; and Mr. Kunte, who has furnished the above account, relates that on one occasion when a Korwa was about to start on a looting expedition his two-year-old child began to cry. He was enraged at the omen, and picking up the child by the feet dashed its brains out against a stone. 10. Dacoity.

Before going out hunting the Korwas tell each other hunting tales, and they think that the effect of doing this is to bring them success in the chase. A specimen of one of these tales is as follows: There were seven brothers and they went out hunting. The youngest brother's name was Chilhra. They had a beat, and four of them lay in ambush with their bows and arrows. A deer came past Chilhra and he shot an arrow at it, but missed. Then all the brothers 11. Folk-tales.

[1] *Ethnology of Bengal*, pp. 228, 229.

were very angry with Chilhra and they said to him, "We have been wandering about hungry for the whole day, and you have let our prey escape." Then the brothers got a lot of *māhul*[1] fibre and twisted it into rope, and from the rope they wove a bag. And they forced Chilhra into this bag, and tied up the mouth and threw it into the river where there was a whirlpool. Then they went home. Now Chilhra's bag was spinning round and round in the whirlpool when suddenly a sāmbhar stag came out of the forest and walked down to the river to drink opposite the pool. Chilhra cried out to the sāmbhar to pull his bag ashore and save him. The sāmbhar took pity on him, and seizing the bag in his teeth pulled it out of the water on to the bank. Chilhra then asked the sāmbhar after he had quenched his thirst to free him from the bag. The sāmbhar drank and then came and bit through the *māhul* ropes till Chilhra could get out. He then proposed to the sāmbhar to try and get into the bag to see if it would hold him. The sāmbhar agreed, but no sooner had he got inside than Chilhra tied up the bag, threw it over his shoulder and went home. When the brothers saw him they were greatly astonished, and asked him how he had got out of the bag and caught a sāmbhar, and Chilhra told them. Then they killed and ate the sāmbhar. Then all the brothers said to Chilhra that he should tie them up in bags as he had been tied and throw them into the river, so that they might each catch and bring home a sāmbhar. So they made six bags and went to the river, and Chilhra tied them up securely and threw them into the river, when they were all quickly drowned. But Chilhra went home and lived happily ever afterwards.

In this story we observe the low standard of moral feeling noticeable among many primitive races, in the fact that the ingratitude displayed by Chilhra in deceiving and killing the sāmbhar who had saved his life conveys no shock to the moral sense of the Korwas. If the episode had been considered discreditable to the hero Chilhra, it would not have found a place in the tale.

The following is another folk-tale of the characteristic

[1] *Bauhinia Vahlii.*

type of fairy story found all over the world. This as well as the last has been furnished by Mr. Narbad Dhanu Sao, Assistant Manager, Uprora:

A certain rich man, a banker and moneylender (Sāhu), had twelve sons. He got them all married and they went out on a journey to trade. There came a holy mendicant to the house of the rich man and asked for alms. The banker was giving him alms, but the saint said he would only take them from his son or son's wife. As his sons were away the rich man called his daughter-in-law, and she began to give alms to the saint. But he caught her up and carried her off. Then her father-in-law went to search for her, saying that he would not return until he had found her. He came to the saint's house upon a mountain and said to him, 'Why did you carry off my son's wife?' The saint said to him, 'What can you do?' and turned him into stone by waving his hand. Then all the other brothers went in turn to search for her down to the youngest, and all were turned into stone. At last the youngest brother set out to search but he did not go to the saint, but travelled across the sea and sat under a tree on the other side. In that tree was the nest with young of the Raigidan and Jatagidan[1] birds. A snake was climbing up the tree to eat the nestlings, and the youngest brother saw the snake and killed it. When the parent birds returned the young birds said, "We will not eat or drink till you have rewarded this boy who killed the snake which was climbing the tree to devour us." Then the parent birds said to the boy, 'Ask of us whatever you will and we will give it to you.' And the boy said, 'I want only a gold parrot in a gold cage.' Then the parent birds said, "You have asked nothing of us, ask for something more; but if you will accept only a gold parrot in a gold cage wait here a little and we will fly across the sea and get it for you." So they brought the parrot and cage, and the youngest brother took them and went home. Immediately the saint came to him and asked him for the gold parrot and cage because the saint's soul was in that parrot. Then the youngest brother told him to dance and he would give him the parrot; and the saint danced, and his legs and

[1] Believed to be some kind of vulture.

arms were broken one after the other, as often as he asked for the parrot and cage. Then the youngest brother buried the saint's body and went to his house and passed his hands before all the stone images and they all came to life again.

KOSHTI

LIST OF PARAGRAPHS

Koshti, Koshta, Sālewār.[1]—The Marātha and Telugu caste of weavers of silk and fine cotton cloth. They belong principally to the Nāgpur and Chhattīsgarh Divisions of the Central Provinces, where they totalled 157,000 persons in 1901, while 1300 were returned from Berār. Koshti is the Marāthi and Sālewār the Telugu name. Koshti may perhaps have something to do with *kosa* or tasar silk; Sālewār is said to be from the Sanskrit Sālika, a weaver,[2] and to be connected with the common word *sāri*, the name for a woman's cloth; while the English 'shawl' may be a derivative from the same root. The caste suppose themselves to be descended from the famous Saint Mārkandi Rishi, who, they say, first wove cloth from the fibres of the lotus flower to clothe the nakedness of the gods. In reward for this he was married to the daughter of Sūrya, the sun, and received with her as dowry a giant named Bhavāni and a tiger. But the giant was disobedient, and so Mārkandi killed him, and from his bones fashioned the first weaver's loom.[3] The tiger remained obedient to Mārkandi, and the

1. General notice.

[1] This article is based on a good paper by Mr. Raghunāth Wāman Vaidya, schoolmaster, Hinganghāt, and others by Mr. M. E. Hardās, Tahsildar, Umrer, and Messrs. Adurām Chaudhri and Pyāre Lāl Misra of the Gazetteer Office.

[2] V. Nanjundayya, *Monograph on the Sāle Caste* (Mysore Ethnographical Survey).

[3] With this may be compared the tradition of the sweeper caste that winnowing fans and sieves were first made out of bones and sinews.

Koshtis think that he still respects them as his descendants; so that if a Koshti should meet a tiger in the forest and say the name of Mārkandi, the tiger will pass by and not molest him; and they say that no Koshti has ever been killed by a tiger. On their side they will not kill or injure a tiger, and at their weddings the Bhāt or genealogist brings a picture of a tiger attached to his sacred scroll, known as Padgia, and the Koshtis worship the picture. A Koshti will not join in a beat for tiger for the same reason; and other Hindus say that if he did the tiger would single him out and kill him, presumably in revenge for his breaking the pact of peace between them. They also worship the Singhwāhini Devi, or Devi riding on a tiger, from which it may probably be deduced that the tiger itself was formerly the deity, and has now developed into an anthropomorphic goddess.

2. Sub-divisions. The caste have several subdivisions of different types. The Halbis appear to be an offshoot of the primitive Halba tribe, who have taken to weaving; the Lād Koshtis come from Gujarāt, the Gadhewāl from Garha or Jubbulpore, the Deshkar and Martha from the Marātha country, while the Dewangān probably take their name from the old town of that name on the Wardha river. The Patwis are dyers, and colour the silk thread which the weavers use to border their cotton cloth. It is usually dyed red with lac. They also make braid and sew silk thread on ornaments like the separate Patwa caste. And the Onkule are the offspring of illegitimate unions. In Berār there is a separate subcaste named Hatghar, which may be a branch of the Dhangar or shepherd caste. Berār also has a group known as Jain Koshtis, who may formerly have professed the Jain religion, but are now strict Sivites.[1] The Sālewārs are said to be divided into the Sūtsāle or thread-weavers, the Padmasāle or those who originally wove the lotus flower and the Sagunsāle, a group of illegitimate descent. The above names show that the caste is of mixed origin, containing a large Telugu element, while a body of the primitive Halbas has been incorporated into it. Many of the Marātha Koshtis are probably Kunbis (cultivators) who have taken up weaving. The caste has

[1] Kitts, *Berār Census Report* (1881), p. 127.

Bemrose, Collo., Derby.

KOSHTI MEN DANCING A FIGURE, HOLDING STRINGS AND BEATING STICKS.

also a number of exogamous divisions of the usual type which serve to prevent the marriage of near relatives.

3. Marriage.

At a Koshti wedding in Nāgpur, the bride and bridegroom with their parents sit in a circle, and round them a long hempen rope is drawn seven times; the bride's mother then holds a lamp, while the bridegroom's mother pours water from a vessel on to the floor. The Sālewārs perform the wedding ceremony at the bridegroom's house, to which the bride is brought at midnight for this purpose. A display of fireworks is held and the *thūn* or log of wood belonging to the loom is laid on the ground between the couple and covered with a black blanket. The bridegroom stands facing the east and places his right foot on the *thūn*, and the bride stands opposite to him with her left foot upon it. A Brāhman holds a curtain between them and they throw rice upon each other's heads five times and then sit on the log. The bride's father washes the feet of the bridegroom and gives him a cloth and bows down before him. The wedding party then proceed with music and a display of fireworks to the bridegroom's house and a round of feasts is given continuously for five days.

The remarriage of widows is freely permitted. In Chānda if the widow is living with her father he receives Rs. 40 from the second husband, but if with her father-in-law no price is given. On the day fixed for the wedding he fills her lap with nuts, cocoanuts, dates and rice, and applies vermilion to her forehead. During the night she proceeds to her new husband's house, and, emptying the fruit from her lap into a dish which he holds, falls at his feet. The wedding is completed the next day by a feast to the caste-fellows. The procedure appears to have some symbolical idea of transferring the fruit of her womb to her new husband. Divorce is allowed, but is very rare, a wife being too valuable a helper in the Koshti's industry to be put away except as a last resort. For a Koshti who is in business on his own account it is essential to have a number of women to assist in sizing the thread and fixing it on the loom. A wife is really a factory-hand and a well-to-do Koshti will buy or occasionally steal as many women as he can. In Bhandāra a recent case is known where a man bought a girl and married her to his son and eight months afterwards sold her to another family for an increased price. In another case a man mortgaged his wife as security for a debt and in lieu of interest, and she lived with his creditor until he paid off the principal. Quarrels over women not infrequently result in cases of assault and riot.

4. Funeral customs.

Members of the Lingāyat and Kabīrpanthi sects bury their dead and the others cremate them. With the Tirmendār Koshtis on the fifth day the Ayawār priest goes to the cremation-ground accompanied by the deceased's family and worships the image of Vishnu and the Tulsi or basil upon the grave; and after this the whole party take their food at the place. Mourning is observed during five days for married and three for unmarried persons; and when a woman has lost her husband she is taken on the fifth day to the bank of some river or tank and her bangles are broken, her bead necklace is taken off, the vermilion is rubbed off her forehead, and her foot ornaments are removed; and these things she must not wear again while she is a widow. On the fourth day the Panch or caste elders come and place a new turban on the head of the chief mourner or deceased's heir; they then take him round the bazār and seat him at his loom, where he weaves a little. After this he goes and sits with the Panch and they take food together. This ceremony indicates that the impurity caused by the death is removed, and the mourners return to common life. The caste do not perform the *shrāddh* ceremony, but on the Akhātij day or commencement of the agricultural year a family which has lost a male member will invite a man from some other family of the caste, and one which has lost a female member a woman, and will feed the guest with good food in the name of the dead. In Chhindwāra during the fortnight of Pitripaksh or the worship of ancestors, a Koshti family will have a feast and invite guests of the caste. Then the host stands in the doorway with a pestle and as the guest comes he bars his entrance, saying: 'Are you one of my ancestors; this feast is for my ancestors?' To which the guest will reply: 'Yes, I am your great-grandfather; take away the pestle.' By this ingenious device the resourceful Koshti combines the difficult filial duty of the feeding of his ancestors with the entertainment of his friends.

The principal deity of the Koshtis is Gajānand or Ganpati, whom they revere on the festival of Ganesh Chathurthi or the fourth day of the month of Bhādon (August). They clean all their weaving implements and worship them and make an image of Ganpati in cowdung to which they make offerings of flowers, rice and turmeric. On this day they do not work and fast till evening, when the image of Ganpati is thrown into a tank and they return home and eat delicacies. Some of them observe the *Tīj* or third day of every month as a fast for Ganpati, and when the moon of the fourth day rises they eat cakes of dough roasted on a cowdung fire and mixed with butter and sugar, and offer these to Ganpati. Some of the Sālewārs are Vaishnavas and others Lingāyats: the former employ Ayawārs for their *gurus* or spiritual preceptors and are sometimes known as Tirmendār; while the Lingāyats, who are also called Woheda, have Jangams as their priests. In Bālāghāt and Chhattīsgarh many of the Koshtis belong to the Kabīrpanthi sect, and these revere the special priests of the sect and abstain from the use of flesh and liquor. They are also known as Ghātibandhia, from the *ghāt* or string of beads of basil-wool (*tulsi*) which they tie round their necks. In Mandla the Kabīrpanthi Koshtis eat flesh and will intermarry with the others, who are known distinctively as Saktaha. The Gurmukhis are a special sect of the Nāgpur country and are the followers of a saint named Koliba Bāba, who lived at Dhāpewāra near Kalmeshwar. He is said to have fed five hundred persons with food which was sufficient for ten and to have raised a Brāhman from the dead in Umrer. Some Brāhmans wished to test him and told him to perform a miracle, so he had a lot of brass pots filled with water and put a cloth over them, and when he withdrew it the water had changed into curded milk. The Gurmukhis have a descendant of Koliba Bāba for their preceptor, and each of them keeps a cocoanut in his house, which may represent Koliba Bāba or else the unseen deity. To this he makes offerings of sandalwood, rice and flowers. The Gurmukhis are forbidden to venerate any of the ordinary Hindu deities, but they cannot refrain from making offerings to Māta Mai when smallpox breaks out, and if any person has the disease in his house they refrain from worshipping

5. Religion.

the cocoanut so long as it lasts, because they think that this would be to offer a slight to the smallpox goddess who is sojourning with them. Another sect is that of the Matwāles who worship Vishnu as Nārāyan, as well as Siva and Sakti. They are so called because they drink liquor at their religious feasts. They have a small platform on which fresh cowdung is spread every day, and they bow to this before taking their food. Once in four or five years after a wedding offerings are made to Nārāyan Deo on the bank of a tank outside the village; chickens and goats are killed and the more extreme of them sacrifice a pig, but the majority will not join with these. Offerings of liquor are also made and must be drunk by the worshippers. Mehras and other low castes also belong to this sect, but the Koshtis will not eat with them. But in Chhindwāra it is said that on the day after the Pola festival in August, when insects are prevalent and the season of disease begins, the Koshtis and Māngs go out together to look for the *nārbod* shrub,[1] and here they break a small piece of bread and eat it together. In Bhandāra the Koshtis worship the spirit of one Kadu, patel or headman of the village of Mohali, who was imprisoned in the fort of Ambāgarh under an accusation of sorcery in Marātha times and died there. He is known as Ambagarhia Deo, and the people offer goats and fowls to him in order to be cured of diseases. The above notice indicates that the caste are somewhat especially inclined to religious feeling and readily welcome reformers striving against Hindu polytheism and Brāhman supremacy. This is probably due in part to the social stigma which attaches to the weaving industry among the Hindus and is resented as an injustice by the Koshtis, and in part also to the nature of their calling, which leaves the mind free for thought during long hours while the fingers are playing on the loom; and with the uneducated serious reflection must almost necessarily be of a religious character. In this respect the Koshti may be said to resemble his fellow-weavers of Thrums. In Nāgpur District the Koshtis observe the Muharram festival, and many of them go out begging on the first day with a green thread tied round their body and a beggar's wallet. They cook the grain which is given

[1] *Bauhīnia Rusa.*

to them on the tenth day of the festival, giving a little to the Muhammadan priest and eating the rest. This observance of a Muhammadan rite is no doubt due to their long association with followers of that religion in Berār.

Before beginning work for the day the Sālewār makes obeisance to his loom and implements, nor may he touch them without having washed his face and hands. A woman must not approach the loom during her periodical impurity, and if anybody sneezes as work is about to be begun, they wait a little time to let the ill luck pass off. In Nāgpur they believe that the posts to which the ends of the loom are fastened have magical powers, and if any one touches them with his leg he will get ulcers up to the knee. If a woman steps on the *kūchi* or loom-brush she is put out of caste and a feast has to be given to the community before she is readmitted. To cure inflammation in the eyes they take a piece of plaited grass and wrap it round with cotton soaked in oil. Then it is held before the sufferer's eyes and set on fire and the drops of oil are allowed to fall into water, and as they get cold and congeal the inflammation is believed to abate. Among some classes of Koshtis the killing of a cat is a very serious offence, almost equivalent to killing a cow. Even if a man touches a dead cat he has to give two feasts and be fully purified. The sanctity of the cat among Hindus is sometimes explained on the ground that it kills rats, which attract snakes into the house. But the real reason is probably that primitive people regard all domestic animals as sacred. The Koshti also reveres the dog and jackal. 6. Superstitions.

The Sālewārs of the Godāvari tract wrap a short rectangular piece of cloth round their head as a turban. Formerly, Mr. Raghunāth Wāman states, the caste had a distinctive form of turban by which it could be recognised, but under British administration these rules of dress are falling into abeyance. A few of the Sālewārs put on the sacred thread, but it is not generally worn. Sālewār women have a device representing a half-moon tattooed on the forehead between the ends of the eyebrows; the cheeks are marked with a small dot and the arms adorned with a representation of the sacred *tulsi* or basil. 7. Clothes, etc.

8. Social rules and status.

The caste eat flesh and fish and drink liquor, and in the Marātha Districts they will eat chickens like most castes of this country. In Mandla they have recently prohibited the keeping of fowls, under pain of temporary expulsion. Those who took food in charity-kitchens during the famine of 1900 were readmitted to the community with the penalty of shaving the beard and moustaches in the case of a man, and cutting a few hairs from the head in that of a woman. In Berār the Lād, Jain and Katghar Koshtis are all strict vegetarians. The Koshtis employ Brāhmans for their ceremonies, but their social status is about on a level with the village menials, below the cultivating castes. This, however, is a very good position for weavers, as most of the weaving castes are stigmatised as impure. But the Koshtis live in towns and not in villages and weave the finer kinds of cloth for which considerable skill is required, while in former times their work also yielded a good remuneration. These facts probably account for their higher status; similarly the Tāntis or weavers of Bengal who produce the fine muslins of Dacca, so famous in Mughal times, have obtained such a high rank there that Brāhmans will take water from their hands;[1] while the few Tāntis who are found in the Central Provinces are regarded as impure and are not touched. The caste are of a turbulent disposition, perhaps on account of their comparatively light work, which does not tire their bodies like cultivation and other manual labour. One or two serious riots have been caused by the Koshtis in recent years.

9. Occupation.

The standard occupation of the caste is the weaving of the fine silk-bordered cloths which are universally worn on the body by Brāhmans and other well-to-do persons of the Marātha country. The cloth is usually white with borders of red silk. They dye their own thread with lac or the flowers of the *palās* tree (*Butea frondosa*). The price of a pair of loin-cloths of this kind is Rs. 14, and of a pair of *dupattas* or shoulder-cloths Rs. 10, while women's *sāris* also are made. Each colony of Koshtis in a separate town usually only weave one kind of cloth of the size for which their looms are made. The silk-bordered loin-cloths of Umrer and Pauni are well known and are sent all over

[1] Sir H. Risley's *Tribes and Castes of Bengal*, art. Tānti.

India. The export of hand-woven cloth from all towns of the Nāgpur plain has been estimated at Rs. 5 lakhs a year. The rich sometimes have the cloths made with gold lace borders. The following account of the caste is given in Sir R. Craddock's Nāgpur Settlement Report: "The Koshti is an inveterate grumbler, and indeed from his point of view he has a great deal to complain of. On the one hand the price of raw cotton and the cost of his living have increased very largely; on the other hand, the product of his loom commands no higher price than it did before, and he cannot rely on selling it when the market is slack. He cannot adapt himself to the altered environment and clings to his loom. He dislikes rough manual labour and alleges, no doubt with truth, that it deprives him of the delicacy of touch needed in weaving the finer cloths. If prices rise he is the first to be distressed, and on relief works he cannot perform the requisite task and has to be treated with special indulgence. The mills have been established many years in Nāgpur, but very few of the older weavers have sought employment there. They have begun to send their children, but work at home themselves, though they really all use machine-spun yarn. The Koshtis are quarrelsome and addicted to drink, and they have generally been the chief instigators of grain riots when prices rise. They often marry several wives and their houses swarm with a proportionate number of children. But although the poorer members of the community are in struggling circumstances and are put to great straits when prices of food rise, those who turn out the fine silk-bordered work are fairly prosperous in ordinary times."

END OF VOL. III